Psychological Dimensions of Organizational Behavior

PSYCHOLOGICAL DIMENSIONS OF ORGANIZATIONAL BEHAVIOR

Second Edition

Edited by
Barry M. Staw
University of California, Berkeley

Prentice Hall

Upper Saddle River, New Jersey 07458

Library of Congress Cataloging-in-Publication Data

Psychological dimensions of organizational behavior / edited by Barry
    M. Staw.—2nd ed.
        p.   cm.
    Includes bibliographical references.
    ISBN 0-02-416153-5
    1. Organizational behavior.   2. Psychology, Industrial.   I. Staw,
Barry M.
HD58.7.P758   1995
158.7—dc20   94-19440
                                                                CIP

Editor: Natalie Anderson
Production Supervisor: Cathi Profitko
Production Manager: Patrice Fraccio
Cover Designer: Bruce Kenselaar
Cover Art (Photo): Carolyn Mazzucca
Editorial-Production Service: Electronic Publishing Services Inc.

 © 1995 by Prentice Hall, Inc.
Upper Saddle River, New Jersey 07458

Printed in the United States of America

10 9

ISBN 0-02-416153-5

Prentice-Hall International (UK) Limited, *London*
Prentice-Hall of Australia Pty. Limited, *Sydney*
Prentice-Hall Canada Inc., *Toronto*
Prentice-Hall Hispanoamericana, S.A., *Mexico*
Prentice-Hall of India Private Limited, *New Delhi*
Prentice-Hall of Japan, Inc., *Tokyo*
Prentice-Hall Asia Pte. Ltd., *Singapore*
Editora Prentice-Hall do Brasil, Ltda., *Rio de Janerio*

CONTENTS

DIMENSION IV. INTERACTING WITH OTHERS: SOCIAL AND GROUP PROCESS   **265**

PREFACE

Welcome to the fascinating world of organizational behavior. Here you will learn about the nature of people and how their behavior is influenced by others in organizations. You will study some basics of individual motivation, attitudes, and decision making, and see how these human tendencies can be forged into productive and ethical actions. You will read about how people are influenced by the politics and culture of an organization, and also how people may themselves shape the environment in which they work. Finally, you will study what it takes to be creative in an organizational setting, with tips about how to lead organizations in new and innovative directions.

This book is organized into five major dimensions. In each, one or more "foundation" readings are presented in which basic knowledge from the behavioral sciences is reviewed. Then "applications" are presented from the literature of organizational behavior. The readings cover most of the major topics of the organizational behavior field and reflect the current state of our knowledge. Some chapters are research summaries; some are think pieces. All have been selected by the combined criteria of writing style and content. Thus, if a piece appears a bit dry, bear with it; it should contain enough content to be worth the effort. If a piece is especially interesting, enjoy the experience. When you finish this anthology, you should not only understand more about how people think and behave, but have some new ideas about how such behavior can be combined to build a productive and healthy organization.

INDIVIDUAL PERFORMANCE: WHY AND HOW WE WORK

Foundations of Work Motivation

1. DRIVES, NEEDS, AND OUTCOMES

Edward E. Lawler III

For centuries, psychologists and philosophers have tried to explain why some objects or outcomes seem to be desired by people while others are not. The concepts of instinct, drive, intrinsic motives, functional autonomy, derived motives, and many others have been used to explain this phenomenon. This chapter will review many of these concepts and present an integrated view of present knowledge about why certain outcomes are desirable or attractive to people.

An adequate explanation of why certain outcomes are desirable must deal with three separate but interrelated questions.

1. What is it about the nature of individuals that causes outcomes to become desirable to them?

2. What general classes or groups of outcomes do people find desirable or undesirable?

3. What factors influence the desirability of outcomes: that is, how does the desirability of outcomes change over time and why do individuals differ in the importance they attach to various outcomes?

Unless the second and third questions are answered, it is impossible to predict the kind of behavior choices a person will make. Although the answer to the first question is not needed in order to predict behavior, most theorists have found that answering it is a prerequisite to answering questions two and three. That is, these theorists have found it necessary to make assumptions about what causes outcomes to be important in the first place in order to make statements about the kinds of outcomes people value and the things that are likely to influence the attractiveness of outcomes.

Our first question has typically been answered by a set of assumptions about man's internal state. For example, some theorists have assumed that man has homeostatic drives, others have talked of instincts, while still others have talked of learned drives. The second question has been answered by the development of a number of need or outcome classification systems. Some of these systems assume only two classes of needs while others assume more than 20. The third question has been answered in many different ways. Maslow (1943), for example, has theorized that needs are arrayed in a hierarchy such that the lower-level needs have to be satisfied before the higher-level needs come into play. Other psychologists have stressed that learned associations can cause change in the attractiveness of outcomes.

Not every theory that has dealt with the attractiveness of outcomes has attempted to answer all of these questions. In fact, some theories have dealt essentially with only one of the questions. For example, in his discussion of the competence motive, White (1959) is concerned with establishing the existence of that motive. He does not present a general classification of motives, nor does he make statements about what influences the importance of other motives. As we discuss the various theories dealing with the attractiveness of outcomes, it is important to note which of the three questions are answered and which are ignored.

Let us now turn to a consideration of some of the more prominent theories.

HISTORICAL APPROACHES

Prior to the 1940s three theoretical approaches to explaining why outcomes are valued dominated the thinking in psychology. The first two, instinct theory and hedonism, do not make scientifically testable predictions of what outcomes people will seek. The third, drive theory, represents an attempt to develop a theory that does make testable predictions.

Instinct Theory

Charles Darwin was the first to call the attention of the scientific world to the possibility that much of human and animal behavior may be determined by instincts. He thought that many "intelligent" actions were inherited, and he provided a number of examples from his research on animals to support this view. William James, Sigmund Freud, and William McDougall developed the instinct doctrine as an important concept in their psychological theories. Some theorists thought of instincts as mechanical and automatic rather than as conscious motivators of behavior, but McDougall, who developed the most exhaustive taxonomy of instincts, thought of them as purposive, inherited, goal-seeking tendencies.

McDougall (1908) wrote that "we may then define an instinct as an inherited or innate psychophysical disposition that determines the possessor to perceive and pay attention to objects of a certain class, to experience an emotional excitement of a particular quality on perceiving such an object, and to act in regard to it in a particular manner, or at least to experience an impulse to such action" (p. 39). Thus, the "pugnacity instinct" was an instinct that manifested itself in fighting when the organism was exposed to appropriate stimuli. At first McDougall thought he could account for all behavior in terms of about a dozen instincts. However, as time progressed he added more and more instincts to his list so that by 1932 his list included 19 instincts. Other psychologists added more, so that by the 1920s the list of instincts totaled nearly 6,000, including the "instinct to avoid eating apples in one's own orchard" (Murray, 1964, p. 6).

In a sense, instinct theory died of its own weight. As more and more instincts were stated, psychologists began to question the explanatory usefulness of the approach. To say that an animal fights because of the instinct of pugnacity or that an individual takes a job because he has an instinct to work is merely to give a redundant description of the observed behavior that adds nothing to our understanding of why the behavior took place. The tendency of some psychologists to add a new instinct to explain each new behavior that was observed also weakened the theory. As instinct theory developed, it seemed to provide unsatisfactory answers to all of our questions. It said that heredity determined which goals or outcomes organisms would seek (which was incomplete and misleading) and that people's goals consisted of the objects they sought (a circular definition). Thus, instinct theory did not allow for the prediction of which outcomes would be sought; it allowed only for the *post hoc* explanation of why certain goals were sought. Instinct theory also failed to provide a useful classification of the type of outcomes people sought. The original list of instincts was too short and the later ones were so long that they proved useless.

Hedonism

The origins of most contemporary conceptions of motivation can be traced to the principle of hedonism (Atkinson, 1964). In turn, hedonism can be traced to the original writings of the English utilitarians. The central assumption is that behavior is directed toward outcomes that provide pleasure and away from those that produce pain. In every situation people strive to obtain those goals or outcomes that provide the most pleasure. Despite its simplicity and popularity, the principle of hedonism fails to answer any of our three questions adequately. Nothing is said about why certain things give pleasure while others don't. There is no specification of the types of outcomes that are pleasurable or painful or even how these outcomes can be determined in advance for a particular individual. Any kind of behavior can be explained after the fact by postulating that particular outcomes were sources of either pain or pleasure. Finally, nothing is said about how the attractiveness of outcomes may be modified by experience or environmental circumstances. In short, the hedonistic assumption has no real empirical content leading to predictions of behavior and, thus, it is untestable.

Despite the fact that hedonism can be described as circular and lacking in content, its influence on

psychology has been extensive. As one psychologist stated, "the study of motivation by psychologists has largely been directed toward filling in the missing empirical content in hedonism" (Vroom, 1964, p. 10). It is certainly true that almost all modern theories assume that people direct their behavior toward outcomes that they find pleasurable and away from those that they find unattractive. However, most modern theories do attempt to overcome the circularity of hedonism. They specify in advance how attractive specific outcomes will be to particular individuals, and they develop models that predict when the attractiveness of outcomes will change.

Drive Theory

Drive theory developed partially as a reaction to instinct theory and hedonism. It is in the tradition of hedonism, but it is more closely tied to empirical events and therefore more testable. In 1918, R. S. Woodworth published a little book entitled *Dynamic Psychology* in which he advanced the view that psychologists should study what induces people to behave in particular ways. He referred to this inducement as drive, and the concept of drive soon replaced the concept of instinct in the psychologist's glossary of important terms. Later, the term "drive" took on a very precise meaning in the writings of C. L. Hull (1943). He assumed that all behavior is motivated by either primary or secondary drives. According to Hull, the primary drives were biologically based; they represented states of homeostatic imbalance. Hull's position was that:

The major primary needs or drives are so ubiquitous that they require little more than to be mentioned. They include the need for foods of various sorts (hunger), the need for water (thirst), the need for air, the need to avoid tissue injury (pain), the need to maintain an optimal temperature, the need to defecate, the need to micturate, the need for rest (after protracted exertion), the need for sleep (after protracted wakefulness), and the need for activity (after protracted inaction). The drives concerned with the maintenance of the species are those which lead to sexual inter-

course and the need represented by nest building and care of the young [pp. 59–60].

In Hull's theory, outcomes become rewards when they are able to reduce primary drives and thereby reduce homeostatic imbalance and the tension that occurs when organisms are in a state of ecological deprivation. Thus, food is a reward to a hungry person and water is a reward to a thirsty person. Hull also stressed that drive strength can be increased by deprivation and reduced as needs become satisfied. Thus, the hungrier a person gets, the more he desires food; but as he eats food, he becomes less hungry and his desire diminishes. Although Hull assumed that all rewards and drives are ultimately based on the reduction of primary drives, he recognized that certain secondary drives and rewards could develop—or be "learned"—if in the past they were associated with food or other primary rewards. Thus, money is a secondary reward because it is often associated with food and other primary rewards. Social approval becomes a reward for children who are praised for eating well, or dressing themselves, and so on. According to Hull's view, most of the rewards used by work organizations would be considered secondary rewards.

Hull's theory represents a significant advance over the previous theories of motivation. It gives a clear-cut answer to the question of what objects or outcomes have value—that is, objects or outcomes that either reduce primary, biologically based drives or have been related to outcomes that do. It also provides a classification of drives that is still commonly used (it divides them into primary and secondary drives, and it specifies what the primary drives are). Finally, it says that deprivation increases drive strength, whereas obtaining the desired outcomes reduces drive strength. Thus, Hull's theory has answers to all three of our questions. But the real significance of Hull's theory rests in the fact that it is empirically testable. Since it specifies in detail the relationship between such measurable things as deprivation, drive, and learning, the theory can be tested, and it has spawned a large number of research studies.

At this point it is safe to say that these studies have found Hull's theory to be inadequate in a number of important respects. The most important shortcomings have to do with the ability of the theory to explain motivation that is not based on primary drives. Hull's basic point about an organism's possessing certain primary drives that become stronger with deprivation and weaker with satisfaction still seems valid. What does not seem valid is his argument that all secondary motives are learned on the basis of primary physiological or homeostatic drives.

There is no solid evidence that drives can be learned on the basis of their association with positive drives such as hunger and thirst (Cravens and Renner, 1970). There is evidence that organisms will work for rewards that have been associated with the reduction of a primary drive if the primary drive is present. However, when the primary drive is not present, there seems to be no "acquired" drive to obtain the reward. For example, in the classic experiments of Wolfe (1936) and Cowles (1937), chimpanzees learned to associate tokens with the acquisition of food. Initially, the chimps learned to operate an apparatus that required lifting a weight to obtain grapes. They continued to operate it when the only visible reward was a token that had been associated with the grapes. However, they didn't seem to develop an acquired need for tokens, since they were willing to work to obtain the tokens only as long as they were hungry and the tokens led to something they desired—that is, food. Hence, it is difficult to see how Hull's explanation can help us understand why workers continue to work for more money even when their basic needs are satisfied.

More damaging to Hull's view than the evidence on the failure of animals to acquire learned drives is the great amount of evidence indicating that people and animals are attracted to many outcomes that do not seem to be directly related to primary needs. Rats will learn mazes in order to explore novel environments, monkeys will solve puzzles even though they receive no extrinsic rewards, and people will work simply in order to develop their skills and abilities and to increase their competence. These and many other phenomena cannot be explained easily by drive theory.

CONTEMPORARY APPROACHES

Recently, many psychologists have rejected the emphasis of drive theory on primary drives and have argued that people have many needs. This argument has come particularly from those psychologists who are interested in studying human behavior. As we shall see, they have proposed a number of needs that do not seem to be directly related to homeostatic imbalance, organism survival, or species survival. This recent work on motivation has produced two somewhat different approaches.

Researchers in one group have focused on establishing the existence of one or two human motives that they consider to be particularly important. Thus, McClelland has focused on the achievement motive and White has focused on the competence motive. They have not tried to develop complex need, or motive, classification systems. In other words, they have not tried to answer our second question. They have contented themselves with trying to understand why one set or type of outcomes is attractive to people. Other researchers have tried to develop need, or motive, classification systems in an attempt to predict which kinds of outcomes will be attractive to people. Murray's (1938) list of needs and Maslow's (1943) statement of a need hierarchy are examples of this approach. But before we consider these classification systems, we need to look at some of the needs that have been proposed as necessary additions to the primary drives observed by Hull.

The Affiliation Motive

A number of researchers have presented evidence to show that an affiliation motive exists. They have shown that social interaction is attractive to people and that it is particularly likely to occur under certain conditions. For example, Schachter (1959) has shown that people seek the companionship of others when they are anxious and confused about their motives. In Schachter's work, college students faced with the prospect of being shocked were given the opportunity to be with another person. The subjects under such anxiety were more likely to accept invitations to be with others than were subjects who were not under such anxiety. This result occurred even when the subjects were not permitted to talk to the person they were to be with. Other research suggests that people are likely to seek social interaction at times when they are doubting their self-esteem.

Harlow (1958) has presented some interesting evidence suggesting that the social motive may be innate. As part of his work with monkeys he raised some infant monkeys, providing them with two surrogate mothers in place of their natural mothers. One surrogate mother consisted of a cylinder of wire mesh with an opening in the center of the "breast" for a bottle. The other was similarly shaped but was covered with cotton terry cloth. In the experiment, baby monkeys were placed in cages containing the two "mothers." Half were fed from the cloth mother, the other half from the wire mother. According to drive theory, the monkeys who were fed by the wire mother should have become attached to the wire mother because it provided the drive reduction—that is, the milk. However, it did not work out that way. The monkeys who were fed on the wire mother spent most of their time clinging to the cloth mother. Thus, it appears that monkeys develop their attachment to their mothers based on contact comfort rather than on primary-drive reduction.

However, the important point for us about the research on the need for social contact is not whether this need is innate or acquired but that it exists in most adult human beings. It clearly is an important motivation—one that has a significant impact on behavior in organizations. Many organizations have discovered—to their sorrow—that jobs that do not provide opportunities for social contact have higher turnover and absenteeism rates because employees simply cannot stand the isolation. Frequently, unnecessary social isolation results from mechanical and architectural designs that do not consider employees' needs for social relationships.

Need for Equity

People want to be treated fairly. They observe what happens to other people and if they receive either "too much" or "too little" in comparison to other people it makes them uncomfortable. For example, one study showed that dissatisfaction with promotion was highest in Army units where promotion rates were high. Why? Because the individuals who weren't promoted in these units felt unfairly treated. Adams (1963, 1965) has developed a theory that makes a number of interesting predictions about the effects of wage inequity on work output, work quality, and attitudes toward work. Although this theory is a general theory of social inequity, it has been tested largely with respect to the effects of wage inequity, and it has some interesting things to say about how equity may affect the attractiveness of rewards. Its predictions seem to be particularly relevant to understanding the effects of offering various sizes of pay increases and the effects of paying different wage rates.

Adams (1965) defines inequity as follows:

Inequity exists for Person when he perceives that the ratio of his outcomes to inputs and the ratio of Other's outcomes to Other's inputs are unequal. This may happen either (a) when he and Other are in a direct exchange relationship or (b) when both are in an exchange relationship with a third party, and Person compares himself to Other [p. 280].

Outcomes in the job situation include pay, fringe benefits, status, the intrinsic interest of the job, and so on. Inputs include how hard the person works, his education level, his general qualifications for the job, and so on. It must be remembered that what determines the equity of a particular input-outcome balance is the individual's perception of what he is giving and receiving; this cognition may or may not correspond to an observer's perception or to reality.

Equity theory states that the presence of inequity will motivate an individual to reduce inequity and that the strength of the motivation to reduce inequity varies directly with the perceived magnitude of the imbalance experienced between inputs and outcomes. Feelings of inequity can be produced in a variety of ways and in a variety of situations. Adams has studied inequity produced by overpayment. His research suggests that overpayment is less attractive to employees than equitable payment is. There is no evidence, for example, that when a person is paid on a piece rate and feels overpaid, he will reduce his productivity in order to reduce the amount of pay he receives. The important thing for this discussion about the research on equity theory is that people tend to seek equity in their work activities, which can affect their job behavior.

Activity and Exploration

Too little stimulation is very uncomfortable for humans. In one study, college students were employed at $20 a day to stay in a low stimulation environment (Bexton, Heron, & Scott, 1954). They were asked to remain for as many days as they could, lying on a cot in a lighted, partially sound-deadened room. They wore translucent goggles, gloves, and cardboard cuffs that minimized tactile stimulation. An air conditioner provided a noise that blocked out other sounds, and the students rested their heads on a U-shaped pillow. After a certain period—usually filled with sleeping—the subjects found this situation impossible to tolerate and asked to leave the experiment. Rarely did a subject endure it for as long as 2 days despite the fact that the pay was relatively high. Other studies have reported similar results, stressing that under these conditions people seem to develop a hunger for stimulation and action leading to such responses as touching the fingers together and twitching the muscles.

Research by Scott (1969) has shown that the results are very similar when people are given repetitive tasks to perform. They develop a negative attitude toward the task, and, as time goes on, they take more breaks and try in many ways to vary their be-

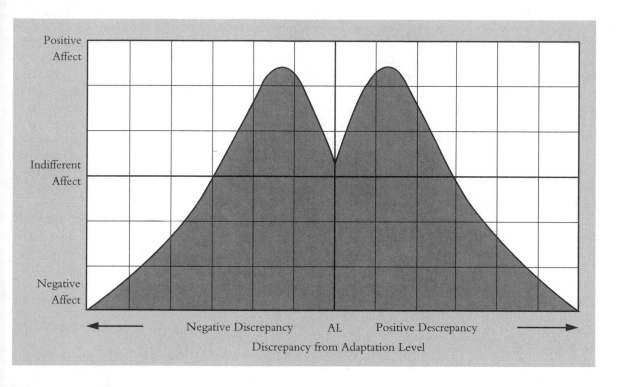

FIGURE 1.1 The Butterfly Curve.
From R. N. Haber "Discrepancy from Adaptation Level as a Source of Affect." *Journal of Experimental Psychology*, 1958, 56, 370–75. Copyright 1958 by the American Psychological Association. Reproduced by permission.

havior. As we shall see, this finding has direct implications for the design of jobs in organizations.

Other studies have shown that both people and animals seek out opportunities to experience novel situations. Butler (1953) has shown that monkeys will learn to push open a window for no reward other than being able to see what is going on in a room, and they will keep doing it. Butler has also shown that the strength of the drive for novel stimulation can be increased by deprivation. An experiment by Smock and Holt (1962) has shown that if children are given a chance to control what they see on a television screen, they will look at objects that offer complex stimuli rather than unconflicting, simple stimuli.

Many studies of rats have shown that they will learn certain behaviors in order to experience novel stimuli. In one experiment, rats preferred a goal box that contained objects to an empty goal box. Miles (1958) found that kittens would learn things when the reward was simply the opportunity to explore a room. There is much evidence that humans and animals will try to solve puzzles simply because of the stimulation provided by working on them. Harlow (1953) has shown that monkeys will persist in solving puzzles for many days. One monkey, who was presented with a square peg and a round hole, persisted for months in trying to get the two to fit together. (The monkey finally died of perforated ulcers.)

Several theorists have suggested that the results of both the stimulus-deprivation studies and the studies of novel-stimulus environments can be explained by considering how novelty affects stimulus attractiveness (Berlyne, 1967). According to activation theory, people become used to a certain level and pattern of stimulation from the environment. For some people this adaptation level may be a relatively low level of stimulation; for others it may be a rather high level. Regardless of where a person's level of adaptation is, however, psychologists hypothesize that deviation from it will have a strong impact on the person. Slight deviations will be experienced as pleasurable and rewarding while large deviations will be experienced as noxious and dissatisfying. Figure 1.1 illustrates this point graphically. According to this approach, the subjects in the stimulus-deprivation experiment were uncomfortable because the situation fell too far below the adaptation level. The animals who wanted to explore new things were attracted to them because these new things represented stimulus situations that were somewhat above their adaptation levels. Presumably if the stimulus situations had been too far above their adaptation levels, the animals would have avoided them, and indeed there is evidence that both animals and people fear situations that are very unfamiliar to them.

One of the problems with activation theory is that it can be very difficult to measure in advance what a person's adaptation level is. Still, the theory and its related research provide some interesting evidence to support the point that not all drives or needs are either primary or learned on the basis of primary drives. It is hard to see how people's reactions to different levels of stimulation can be explained by reference to a drive that has been learned on the basis of a primary drive.

Achievement

The achievement motive has been extensively studied by D. C. McClelland. It is defined by McClelland (1951, 1961) as a desire to perform in terms of a standard of excellence or as a desire to be successful in competitive situations. McClelland stresses that achievement motivation is present in most people but that the amount people have depends on a number of things, including how they were treated during childhood. One study has shown that high-need-achievement people tend to come from families where high demands were made for independence and performance at an early age. Their mothers evaluated their accomplishments favorably and rewarded them liberally.

McClelland measures the strength of people's achievement motive by scoring their responses to a series of pictures. The pictures are shown to individuals who are asked to write a five-minute story about what is going on in the picture. The stories are scored on the basis of how frequently achievement-oriented themes are mentioned (for example, "He will try his best to succeed"). The following is an example of a story showing a young boy in the foreground and a hazy representation of an operation in the background.

A boy is dreaming of being a doctor. He can see himself in the future. He is hoping that he can make the grade. It is more or less a fantasy. The boy has seen many pictures of doctors in books, and it has inspired him. He will try his best *and hopes to become the best doctor in the country. He can see himself as a very important doctor. He is performing a very dangerous operation. He can see himself victorious and is proud of it. He gets world renown for it. He will become the* best doctor in the U.S. *He will be an honest man, too. His name will go down in medical history as one of the* greatest men *[Atkinson, 1958. p. 193].*

McClelland's research has shown that under certain conditions achievement motivation can be an important motivator of good performance in work organizations. When achievement motivation is operating, good job performance becomes very attractive to people; as a result, the motivation to perform well is higher. Achievement motivation typically does not operate when people are performing routine or boring tasks where no competition is involved. However, when challenge and competition are involved, achievement motivation can stimulate good performance. A study by French (1955) clearly illustrates this point. In French's study, Officer Candidate School cadets performed a simple task under three different sets of instructions. Under the "relaxed" instructions the subjects were told that the experimenter was merely interested in determining what kinds of scores people make on the test. The "task-motivated" instructions said that the task was a measure of people's ability to deal rapidly with new materials. The "extrinsically motivated" instructions said that the best performers could leave while the others had to continue performing. Performance was highest under the "task-motivated" instructions and lowest under the "relaxed" instructions. Subjects with high need for achievement performed better on the "task-motivated" instructions but not under the two other kinds of instructions.

Other studies also support the view that people can be motivated simply by a drive to achieve. For example, Alper (1946) gave two groups of subjects a list of nonsense syllables to learn. Only one group was told it was an intelligence test. A test given 24 hours later showed that the "intelligence test" group remembered more of what they had learned. McClelland (1961) showed that successful people in competitive occupations tend to be universally high in achievement motivation. For example, he showed that successful managers from countries such as the United States, Italy, and India tend to be high in achievement motivation.

Overall, the research on achievement motivation suggests that such motivation is most likely to be present when moderately challenging tasks have to be performed (where about a 50-50 chance of success exists), in competitive situations, in situations where performance is perceived to depend upon some important or valued skill, and in situations where performance feedback is given. The research also suggests that people with a high need for achievement tend to seek out situations in which they can achieve, and they tend to find successful performance attractive once they are in these situations. These points have important implications for the design of jobs in organizations and for the kinds of people that are attracted to jobs in different types of work situations.

Judging from the research cited earlier on the effects of child rearing on the strength of need for achievement, it seems certain that achievement motivation is a partly learned drive. McClelland in fact argues that it is differentially present in certain cultures precisely because child-rearing practices differ. However, even though achievement motivation is a learned drive, it is hard to see how it could

TABLE 1.1
List of Theorists Classified as Emphasizing Self-actualization, and the Term Each Uses

Kurt Goldstein (1939): Self-actualization
Erich Fromm (1941): The productive orientation
Prescott Lecky (1945): The unified personality; self-consistency
Donald Snygg and Arthur Combs (1949): The preservation and enhancement of the phenomenal self
Karen Horney (1950): The real self and its realization
David Riesman (1950): The autonomous person
Carl Rogers (1951): Actualization, maintenance, and enhancement of the experiencing organism
Rollo May (1953): Existential being
Abraham Maslow (1954): Self-actualization
Gordon W. Allport (1955): Creative becoming

Adapted from Cofer, C.N., and Appley, M. H., *Motivation: Theory and Research.* Copyright © 1964 by John Wiley & Sons, Inc. Reprinted by permission.

develop because of the primary drives. There may be some relationship here, since success often helps people to obtain primary rewards, such as food; but it is hard to see how the primary drive approach can explain the fact that early independence training leads to a strong need for achievement. Thus, even though achievement is a learned drive, it seems that it is only partially learned on the basis of primary drives.

Competence

Robert W. White (1959) has argued for the existence of a competence motive. He uses competence to refer to an organism's capacity to interact effectively with its environment. In organisms capable of little learning, competence is considered to be innate; however, competence in man—that is, his fitness to interact with the environment—is slowly attained through prolonged feats of learning. The human learning that is needed to gain competence is characterized by high persistence and a strong goal orientation. Because of this dedication to learning, White argues that it is necessary to treat competence as having a motivation aspect that is separate from motivation derived from primary drives or instincts. He presents considerable evidence of organisms trying to cope with their environment seemingly for no other reason than that they want to master it. As White notes, there are repeated references in psychological literature

. . . to the familiar series of learned skills which starts with sucking, grasping, and visual exploration and continues with crawling and walking, acts of focal attention and perception, memory, language and thinking, anticipation, the exploring of novel places and objects, effecting stimulus changes in the environment, manipulating and exploiting the surroundings, and achieving higher levels of motor and mental coordination. . . . Collectively they are sometimes referred to as mechanisms . . . but on the whole we are not accustomed to cast a single name over the diverse feats whereby we learn to deal with the environment. . . . I now propose that we gather the various kinds of behavior just mentioned, all of which had to do with effective interaction with the environment, under the general

heading of competence . . . it is necessary to make competence a motivational concept; there is a competence motivation [1959, pp. 317–318].

White argues that competence motivation is aroused when people are faced with somewhat new situations and wanes when a situation has been explored and mastered to the point at which it no longer presents a challenge.

There is an obvious similarity between White's view of when competence motivation is aroused and the activation theorists' view of how stimulus novelty affects motivation. Both argue for high motivation when somewhat novel situations are encountered. White's theory is also very closely related to the theory of achievement motivation, since both talk of man's need to perform adequately. In fact, White says that achievement may be one outcome of competence motivation. White's theory has some interesting implications for the design of jobs in organizations. It suggests that if presented with the right task people can be motivated to perform effectively without the use of extrinsic rewards such as pay and promotion. However, once the task is mastered, competence motivation will disappear. It is also interesting to note that White, like other recent theorists, argues that the competence motive is not based on any primary drive. Although he does not say exactly where it comes from, he does imply that man's desire to be competent is innate.

Self-Actualization

In the last thirty years a number of psychologists have introduced concepts into their theories that have to do with people's need to grow and develop. Table 1.1 lists some of these theorists and their concepts. The work of Maslow has had by far the greatest impact on the thinking concerned with motivation in organizations. Maslow uses the term "self-actualization" to describe the need people have to grow and develop. According to him, it is the "desire for self-fulfillment, namely . . . the tendency [for a person] to become actualized in what he is potentially . . . the desire to become more and more of what one is, to become everything that one

TABLE 1.2
Murray's List of Needs

Social Motive	Brief Definition
Abasement	To surrender. To comply and accept punishment. To apologize, confess, atone. Self-depreciation. Masochism.
Achievement	To overcome obstacles, to exercise power, to strive to do something difficult as well and as quickly as possible.
Affiliation	To form friendships and associations. To greet, join, and live with others. To cooperate and converse sociably with others. To love. To join groups.
Aggression	To assault or injure an other. To murder. To belittle, harm, blame, accuse or maliciously ridicule a person. To punish severely. Sadism.
Autonomy	To resist influence or coercion. To defy an authority or seek freedom in a new place. To strive for independence.
Blamavoidance	To avoid blame, ostracism or punishment by inhibiting asocial or unconventional impulses. To be well-behaved and obey the law.
Counteraction	Proudly to refuse admission of defeat by restriving and retaliating. To select the hardest tasks. To defend one's honor in action.
Defendance	To defend oneself against blame or belittlement. To justify one's actions. To offer extenuations, explanations and excuses. To resist "probing."
Deference	To admire and willingly follow a superior allied other. To coorperate with a leader. To serve gladly.
Dominance	To influence or control others. To persuade, prohibit, dictate. To lead and direct. To restrain. To organize the behavior of a group.
Exhibition	To attract attention to one's person. To excite, amuse, stir, shock, thrill others. Self-dramatization.
Harmavoidance	To avoid pain, physical injury, illness and death. To escape from a dangerous situation. To take precautionary measures.
Infavoidance	To avoid failure, shame, humiliation, ridicule. To refrain from attempting to do something that is beyond one's powers. To conceal a disfigurement.
Nurturance	To nourish, aid or protect a helpless other. To express sympathy. To "mother" a child.
Order	To arrange, organize, put away objects. To be tidy and clean. To be scrupulously precise.
Play	To relax, amuse oneself, seek diversion and entertainment. To "have fun," to play games. To laugh, joke and be merry. To avoid serious tension.
Rejection	To snub, ignore or exclude an other. To remain aloof and indifferent. To be discriminating.
Sentience	To seek and enjoy sensuous impressions.
Sex	To form and further an erotic relationship. To have sexual intercourse.
Succorance	To seek aid, protection or sympathy. To cry for help. To plead for mercy. To adhere to an affectionate, nurturant parent. To be dependent.
Understanding	To analyze experience, to abstract, to discriminate among concepts, to define relations, to synthesize ideas.

From H. A. Murray, *Explorations in Personality,* New York: Oxford, 1938.

is capable of becoming . . ." (1954, pp. 91–92). Maslow stresses that not all people function on the self-actualization level. He then goes on to describe the characteristics of people who are motivated by self-actualization. According to him, much of the self-actualizing person's behavior is motivated solely by the sheer enjoyment he obtains from using and developing his capacities. He does not necessarily behave in accordance with extrinsic goals or rewards. For him, the goal is simply to behave in a certain way or experience a certain feeling. Maslow makes the point like this:

. . . we must construct a profoundly different psychology of motivation for self-actualizing people, e.g., expression motivation or growth motivation, rather than deficiency motivation. Perhaps it will be useful to make a distinction between living and preparing to live. Perhaps the concept of motivation should apply only to non-self-actualizers. Our subjects no longer strive in the ordinary sense, but rather develop. They attempt to grow to perfection and to develop more and more fully in their own style. The motivation of ordinary men is a striving for the basic need gratifications that they lack. But self-actualizing people in fact lack none of these gratifications; and yet they have impulses. They work, they try, and they are ambitious, even though in an unusual sense. For them motivation is just character growth, character expression, maturation, and development; in a word self-actualization [p. 211].[1]

Thus, like White and others, Maslow is careful to say that all motivation is not tied to the primary drives. Maslow also stresses that people will work to obtain outcomes that are intrinsic, such as feelings of growth. He completely rejects the view that valued outcomes have to be related to such extrinsic rewards as food and water. Maslow probably goes further than any of the other theorists we have reviewed in stressing the differences between motivation based on primary drives and motivation that is independent of primary drives. He says that, unlike motivation based on primary drives, motivation based on growth needs does not decrease as the needs become satisfied. Quite to the contrary, Maslow argues that as people experience growth and self-actualization they simply want more. In his view, obtaining growth cre-

ates a desire for more growth, whereas obtaining food decreases one's desire for food.

Maslow argues that the concept of self-actualization can explain a significant amount of the motivation in organizations. He states that, particularly at the managerial level, many people are motivated by a desire to self-actualize. There is a considerable amount of evidence to support this point. In one study, managers rated the need for self-actualization as their most important need (Porter, 1964). In addition, most large organizations abound with training and development programs designed to help people develop their skills and abilities. Sometimes people do enter these programs in the hope of obtaining a raise or promotion, but on other occasions they do it only because it contributes to their self-development. There is also evidence of people seeking more challenging jobs for no other reason than to develop themselves.

An interesting contrast to Maslow's work on self-actualization is provided by the work of existential psychologists such as Allport (1955) and Rogers (1961). They too talk of people being motivated by desires that are not related to obtaining rewards such as money and status. However, they give less emphasis to the development of skills and abilities and the achievement of goals than does Maslow, and they give more emphasis to new experiences as a way of learning about one's self. Rogers, for example, talks of people being motivated "to be that self which one truly is." He emphasizes self-discovery and the importance of being open to experience. Perhaps because they don't emphasize skill development and accomplishments as much as Maslow, the existential psychologists have not had much impact on the research of psychologists interested in work organizations. This is unfortunate, and it is important to remember that at times people may be motivated by nothing more than self-discovery and a desire to experience.

Need-Classification Theories

Numerous lists and classifications of needs have been presented by psychologists. One of the most important is Henry A. Murray's (1938) list of "psy-chogenic" or "social" needs. This list, which contains more than 20 motives, was arrived at on the basis of the study of a number of "normal" people. Although Murray's list has been very influential in the field of psychology, it has not been applied very much to the study of motivation in organizations, probably because its length greatly reduces its usefulness. Like the early lists of instincts, it is so long that there is almost a separate need for each behavior people demonstrate. A look at Table 1.2, which lists some of Murray's needs, may help the reader gain an impression of the nature of the problem. The issue is not whether Murray has identified separate kinds of behavior (he has) but whether these behaviors might not be better dealt with by a more parsimonious list of needs.

Maslow's hierarchical classification of needs has been by far the most widely used classification system in the study of motivation in organizations. Maslow differs from Murray in two important ways: first, his list is shorter; second, he argues that needs are arranged in a hierarchy.

Maslow's (1943, 1954, 1970) hierarchical model is composed of a five-level classification of human needs and a set of hypotheses about how the satisfaction of these needs affects their importance.

The five need categories are as follows:

1. *Physiological needs*, including the need for food, water, air, and so on.

2. *Safety needs*, or the need for security, stability, and the absence from pain, threat, or illness.

3. *Belongingness and love needs*, which include a need for affection, belongingness, love, and so on.

4. *Esteem needs*, including both a need for personal feelings of achievement or self-esteem and also a need for recognition or respect from others.

5. *The need for self-actualization*, a feeling of self-fulfillment or the realization of one's potential.

More important than the definition of these five need groups, however, is the *process* by which each class of needs becomes important or active. According to Maslow, the five need categories exist in a hierarchy of prepotency such that the lower or more basic needs are inherently more important (prepotent) than the higher or less basic needs. This means that before any of the higher-level needs will become important, a person's physiological needs must be satisfied. Once the physiological needs have been satisfied, however, their strength or importance decreases, and the next-higher-level need becomes the strongest motivator of behavior. This process of "increased satisfaction/decreased importance/increased importance of the next higher need" repeats itself until the highest level of the hierarchy is reached. Maslow has proposed in later revisions of his theory (1968, 1970) that at the highest level of the hierarchy a reversal occurs in the satisfaction-importance relationship. He states that for self-actualization, increased satisfaction leads to *increased* need strength. "Gratification breeds increased rather than decreased motivation, heightened rather than lessened excitement" (1968, p. 30).

In short, individual behavior is motivated by an attempt to satisfy the need that is *most important* at that point in time. Further, the strength of any need is determined by its position in the hierarchy and by the degree to which it and all lower needs have been satisfied. Maslow's theory predicts a dynamic, step-by-step, casual process of human motivation in which behavior is governed by continuously changing (though predictable) set of "important" needs. An increase (change) in the satisfaction of the needs in one category *causes* the strength of these needs to decrease, which results in an increase in the importance of the needs at the next-higher level. Maslow does say that the hierarchy of needs is not a rigidly fixed order that is the same for all individuals. Especially in the case of needs in the middle of the hierarchy, the order varies somewhat from person to person. However, this view clearly states that physiological needs are the most prepotent and that self-actualization needs are usually the least.

Two other need-hierarchy theories have been stated. One is by Langer (1937)—predating Maslow's—and another by Alderfer (1969). Alderfer's (1972) theory is the best developed of these two theories. Alderfer argues for three levels

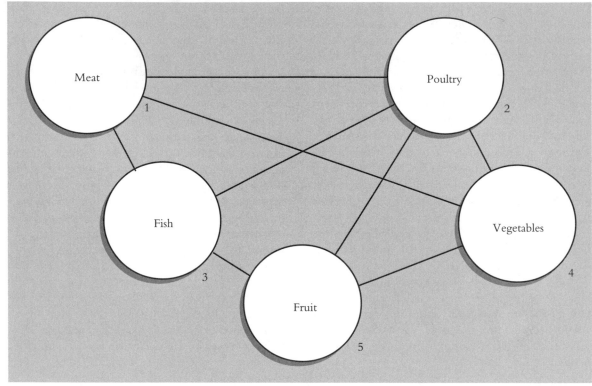

FIGURE 1.2   An Outcome Cluster.

of needs: existence, relatedness, and growth. Like Maslow, he argues that the satisfaction of a need influences its importance and the importance of higher-level needs. He agrees with Maslow's hypothesis that the satisfaction of growth needs makes them more important rather than less important to people; however, he also hypothesizes that the lack of satisfaction of higher-order needs can lead to lower-order needs becoming more important to people. He then argues that the importance of any need is influenced by the satisfaction/frustration of the needs above and below it in the hierarchy. He also assumes that all needs can be simultaneously active; thus, prepotency does not play as major a role in his theory as it does in Maslow's.

From the point of view of the three questions we asked at the beginning of the chapter, the hierarchical theories of Maslow and Alderfer provide rather complete answers to the last two questions. These theories make specific statements about what outcomes people will value (outcomes that satisfy whatever need or needs are active). They also make specific predictions about what will influence the attractiveness of various outcomes—for example, satisfaction of relevant needs including those lower on the hierarchy. They provide less complete answers to our first question, since they are not clear on why needs originate. They do, however, imply that the lower-order needs are innate and that the higher-order needs are present in most people and will appear if not blocked from appearing.

The hierarchical concept has received a great deal of attention among those interested in organizations. This interest is undoubtedly because the concept, if valid, provides a powerful tool for predicting how the importance of various outcomes will change in response to certain actions by organizations. It also can provide some important clues concerning what is likely to be important to employees. It suggests, for example, that as people get promoted in organizations and their lower-level needs become satisfied, they will become concerned with self-actualization and growth. It also suggests that if a person's job security is threatened, he will abandon all else in order to protect it. Finally, it suggests that an organization can give an employee enough of the lower-level rewards, such as security, but that it cannot give him enough growth and development. Thus, as employees receive more valued outcomes from organizations, they will *want* more; although the nature of what they want may change from things that satisfy their lower-order needs to things that satisfy their higher-order needs. As more than one manager has noted, "we have given our employees good working conditions, high pay, and a secure future. Now they want more interesting jobs and a chance to make more decisions. Won't they ever be satisfied?" Need hierarchy suggests that they won't!

AN APPROACH TO OUTCOME ATTRACTIVENESS

The approaches of Maslow, McClelland, and others are useful in thinking about motivation in organizations. They clearly indicate a number of important points that need to be included in any approach that tries to deal with the issue of why certain outcomes are attractive to people. However, there are still many questions. The rest of this chapter will be concerned with answering these questions and with developing an approach to explaining outcome attractiveness.

Drives, Needs, Motives, or Just Outcomes?

All of the theorists discussed so far have assumed that outcomes are attractive to a person because of

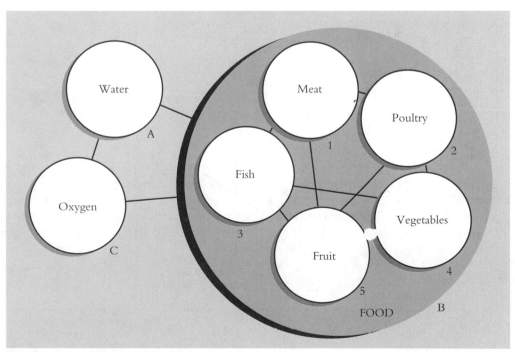

FIGURE 1.3 An Existence-Need Cluster.

some drive, motive, or need the person has. On the other hand, Vroom (1964) has taken a different approach. He does not use the terms drive, need or motive in his theory. He simply says that outcomes have value if they lead to other valued outcomes. Nothing is said about what causes people to value those other outcomes nor about what other outcomes are likely to be valued. Although it does solve the problem of trying to understand why individual outcomes are attractive, a theory that deals with the problem as Vroom's does sacrifices predictive power, in contrast to a theory of needs that states in advance what outcomes are likely to be valued and what affects their value.

A theory of needs can make some predictions—such as when outcomes will be important and what will be the effects of certain events—that Vroom's theory cannot make. For example, if it is known that pay is important to an individual because it leads to prestige, Vroom's theory can only predict that, as prestige outcomes become less important, so will pay. On the other hand, a need theory such as

Maslow's can make further predictions. It can predict what conditions will affect the importance of prestige outcomes—that is, satisfaction of esteem needs or lower-level needs—and can then predict what the effect of a number of factors, such as a promotion, will be on the importance of pay.

The issue of whether needs are innate or learned is an important one; but since we are dealing with adults whose need structures are already developed, it is not crucial for us. This issue is important for us only in the sense that it might provide information about how common it is for people to have a need. Innate needs should be present in a greater proportion of the society than learned needs. Of course, at this point no one seriously argues that any needs other than the basic ones are either purely learned or purely innate. Still, it does seem that the needs that are lower on Maslow's hierarchy are more innate and, therefore, more universally present than are those that are at the top of the hierarchy.

For our purposes a theory of needs does not have to specify why people have needs, since it can

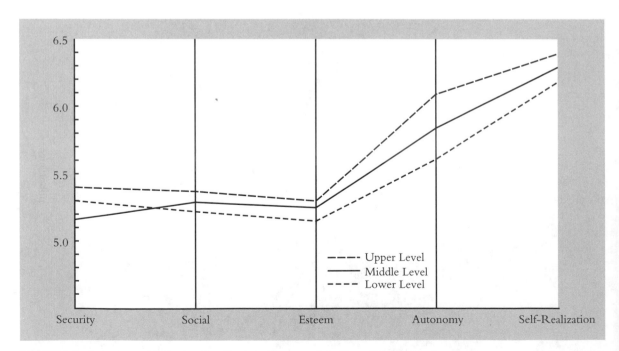

FIGURE 1.4 Importance Attached to Five Needs by Managers from Three Organization Levels.

say something about the needs people have and the conditions under which certain needs operate without doing this. All it has to say is that certain outcomes can be grouped together because when one is sought the others are sought and when one is obtained the others are no longer sought. People often have several groups of such outcomes. The groups can be called "needs," and, if the same ones are sought by most people, then it is reasonable to speak of a "human need" for the group of outcomes. Perhaps it should be added that before a group of outcomes is called a need the outcomes should be sought as ends in themselves rather than as instruments for obtaining other outcomes. For example, food outcomes are sought as an end in themselves, and thus we speak of a *need* for food; a big office is not an end in itself, and thus cannot be called a need. Once it is decided that people have needs, the question is "how many needs?"

How Many Needs?

Interestingly, theorists defining different categories of human needs usually don't disagree over which specific outcomes are likely to be goals for people, but they do disagree on what kinds of needs lead to outcomes taking on goal characteristics. Psychologists have argued that people have from three to several hundred needs. Part of the reason for this variance rests in the way needs are defined. Originally, the criterion was simple; needs or drives were only said to exist when it could be established that a physiological basis could be found for the attractiveness of the outcomes sought by a person.

The recent research on higher-level needs has clearly shown this approach to be too restrictive. A suggested alternative is to use the term "need" to refer to clusters of outcomes that people seek as ends in themselves. This definition, however, does not solve the problem of how to determine what constitutes a valid cluster. Different foods provide a simple example of the problem. Various food objects can be grouped together in the sense that when a person wants one he often wants the oth-

ers and when he gets enough of one he may lose interest in the others. Thus, we can say that people have a need for meat rather than saying that people have a need for roast beef or steak. By thinking in terms of outcome clusters such as the one just described, we move to a more general level and begin to group outcomes more parsimoniously. The question that arises now, however, is where to stop. That is, at what level of abstraction or generality should we stop grouping outcomes. Should we, for example, stop at the level of meat or put all food outcomes together and speak of a need for food, since food objects are somewhat similar in attractiveness as shown in Figure 1.2. The former is a tighter cluster in the sense that the attractiveness of different kinds of meat is probably more closely related than is the attractiveness of meat to the attractiveness of fruit. However, there are still tighter clusters (different kinds of steak), and thus there is no final answer to the question of how tight a cluster should be.

It is also possible to go to a higher level of abstraction and combine food outcomes with water and oxygen and call this combination an existence need (see Figure 1.3). This existence need includes all the outcomes that people need to sustain life. The criterion for grouping at this level is different from the criterion stated earlier (when one outcome is sought the other will be sought, and when one is obtained the attractiveness of the other is affected). The grouping in Figure 1.3 is based on the fact that all the outcomes have a common property: they are necessary for existence. Unlike the cluster shown in Figure 1.2, the attractiveness of one is not necessarily related to the other. Using this system, we would say that people desire food objects because of a basic need to exist; whereas, if we operated at a lower level, we would say people desire food objects because of a need for nourishment. A somewhat similar grouping problem occurs with achievement, self-actualization, and competence. Although it is possible to say that these concepts each represent separate needs, they also overlap in many respects. They all focus on the attractiveness to people of dealing effectively with challenging problems. Thus, they can be grouped and labeled as

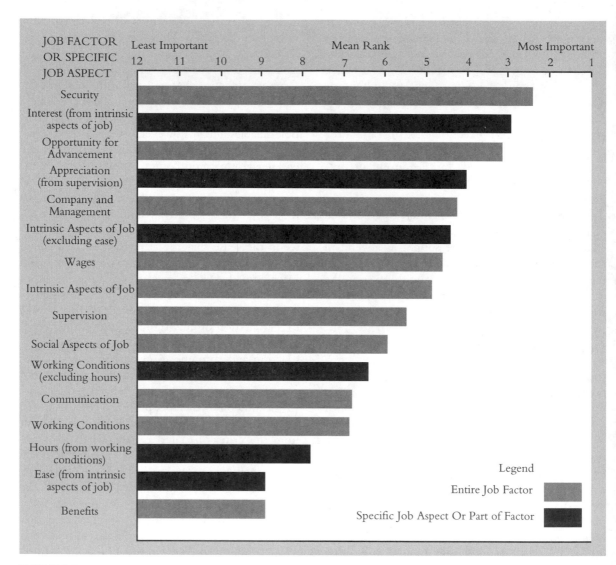

FIGURE 1.5 Average Importance of Factors in Employee Attitudes (Compiled from 16 Studies, Including Over 11,000 Employees).

From Herzberg et al., *Job Attitudes: Review of Research and Opinion.* Copyright 1957 by the PSP Human Resource Development, Inc. Reprinted by permission.

"a need for competence and growth" or they can be treated separately.

Ultimately, the best approach to categorizing needs is that which allows the greatest prediction of behavior in organizations. Unfortunately, at the moment there is not enough research evidence to allow us to state conclusively which listing of needs leads to the greatest predictability. Because of this lack of evidence, the best approach would seem to be grouping only those outcomes that have a strong empirical relationship to each other. By this condition we mean those outcomes that can be observed to have common degrees of attractiveness to people. Using this criterion and thinking in terms of organizations, the following needs can be identified:

1. A number of existence needs—primarily sex, hunger, thirst, and oxygen.

2. A security need.

3. A social need.

4. A need for esteem and reputation.

5. An autonomy or freedom need.

6. A need for competence and self-actualization.

Is There a Need Hierarchy?

Now that we have identified a specific set of human needs, we must consider whether these needs should be arranged in a hierarchy. What does the evidence show about the existence of a need hierarchy?

There is strong evidence to support the view that unless existence needs are satisfied, none of the higher-order needs will come into play. There is also evidence that unless security needs are satisfied, people will not be concerned with higher-order needs. One report shows that subjects kept in a state of hunger think of little else than food (Keys, Brozek, Henschel, Mickelsen, & Taylor, 1950). Similar data is available in the literature on brainwashing and concentration camps (Lawler & Suttle, 1972).

There is, however, very little evidence to support the view that a hierarchy exists above the security level. Thus, it probably is not safe to assume more than a two-step hierarchy with existence and security needs at the lowest level and all the higher-order needs at the next level. This line of thinking leads to the prediction that unless these lower-order needs are satisfied, the others will not come into play. However, which higher-order needs come into play after the lower ones are satisfied and in what order they will come into play cannot be predicted. If anything, it seems that most people are simultaneously motivated by several of the same-level needs. On the other hand, people do not seem to be simultaneously motivated by needs from the two different levels. One person might, for example, be motivated by so-

cial and autonomy needs, while another might be motivated by hunger and thirst. Once a need appears, it does seem to persist until it is satisfied or the satisfaction of the lower-order needs is threatened. The one exception to this rule is the need for self-actualization and competence. Unlike the other needs, evidence shows that this need does not appear to be satiable and, thus, is not likely to cease to be important unless the satisfaction of one of the lower-level needs is threatened.

Can Outcomes Satisfy More Than One Need?

There is a considerable amount of research evidence indicating that some outcomes are relevant to the satisfaction of more than one need. That is, when these outcomes are obtained they affect the attractiveness of more than one cluster of outcomes. A classic example is pay (Lawler, 1971). Pay appears to have the ability to satisfy not only existence needs but also security and esteem needs. For example, Lawler and Porter (1963) report that the more a manager is paid, the higher is his security- and esteem-need satisfaction. This statement means that when a person is trying to satisfy either security or esteem needs, pay will be important. It is not difficult to see why pay has the ability to satisfy a number of needs. Pay can be used to buy articles, such as food, that satisfy existence needs, and high pay also earns a certain amount of esteem and respect in our society.

How Important Are Different Needs?

Literally hundreds of studies have tried to measure the importance of different needs and outcomes to employees. Some idea of the importance of different needs can be obtained by looking at the data collected by Porter (1964), which appears in Figure 1.4. These data show that for over 1,900 managers sampled the higher-order needs are clearly the most important. Other data from the study show that the managers are most satisfied with the lower-order needs. Thus, it follows that these lower-order needs should be the least important. Whether this same concern with higher-order need satisfaction exists at the lower levels in organizations is not clear. The data presented in Figure 1.4 show that higher-order needs do seem to be somewhat less important to lower-level managers than to higher-level managers. Other data suggest that pay and certain lower-level needs are rated as more important by workers than by managers (Porter & Lawler, 1965). Dubin (1956), for example, argues that the work place is not a central part of the life of most industrial workers and that it is unwise to expect the workers to be concerned with fulfilling their higher-order needs within the context of their jobs.

Figure 1.5 shows the average ratings of the importance of job factors in a large number of studies (16 studies and 11,000 employees). Most of these studies were done on nonmanagerial employees. It shows job security and intrinsic job interest to be the most important factors to the employees. Lawler (1971) reviewed 43 studies in which pay was rated and found that its average rating was third. This is an interesting finding, but, like other findings that are based on employee ratings of how important various needs and job characteristics are, it must be interpreted very cautiously. These ratings are difficult for people to make and are strongly influenced by how the questions are worded. Thus, it is impossible to reach any strong conclusions about which job factors are the most important. Perhaps the most significant thing to remember from these studies is that employees rate a number of factors as very important. Some of these factors seem to be most strongly related to lower-order needs, while others are related to higher-order needs.

Individual Differences in Need Strength

Large differences clearly exist in the goals and needs people have, and these differences must be considered when viewing individual motivation in organizations. For example, Lawler reports that in about ¼ of the cases he analyzed, pay was rated as first in importance, while in many other cases it was rated

sixth or lower in importance. Because of these differences a pay system that will motivate one person is often seen as irrelevant by others. Porter's (1963) data show that managers at different organization levels differ in the degree to which they are motivated by higher-order needs. Other data show that managers are motivated by self-actualization, while others are motivated by autonomy. There is also evidence that some people seem to be fixated on such lower-order needs as security.

Many individual differences in need strength are understandable if we relate them to personal characteristics and situations. Hulin and Blood (1968), for example, point out that urban workers have different values from those of rural workers. Urban workers seem to be more alienated from work and apparently are less concerned with fulfilling higher-order needs on the job. For an interesting example of the type of individual profile that can be drawn from the research on need strength, consider the profile of a person to whom money is likely to be very important (Lawler, 1971).

The employee is a male, young (probably in his twenties); his personality is characterized by low self-assurance and high neuroticism; he comes from a small town or farm background; he belongs to few clubs and social groups, and he owns his own home and probably is a Republican and a Protestant [p. 51].

In summary then, there are significant individual differences among employees in the importance of different needs and outcomes. These differences are not surprising; in fact, many are predictable from what has been said about how the importance of needs is affected by the satisfaction of needs and by certain child-rearing experience. There is also evidence that these individual differences are related in meaningful ways to a number of organizational factors, such as management level, and to personal characteristics, such as age, sex, and education level. This point has some interesting implications for the management of organizations, since it means that it is possible to identify those people for whom a particular reward is likely to be important.

How Changeable Is the Importance of Needs?

There is evidence to indicate that some things can and do influence the importance of needs. Still, the evidence suggests that organizations have relatively little influence over how important various outcomes will be to their members. The importance of needs is determined partly by hereditary factors and partly by childhood experiences—things over which organizations have no control. Organizations can influence only two of the factors that determine need importance: need satisfaction and need arousal. Satisfaction influences importance, and organizational practices strongly influence satisfaction. Achievement motivation can be aroused by certain tasks and situations, as can competence motivation. Since organizations do have partial control over the situation in which their employees work, they can create conditions that will arouse certain needs. However, these needs must be present in the individual in order to be aroused, and whether the needs are present is a function of many things beyond the control of the organization.

Probably the best opportunity organizations have to influence the needs of their employees is provided by the selection process. Since need importance is relatively fixed and it is possible to identify people who are high on particular needs, organizations can select people who have the kinds of need-strength patterns they want. This would seem to be a much better approach than trying to change people's needs once they join the organization. This point also has some interesting implications for managers who have to motivate employees. It suggests that rather than trying to change the needs of their subordinates, managers should concentrate on placing people in jobs where their need structure is appropriate. The motivation system that is used must fit the needs of the person or it will not work. If pay is not important to an employee, he or she will never be motivated by a pay-incentive system.

Has There Been an Overall Change in the Relative Importance of Needs?

Many writers (for example, Roszak, 1969) have speculated that the strength of the various needs in the population has been changing over the past 60 years. They argue that only recently has a significant proportion of the population been concerned with needs such as self-actualization and autonomy. (And it is interesting to note that only recently have psychologists been concerned with needs such as self-actualization.) The concept of man as a self-actualizing organism is essentially a development of the 1960s.

Two reasons are generally advanced for the emergence of higher-order needs. First, there is the rising level of education in our society; approximately 40 percent of the high school graduates in the United States go to college. Second, the standard of living has constantly increased so that fewer and fewer people are concerned with satisfying their existence needs and, thus, can focus on satisfying their higher-order needs.

Unfortunately, there is very little evidence to either support or disprove the view that the strength of needs is changing. To test this view adequately we would have to compare need-strength data collected 60 years ago from a random population sample with data collected recently. Unfortunately, such data do not exist. There are, however, some data that can be said to support the view that higher-order needs have become more important. We've already seen that there is evidence to support a two-step hierarchy. If we accept the fact that the standard of living is higher, then, on the basis of a two-step hierarchy, this higher standard of living supports the view that higher-order needs probably are more important. In addition, Porter's (1962) data show that younger managers place greater importance on self-actualization than older managers do. This could, of course, be simply a function of age, but it could also be due to the higher education level of these younger managers and the fact that they never experienced a depression.

There is also some direct evidence that higher-educated people are more concerned with self-actualization. Finally, there is the fact that the idea of self-actualization has gained fairly wide attention in our society. It now seems "in" to talk about self-actualization; and, as we pointed out, the concept of "self-actualization" is now prominent in psychology. Although this evidence is only indirect, it does support the view that concern with self-actualization has increased recently. In summary, although there is little direct data to support the view, it probably is true that, in general, people are somewhat more concerned with satisfying higher-order needs than they used to be.

SUMMARY AND CONCLUSIONS

The following statements summarize the major points that have been made so far about human needs.

1. Needs can be thought of as groups of outcomes that people seek.

2. Man's needs are arranged in a two-level hierarchy. At the lowest level are existence and security needs; at the other level are social, esteem, autonomy, and self-actualization needs.

3. The higher-level needs will appear only when the lower-level ones are satisfied.

4. All needs except self-actualization are satiable, and as needs become satisfied they decrease in importance.

5. A person can be motivated by more than one need at a given point in time and will continue to be motivated by a need until either it is satisfied or satisfaction of the lower-order needs is threatened.

Thus, we have answered two of the three questions asked at the beginning of the chapter. A classification system for needs has been developed, and statements have been made about what influences the importance of needs. No conclusions have been reached about why people develop needs or about whether needs are innate or learned because these questions don't seem to be answerable at this time.

REFERENCES

Adams, J. S. Toward an understanding of inequity. *Journal of Abnormal Psychology*, 1963, 67, 422–436.

Adams, J. S. Injustice in social exchange. In L. Berkowitz (Ed.), *Advances in experimental social psychology*. Vol. 2. New York: Academic Press, 1965.

Alderfer, C. P. An empirical test of a new theory of human needs. *Organizational Behavior and Human Performance*. 1969, 4, 142–175.

Alderfer, C. P. *Existence, relatedness, and growth: Human needs in organizational settings*. New York: The Free Press, 1972.

Allport, G. W. *Becoming: Basic considerations for a psychology of personality*. New Haven: Yale University Press, 1955.

Alper, T. G. Task-orientation vs. ego-orientation in learning and retention. *American Journal of Psychology*. 1946, 38, 224–238.

Atkinson, J. W. Towards experimental analysis of human motivation in terms of motives, expectancies, and incentives. In J. W. Atkinson (Ed.), *Motives in fantasy, action, and society*. Princeton, N.J.: Van Nostrand Reinhold, 1958.

Atkinson, J. W. *An introduction to motivation*. Princeton, N.J.: Van Nostrand Reinhold, 1964.

Berlyne, D. E. Arousal and reinforcement. In D. Levine (Ed.), *Nebraska symposium on motivation*. Lincoln: University of Nebraska Press, 1967.

Bexton, W. H., Heron, W., & Scott, T. H. Effects of decreased variation in the sensory environment. *Canadian Journal of Psychology*. 1954, *8*, 70–76.

Butler, R. A. Discrimination learning by rhesus monkeys to visual-exploration motivation. *Journal of Comparative and Physiological Psychology*, 1953, *46*, 95–98.

Cofer, C. N., & Appley, M. H. *Motivation: Theory and research*. New York: John Wiley & Sons, 1964.

Cowles, J. T. Food tokens as incentives for learning by chimpanzees. *Comparative Psychology Monograph*, 1937, *14* (No. 71).

Cravens, R. W., & Renner, K. E. Conditioned appetitive drive states: Empirical evidence and theoretical status. *Psychological Bulletin*, 1970, *73*, 212–220.

Dubin, R. Industrial workers' worlds: A study of the "central life interests" of industrial workers. *Social Problems*, 1956, **3**, 131–142.

French, E. G. Some characteristics of achievement motivation. *Journal of Experimental Psychology*, 1955, *50*, 232–236.

Fromm, E. *Escape from freedom*. New York: Rinehart & Winston, 1941.

Goldstein, K. *The organism*. New York: American Book, 1939.

Haber, R. N. Discrepancy from adaptation level as a source of affect. *Journal of Experimental Psychology*, 1958, *56*, 370–375.

Hall, C. S. & Lindzey, G. *Theories of personality*. New York: John Wiley & Sons, 1957.

Harlow, H. F. Mice, monkeys, men, and motives. *Psychological Review*, 1953, *60*, 23–32.

Harlow, H. F. The nature of love. *American Psychologist*, 1958, *13*, 673–685.

Herzberg, F., Mausner, B., Peterson, R. O., & Capwell, D. F. *Job attitudes: Review of research and opinion*. Pittsburgh: Psychological Service of Pittsburgh, 1957.

Horney, K. *Neurosis and human growth*. New York: W. W. Norton, 1950.

Hulin, C. L., & Blood, M. R. Job enlargement, individual differences, and worker responses. *Psychological Bulletin*. 1968, *69*, 41–55.

Hull, C. L. *Principles of Behavior*. New York: Appleton-Century-Crofts, 1943.

Keys, A., Brozek, J., Henschel, A., Mickelsen, O., & Taylor, H. *The biology of human starvation*. Minneapolis: University of Minnesota Press, 1950. 2 vols.

Langer, W. C. *Psychology and human living*. New York: Appleton-Century-Crofts, 1937.

Lawler, E. E. *Pay and organizational effectiveness: A psychological view*. New York: McGraw-Hill, 1971.

Lawler, E. E., & Porter, L. W. Perceptions regarding management compensation. *Industrial Relations*, 1963, *3*, 41–49.

Lawler, E. E., & Suttle, J. L. A causal correlational test of the need hierarchy concept. *Organizational Behavior and Human Performance*, 1972, 7, 265–287.

Lecky, P. *Self-consistency: A theory of personality*. New York: Island Press, 1945.

McClelland, D. C. Measuring motivation in phantasy: The achievement motive. In H. Guetzkow (Ed.), *Groups, leadership, and men*. Pittsburgh: Carnegie Press, 1951.

McClelland, D. C. *The achieving society*. Princeton: Van Nostrand Reinhold, 1961.

McDougall, W. *An introduction to social psychology*. London: Methuen & Co., 1908.

Maslow, A. H. A theory of human motivation. *Psychological Review*, 1943, *50*, 370–396.

Maslow, A. H. *Motivation and personality*. New York: Harper & Row, 1954.

Maslow, A. H. *Toward a psychology of being*. (2nd ed.) Princeton, N. J.: Van Nostrand Reinhold, 1968.

Maslow, A. H. *Motivation and personality*. (2nd ed.) New York: Harper & Row, 1970.

May, R. *Man's search for himself*. New York: W. W. Norton, 1953.

Miles, R. C. Learning in kittens with manipulatory, exploratory, and food incentives. *Journal of Comparative and Physiological Psychology*, 1958, *51*, 39–42.

Murray, E. J. *Motivation and emotion*. Englewood Cliffs, N.J.: Prentice-Hall, 1964.

Murray, H. A. *Explorations in personality*. New York: Oxford University Press, 1938.

Porter, L. W. Job attitudes in management: I. Perceived deficiencies in need fulfillment as a function of job level. *Journal of Applied Psychology*, 1962, *46*, 375–384.

Porter, L. W. Job attitudes in management: II. Perceived importance of needs as a function of job level. *Journal of Applied Psychology*, 1963, *47*, 141–148.

Porter, L. W. *Organizational patterns of managerial job attitudes*. New York: American Foundation for Management Research, 1964.

Porter, L. W., & Lawler, E. E. Properties of organization structure in relation to job attitudes and job behavior. *Psychological Bulletin*, 1965, *64*, 23–51.

Riesman, D. *The lonely crowd*. New Haven: Yale University Press, 1950.

Rogers, C. R. *Client-centered therapy: Its current practice, implications and theory*. Boston: Houghton Mifflin, 1951.

Rogers, C. R. *On becoming a person*. Boston: Houghton Mifflin, 1961.

Roszak, Theodore. *The making of a counter culture*. Garden City, N.Y.: Doubleday, 1969.

Schachter, S. *The psychology of affiliation*. Stanford, Calif.: Stanford University Press, 1959.

Scott, W. E. The behavioral consequences of repetitive task design: Research and theory. In L. L. Cummings & W. E. Scott (Eds.), *Readings in organizational behavior and human performance*. Homewood, Ill.: Richard D. Irwin, 1969.

Smock, C. D., & Holt, B. G. Children's reactions to novelty: An experimental study of "curiosity motivation." *Child Development*, 1962, *33*, 631–642.

Snygg, D., & Combs, A. W. *Individual behavior*. New York: Harper & Row, 1949.

Vroom, V. H. *Work and motivation*. New York: John Wiley & Sons, 1964.

White, R. W. Motivation reconsidered: The concept of competence. *Psychological Review*, 1959, *66*, 297–333.

Wolfe, J. B. Effectiveness of token-rewards for chimpanzees. *Comparative Psychology Monograph*, 1936, *12*, 15.

Woodworth, R. S. *Dynamic psychology*. New York: Columbia University Press, 1918.

NOTES

1. From *Motivation and Personality* (2nd ed.) by A. H. Maslow. Copyright © 1970 by Harper & Row, Publishers, Inc. Reprinted by permission of the publishers.

Motivating Individuals in Organizational Settings

2.   MOTIVATION: A DIAGNOSTIC APPROACH

David A. Nadler and Edward E. Lawler III

- What makes some people work hard while others do as little as possible?

- How can I, as a manager, influence the performance of people who work for me?

- Why do people turn over, show up late to work, and miss work entirely?

These important questions about employees' behavior can only be answered by managers who have a grasp of what motivates people. Specifically, a good understanding of motivation can serve as a valuable tool for *understanding* the causes of behavior in organizations, for *predicting* the effects of any managerial action, and for *directing* behavior so that organizational and individual goals can be achieved.

EXISTING APPROACHES

During the past twenty years, managers have been bombarded with a number of different approaches to motivation. The terms associated with these approaches are well known—"human relations," "scientific management," "job enrichment," "need hierarchy," "self-actualization," etc. Each of these approaches has something to offer. On the other hand, each of these different approaches also has its problems in both theory and practice. Running through almost all of the approaches with which managers are familiar are a series of implicit but clearly erroneous assumptions.

Assumption 1: All Employees Are Alike. Different theories present different ways of looking at people, but each of them assumes that all employees are

---

basically similar in their makeup: Employees all want economic gains, or all want a pleasant climate, or all aspire to be self-actualizing, etc.

Assumption 2: All Situations Are Alike. Most theories assume that all managerial situations are alike, and that the managerial course of action for motivation (for example, participation, job enlargement, etc.) is applicable in all situations.

Assumption 3: One Best Way. Out of the other two assumptions there emerges a basic principle that there is "one best way" to motivate employees.

When these "one best way" approaches are tried in the "correct" situation they will work. However, all of them are bound to fail in some situations. They are therefore not adequate managerial tools.

A NEW APPROACH

During the past ten years, a great deal of research has been done on a new approach to looking at motivation. This approach, frequently called "expectancy theory," still needs further testing, refining, and extending. However, enough is known that many behavioral scientists have concluded that it represents the most comprehensive, valid, and useful approach to understanding motivation. Further, it is apparent that it is a very useful tool for understanding motivation in organizations.

The theory is based on a number of specific assumptions about the causes of behavior in organizations.

Assumption 1: Behavior Is Determined by a Combination of Forces in the Individual and Forces in the Environment. Neither the individual nor the environment alone determines behavior. Individuals come into organizations with certain "psychological baggage." They have past experiences and a developmental history which has given them unique sets of needs, ways of looking at the world, and expectations about how organizations will treat them. These all influence how individuals respond to their work environment. The work environment provides

structures (such as a pay system or a supervisor) which influence the behavior of people. Different environments tend to produce different behavior in similar people just as dissimilar people tend to behave differently in similar environments.

Assumption 2: People Make Decisions About Their Own Behavior in Organizations. While there are many constraints on the behavior of individuals in organizations, most of the behavior that is observed is the result of individuals' conscious decisions. These decisions usually fall into two categories. First, individuals make decisions about *membership behavior* —coming to work, staying at work, and in other ways being a member of the organization. Second, individuals make decisions about the amount of effort they will direct *towards performing their jobs.* This includes decisions about how hard to work, how much to produce, at what quality, etc.

Assumption 3: Different People Have Different Types of Needs, Desires and Goals. Individuals differ on what kinds of outcomes (or rewards) they desire. These differences are not random; they can be examined systematically by an understanding of the differences in the strength of individuals' needs.

Assumption 4: People Make Decisions Among Alternative Plans of Behavior Based on Their Perceptions (Expectancies) of the Degree to Which a Given Behavior Will Lead to Desired Outcomes. In simple terms, people tend to do those things which they see as leading to outcomes (which can also be called "rewards") they desire and avoid doing those things they see as leading to outcomes that are not desired.

In general, the approach used here views people as having their own needs and mental maps of what the world is like. They use these maps to make decisions about how they will behave, behaving in those ways which their mental maps indicate will lead to outcomes that will satisfy their needs. Therefore, they are inherently neither motivated nor unmotivated; motivation depends on the situation they are in, and how it fits their needs.

THE THEORY

Based on these general assumptions, expectancy theory states a number of propositions about the process by which people make decisions about their own behavior in organizational settings. While the theory is complex at first view, it is in fact made of a series of fairly straightforward observations about behavior. (The theory is presented in more technical terms in Appendix A.) Three concepts serve as the key building blocks of the theory.

Performance-Outcome Expectancy. Every behavior has associated with it, in an individual's mind, certain outcomes (rewards or punishments). In other words, the individual believes or expects that if he or she behaves in a certain way, he or she will get certain things.

Examples of expectancies can easily be described. An individual may have an expectancy that if he produces ten units he will receive his normal hourly rate while if he produces fifteen units he will receive his hourly pay rate plus a bonus. Similarly an individual may believe that certain levels of performance will lead to approval or disapproval from members of her work group or from her supervisor. Each performance can be seen as leading to a number of different kinds of outcomes and outcomes can differ in their types.

Valence. Each outcome has a "valence" (value, worth, attractiveness) to a specific individual. Outcomes have different valences for different individuals. This comes about because valences result from individual needs and perceptions, which differ because they in turn reflect other factors in the individual's life.

For example, some individuals may value an opportunity for promotion or advancement because of their needs for achievement or power, while others may not want to be promoted and leave their current work group because of needs for affiliation with others. Similarly, a fringe benefit such as a pension plan may have great valence for an older worker but little valence for a young employee on his first job.

Effort-Performance Expectancy. Each behavior also has associated with it in the individual's mind a certain expectancy or probability of success. This expectancy represents the individual's perception of how hard it will be to achieve such behavior and the probability of his or her successful achievement of that behavior.

For example, you may have a strong expectancy that if you put forth effort, you can produce ten units an hour, but that you have only a fifty-fifty chance of producing fifteen units an hour if you try.

Putting these concepts together, it is possible to make a basic statement about motivation. In general, the motivation to attempt to behave in a certain way is greatest when:

a. The individual believes that the behavior will lead to outcomes (performance-outcome expectancy)

b. The individual believes that these outcomes have positive value for him or her (valence)

c. The individual believes that he or she is able to perform at the desired level (effort-performance expectancy)

Given a number of alternative levels of behavior (ten, fifteen, and twenty units of production per hour, for example) the individual will choose that level of performance which has the greatest motivational force associated with it, as indicated by the expectancies, outcomes, and valences.

In other words, when faced with choices about behavior, the individual goes through a process of considering questions such as, "Can I perform at that level if I try?" "If I perform at that level, what will happen?" "How do I feel about those things that will happen?" The individual then decides to behave in that way which seems to have the best chance of producing positive, desired outcomes.

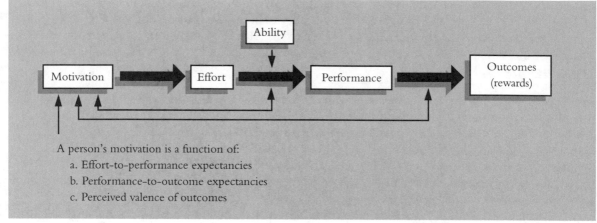

FIGURE 2.1 The Basic Motivation-Behavior Sequence.

A General Model

On the basis of these concepts, it is possible to construct a general model of behavior in organizational settings (see Figure 2.1). Working from left to right in the model, motivation is seen as the force on the individual to expend effort. Motivation leads to an observed level of effort by the individual. Effort, alone, however, is not enough. Performance results from a combination of the effort that an individual puts forth *and* the level of ability which he or she has (reflecting skills, training, information, etc.) Effort thus combines with ability to produce a given level of performance. As a result of performance, the individual attains certain outcomes. The model indicates this relationship in a dotted line, reflecting the fact that sometimes people perform but do not get desired outcomes. As this process of performance-reward occurs, time after time, the actual events serve to provide information which influences the individual's perceptions (particularly expectancies) and thus influences motivation in the future.

Outcomes, or rewards, fall into two major categories. First, the individual obtains outcomes from the environment. When an individual performs at a given level he or she can receive positive or negative outcomes from supervisors, coworkers, the organization's rewards systems, or other sources. These environmental rewards are thus one source of out-

comes for the individual. A second source of outcomes is the individual. These include outcomes which occur purely from the performance of the task itself (feelings of accomplishment, personal worth, achievement, etc.) In a sense, the individual gives these rewards to himself or herself. The environment cannot give them or take them away directly; it can only make them possible.

Supporting Evidence

Over fifty studies have been done to test the validity of the expectancy-theory approach to predicting employee behavior.[1] Almost without exception, the studies have confirmed the predictions of the theory. As the theory predicts, the best performers in organizations tend to see a strong relationship between performing their jobs well and receiving rewards they value. In addition they have clear performance goals and feel they can perform well. Similarly, studies using the expectancy theory to predict how people choose jobs also show that individuals tend to interview for and actually take those jobs which they feel will provide the rewards they value. One study, for example, was able to correctly predict for 80 percent of the people studied which of several jobs they would take.[2] Finally, the theory correctly predicts that beliefs about the outcomes associated with performance (expectancies) will be better predictors of performance than will feelings of job satisfaction since expectancies are the critical causes of performance and satisfaction is not.

Questions About the Model

Although the results so far have been encouraging, they also indicate some problems with the model. These problems do not critically affect the managerial implications of the model, but they should be noted. The model is based on the assumption that individuals make very rational decisions after a thorough exploration of all the available alternatives and on weighing the possible outcomes of all these alternatives. When we talk to or observe individuals, however, we find that their decision processes are frequently less thorough. People often stop considering alternative behavior plans when they find one that is at least moderately satisfying, even though more rewarding plans remain to be examined.

People are also limited in the amount of information they can handle at one time, and therefore the model may indicate a process that is much more complex than the one that actually takes place. On the other hand, the model does provide enough information and is consistent enough with reality to present some clear implications for managers who are concerned with the question of how to motivate the people who work for them.

Implications for Managers

The first set of implications is directed toward the individual manager who has a group of people working for him or her and is concerned with how to motivate good performance. Since behavior is a result of forces both in the person and in the environment, you as manager need to look at and diagnose both the person and the environment. Specifically, you need to do the following:

Figure Out What Outcomes Each Employee Values. As a first step, it is important to determine what kinds of outcomes or rewards have valence for your employees. For each employee you need to determine "what turns him or her on." There are various ways of finding this out, including (a) finding out employees' desires through some structured method of data collection, such as a questionnaire, (b) observing the employees' reactions to different situations or rewards, or (c) the fairly simple act of asking them what kinds of rewards they want, what kind of career goals they have, or "what's in it for them." It is important to stress here that it is very difficult to change what people want, but fairly easy to find out what they want. Thus, the skillful manager emphasizes diagnosis of needs, not changing the individuals themselves.

Determine What Kinds of Behavior You Desire. Managers frequently talk about "good performance" without really defining what good performance is. An important step in motivating is for you yourself to figure out what kinds of performance are required and what are adequate measures or indicators of performance (quantity, quality, etc.). There is also a need to be able to define those performances in fairly specific terms so that observable and measurable behavior can be defined and subordinates can understand what is desired of them (e.g., produce ten products of a certain quality standard— rather than only produce at a high rate).

Make Sure Desired Levels of Performance Are Reachable. The model states that motivation is determined not only by the performance-to-outcome expectancy, but also by the effort-to-performance expectancy. The implication of this is that the levels of performance which are set as the points at which individuals receive desired outcomes must be reachable or attainable by these individuals. If the employees feel that the level of performance required to get a reward is higher than they can reasonably achieve, then their motivation to perform well will be relatively low.

Link Desired Outcomes to Desired Performances. The next step is to directly, clearly, and explicitly link those outcomes desired by employees to the specific performances desired by you. If your employee values external rewards, then the emphasis should be on the rewards systems concerned with promotion, pay, and approval. While the linking of these rewards can be initiated through your making statements to your employees, it is extremely important that employees see a clear example of the reward process working in a fairly short period of time if the motivating "expectancies" are to be created in the employees' minds. The linking must be done by some concrete public acts, in addition to statements of intent.

If your employee values internal rewards (e.g., achievement), then you should concentrate on changing the nature of the person's job, for he or she is likely to respond well to such things as increased autonomy, feedback, and challenge, because these things will lead to a situation where good job performance is inherently rewarding. The best way to check on the adequacy of the internal and external reward system is to ask people what their perceptions of the situation are. Remember it is the perceptions of people that determine their motivation, not reality. It doesn't matter for example whether you feel a subordinate's pay is related to his or her motivation. Motivation will be present only if the subordinate sees the relationship. Many managers are misled about the behavior of their subordinates because they rely on their own perceptions of the situation and forget to find out what their subordinates feel. There is only one way to do this: ask. Questionnaires can be used here, as can personal interviews.

Analyze the Total Situation for Conflicting Expectancies. Having set up positive expectancies for employees, you then need to look at the entire situation to see if other factors (informal work groups, other managers, the organization's reward systems) have set up conflicting expectancies in the minds of the employees. Motivation will only be high when people see a number of rewards associated with good performance and few negative outcomes. Again, you can often gather this kind of information by asking your subordinates. If there are major conflicts, you need to make adjustments, either in your own performance and reward struc-

ture, or in the other sources of rewards or punishments in the environment.

Make Sure Changes in Outcomes Are Large Enough. In examining the motivational system, it is important to make sure that changes in outcomes or rewards are large enough to motivate significant behavior. Trivial rewards will result in trivial amounts of effort and thus trivial improvements in performance. Rewards must be large enough to motivate individuals to put forth the effort required to bring about significant changes in performance.

Check the System for Its Equity. The model is based on the idea that individuals are different and therefore different rewards will need to be used to motivate different individuals. On the other hand, for a motivational system to work it must be a fair one—one that has equity (not equality). Good performers should see that they get more desired rewards than do poor performers, and others in the system should see that also. Equity should not be confused with a system of equality where all are rewarded equally, with no regard to their performance. A system of equality is guaranteed to produce low motivation.

Implications for Organizations

Expectancy theory has some clear messages for those who run large organizations. It suggests how organizational structures can be designed so that they increase rather than decrease levels of motivation of organization members. While there are many different implications, a few of the major ones are as follows:

Implication 1: The Design of Pay and Reward Systems. Organizations usually get what they reward, not what they want. This can be seen in many situations, and pay systems are a good example.[3] Frequently, organizations reward people for membership (through pay tied to seniority, for example) rather than for performance. Little wonder that what the organization gets is behavior oriented towards "safe," secure employment rather than effort directed at performing well. In addition, even where organizations do pay for performance as a motivational device, they frequently negate the motivational value of the system by keeping pay secret, therefore preventing people from observing the pay-to-performance relationship that would serve to create positive, clear, and strong performance-to-reward expectancies. The implication is that organizations should put more effort into rewarding people (through pay, promotion, better job opportunities, etc.) for the performances which are desired, and that to keep these rewards secret is clearly self-defeating. In addition, it underscores the importance of the frequently ignored performance evaluation or appraisal process and the need to evaluate people based on how they perform clearly defined specific behaviors, rather than on how they score on ratings of general traits such as "honesty," "cleanliness," and other, similar terms which frequently appear as part of the performance appraisal form.

Implication 2: The Design of Tasks, Jobs, and Roles. One source of desired outcomes is the work itself. The expectancy-theory model supports much of the job enrichment literature, in saying that by designing jobs which enable people to get their needs fulfilled, organizations can bring about higher levels of motivation.[4] The major difference between the traditional approaches to job enlargement or enrichment and the expectancy-theory approach is the recognition by the expectancy theory that different people have different needs and, therefore, some people may not want enlarged or enriched jobs. Thus, while the design of tasks that have more autonomy, variety, feedback, meaningfulness, etc., will lead to higher motivation in some, the organization needs to build in the opportunity for individuals to make choices about the kind of work they will do so that not everyone is forced to experience job enrichment.

Implication 3: The Importance of Group Structures. Groups, both formal and informal, are powerful and potent sources of desired outcomes for individuals. Groups can provide or withhold accep-

tance, approval, affection, skill training, needed information, assistance, etc. They are a powerful force in the total motivational environment of individuals. Several implications emerge from the importance of groups. First, organizations should consider the structuring of at least a portion of rewards around group performance rather than individual performance. This is particularly important where group members have to cooperate with each other to produce a group product or service, and where the individual's contribution is often hard to determine. Second, the organization needs to train managers to be aware of how groups can influence individual behavior and to be sensitive to the kinds of expectancies which informal groups set up and their conflict or consistency with the expectancies that the organization attempts to create.

Implication 4: The Supervisor's Role. The immediate supervisor has an important role in creating, monitoring, and maintaining the expectancies and reward structures which will lead to good performance. The supervisor's role in the motivation process becomes one of defining clear goals, setting clear reward expectancies, and providing the right rewards for different people (which could include both organizational rewards and personal rewards such as recognition, approval, or support from the supervisor). Thus, organizations need to provide supervisors with an awareness of the nature of motivation as well as the tools (control over organizational rewards, skill in administering those rewards) to create positive motivation.

Implication 5: Measuring Motivation. If things like expectancies, the nature of the job, supervisor-controlled outcomes, satisfaction, etc., are important in understanding how well people are being motivated, then organizations need to monitor employee perceptions along these lines. One relatively cheap and reliable method of doing this is through standardized employee questionnaires. A number of organizations already use such techniques, surveying employees' perceptions and attitudes at regular intervals (ranging from once a month to once every year-and-a-half) using either standardized

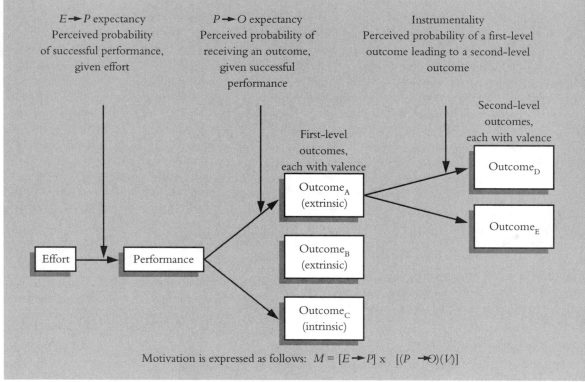

FIGURE 2.2   *Major Terms in Expectancy Theory.*

surveys or surveys developed specifically for the organization. Such information is useful both to the individual manager and to top management in assessing the state of human resources and the effectiveness of the organization's motivation systems.[5]

Implication 6: Individualizing Organizations. Expectancy theory leads to a final general implication about a possible future direction for the design of organizations. Because different people have different needs and therefore have different valences, effective motivation must come through the recognition that not all employees are alike and that organizations need to be flexible in order to accommodate individual differences. This implies the "building in" of choice for employees in many areas, such as reward systems, fringe benefits, job as-

signments, etc., where employees previously have had little say. A successful example of the building in of such choice can be seen in the experiments at TRW and the Educational Testing Service with "cafeteria fringe-benefits plans" which allow employees to choose the fringe benefits they want, rather than taking the expensive and often unwanted benefits which the company frequently provides to everyone.[6]

SUMMARY

Expectancy theory provides a more complex model of man for managers to work with. At the same time, it is a model which holds promise for the more effective motivation of individuals and the more effective design of organizational systems. It implies, however, the need for more exacting and thorough diagnosis by the manager to determine (a) the relevant forces in the individual, and (b) the relevant forces in the environment, both of which combine to motivate different kinds of behavior. Following diagnosis, the model implies a need to act—to develop a system of pay, promotion, job assignments, group structures, supervision, etc.—to bring about effective motivation by providing different outcomes for different individuals.

Performance of individuals is a critical issue in making organizations work effectively. If a manager is to influence work behavior and performance, he or she must have an understanding of motivation and the factors which influence an individual's motivation to come to work, to work hard, and to work well. While simple models offer easy answers, it is the more complex models which seem to offer more promise. Managers can use models (like expectancy theory) to understand the nature of behavior and build more effective organizations.

APPENDIX A: THE EXPECTANCY THEORY MODEL IN MORE TECHNICAL TERMS

A person's motivation to exert effort towards a specific level of performance is based on his or her perceptions of associations between actions and outcomes. The critical perceptions which contribute to motivation are graphically presented in Figure 2.2. These perceptions can be defined as follows:

a. The effort-to-performance expectancy ($E{\rightarrow}P$): This refers to the person's subjective probability about the likelihood that he or she can perform at a given level, or that effort on his or her part will lead to successful performance. This term can be thought of as varying from 0 to 1. In general, the less likely a person feels that he or she can perform at a given level, the less likely he or she will be to try to perform at that level. A person's $E \rightarrow P$ probabilities are

also strongly influenced by each situation and by previous experience in that and similar situations.

b. The performance-to-outcomes expectancy ($P \rightarrow 0$) and valence (V): This refers to a combination of a number of beliefs about what the outcomes of successful performance will be and the value or attractiveness of these outcomes to the individual. Valence is considered to vary from +1 (very desirable) to −1 (very undesirable) and the performance-to-outcomes probabilities vary from +1 (performance sure to lead to outcome) to 0 (performance not related to outcome). In general, the more likely a person feels that performance will lead to valent outcomes, the more likely he or she will be to try to perform at the required level.

c. Instrumentality: As Figure 2.2 indicates, a single level of performance can be associated with a number of different outcomes, each having a certain degree of valence. Some outcomes are valent because they have direct value or attractiveness. Some outcomes, however, have valence because they are seen as leading to (or being "instrumental" for) the attainment of other "second level" outcomes which have direct value or attractiveness.

d. Intrinsic and extrinsic outcomes: Some outcomes are seen as occurring directly as a result of performing the task itself and are outcomes which the individual thus gives to himself (i.e., feelings of accomplishment, creativity, etc.). These are called "intrinsic" outcomes. Other outcomes that are associated with performance are provided or mediated by external factors (the organization, the supervisor, the work group, etc.). These outcomes are called "extrinsic" outcomes.

Along with the graphic representation of these terms presented in Figure 2.2, there is a simplified formula for combining these perceptions to arrive at a term expressing the relative level of motivation to exert effort towards performance at a given level. The formula expresses these relationships:

a. The person's motivation to perform is determined by the $P \rightarrow O$ expectancy multiplied by the valence (V) of the outcome. The valence of the first order outcome subsumes the instrumentalities and valences of

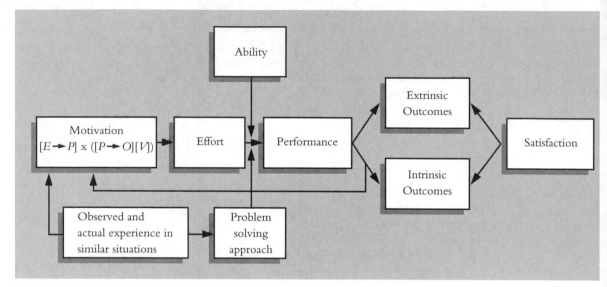

FIGURE 2.3 *Simplified Expectancy-Theory Model of Behavior.*

second order outcomes. The relationship is multiplicative since there is no motivation to perform if either of the terms is zero.

b. Since a level of performance has multiple outcomes associated with it, the products of all probability-times-valence combinations are added together for all the outcomes that are seen as related to the specific performance.

c. This term (the summed $P \rightarrow O$ expectancies times valences) is then multiplied by the $E \rightarrow P$ expectancy. Again the multiplicative relationship indicates that if either term is zero, motivation is zero.

d. In summary, the strength of a person's motivation to perform effectively is influenced by (1) the person's belief that effort can be converted into performance, and (2) the net attractiveness of the events that are perceived to stem from good performance.

So far, all the terms have referred to the individual's perceptions which result in motivation and thus an intention to behave in a certain way. Figure 2.3 is a simplified representation of the total model, showing how these intentions get translated into actual

behavior.[7] The model envisions the following sequence of events:

a. First, the strength of a person's motivation to perform correctly is most directly reflected in his or her effort—how hard he or she works. This effort expenditure may or may not result in good performance, since at least two factors must be right if effort is to be converted into performance. First, the person must possess the necessary abilities in order to perform the job well. Unless both ability and effort are high, there cannot be good performance. A second factor is the person's perception of how his or her effort can best be converted into performance. It is assumed that this perception is learned by the individual on the basis of previous experience in similar situations. This "how to do it" perception can obviously vary widely in accuracy, and—where erroneous perceptions exist—performance is low even though effort or motivation may be high.

b. Second, when performance occurs, certain amounts of outcomes are obtained by the individual. Intrinsic outcomes, not being mediated by outside forces, tend to occur regularly as a result of performance, while extrinsic outcomes may or may not accrue to the individual (indicated by the wavy line of the model).

c. Third, as a result of the obtaining of outcomes and the perceptions of the relative value of the outcomes obtained, the individual has a positive or negative affec-

tive response (a level of satisfaction or dissatisfaction).

d. Fourth, the model indicates that events which occur influence future behavior by altering the $E \to P, P \to O$, and V perceptions. This process is represented by the feedback loops running from actual behavior back to motivation.

NOTES

1. For reviews of the expectancy theory research see Mitchell, T. R. Expectancy models of job satisfaction, occupational preference and effort: A theoretical, methodological, and empirical appraisal. *Psychological Bulletin*, 1974, 81, 1053–1077. For a more general discussion of expectancy theory and other approaches to motivation see Lawler, E. E. *Motivation in work organizations*. Belmont, Calif. Brooks/Cole, 1973.

2. Lawler, E. E., Kuleck, W. J., Rhode, J. G., & Sorenson, J. E. Job choice and post-decision dissonance. *Organizational Behavior and Human Performance*, 1975, 13, 133–145.

3. For a detailed discussion of the implications of expectancy theory for pay and reward systems, see Lawler, E. E. *Pay and organizational effectiveness: A psychological view*. New York: McGraw-Hill, 1971.

4. A good discussion of job design with an expectancy-theory perspective is in Hackman, J. R., Oldham, G. R., Janson, R., & Purdy, K. A new strategy for job enrichment. *California Management Review*, Summer, 1975, p. 57.

5. The use of questionnaires for understanding and changing organizational behavior is discussed in Nadler, D. A. *Feedback and organizational development: Using data-based methods*. Reading, Mass.: Addison-Wesley, 1977.

6. The whole issue of individualizing organizations is examined in Lawler, E. E. The individualized organization: Problems and promise. *California Management Review*, 1974, 17 (2), 31–39.

7. For a more detailed statement of the model see Lawler, E. E. Job attitudes and employee motivation: Theory, research and practice. *Personnel Psychology*, 1970, 23, 223–237.

3.   GOAL-SETTING—A MOTIVATIONAL TECHNIQUE THAT WORKS

Gary P. Latham and Edwin A. Locke

The problem of how to motivate employees has puzzled and frustrated managers for generations. One reason the problem has seemed difficult, if not mysterious, is that motivation ultimately comes from within the individual and therefore cannot be observed directly. Moreover, most managers are not in a position to change an employee's basic personality structure. The best they can do is try to use incentives to direct the energies of their employees toward organizational objectives.

Money is obviously the primary incentive, since without it few if any employees would come to work. But money alone is not always enough to motivate high performance. Other incentives, such as participation in decision making, job enrichment, behavior modification, and organizational development, have been tried with varying degrees of success. A large number of research studies have shown, however, that one very straightforward technique—goal setting—is probably not only more effective than alternative methods, but may be the major mechanism by which these other incentives affect motivation. For example, a recent experiment on job enrichment demonstrated that unless employees in enriched jobs set higher, more specific goals than do those with unenriched jobs, job enrichment has absolutely no effect on productivity. Even money has been found most effective as a motivator when the bonuses offered are made contingent on attaining specific objectives.

THE GOAL-SETTING CONCEPT

The idea of assigning employees a specific amount of work to be accomplished—a specific task, a quota, a performance standard, an objective, or a deadline—is not new. The task concept, along with time and motion study and incentive pay, was the cornerstone of scientific management, founded by Frederick W. Taylor more than 70 years ago. He used his system to increase the productivity of blue-collar workers. About 20 years ago the idea of goal setting reappeared under a new name, management by objectives, but this technique was designed for managers.

In a 14-year program of research, we have found that goal setting does not necessarily have to be part of a wider management system to motivate performance effectively. It can be used as a technique in its own right.

Laboratory and Field Research

Our research program began in the laboratory. In a series of experiments, individuals were assigned different types of goals on a variety of simple tasks—addition, brainstorming, assembling toys. Repeatedly it was found that those assigned hard goals performed better than did people assigned moderately difficult or easy goals. Furthermore, individuals who had specific, challenging goals outperformed those who were given such vague goals as to "do your best." Finally, we observed that pay and performance feedback led to improved performance only when these incentives led the individual to set higher goals.

While results were quite consistent in the laboratory, there was no proof that they could be applied to actual work settings. Fortunately, just as Locke published a summary of the laboratory studies in 1968, Latham began a separate series of experiments in the wood products industry that demonstrated the practical significance of these findings. The field studies did not start out as a validity test of a laboratory theory, but rather as a response to a practical problem.

In 1968, six sponsors of the American Pulpwood Association became concerned about increasing the productivity of independent loggers in the South. These loggers were entrepreneurs on whom the multimillion-dollar companies are largely dependent for their raw material. The problem was twofold. First, these entrepreneurs did not work for a single company; they worked for themselves. Thus they were free to (and often did) work two days one week, four days a second week, five half-days a third week, or whatever schedule they preferred. In short, these workers could be classified as marginal from the standpoint of their productivity and attendance, which were considered highly unsatisfactory by conventional company standards. Second, the major approach taken to alleviate this problem had been to develop equipment that would make the industry less dependent on this type of worker. A limitation of this approach was that many of the logging supervisors were unable to obtain the financing necessary to purchase a small tractor, let alone a rubber-tired skidder.

Consequently, we designed a survey that would help managers determine "what makes these people tick." The survey was conducted orally in the field with 292 logging supervisors. Complex statistical analyses of the data identified three basic types of supervisor. One type stayed on the job with their men, gave them instructions and explanations, provided them with training, read the trade magazines, and had little difficulty financing the equipment

they needed. Still, the productivity of their units was at best mediocre.

The operation of the second group of supervisors was slightly less mechanized. These supervisors provided little training for their workforce. They simply drove their employees to the woods, gave them a specific production goal to attain for the day or week, left them alone in the woods unsupervised, and returned at night to take them home. Labor turnover was high and productivity was again average.

The operation of the third group of supervisors was relatively unmechanized. These leaders stayed on the job with their men, provided training, gave instructions and explanations, and in addition, set a specific production goal for the day or week. Not only was the crew's productivity high, but their injury rate was well below average.

Two conclusions were discussed with the managers of the companies sponsoring this study. First, mechanization alone will not increase the productivity of logging crews. Just as the average tax payer would probably commit more mathematical errors if he were to try to use a computer to complete his income tax return, the average logger misuses, and frequently abuses, the equipment he purchases (for example, drives a skidder with two flat tires, doesn't change the oil filter). This increases not only the logger's downtime, but also his costs which, in turn, can force him out of business. The second conclusion of the survey was that setting a specific production goal combined with supervisory presence to ensure goal commitment will bring about a significant increase in productivity.

These conclusions were greeted with the standard, but valid, cliché, "Statistics don't prove causation." And our comments regarding the value of machinery were especially irritating to these managers, many of whom had received degrees in engineering. So one of the companies decided to replicate the survey in order to check our findings.

The company's study placed each of 892 independent logging supervisors who sold wood to the company into one of three categories of supervisory styles our survey had identified—namely, (1) stays on the job but does not set specific production goals; (2) sets specific production goals but does not stay on the job; and (3) stays on the job and sets specific production goals. Once again, goal setting, in combination with the on-site presence of a supervisor, was shown to be the key to improved productivity.

TESTING FOR THE HAWTHORNE EFFECT

Management may have been unfamiliar with different theories of motivation, but it was fully aware of one label—the Hawthorne effect. Managers in these wood products companies remained unconvinced that anything so simple as staying on the job with the men and setting a specific production goal could have an appreciable effect on productivity. They pointed out that the results simply reflected the positive effects any supervisor would have on the work unit after giving his crew attention. And they were unimpressed by the laboratory experiments we cited—experiments showing that individuals who have a specific goal solve more arithmetic problems or assemble more tinker toys than do people who are told to "do your best." Skepticism prevailed.

But the country's economic picture made it critical to continue the study of inexpensive techniques to improve employee motivation and productivity. We were granted permission to run one more project to test the effectiveness of goal setting.

Twenty independent logging crews who were all but identical in size, mechanization level, terrain on which they worked, productivity, and attendance were located. The logging supervisors of these crews were in the habit of staying on the job with their men, but they did not set production goals. Half the crews were randomly selected to receive training in goal setting; the remaining crews served as a control group.

The logging supervisors who were to set goals were told that we had found a way to increase productivity at no financial expense to anyone. We gave the ten supervisors in the training group production tables developed through time-and-motion

studies by the company's engineers. These tables made it possible to determine how much wood should be harvested in a given number of man hours. They were asked to use these tables as a guide in determining a specific production goal to assign their employees. In addition, each sawhand was given a tallymeter (counter) that he could wear on his belt. The sawhand was asked to punch the counter each time he felled a tree. Finally, permission was requested to measure the crew's performance on a weekly basis.

The ten supervisors in the control group—those who were not asked to set production goals—were told that the researchers were interested in learning the extent to which productivity is affected by absenteeism and injuries. They were urged to "do your best" to maximize the crew's productivity and attendance and to minimize injuries. It was explained that the data might be useful in finding ways to increase productivity at little or no cost to the wood harvester.

To control for the Hawthorne effect, we made an equal number of visits to the control group and the training group. Performance was measured for 12 weeks. During this time, the productivity of the goal-setting group was significantly higher than that of the control group. Moreover, absenteeism was significantly lower in the groups that set goals than in the groups who were simply urged to do their best. Injury and turnover rates were low in both groups.

Why should anything so simple and inexpensive as goal setting influence the work of these employees so significantly? Anecdotal evidence from conversations with both the loggers and the company foresters who visited them suggested several reasons.

Harvesting timber can be a monotonous, tiring job with little or no meaning for most workers. Introducing a goal that is difficult, but attainable, increases the challenge of the job. In addition, a specific goal makes it clear to the worker what it is he is expected to do. Goal feedback via the tallymeter and weekly recordkeeping provide the worker with a sense of achievement, recognition, and accomplishment. He can see how well he is doing now as against his past performance and, in some cases, how well he is doing in comparison with others. Thus the worker not only may expend greater effort, but may also devise better or more creative tactics for attaining the goal than those he previously used.

NEW APPLICATIONS

Management was finally convinced that goal setting was an effective motivational technique for increasing the productivity of the independent woods worker in the South. The issue now raised by the management of another wood products company was whether the procedure could be used in the West with company logging operations in which the employees were unionized and paid by the hour. The previous study had involved employees on a piecerate system, which was the practice in the South.

The immediate problem confronting this company involved the loading of logging trucks. If the trucks were underloaded, the company lost money. If the trucks were overloaded, however, the driver could be fined by the Highway Department and could ultimately lose his job. The drivers opted for underloading the trucks.

For three months management tried to solve this problem by urging the drivers to try harder to fill the truck to its legal net weight, and by developing weighing scales that could be attached to the truck. But this approach did not prove cost effective, because the scales continually broke down when subjected to the rough terrain on which the trucks traveled. Consequently, the drivers reverted to their former practice of underloading. For the three months in which the problem was under study the trucks were seldom loaded in excess of 58 to 63 percent of capacity.

At the end of the three-month period, the results of the previous goal-setting experiments were explained to the union. They were told three things— that the company would like to set a specific net weight goal for the drivers, that no monetary reward or fringe benefits other than verbal praise could be expected for improved performance, and that no one would be criticized for failing to attain the goal. Once again, the idea that simply setting a specific goal would solve a production problem seemed too incredible to be taken seriously by the union. However, they reached an agreement that a difficult, but attainable, goal of 94 percent of the truck's legal net weight would be assigned to the drivers, provided that no one could be reprimanded for failing to attain the goal. This latter point was emphasized to the company foremen in particular.

Within the first month, performance increased to 80 percent of the truck's net weight. After the second month, however, performance decreased to 70 percent. Interviews with the drivers indicated that they were testing management's statement that no punitive steps would be taken against them if their performance suddenly dropped. Fortunately for all concerned, no such steps were taken by the foremen, and performance exceeded 90 percent of the truck's capacity after the third month. Their performance has remained at this level to this day, seven years later.

The results over the nine-month period during which this study was conducted saved the company $250,000. This figure, determined by the company's accountants, is based on the cost of additional trucks that would have been required to deliver the same quantity of logs to the mill if goal setting had not been implemented. The dollars-saved figure is even higher when you factor in the cost of the additional diesel fuel that would have been consumed and the expenses incurred in recruiting and hiring the additional truck drivers.

Why could this procedure work without the union's demanding an increase in hourly wages? First, the drivers did not feel that they were really doing anything differently. This, of course, was not true. As a result of goal setting, the men began to record their truck weight in a pocket notebook, and they found themselves bragging about their accomplishments to their peers. Second, they viewed goal setting as a challenging game: "It was great to beat the other guy."

Competition was a crucial factor in bringing about goal acceptance and commitment in this study. However, we can reject the hypothesis that improved performance resulted solely from competition, because no special prizes or formal recognition programs were provided for those who came closest to, or exceeded, the goal. No effort was made by the company to single out one "winner." More important, the opportunity for competition among drivers had existed before goal setting was instituted; after all, each driver knew his own truck's weight, and the truck weight of each of the 36 other drivers every time he hauled wood into the yard. In short, competition affected productivity only in the sense that it led to the acceptance of, and commitment to, the goal. It was the setting of the goal itself and the working toward it that brought about increased performance and decreased costs.

PARTICIPATIVE GOAL SETTING

The inevitable question always raised by management was raised here: "We know goal setting works. How can we make it work better?" Was there one best method for setting goals? Evidence for a "one best way" approach was cited by several managers, but it was finally concluded that different approaches would work best under different circumstances.

It was hypothesized that the woods workers in the South, who had little or no education, would work better with assigned goals, while the educated workers in the West would achieve higher productivity if they were allowed to help set the goals themselves. Why the focus on education? Many of the uneducated workers in the South could be classified as culturally disadvantaged. Such persons often lack self-confidence, have a poor sense of time, and are not very competitive. The cycle of skill mastery, which in turn guarantees skill levels high enough to prevent discouragement, doesn't apply to these employees. If, for example, these people were allowed to participate in goal setting, the goals might be too difficult or they might be too easy. On the other hand, participation for the educated worker was considered critical in effecting maximum goal acceptance. Since these conclusions appeared logical, management initially decided that no research was necessary. This decision led to hours of further discussion.

The same questions were raised again and again by the researchers. What if the logic were wrong? Can we afford to implement these decisions without evaluating them systematically? Would we implement decisions regarding a new approach to tree planting without first testing it? Do we care more about trees than we do about people? Finally, permission was granted to conduct an experiment.

Logging crews were randomly appointed to either participative goal setting, assigned (non-participative) goal setting, or a do-your-best condition. The results were startling. The uneducated crews, consisting primarily of black employees who participated in goal setting, set significantly higher goals and attained them more often than did those whose goals were assigned by their supervisor. Not surprisingly, their performance was higher. Crews with assigned goals performed no better than did those who were urged to do their best to improve their productivity. The performance of white, educationally advantaged workers was higher with assigned rather than participatively set goals, although the difference was not statistically significant. These results were precisely the opposite of what had been predicted.

Another study comparing participative and assigned goals was conducted with typists. The results supported findings obtained by researchers at General Electric years before. It did not matter so much *how* the goal was set. What mattered was *that* a goal was set. The study demonstrated that both assigned and participatively set goals led to substantial improvements in typing speed. The process by which these gains occurred, however, differed in the two groups.

In the participative group, employees insisted on setting very high goals regardless of whether they had attained their goal the previous week. Nevertheless, their productivity improved—an outcome consistent with the theory that high goals lead to high performance.

In the assigned-goal group, supervisors were highly supportive of employees. No criticism was given for failure to attain the goals. Instead, the supervisor lowered the goal after failure so that the

TABLE 3.1
Representative Field Studies of Goal Setting

Researcher(s)	Task	Duration of Study or of Significant Effects	Percent of Change in Performance*
Blumenfeld and Leidy	Servicing soft drink coolers	Unspecified	+27
Dockstader	Keypunching	3 mos.	+27
Ivancevich	Skilled technical jobs	9 mos.	+15
Ivancevich	Sales	9 mos.	+24
Kim and Hamner	Five telephone service jobs	3 mos.	+13
Latham and Baldes	Loading trucks	9 mos.†	+26
Latham and Yukl	Logging	2 mos.	+18
Latham and Yukl	Typing	5 weeks	+11
Migliore	Mass production	2 years	+16
Umstot, Bell, and Mitchell	Coding land parcels	1–2 days‡	+16

*Percentage of changes were obtained by subtracting pre-goal-setting performance from post-goal-setting performance and dividing by pre-goal setting performance. Differenct experiemental groups were combined where appropriate. If a control group was available, the percentage figure represents the difference of the percentage changes between the experimental and control groups. If multiple performance measures were used, the median improvement on all measures was used. The authors would like to thank Dena Feren and Vicki McCaleb for performing these calculations.

†Performance remained high for seven years.

‡Simulated organization.

employee would be certain to attain it. The goal was then raised gradually each week until the supervisor felt the employee was achieving his or her potential. The result? Feelings of accomplishment and achievement on the part of the worker and improved productivity for the company.

These basic findings were replicated in a subsequent study of engineers and scientists. Participative goal setting was superior to assigned goal setting only to the degree that it led to the setting of higher goals. Both participative and assigned-goal groups outperformed groups that were simply told to "do your best."

An additional experiment was conducted to validate the conclusion that participation in goal setting may be important only to the extent that it leads to the setting of difficult goals. It was performed in a laboratory setting in which the task was to brainstorm uses of wood. One group was asked to "do your best" to think of as many ideas as possible. A second group took part in deciding, with the experimenter, the specific number of ideas each person would generate. These goals were, in turn, assigned to individuals in a third group. In this way, goal difficulty was held constant between the assigned-goal and participative groups. Again, it was found that specific, difficult goals—whether assigned or set through participation—led to higher performance than did an abstract or generalized goal such as "do your best." And, when goal difficulty was held constant, there was no significant difference in the performance of those with assigned as compared with participatively set goals.

These results demonstrate that goal setting in industry works just as it does in the laboratory. Specific, challenging goals lead to better performance than do easy or vague goals, and feedback motivates higher performance only when it leads to the setting of higher goals.

It is important to note that participation is not only a motivational tool. When a manager has competent subordinates, participation is also a useful device for increasing the manager's knowledge and thereby improving decision quality. It can lead to better decisions through input from subordinates.

A representative sample of the results of field studies of goal setting conducted by Latham and others is shown in Table 3.1. Each of these ten studies compared the performance of employees given specific challenging goals with those given "do best" or no goals. Note that goal setting has been successful across a wide variety of jobs and industries. The effects of goal setting have been recorded for as long as seven years after the onset of the program, although the results of most studies have been followed up for only a few weeks or months. The median improvement in performance in the ten studies shown in Table 3.1 was 17 percent.

A CRITICAL INCIDENTS SURVEY

To explore further the importance of goal setting in the work setting, Dr. Frank White conducted another study in two plants of a high-technology, multinational corporation on the East Coast. Seventy-one engineers, 50 managers, and 31 clerks were asked to describe a specific instance when they were especially productive and a specific instance when they were especially unproductive on their present jobs. Responses were classified according to a reliable coding scheme. Of primary interest here are the external events perceived by employees as being responsible for the high-productivity and low-productivity incidents. The results are shown in Table 3.2.

The first set of events—pursuing a specific goal, having a large amount of work, working under a deadline, or having an uninterrupted routine—accounted for more than half the high-productivity events. Similarly, the converse of these—goal blockage, having a small amount of work, lacking a deadline, and suffering work in-terruptions—accounted for nearly 60 percent of the low-productivity events. Note that the first set of four categories are all relevant to goal setting and the second set to a lack of goals or goal blockage. The goal category itself—that of pursuing an attainable goal or goal blockage—was the one most frequently used to describe high- and low-productivity incidents.

The next four categories, which are more pertinent to Frederick Herzberg's motivator-hygiene theory—task interest, responsibility, promotion, and recognition—are less important, accounting for 36.8 percent of the high-productivity incidents (the opposite of these four categories accounted for 19.1 percent of the lows). The remaining categories were even less important.

Employees were also asked to identify the responsible agent behind the events that had led to high and low productivity. In both cases, the employees themselves, their immediate supervisors, and the organization were the agents most frequently mentioned.

The concept of goal setting is a very simple one. Interestingly, however, we have gotten two contradictory types of reaction when the idea was introduced to managers. Some claimed it was so simple and self-evident that everyone, including themselves, already used it. This, we have found, is not true. Time after time we have gotten the following response from subordinates after goal setting was introduced: "This is the first time I knew what my supervisor expected of me on this job." Conversely, other managers have argued that the idea would not work, precisely *because* it is so simple (implying that something more radical and complex was needed). Again, results proved them wrong.

But these successes should not mislead managers into thinking that goal setting can be used without careful planning and forethought. Research and experience suggest that the best results are obtained when the following steps are followed

Setting the Goal. The goal set should have two main characteristics. First, it should be specific rather than vague: "Increase sales by 10 percent" rather than "Try

TABLE 3.2
Events Perceived as Causing High and Low Productivity*

	Percentage of Times Event Caused	
Event	High Productivity	Low Productivity
Goal pursuit/Goal blockage	17.1	23.0
Large amount of work/Small amount of work	12.5	19.0
Deadline or schedule/No deadline	15.1	3.3
Smooth work routine/Interrupted routine	5.9	14.5
Intrinsic/Extrinsic factors	50.6	59.8
Interesting task/Uninteresting task	17.1	11.2
Increased responsibility/Decreased responsibility	13.8	4.6
Anticipated promotion/Promotion denied	1.3	0.7
Verbal recognition/Criticism	4.6	2.6
People/Company conditions	36.8	19.1
Pleasant personal relationships/Unpleasant personal relationships	10.5	9.9
Anticipated pay increase/Pay increase denied	1.3	1.3
Pleasant working conditions/Unpleasant working conditions	0.7	0.7
Other (miscellaneous)	–	9.3

*N = 152 in this study by Frank White.

to improve sales." Whenever possible, there should be a time limit for goal accomplishment: "Cut costs by 3 percent in the next six months."

Second, the goal should be challenging yet reachable. If accepted, difficult goals lead to better performance than do easy goals. In contrast, if the goals are perceived as unreachable, employees will not accept them. Nor will employees get a sense of achievement from pursuing goals that are never attained. Employees with low self-confidence or ability should be given more easily attainable goals than those with high self-confidence and ability.

There are at least five possible sources of input, aside from the individual's self-confidence and ability, that can be used to determine the particular goal to set for a given individual.

The scientific management approach pioneered by Frederick W. Taylor uses time and motion study to determine a fair day's work. This is probably the most objective technique available, but it can be used only where the task is reasonably repetitive and standardized. Another drawback is that this method often leads to employee resistance, espe-cially in cases where the new standard is substantially higher than previous performance and where rate changes are made frequently.

More readily accepted, although less scientific than time and motion study, are standards based on the average past performance of employees. This method was used successfully in some of our field studies. Most employees consider this approach fair but, naturally, in cases where past performance is far below capacity, beating that standard will be extremely easy.

Since goal setting is sometimes simply a matter of judgment, another technique we have used is to allow the goal to be set jointly by supervisor and subordinate. The participative approach may be less scientific than time and motion study, but it does lead to ready acceptance by both employee and immediate superior in addition to promoting role clarity.

External constraints often affect goal setting, especially among managers. For example, the goal to produce an item at a certain price may be dictated by the actions of competitors, and deadlines may be imposed externally in line with contract agreements. Legal regulations, such as attaining a certain reduction in pollution levels by a certain date, may affect goal setting as well. In these cases, setting the goal is not so much the problem as is figuring out a method of reaching it.

Finally, organizational goals set by the board of directors or upper management will influence the goals set by employees at lower levels. This is the essence of the MBO process.

Another issue that needs to be considered when setting goals is whether they should be designed for individuals or for groups. Rensis Likert and a number of other human relations experts argue for group goal setting on grounds that it promotes cooperation and team spirit. But one could argue that individual goals better promote individual responsibility and make it easier to appraise individual performance. The degree of task interdependence involved would also be a factor to consider.

Obtaining Goal Commitment. If goal setting is to work, then the manager must ensure that subordinates will accept and remain committed to the goals. Simple instruction backed by positive support and an absence of threats or intimidation were enough to ensure goal acceptance in most of our studies. Subordinates must perceive the goals as fair and reasonable and they must trust management, for if they perceive the goals as no more than a means of exploitation, they will be likely to reject the goals.

It may seem surprising that goal acceptance was achieved so readily in the field studies. Remember, however, that in all cases the employees were receiving wages or a salary (although these were not necessarily directly contingent on goal attainment). Pay in combination with the supervisor's benevolent authority and supportiveness were sufficient to bring about goal acceptance. Recent research indicates that whether goals are assigned or set participatively, supportiveness on the part of the immediate superior is critical. A supportive manager or supervisor does not use goals to threaten subordinates, but rather to clarify what is expected of them. His or her role is that of a helper and goal facilitator.

As noted earlier, the employee gets a feeling of pride and satisfaction from the experience of reaching a challenging but fair performance goal. Success in reaching a goal also tends to reinforce acceptance of future goals. Once goal setting is introduced, informal competition frequently arises among the employees. This further reinforces commitment and may lead employees to raise the goals spontaneously. A word of caution here, however: We do not recommend setting up formal competition, as this may lead employees to place individual goals ahead of company goals. The emphasis should be on accomplishing the task, getting the job done, not "beating" the other person.

When employees resist assigned goals, they generally do so for one of two reasons. First, they may think they are incapable of reaching the goal because they lack confidence, ability, knowledge, and the like. Second, they may not see any personal benefit—either in terms of personal pride or in terms of external rewards like money, promotion, recognition—in reaching assigned goals.

There are various methods of overcoming employee resistance to goals. One possibility is more training designed to raise the employee's level of skill and self-confidence. Allowing the subordinate to participate in setting the goal—deciding on the goal level—is another method. This was found most effective among uneducated and minority group employees, perhaps because it gave them a feeling of control over their fate. Offering monetary bonuses or other rewards (recognition, time off) for reaching goals may also help.

The last two methods may be especially useful where there is a history of labor-management conflict and where employees have become accustomed to a lower level of effort than currently considered acceptable. Group incentives may also encourage goal acceptance, especially where there is a group goal, or when considerable cooperation is required.

Providing Support Elements. A third step to take when introducing goal setting is to ensure the availability of necessary support elements. That is, the employee

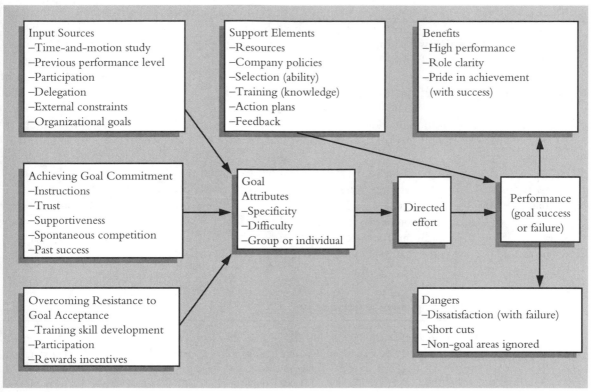

FIGURE 3.1   Goal-Setting Model.

must be given adequate resources—money, equipment, time, help—as well as the freedom to utilize them in attaining goals, and company policies must not work to block goal attainment.

Before turning an employee loose with these resources, however, it's wise to do a quick check on whether conditions are optimum for reaching the goal set. First, the supervisor must make sure that the employee has sufficient ability and knowledge to be able to reach the goal. Motivation without knowledge is useless. This, of course, puts a premium on proper selection and training and requires that the supervisor know the capabilities of subordinates when goals are assigned. Asking an employee to formulate an action plan for reaching the goal, as in MBO, is very useful, as it will indicate any knowledge deficiencies.

Second, the supervisor must ensure that the employee is provided with precise feedback to that he will know to what degree he's reaching or falling short of his goal and can thereupon adjust his level of effort or strategy accordingly. Recent research indicates that, while feedback is not a sufficient condition for improved performance, it is a necessary condition. A useful way to present periodic feedback is through the use of charts or graphs that plot performance over time.

Elements involved in taking the three steps described are shown in Figure 3.1, which illustrates in outline form our model of goal setting.

CONCLUSION

We believe that goal setting is a simple, straightforward, and highly effective technique for motivating employee performance. It is a basic technique, a method on which most other methods depend for their motivational effectiveness. The currently popular technique of behavior modification, for example, is mainly goal setting plus feedback, dressed up in academic terminology.

However, goal setting is no panacea. It will not compensate for underpayment of employees or for poor management. Used incorrectly, goal setting may cause rather than solve problems. If, for example, the goals set are unfair, arbitrary, or unreachable, dissatisfaction and poor performance may result. If difficult goals are set without proper quality controls, quantity may be achieved at the expense of quality. If pressure for immediate results is exerted without regard to how they are attained, short-term improvement may occur at the expense of long-run profits. That is, such pressure often triggers the use of expedient and ultimately costly methods—such as dishonesty, high-pressure tactics, postponing of maintenance expenses, and so on—to attain immediate results. Furthermore, performance goals are more easily set in some areas than in others. It's all too easy, for example, to concentrate on setting readily measured production goals and ignore employee development goals. Like any other management tool, goal setting works only when combined with good managerial judgment.

SELECTED BIBLIOGRAPHY

A summary of the early (mainly laboratory) research on goal setting may be found in E. A. Locke's "Toward a Theory of Task Motivation and Incentives" (*Organization Behavior and Human Performance*, May 1968). More recent reviews that include some of the early field studies are reported by G. P. Latham and G. A. Yukl's "Review of Research on the Application of Goal Setting in Organizations" (*Academy of Management Journal*, December 1975) and in R. M. Steers and L. W. Porter's "The Role of Task-Goal Attributes in Employee Performance" (*Psychological Bulletin*, July 1974).

An excellent historical discussion of management by objectives, including its relationship to goal-setting research, can be found in G. S. Odiorne's "MBO: A Backward Glance" (*Business Horizons*, October 1978).

A thorough review of the literature on participation, including the relationship of participation and goal setting, can be found in a chapter by E. A. Locke and D. M. Schweiger, "Participation in Decision-Making: One More Look," in B. M. Staw's edited work, *Research in Organizational Behavior* (Vol. 1, Greenwich, JAI Press, 1979). General Electric's famous research on the effect of participation in the appraisal interview is summarized in H. H. Meyer, E. Kay, and J. R. P. French, Jr.'s "Split Roles in Performance Appraisal" (*Harvard Business Review*, January-February 1965).

The relationship of goal setting to knowledge of results is discussed in E. A. Locke, N. Cartledge, and J. Koeppel's "Motivational Effects of Knowledge of Results: A Goal Setting Phenomenon?" (*Psychological Bulletin*, December 1968) and L. J. Becker's "Joint Effect of Feedback and Goal Setting on Performance: A Field Study of Residential Energy Conservation" (*Journal of Applied Psychology*, August 1978). Finally, the role of goal setting in virtually all theories of work motivation is documented in E. A. Locke's "The Ubiquity of the Technique of Goal Setting in Theories of and Approaches to Employee Motivation" (*Academy of Management Review*, July 1978).

4.   ON THE FOLLY OF REWARDING A, WHILE HOPING FOR B

Steven Kerr

Whether dealing with monkeys, rats, or human beings, it is hardly controversial to state that most organisms seek information concerning what activities are rewarded and then seek to do (or at least pretend to do) those things, often to the virtual exclusion of activities not rewarded. The extent to which this occurs of course will depend on the perceived attractiveness of the rewards offered, but neither operant nor expectancy theorists would quarrel with the essence of this notion.

Nevertheless, numerous examples exist of reward systems that are fouled up in that behaviors which are rewarded are those which the rewarder is trying to discourage, while the behavior he desires is not being rewarded at all.

In an effort to understand and explain this phenomenon, this paper presents examples from society, from organizations in general, and from profit-making firms in particular. Data from a manufacturing company and information from an insurance firm are examined to demonstrate the consequences of such reward systems for the organizations involved, and possible reasons why such reward systems continue to exist are considered.

SOCIETAL EXAMPLES

Politics

Official goals are "purposely vague and general and do not indicate . . . the host of decisions that must be made among alternative ways of achieving official goals and the priority of multiple goals . . ." (8, p. 66). They usually may be relied on to offend absolutely no one, and in this sense can be considered high-acceptance, low-quality goals. An example might be "build better schools." Operative goals are higher in quality but lower in acceptance, since they specify where the money will come from, what alternative goals will be ignored, etc.

The American citizenry supposedly wants its candidates for public office to set forth operative goals, making their proposed programs "perfectly clear," specifying sources and uses of funds, etc. However, since operative goals are lower in acceptance, and since aspirants to public office need acceptance (from at least 50.1 percent of the people), most politicians prefer to speak only of official goals, at least until after the election. They of course would agree to speak at the operative level if "punished" for not doing so. The electorate could do this by refusing to support candidates who do not speak at the operative level.

Instead, however, the American voter typically punishes (withholds support from) candidates who frankly discuss where the money will come from, rewards politicians who speak only of official goals, but hopes that candidates (despite the reward system) will discuss the issues operatively. It is academic whether it was moral for Nixon, for example, to refuse to discuss his 1968 "secret plan" to end the Vietnam war, his 1972 operative goals concerning the lifting of price controls, the reshuffling of his cabinet, etc. The point is that the reward system made such refusal rational.

It seems worth mentioning that no manuscript can adequately define what is "moral" and what is not. However, examination of costs and benefits,

"On the Folly of Rewarding A, While Hoping for B" by Steven Kerr from *Academy of Management Journal*, 1975, 18, No. 4:769–83. Reprinted with permission.

combined with knowledge of what motivates a particular individual, often will suffice to determine what for him is "rational."[1] If the reward system is so designed that it is irrational to be moral, this does not necessarily mean that immorality will result. But is this not asking for trouble?

War

If some oversimplification may be permitted, let it be assumed that the primary goal of the organization (Pentagon, Luftwaffe, or whatever) is to win. Let it be assumed further that the primary goal of most individuals on the front lines is to get home alive. Then there appears to be an important conflict in goals—personally rational behavior by those at the bottom will endanger goal attainment by those at the top.

But not necessarily! It depends on how the reward system is set up. The Vietnam war was indeed a study of disobedience and rebellion, with terms such as "fragging" (killing one's own commanding officer) and "search and evade" becoming part of the military vocabulary. The difference in subordinates' acceptance of authority between World War II and Vietnam is reported to be considerable, and veterans of the Second World War often have been quoted as being outraged at the mutinous actions of many American soldiers in Vietnam.

Consider, however, some critical differences in the reward system in use during the two conflicts. What did the GI in World War II want? To go home. And when did he get to go home? When the war was won! If he disobeyed the orders to clean out the trenches and take the hills, the war would not be won and he would not go home. Furthermore, what were his chances of attaining his goal (getting home alive) if he obeyed the orders compared to his chances if he did not? What is being suggested is that the rational soldier in World War II, *whether patriotic or not*, probably found it expedient to obey.

Consider the reward system in use in Vietnam. What did the man at the bottom want? To go home. And when did he get to go home? When his tour of duty was over! This was the case *whether or not* the war was won. Furthermore, concerning the relative chance of getting home alive by obeying orders compared to the chance if they were disobeyed, it is worth noting that a mutineer in Vietnam was far more likely to be assigned rest and rehabilitation (on the assumption that fatigue was the cause) than he was to suffer any negative consequence.

In his description of the "zone of indifference," Barnard stated that "a person can and will accept a communication as authoritative only when . . . at the time of his decision, he believes it to be compatible with his personal interests as a whole" (1, p. 165). In light of the reward system used in Vietnam, would it not have been personally irrational for some orders to have been obeyed? Was not the military implementing a system which *rewarded* disobedience, while *hoping* that soldiers (despite the reward system) would obey orders?

Medicine

Theoretically, a physician can make either of two types of error, and intuitively one seems as bad as the other. A doctor can pronounce a patient sick when he is actually well, thus causing him needless anxiety and expense, curtailment of enjoyable foods and activities, and even physical danger by subjecting him to needless medication and surgery. Alternatively, a doctor can label a sick person well and thus avoid treating what may be a serious, even fatal ailment. It might be natural to conclude that physicians seek to minimize both types of error.

Such a conclusion would be wrong.[2] It is estimated that numerous Americans are presently afflicted with iatrogenic (physician *caused*) illnesses (9). This occurs when the doctor is approached by someone complaining of a few stray symptoms. The doctor classifies and organizes these symptoms, gives them a name, and obligingly tells the patient what further symptoms may be expected. This information often acts as a self-fulfilling prophecy, with the result that from that day on the patient for all practical purposes is sick.

Why does this happen? Why are physicians so reluctant to sustain a type 2 error (pronouncing a sick person well) that they will tolerate many type 1 errors? Again, a look at the reward system is needed. The punishments for a type 2 error are real: guilt, embarrassment, and the threat of lawsuit and scandal. On the other hand, a type 1 error (labeling a well person sick) "is sometimes seen as sound clinical practice, indicating a healthy conservative approach to medicine" (9, p. 69). Type 1 errors also are likely to generate increased income and a stream of steady customers who, being well in a limited physiological sense, will not embarrass the doctor by dying abruptly.

Fellow physicians and the general public therefore are really *rewarding* type 1 errors and at the same time *hoping* fervently that doctors will try not to make them.

GENERAL ORGANIZATIONAL EXAMPLES

Rehabilitation Centers and Orphanages

In terms of the prime beneficiary classification (2, p. 42) organizations such as these are supposed to exist for the "public-in-contact," that is, clients. The orphanage therefore theoretically is interested in placing as many children as possible in good homes. However, often orphanages surround themselves with so many rules concerning adoption that it is nearly impossible to pry a child out of the place. Orphanages may deny adoption unless the applicants are a married couple, both of the same religion as the child, without history of emotional or vocational instability, with a specified minimum income and a private room for the child, etc.

If the primary goal is to place children in good homes, then the rules ought to constitute means toward that goal. Goal displacement results when these "means become ends-in-themselves that displace the original goals" (2, p. 229).

To some extent these rules are required by law. But the influence of the reward system on the orphanage's management should not be ignored. Consider, for example, that the:

1. Number of children enrolled often is the most important determinant of the size of the allocated budget.

2. Number of children under the director's care also will affect the size of his staff.

3. Total organizational size will determine largely the director's prestige at the annual conventions, in the community, etc.

Therefore, to the extent that staff size, total budget, and personal prestige are valued by the orphanage's executive personnel, it becomes rational for them to make it difficult for children to be adopted. After all, who wants to be the director of the smallest orphanage in the state?

If the reward system errs in the opposite direction, paying off only for placements, extensive goal displacement again is likely to result. A common example of vocational rehabilitation in many states, for example, consists of placing someone in a job for which he has little interest and few qualifications, for two months or so, and then "rehabilitating" him again in another position. Such behavior is quite consistent with the prevailing reward system, which pays off for the number of individuals placed in any position for 60 days or more. Rehabilitation counselors also confess to competing with one another to place relatively skilled clients, sometimes ignoring persons with few skills who would be harder to place. Extensively disabled clients find that counselors often prefer to work with those whose disabilities are less severe.[3]

Universities

Society *hopes* that teachers will not neglect their teaching responsibilities but *rewards* them almost entirely for research and publications. This is most true at the large and prestigious universities. Clichés such as "good research and good teaching go together" notwithstanding, professors often find that they must choose between teaching and research oriented activities when allocating their time. Rewards for good teaching usually are limited to outstanding teacher awards, which are given to only a small percentage of good teachers and which usually bestow little money and fleeting prestige. Punishments for poor teaching also are rare.

Rewards for research and publications, on the other hand, and punishments for failure to accomplish these, are commonly administered by universities at which teachers are employed. Furthermore, publication oriented resumés usually will be well received at other universities, whereas teaching credentials, harder to document and quantify, are much less transferable. Consequently, it is rational for university teachers to concentrate on research, even if to the detriment of teaching and at the expense of their students.

By the same token, it is rational for students to act based upon the goal displacement which has occurred within universities concerning what they are rewarded for. If it is assumed that a primary goal of a university is to transfer knowledge from teacher to student, then grades become identifiable as a means toward that goal, serving as motivational, control, and feedback devices to expedite the knowledge transfer. Instead, however, the grades themselves have become much more important for entrance to graduate school, successful employment, tuition refunds, parental respect, etc., than the knowledge or lack of knowledge they are supposed to signify.

It therefore should come as no surprise that information has surfaced in recent years concerning fraternity files for examinations, term paper writing services, organized cheating at the service academies, and the like. Such activities constitute a personally rational response to a reward system which pays off for grades rather than knowledge.

BUSINESS RELATED EXAMPLES

Ecology

Assume that the president of XYZ Corporation is confronted with the following alternatives:

1. Spend $11 million for antipollution equipment to keep from poisoning fish in the river adjacent to the plant; or

2. Do nothing, in violation of the law, and assume a one-in-ten chance of being caught, with a resultant $1 million fine plus the necessity of buying the equipment.

Under this not unrealistic set of choices it requires no linear program to determine that XYZ Corporation can maximize its probabilities by flouting the law. Add the fact that XYZ's president is probably being rewarded (by creditors, stockholders, and other salient parts of his task environment) according to criteria totally unrelated to the number of fish poisoned, and his probable course of action becomes clear.

Evaluation of Training

It is axiomatic that those who care about a firm's well-being should insist that the organization get fair value for its expenditures. Yet it is commonly known that firms seldom bother to evaluate a new GRID, MBO, job enrichment program, or whatever, to see if the company is getting its money's worth. Why? Certainly it is not because people have not pointed out that this situation exists; numerous practitioner oriented articles are written each year to just this point.

The individuals (whether in personnel, manpower planning, or wherever) who normally would be responsible for conducting such evaluations are the same ones often charged with introducing the change effort in the first place. Having convinced top management to spend the money, they usually are quite animated afterwards in collecting arigorous vignettes and anecdotes about how successful the program was. The last thing many desire is a formal, systematic, and revealing evaluation. Although members of top management may actually *hope* for such systematic evaluation, their reward systems continue to *reward* ignorance in this area. And if the personnel department abdicates its responsibility, who is to step into the breach? The change agent himself? Hardly! He is likely to be too busy collecting anecdotal "evidence" of his own, for use with his next client.

Miscellaneous

Many additional examples could be cited of systems which in fact are rewarding behaviors other than those supposedly desired by the rewarder. A few of these are described briefly below.

Most coaches disdain to discuss individual accomplishments, preferring to speak of teamwork, proper attitude, and a one-for-all spirit. Usually, however, rewards are distributed according to individual performance. The college basketball player who feeds his teammates instead of shooting will not compile impressive scoring statistics and is less likely to be drafted by the pros. The ballplayer who hits to right field to advance the runners will win neither the batting nor home run titles and will be offered smaller raises. It therefore is rational for players to think of themselves first and the team second.

In business organizations where rewards are dispensed for unit performance or for individual goals achieved without regard for overall effectiveness, similar attitudes often are observed. Under most Management by Objectives (MBO) systems, goals in areas where quantification is difficult often go unspecified. The organization therefore often is in a position where it *hopes* for employee effort in the areas of team building, interpersonal relations, creativity, etc., but it formally *rewards* none of these. In cases where promotions and raises are formally tied to MBO, the system itself contains a paradox in that it "asks employees to set challenging, risky goals, only to face smaller paychecks and possibly damaged careers if these goals are not accomplished" (5, p. 40).

It is *hoped* that administrators will pay attention to long-run costs and opportunities and will institute programs which will bear fruit later on. However, many organizational reward systems pay off for short-run sales and earnings only. Under such circumstances it is personally rational for officials to sacrifice long-term growth and profit (by selling off equipment and property, or by stifling research and development) for short-term advantages. This probably is most pertinent in the public sector, with the result that many public officials are unwilling to implement programs which will not show benefits by election time.

As a final, clear-cut example of a fouled-up reward system, consider the cost-plus contract or its next of kin, the allocation of next year's budget as a direct function of this year's expenditures. It probably is conceivable that those who award such budgets and contracts really hope for economy and prudence in spending. It is obvious, however, that adopting the proverb "to him who spends shall more be given," rewards not economy, but spending itself.

TWO COMPANIES' EXPERIENCES

A Manufacturing Organization

A Midwestern manufacturer of industrial goods had been troubled for some time by aspects of its organizational climate it believed dysfunctional. For research purposes, interviews were conducted with many employees, and a questionnaire was administered on a companywide basis, including plants and offices in several American and Canadian locations. The company strongly encouraged employee participation in the survey and made available time and space during the workday for completion of the instrument. All employees in attendance during the day of the survey completed the questionnaire. All instruments were collected directly by the researcher, who personally administered each session. Since no one employed by the firm handled the questionnaires, and since respondent names were not asked for, it seems likely that the pledge of anonymity given was believed.

A modified version of the Expect Approval scale (7) was included as part of the questionnaire. The instrument asked respondents to indicate the degree of approval or disapproval they could expect if they performed each of the described actions. A seven point Likert scale was used, with one indicating that the action would probably bring strong disapproval and seven signifying likely strong approval.

Although normative data for this scale from studies of other organizations are unavailable, it is

TABLE 4.1

Summary of Two Divisions' Data Relevant to Conforming and Risk-Avoidance Behaviors
(extent to which subjects expect approval)

Dimension	Item	Division and Sample	Total Responses	1, 2, or 3 Disapproval	4	5, 6, or 7 Approval
				Percentage of Workers Responding		
Risk avoidance	Making a risky decision based	A, levels 1–4 (lowest)	127	61	25	14
	on the best	A, levels 5–8	172	46	31	23
	information	A, levels 9, and above	17	41	30	30
	available at					
	the time, but	B, levels 1–4 (lowest)	31	58	26	16
	which turns	B, levels 5–8	19	42	42	16
	out wrong	B, levels 9 and above	10	50	20	30
	Setting extreme-	A, levels 1–4	122	47	28	25
	ly high and	A, levels 5–8	168	33	26	41
	challenging	A, levels 9+	17	24	6	70
	standards and	B, levels 1–4	31	48	23	29
	goals and then	B, levels 5–8	18	17	33	50
	narrowly failing to make them	B, levels 9+	10	30	0	70
	Setting goals	A, levels 1–4	124	35	30	35
	which are	A, levels 5–8	171	47	27	26
	extremely easy	A, levels 9+	17	70	24	6
	to make and	B, levels 1–4	31	58	26	16
	then making	B, levels 5–8	19	63	16	21
	them	B, levels 9+	10	80	0	20
Conformity	Being a "yes man"	A, levels 1–4	126	46	17	37
	and always	A, levels 5–8	180	54	14	31
	agreeing with	A, levels 9+	17	88	12	0
	the boss	B, levels 1–4	32	53	28	19
		B, levels 5–8	19	68	21	11
		B, levels 9+	10	80	10	10
	Always going	A, levels 1–4	125	40	25	35
	along with the	A, levels 5–8	173	47	21	32
	majority	A, levels 9+	17	70	12	18
		B, levels 1–4	31	61	23	16
		B, levels 5–8	19	68	11	21
		B, levels 9+	10	80	10	10
	Being careful to	A, levels 1–4	124	40	18	37
	stay on the good	A, levels 5–8	173	47	22	33
	side of everyone,	A, levels 9+	17	70	6	30
	so that everyone	B, levels 1–4	31	61	23	23
	agrees that you	B, levels 5–8	19	68	11	16
	are a great guy	B, levels 9+	10	80	10	10

possible to examine fruitfully the data obtained from this survey in several ways. First, it may be worth noting that the questionnaire data corresponded closely to information gathered through interviews. Furthermore, as can be seen from the results summarized in Table 4.1, sizable differences between various work units, and between employ-ees at different job levels within the same work unit, were obtained. This suggests that response bias effects (social desirability in particular loomed as a potential concern) are not likely to be severe.

Most importantly, comparisons between scores obtained on the Expect Approval scale and a statement of problems which were the reason for the survey revealed that the same behaviors which managers in each division thought dysfunctional were those which lower-level employees claimed were rewarded. As compared to job levels 1 to 8 in Division B (see Table 4.1), those in Division A claimed a much higher acceptance by management of "conforming" activities. Between 31 and 37 percent of Division A employees at levels 1–8 stated that going along with the majority, agreeing with the boss, and staying on everyone's good side brought approval; only once (level 5–8 responses to one of the three items) did a majority suggest that such actions would generate disapproval.

Furthermore, responses from Division A workers at levels 1–4 indicate that behaviors geared toward risk avoidance were as likely to be rewarded as to be punished. Only at job levels 9 and above was it apparent that the reward system was positively reinforcing behaviors desired by top management. Overall, the same "tendencies toward conservatism and apple-polishing at the lower levels" which divisional management had complained about during the interviews were those claimed by subordinates to be the most rational course of action in light of the existing reward system. Management apparently was not getting the behaviors it was *hoping* for, but it certainly was getting the behaviors it was perceived by subordinates to be *rewarding*.

An Insurance Firm

The Group Health Claims Division of a large eastern insurance company provides another rich illustration of a reward system which reinforces behaviors not desired by top management.

Attempting to measure and reward accuracy in paying surgical claims, the firm systematically keeps track of the number of returned checks and letters of complaint received from policyholders. However, underpayments are likely to provoke cries of outrage from the insured, while overpayments often are accepted in courteous silence. Since it often is impossible to tell from the physician's statement which of two surgical procedures, with different allowable benefits, was performed, and since writing for clarifications will interfere with other standards used by

the firm concerning "percentage of claims paid within two days of receipt," the new hire in more than one claims section is soon acquainted with the informal norm: "When in doubt, pay it out!"

The situation would be even worse were it not for the fact that other features of the firm's reward system tend to neutralize those described. For example, annual "merit" increases are given to all employees, in one of the following three amounts:

1. If the worker is "outstanding" (a select category, into which no more than two employees per section may be placed): 5 percent.

2. If the worker is "above average" (normally all workers not "outstanding" are so rated): 4 percent.

3. If the worker commits gross acts of negligence and irresponsibility for which he might be discharged in many other companies: 3 percent.

Now, since (a) the difference between the 5 percent theoretically attainable through hard work and the 4 percent attainable merely by living until the review date is small and (b) since insurance firms seldom dispense much of a salary increase in cash (rather, the worker's insurance benefits increase, causing him to be further overinsured), many employees are rather indifferent to the possibility of obtaining the extra one percent reward and therefore tend to ignore the norm concerning indiscriminate payments.

However, most employees are not indifferent to the rule which states that, should absences or latenesses total three or more in any six-month period, the entire 4 or 5 percent due at the next "merit" review must be forfeited. In this sense the firm may be described as *hoping* for performance, while *rewarding* attendance. What it gets, of course, is attendance. (If the absence-lateness rule appears to the reader to be stringent, it really is not. The company counts "times" rather than "days" absent, and a ten-day absence therefore counts the same as one lasting two days. A worker in danger of accumulating a third absence within six months merely has to remain ill (away from work) during his second absence until his first absence is more than six months old. The limiting factor is that at some point his salary ceases, and his sickness benefits take over. This usually is sufficient to get the younger workers to return, but for those with 20 or more years' service, the company provides sickness benefits of 90 percent of normal salary, tax-free! Therefore. . . .)

CAUSES

Extremely diverse instances of systems which reward behavior A although the rewarder apparently hopes for behavior B have been given. These are useful to illustrate the breadth and magnitude of the phenomenon, but the diversity increases the difficulty of determining commonalities and establishing causes. However, four general factors may be pertinent to an explanation of why fouled up reward systems seem to be so prevalent.

Fascination with an "Objective" Criterion

It has been mentioned elsewhere that:

Most "objective" measures of productivity are objective only in that their subjective elements are (a) determined in advance, rather than coming into play at the time of the formal evaluation, and (b) well concealed on the rating instrument itself. Thus industrial firms seeking to devise objective rating systems first decide, in an arbitrary manner, what dimensions are to be rated, ... usually including some items having little to do with organizational effectiveness while excluding others that do. Only then does Personnel Division churn out official-looking documents on which all dimensions chosen to be rated are assigned point values, categories, or whatever (6, p. 92).

Nonetheless, many individuals seek to establish simple, quantifiable standards against which to measure and reward performance. Such efforts may be successful in highly predictable areas within an organization but are likely to cause goal displacement when applied anywhere else. Overconcern with attendance and lateness in the insurance firm and with the number of people placed in the vocational rehabilitation division may have been largely responsible for the problems described in those organizations.

Overemphasis on Highly Visible Behaviors

Difficulties often stem from the fact that some parts of the task are highly visible while other parts are not. For example, publications are easier to demonstrate than teaching, and scoring baskets and hitting home runs are more readily observable than feeding teammates and advancing base runners. Similarly, the adverse consequences of pronouncing a sick person well are more visible than those sustained by labeling a well person sick. Team-building and creativity are other examples of behaviors which may not be rewarded simply because they are hard to observe.

Hypocrisy

In some of the instances described the rewarder may have been getting the desired behavior, notwithstanding claims that the behavior was not desired. This may be true, for example, of management's attitude toward apple-polishing in the manufacturing firm (a behavior which subordinates felt was rewarded, despite management's avowed dislike of the practice). This also may explain politicians' unwillingness to revise the penalties for disobedience of ecology laws, and the failure of top management to devise reward systems which would cause systematic evaluation of training and development programs.

Emphasis on Morality or Equity Rather than Efficiency

Sometimes consideration of other factors prevents the establishment of a system which rewards behaviors desired by the rewarder. The felt obligation of many Americans to vote for one candidate or another, for example, may impair their ability to withhold support from politicians who refuse to discuss the issues. Similarly, the concern for spreading the risks and costs of wartime military service may outweigh the advantage to be obtained by committing personnel to combat until the war is over.

It should be noted that only with respect to the first two causes are reward systems really paying off for other than desired behaviors. In the case of the third and fourth causes the system *is* rewarding behaviors desired by the rewarder, and the systems are fouled up only from the standpoints of those who believe the rewarder's public statements (cause 3), or those who seek to maximize efficiency rather than other outcomes (cause 4).

CONCLUSIONS

Modern organization theory requires a recognition that the members of organizations and society possess divergent goals and motives. It therefore is unlikely that managers and their subordinates will seek the same outcomes. Three possible remedies for this potential problem are suggested.

Selection

It is theoretically possible for organizations to employ only those individuals whose goals and motives are wholly consonant with those of management. In such cases the same behaviors judged by subordinates to be rational would be perceived by management as desirable. State-of-the-art reviews of selection techniques, however, provide scant grounds for hope that such an approach would be successful (for example, see 12).

Training

Another theoretical alternative is for the organization to admit those employees whose goals are not consonant with those of management and then, through training, socialization, or whatever, alter employee goals to make them consonant. However, research on the effectiveness of such training programs, though limited, provides further grounds for pessimism (for example, see 3).

Altering the Reward System

What would have been the result if:

1. Nixon had been assured by his advisors that he could not win reelection except by discussing the issues in detail?

2. Physicians' conduct was subjected to regular examination by review boards for type 1 errors (calling healthy people ill) and to penalties (fines, censure, etc.) for errors of either type?

3. The President of XYZ Corporation had to choose between (*a*) spending $11 million dollars for antipollution equipment, and (*b*) incurring a 50-50 chance of going to jail for five years?

Managers who complain that their workers are not motivated might do well to consider the possibility that they have installed reward systems which are paying off for behaviors other than those they are seeking. This, in part, is what happened in Vietnam, and this is what regularly frustrates societal efforts to bring about honest politicians, civic-minded managers, etc. This certainly is what happened in both the manufacturing and the insurance companies.

A first step for such managers might be to find out what behaviors currently are being rewarded. Perhaps an instrument similar to that used in the manufacturing firm could be useful for this purpose. Chances are excellent that these managers will be surprised by what they find—that their firms are not rewarding what they assume they are. In fact, such undesirable behavior by organizational members as they have observed may be explained largely by the reward systems in use.

This is not to say that all organizational behavior is determined by formal rewards and punishments. Certainly it is true that in the absence of formal reinforcement some soldiers will be patriotic, some presidents will be ecology minded, and some orphanage directors will care about children. The point, however, is that in such cases the rewarder is not *causing* the behaviors desired but is only a fortunate bystander. For an organization to *act* upon its members, the formal reward system should positively reinforce desired behaviors, not constitute an obstacle to be overcome.

It might be wise to underscore the obvious fact that there is nothing really new in what has been said. In both theory and practice these matters have been mentioned before. Thus in many states Good

Samaritan laws have been installed to protect doctors who stop to assist a stricken motorist. In states without such laws it is commonplace for doctors to refuse to stop, for fear of involvement in a subsequent lawsuit. In college basketball additional penalties have been instituted against players who foul their opponents deliberately. It has long been argued by Milton Friedman and others that penalties should be altered so as to make it irrational to disobey the ecology laws, and so on.

By altering the reward system the organization escapes the necessity of selecting only desirable people or of trying to alter undesirable ones. In Skinnerian terms (as described in 11, p. 704), "As for responsibility and goodness—as commonly defined—no one . . . would want or need them. They refer to a man's behaving well despite the absence of positive reinforcement that is obviously sufficient to explain it. Where such reinforcement exists, 'no one needs goodness.'"

REFERENCE NOTES

1. Barnard, Chester I. *The functions of the executive.* Cambridge, Mass.: Harvard University Press, 1964.

2. Blau, Peter M., and Scott, W. Richard. *Formal organizations.* San Francisco: Chandler, 1962.

3. Fiedler, Fred E. Predicting the effects of leadership training and experience from the contingency model, *Journal of Applied Psychology,* 1972, 56:114–19.

4. Garland, L. H. Studies of the accuracy of diagnostic procedures, *American Journal Roentgenological, Radium Therapy Nuclear Medicine,* 1959, 82:25–38.

5. Kerr, Steven. Some modifications in MBO as an OD strategy, *Academy of Management Proceedings,* 1973:39–42.

6. Kerr, Steven. What price objectivity? *American Sociologist,* 1973, 8:92–93.

7. Litwin, G. H., and Stringer, R. A., Jr. *Motivation and organizational climate.* Boston: Harvard University Press, 1968.

8. Perrow, Charles. The analysis of goals in complex organizations, in A. Etzioni (ed.), *Readings on modern organizations.* Englewood Cliffs, N.J.: Prentice-Hall, 1969.

9. Scheff, Thomas J. Decision rules, types of error, and their consequences in medical diagnosis, in F. Massarik and P. Ratoosh (eds.), *Mathematical explorations in behavioral science.* Homewood, Ill.: Richard D. Irwin, Inc., 1965.

10. Simon, Herbert A. *Administrative behavior.* New York: Free Press, 1957.

11. Swanson, G. E. Review symposium: Beyond freedom and dignity, *American Journal of Sociology,* 1972, 78:702–705.

12. Webster, E. *Decision making in the employment interview.* Montreal Industrial Relations Center, McGill University, 1964.

NOTES

1. In Simon's (10, pp. 76–77) terms, a decision is "subjectively rational" if it maximizes an individual's valued outcomes so far as his knowledge permits. A decision is "personally rational" if it is oriented toward the individual's goals.

2. In one study (4) of 14,867 films for signs of tuberculosis, 1,216 positive readings turned out to be clinically negative; only 24 negative readings proved clinically active, a ratio of 50 to 1.

3. Personal interviews conducted during 1972–1973.

5. A NEW STRATEGY FOR JOB ENRICHMENT

J. Richard Hackman, Greg Oldham, Robert Janson, and Kenneth Purdy

Practitioners of job enrichment have been living through a time of excitement, even euphoria. Their craft has moved from the psychology and management journals to the front page and the Sunday supplement. Job enrichment, which began with the pioneering work of Herzberg and his associates, originally was intended as a means to increase the motivation and satisfaction of people at work—and to improve productivity in the bargain.[1-5] Now it is being acclaimed in the popular press as a cure for problems ranging from inflation to drug abuse.

Much current writing about job enrichment is enthusiastic, sometimes even messianic, about what it can accomplish. But the hard questions of exactly what should be done to improve jobs, and how, tend to be glossed over. Lately, because the harder questions have not been dealt with adequately, critical winds have begun to blow. Job enrichment has been described as yet another "management fad," as "nothing new," even as a fraud. And reports of job-enrichment failures are beginning to appear in management and psychology journals.

This article attempts to redress the excesses that have characterized some of the recent writings about job enrichment. As the technique increases in popularity as a management tool, top managers inevitably will find themselves making decisions about its use. The intent of this paper is to help both managers and behavioral scientists become better able to make those decisions on a solid basis of fact and data.

Succinctly stated, we present here a new strategy for going about the redesign of work. The strategy is based on three years of collaborative work and cross-fertilization among the authors—two of whom are academic researchers and two of whom are active practitioners in job enrichment. Our approach is new, but it has been tested in many organizations. It draws on the contributions of both management practice and psychological theory, but it is firmly in the middle ground between them. It builds on and complements previous work by Herzberg and others, but provides for the first time a set of tools for *diagnosing* existing jobs—and a map for translating the diagnostic results into specific action steps for change.

What we have, then, is the following:

1. A theory that specifies when people will get personally "turned on" to their work. The theory shows what kinds of jobs are most likely to generate excitement and commitment about work, and what kinds of employees it works best for.

2. A set of action steps for job enrichment based on the theory, which prescribe in concrete terms what to do to make jobs more motivating for the people who do them.

3. Evidence that the theory holds water and that it can be used to bring about measurable—and sometimes dramatic—improvements in employee work behavior, in job satisfaction and in the financial performance of the organizational unit involved.

THE THEORY BEHIND THE STRATEGY

What Makes People Get Turned on to Their Work?

For workers who are really prospering in their jobs, work is likely to be a lot like play. Consider, for example, a golfer at a driving range, practicing to get rid of a hook. His activity is *meaningful* to him; he has chosen to do it because he gets a "kick" from testing his skills by playing the game. He knows that he alone is *responsible* for what happens when he hits the ball. And he has *knowledge of the results* within a few seconds.

Behavioral scientists have found that the three "psychological states" experienced by the golfer in

the above example also are critical in determining a person's motivation and satisfaction on the job.

1. *Experienced meaningfulness*: The individual must perceive his work as worthwhile or important by some system of values he accepts.

2. *Experienced responsibility*: He must believe that he personally is accountable for the outcomes of his efforts.

3. *Knowledge of results*: He must be able to determine, on some fairly regular basis, whether or not the outcomes of his work are satisfactory.

When these three conditions are present, a person tends to feel very good about himself when he per-

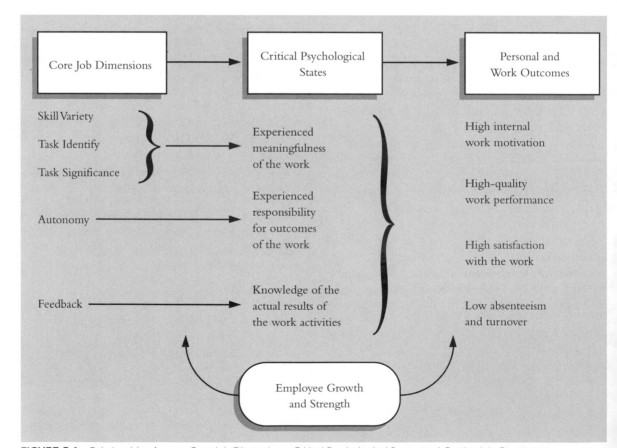

FIGURE 5.1   Relationships Among Core Job Dimensions, Critical Psychological States, and On-the-Job Outcomes.

forms well. And those good feelings will prompt him to try to continue to do well—so he can continue to earn the positive feelings in the future. That is what is meant by "internal motivation"—being turned on to one's work because of the positive internal feelings that are generated by doing well, rather than being dependent on external factors (such as incentive pay or compliments from the boss) for the motivation to work effectively.

What if one of the three psychological states is missing? Motivation drops markedly. Suppose, for example, that our golfer has settled in at the driving range to practice for a couple of hours. Suddenly a fog drifts in over the range. He can no longer see if the ball starts to tail off to the left a hundred yards out. The satisfaction he got from hitting straight down the middle—and the motivation to try to correct something whenever he didn't—are both gone. If the fog stays, it's likely that he soon will be packing up his clubs.

The relationship between the three psychological states and on-the-job outcomes is illustrated in Figure 5.1. When all three are high, then internal work motivation, job satisfaction, and work quality are high, and absenteeism and turnover are low.

What Job Characteristics Make It Happen?

Recent research has identified five "core" characteristics of jobs that elicit the psychological states described above.[6-8] These five core job dimensions provide the key to objectively measuring jobs and to changing them so that they have high potential for motivating people who do them.

Toward Meaningful Work. Three of the five core dimensions contribute to a job's meaningfulness for the worker:

1. Skill variety—the degree to which a job requires the worker to perform activities that challenge his skills and abilities. When even a single skill is involved, there is at least a seed of potential meaningfulness. When several are involved, the job has the potential of appealing to more of the whole person, and also of avoiding the monotony of performing the same task repeatedly, no matter how much skill it may require.

2. Task identity—the degree to which the job requires completion of a "whole" and identifiable piece of work—doing a job from beginning to end with a visible outcome. For example, it is clearly more meaningful to an employee to build complete toasters than to attach electrical cord after electrical cord, especially if he never sees a completed toaster. (Note that the whole job, in this example, probably would involve greater skill variety as well as task identity.)

3. Task significance—the degree to which the job has a substantial and perceivable impact on the lives of other people, whether in the immediate organization or the world at large. The worker who tightens nuts on aircraft brake assemblies is more likely to perceive his work as significant than the worker who fills small boxes with paper clips—even though the skill levels involved may be comparable.

Each of these three job dimensions represents an important route to experienced meaningfulness. If the job is high in all three, the worker is quite likely to experience his job as very meaningful. It is not necessary, however, for a job to be very high in all three dimensions. If the job is low in any one of them, there will be a drop in overall experienced meaningfulness. But even when two dimensions are low the worker may find the job meaningful if the third is high enough.

Toward Personal Responsibility. A fourth core dimension leads a worker to experience increased responsibility in his job. This is *autonomy*, the degree to which the job gives the worker freedom, independence, and discretion in scheduling work and determining how he will carry it out. People in highly autonomous jobs know that they are personally responsible for successes and failures. To the extent that their autonomy is high, then, how the work goes will be felt to depend more on the indi-

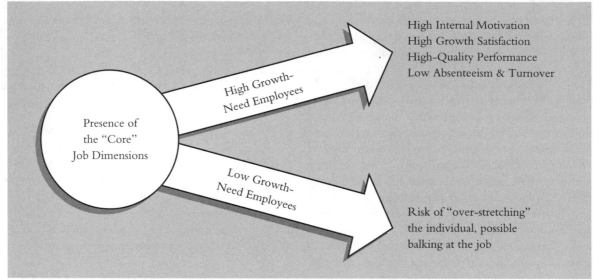

FIGURE 5.2 *The Moderating Effect of Employee Growth-Need Strength.*

vidual's own efforts and initiatives—rather than on detailed instructions from the boss or from a manual of job procedures.

Toward Knowledge of Results. The fifth and last core dimension is *feedback*. This is the degree to which a worker, in carrying out the work activities required by the job, gets information about the effectiveness of his efforts. Feedback is most powerful when it comes directly from the work itself—for example, when a worker has the responsibility for gauging and otherwise checking a component he has just finished, and learns in the process that he has lowered his reject rate by meeting specifications more consistently.

The Overall "Motivating Potential" of a Job. Figure 5.1 shows how the five core dimensions combine to affect the psychological states that are critical in determining whether or not an employee will be internally motivated to work effectively. Indeed, when using an instrument to be described later, it is possible to compute a "motivating potential score" (MPS)

for any job. The MPS provides a single summary index of the degree to which the objective characteristics of the job will prompt high internal work motivation. Following the theory outlined above, a job high in motivating potential must be high in at least one (and hopefully more) of the three dimensions that lead to experienced meaningfulness and high in both autonomy and feedback as well. The MPS provides a quantitative index of the degree to which this is in fact the case (see Appendix for detailed formula). As will be seen later, the MPS can be very useful in diagnosing jobs and in assessing the effectiveness of job-enrichment activities.

Does the Theory Work for Everybody?

Unfortunately not. Not everyone is able to become internally motivated in his work, even when the motivating potential of a job is very high indeed.

Research has shown that the *psychological needs* of people are very important in determining who can (and who cannot) become internally motivated at work. Some people have strong needs for personal accomplishment, for learning and developing themselves beyond where they are now, for being stimulated and challenged, and so on. These people are high in "growth-need strength."

Figure 5.2 shows diagrammatically the proposition that individual growth needs have the power to moderate the relationship between the characteristics of jobs and work outcomes. Many workers with high growth needs will turn on eagerly when they have jobs that are high in the core dimensions. Workers whose growth needs are not so strong may respond less eagerly—or, at first, even balk at being "pushed" or "stretched" too far.

Psychologists who emphasize human potential argue that everyone has within him at least a spark of the need to grow and develop personally. Steadily accumulating evidence shows, however, that unless that spark is pretty strong, chances are it will get snuffed out by one's experiences in typical organizations. So, a person who has worked for twenty years in stultifying jobs may find it difficult or impossible to become internally motivated overnight when given the opportunity.

We should be cautious, however, about creating rigid categories of people based on their measured growth-need strength at any particular time. It is true that we can predict from these measures who is likely to become internally motivated on a job and who will be less willing or able to do so. But what we do not know yet is whether or not the growth-need "spark" can be rekindled for those individuals who have had their growth needs dampened by years of growth-depressing experience in their organizations.

Since it is often the organization that is responsible for currently low levels of growth desires, we believe that the organization also should provide the individual with the chance to reverse that trend whenever possible, even if that means putting a person in a job where he may be "stretched" more than he wants to be. He can always move back later to the old job—and in the meantime the embers of his growth needs just might burst back into flame, to his surprise and pleasure, and for the good of the organization.

FROM THEORY TO PRACTICE: A TECHNOLOGY FOR JOB ENRICHMENT

When job enrichment fails, it often fails because of inadequate *diagnosis* of the target job and employees' reactions to it. Often, for example, job enrichment is assumed by management to be a solution to "people problems" on the job and is implemented even though there has been no diagnostic activity to indicate that the root of the problem is in fact how the work is designed. At other times, some diagnosis is made—but it provides no concrete guidance about what specific aspects of the job require change. In either case, the success of job enrichment may wind up depending more on the quality of the intuition of the change agent—or his luck—than on a solid base of data about the people and the work.

In the paragraphs to follow, we outline a new technology for use in job enrichment which explicitly addresses the diagnostic as well as the action components of the change process. The technology has two parts: (1) a set of diagnostic tools that are useful in evaluating jobs and people's reactions to them prior to change—and in pinpointing exactly what aspects of specific jobs are most critical to a successful change attempt; and (2) a set of "implementing concepts" that provide concrete guidance for action steps in job enrichment. The implementing concepts are tied directly to the diagnostic tools; the output of the diagnostic activity specifies which action steps are likely to have the most impact in a particular situation.

The Diagnostic Tools

Central to the diagnostic procedure we propose is a package of instruments to be used by employees, supervisors, and outside observers in assessing the target job and employees' reactions to it.[9] These instruments gauge the following:

1. The objective characteristics of the jobs themselves, including both an overall indication of the "motivating potential" of the job as it exists (that is, the MPS

score) and the score of the job on each of the five core dimensions described previously. Because knowing the strengths and weaknesses of the job is critical to any work-redesign effort, assessments of the job are made by supervisors and outside observers as well as the employees themselves—and the final assessment of a job uses data from all three sources.

2. The current levels of motivation, satisfaction, and work performance of employees on the job. In addition to satisfaction with the work itself, measures are taken of how people feel about other aspects of the work setting, such as pay, supervision, and relationships with coworkers.

3. The level of growth-need strength of the employees. As indicated earlier, employees who have strong growth needs are more likely to be more responsive to job enrichment than employees with weak growth needs. Therefore, it is important to know at the outset just what kinds of satisfactions the people who do the job are (and are not) motivated to obtain from their work. This will make it possible to identify which persons are best to start changes with and which may need help in adapting to the newly enriched job.

What then, might be the actual steps one would take in carrying out a job diagnosis using these tools? Although the approach to any particular diagnosis depends upon the specifics of the particular work situation involved, the sequence of questions listed below is fairly typical.

Step 1. Are Motivation and Satisfaction Central to the Problem? Sometimes organizations undertake job enrichment to improve the work motivation and satisfaction of employees when in fact the real problem with work performance lies elsewhere— for example, in a poorly designed production system, in an error-prone computer, and so on. The first step is to examine the scores of employees on the motivation and satisfaction portions of the diagnostic instrument. (The questionnaire taken by the employees is called the Job Diagnostic Survey and will be referred to hereafter as the JDS.) If motivation and satisfaction are problematic, the change

agent would continue to Step 2; if not, he would look to other aspects of the work situation to identify the real problem.

Step 2. Is the Job Low in Motivating Potential? To answer this question, one would examine the motivating potential score of the target job and compare it to the MPS's of other jobs to determine whether or not *the job itself* is a probable cause of the motivational problems documented in Step 1. If the job turns out to be low on the MPS, one would continue to Step 3; if it scores high, attention should be given to other possible reasons for the motivational difficulties (such as the pay system, the nature of supervision, and so on).

Step 3. What Specific Aspects of the Job Are Causing the Difficulty? This step involves examining the job on each of the five core dimensions to pinpoint the specific strengths and weaknesses of the job as it is currently structured. It is useful at this stage to construct a "profile" of the target job, to make visually apparent where improvements need to be made. An illustrative profile for two jobs (one "good" job and one job needing improvement) is shown in Figure 5.3.

Job A is an engineering maintenance job and is high on all of the core dimensions; the MPS of this job is a very high 260. (MPS scores can range from 1 to about 350; an "average" score would be about 125.) Job enrichment would not be recommended for this job; if employees working on the job were unproductive and unhappy, the reasons are likely to have little to do with the nature or design of the work itself.

Job B, on the other hand, has many problems. This job involves the routine and repetitive processing of checks in the "back room" of a bank. The MPS is 30, which is quite low—and indeed, would be even lower if it were not for the moderately high task significance of the job. (Task significance is moderately high because the people are handling large amounts of other people's money, and therefore the quality of their efforts potentially has important consequences for their unseen clients.) The job provides the individuals with very little direct feedback about how effectively they are doing it; the employees have little autonomy in how they go about doing the job; and the job is moderately low in both skill variety and task identity.

For Job B, then, there is plenty of room for improvement—and many avenues to examine in planning job changes. For still other jobs, the avenues for change often turn out to be considerably more specific: for example, feedback and autonomy may be reasonably high, but one or more of the core dimensions that contribute to the experienced meaningfulness of the job (skill variety, task identity, and task significance) may be low. In

such a case, attention would turn to ways to increase the standing of the job on these latter three dimensions.

Step 4. How "Ready" Are the Employees for Change? Once it has been documented that there is need for improvement in the job—and the particularly troublesome aspects of the job have been identified then it is time to begin to think about the specific action steps which will be taken to enrich the job. An important factor in such planning is the level of growth needs of the employees, since employees high on growth needs usually respond more readily to job enrichment than do employees with little need for growth. The JDS provides a direct measure of the

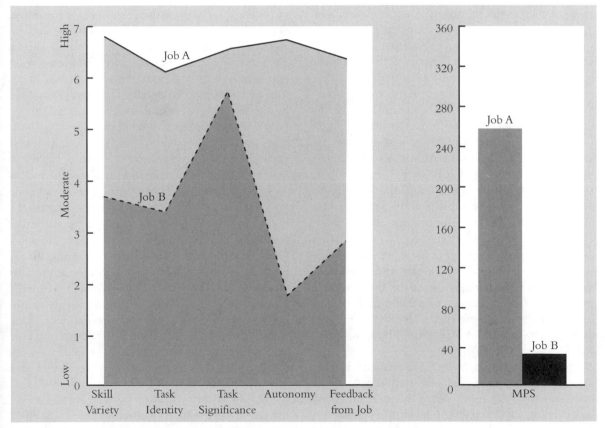

FIGURE 5.3 The JDS Diagnostic Profile for a "Good" and a "Bad" Job.

growth-need strength of the employees. This measure can be very helpful in planning how to introduce the changes to the people (for instance, cautiously versus dramatically), and in deciding who should be among the first group of employees to have their jobs changed.

In actual use of the diagnostic package, additional information is generated which supplements and expands the basic diagnostic questions outlined above. The point of the above discussion is merely to indicate the kinds of questions which we believe to be most important in diagnosing a job prior to changing it. We now turn to how the diagnostic conclusions are translated into specific job changes.

The Implementing Concepts

Five "implementing concepts" for job enrichment are identified and discussed below.[10] Each one is a specific action step aimed at improving both the quality of the working experience for the individual and his work productivity. They are (1) forming natural work units; (2) combining tasks; (3) establishing client relationships; (4) vertical loading; (5) opening feedback channels.

The links between the implementing concepts and the core dimensions are shown in Figure 5.4—which illustrates our theory of job enrichment, ranging from the concrete action steps through the core dimensions and the psychological states to the actual personal and work outcomes.

After completing the diagnosis of a job, a change agent would know which of the core dimensions were most in need of remedial attention. He could then turn to Figure 5.4 and select those implementing concepts that specifically deal with the most troublesome parts of the existing job. How this would take place in practice will be seen below.

Forming Natural Work Units. The notion of distributing work in some logical way may seem to be an obvious part of the design of any job. In many cases, however, the logic is one imposed by just about any consideration except job-holder satisfaction and motivation. Such considerations include technological dictates, level of worker training or experience, "efficiency" as defined by industrial engineering, and current workload. In many cases the cluster of tasks a worker faces during a typical day or week is natural to anyone *but* the worker.

For example, suppose that a typing pool (consisting of one supervisor and ten typists) handles all work for one division of a company. Jobs are delivered in rough draft or dictated form to the supervisor, who distributes them as evenly as possible among the typists. In such circumstances the individual letters, reports, and other tasks performed by a given typist in one day or week are randomly assigned. There is no basis for identifying with the work or the person or department for whom it is performed, or for placing any personal value upon it.

The principle underlying natural units of work, by contrast, is "ownership"—a worker's sense of continuing responsibility for an identifiable body of work. Two steps are involved in creating natural work units. The first is to identify the basic work items. In the typing pool, for example, the items might be "pages to be typed." The second step is to group the items in natural categories. For example, each typist might be assigned continuing responsibility for all jobs requested by one or several specific departments. The assignments should be made, of course, in such a way that workloads are about equal in the long run. (For example, one typist might end up with all the work from one busy department, while another handles jobs from several smaller units.)

At this point we can begin to see specifically how the job-design principles relate to the core dimensions (cf. Figure 5.4). The ownership fostered by natural units of work can make the difference between a feeling that work is meaningful and rewarding and the feeling that it is irrelevant and boring. As the diagram shows, natural units of work are directly related to two of the core dimensions: task identity and task significance.

A typist whose work is assigned naturally rather than randomly—say, by departments—has a much greater chance of performing a whole job to com-

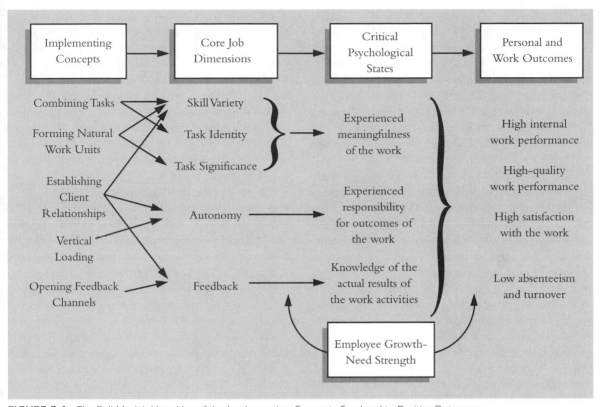

FIGURE 5.4   The Full Model: How Use of the Implementing Concepts Can Lead to Positive Outcomes.

pletion. Instead of typing one section of a large report, the individual is likely to type the whole thing, with knowledge of exactly what the product of the work is (task identity). Furthermore, over time the typist will develop a growing sense of how the work affects coworkers in the department serviced (task significance).

Combining Tasks. The very existence of a pool made up entirely of persons whose sole function is typing reflects a fractionalization of jobs that has been a basic precept of "scientific management." Most obvious in assembly-line work, fractionalization has been applied to nonmanufacturing jobs as

well. It is typically justified by efficiency, which is usually defined in terms of either low costs or some time-and-motion type of criteria.

It is hard to find fault with measuring efficiency ultimately in terms of cost-effectiveness. In doing so, however, a manager should be sure to consider *all* the costs involved. It is possible, for example, for highly fractionalized jobs to meet all the time-and-motion criteria of efficiency, but if the resulting job is so unrewarding that performing it day after day leads to high turnover, absenteeism, drugs and alcohol, and strikes, then productivity is really lower (and costs higher) than data on efficiency might indicate.

The principle of combining tasks, then, suggests that whenever possible existing and fractionalized tasks should be put together to form new and larger modules of work. At the Medfield, Massachusetts plant of Corning Glass Works the assembly of a laboratory hot plate has been redesigned along the lines suggested here. Each hot plate now is assembled from start to finish by one operator, instead of going through several separate operations that are performed by different people.

Some tasks, if combined into a meaningfully large module of work, would be more than an individual could do by himself. In such cases, it is often useful to consider assigning the new, larger task to a small *team* of workers—who are given great autonomy for its completion. At the Racine, Wisconsin plant of Emerson Electric, the assembly process for trash disposal appliances was restructured this way. Instead of a sequence of moving the appliance from station to station, the assembly now is done from start to finish by one team. Such teams include both men and women to permit switching off the heavier and more delicate aspects of the work. The team responsible is identified on the appliance. In case of customer complaints, the team often drafts the reply.

As a job-design principle, task combination, like natural units of work, expands the task identity of the job. For example, the hot-plate assembler can see and identify with a finished product ready for shipment, rather than a nearly invisible junction of solder. Moreover, the more tasks that are combined into a single worker's job, the greater the variety of skills he must call on in performing the job. So task combination also leads directly to greater skill variety—the third core dimension that contributes to the overall experienced meaningfulness of the work.

Establishing Client Relationships. One consequence of fractionalization is that the typical worker has little or no contact with (or even awareness of) the ultimate user of his product or service. By encouraging and enabling employees to establish direct relationships with the clients of their work, im-

provements often can be realized simultaneously on three of the core dimensions. Feedback increases because of additional opportunities for the individual to receive praise or criticism of his work outputs directly. Skill variety often increases because of the necessity to develop and exercise one's interpersonal skills in maintaining the client relationship. And autonomy can increase because the individual often is given personal responsibility for deciding how to manage his relationships with the clients of his work.

Creating client relationships is a three-step process. First, the client must be identified. Second, the most direct contact possible between the worker and the client must be established. Third, criteria must be set up by which the client can judge the quality of the product or service he receives. And whenever possible, the client should have a means of relaying his judgments directly back to the worker.

The contact between worker and client should be as great as possible and as frequent as necessary. Face-to-face contact is highly desirable, at least occasionally. Where that is impossible or impractical, telephone and mail can suffice. In any case, it is important that the performance criteria by which the worker will be rated by the client must be mutually understood and agreed upon.

Vertical Loading. Typically the split between the "doing" of a job and the "planning" and "controlling" of the work has evolved along with horizontal fractionalization. Its rationale, once again, has been "efficiency through specialization." And once again, the excess of specialization that has emerged has resulted in unexpected but significant costs in motivation, morale, and work quality. In vertical loading, the intent is to partially close the gap between the doing and the controlling parts of the job—and thereby reap some important motivational advantages.

Of all the job-design principles, vertical loading may be the single most crucial one. In some cases, where it has been impossible to implement any other changes, vertical loading alone has had significant motivational effects.

When a job is vertically loaded, responsibilities and controls that formerly were reserved for higher levels of management are added to the job. There are many ways to accomplish this:

1. Return to the job holder greater discretion in setting schedules, deciding on work methods, checking on quality, and advising or helping to train less experienced workers.

2. Grant additional authority. The objective should be to advance workers from a position of no authority or highly restricted authority to positions of reviewed, and eventually, near-total authority for their own work.

3. Time management. The job holder should have the greatest possible freedom to decide when to start and stop work, when to break, and how to assign priorities.

4. Troubleshooting and crisis decisions. Workers should be encouraged to seek problem solutions on their own, rather than calling immediately for the supervisor.

5. Financial controls. Some degree of knowledge and control over budgets and other financial aspects of a job can often be highly motivating. However, access to this information frequently tends to be restricted. Workers can benefit from knowing something about the costs of their jobs, the potential effect upon profit, and various financial and budgetary alternatives.

When a job is vertically loaded it will inevitably increase in *autonomy*. And as shown in Figure 5.4, this increase in objective personal control over the work will also lead to an increased feeling of personal responsibility for the work, and ultimately to higher internal work motivation.

Opening Feedback Channels. In virtually all jobs there are ways to open channels of feedback to individuals or teams to help them learn whether their performance is improving, deteriorating, or remaining at a constant level. While there are numerous channels through which information about performance can be provided, it generally is better for a worker to learn about his performance directly

as he does his job—rather than from management on an occasional basis.

Job-provided feedback usually is more immediate and private than supervisor-supplied feedback, and it increases the worker's feelings of personal control over his work in the bargain. Moreover, it avoids many of the potentially disruptive interpersonal problems that can develop when the only way a worker has to find out how he is doing is through direct messages or subtle cues from the boss.

Exactly what should be done to open channels for job-provided feedback will vary from job to job and organization to organization. Yet in many cases the changes involve simply removing existing blocks that isolate the worker from naturally occurring data about performance—rather than generating entirely new feedback mechanisms. For example:

1. Establishing direct client relationships often removes blocks between the worker and natural external sources of data about his work.

2. Quality-control efforts in many organizations often eliminate a natural source of feedback. The quality check on a product or service is done by persons other than those responsible for the work. Feedback to the workers—if there is any—is belated and diluted. It often fosters a tendency to think of quality as "someone else's concern." By placing quality control close to the worker (perhaps even in his own hands), the quantity and quality of data about performance available to him can dramatically increase.

3. Tradition and established procedure in many organizations dictate that records about performance be kept by a supervisor and transmitted up (not down) in the organization hierarchy. Sometimes supervisors even check the work and correct any errors themselves. The worker who made the error never knows it occurred—and is denied the very information that could enhance both his internal work motivation and the technical adequacy of his performance. In many cases it is possible to provide standard summaries of performance records directly to the worker (as well

as to his superior), thereby giving him personally and regularly the data he needs to improve his performance.

4. Computers and other automated operations sometimes can be used to provide the individual with data now blocked from him. Many clerical operations, for example, are now performed on computer consoles. These consoles often can be programmed to provide the clerk with immediate feedback in the form of a CRT display or a print-out indicating that an error has been made. Some systems even have been programmed to provide the operator with a positive feedback message when a period of error-free performance has been sustained.

Many organizations simply have not recognized the importance of feedback as a motivator. Data on quality and other aspects of performance are viewed as being of interest only to management. Worse still, the *standards* for acceptable performance often are kept from workers as well. As a result, workers who would be interested in following the daily or weekly ups and downs of their performance, and in trying accordingly to improve, are deprived of the very guidelines they need to do so. They are like the golfer we mentioned earlier, whose efforts to correct his hook are stopped dead by fog over the driving range.

THE STRATEGY IN ACTION: HOW WELL DOES IT WORK?

So far we have examined a basic theory of how people get turned on to their work; a set of core dimensions of jobs that create the conditions for such internal work motivation to develop on the job; and a set of five implementing concepts that are the action steps recommended to boost a job on the core dimensions and thereby increase employee motivation, satisfaction, and productivity.

The remaining question is straightforward and important: *Does it work?* In reality, that question is twofold. First, does the theory itself hold water, or are we barking up the wrong conceptual tree? And second, does the change strategy really lead to measurable differences when it is applied in an actual organizational setting?

This section summarizes the findings we have generated to date on these questions.

Is the Job-Enrichment Theory Correct?

In general, the answer seems to be yes. The JDS instrument has been taken by more than 1,000 employees working on about 100 diverse jobs in more than a dozen organizations over the last two years. These data have been analyzed to test the basic motivational theory—and especially the impact of the core job dimensions on worker motivation, satisfaction, and behavior on the job. An illustrative overview of some of the findings is given below.[11]

1. People who work on jobs high on the core dimensions are more motivated and satisfied than are people who work on jobs that score low on the dimensions. Employees with jobs high on the core dimensions (MPS scores greater than 240) were compared to those who held unmotivating jobs (MPS scores less than 40). As shown in Figure 5.5, employees with high MPS jobs were higher on (a) the three psychological states, (b) internal work motivation, (c) general satisfaction, and (d) "growth" satisfaction.

2. Figure 5.6 shows that the same is true for measures of actual behavior at work—absenteeism and performance effectiveness—although less strongly so for the performance measure.

3. Responses to jobs high in motivating potential are more positive for people with weak needs for growth. In Figure 5.7 the linear relationship between the motivating potential of a job and employees' level of internal work motivation is shown, separately for people with high versus low growth needs as measured by the JDS. While both groups of employees show increases in internal motivation as MPS increases, the *rate* of in-

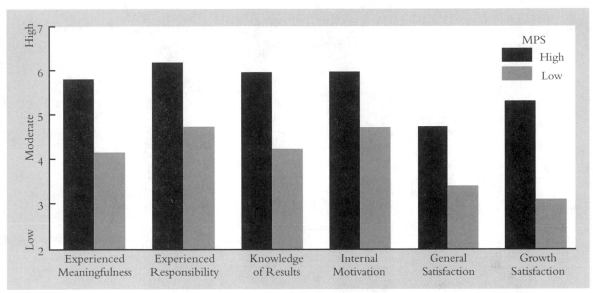

FIGURE 5.5 *Employee Reactions to Jobs High and Low in Motivating Potential for Two Banks and a Steel Firm.*

crease is significantly greater for the group of employees who have strong needs for growth.

How Does the Change Strategy Work in Practice?

The results summarized above suggest that both the theory and the diagnostic instrument work when used with real people in real organizations. In this section, we summarize a job-enrichment project conducted at The Travelers Insurance Companies, which illustrates how the change procedures themselves work in practice.

The Travelers project was designed with two purposes in mind. One was to achieve improvements in morale, productivity, and other indicators of employee well-being. The other was to test the general effectiveness of the strategy for job enrichment we have summarized in this article.

The work group chosen was a keypunching operation. The group's function was to transfer information from printed or written documents onto punched cards for computer input. The work group

consisted of ninety-eight keypunch operators and verifiers (both in the same job classification), plus seven assignment clerks. All reported to a supervisor who, in turn, reported to the assistant manager and manager of the data-input division.

The size of individual punching orders varied considerably, from a few cards to as many as 2,500. Some work came to the work group with a specified delivery date, while other orders were to be given routine service on a predetermined schedule.

Assignment clerks received the jobs from the user departments. After reviewing the work for obvious errors, omissions, and legibility problems, the assignment clerk parceled out the work in batches expected to take about one hour. If the clerk found the work not suitable for punching it went to the supervisor, who either returned the work to the user department or cleared up problems by phone. When work went to operators for punching, it was with the instruction, "Punch only what you see. Don't correct errors, no matter how obvious they look."

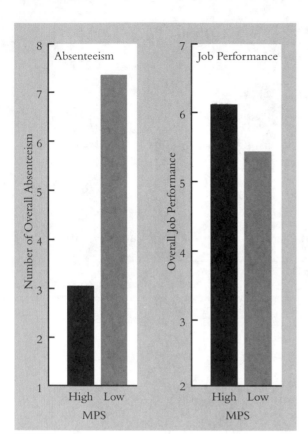

FIGURE 5.6 Absenteeism and Job Performance for Employees with Jobs High and Low in Motivating Potential.

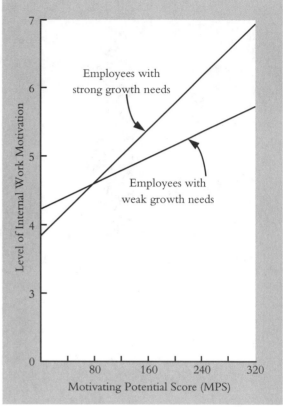

FIGURE 5.7 Relationship Between the Motivating Potential of a Job and the Internal Work Motivation of Employees. (Shown Separately for Employees with Strong versus Weak Growth-Need Strength.)

Because of the high cost of computer time, key-punched work was 100 percent verified—a task that consumed nearly as many man-hours as the punching itself. Then the cards went to the supervisor, who screened the jobs for due dates before sending them to the computer. Errors detected in verification were assigned to various operators at random to be corrected.

The computer output from the cards was sent to the originating department, accompanied by a printout of errors. Eventually the printout went back to the supervisor for final correction.

A great many phenomena indicated that the problems being experienced in the work group might be the result of poor motivation. As the only person performing supervisory functions of any kind, the supervisor spent most of his time responding to crisis situations, which recurred continually. He also had to deal almost daily with employees' salary grievances or other complaints. Employees frequently showed apathy or outright hostility toward their jobs.

Rates of work output, by accepted work-measurement standard, were inadequate. Error rates were high. Due dates and schedules frequently were missed. Absenteeism was higher than average, especially before and after weekends and holidays.

The single, rather unusual exception was turnover. It was lower than the companywide average for similar jobs. The company has attributed this fact to poor job market in the base period just before the product began, and to an older, relatively more settled work force—made up, incidentally, entirely of women.

The Diagnosis. Using some of the tools and techniques we have outlined, a consulting team from the Management Services Department and from Roy W. Walters & Associates concluded that the keypunch-operator's job exhibited the following serious weaknesses in terms of the core dimensions.

1. Skill variety: there was none. Only a single skill was involved—the ability to punch adequately the data on the batch of documents.

2. Task identity: virtually nonexistent. Batches were assembled to provide an even workload, but not whole identifiable jobs.

3. Task significance: not apparent. The keypunching operation was a necessary step in providing service to the company's customers. The individual operator was isolated by an assignment clerk and a supervisor from any knowledge of what the operation meant to the using department, let alone its meaning to the ultimate customer.

4. Autonomy: none. The operators had no freedom to arrange their daily tasks to meet schedules, to resolve problems with the using department, or even to correct, in punching, information that was obviously wrong.

5. Feedback: none. Once a batch was out of the operator's hands, she had no assured chance of seeing evidence of its quality or inadequacy.

Design of the Experimental Trial. Since the diagnosis indicated that the motivating potential of the job was extremely low, it was decided to attempt to improve the motivation and productivity of the work group through job enrichment. Moreover, it was possible to design an experimental test of the effects of the changes to be introduced: the results of the changes made in the target work group were to be compared with trends in a control work group of similar size and demographic makeup. Since the control group was located more than a mile away, there appeared to be little risk of communication between members of the two groups.

A base period was defined before the start of the experimental trial period, and appropriate data were gathered on the productivity, absenteeism, and work attitudes of members of both groups. Data also were available on turnover; but since turnover was already below average in the target group, prospective changes in this measure were deemed insignificant.

An educational session was conducted with supervisors, at which they were given the theory and implementing concepts and actually helped to design the job changes themselves. Out of this session came an active plan consisting of about twenty-five change items that would significantly affect the design of the target jobs.

The Implementing Concepts and the Changes. Because the job as it existed was rather uniformly low on the core job dimensions, all five of the implementing concepts were used in enriching it.

1. Natural units of work. The random batch assignment of work was replaced by assigning to each operator continuing responsibility for certain accounts—either particular departments or particular recurring jobs. Any work for those accounts now always goes to the same operator.

2. Task combination. Some planning and controlling functions were combined with the central task of keypunching. In this case, however, these additions can be more suitably discussed under the remaining three implementing concepts.

3. Client relationships. Each operator was given several channels of direct contact with clients. The operators, not their assignment clerks, now inspect their

documents for correctness and legibility. When problems arise, the operator, not the supervisor, takes them up with the client.

4. Feedback. In addition to feedback from client contact, the operators were provided with a number of additional sources of data about their performance. The computer department now returns incorrect cards to the operators who punched them, and operators correct their own errors. Each operator also keeps her own file of copies of her errors. These can be reviewed to determine trends in error frequency and types of errors. Each operator receives weekly a computer printout of her errors and productivity, which is sent to her directly, rather than given to her by the supervisor.

5. Vertical loading. Besides consulting directly with clients about work questions, operators now have the authority to correct obvious coding errors on their own. Operators may set their own schedules and plan their daily work, as long as they meet schedules. Some competent operators have been given the option of not verifying their work and making their own program changes.

Results of the Trial. The results were dramatic. The number of operators declined from ninety-eight to sixty. This occurred partly through attrition and partly through transfer to other departments. Some of the operators were promoted to higher-paying jobs in departments whose cards they had been handling—something that had never occurred before. Some details of the results are given below.

1. Quantity of work. The control group, with no job changes made, showed an increase in productivity of 8.1 percent during the trial period. The experimental group showed an increase of 39.6 percent.

2. Error rates. To assess work quality, error rates were recorded for about forty operators in the experimental group. All were experienced, and all had been in their jobs before the job-enrichment program began. For two months before the study, these operators had a collective error rate of 1.53 percent. For two months toward the end of the study, the collec-

tive error rate was 0.99 percent. By the end of the study the number of operators with poor performance had dropped from 11.1 percent to 5.5 percent.

3. Absenteeism. The experimental group registered a 24.1 percent decline in absences. The control group, by contrast, showed a 29 percent increase.

4. Attitudes toward the job. An attitude survey given at the start of the project showed that the two groups scored about average, and nearly identically, in nine different areas of work satisfaction. At the end of the project the survey was repeated. The control group showed an insignificant 0.5 percent improvement, while the experimental group's overall satisfaction score rose 16.5 percent.

5. Selective elimination of controls. Demonstrated improvements in operator proficiency permitted them to work with fewer controls. Travelers estimates that the reduction of controls had the same effect as adding seven operators—a saving even beyond the effects of improved productivity and lowered absenteeism.

6. Role of the supervisor. One of the most significant findings in the Travelers experiment was the effect of the changes on the supervisor's job, and thus on the rest of the organization. The operators took on many responsibilities that had been reserved at least to the unit leaders and sometimes to the supervisor. The unit leaders, in turn, assumed some of the day-to-day supervisory functions that had plagued the supervisor. Instead of spending his days supervising the behavior of subordinates and dealing with crises, he was able to devote time to developing feedback systems, setting up work modules and spearheading the enrichment effort—in other words, managing. It should be noted, however, that helping supervisors change their own work activities when their subordinates' jobs have been enriched is itself a challenging task. And if appropriate attention and help are not given to supervisors in such cases, they rapidly can become disaffected—and a job-enrichment "backlash" can result.[12]

Summary. By applying work-measurement standards to the changes wrought by job enrichment—

attitude and quality, absenteeism, and selective administration of controls—Travelers was able to estimate the total dollar impact of the project. Actual savings in salaries and machine rental charges during the first year totaled $64,305. Potential savings by further application of the changes were put at $91,937 annually. Thus, by almost any measure used—from the work attitudes of individual employees to dollar savings for the company as a whole—The Travelers test of the job-enrichment strategy proved a success.

CONCLUSIONS

In this article we have presented a new strategy for the redesign of work in general and for job enrichment in particular. The approach has four main characteristics:

1. It is grounded in a basic psychological theory of what motivates people in their work.

2. It emphasizes that planning for job changes should be done on the basis of *data* about the jobs and the people who do them—and a set of diagnostic instruments is provided to collect such data.

3. It provides a set of specific implementing concepts to guide actual job changes, as well as a set of theory-based rules for selecting *which* action steps are likely to be most beneficial in a given situation.

4. The strategy is buttressed by a set of findings showing that the theory holds water, that the diagnostic procedures are practical and informative, and that the implementing concepts can lead to changes that are beneficial both to organizations and to the people who work in them.

We believe that job enrichment is moving beyond the stage where it can be considered "yet another management fad." Instead, it represents a potentially powerful strategy for change that can help organizations achieve their goals for higher quality work—and at the same time further the equally legitimate needs of contemporary employees for a more meaningful work experience. Yet there are pressing questions about job enrichment and its use that remain to be answered.

Prominent among these is the question of employee participation in planning an implementing work redesign. The diagnostic tools and implementing concepts we have presented are neither designed nor intended for use only by management. Rather, our belief is that the effectiveness of job enrichment is likely to be enhanced when the tasks of diagnosing and changing jobs are undertaken *collaboratively* by management and by the employees whose work will be affected.

Moreover, the effects of work redesign on the broader organization remain generally uncharted. Evidence now is accumulating that when jobs are changed, turbulence can appear in the surrounding organization—for example, in supervisory-subordinate relationships, in pay and benefit plans, and so on. Such turbulence can be viewed by management either as a problem with job enrichment, or as an opportunity for further and broader organizational development by teams of managers and employees. To the degree that management takes the latter view, we believe, the oft-espoused goal of achieving basic organizational change through the redesign of work may come increasingly within reach.

The diagnostic tools and implementing concepts we have presented are useful in deciding on and designing basic changes in the jobs themselves. They do not address the broader issues of who plans the changes, how they are carried out, and how they are followed up. The way these broader questions are dealt with, we believe, may determine whether job enrichment will grow up—or whether it will die an early and unfortunate death, like so many other fledgling behavioral-science approaches to organizational change.

APPENDIX

For the algebraically inclined, the motivating Potential Score is computed as follows:

$$MPS = \frac{\dfrac{\text{Skill} \atop \text{Variety}} + \dfrac{\text{Task} \atop \text{Identity}} + \dfrac{\text{Task} \atop \text{Significance}}}{3} \times \text{Autonomy} \times \text{Feedback}$$

It should be noted that in some cases the MPS score can be *too* high for positive job satisfaction and effective performance—in effect overstimulating the person who holds the job. This paper focuses on jobs which are toward the low end of the scale—and which potentially can be improved through job enrichment.

Acknowledgments

The authors acknowledge with great appreciation the editorial assistance of John Hickey in the preparation of this paper, and the help of Kenneth Brousseau, Daniel Feldman, and Linda Frank in collecting the data that are summarized here. The research activities reported were supported in part by the Organizational Effectiveness Research Program of the Office of Naval Research, and the Manpower Administration of the U.S. Department of Labor, both through contracts to Yale University.

NOTES

1.   F. Herzberg, B. Mausner, and B. Snyderman, *The Motivation to Work* (New York: John Wiley & sons, 1959).

2.   F. Herzberg, *Work and the Nature of Man* (Cleveland: World, 1966).

3.   F. Herzberg, "One More Time: How Do You Motivate Employees?" *Harvard Business Review* (1968): 53–62.

4.   W. J. Paul, Jr., K. B. Robertson, and F. Herzberg, "Job Enrichment Pays Off." *Harvard Business Review* (1969): 61–78.

5.   R. N. Ford, *Motivation Through the Work Itself* (New York: American Management Association, 1969).

6.   A. N. Turner and P. R. Lawrence, *Industrial Jobs and the Worker* (Cambridge, Mass.: Harvard Graduate School of Business Administration, 1965).

7.   J. R. Hackman and E. E. Lawler, "Employee Reactions to Job Characteristics," *Journal of Applied Psychology Monograph* (1971): 259–86.

8.   J. R. Hackman and G. R. Oldham, *Motivation Through the Design of Work: Test of a Theory*, Technical Report No. 6, Department of Administrative Sciences, Yale University, 1974.

9.   J. R. Hackman and G. R. Oldham, "Development of the Job Diagnostic Survey," *Journal of Applied Psychology* (1975): 159–70.

10.   R. W. Walters and Associates, *Job Enrichment for Results* (Cambridge, Mass.: Addison-Wesley, 1975).

11.   Hackman and Oldham, "Development of the Job Diagnostic Survey."

12.   E. E. Lawler III, J. R. Hackman, and S. Kaufman; "Effects of Job Redesign: A Field Experiment," *Journal of Applied Social Psychology* (1973): 49–62.

SATISFACTION AND EMOTION: THE AFFECTIVE SIDE OF ORGANIZATIONAL LIFE

Foundations of Job Satisfaction

6.   SATISFACTION AND BEHAVIOR

Edward E. Lawler III

. . . During the last 30 years, thousands of studies have been done on job satisfaction. Usually, these studies have not been theoretically oriented; instead, researchers have simply looked at the relationship between job satisfaction and factors such as age, education, job level, absenteeism rate, productivity, and so on. Originally, much of the research seemed to be stimulated by a desire to show that job satisfaction is important because it influences productivity. Underlying the earlier articles on job satisfaction was a strong conviction that "happy workers are productive workers." Recently, however, this theme has been disappearing, and many organizational psychologists seem to be studying job satisfaction simply because they are interested in finding its causes. This approach to studying job satisfaction is congruent with the increased promi-nence of humanistic psychology, which emphasizes human affective experience.

The recent interest in job satisfaction also ties in directly with the rising concern in many countries about the quality of life. There is an increasing acceptance of the view that material possessions and economic growth do not necessarily produce a high quality of life. Recognition is now being given to the importance of the kinds of affective reactions that people experience and to the fact that these are not always tied to economic or material accomplishments. Through the Department of Labor and the Department of Health, Education, and Welfare, the United States government has recently become active in trying to improve the affective quality of work life. Job satisfaction is one measure of the quality of life in organizations and is worth understanding and increasing even if it doesn't relate to performance. This reason for studying satisfaction is likely to be an increasingly prominent one as we begin to worry more about the effects working in organizations has on people and as our humanitarian concern for the kind of psychological experiences people have during their lives increases. What happens to people during the work day has profound effects both on the individual employee's life and on the society as a whole, and thus these events cannot be ignored if the quality of life in a society is to be high. As John Gardner has said:

Of all the ways in which society serves the individual, few are more meaningful than to provide him with a decent job. . . . It isn't going to be a decent society for any of us until it is for all of us. If our sense of responsibility fails us, our sheer self-interest should come to the rescue. [1968, p. 25]

As it turns out, satisfaction is related to absenteeism and turnover, both of which are very costly to organizations. Thus, there is a very "practical" economic reason for organizations to be concerned with job satisfaction, since it can influence organizational effectiveness. However, before any practical use can be made of the finding that job dissatisfaction causes absenteeism and turnover, we must understand what factors cause and influence job satisfaction. Organizations can influence job satisfaction and prevent absenteeism and turnover only if the organizations can pinpoint the factors causing and influencing these effective responses.

THEORIES OF JOB SATISFACTION

Four approaches can be identified in the theoretical work on satisfaction. Fulfillment theory was the first approach to develop. Equity theory and discrepancy theory developed later, partially as reactions against the shortcomings of fulfillment theory. Two-factor theory, the fourth approach, represents an attempt to develop a completely new approach to thinking about satisfaction.

Fulfillment Theory

Schaffer (1953) has argued that "job satisfaction will vary directly with the extent to which those needs of an individual which can be satisfied are actually satisfied" (p. 3). Vroom (1964) also sees job satisfaction in terms of the degree to which a job provides the person with positively valued outcomes. He equates satisfaction with valence and adds, "If we describe a person as satisfied with an object, we mean that the object has positive valence for him. However, satisfaction has a much more restricted usage. In common parlance, we refer to a person's satisfaction only with reference to objects which he possesses" (p. 100).[1] Researchers who have adopted the fulfillment approach measure people's satisfaction by simply asking how much of a given facet or outcome they are receiving. Thus, these researchers view satisfaction as depending on how much of a given outcome or group of outcomes a person receives.

Fulfillment theorists have considered how facet-satisfaction measures combine to determine overall satisfaction. The crucial issue is whether the facet-satisfaction measures should be weighted by their importance to the person when combined. We know that some job factors are more important than other job factors for each individual; therefore, the important factors need to be weighted more in determining the individual's total satisfaction. However, there is evidence that the individual's facet satisfaction scores reflect this emphasis already and thus do not need to be further weighted (Mobley & Locke, 1970).

A great deal of research shows that people's satisfaction is a function both of how much they receive and of how much they feel they should and/or want to receive (Locke, 1969). A foreman, for example, may be satisfied with a salary of $12,000, while a company president may be dissatisfied with a salary of $100,000, even though the president correctly perceives that he receives more than the foreman. The point is that people's reactions to what they receive are not simply a function of how much they receive; their reactions are strongly influenced by such individual-difference factors as what they want and what they feel they should receive. Individual-difference factors suggest that the fulfillment-theory approach to job satisfaction is not valid, since this approach fails to take into account differences in people's feelings about what outcomes they should receive.

Morse (1953) stated this point of view as follows:

At first we thought that satisfaction would simply be a function of how much a person received from the situation or what we have called the amount of environmental return. It made sense to feel that those who were in more need-fulfilling environments would be more satisfied. But the amount of environmental return did not seem to be the only factor involved. Another factor obviously had to be included in order to predict satisfaction accurately. This variable was the strength of an individual's desires, or his level of aspiration in a particular area. If the environment provided little possibility for need satisfaction, those with the strongest desires, or highest aspirations, were the least happy [pp. 27–28].

Discrepancy theory, which will be discussed next, represents an attempt to take into account the fact that people do differ in their desires.

Discrepancy Theory

Recently many psychologists have argued for a discrepancy approach to thinking about satisfaction. They maintain that satisfaction is determined by the differences between the actual outcomes a person receives and some other outcome level. The theories differ widely in their definitions of this other outcome level. For some theories it is the outcome level the person feels should be received, and for other theories it is the outcome level the person expects to receive. All of the theoretical approaches argue that what is received should be compared with another outcome level, and when there is a difference—when received outcome is below the other outcome level—dissatisfaction results. Thus, if a person expects or thinks he should receive a salary of $10,000 and he receives one of only $8,000, the prediction is that he will be dissat-

isfied with his pay. Further, the prediction is that he will be more dissatisfied than the person who receives a salary of $9,000 and expects or thinks he should receive a salary of $10,000.

Katzell (1964) and Locke (1968, 1969) have probably presented the two most completely developed discrepancy-theory approaches to satisfaction. According to Katzell, satisfaction = $1 - (|X - V|/V)$, where X equals the actual amount of the outcome and V equals the desired amount of the outcome. Like many discrepancy theorists, Katzell sees satisfaction as the difference between an actual amount and some desired amount; but, unlike most discrepancy theorists, he assumes that this difference should be divided by the desired amount of the outcome. If we use Katzell's formula, we are led to believe that the more a person wants of an outcome the less dissatisfied he will be with a given discrepancy. Katzell offers no evidence for this assumption, and it is hard to support logically. A discrepancy from what is desired would seem to be equally dissatisfying regardless of how much is desired. Katzell also speaks of "actual" discrepancies, while most discrepancy theorists talk of "perceived" discrepancies. Note also that by Katzell's formula, getting more than the desired amount should produce less satisfaction than getting the desired amount.

Locke (1969) has stated a discrepancy theory that differs from Katzell's in several ways. First, Locke emphasizes that the perceived discrepancy, not the actual discrepancy, is important. He also argues that satisfaction is determined by the simple difference between what the person wants and what he perceives he receives. The more his wants exceed what he receives, the greater his dissatisfaction. Locke says, "job satisfaction and dissatisfaction are a function of the perceived relationship between what one wants from one's job and what one perceives it is offering" (p. 316).

Porter (1961), in measuring satisfaction, asks people how much of a given outcome there should be for their job and how much of a given outcome there actually is; he considers the discrepancy between the two answers to be a measure of satisfaction. This particular discrepancy approach has been the most widely used. It differs from Locke's approach since it sees satisfaction as influenced not by how much a person wants but by how much he feels he should receive.

A few researchers have argued that satisfaction is determined by what a person expects to receive rather than by what he wants or feels he should receive. Thus, the literature on job satisfaction contains three different discrepancy approaches; the first looks at what people want, the second at what people feel they should receive, and the third at what people expect to receive. The last of these approaches has seldom been used and can be dismissed. As Locke (1969) points out, the expectation approach is hard to defend logically. Admittedly, getting what is not expected may lead to surprise, but it hardly need lead to dissatisfaction. What if, for example, it exceeds expectations? What if it exceeds expectations but still falls below what others are getting?

It is not obvious on logical grounds that either of the first two approaches can be rejected as meaningless. Both approaches seem to be addressing important but perhaps different affective reactions to a job. There clearly is a difference between asking people how much they want and how much they think they should receive. People do respond differently to those questions (Wanous & Lawler, 1972). In a sense, the two questions help us understand different aspects of a person's feelings toward his present situation. A person's satisfaction with the fairness of what he receives for his present job would seem to be more influenced by what he feels he should receive than by what he ultimately aspires to. The difference between what the person aspires to or wants and what he receives gives us an insight into his satisfaction with his present situation relative to his long-term aspired to, or desired, situation. These two discrepancy measures can and do yield different results. For example, a person can feel that his present pay is appropriate for his present job, and in this sense he can be satisfied; however, he can feel that his present pay is much below what he wants, and in this sense he can be dissatisfied. In most cases, however, these two discrepancies probably are closely related and influence each other. Thus, the difference between the two discrepancies may not be as large or as important as some theorists have argued.

Like the fulfillment theorists, many discrepancy theorists argue that total job satisfaction is influenced by the sum of the discrepancies that are present for each job factor. Thus, a person's overall job satisfaction would be equal to his pay-satisfaction discrepancy plus his supervision-satisfaction discrepancy, and so on. It has been argued that in computing such a sum it is important to weight each of the discrepancies by the importance of that factor to the person, the argument being that important factors influence job satisfaction more strongly than unimportant ones. Locke (1969), however, argues that such a weighting is redundant, since the discrepancy score is a measure of importance in itself because large discrepancies tend to appear only for important items.

Most discrepancy theories allow for the possibility of a person saying he is receiving more outcomes than he should receive, or more outcomes than he wants to receive. However, the theories don't stress this point, which presents some problems for them. It is not clear how to equate dissatisfaction (or whatever this feeling might be called) due to over-reward with dissatisfaction due to under-reward. Are they produced in the same way? Do they have the same results? Do they both contribute to overall job dissatisfaction? These are some of the important questions that discrepancy theories have yet to answer. Equity theory, which will be discussed next, has dealt with some of these questions.

Equity Theory

Equity theory is primarily a motivation theory, but it has some important things to say about the causes of satisfaction/dissatisfaction. Adams (1963, 1965) argues in his version of equity theory that satisfaction is determined by a person's perceived input-outcome balance in the following manner: the perceived equity of a person's rewards is determined by his input-outcome balance; this perceived equity, in turn, determines satisfaction. Satisfaction results when perceived equity exists, and dissatisfaction results when perceived inequity exists. Thus, satisfaction is determined by the perceived ratio of what a person receives from his job relative to what a person puts into his job. According to equity theory, either under-reward or over-reward can lead to dissatisfaction, although the feelings are somewhat different. The theory emphasizes that over-reward leads to feelings of guilt, while under-reward leads to feelings of unfair treatment.

Equity theory emphasizes the importance of other people's input-outcome balance in determining how a person will judge the equity of his own input-outcome balance. Equity theory argues that people evaluate the fairness of their own input-outcome balance by comparing it with their perception of input-outcome balance of their "comparison-other" (the person they compare with). This emphasis does not enter into either discrepancy theory or fulfillment theory as they are usually stated. Although there is an implied reference to "other" in the discussion of how people develop their feelings about what their outcomes should be, discrepancy theory does not explicitly state that this perception is based on perceptions of what other people contribute and receive. This difference points up a strength of equity theory relative to discrepancy theory. Equity theory rather clearly states how a person assesses his inputs and outcomes in order to develop his perception of the fairness of his input-outcome balance. Discrepancy theory, on the other hand, is vague about how people decide what their outcomes should be.

Two-Factor Theory

Modern two-factor theory was originally developed in a book by Herzberg, Mausner, Peterson, and Capwell (1957), in which the authors stated that job factors could be classified according to whether the factors contribute primarily to satisfaction or to dissatisfaction. Two years later, Herzberg, Mausner, and Snyderman (1959) published the results of a research study, which they interpreted as supportive of the theory. Since 1959, much research has been directed toward testing two-factor theory. Two aspects of the theory are unique and account for the attention it has received. First, two-factor theory says that satisfaction and dissatisfaction do not exist on a continuum running from satisfaction through neutral to dissatisfaction. Two independent continua exist, one running from satisfied to neutral and another running from dissatisfied to neutral (see Figure 6.1). Second, the theory stresses that different job facets influence feelings of satisfaction and dissatisfaction. Figure 6.2 presents the results of a study by Herzberg et al., which show that factors such as achievement, recognition, work itself, and responsibility are mentioned in connection with satisfying experiences, while working conditions, interpersonal relations, supervision, and company policy are usually mentioned in connection with dissatisfying experiences. The figure shows the frequency with which each factor is mentioned in connection with high (satisfying) and low (dissatisfying) work experiences. As can be seen, achievement was present in over 40 percent of the satisfying experiences and less than 10 percent of the dissatisfying experiences.

Perhaps the most interesting aspect of Herzberg's theory is that at the same time a person can be very satisfied and very dissatisfied. Also the theory implies that factors such as better working conditions cannot increase or cause satisfaction, they can only

FIGURE 6.1 *Two-Factor Theory: Satisfaction Continua.*

Satisfied	Neutral

Dissatisfied	Neutral

FIGURE 6.2 *Comparison of Satisfiers and Dissatisfiers.*

Satisfied	Neutral

Dissatisfied	Neutral

Source: Adapted from Herzberg et al. *The Motivation to Work*, 2d ed. Copyright © 1959 by John Wiley & Sons, Inc. Reprinted by permission.

affect the amount of dissatisfaction that is experienced. The only way satisfaction can be increased is by effecting changes in those factors that are shown in Figure 6.2 as contributing primarily to satisfaction.

The results of the studies designed to test two-factor theory have not provided clear-cut support for the theory, nor have these studies allowed for total rejection of the theory. In many cases, the studies have only fueled the controversy that surrounds the theory. It is beyond the scope of this reading to review the research that has been done on the theory. What we can do, however, is to consider some of the conclusions to which two-factor theory has led. Perhaps the most negative summary of the evidence is the account presented by Dunnette, Campbell, and Hakel (1967). According to them:

It seems that the evidence is now sufficient to lay the two-factor theory to rest, and we hope that it may be buried peaceably. We believe that it is important that this be done so that researchers will address themselves to studying the full complexities of human motivation, rather than continuing to allow the direction of motivational research or actual administrative decisions to be dictated by the seductive simplicity of two-factor theory [p. 173].

This opinion has been rejected by many researchers as too harsh and negative, and indeed research on the theory has continued since the publication of the Dunnette et al. study. Still, research on the theory has raised serious doubts about its validity. Even proponents of the theory admit that the same factors can cause both satisfaction and dissatisfaction and that a given factor can cause satisfaction in one group of people and dissatisfaction in another group of people. Other researchers have pointed out that results supporting the theory seem to be obtainable only when certain limited research methodologies are used.

The major unanswered question with respect to two-factor theory is whether satisfaction and dissatisfaction really are two separate dimensions. The evidence is not sufficient to establish that satisfaction and dissatisfaction are separate, making this the crucial unproven aspect of the theory. Neither the fact that some factors can contribute to both satisfaction and dissatisfaction nor the fact that, in some populations, factors contribute to satisfaction while, in other populations, these factors contribute to dissatisfaction is sufficient reason to reject the theory. Although these findings raise questions about the theory, they do not destroy its core concept, which is that satisfaction and dissatisfaction are, in fact, on different continua.

Significantly, while considerable research has tried to determine which factors contribute to satisfaction and dissatisfaction, little attention has been directed toward testing the motivation and performance implications of the theory. The study of Herzberg et al. (1959) did ask the subjects (engineers and accountants) to report how various job factors affected their performance. In agreement with the theory, the subjects reported that the presence of satisfiers boosted performance, while the presence of dissatisfiers reduced performance. At best, the results of this study give weak evidence that these job factors influence performance as suggested by the theory. Only self-reports of performance were used, and in many cases the subjects were reporting on events that had happened some time prior to the date of the interviews. The evidence, although not at all conclusive, at least suggests the kinds of experiences that might lead to a strong motivation to perform effectively. Unfortunately, Herzberg et al. did not develop any theoretical concepts to explain why the job factors should affect performance. Their theory contains little explanation of why outcomes are attractive, and it fails to consider the importance of associative connections in determining which of a number of behaviors a person will choose to perform in order to obtain a desired outcome. Thus, it is not a theory of motivation; rather, it is a theory primarily concerned with explaining the determinants of job satisfaction and dissatisfaction.

Equity Theory and/or Discrepancy Theory

Equity and theory and discrepancy theory are the two strongest theoretical explanations of satisfaction. Either theory could be used as a basis for thinking about the determinants of satisfaction. Fortunately it is not necessary to choose between the theories, since it is possible to build a satisfaction model that capitalizes on the strengths of each theory. In this reading, we will try to build such a model. In many ways, equity theory and discrepancy theory are quite similar. Both theories stress the importance of a person's perceived outcomes, along with the relationship of these outcomes to a second perception. In discrepancy theory, the second perception is what the outcomes should be or what the person wants the outcomes to be; in equity theory, the second perception is what a person's perceived inputs are in relation to other people's inputs and outcomes. Clearly, it could be argued that the two theories are talking about very similar concepts when they talk about perceived inputs and what the subject's feeling about what his outcomes should be. A person's perception of what his outcomes should be is partly determined by what he feels his inputs are. Thus, the "should be" phrase from discrepancy theory and the "perceived inputs relative to other people's inputs and outcomes" phrase from equity theory are very similar.

Equity theory and discrepancy theory do differ in that equity theory places explicit emphasis on the importance of social comparison, while discrepancy theory does not. This is a strength of equity theory because it helps to make explicit what influences a person's "should be" judgment. Finally, discrepancy theory talks in terms of a *difference*, while equity theory talks in terms of a *ratio*. For example, equity theory would predict that a person with 16 units of input and 4 units of outcome would feel the same as a person with 8 units of input and 2 units of outcome (same ratio, 1 to 4). Although discrepancy theory does not talk specifically in terms of inputs, if we consider input as one determinant of what outcomes should be, then discrepancy theory would not go along with equity theory. Discrepancy theory would argue that the person with 16 units of input will be more dissatisfied than the person with 8 units of input because the difference between his input and outcomes is greater. The two theories also

suggest different types of relationships between dissatisfaction and feelings of what rewards should be. Discrepancy theory would predict a linear relationship such that, rewards being constant, increases in a person's perception of what his outcomes should be would be directly proportionate to increases in dissatisfaction. Equity theory, on the other hand, would predict a nonlinear relationship [satisfaction = (is getting/should be getting)] such that if a poor ratio exists, a further increase in "should be getting" will have little effect on satisfaction.

In building our "model of satisfaction," we will use the difference approach rather than the ratio approach. This choice is one of the few either/or choices that must be made between the two theories. It is not a particularly crucial choice from the point of view of measurement because methods of measurement in the field of psychology are not precise enough so that discrepancy theory and equity theory would yield very different results. Measurement scales with true zero points and equal distances between all points on the scale (for example, as in measuring weight and height) are required, and such scales are not used when attitudes are measured.

Once it has been decided to think of satisfaction in terms of a difference, the key question becomes what difference or differences should be considered. There is clear agreement that one element in the discrepancy should be what the person perceives that he actually receives. The second element could be one of two other perceptions: (1) what a person thinks he should receive, or (2) what a person wants to receive. As we've already seen, these two perceptions are closely related. However, there is a difference. Overall, it seems preferable to focus more on what a person feels he should receive than on what a person wants to receive.

If satisfaction is conceptualized as the difference between what one receives and what one wants, it is difficult to talk meaningfully about satisfaction with one's present job. Such an approach partially removes satisfaction from the context of the job and the situation. The question "How much do you want?" is an aspiration-level variable, which is not as closely related to the job situation as the question "How much should there be?" An answer to the first question is more a statement of personal goals than a statement of what is appropriate in a particular situation. Research data show that employees consistently give higher answers to the "how much do you want" question than to the "how much should there be" question (Wanous & Lawler, 1972); answers to the "should be" question seem to vary more with such organization factors as job level. Thus, in studying people's feelings about their jobs, it seems logical to focus on what employees feel they should receive from their jobs. This perception would seem to be strongly influenced by organization practices, and it would seem to be a perception that must be studied if we are to understand employees' affective reactions to their jobs and the behavioral responses these reactions produce.

A MODEL OF FACET SATISFACTION

Figure 6.3 presents a model of the determinants of facet satisfaction. The model is intended to be applicable to understanding what determines a person's satisfaction with any facet of the job. The model assumes that the same psychological processes operate to determine satisfaction with job factors ranging from pay to supervision and satisfaction with the work itself. The model in Figure 6.3 is a discrepancy model in the sense that it shows satisfaction as the difference between *a*, what a person feels he should receive, *b*, what he perceives that

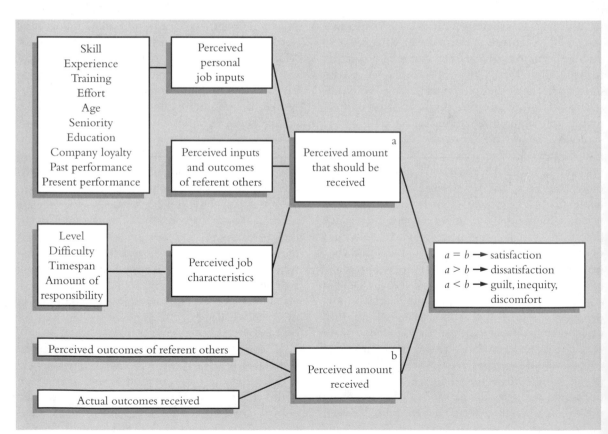

FIGURE 6.3 Model of the Determinants of Satisfaction.

he actually receives. The model indicates that when the person's perception of what his outcome level is and his perception of what his outcome level should be are in agreement, the person will be satisfied. When a person perceives his outcome level as falling below what he feels it should be, he will be dissatisfied. However, when a person's perceived outcome level exceeds what he feels it should be, he will have feelings of guilt and inequity and perhaps some discomfort (Adams, 1965). Thus, for any job factor, the assumption is that satisfaction with the factor will be determined by the difference between how much of the factor there is and how much of the factor the person feels there should be.

Present outcome level is shown to be the key influence on a person's perception of what rewards he receives, but his perception is also shown to be influenced by his perception of what his "referent others" receive. The higher the outcome levels of his referent others, the lower his outcome level will appear. Thus, a person's psychological view of how much of a factor he receives is said to be influenced by more than just the objective amount of the factor. Because of this psychological influence, the same amount of reward often can be seen quite differently by two people; to one person it can be a large amount, while to another person it can be a small amount.

The model in Figure 6.3 also shows that a person's perception of what his reward level should be is influenced by a number of factors. Perhaps the most important influence is perceived job inputs. These inputs include all of the skills, abilities, and training a person brings to the job as well as the behavior he exhibits on the job. The greater he perceives his inputs to be, the higher will be his perception of what his outcomes should be. Because of this relationship, people with high job inputs must receive more rewards than people with low job inputs or they will be dissatisfied. The model also shows that a person's perception of what his outcomes should be is influenced by his perception of the job demands. The greater the demands made by the job, the more he will perceive he should receive. Job demands include such things as job difficulty, responsibilities, and organization level. If outcomes do not rise along with these factors, the clear prediction of the model is that the people who perceive they have the more difficult, higher-level jobs will be the most dissatisfied.

The model shows that a person's perception of what his outcomes should be is influenced by what the person perceives his comparison-other's inputs and outcomes to be. This aspect of the model is taken directly from equity theory and is included to stress the fact that people look at the inputs and outcomes of others in order to determine what their own outcome level should be. If a person's comparison-other's inputs are the same as the person's inputs but the other's outcomes are much higher, the person will feel that he should be receiving more outcomes and will be dissatisfied as a result.

The model allows for the possibility that people will feel that their outcomes exceed what they should be. The feelings produced by this condition are quite different from those produced by under-reward. Because of this difference, it does not make sense to refer to a person who feels over-rewarded as being dissatisfied. There is considerable evidence that very few people feel over-rewarded, and this fact can be explained by the model. Even when people are highly rewarded, the social-comparison aspect of satisfaction means that people can avoid feeling over-rewarded by looking around and finding someone to compare with who is doing equally well. Also, a person tends to value his own inputs much higher than they are valued by others (Lawler, 1967). Because of this discrepancy, a person's perception of what his outcomes should be is often not shared by those administering his rewards, and is often above what he actually receives. Finally, the person can easily increase his perception of his inputs and thereby justify a high reward level.

As a way of summarizing some of the implications of the model, let us briefly make some statements about who should be dissatisfied if the model is correct. Other things being equal:

1. People with high perceived inputs will be more dissatisfied with a given facet than people with low perceived inputs.

2. People who perceive their job to be demanding will be more dissatisfied with a given facet than people who perceive their jobs as undemanding.

3. People who perceive similar others as having a more favorable input-outcome balance will be more dissatisfied with a given facet than people who perceive their own balance as similar to or better than that of others.

4. People who receive a low outcome level will be more dissatisfied than those who receive a high outcome level.

5. The more outcomes a person perceives his comparison-other receives, the more dissatisfied he will be with his own outcomes. This should be particularly true when the comparison-other is seen to hold a job that demands the same or fewer inputs.

OVERALL JOB SATISFACTION

Most theories of job satisfaction argue that overall job satisfaction is determined by some combination of all facet-satisfaction feelings. This could be expressed in terms of the facet-satisfaction model in Figure 6.3 as a simple sum of, or average of, all $a - b$ discrepancies. Thus, overall job satisfaction is determined by the difference between all the

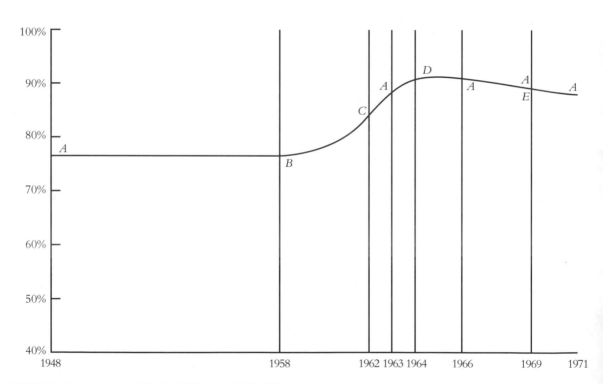

FIGURE 6.4 Percentage of "Satisfied" Workers, 1948–1971.
Source: From Quinn, Staines, and McCullough, 1973.
Note: "Don't know" and "Uncertain" have been excluded from the base of the percentages. Sources: A = Gallup, or Gallup as reported by Roper; B = Survey Research Center (Michigan); C = NORC; D = Survey Research Center (Berkeley); E = 1969–1970 Survey of Working Conditions.

things a person feels he should receive from his job and all the things he actually does receive.

A strong theoretical argument can be made for weighting the facet-satisfaction scores according to their importance. Some factors do make larger contributions to overall satisfaction than others. Pay satisfaction, satisfaction with the work itself, and satisfaction with supervision seem to have particularly strong influences on overall satisfaction for most people. Also, employees tend to rate these factors as important. Thus, there is a connection between how important employees say job factors are and how much job factors influence overall job satisfaction (Vroom, 1964). Conceptually, therefore, it seems worthwhile to think of the various job-facet-satisfaction scores as influencing total satisfaction in terms of their importance. One way to express this relationship is by defining overall job satisfaction as being equal to Σ (facet satisfaction × facet importance). However, as stressed earlier, actually measuring importance and multiplying it by measured facet satisfaction often isn't necessary because the satisfaction scores themselves seem to take importance into account. (The most important items tend to be scored as either very satisfactory or very dissatisfactory; thus, these items have the most influence on any sum score.) Still, on a conceptual level, it is important to remember that facet-satisfaction scores do differentially contribute to the feeling of overall job satisfaction.

A number of studies have attempted to determine how many workers are actually satisfied with their jobs. Our model does not lead to any predictions in this area. The model simply gives the conditions that lead to people experiencing feelings of satisfaction or dissatisfaction. Not surprisingly, the studies that have been done do not agree on the percentage of dissatisfied workers. Some suggest figures as low as 13 percent, others give figures as high as 80 percent. The range generally reported is from 13 to 25 percent dissatisfied. Herzberg et al. (1957) summarized the findings of research studies conducted from 1946 through 1953. The figures in their report showed a yearly increase in the median percentage of job-satisfied persons (see Table 6.1). Figure 6.4 presents satisfaction-trend data for 1948

through 1971. These data also show an overall increase in the number of satisfied workers, which is interesting because of recent speculation that satisfaction is decreasing. However, due to many measurement problems, it is impossible to conclude that a real decline in number of dissatisfied workers has taken place.

The difficulty in obtaining meaningful conclusions from the data stems from the fact that different questions yield very different results. For example, a number of studies, instead of directly asking workers "How satisfied are you?," have asked "If you had it to do over again, would you pick the same job?" The latter question produces much higher dissatisfaction scores than does the simple "how satisfied are you" question. One literature review showed that 54 percent of the workers tended to say that they were sufficiently dissatisfied with their jobs that they would not choose them again. On the other hand, the straight satisfaction question shows between 13 and 25 percent dissatisfied. However, even this figure is subject to wide variation depending on how the question is asked. When the question is asked in the simple form, "Are you satisfied, yes or no?," the number of satisfied responses is large. When the question is changed so that the employees can respond yes, no, or undecided—or satisfied, dissatisfied, or neutral—the number of satisfied responses drops.

Because of these methodological complexities, it is difficult to draw conclusions about the number of workers who are or are not satisfied with their jobs or with some facet of their jobs. This drawback does not mean, however, that meaningful research on satisfaction is impossible. On the contrary, interesting and important research has been and can be done on the determinants of job satisfaction. For example, the relationship between personal-input factors—such as education level, sex, and age and seniority—and job or facet satisfaction can be ascertained by simply comparing those people who report they are satisfied with those people who report they are dissatisfied and checking the results to see if the two groups differ in any systematic manner. The number of people reporting satisfaction is

TABLE 6.1
Median Percentages of Job-Dissatisfied Persons Reported
from 1946 to 1953

Year	Median Percentage of Job Dissatisfied
1953	13
1952	15
1951	18
1950	19
1949	19
1948	19
1946–1947	21

Source: From Herzberg et al., *Job Attitudes: Review of Research and Opinion.* Copyright 1957 by the Psychological Service of Pittsburgh. Reprinted by permission.

not crucial for this purpose. What is important is that we distinguish those people who tend to be more satisfied from those people who tend to be less satisfied. This distinction can be made with many of the better-known satisfaction-measuring instruments, such as the Job Description Index (Smith, Kendall, & Hulin, 1969) and Porter's (1961) need-satisfaction instrument.

A number of studies have tried to determine the amount of employee dissatisfaction that is associated with different job facets. Although these studies have yielded interesting results, some serious methodological problems are involved in this work. As with overall job satisfaction, factors such as type of measurement scale used and manner of wording questions seriously affect the number of people who express dissatisfaction with a given facet. For example, a question about pay satisfaction can be asked in a way that will cause few people to express dissatisfaction, while a question about security satisfaction can be asked in a way that will cause many people to express dissatisfaction. In this situation, comparing the number of people expressing security satisfaction with the number of people expressing pay dissatisfaction might produce very misleading conclusions. This problem is always present no matter how carefully the various items are worded because it is impossible to balance the items so they are comparable for all factors.

Despite methodological problems, the data on relevant satisfaction levels with different job factors are interesting. These data show that the factors mentioned earlier as being most important—that is, pay, promotion, security, leadership, and the work itself—appear in these studies as the major sources

TABLE 6.2
Differences Between Management Levels in Percentage of Subjects Indicating Need-Fulfillment Deficiencies

Questionnaire Items	% Bottom Management (N = 64)	% Middle Management (N = 75)	% Difference
Security needs	42.2	26.7	15.5
Social needs	35.2	32.0	3.2
Esteem needs	55.2	35.6	19.6
Autonomy needs	60.2	47.7	12.5
Self-actualization needs	59.9	53.3	6.6
Pay	79.7	80.0	0.3
Communications	78.1	61.3	16.8

Source: Adapted from Porter, 1961.

of dissatisfaction. Porter (1961) designed items using Maslow's needs as a measure of satisfaction. With these items, he collected data from various managers. The results of his study (see Table 6.2) show that more managers express high-order-need dissatisfaction than express lower-order-need dissatisfaction. The results also show that a large number of managers are dissatisfied with their pay and with the communications in their organizations and that middle-level managers tend to be better satisfied in all areas than lower-level managers.

Porter's data also show that managers consider the areas of dissatisfaction to be the most important areas. It is not completely clear whether the dissatisfaction causes the importance or the importance causes the dissatisfaction. The research reviewed earlier suggests that the primary causal direction is from dissatisfaction to importance, although there undoubtedly is a two-way influence process operating. The important thing to remember is that employees do report varying levels of satisfaction with different job factors, and the factors that have come out high on dissatisfaction have also been rated high on importance and have the strongest influence on overall job satisfaction.

A study by Grove and Kerr (1951) illustrates how strongly organizational conditions can affect factor satisfaction. Grove and Kerr measured employee satisfaction in two plants where normal work conditions prevailed and found that 88 percent of the workers were satisfied with their job security, which indicated that security was one of the least dissatisfying job factors for employees in these two plants. In another plant where layoffs had occurred, only 17 percent of the workers said they were satisfied with the job security, and job security was one of the most dissatisfying job factors for this plant's employees.

DETERMINANTS OF SATISFACTION

The research on the determinants of satisfaction has looked primarily at two relationships: (1) the relationship between satisfaction and the characteristics of the job, and (2) the relationship between satisfaction and the characteristics of the person. Not sur-prisingly, the research shows that satisfaction is a function of both the person and the environment. These results are consistent with our approach to thinking about satisfaction, since our model (shown in Figure 6.3) indicates that personal factors influence what people feel they should receive and that job conditions influence both what people perceive they actually receive and what people perceive they should receive. . . .

The evidence on the effects of personal-input factors on satisfaction is voluminous and will be only briefly reviewed. The research clearly shows that personal factors do affect job satisfaction, basically because they influence perceptions of what outcomes should be. As predicted by the satisfaction model in Figure 6.3, the higher a person's perceived personal inputs—that is, the greater his education, skill, and performance—the more he feels he should receive. Thus, unless the high-input person receives more outcomes, he will be dissatisfied with his job and the rewards his job offers. Such straightforward relationships between inputs and satisfaction appear to exist for all personal-input factors except age and seniority. Evidence from the study of age and seniority suggests a curvilinear relationship (that is, high satisfaction among young and old workers, low satisfaction among middle-age workers) or even a relationship of increasing satisfaction with old age and tenure. The tendency of satisfaction to be high among older, long-term employees seems to be produced by the effects of selective turnover and the development of realistic expectations about what the job has to offer.

CONSEQUENCES OF DISSATISFACTION

Originally much of the interest in job satisfaction stemmed from the belief that job satisfaction influenced job performance. Specifically, psychologists thought that high job satisfaction led to high job performance. This view has now been discredited and most psychologists feel that satisfaction influences absenteeism and turnover but not job performance. However, looking at the relationship among satisfaction, absenteeism, and turnover, let's review the work on satisfaction and performance.

Job Performance

In the 1950s two major literature reviews showed that in most studies only a slight relationship had been found between satisfaction and performance. A later review by Vroom (1964) also showed that studies had not found a strong relationship between satisfaction and performance; in fact, most studies had found a very low positive relationship between the two. In other words, better performers did seem to be slightly more satisfied than poor performers. A considerable amount of recent work suggests that the slight existing relationship is probably due to better performance indirectly causing satisfaction rather than the reverse. Lawler and Porter (1967) explained this "performance causes satisfaction" viewpoint as follows:

If we assume that rewards cause satisfaction, and that in some cases performance produces rewards, then it is possible that the relationship found between satisfaction and performance comes about through the action of a third variable—rewards. Briefly stated, good performance may lead to rewards, which in turn lead to satisfaction; this formulation then would say that satisfaction, rather than causing performance, as was previously assumed, is caused by it.

[Figure 6.5] shows that performance leads to rewards, and it distinguishes between two kinds of rewards and their connection to performance. A wavy line between performance and extrinsic rewards indicates that such rewards are likely to be imperfectly related to performance. By extrinsic rewards is meant such organizationally controlled rewards as pay, promotion, status, and security—rewards that are often referred to as satisfying mainly lower-level needs. The connection is relatively weak because of the difficulty of tying extrinsic rewards directly to performance. Even though an organization may have a policy of rewarding merit, performance is difficult to measure, and in dispensing rewards like pay, many other factors are frequently taken into consideration.

Quite the opposite is likely to be true for intrinsic rewards, however, since they are given to the individual by himself for good performance. Intrinsic or internally mediated re-

wards are subject to fewer disturbing influences and thus are likely to be more directly related to good performance. This connection is indicated in the model by a semi-wavy line. Probably the best example of an intrinsic reward is the feeling of having accomplished something worthwhile. For that matter any of the rewards that satisfy self-actualization needs or higher-order growth needs are good examples of intrinsic rewards [pp. 23–24].[2]

Figure 6.5 shows that intrinsic and extrinsic rewards are not directly related to job satisfaction, since the relationship is moderated by perceived equitable rewards (what people think they should receive). The model in Figure 6.5 is similar to the model in Figure 6.3, since both models show that satisfaction is a function of the amount of rewards a person receives and the amount of rewards he feels he should receive.

Because of the imperfect relationship between performance and rewards and the important effect of perceived equitable rewards, a low but positive relationship should exist between job satisfaction and job performance in most situations. However, in certain situations, a strong positive relationship may exist; while in other situations, a negative relationship may exist. A negative relationship would be expected where rewards are unrelated to performance or negatively related to performance.

To have the same level of satisfaction for good performers and poor performers, the good performers must receive more rewards than the poor performers. The reason for this, as stressed earlier, is that performance level influences the amount of rewards a person feels he should receive. Thus, when rewards are not based on performance—when poor performers receive equal rewards or a larger amount of rewards than good performers—the best performers will be the least satisfied, and a negative satisfaction–performance relationship will exist. If, on the other hand, the better performers are given significantly more rewards, a positive satisfaction–performance relationship should exist. If it is assumed that most organizations are partially successful in relating rewards to performance, it follows that most studies should find a low but positive relationship between satisfaction and performance. Lawler and Porter's (1967) study was among those that found this relationship; their study also found that, as predicted, intrinsic-need satisfaction was more closely related to performance than was extrinsic-need satisfaction.

In retrospect, it is hard to understand why the belief that high satisfaction causes high performance was so widely accepted. There is nothing in the literature on motivation that suggests this causal relationship. In fact, such a relationship is opposite to the concepts developed by both drive theory and expectancy theory. If anything, these two theories would seem to predict that high satisfaction might reduce motivation because of a consequent reduction in the importance of various rewards that may have provided motivational force. Clearly, a more logical view is that performance is determined by people's efforts to obtain the goals and outcomes they desire, and satisfaction is determined by the outcomes people actually obtain. Yet for some reason, many people believed—and some people still do believe—that the "satisfaction causes performance" view is best.

Turnover

The relationship between satisfaction and turnover has been studied often. In most studies, researchers have measured the job satisfaction among a number of employees and then waited to see which of the employees studied left during an ensuing time period (typically, a year). The satisfaction scores of the employees who left have then been compared with the remaining employees' scores. Although relationships between satisfaction scores and turnover have not always been very strong, the studies in this area have consistently shown that dissatisfied workers are more likely than satisfied workers to terminate employment; thus, satisfaction scores can predict turnover.

A study by Ross and Zander (1957) is a good example of the kind of research that has been done. Ross and Zander measured the job satisfaction of 2,680 female workers in a large company. Four months later, these researchers found that 169 of these employees had resigned; those who left were significantly more dissatisfied with the amount of recognition they received on their

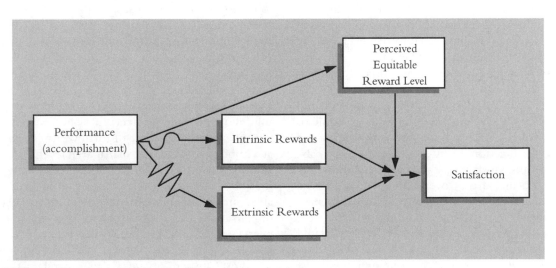

FIGURE 6.5 *Model of the Relationship of Performance to Satisfaction.*
Source: From E. E. Lawler and L. W. Porter, "The Effect of Performance on Job Satisfaction," *Industrial Relations* 7 (1967): 20–28. Reprinted by permission of the publisher, Industrial Relations.

jobs, with the amount of achievement they experienced, and with the amount of autonomy they had.

Probably the major reason that turnover and satisfaction are not more strongly related is that turnover is very much influenced by the availability of other positions. Even if a person is very dissatisfied with his job, he is not likely to leave unless more attractive alternatives are available. This observation would suggest that in times of economic prosperity, turnover should be high, and a strong relationship should exist between turnover and satisfaction; but in times of economic hardship, turnover should be low, and little relationship should exist between turnover and satisfaction. There is research evidence to support the argument that voluntary turnover is much lower in periods of economic hardship. However, no study has compared the relationship between satisfaction and turnover under different economic conditions to see if it is stronger under full employment.

Absenteeism

Like turnover, absenteeism has been found to be related to job satisfaction. If anything, the relationship between satisfaction and absenteeism seems to be stronger than the relationship between satisfaction and turnover. However, even in the case of absenteeism, the relationship is far from being isomorphic. Absenteeism is caused by a number of factors other than a person's voluntarily deciding not to come to work; illness, accidents, and so on can prevent someone who wants to come to work from actually coming to work. We would expect satisfaction to affect only voluntary absences; thus, satisfaction can never be strongly related to a measure of overall absence rate. Those studies that have separated voluntary absences from overall absences have, in fact, found that voluntary absence rates are much more closely related to satisfaction than are overall absence rates (Vroom, 1964). Of course, this outcome would be expected if satisfaction does influence people's willingness to come to work.

Organization Effectiveness

The research evidence clearly shows that employees' decisions about whether they will go to work on any given day and whether they will quit are affected by their feelings of job satisfaction. All the literature reviews on the subject have reached this conclusion. The fact that present satisfaction influences future absenteeism and turnover clearly indicates that the causal direction is from satisfaction to behavior. This conclusion is in marked contrast to our conclusion with respect to performance—that is, behavior causes satisfaction. . . .

The research evidence on the determinants of satisfaction suggests that satisfaction is very much influenced by the actual rewards a person receives; of course, the organization has a considerable amount of control over these rewards. The research also shows that, although not all people will react to the same reward level in the same manner, reactions are predictable if something is known about how people perceive their inputs. The implication is that organizations can influence employees' satisfaction levels. Since it is possible to know how employees will react to different outcome levels, organizations can allocate outcomes in ways that will either cause job satisfaction or job dissatisfaction.

Absenteeism and turnover have a very direct influence on organizational effectiveness. Absenteeism is very costly because it interrupts scheduling, creates a need for over-staffing, increases fringe-benefit costs, and so on. Turnover is expensive because of the many costs incurred in recruiting and training replacement employees. For lower-level jobs, the cost of turnover is estimated at $2,000 a person; at the managerial level, the cost is at least five to ten times the monthly salary of the job involved. Because satisfaction is manageable and influences absenteeism and turnover, organizations can control absenteeism and turnover. Generally, by keeping satisfaction high and, specifically, by seeing that the best employees are the most satisfied, organizations can retain those employees they need the most. In effect, organizations can manage turnover so that, if it occurs, it will occur among employees the organization can most afford to lose. However, keeping the better performers more satisfied is not easy, since they must be rewarded very well . . . although identifying and rewarding the better performers is not always easy, the effort may have significant payoffs in terms of increased organizational effectiveness.

REFERENCES

Adams, J. S. "Toward an Understanding of Inequity." *Journal of Abnormal Psychology* 67 (1963); 422–36.

Adams, J. S. "Injustice in Social Exchange," In *Advances in Experimental Social Psychology*, vol. 2, edited by L. Berkowitz. New York: Academic Press, 1965.

Dunnette, M. D.; Campbell, J. P.; and Hakel, M. D. "Factors Contributing to Job Satisfaction and Job Dissatisfaction in Six Occupational Groups." *Organizational Behavior and Human Performance* 2 (1967): 143–74.

Gardner, J. W. *No Easy Victories*. New York: Harper & Row, 1968.

Grove, E. A., and Kerr, W. A. "Specific Evidence on Origin of Halo Effect in Measurement of Employee Morale." *Journal of Social Psychology* 34 (1951): 165–70.

Herzberg, F.; Mausner, B.; Peterson, R. O.; and Capwell, D. F. *Job Attitudes: Review of Research and Opinion*. Pittsburgh: Psychological Service of Pittsburgh. 1957.

Herzberg, F.; Mausner, B., and Snyderman, B. *The Motivation to Work*, 2nd ed. New York; John Wiley & Sons, 1959.

Katzell, R. A. "Personal Values, Job Satisfaction, and Job Behavior." In *Man in a World of Work*, edited by H. Borow. Boston; Houghton Mifflin, 1964.

Lawler, E. E. "The Multitrait-Multirater Approach to Measuring Managerial Job Performance." *Journal of Applied Psychology* 51 (1967). 369–81.

Lawler, E. E., and Porter, L. W. "The Effect of Performance on Job Satisfaction." *Industrial Relations* 7 (1967) 20–28.

Locke, E. A. "What Is Job Satisfaction?" Paper presented at the APA Convention, San Francisco, September 1968.

Locke, E. A. "What Is Job Satisfaction?" *Organizational Behavior and Human Performance* 4 (1969): 309–36.

Mobley, W. H., and Locke, E. A. "The Relationship of Value Importance to Satisfaction." *Organizational Behavior and Human Performance* 5 (1970): 463–83.

Morse, N. C. *Satisfactions in the White-Collar Job*. Ann Arbor: University of Michigan, Institute for Social Research, Survey Research Center, 1953.

Porter, L. W. "A Study of Perceived Need Satisfactions in Bottom and Middle Management Jobs." *Journal of Applied Psychology* 45 (1961): 1–10.

Ross, I. E., and Zander, A. F. "Need Satisfaction and Employee Turnover." *Personnel Psychology* 10 (1957): 327–38.

Schaffer, R. H. "Job Satisfaction as Related to Need Satisfaction in Work." *Psychological Monographs* 67 (1953): 14, whole no. 364.

Smith, P.; Kendall, L.; and Hulin, C. *The Measurement of Satisfaction in Work and Retirement*. Chicago: Rand McNally & Company, 1969.

Vroom, V. H. *Work and Motivation*. New York: John Wiley & Sons, 1964.

Wanous, J. P., and Lawler, E. E. "Measurement and Meaning of Job Satisfaction." *Journal of Applied Psychology* 56 (1972): 95–105.

NOTES

1. V. Vroom, *Work and Motivation.* Copyright © 1964 by John Wiley & Sons, Inc. This and all other quotes from the same source are reprinted by permission.

2. E. E. Lawler and L. W. Porter, "The Effect of Performance on Job Satisfaction," *Industrial Relations* 7 (1967): 20–28. Reprinted by permission of the publisher, *Industrial Relations*.

Expressing Emotions in Organizations

7. ORGANIZATIONAL PSYCHOLOGY AND THE PURSUIT OF THE HAPPY/PRODUCTIVE WORKER

Barry M. Staw

What I am going to talk about in this article is an old and overworked topic, but one that remains very much a source of confusion and controversy. It is also a topic that continues to attract the attention of managers and academic researchers alike, frequently being the focus of both popular books and scholarly articles. The issue is how to manage an organization so that employees can be both happy and productive—a situation where workers and managers are both satisfied with the outcomes.

The pursuit of the happy/productive worker could be viewed as as impossible dream from the Marxist perspective of inevitable worker-management conflict. Such a goal could also be seen as too simple or naive from the traditional industrial relations view of outcomes being a product of necessary bargaining and compromise. Yet, from the psychological perspective, the pursuit of the happy/productive worker has seemed a worthwhile though difficult endeavor, one that might be achieved if we greatly increase our knowledge of work attitudes and behavior. In this article, I will examine this psychological perspective and try to provide a realistic appraisal of where we now stand in the search for satisfaction and productivity in work settings.

APPROACHES TO THE HAPPY/PRODUCTIVE WORKER

One of the earliest pursuits of the happy/productive worker involved the search for a relationship between satisfaction and productivity. The idea was that the world might be neatly divided into situations where workers are either happy and productive or unhappy and unproductive. If this were true, then it would be a simple matter to specify the differences between management styles present in the two sets of organizations and to come up with a list of prescriptions for improvement. Unfortunately, research has never supported such a clear relationship between individual satisfaction and productivity. For over thirty years, starting with Brayfield and Crockett's classic review of the job satisfaction-performance literature,[1] and again with Vroom's discussion of satisfaction-performance research,[2] organizational psychologists have had to contend with the fact that happiness and productivity may not necessarily go together. As a result, most organizational psychologists have come to accept the argument that satisfaction and performance may relate to two entirely different individual decisions—decisions to participate and to produce.[3]

Though psychologists have acknowledged the fact that satisfaction and performance are not tightly linked, this has not stopped them from pursuing the happy/productive worker. In fact, over the last thirty years, an enormous variety of theories have attempted to show how managers can reach the promised land of high satisfaction and productivity. The theories shown in Table 7.1 constitute only an abbreviated list of recent attempts to reach this positive state.

None of the theories in Table 7.1 have inherited the happy/productive worker hypothesis in the simple sense of believing that job satisfaction and performance generally co-vary in the world *as it now exists*. But, these models all make either indirect or direct assumptions that *it is possible* to achieve a world where both satisfaction and performance will be present. Some of the theories focus on ways to increase job satisfaction, with the implicit assumption that performance will necessarily follow; some strive to directly increase performance, with the assumption that satisfaction will result; and some note that satisfaction and performance will be a joint product of implementing certain changes in the organization.

Without going into the specifics of each of these routes to the happy/productive worker, I think it is fair to say that most of the theories in Table 7.1 have been oversold. Historically, they each burst on the scene with glowing and almost messianic predictions, with proponents tending to simplify the process of change, making it seem like a few easy tricks will guarantee benefits to workers and management alike. The problem, of course, is that as results have come in from both academic research and from wider practical application, the benefits no longer have appeared so strong nor widespread. Typically, the broader the application and the more well-documented the study (with experimental controls and measures of expected costs and benefits), the weaker have been the empirical results.

TABLE 7.1
Paths to the Happy/Product Worker

Worker Participation	The Pursuit of Excellence
Supportive Leadership	Socio-Technical Systems
9–9 Systems	Organizational Commitment
Job Enrichment	High Performing Systems
Behavior Modification	Theory Z
Goal Setting	Strong Culture

Thus, in the end, both managers and researchers have often been left disillusioned, sceptical that any part of these theories are worth a damn and that behavioral science will ever make a contribution to management.

My goal with this article is to *lower our expectations*—to show why it is so difficult to make changes in both satisfaction and performance. My intention is not to paint such a pessimistic picture as to justify not making any changes at all, but to innoculate us against the frustrations of slow progress. My hope is to move us toward a reasoned but sustainable pursuit of the happy/productive worker—away from the alternating practice of fanfare and despair.

CHANGING JOB ATTITUDES

Although organizational psychologists have accepted the notion that job satisfaction and performance do not necessarily co-vary, they have still considered job attitudes as something quite permeable or subject to change. This "blank slate" approach to job attitudes comes from prevailing psychological views of the individual, where the person is seen as a creature who constantly appraises the work situation, evaluates the merits of the context, and formulates an attitude based on these conditions. As the work situation changes, individuals are thought to be sensitive to the shifts adjusting their attitudes in a positive or negative direction. With such an approach to attitudes, it is easy to see why job satisfaction has been a common target of organizational change, and why attempts to redesign work have evolved as a principal mechanism for improving job satisfaction.

Currently, the major debate in the job design area concerns whether individuals are more sensitive to objective job conditions or social cues. In one camp are proponents of job redesign who propose that individuals are highly receptive to concrete efforts to improve working conditions. Hackman and Oldham, for example, argue that satisfaction can be increased by improving a job in terms of its variety (doing a wider number of things), identity (seeing how one's various tasks make a meaningful whole), responsibility (being in charge of one's own work and its quality), feedback (knowing when one has done a good job), and significance (the meaning or relative importance of one's contribution to the organization or society in general).[4] In the opposing camp are advocates of social information processing. These researchers argue that jobs are often ambiguous entities subject to multiple interpretations and perceptions.[5] Advocates of social information processing have noted that the positive or negative labeling of a task can greatly determine one's attitude toward the job, and that important determinants of this labeling are the opinions of co-workers who voice positive or negative views of the work. These researchers have shown that it may be as easy to persuade workers that their jobs are interesting by influencing the *perception* of a job as it is to make objective changes in the work role.

The debate between job design and social information processing has produced two recent shifts in the way we think about job attitudes. First, organizational psychology now places greater emphasis on the role of cognition and subjective evaluation in the way people respond to jobs. This is probably helpful, because even though we have generally measured job conditions with perceptual scales, we have tended to confuse these perceptions with objective job conditions. We need to be reminded that perceptions of job characteristics do not necessarily reflect reality, yet they can determine how we respond to that reality.

The second shift in thinking about job attitudes is a movement toward situationalism, stressing how even slight alterations in job context can influence one's perception of a job. It is now believed that people's job attitudes may be influenced not only by the objective properties of the work, but also by subtle cues given off by co-workers or supervisors that the job is dull or interesting. I think this new view is a mistake since it overstates the role of external influence in the determination of job attitudes. The reality may be that individuals are quite resistant to change efforts, with their attitudes coming more as a function of personal disposition than situational influence.

THE CONSISTENCY OF JOB ATTITUDES

Robert Kahn recently observed that, although our standard of living and working conditions have improved dramatically since World War II, reports of satisfaction on national surveys have not changed dramatically.[6] This implies that job satisfaction might be something of a "sticky variable," one that is not easily changed by outside influence. Some research on the consistency of job attitudes leads to the same conclusion. Schneider and Dachler, for example, found very strong consistency in satisfaction scores over a 16-month longitudinal study (averaging .56 for managers and .58 for non-managers).[7] Pulakos and Schmitt also found that high school students' pre-employment expectations of satisfaction correlated significantly with ratings of their jobs several years later.[8] These findings, along with the fact that job satisfaction is generally intertwined with both life satisfaction and mental health, imply that there is some ongoing consistency in job attitudes, and that job satisfaction may be determined as much by dispositional properties of the individual as any changes in the situation.

A Berkeley colleague, Joseph Garbarino, has long captured this notion of a dispositional source of job attitudes with a humorous remark, "I always told my children at a young age that their most important decision in life would be whether they wanted to be happy or not; everything else is malleable enough to fit the answer to this question." What Garbarino implies is that job attitudes are fairly constant, and when reality changes for either the better or worse, we can easily distort that reality to fit our underlying disposition. Thus, individuals may think a great deal about the nature of their jobs, but satisfaction can result as much from the unique way a person views the world around him as from any social influence or objective job characteristics. That is, individuals predisposed to be happy may interpret their jobs in a much different way than those with more negative predispositions.

The Attitudinal Consistency Study

Recently, I have been involved with two studies attempting to test for dispositional sources of job attitudes. In the first study, Jerry Ross and I reanalyzed data from the National Longitudinal Survey, a study conducted by labor economists at Ohio State.[9] We used this survey to look at the stability of job attitudes over time and job situations. The survey's measures of attitudes were not very extensive but did provide one of the few available sources of data on objective job changes.

The National Longitudinal Survey data revealed an interesting pattern of results. We found that job satisfaction was fairly consistent over time, with significant relationships among job attitudes over three- and five-year time intervals. We also found that job satisfaction showed consistency *even when people changed jobs*. This later finding is especially important, since it directly contradicts the prevailing assumptions of job attitude research.

Most job design experiments and organizational interventions that strive to improve job attitudes change a small aspect of work, but look for major changes in job satisfaction. However, the National Longitudinal Survey data showed that when people changed their place of work (which would naturally include one's supervisor, working conditions, and procedures), there was still significant consistency in attitudes. One could, of course, argue that people leave one terrible job for another, and this is why such consistency in job attitude arises. Therefore, we checked for consistency across occupational changes. The National Longitudinal Survey showed consistency not only across occupational changes, but also when people changed *both* their employers and their occupations. This evidence of consistency tells us that people may not be as malleable as we would like to think they are, and that there may be some underlying tendency toward equilibrium in job attitudes. If you are dissatisfied in one job context, you are also likely to be dissatisfied in another (perhaps better) environment.

The Dispositional Study

The consistency data from the National Longitudinal Survey, while interesting, do not tell us what it is that may underlie a tendency to be satisfied or dissatisfied on the job. Therefore, Nancy Bell (a doctoral student at the Berkeley Business School), John Clausen (a developmental sociologist at Berkeley), and I undertook a study to find some of the dispositional sources of job satisfaction.[10] We sought to relate early personality characteristics to job attitudes later in life, using a very unusual longitudinal data source.

There are three longitudinal personality projects that have been running for over fifty years at Berkeley (the Berkeley Growth Study, the Oakland Growth Study, and the Guidance Study), and they have since been combined into what is now called the Intergenerational Study. Usually when psychologists speak of longitudinal studies, they mean data collected from one or two year intervals. These data span over 50 years. Usually, when psychologists refer to personality ratings, they mean self-reports derived from the administration of various questionnaires. Much of the Intergenerational Study data are clinical ratings derived from questionnaires, observation, and interview materials evaluated by a different set of raters for each period of the individual's life. Thus, these data are of unusual quality for psychological research.

Basically what we did with data from the Intergenerational Study was to construct an affective disposition scale that measured a very general positive-negative orientation of people. We then related this scale to measures of job attitudes at different periods in people's lives. The ratings used for our affective disposition scale included items such as "cheerful," "satisfied with self," and "irritable" (reverse coded), and we correlated this scale with measures of job and career satisfaction. The results were very provocative. We found that affective dispositions, from as early as the junior-high-school years, significantly predicted job attitudes during middle and late adulthood (ages 40–60). The magnitude of correlations was not enormous (in the .3 to .4 range).

But, these results are about as strong as we usually see between two attitudes measured on the same questionnaire by the same person at the same time—yet, these data cut across different raters and over fifty years in time.

What are we to conclude from this personality research as well as our reanalyses of the National Longitudinal Survey? I think we can safely conclude that there is a fair amount of consistency in job attitudes and that there may be dispositional as well as situational sources of job satisfaction. Thus, it is possible that social information processing theorists have been on the right track in viewing jobs as ambiguous entities that necessitate interpretation by individuals. But, it is also likely that the interpretation of jobs (whether they are perceived as positive or negative) can come as much from internal, dispositional causes (e.g., happiness or depression) as external sources. Consequently, efforts to improve job satisfaction via changes in job conditions will need to contend with stable personal dispositions toward work—forces that may favor consistency or equilibrium in the way people view the world around them.

THE INTRANSIGENCE OF JOB PERFORMANCE

Although we have not conducted research on the consistency of performance or its resistance to change, I think there are some parallels between the problems of changing attitudes and performance. Just as job attitudes may be constrained by individual dispositions, there are many elements of both the individual and work situation that can make improvements in job performance difficult.[11]

Most of the prevailing theories of work performance are concerned with individual motivation. They prescribe various techniques intended to stimulate, reinforce, or lure people into working harder. Most of these theories have little to say about the individual's limits of task ability, predisposition for working hard, or the general energy or activity level of the person. Somewhat naively, our theories have maintained that performance is under the complete control of the individual. Even through there are major individual differences affecting the quantity or quality of work produced, we have assumed that *if the employee really wants to perform better, his or her performance will naturally go up.*

There already exist some rather strong data that refute these implicit assumptions about performance. A number of studies[12] have shown that mental and physical abilities can be reliable predictors of job performance, and it is likely that other dispositions (e.g., personality characteristics) will eventually be found to be associated with effective performance of certain work roles. Thus, influencing work effort may not be enough to cause wide swings in performance, unless job performance is somewhat independent of ability (e.g., in a low skill job). Many work roles may be so dependent on ability (such as those of a professional athlete, musician, inventor) that increases in effort may simply not cause large changes in the end product.

In addition to ability, there may also be other individual factors that contribute to the consistency of performance. People who work hard in one situation are likely to be the ones who exert high effort in a second situation. If, for example, the person's energy level (including need for sleep) is relatively constant over time, we should not expect wide changes in available effort. And, if personality dimensions such as dependability and self-confidence can predict one's achievement level over the lifecourse,[13] then a similar set of personal attributes may well constitute limitations to possible improvements in performance. Already, assessment centers have capitalized on this notion by using personality measures to predict performance in many corporate settings.

Performance may not be restricted just because of the individual's level of ability and effort, however. Jobs may *themselves* be designed so that performance is not under the control of the individual, regardless of ability or effort. Certainly we are aware of the fact that an assembly line worker's output is more a product of the speed of the line than any personal preference. In administrative jobs too, what one does may be constrained by the work cycle or technical procedures. There may be many people with interlocking tasks so that an increase in the performance of one employee doesn't mean much if several tasks must be completed sequentially or simultaneously in order to improve productivity. Problems also arise in situations where doing one's job better may not be predicted upon a burst of energy or desire, but upon increases in materials, financial support, power, and resources. As noted by Kanter, the administrator must often negotiate, hoard, and form coalitions to get anything done on the job, since there are lots of actors vying for the attention and resources of the organization.[14] Thus, the nature of the organization, combined with the abilities and efforts of individuals to maneuver in the organization, may serve to constrain changes in individual performance.

ASSESSING THE DAMAGE

So far I have taken a somewhat dark or pessimistic view of the search for the happy/productive worker. I have noted that in terms of satisfaction and performance, it may not be easy to create perfect systems because both happiness and performance are constrained variables, affected by forces not easily altered by our most popular interventions and prescriptions for change. Should organizational psychologists therefore close up shop and go home? Should we move to a more descriptive study of behavior as opposed to searching for improvements in work attitudes and performance?

I think such conclusions are overly pessimistic. We need to interpret the stickiness of job attitudes and performance not as an invitation to complacency or defeat, but as a realistic assessment that it will take very strong treatments to move these entrenched variables. Guzzo, Jackson, and Katzell have recently made a similar point after a statistical examination (called meta-analysis) of organizational interventions designed to improve productivity.[15] They noted that the most effective changes are often *multiple treatments*, where several things are changed at once in a given organization. Thus, instead of idealistic and optimistic promises, we may literally need to throw the kitchen sink at the problem.

The problem of course is that we have more than one kitchen sink! As noted earlier, nearly every theory of organizational behavior has been devoted to predicting and potentially improving job attitudes and performance. And, simply aggregating these treatments is not likely to have the desired result, since many of these recommendations consist of conflicting prescriptions for change. Therefore, it would be wiser to look for compatible *systems* of variables that can possibly be manipulated in concert. Let us briefly consider three systems commonly used in organizational change efforts and then draw some conclusions about their alternative uses.

THREE SYSTEMS OF ORGANIZATIONAL CHANGE

The Individually-Oriented System

The first alternative is to build a strong individually-oriented system, based on the kind of traditional good management that organizational psychologists have been advocating for years. This system would emphasize a number of venerable features of Western business organizations such as:

- Tying extrinsic rewards (such as pay) to performance.

- Setting realistic and challenging goals.

- Evaluating employee performance accurately and providing feedback on performance

- Promoting on the basis of skill and performance rather than personal characteristics, power, or connections.

- Building the skill level of the workforce through training and development.

- Enlarging and enriching jobs through increases in responsibility, variety, and significance.

All of the above techniques associated with the individually-oriented system are designed to promote both satisfaction and productivity. The major principle underlying each of these features is to structure the work and/or reward system so that high performance is either intrinsically or extrinsically rewarding to the individual, thus creating a situation where high performance contributes to job satisfaction.

In practice, there can be numerous bugs in using an individually-oriented system to achieve satisfaction and performance. For example, just saying that rewards should be based on performance is easier than knowing what the proper relationship should be or whether there should be discontinuities at the high or low end of that relationship. Should we, for instance, lavish rewards on the few highest performers, deprive the lowest performers, or establish a constant linkage between pay and performance? In terms of goal-setting, should goals be set by management, workers, or joint decision making, and what should be proper baseline be for measuring improvements? In terms of job design, what is the proper combination of positive social cues and actual job enrichment that will improve motivation and satisfaction?

These questions are important and need to be answered in order to "fine-tune" or fully understand an individually-oriented system. Yet, even without answers to these questions, we already know that a well-run organization using an individually-oriented system *can* be effective. The problem is we usually don't implement such a system, either completely or very well, in most organizations. Instead, we often compare poorly managed corporations using individually-oriented systems (e.g., those with rigid bureaucratic structures) with more effectively run firms using another motivational system (e.g., Japanese organizations), concluding that the individual model is wrong. The truth may be that the individual model may be just as correct as other approaches, but we simply don't implement it as well.

The Group-Oriented System

Individually-oriented systems are obviously not the only way to go. We can also have a group-oriented system, where satisfaction and performance are derived from group participation. In fact, much of organizational life could be designed around groups, if we wanted to capitalize fully on the power of groups to influence work attitudes and behavior.[16] The basic idea would be to make group participation so important that groups would be capable of controlling both satisfaction and performance. Some of the most common techniques would be:

• Organizing work around intact groups.
• Having groups charged with selection, training, and rewarding of members.
• Using groups to enforce strong norms for behavior, with group involvement in off-the-job as well as on-the-job behavior.
• Distributing resources on a group rather than individual basis.
• Allowing and perhaps even promoting intergroup rivalry so as to build within-group solidarity.

Group-oriented systems may be difficult for people at the top to control, but they can be very powerful and involving. We know from military research that soldiers can fight long and hard, not out of special patriotism, but from devotion and loyalty to their units. We know that participation in various high-tech project groups can be immensely involving, both in terms of one's attitudes and performance. We also know that people will serve long and hard hours to help build or preserve organizational divisions or departments, perhaps more out of loyalty and altruism than self-interest. Thus, because individuals will work to achieve group praise and adoration, a group oriented system, effectively managed, can potentially contribute to high job performance and satisfaction.

The Organizationally-Oriented System

A third way of organizing work might be an organizationally-oriented system, using the principles of Ouchi's Theory Z and Lawler's recommendations for developing high-performing systems.[17] The basic goal would be to arrange working conditions so that individuals gain satisfaction from contributing to the entire organization's welfare. If individuals were to identify closely with the organization as a whole, then organizational performance would be intrinsically rewarding to the individual. On a less altruistic basis, individuals might also gain extrinsic rewards from association with a high-performing organization, since successful organizations may provide greater personal opportunities in terms of salary and promotion. Common features of an organizationally-oriented system would be:

• Socialization into the organization as a whole to foster identification with the entire business and not just a particular subunit.
• Job rotation around the company so that loyalty is not limited to one subunit.
• Long training period with the development of skills that are specific to the company and not transferable to other firms in the industry or profession, thus committing people to the employing organization.
• Long-term or protected employment to gain organizational loyalty, with concern for survival and welfare of the firm.
• Decentralized operations, with few departments or subunits to compete for the allegiance of members.
• Few status distinctions between employees so that dissension and separatism are not fostered.
• Economic education and sharing of organizational information about products, financial condition, and strategies of the firm.
• Tying individual rewards (at all levels in the firm) to organizational performance through various forms of profit sharing, stock options, and bonuses.

The Japanese have obviously been the major proponents of organizationally-oriented systems, although some of the features listed here (such as profit sharing) are very American in origin. The odd thing is that Americans have consistently followed an organizationally-oriented system for middle and upper management and for members of professional organizations such as law and accounting firms. For these high-level employees, loyalty may be as valued as immediate performance, with the firm expecting the individual to defend the organization, even if there does not seem to be any obvious self-interest involved. Such loyalty is rarely demanded or expected from the lower levels of traditional Western organizations.

EVALUATING THE THREE SYSTEMS

I started this article by noting that it may be very difficult to change job performance and satisfaction. Then I noted that recognition of this difficulty should not resign us to the present situation, but spur us to stronger and more systemic actions—in a sense, throwing more variables at the problem. As a result, I have tried to characterize three syndromes of actions that might be effective routes toward the happy/productive worker.

One could build a logical case for the use of any of the three motivational systems. Each has the potential for arousing individuals, steering their behavior in desired ways, and building satisfaction as a consequence of high performance. Individually-oriented systems work by tapping the desires and goals of individuals and by taking advantage of our cultural affinity for independence. Group-oriented systems work by taking advantage of our more social selves, using group pressures and loyalty as the means of enforcing desired behavior and dispensing praise for accomplishments. Finally, organizationally-oriented systems function by building intense attraction to the goals of an institution, where individual pleasure is desired from serving the collective welfare.

If we have three logical and defensible routes toward achieving the happy/productive worker, which is the best path? The answer to this question will obviously depend on how the question is phrased. If "best" means appropriate from a cultural point of view, we will get one answer. As Americans, although we respect organizational loyalty, we often become suspicious of near total

institutions where behavior is closely monitored and strongly policed—places like the company town and religious cult. If we define "best" as meaning the highest level of current performance, we might get a different answer, since many of the Japanese-run plants are now outperforming the American variety. Still, if we phrase the question in terms of *potential* effectiveness, we may get a third answer. Cross-cultural comparisons, as I mentioned, often pit poorly managed individually-oriented systems (especially those with non-contingent rewards and a bureaucratic promotion system) against more smoothly running group or organizationally-oriented systems. Thus, we really do not know which system, managed to its potential, will lead to the greatest performance.

Mixing the Systems

If we accept the fact that individual, group, and organizationally-oriented systems may each do *something* right, would it be possible to take advantage of all three? That is, can we either combine all three systems into some suprasystem or attempt to build a hybrid system by using the best features of each?

I have trepidations about combining the three approaches. Instead of a stronger treatment, we may end up with either a conflicted or confused environment. Because the individually-oriented system tends to foster competition among individual employees, it would not, for example, be easily merged with group-oriented systems that promote intragroup solidarity. Likewise, organizationally-oriented systems that emphasize how people can serve a common goal may not blend well with group-oriented systems that foster intergroup rivalry. Finally, the use of either a group- or organizationally-oriented reward system may diminish individual motivation, since it becomes more difficult for the person to associate his behavior with collective accomplishments and outcomes. Thus, by mixing the motivational approaches, we may end up with a watered-down treatment that does not fulfill the potential of *any* of the three systems.

In deciding which system to use, we need to face squarely the costs as well as benefits of the three approaches. For example, firms considering an individually-oriented system should assess not only the gains associated with increases in individual motivation, but also potential losses in collaboration that might result from interpersonal competition. Similarly, companies thinking of using a group-oriented system need to study the trade-offs of intergroup competition that can be a byproduct of increased intragroup solidarity. And, before thinking than an organizationally-oriented system will solve all the firm's problems, one needs to know whether motivation to achieve collective goals can be heightened to the point where it outweighs potential losses in motivation toward personal and group interests. These trade-offs are not trivial. they trigger considerations of human resource policy as well as more general philosophical issues of what the organization wants to be. They also involve technical problems for which current organizational research has few solutions, since scholars have tended to study treatments in isolation rather than the effect of larger systems of variables.

So far, all we can be sure of is that task structure plays a key role in formulating the proper motivational strategy. As an example, consider the following cases: a sales organization can be divided into discrete territories (where total performance is largely the sum of individual efforts), a research organization where several product groups are charged with making new developments (where aggregate performance is close to the sum of group efforts), and a high-technology company where success and failure is due to total collaboration and collective effort. In each of these three cases, the choice of the proper motivational system will be determined by whether one views individual, group, or collective effort as the most important element. Such a choice is also determined by the degree to which one is willing to sacrifice (or trade-off) a degree of performance from other elements of the system, be they the behavior of individuals, groups, or the collective whole. Thus, the major point is that each motivational system has its relative strengths and weaknesses—that despite the claims of many of our theories of management, there is no simple or conflict-free road to the happy/productive worker.

CONCLUSION

Although this article started by noting that the search for the happy/productive worker has been a rather quixotic venture, I have tried to end the discussion with some guarded optimism. By using individual, group, and organizational systems, I have shown how it is *at least possible* to create changes than can overwhelm the forces for stability in both job attitudes and performance. None of these three approaches are a panacea that will solve all of an organization's problems, and no doubt some very hard choices must be made between them. Yet, caution need not preclude action. Therefore, rather than the usual academic's plea for further research or the consultant's claim for bountiful results, we need actions that are flexible enough to allow for mistakes and adjustments along the way.

REFERENCES

1. A. H. Brayfield and W. H. Crockett, "Employee Attitudes and Employee Performance," *Psychological Bulletin*, 51 (1955):396–424.

2. Victor H. Vroom, *Work and Motivation* (New York, NY: Wiley, 1969).

3. James G. March and Herbert A. Simon, *Organizations* (New York, NY: Wiley, 1958).

4. Richard J. Hackman and Greg R. Oldham, *Work Redesign* (Reading, MA: Addison-Wesley, 1980).

5. E.g., Gerald R. Salancik and Jeffrey Pfeffer, "A Social Information Processing Approach to Job Attitudes and Task Design," *Administrative Science Quarterly*, 23 (1978):224–253.

6. Robert Kahn, (1985).

7. Benjamin Schneider and Peter Dachler, "A Note on the Stability of the Job Description Index," *Journal of Applied Psychology*, 63 (1978):650–653.

8. Elaine D. Pulakos and Neil Schmitt, "A Longitudinal Study of a Valance Model Approach for the Prediction of Job Satisfaction of New Employees," *Journal of Applied Psychology*, 68 (1983):307–312.

9. Barry M. Staw and Jerry Ross, "Stability in the Midst of Change: A Dispositional Approach to Job Attitudes," *Journal of Applied Psychology*, 70 (1985):469–480.

10. Barry M. Staw, Nancy E. Bell, and John A. Clausen, "The Dispositional Approach to Job Attitudes: A Lifetime Longitudinal Test," *Administrative Science Quarterly* (March 1986).

11. See, Lawrence H. Peters, Edward J. O'Connor, and Joe R. Eulberg, "Situational Constraints: Sources, Consequences, and Future Considerations," in Kendreth M. Rowland and Gerald R. Ferris, eds., *Research in Personnel and Human Resources Management*, Vol. 3 (Greenwich, CT: JAI Press, 1985).

12. For a review, see Marvin D. Dunnette, "Aptitudes, Abilities, and Skills" in Marvin D. Dunnette, ed., *Handbook of Industrial and Organizational Psychology* (Chicago, IL: Rand McNally, 1976).

13. As found by John Clausen, personal communications, 1986.

14. Rosabeth M. Kanter, *The Change Masters* (New York, NY: Simon & Schuster, 1983).

15. Richard A. Guzzo, Susan E. Jackson, and Raymond A. Katzell, "Meta-analysis Analysis," in Barry M. Staw and Larry L. Cummings, eds., *Research in Organizational Behavior*, Volume 9 (Greenwich, CT: JAI Press, 1987).

16. See, Harold J. Leavitt, "Suppose We Took Groups Seriously," in E. L. Cass and F. G. Zimmer, eds., *Man and Work in Society* New York, NY: Van Nostrand, 1975).

17. William Ouchi, *Theory Z: How American Business Can Meet the Japanese Challenge* (Reading, MA: Addison-Wesley, 1981); Edward E. Lawler, III, "Increasing Worker Involvement to Enhance Organizational Effectiveness," in Paul Goodman, ed., *Change in Organizations* (San Francisco, CA: Jossey-Bass, 1982).

8.   THE SUBTLE SIGNIFICANCE OF JOB SATISFACTION

Dennis W. Organ

Imagine that Michael Jordan were to become dissatisfied with the Chicago Bulls organization. Suppose, for example, Jordan felt that the team's management had reneged on some promise, or violated some understanding, or sullied his reputation. How would Jordan act out his dissatisfaction? Would he deliberately turn over the ball, let an opposing player score an easy uncontested basket, commit silly fouls to exit the game early?

I submit that it is virtually unthinkable that Jordan or any other professional athlete would respond this way, for two reasons. First, to do so would severely compromise the player's own interests— the "stats" would suffer, and, with that, the bargaining wedge for future contracts. Second, and more important, true professionals cannot bear the intrinsic pain of deliberately botching their individual performance. Whatever grievance Jordan might have against the Bulls, he would inflict unbearable grief on himself as he mentally replayed episodes of shoddy workmanship.

So, given the prohibitive personal and psychic costs of betraying one's craft, how does a professional act out dissatisfaction—aside from merely voicing it? Perhaps voicing dissatisfaction is as far as some would go. But athletes, like other professionals—including those in the clinical laboratory—have some other options. They can choose to define their obligations and their roles narrowly; they will do what they contractually must do. They will do what redounds directly to their self-interests, but contribute only grudgingly (if at all) in other ways.

They can choose not to help teammates improve their skills, not to sacrifice leisure hours to "rubber chicken" banquets for community groups, not to take part in (or not even to attend) informal discussions off the playing arena, not to make suggestions for improving the organization, not to sign autographs. They can tie up valuable management time by pressing every imaginable petty grievance, sour the whole atmosphere for players and staff, and undermine confidence in the organization.

Research now indicates that precisely these effects on Organizational Citizenship Behavior, rather than in-role performance or productivity as traditionally defined, are the casualty of dissatisfaction.

SATISFACTION CAUSES PRODUCTIVITY— AN APPEALING BUT DISCREDITED PREMISE

The notion that "a happy employee is a productive employee" lay for a long time at the center of one popular school of management thought. This concept of worker motivation, probably traceable to some distorted accounts of the legendary Hawthorne research of the 1920s and 1930s, certainly has its appeal. Most managers want productivity, and they prefer a satisfied work force over one that is dissatisfied. So practitioners espouse that whatever makes people happy is justifiable as "an investment in higher productivity." Not surprisingly, surveys have shown a strong tendency by hu-

From *Clinical Laboratory Management Review* (Jan/Feb 1990) *4*, no. 1, 94–98. Copyright © 1990 by Clinical Laboratory Management Association, Inc.

man resource and line managers and union leaders to agree that an individual's job satisfaction translates into a corresponding level of productivity.[1,2]

Unfortunately, researchers began to discredit this theory almost from the start. Nearly 35 years ago, Brayfield and Crockett[3] reviewed an already large body of empirical study of the relationship between job attitudes and productivity. They concluded that no "appreciable" relationships existed. Periodic updates have found no reason to modify this general assessment.

THE PENDULUM TURNS

Interestingly, the findings of "rigorous research" have not disturbed practicing managers. Well into the 1970s, possibly into the early 1980s, most managers—either because they did not know about the results of behavioral research, or perhaps because they chose to believe evidence from their own experience—held to the premise that satisfaction does significantly affect productivity. In retrospect, it is doubtful if management science research alone would have ever seriously undermined that premise.

A much more powerful stimulus to revising management opinion was the combined form of double-digit inflation in the late 1970s and the recession of the early 1980s. Malaise about the state of the "body economic" saturated the financial tabloids and the after-dinner speeches of corporate CEOs. We must wake up, it was argued, to the dawning of a new era—one of global competition, deregulation, and accountability. "Country-club-style" management led to creeping costs—costs that only begat more costs rather than increasing output. The ethos of the day was for organizations to hack away the dead wood, downsize to a lean and mean profile, and get more bang for the buck. That meant *every* buck, including the one spent on amenities to make people happy or put into their pay checks.

Tough-minded management came to the fore. Its rationale was the rigorous research showing no consistent or "appreciable" effect of satisfaction on productivity. The old model that a happy worker is a productive worker was rejected as simplistic, if not soft-headed. The new model emphasized performance; let satisfaction fall where it may. The important consideration was not *how many* people were happy but *which* people. The underlying logic was to obtain results from those able and willing to supply them and to ensure that those people, and only those, had any reason for satisfaction.

The new, tough-minded management doctrine was evident in a variety of reforms in human resource practices. For example, many firms took steps to ensure that performance appraisals differentiated among people to a much greater extent. Supervisors could no longer rate a few people as, for example, a 5 on a 5-point scale and everyone else a 4. They had to use the 1s and 2s on the scale. Some programs required every manager to rank people from top to bottom. By definition every department had 50 percent of its people "below average." Moreover, performance measurement was not based on the subjective impressions of supervisors. Feverish activity went into the design of quantitative indicators of specific accomplishments. The message was clear and emphatic: "Let's see your stats as they relate to the bottom line." Merit-pay plans, although nominally in effect in most organizations for many years, acquired new and sharp teeth. Those in the top quartile of ratings and statistical categories received substantial raises; those in the bottom quartile were "zeroed out."

How did such reforms affect job satisfaction? For some, the effect was positive. Overall, as some research suggests (4, 5), the effect was reduced satisfaction. But so what? Job satisfaction doesn't affect a person's productivity, so it doesn't matter. Or does it?

SATISFACTION AND ORGANIZATIONAL CITIZENSHIP BEHAVIOR

Research currently distinguishes between *in-role* performance and productivity and *extra-role* contributions in the form of Organizational Citizenship Behavior (OCB). Individual in-role performance consists of well-specified job requirements—what the person must do according to the job description—and accomplishments (such as meeting certain quotas or statistical norms) that contractually qualify the individual for incremental rewards, such as bonus pay or prizes. Such performance is to some degree a function of attitude, but also of aptitude, expertise, work flow, dependence on others, and resources (such as equipment, budget, staff). Positive attitudes can add little to a person's in-role performance once the limits of those other constraints are reached.

Negative attitudes that might otherwise cause reduced effort for this kind of performance often will not have this effect—people can be disciplined (even terminated) for unsatisfactory in-role performance. And, negative attitudes toward management notwithstanding, someone who needs bonus pay and qualifies for it will perform accordingly.

But for the professional—not only the Michael Jordans but also the highly skilled specialists in the laboratory—there is an even more compelling reason why in-role performance will not suffer because of dissatisfaction. The reason is ego-involvement. For the ego-involved professional, poor or even mediocre performance is intrinsically painful. It arouses feelings of guilt, embarrassment, and self-reproach.

So neither satisfaction nor dissatisfaction will necessarily manifest itself by effects on individual in-role performance.

The problem is that in-role performance is never enough. As Daniel Katz noted:

An organization which depends solely upon its blueprints of prescribed behavior is a very fragile system. . . . The patterned activity which makes up an organization is so intrinsically a cooperative set of interrelationships, that we are not aware of the cooperative nexus any more than we are of any habitual behavior like walking. Within every work group in a factory, within every division in a government bureau, or within any department of a university are countless acts of cooperation without which the system would break down. We take these everyday acts for granted. . . .[6]

An effective organization depends on many forms of discretionary, voluntary contributions for which people seldom get direct credit. These contributions make up OCB. Satisfied people do more of these things (because OCB is primarily a function of attitude and not very dependent on ability or resources); dissatisfied people can choose to do less of them without incurring the risk of sanctions or lost benefits. Because OCB includes many humble and mundane gestures, cutting back on OCB does not hurt the ego as would inferior task performance.

Characteristics of OCB

The concept of OCB becomes less abstract, and much more intuitively familiar to the practicing manager, by understanding some of its characteristics.

Altruism consists of those voluntary actions that help another person with a work problem—instructing a new hire on how to use equipment, helping a co-worker catch up with a backlog of work, fetching materials that a colleague needs and cannot procure on his own.

Courtesy subsumes all of those foresightful gestures that help someone else prevent a problem—touching base with people before committing to action that will affect them, providing advance notice to someone who needs to know to schedule work.

Sportsmanship is a citizen-like posture of tolerating the inevitable inconveniences and impositions of work without whining and grievances—for example, the forbearance shown by a technician whose vacation schedule must yield to unexpected contingencies, or by the programmer who must temporarily endure cramped work quarters.

Conscientiousness is a pattern of going well beyond minimally required levels of attendance, punctuality, housekeeping, conserving resources, and related matters of internal maintenance.

Civic virtue is responsible, constructive involvement in the political process of the organization, including not just expressing opinions but reading one's mail, attending meetings, and keeping abreast of larger issues involving the organization.

At Indiana University, we have developed reliable research instruments for rating people's contributions in these forms. Two other categories for which we do not presently have measures, but which logically relate to OCB, are *Peacemaking*—actions that help to prevent, resolve, or mitigate unconstructive interpersonal conflict—and *Cheerleading*—the words and gestures of encouragement and reinforcement of co-workers' accomplishments and professional development.

A key point is that the person who shows these characteristics of OCB seldom sees it register in his or her individual productivity or "stats" (an exception, perhaps, would be an outstanding attendance record). More often, OCB contributes either to a colleague's performance or to improving the efficiency of the system. A manager, for example, has more time and stamina for important business when not mediating protracted grievances by a staff lacking in sportsmanship. The operator who ignores matters of courtesy generally does not sacrifice his or her individual productivity but creates snafus farther down the line, eventually hurting other's work.

The experienced administrator may, as Katz suggested, take OCB for granted. But if, for whatever reasons, OCB diminishes, the perceptive manager either sees or foresees the eventual effects. As Max Depree, chairman of Herman Miller, Inc., observed,[7] one of the warning signs of a company in decline is a "general loss of grace and civility."

Research at Indiana University[8] and elsewhere confirms that OCB is where we must look for the effects of dissatisfaction. The effects are indirect and not generally visible in lower in-role performance. The loss is in those discretionary forms of citizenship on which effective systems depend.

Interdependence and OCB

Management theorists have always noted the essential condition of interdependence created by organization. Much of their creative energies have involved formulating principles, rules, and design structures that address this condition.

James D. Thompson[9] pointed out that formal structure suffices for only certain types of interdependence as they arise from the basic technology of organization. *Mediating technologies*—common to banks, telephone exchanges, libraries, and retail establishments—link clients or customers who wish to be interdependent. This technology creates what Thompson termed "pooled interdependence," which can be managed by standardized rules and procedures. *Long-linked technologies*, of which the archetype is the assembly line, give rise to serial or "linear interdependence." Detailed plans and forecasts are needed to cope with long-linked technologies.

Thompson's third form, *intensive technology*, perhaps best describes the clinical laboratory. Thompson defines this form to "signify that a variety of techniques is drawn upon in order to achieve a change in some specific object; but the selection, combination, and order of application are determined by feedback from the object itself."[9] This type of technology breeds complex, often unforeseeable, reciprocal interdependence. Thompson argued that formal structure, standardized procedures, and elaborate plans are not sufficient to manage this dependence. It requires "mutual adjustment," spontaneous give-and-take, informal helping, teamwork, and cooperation—in other words, OCB. OCB always matters, but especially when intensive technologies breed complex reciprocal interdependence among people, managers, and departments.

SATISFACTION: FAIRNESS, NOT HAPPINESS

So job satisfaction is important after all. Does this mean reverting to country-club-style management, with all its attendant concern for making people happy? The answer is "no" because recent research[10] suggests that happiness has little to do with job satisfaction. When people answer questions about their satisfaction—with work, pay, supervision, promotion—they think about fairness. They compare what they might reasonably have expected and what they actually experience.

Fairness certainly is an inherently subjective and complex issue. People have different ideas about what makes an arrangement fair or unfair. One person will think in terms of visible accomplishments; another will think in terms of loyalty and commitment (e.g., seniority). Still others think of ability, effort, external markets (such as supply and demand for specific expertise), precedent (the fact that certain groups "have always rated a premium"), or education. Seldom is there consensus about the relative weights of these criteria. Fortunately, most people have a reasonably high threshold for perceiving inequity. A system need not match any one person's preferred formula so long as the rank and file understand that an array of relevant criteria have been considered. Most employees expect the technically excellent performer to command a differential in pay or status; they just don't want other criteria of worthiness to be totally ignored. When differentials become marked, and when they are determined by unduly narrow conceptions or measures of contribution, the threshold of unfairness is breached. Dissatisfaction mounts, OCB suffers, and eventually, so does the organization.

Any discussion of fairness at work must reckon with procedural and distributive justice. The process in which decisions are made and benefits determined can affect satisfaction just as much as the decisions and benefits themselves. Studies of employee personnel systems and managerial leadership point to four critical factors in perceptions of fairness:

- *Feedback*—ample and prompt.
- *Recourse*—the option of appeal.
- *Fundamental respect for human dignity*—Even the most incompetent and incorrigible subordinate has the right to be addressed civilly.
- *Some form of input*—We do not mean pure democracy, but simply the opportunity to be heard. As one CEO put it, "having a voice does not mean having a vote."

CONCLUSION

Management research and theory have taken a long time and a torturous path in catching up with the insights of Chester Barnard. More than half a century ago, Barnard[11] noted the essential condition of the *"willingness* of persons to contribute efforts to the cooperative system." This quality of willingness "is something different from effectiveness, ability, or value of personal contributions. . . . [it] means self-abnegation." Willingness is characterized by "[an] indefinitely large range of variation in its intensity among individuals" and, within individuals, "it cannot be constant in degree." Finally, this "willingness to cooperate, positive or negative, is the expression of the net satisfactions and dissatisfactions experienced or anticipated."

Barnard underscored the very nature of organizations as cooperative systems. Rules, structures, policies, job descriptions, sanctions, incentives—they all play necessary roles in collaborative endeavors, but as derivatives of, not as substitutes for, the underlying disposition to cooperate. Such a disposition can be sustained only by a sense of the organization as a microcosm of a just world. Occasional inequities can be tolerated if there is faith that the system works fairly over the long run, with self-correcting tendencies. When faith yields to a narrowly defined, *quid pro quo* contractual relationship, the disposition to cooperate ebbs. Surveys show that most of the nation's labor force begins work with a fairly high degree of job satisfaction and that most of the people, most of the time, will describe themselves as "all in all, satisfied." There is a generally prevalent inclination to give the employer the benefit of the doubt—"I'll assume you're treating me fairly until you persuade me otherwise." So the disposition is generally present to render a substantial contribution via OCB. A good-faith effort by managers to provide a "square deal" will do much to ensure the quality of OCB.

REFERENCES

1. Gannon, M. J., and J. P. Noon. "Management's critical deficiency." *Business Horizons* (1971) *14*, 49–56.

2. Katzell, R. A., and D. Yankelovich. *Work, productivity, and job satisfaction.* New York: The Psychological Corporation, 1975.

3. Brayfield, A. H., and W. H. Crockett. "Employee attitudes and employee performance." *Psychological Bulletin* (1955) *52*, 396–424.

4. Baird L. S., and W. C. Hammer. "Individual versus system rewards: Who's dissatisfied, why and what is their likely response?" *Academy of Management Journal* (1979) *22*, 783–92.

5. Pearce, J. L. and L. W. Porter. "Employee responses to formal performance appraisal feedback." *Journal of Applied Psychology* (1986) *71*, 211–18.

6. Katz, D. "The motivational basis of organizational behavior." *Behavioral Science* (1964) *9*, 131–46.

7. Labich, K. "Hot company, warm culture." *Fortune* (February 27, 1989), 74–78.

8. Organ, D. W. *Organizational citizenship behavior.* Lexington, Mass.: Lexington Books, 1988.

9. Thompson, J. D. *Organizations in action.* New York: McGraw-Hill, 1967.

10. Organ, D. W., and J. P. Near. "Cognition vs. affect in measures of job satisfaction." *International Journal of Psychology* (1985) *20*, 241–53.

11. Barnard, C. I. *The functions of the executive.* Cambridge, Mass.: Harvard University Press, 1938.

9.   EXPRESSION OF EMOTION AS PART OF THE WORK ROLE

Anat Rafaeli and Robert I. Sutton

Research on feelings experienced and expressed by organizational members emphasizes emotions as indicators of well-being and happiness. Writings on job stress, for example, view affective responses primarily as dependent variables that change in response to objective or subjective threats to well-being (Kahn, 1981). Related writings convey that "burnout" is a syndrome of emotional exhaustion among workers in the helping professions (Maslach, 1978a). Perhaps the greatest attention to emotion as a dependent variable is found in the job satisfaction literature. Locke's (1976) widely cited review defines job satisfaction as "a pleasurable or positive emotional state resulting from the appraisal of one's job or job experiences" (p. 1300).

Yet viewing emotion only as an intrapsychic outcome masks the complex role it plays in organizational life. In service organizations, for example, effectiveness is thought to hinge partly on the emotions expressed by employees (Czepiel, Solomon, & Surprenant, 1985). To illustrate, check-out clerks working at one chain of supermarkets are issued a handbook that commands:

YOU are the company's most effective representative. Your customers judge the entire company by your actions. A cheerful "Good Morning" and "Good Evening" followed by courteous, attentive treatment, and a sincere "Thank you, please come again," will send them away with a friendly feeling and a desire to return. A friendly smile is a must.

The feelings offered by this employee to customers are not indicators of well-being. Rather, smiling and acting "friendly" are part of the work role.

The display of friendliness and good cheer are expected in an array of service occupations including flight attendants, servants, and sales clerks. In contrast, bill collectors and bouncers are paid to convey hostility. Funeral directors express sadness. Other roles call for the suppression of emotion: "good" academic deans display neutrality, especially around budget time. Many roles call for variation in expressed emotions. For example, a case study of a team of surgical nurses (Denison & Sutton, in press) revealed that members were expected to present an emotionally flat demeanor in the operating room, to be warm when talking with patients and their families, and to encourage one another to express "true feelings" such as rage and disgust during breaks and informal meetings with other nurses.

Yet expectations about emotional expression have been largely ignored by organizational theorists who have adopted role theory. The widely cited work by Kahn and his colleagues (Kahn, Wolfe, Quinn, Snoek, & Rosenthal, 1964; Katz & Kahn, 1978) focused on sent and received role expectations that are excessive, ambiguous, or in conflict. The sources of expectations about emotional expressions and the effects of displayed feelings are not addressed explicitly in Kahn's work, or in the more general writings on role theory (Biddle, 1979). Goffman's (1969) work, however, addressed the causes and consequences of expressed emotions. His writings on strategic interaction focus on how people manipulate emotional

Anat Rafaeli and Robert I. Sutton, "Expression of Emotion as Part of the Work Role" in *Academy of Management Review*, 1987, vol. 12, no. 1, p.p. 23–27. Reprinted by permission.

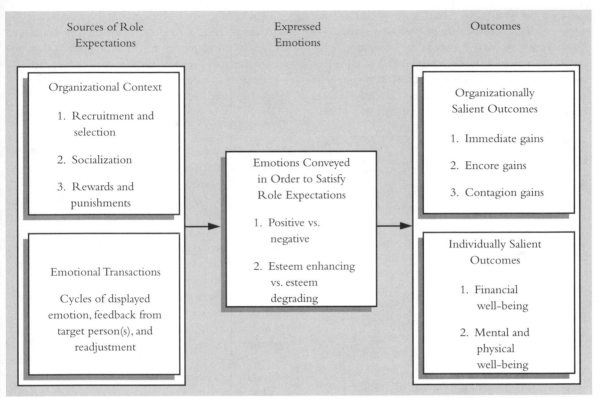

FIGURE 9.1   Expression of emotion as part of the work role: A conceptual framework.

expression to promote their own interests. But employees also display feelings to promote the interests of other role senders including clients and co-workers. This paper follows the spirit of Goffman's writings and considers work settings in which employees display emotions in order to fulfill role expectations.

CONCEPTUAL FRAMEWORK

The conceptual territory covered by the framework proposed here includes the sources of role expectations about emotional expression, the range of such emotional expressions, and the influence expressed feelings have on the organization and on the role occupant (see Figure 9.1). The underlying assumption is that many of the emotions conveyed by employees can be thought of as "control moves"

(Goffman, 1969), which refer to "the intentional effort of an informant to produce expressions that he thinks will improve his situation if they are gleaned by the observer" (p. 12). It is further proposed that emotions expressed without the intention of influencing others can serve as control moves.

The attributes of expressed emotions are central to our framework. Developing a complete theory of emotion is a task that has intrigued and puzzled writers from a variety of disciplines. Such theories are sometimes the subject of entire books (Darwin, 1965; DeRivera, 1977; Hillman, 1961); identifying the full range of human emotion is beyond the scope of this paper. Nonetheless, a pair of imperfect dimensions is useful for developing theory about emotions conveyed as part of the job. First, emotions can be arrayed on a continuum ranging from positive, through neutral, to negative. Expression of positive affect includes smiling and enthusiasm. Negative affect includes frowning and disgust.

One limitation of this continuum is that some emotions are difficult to classify. Is the sadness expressed by a funeral director positive or negative? Further, depending on which perspective is adopted, the same expressed emotion can be positive or negative. The friendly smile of, say a waitress, may be positive from the customer's point of view, but may be construed as artificial and thus negative by the waitress.

The second continuum is the extent that expressed emotions reinforce the target person's self-esteem. Some occupations require employees to support co-workers or clients (social workers, physicians, receptionists); others require employees to remain neutral (judges and referees); and some jobs require the role occupant to degrade the self-esteem of others (drill sergeants, poker players).

This second continuum is also imperfect; because of differences in cultural backgrounds and personality, it is difficult to predict the influence an expressed emotion will have on a person's self-esteem. Taken together, however, these continua indicate that for expressed emotions (or any other human communication) to convey meaning, the message must be encoded by a source and decoded by a receiver (Osgood, Suci, & Tannenbaum, 1957). The positive-negative continuum highlights feelings encoded by the role occupant; the esteem enhancing-degrading continuum accentuates expressed emotions decoded by the audience.

SOURCES OF ROLE EXPECTATIONS

Two sources of role expectations are proposed that create, influence, and maintain the emotions expressed in organizational life: the *organizational context* and *emotional transactions*. The organizational context comprises formal and informal practices used by a larger organization to influence emotions displayed by members. Following Trist's (1977) distinction between contextual and transactional environments, the organizational context can be distinguished from emotional transactions. The organizational context includes selection, socialization, and reward systems; emotional transactions comprise the sequence of communication that occurs when an employee displays emotion, notes the reaction of a "target" person, and adjusts or maintains expressed feelings.

Organizational Context

The present authors propose that three dimensions of the organizational context create and maintain expectations about emotional expression: recruitment and selection, socialization, and rewards and punishments. For the sake of simplicity, most of this discussion considers incumbents who are influenced by the context of a single organization. Nevertheless, in practice, a person may be affected by the selection, socialization, and reward systems of more than one organization. Some people are members of more than one organization. Boundary-spanners are influenced by the norms of outside organizations encountered in their work. Moreover, contexts encountered in prior organizational memberships (schools attended, previous jobs) may influence emotions that are expressed in current roles.

Recruitment and Selection. Organizations seek to employ people who can convey emotions deemed to be appropriate for the role. For example, a manual produced by McDonald's "Hamburger University" urges store managers "Your window-men and outside order-takers must impress customers as being 'All-American' boys. They must display desirable traits such as sincerity, enthusiasm, confidence, and a sense of humor" (Boas & Chain, 1976, p. 84). Newspaper ads solicit sales people who are "young-minded with a positive attitude," "personable," "aggressive," and "convincing." Also, Playboy bunnies were required to be charming as well as sexy (Steinem, 1983).

Although emotional expression is not discussed explicitly in the literature on job analysis, some job analysis techniques imply that displayed feelings are job requirements (McCormick, 1979). For example, the traits required to deal with other people such as diverting, serving, and persuading are included in the rating scales used by the United States Employment Service (U.S. Department of Labor, 1972).

Hypothesis testing studies on the recruitment and selection of incumbents on the basis of emotional skills are rare, but some research suggests that job prospects are brighter for interviewees who convey positive emotions and hide negative feelings. Forbes and Jackson (1980) reported that interviewees who smiled, maintained eye contact, and nodded their heads were most likely to be offered jobs. In contrast, rejected candidates in this study "were characterized by more avoidance gaze; eye wandering, more neutral facial expression, and less smiling" (p. 70). Similar findings were reported by Imada and Hakel (1977), as well as McGovern and Tinsley (1978).

Research is needed, however, on whether such decisions are intentional. Moreover, these studies do not distinguish between the emotions required to get a job and the emotions needed to do the job.

Socialization. Organizational socialization often includes learning norms, or "feeling rules" (Hochschild, 1979), about which emotions ought to be displayed and which ought to be hidden. Feeling rules can be learned in an organization other than the one in which a member practices his or her occupation. The "University of Santa Claus," for example, teaches Santas who will work in department stores to smile and be jolly "even when a kid who isn't quite potty trained has an accident" ("Rules for Santas," 1984). Similarly, law schools and medical schools teach professional norms, including norms about emotional expression.

Many organizations provide internal training about feeling rules. Walt Disney World uses classes, handbooks, and billboards to teach newcomers that they must convey positive and esteem-enhancing emotions to customers. A handbook advises:

First, we practice a friendly smile *at all times with our guests and among ourselves. Second, we use friendly, courteous phrases. "May I help you." . . . "Thank*

you." . . . "Have a nice day." . . . "Enjoy the rest of your stay." and many others are all part of our daily working vocabulary (Walt Disney Productions, 1982, p. 6, emphasis in the original).

In the Disney tradition, newcomers learn the sharp distinction between being "onstage" (where Disney patrons can go) and being "off-stage" (where only employees are allowed). When onstage, employees must follow concise guidelines about which emotions can, and cannot, be expressed (Peters & Waterman, 1982; Tyler & Nathan, 1985). Newcomers hear in lectures at Disney University and read in handbooks (Walt Disney Productions, 1982, p. 2): "You were cast for a role, not hired for a job" and "Our audience is composed of *guests* not customers . . . and we as cast members are *hosts* and *hostesses*" (emphasis in original). Such metaphors teach and maintain an organizational culture that emphasizes the display of good cheer and the skilled utterance of social amenities, perhaps above all else.

Disney's approach may seem extreme, but socialization practices used by other service organizations place similar emphasis on the display of appropriate feelings. Examples include Mrs. Fields' Cookies (Richman, 1984), Delta Airlines (Hochschild, 1983), and McDonald's Hamburgers (Boas & Chain, 1976).

Some organizations even use operant conditioning to teach employees how to express appropriate emotions. Behavioral modification was used by Komaki, Blood, and Holder (1980) to teach employees in a fast food restaurant how to be friendly. Friendliness was operationalized as smiling at customers and exchanging polite remarks such as "Is this your first visit?"

Perhaps more powerful than formal socialization practices are lessons about emotional display learned through the informal organization. The stories told and actions taken by role models provide opportunities for social learning (Bandura, 1977). Bandura's work suggests that newcomers learn norms about emotional expression through both vicarious processes and imitation. The expression and control of emotions is frequently mentioned in the "war stories" that experienced street cops tell to rookie officers (Van Maanen, 1973, 1978). Storytelling provides an opportunity for vicarious learning about feeling rules; as role models tell stories, rookies imagine how *they* would have acted.

Social learning theory also suggests that newcomers learn about the display of emotion by observing and then imitating more experienced co-workers. By watching experienced physicians, for example, medical interns learn that mild compassion is the expected emotional posture and that there is a permissive attitude about physicians who express indifference toward patients (Daniels, 1960).

Explicit feedback from insiders and other newcomers is another means through which feeling rules are learned. A medical intern writes in the *Journal of The American Medical Association*:

In my first months as a medical student, I was called a "softie" when I cried about patients; being a woman made it only worse. Classmates and physicians told me "You get too emotionally involved with patients. You will never be a 'good' doctor." (Bell, 1984, p. 2684).

Employees not only learn which feelings should be expressed to clients or other outsiders; they also learn which feelings should be displayed in the presence of co-workers. The medical intern in the above example learned that fellow interns and teaching physicians did not want to see her cry.

The treatment of socialization presented here emphasizes the expression of emotion. Yet socialization in some roles entails learning how to suppress or disguise feelings—examples include judges, academic deans, and referees. Margaret Mead (1951) described a technique used by a communist party member to suppress his emotions:

By smoking a heavy pipe, you are sure of yourself. Through the heaviness of the pipe, the lips become deformed and cannot react spontaneously (pp. 65–66).

Rewards and Punishments. Reward and solicitation processes overlap since learning a role includes encounters with the reward system. Yet it is useful to discuss these processes separately: Socialization

teaches newcomers which emotions are expected, while rewards and punishments maintain (or alter) such behaviors.

As with socialization, rewards and punishments are supplied by both the formal and informal organization. Many organizations monitor employees to assure that displayed feelings are "correct." To illustrate, The University of Michigan's Survey Research Center monitors telephone interviewers (see Groves & Kahn, 1979; Survey Research Center, 1976). Feedback to interviewers includes comments about the quality of their emotion work. Interviewers are encouraged to say kind things when respondent's answers are "acceptable" (e.g., "Thanks" or "That's helpful"), and to withhold positive affect when the respondent's actions are unacceptable. Moreover, interviewers are forbidden to express certain emotions such as anger. Data gatherers who convey a "professional attitude of neutrality and acceptance" (Survey Research Center, 1976, p. 130) are more likely to receive pay increases; those who do not express required emotions are reprimanded.

Similarly, conversations with executives from a national chain of grocery stores reveal that "employee courtesy" is monitored by "mystery shoppers." Ratings provided by such shoppers are entered into the employee's personnel file. A recent study by another chain of stores indicated that, in over 2000 interactions between "mystery shoppers" and clerks, only 21 percent of the clerks smiled and only 25 percent greeted customers. These findings disappointed top executives. As a result, employee courtesy contests are being held in some regions. Clerks who are "caught" smiling, greeting customers, and expressing thanks may receive prizes including a new car.

Emotional Transactions

An organization may use selection, socialization, and rewards to encourage the display of certain emotions. But the verbal and nonverbal cues sent by target persons also may influence the feelings conveyed by an employee. Thus, the organizational context can be distinguished from emotional trans-actions. Emotional transactions are a sequence of communication between sender and receiver. The organizational context has the strongest influence over feelings conveyed at the outset of an emotional transaction. Yet the emotions sent by an employee may be modified as the sequence of communication unfolds; the reactions of "receivers" or "targets" serve as feedback that can influence and constrain subsequent sent emotions.

Emotional transactions can be viewed as "double interacts" (Weick, 1979). According to Weick (1979, p. 115), the initial emotions sent by a focal employee (an "act") stimulate the target person to respond with implicit or explicit feedback about the con-tinuation of the displayed emotion (an "interact"). The sender of emotion reacts to such feedback by readjustments including abandoning, revising, or maintaining the displayed emotion (completing a "double interact"). The sender and receiver of dis-played emotion use one or more double interacts to reach agreement, or reduce equivocality (Weick, 1979), about which feelings should be conveyed and which should be hidden.

Clark and LaBeef (1982), for example, studied the tactics used by physicians, nurses, police offi-cers, and clergy in delivering the news of a per-son's death. Their qualitative research suggests that "death tellers" first deliver the news of death to the friend or relative in a somber manner (an ini-tial emotional "act"). Next, the reactions of people who receive the bad news can influence the "death tellers" subsequent emotion work (an "in-teract"). Finally, the death teller continues, modi-fies, or abandons displayed emotions in response to such cues (a "double interact"). Reactions by friends or relatives to the sad news range from cry-ing, to silence, to expressing anger and blame to-ward the death teller. The professionals studied by Clark and LaBeef made a similarly wide range of adjustments in the emotions they expressed. They sometimes hugged crying relatives and friends, or even cried along with them. In contrast, when family or friends became angry, death tellers tended to withdraw.

The cycles of displayed emotion, reaction, and readjustment may reinforce or weaken the effects of feeling rules as an emotional transaction unfolds. For example, Hochschild (1983) described a double interact in which a somewhat insulting customer encourages an unsmiling flight attendant to con-form to organizational rules.

On a 15-hour flight from Hong Kong to New York, a young businessman put his drink down, leans back, and takes in a flight attendant. . . . "Hey honey," he calls out, "give me a smile." (p. 35).

Reactions by the targets of emotion also can en-courage employees to abandon required emotional displays. Consider the advice offered by two restau-rant reviewers (Unterman & Sesser, 1984) who are appalled by food servers who offer organizationally specified emotions:

Nothing can put a damper on a meal quicker than having a waiter bug you with "Hi, my name's Bruce" and con-tinuing with "Is everything satisfactory?" about twenty times. When you see that sort of behavior going on at other tables, bring out a good put-down line. We've found one that works: as soon as the waiter walks up, stick out your hand and say in as cheerful a voice you can manage, "Hi, my name's Dave and I'm your customer tonight." That's guaranteed to stop them speechless (p. vi).

OUTCOMES OF EXPRESSED EMOTIONS

Organizationally Salient Outcomes

The expression of emotions by organizational members may, in the aggregate, have a positive or a negative influence on organizational performance. The present authors propose that emotion work can bring about immediate, encore, and contagion gains (or losses) for the organization (see Figure 9.1).

Immediate Gains. Emotions can have an immediate impact on organizationally salient outcomes. Such effects are obvious in sales jobs. Rosci (1981) urged vendors to "Grin and Sell it" because "salespeople profit by combining the principles of body language with professional selling skills" (p. 106). Rosci described a training course that teaches salespeople to employ nonverbal signals such as "friendly, smiling, enthusiastic face, arms and hands that are relaxed and open" (p. 107) to enhance sales. The consultants who offer the course claim that 2,400 salespeople have taken the course and average sales for these people have increased by 41 percent.

Arthur and Caputo (1959) also illustrated how employees can use emotional expressions to garner immediate gains. Their book *Interrogation for Investigators* provides guidance for police officers who seek to gain confessions from criminals. They suggest using the "Silent Approach" on "The Cool Customer":

Using this approach, you enter the interrogation room with a slight smile on your face, sit comfortably down in your chair, look him straight in the eye, and say absolutely nothing. . . . The senior author once sat for some 25 minutes without moving or taking his gaze from the suspect's face. The suspect, who was very loud before the interrogation, suddenly broke down and began to cry. Within 3 minutes he gave a full confession (pp. 75–76).

To use Goffman's (1969) terminology, such police interrogation techniques are a rich example of "control moves" that influence the actions of others.

In contrast, Driscoll, Meyer, and Schanie (1973) described how other police officers used positive and esteem-enhancing emotions to garner immediate gains. They used presentations, films, roleplays, and feedback sessions to train six teams in the skills required for family crisis investigations. Much of the training focused on emotion work. The program was evaluated with telephone interviews and questionnaires completed by complaining citizens. The study compared 129 "domestic trouble" calls answered by trained officers to 292 calls answered by untrained officers. The trained officers were perceived to be more supportive of citizens and to have greater overall effectiveness at crisis intervention.

The link between emotion work and immediate gains does not always depend on formal training. Consider the following example:

Bradshaw (1980) noticed that nuns who regularly solicit alms in Grand Central Terminal in New York customarily look rather glum. One day, however, Bradshaw saw one nun smiling brightly and "the activity at her basket seemed unusually brisk." Bradshaw subsequently disguised herself as a nun and positioned herself in the terminal. She spent the first day with a suitable glum visage and collected $143 . . . and the second day with a smile which resulted in a total contribution of $186 (described in Webb, Campbell, Schwartz, Sechrest, & Grove, 1981, p. 154).

Encore Gains. The emotions conveyed by role occupants also have long-term effects on the organization. Emotion work may lead to further gains either by repeat encounters with the same 'other' (i.e., encore gains), or through the comments that are passed by him or her to a third party (i.e., contagion gains).

Skilled emotion work can bring encore gains even when the organization's product is of questionable quality:

This is hard for some restaurant reviewers to stomach, but there are some restaurants where it just doesn't seem to matter whether the food is good or not. While we may be sitting at a table with plates of barely tasted food everyone in the place seems to be having a great time. The North Beach Restaurant, almost a San Francisco institution, is a prime example. . . . The waiters, probably the best group we've ever seen in a large restaurant, don't hurt any. No matter how pressed they are, they're resolutely cheerful and always willing to explain and offer suggestions. However, this book is about food and not about atmosphere, and here the North Beach Restaurant strikes out (Unterman & Sesser, 1984, p. 118).

Quantitative evidence for the influence of emotion work on encore gains was found in the police training intervention mentioned earlier (Driscoll, Meyer, & Schanie, 1973). The evaluation indicated that, in addition to greater immediate success at crisis intervention, families treated by trained police were more likely to ask for assistance the next time that they faced a crisis.

Contagion Gains. The long-term effects of emotion work also transcend the reactions of the target person. The reputation of a sales clerk or a university administrator may spread through word of mouth. Advertising research suggests that word of mouth is among the most potent of communication sources. In a study of the effectiveness of a bank advertising campaign, for example, Anderson and Golden (1984) found that word of mouth communication (in comparison to other sources) was associated with the highest believability and increased likelihood of bank patronage.

Individually Salient Outcomes

Expressed emotions also influence outcomes that are salient to the role occupant (see Figure 9.1). Here, the influence of emotion work on individual financial well-being and on mental and physical well-being are explored.

Financial Well-being. The link between emotion work and financial well-being is explicit when employees depend on tips from customers. We have all noticed how friendly even the most incompetent food server can become as "tip time" approaches. And empirical research suggests that such friendliness is rewarded. Tidd and Lockard (1978), for example, described the "Monetary Significance of the Affiliative Smile." They examined the influence of a "maximal" versus a "minimal" smile on the tips received by a cocktail waitress who served 48 men and 48 women. The waitress:

approached each individual with either a minimal smile (mouth corners noticably turned up but no teeth showing) or a maximal smile (mouth corners turned up to extensively expose the closed front on a "natural" appearing broad smile) (p. 344).

Tidd and Lockard (1978) reported that the degree of smiling had no effect on the number of drinks ordered. But broad smiles yielded bigger tips. In the aggregate, the maximal smile brought $23.20, while the 48 victims of the minimal smile tipped a total of $9.40.

Emotion work also includes physical contact. Crusco and Wetzel (1984) described "The Midas Touch"—the positive effect of touching (by 2 waitresses) on tipping (by 114 diners). Customers who were not touched tipped an average of 12.2 percent. Customers who received a fleeting touch on the palm tipped an average of 16.7 percent, while the diners given longer touches on a shoulder tipped an average tip of 14.4 percent.

Professional poker players use an array of emotion work techniques to influence opponents (Goffman, 1967). Hayano's (1982) participant-observation research on *poker faces* indicates that successful players are skilled at "stifling emotions when defeated, tired, or angry" (p. 89). Further, while the exchange of ritualistic insults may ease tension, Hayano contended:

Insults may also have the intended or unintended effect of changing, destroying, or weakening opponents thereby making them more likely to commit errors or begin "steaming." ["Steaming" is the expression used by poker players to describe what happens when a poker player loses his or her temper.] Raking in the chips the winner tells the loser to "get a job" or threatens to send him and the other "poker bums" back to the freeway forever. These gabby methods of intimidation are highly effective in many instances, especially against players who are easily flustered (p. 56).

Hayano also reported that insults are used to convince "tight" players or "rocks" (i.e., financially conservative players) to bet their money more freely.

The influence of displayed emotions on financial well-being is sometimes more subtle. A pediatrician who does not express warmth and empathy may lose clients and a lawyer who is cold and abrupt may alienate juries, hence losing his or her share of the damages awarded.

Mental and Physical Well-being. Hochschild (1983) is perhaps most adamant about the negative impact of emotion work on psychological well-being. She compares the physical exploitation of a child laborer in the 19th century to the emotional exploitation of a female flight attendant in the 20th century. Hochschild argued that, while the hours of work and physical conditions for the flight attendant are superior to those of the child laborer, the flight attendant gives even more of herself to the organization than did the child laborer; the employer controls not only her physical activities, but also her feelings.

Hochschild's qualitative evidence from flight attendants at Delta Airlines leads her to argue that, in the short-term, the strain of emotional labor can cause a loss of emotional control:

A young businessman said to a flight attendant, "Why aren't you smiling?" She put her tray back on the food cart, looked him in the eye, and said, "I'll tell you what. You smile first, then I'll smile." The businessman smiled at her. "Good," she replied. "Now freeze and hold that smile for fifteen hours." (Hochschild, 1983, p. 127).

In the long-term, Hochschild contended, the constant pressure of emotional labor may lead to drug use, excessive drinking, headaches, absenteeism, and sexual dysfunction.

The display of expected emotion is not always detrimental to well-being. The financial gains described above for food servers and poker players likely evoke feelings of satisfaction and security. Moreover, despite Hochschild's emphasis on the damage caused by emotion work, flight attendants whom the present authors have spoken with take pride in their ability to cope with airborne emergencies by hiding their own fears and offering calm faces to passengers.

The display of normative emotions may also protect incumbents from ill-being. The professional socialization of physicians, for example, entails learning how to appear concerned, but not so concerned that it causes severe psychological distress (Daniels, 1960). Thus, the physicians' ability to distinguish between the emotions they feel and those they convey to others helps them to continue performing effectively.

Further, Zajonc (1985) argued that smiling brings about physiological changes that cause the experience of subjective well-being. In other words, smiling makes us feel happy. Zajonc re-

claimed a theory first proposed by Wynbaum in 1906. In brief, Wynbaum pointed out that the face has over 80 muscles and that all changes in facial expression influence the flow of blood to the brain. Smiling and laughing entail contraction of the zygomatic muscle, which increases blood flow to the brain. Zajonc contended that "It is like taking an oxygen bath. The cells and tissues receive an increased supply of oxygen, causing a feeling of exuberance" (p. 10). This creative argument suggests that employees who are expected to smile may benefit from feelings of elation and exuberance. We must learn more about this interesting hypothesis, but implications for the link between emotional labor and subjective well-being are intriguing.

EXPERIENCED EMOTIONS, FEELING RULES, AND INTERNALIZED FEELING RULES

The framework presented here emphasizes emotional expression, not emotions as intrapsychic states. But the discussion of well-being suggests that the match between felt emotions and expectations about emotional display is a promising area for future research. Specifically, expressed feelings may match well or poorly with: (a) experienced feelings, especially "true" feelings about the target of emotional expression; (b) external feeling rules; and (c) internalized feeling rules. Building on Hochschild (1979, 1983) and Thoits (1985), the match between feelings expressed in the role and these three demands on expression can lead to: *emotional harmony, emotional dissonance,* or *emotional deviance.*

Emotional harmony occurs when expressed feelings are congruent with experienced emotions, feeling rules, and expectations the incumbent holds for himself or herself about emotional expression. To illustrate, Mary Kay Ash, the founder of Mary Kay Cosmetics, insists that her salespeople exude enthusiasm (Ash, 1984). They are expected to take a "Vow of Enthusiasm" and sing the lyrics to "I've got the Mary Kay Enthusiasm." Emotional harmony is experienced by a salesperson who expresses normative enthusiasm, feels enthusiastic, and expects himself or herself to act enthusiastic.

Emotional harmony is an indicator of good fit between person and environment. More specifically, according to person-environment fit theory (Caplan, 1983), an employee will be free from occupational stress to the extent there is congruence among the behavior expected by role senders, the behavior that an employee expects of himself or herself, and the employee's personal characteristics. Thoits (1985) made a stronger argument: she contended that freedom from mental illness depends, in part, on the belief that one is acting in concert with feeling norms. Both perspectives lead to the hypothesis that emotional harmony is associated with well-being.

Emotional dissonance, according to Hochschild (1983), occurs when expressed emotions satisfy feeling rules, but clash with inner feelings. The effects of emotional dissonance depend on the internalization of feeling rules. Some people display "fake" emotions, yet believe that such acting should *not* be part of the job; this is *faking in bad faith*. To illustrate, a check-out clerk who was interviewed resented acting friendly to customers because "pasting on a smile should not be part of the job." The present authors are unable to find quantitative research on such emotional dissonance. But this is an example of person-role conflict, or a clash between personal values and role requirements. Research indicates that person-role conflict is a clear threat to employee well-being (Caplan, Cobb, French, Harrison, & Pinneau, 1975; Kahn et al., 1964). Moreover, since people who fake in bad faith have not internalized feeling rules, they are likely to be poor employees because they may comply with feeling rules only when monitored closely.

In contrast, the effects of suppressing true feelings are less clear when feeling rules are internalized. Some people display "fake" normative emotions and believe that such expressions should be part of the job; this is *faking in good faith*. Hochschild (1983) argued that faking in good faith is a threat to well-being because it causes estrangement between felt and expressed emotions. She contended, for example, that poor mental health may be suffered by outwardly cheerful flight attendants who have internalized norms about acting friendly, and who hide their contempt for passengers.

Yet writings on the burnout syndrome (e.g., Maslach, 1978a, 1978b, 1982) identify settings in which faking in good faith can enhance well-being. Mashlach (1978a) argued that members of helping professions can cope with burnout by acting concerned about clients, but allowing themselves to feel emotionally detached. Perhaps these are competing hypotheses. Or perhaps faking in good faith decreases stress only when it helps an employee cope with emotions that are felt too deeply.

Emotional deviance occurs when expressed emotions clash with local norms. Emotional deviance is the opposite of emotional dissonance because the organization member express inner feelings and disregards feeling rules. Again, however, internalization of feeling rules may influence the effects of incongruence between felt and expressed emotions.

Employees who express inner feelings and who reject local feeling rules may be punished. A rude flight attendant is likely to be fired, as is a funeral director who displays good cheer. Or such employees may quit. One student quit working as a Mary Kay Cosmetics salesperson because she thought that the norms were silly and "I couldn't bring myself to act happy and enthusiastic enough."

However, more serious consequences may haunt employees who express inner feelings that clash with role expectations, but have internalized those expectations. One sign of the burnout syndrome is that a person is unable to express empathy and concern, even though he or she believes that expressing such feelings is part of the job (Maslach, 1978a, 1978b). Similarly, Thoits (1985) maintained that people who perceive themselves as consistently expressing deviant emotions may label themselves as mentally ill. Essential to Thoits' argument is that the emotional deviant has internalized feeling rules. Both perspectives suggest that such emotional deviants risk poor mental health because they want to control the expression of inner feelings, but are unable to do so. Research is needed on emotional deviance in organizations. Is it as damaging as Thoits implies? Or are there unrecognized advantages?

Emotional harmony, dissonance, and deviance are thought to influence behavior in all work roles. Nevertheless, the most valuable occupations for research are those in which the demands on emotional expression or experience are strongest. Occupations with strong external demands for emotional display discussed here include flight attendants, "performers" at Disney World, and bill collectors. Perhaps the most revealing occupations, however, are those in which the internal feelings evoked by the job clash with feeling rules. Examples include poker players, judges, and referees; performing these jobs requires tolerating, and even enjoying, emotional dissonance.

TOWARD FUTURE RESEARCH

The perspective outlined here is intended to encourage and guide further research on emotions displayed as part of the job. Future research on the match between experienced and expressed emotions has been discussed. Subsequent work in this area may also benefit from consideration of three additional questions: How should expressed emotions be measured? How powerful are the effects of displayed emotions? How should emotion work be managed?

How Should Expressed Emotions Be Measured?

The study of displayed feelings is fraught with methodological hazards. Distinguishing between varieties of expressed emotions will be essential for future research. But this task may prove impossible because scholars do not agree about how long the list of emotions should be, nor do they agree about the boundaries between types of emotions (Kemper, 1981).

Studies also may be hampered because questionnaires, interviews, and records data—the staples of organizational research—will be of limited use. Employee self-reports about displayed emotions are suspect and few organizations keep records about such behaviors. Structured observation, the most promising method, could be difficult because emotions are displayed through a complex combination of facial expression, body language, spoken words, and tone of voice. Thus, a comprehensive method would require elaborate coding schemes for all four of these modes of emotional expression.

Some evidence suggests that initial efforts at structured observation may benefit from focusing on facial expressions. Leathers and Emigh (1980) reported that laboratory subjects who examined photographs could reliably associate emotion labels with facial expressions. For example, happiness, sadness, and surprise were decoded with over 95 percent accuracy. These results imply that structured observation could be used to reliably decode the facial expressions of organizational members. But field research poses the additional problem of rating the variable behavior of live subjects rather than the constant stimuli provided by photographs. Perhaps this hazard could be overcome by using multiple raters and video tape.

How Powerful Are the Effects of Displayed Emotions?

A causal link between emotional display and outcomes for organizations and individuals has been proposed. These links require further empirical support. Managers of retail stores, for example, assume that "friendly" employees produce profits. Is this a valid assumption? Or are sales only influenced by variables such as store location or prices? A field study could be conducted to test the hypothesis that organizational gains are greater in stores where employees act friendlier.

That emotional transactions between members of the same organization may influence organizational performance also was suggested. For example, members of the team that designed Apple's Macintosh computer only selected newcomers who displayed wild enthusiasm about the machine (Tyler & Nathan, 1985). They claimed that shared enthusiasm about the machine and each other was essential to the team's success. Research could be conducted to discover if effort and creativity is higher among product design teams in which members act more enthusiastic. Or perhaps a curvilinear relationship between enthusiasm and creativity should be hypothesized—teams in which members feel compelled to express constant enthusiasm may suffer from groupthink (Janis, 1982).

The relationship between expressed emotion and organizational outcomes may be influenced by a host of contingencies; two are offered as a start for future research. The first contingency is the extent to which attributes other than expressed emotions do not vary. For example, the prices of airline tickets were strictly controlled by the Civil Aeronautics Board before the Airline Deregulation Act was passed in 1978. Before deregulation, advertisements focused heavily on the quality of service because all airlines were required to charge identical prices. The 1978 Act enabled airlines to compete on the basis of ticket prices. It is hypothesized that the strength of relationship between employee courtesy and ticket sales has been weakened by deregulation since the prices of tickets are no longer held constant.

The second contingency is the extent to which employees experience role overload, particularly when employees have too many customers or clients. Customers of uncrowded stores and patrons of empty restaurants expect employees to act friendly and relaxed. In contrast, customers who have been waiting for a clerk in a store or a seat in a restaurant may care only about the speed of the service, and may become irritated by employees who take time for polite conversation with each customer.

How Should Emotion Work Be Managed?

There is a dearth of literature about how management can best influence the emotions conveyed in organizational settings. The emerging literature on interactions between employees and customers addresses a range of issues including the structure of verbal exchanges (Stiles, 1985), control over employee behavior (Mills, 1985), and the psychology of waiting in lines (Maister, 1985). The management of

emotional display is addressed indirectly in this literature, but little research explores this subject explicitly. Hypotheses testing is rare, and to what extent emotion work can be managed is not even known.

If organizations seek to hire employees who can convey certain emotions, then more questions arise. Can the ability to display such emotions be predicted? If so, how? Previous research suggests that behavior in the employment interview does not generalize well to the work role (Arvey & Campion, 1982). Thus, emotions displayed in the interview may not be expressed on the job. Moreover, as argued earlier, the emotions that enable an interviewee to *get* a job may be different than the emotions needed to *do* the job. Can interviewers be trained to overcome these weaknesses of the selection interview? Or perhaps other tools can be developed to identify a candidate's emotional skills.

A related question is how to teach emotion work skills, or perhaps such skills cannot be taught. Classroom programs often are used to teach employees to display expected emotions (Hochschild, 1983; Tyler & Nathan, 1985). Transfer of such behaviors from the classroom to the job is unlikely (Goldstein, 1974), but the present authors are not aware of any evaluation reports. Komaki, Blood, and Holder (1980) reported that behavior modification techniques can be used to enhance emotion work, but additional evidence is needed.

CONCLUSION

The proposed framework is best viewed as a point of departure for both theory testing and theory building. The discussion suggests testable hypotheses. But it also suggests that more inductive work is needed so that our theories can capture the complexities of emotional expression in organizational life. And such inductive work ought to include field research. As Sherlock Holmes put it, "The temptation to form premature theories upon insufficient data is the bane of our profession" (Barring-Gould, 1967; cited in Van Maanen, 1979, p. 539).

REFERENCES

Anderson, W. T., & Golden, L. (1984) Bank promotion strategy. *Journal of Advertising Research*, 24(2), 53–65.

Arther, R. O., & Caputo, R. R. (1959) *Interrogation for investigators*. New York: William C. Copp and Associates.

Arvey, R. P., & Campoin, J. E. (1982) The employment interview: A summary and review of recent research. *Personnel Psychology*, 35, 281–322.

Ash, M. K. (1984) *Mary Kay on people management*. New York: Warner Books.

Bandura, A. (1977) *Social learning theory*. Englewood Cliffs, NJ: Prentice-Hall.

Bell, M. (1984) Teaching of the heart. *The Journal of the American Medical Association*, 252, 2684.

Biddle, B. J. (1979) *Role theory: Expectations, identities, and behaviors*. San Francisco: Academic Press.

Boas, M., & Chain, S. (1976) *Big Mac: The unauthorized story of McDonald's*. New York: Dutton.

Caplan, R. D. (1983) Person-environment fit: Past, present and future. In C. L. Cooper (Ed.), *Stress research: Issues for the eighties* (pp. 35–77). Ann Arbor, MI: Institute for Social Research.

Caplan, R. D., Cobb, S., French, J. R. P., Harrison, R. V., & Pinneau, S. R. (1975) *Job demands and worker health* (Report No. 75–160). Washington, DC: U.S. Department of Health, Education, & Welfare.

Clark, R. E., & LaBeef, E. E. (1982) Death telling: Managing the delivery of bad news. *Journal of Health and Social Behavior*, 23, 366–380.

Crusco, A. H., & Wetzel, C. G. (1984) The Midas touch: The effects of interpersonal touch on restaurant tipping. *Personality and Social Psychology Bulletin*, 10(4), 512–517.

Czepiel, J. A., Solomon, M. E., & Surprenant, C. F. (1985) *The service encounter*. Lexington, MA: Lexington Books.

Daniels, M. J. (1960) Affect and its control in the medical intern. *American Journal of Sociology*, 66, 259–267.

Darwin, C. (1965) *The expression of emotions in man and animals*. Chicago: University of Chicago Press.

Denison, D. R., & Sutton, R. I. (in press) Surgical nurses: Issues in the design of a loosely-bounded team. In J. R. Hackman (Ed.), *Groups that work*.

De Rivera, J. (1977) *A structural theory of emotions*. New York: International Universities Press.

Driscoll, J. M., Meyer, R. G., & Schanie, C. F. (1973) Training police in family crisis intervention. *Journal of Applied Behavioral Science*, 9, 62–82.

Forbes, R. J., & Jackson, P. R. (1980) Non-verbal behavior and the outcome of selection interviews. *Journal of Occupational Psychology*, 53, 65–72.

Goffman, E. (1959) *The presentation of self in everyday life*. New York: Doubleday Anchor.

Goffman, E. (1967) *Interaction ritual*. New York: Doubleday Anchor.

Goffman, E. (1969) *Strategic interaction*. Philadelphia: University of Pennsylvania Press.

Goldstein, I. I. (1974) *Training: Program development and evaluation*. Monterey, CA: Brooks/Cole.

Groves, R., & Kahn, R. L. (1979) *Surveys by telephone: A national comparison with personal interviews*. New York: Academic Press.

Hayano, D. M. (1982) *Poker faces*. Berkeley: University of California Press.

Hillman, J. (1961) *Emotion*. Evanston, IL: Northwestern University Press.

Hochschild, A. (1979) Emotion work, feeling rules and social structure. *American Journal of Sociology*, 85, 551–575.

Hochschild, A. R. (1983) *The managed heart*. Berkeley: University of California Press.

Imada, A. S., & Hakel, M. D. (1977) Influence of nonverbal communication and rater proximity on impressions and decisions in simulated employment interviews. *Journal of Applied Psychology*, 62, 295–300.

Janis, I. L. (1982) *Groupthink*. Boston: Houghton Mifflin.

Kahn, R. L. (1981) *Work and health*. New York: Wiley.

Kahn, R. L., Wolfe, D. M., Quinn, R. P., Snoek, J. D., & Rosenthal, R. A. (1964) *Organizational stress: Studies in role conflict and ambiguity*. New York: Wiley.

Katz, D., & Kahn, R. L. (1978) *Social psychology of organizations* (2nd ed.). New York: Wiley.

Kemper, T. D. (1981) Social constructionist and positivist approaches to the sociology of emotions. *American Journal of Sociology*, 87, 336–362.

Komaki, J., Blood, M. R., & Holder, D. (1980) Fostering friendliness in a fast food franchise. *Journal of Organizational Behavior Management*, 2, 151–164.

Leathers, D. G., & Emigh, T. H. (1980) Decoding facial expressions: A new test with decoding norms. *Quarterly Journal of Speech*, 66, 418–436.

Locke, E. A. (1976) The nature and causes of job satisfaction. In M. D. Dunnette (Ed.), *Handbook of industrial and organizational psychology* (pp. 1297–1350). Chicago: Rand McNally.

Maister, D. H. (1985) The psychology of waiting in lines. In J. A. Cziepiel, M. R. Solomon, & C. F. Surprenant (Eds.), *The service encounter* (pp. 113–123). Lexington, MA: Lexington Books.

Maslach, C. (1978a, Spring) How people cope. *Public Welfare*, 36, 56–58.

Maslach, C. (1978b) The client role in staff burnout. *Journal of Social Issues*, 34, 4.

Maslach, C. (1982) Understanding burnout: Definitional issues in analyzing a complex phenomenon. In W. S. Paine (Ed.), *Job stress and burnout* (pp. 111–124). Beverly Hills, CA: Sage.

McCormick, E. J. (1979) *Job analysis: Methods and applications*. New York: American Management Association.

McGovern, T. V., & Tinsley, H. E. (1978) Interviewer evaluations of interviewee nonverbal behavior. *Journal of Vocational Behavior*, 13, 163–171.

Mead, M. (1951) *Soviet attitudes toward authority*. New York: McGraw-Hill.

Mills, P. K. (1985) The control mechanisms of employees at the encounter of service organizations. In J. A. Cziepiel, M. R. Solomon, & C. F. Surprenant (Eds.), *The service encounter* (pp. 163–178). Lexington, MA: Lexington Books.

Osgood, C. E., Suci, G. J., & Tannenbaum, P. H. (1957) *The measurement of meaning*. Urbana: University of Illinois Press.

Peters, T. J., & Waterman, R. H., Jr. (1982) *In search of excellence*. New York: Harper & Row.

Richman, T., (1984, July) A tale of two companies. *Inc.*, pp. 38–43.

Rosci, F. (1981 June) Grin and sell it. *Successful Meetings*, 106–107.

Rules for Santas—Don't say "ho, ho, ho." (1984, November 15) *San Francisco Chronicle*, p. 3.

Steinem, G. (1983) *Outrageous acts and everyday rebellions*. New York: Holt, Rinehart and Winston.

Stiles, W. B. (1985) Measuring roles in service encounters: The verbal exchange structure. In J. A. Cziepiel, M. R. Solomon, & C. F. Surprenant (Eds.), *The service encounter* (pp. 213–224). Lexington, MA: Lexington Books.

Survey Research Center (1976) *Interviewer's manual* (rev. ed.). Ann Arbor, MI: Institute for Social Research.

Thoits, P. A. (1985) Self-labeling processes in mental illness: The role of emotional deviance. *American Journal of Sociology*, 91, 221–247.

Tidd, K. L., & Lockard, J. S. (1978) Monetary significance of the affiliative smile. *Bulletin of the Psychonomic Society*, 11, 344–346.

Trist, E. (1977) Collaboration in work settings: A personal perspective. *Journal of Applied Behavioral Science*, 13, 268–278.

Tyler, S. (Producer), & Nathan, J. (Producer) (1985) *In search of excellence* [Film]. New York: Public Broadcast System.

Unterman, P., & Sesser, S. (1984) *Restaurants of San Francisco*. San Francisco: Chronicle Books.

U.S. Department of Labor, Manpower Administration (1972) *Handbook for analyzing jobs*. (Stock No. 2900–0131) Washington, DC: U.S. Government Printing Office.

Van Maanen, J. (1973) Observations on the making of policemen. *Human Organizations*, 32, 407–417.

Van Maanen, J. (1978) The asshole. In P. K. Manning & J. Van Maanen (Eds.), *Policing: A view from the streets* (pp. 231–238). Santa Monica, CA: Goodyear.

Van Maanen, J. (1979) The fact of fiction in organizational ethnography. *Administrative Science Quarterly*, 24, 539–550.

Walt Disney Productions (1982) *Your role in the Walt Disney World show*. Orlando, FL: Walt Disney Productions.

Webb, E. J., Campbell, D. T., Schwartz, D. S., Sechrest, L., & Grove, J. B. (1981) *Nonreactive measures in the social sciences*. Boston: Houghton Mifflin.

Weick, K. (1979) *The social psychology of organizing* (2nd ed.). Reading, MA: Addison-Wesley.

Zajonc, R. B. (1985, April 5) Emotion and facial efference: An ignored theory reclaimed. *Science*, pp. 15–21.

THINKING AND MAKING DECISIONS: SOURCES OF RATIONAL, IRRATIONAL, ETHICAL, AND UNETHICAL ACTIONS

Foundations of Social Cognition

Two conflicting beliefs in a single mind don't cohabit comfortably. To defend his ego, man becomes

10.   THE RATIONALIZING ANIMAL

Elliot Aronson

Man likes to think of himself as a rational animal. However, it is more true that man is a *rationalizing* animal, that he attempts to appear reasonable to himself and to others. Albert Camus even said that man is a creature who spends his entire life in an attempt to convince himself that he is not absurd.

Some years ago a woman reported that she was receiving messages from outer space. Word came to her from the planet Clarion that her city would be destroyed by a great flood on December 21. Soon a considerable number of believers shared her deep commitment to the prophecy. Some of them quit their jobs and spent their savings freely in anticipation of the end.

On the evening of December 20, the prophet and her followers met to prepare for the event. They believed that flying saucers would pick them up, thereby sparing them from disaster. Midnight arrived, but no flying saucers. December 21 dawned, but no flood.

What happens when prophecy fails? Social psychologists Leon Festinger, Henry Riecken, and Stanley Schachter infiltrated the little band of believers to see how they would react. They predicted that persons who had expected the disaster, but awaited it alone in their homes, would simply lose faith in the prophecy. But those who awaited the outcome in a group, who had thus admitted their belief publicly, would come to believe even more strongly in the prophecy and turn into active proselytizers.

This is exactly what happened. At first the faithful felt despair and shame because all their predictions had been for nought. Then, after waiting nearly five hours for the saucers, the prophet had a new vision. The city had been spared, she said, because of the trust and faith of her devoted group. This revelation was elegant in its simplicity, and the believers accepted it enthusiastically. They now sought the press that they had previously avoided. They turned from believers into zealots.

LIVING ON THE FAULT

In 1957 Leon Festinger proposed his theory of *cognitive dissonance*, which describes and predicts man's rationalizing behavior. Dissonance occurs whenever a person simultaneously holds two inconsistent cognitions (ideas, beliefs, opinions). For example, the belief that the world will end on a certain day is dissonant with the awareness, when the day breaks, that the world has not ended. Festinger maintained that this state of inconsistency is so uncomfortable that people strive to reduce the conflict in the easiest way possible. They will change one or both cognitions so that they will "fit together" better.

Consider what happens when a smoker is confronted with evidence that smoking causes cancer. He will become motivated to change either his attitudes about smoking or his behavior. And as anyone who has tried to quit knows, the former alternative is easier.

The smoker may decide that the studies are lousy. He may point to friends ("If Sam, Jack and Harry smoke, cigarettes can't be all that dangerous"). He may conclude that filters trap all the cancer-producing materials. Or he may argue that he would rather live a short and happy life with cigarettes than a long and miserable life without them.

The more a person is committed to a course of action, the more resistant he will be to information that threatens that course. Psychologists have reported that the couple who are least likely to believe the dangers of smoking are those who tried to quit—and failed. They have become more committed to smoking. Similarly, a person who builds a $100,000 house astride the San Andreas Fault will be less receptive to arguments about imminent earthquakes than would a person who is renting the house for a few months. The new homeowner is committed; he doesn't want to believe that he did an absurd thing.

When a person reduces his dissonance, he defends his ego, and keeps a positive self-image. But self-justification can reach startling extremes; people will ignore danger in order to avoid dissonance, even when that ignorance can cause their deaths. I mean that literally.

Suppose you are Jewish in a country occupied by Hitler's forces. What should you do? You could try to leave the country; you could try to pass as "Aryan"; you could do nothing and hope for the best. The first two choices are dangerous: if you are caught you will be executed. If you decide to sit tight, you will try to convince yourself that you made the best decision. You may reason that while Jews are indeed being treated unfairly, they are not being killed unless they break the law.

Now suppose that a respected man from your town announces that he has seen Jews being butchered mercilessly, including everyone who had recently been deported from your village. If you believe him, you might have a chance to escape. If you don't believe him, you and your family will be slaughtered.

Dissonance theory would predict that you will not listen to the witness, because to do so would be to admit that your judgment and decisions were wrong. You will dismiss his information as untrue, and decide that he was lying or hallucinating. Indeed, Eli Wiesel reported that this happened to the Jews in Sighet, a small town in Hungary, in 1944. Thus people are not passive receptacles for the deposit of information. The manner in which they view and distort the objective world in order to avoid and reduce dissonance is entirely predictable. But one cannot divide the world into rational people on one side and dissonance reducers on the other. While people vary in their ability to tolerate dissonance, we are all capable of rational or irrational behavior, depending on the circumstances— some of which follow.

DISSONANCE BECAUSE OF EFFORT

Judson Mills and I found that if people go through a lot of trouble to gain admission to a group, and the group turns out to be dull and dreary, they will experience dissonance. It is a rare person who will accept this situation with an "Oh, pshaw. I worked hard for nothing. Too bad." One way to resolve the dissonance is to decide that the group is worth the effort it took to get admitted.

We told a number of college women that they would have to undergo an initiation to join a group that would discuss the psychology of sex. One third of them had severe initiation: they had to recite a list of obscene words and read some lurid sexual passages from novels in the presence of a male experimenter (in 1959, this really was a "severe" and embarrassing task). One third went through a mild initiation in which they read words that were sexual but not obscene (such as "virgin" and "petting"); and the last third had no initiation at all. Then all of the women listened to an extremely boring taped discussion of the group they had presumably joined. The women in the severe initiation group rated the discussion and its drab participants much more favorably than those in the other groups.

I am not asserting that people enjoy painful experiences, or that they enjoy things that are associated with painful experiences. If you got hit on the head by a brick on the way to a fraternity initiation, you would not like that group any better. But if you volunteered to get hit with a brick *in order to join* the fraternity, you definitely would like the group more than if you had been admitted without fuss.

After a decision—especially a difficult one that involves much time, money, or effort—people almost always experience dissonance. Awareness of defects in the preferred object is dissonance with having chosen it; awareness of positive aspects of the unchosen object is dissonant with having rejected it.

Accordingly, researchers have found that *before* making a decision, people seek as much information as possible about the alternatives. Afterwards, however, they seek reassurance that they did the right thing, and do so by seeking information in support of their choice or by simply changing the information that is already in their heads. In one of the earliest experiments on dissonance theory, Jack Brehm gave a group of women their choice between two appliances, such as a toaster or a blender, that they had previously rated for desirability. When the subjects reevaluated the appliances after choosing one of them, they increased their liking for the one they had chosen and downgraded their evaluation of the rejected appliance. Similarly, Danuta Ehrlich and her associates found that a person about to buy a new car does so carefully, reading all ads and accepting facts openly on advertisements more selectively, and he will tend to avoid ads for Volkswagens, Chevrolets, and so on.

THE DECISION TO BEHAVE IMMORALLY

Your conscience, let us suppose, tells you that it is wrong to cheat, lie, steal, seduce your neighbor's husband or wife, or whatever. Let us suppose further that you are in a situation in which you are sorely tempted to ignore your conscience. If you give in to temptation, the cognition "I am a decent moral person" will be dissonant with the cognition "I have committed an immoral act." If you resist, the cognition "I want to get a good grade (have that money, seduce that person)" is dissonant with the cognition "I could have acted so as to get that grade, but I chose not to."

The easiest way to reduce dissonance in either case is to minimize the negative aspects of the action one has chosen, and to change one's attitude about its immorality. If Mr. C. decides to cheat, he will probably decide that cheating isn't really so bad. It hurts no one; everyone does it; it's part of human nature. If Mr. D. decides not to cheat, he will no doubt come to believe that cheating is a sin, and deserves severe punishment.

The point here is that the initial attitudes of these men is virtually the same. Moreover, their decisions could be a hair's breadth apart. But once the action is taken, their attitudes diverge sharply.

Judson Mills confirmed these speculations in an experiment with sixth-grade children. First he measured their attitudes toward cheating, and then put them in a competitive situation. He arranged the test so that it was impossible to win without cheating, and so it was easy for the children to cheat, thinking they would be unwatched. The next day, he asked the children again how they felt about cheating. Those who had cheated on the test had become more lenient in their attitudes; those who had resisted the temptation adopted harsher attitudes.

These data are provocative. They suggest that the most zealous crusaders are not those who are removed from the problem they oppose. I would hazard to say that the people who are most angry about "the sexual promiscuity of the young" are *not* those who have never dreamed of being promiscuous. On the contrary, they would be persons who had been seriously tempted by illicit sex, who came very close to giving in to their desires, but who finally resisted. People who almost live in glass houses are the ones who are most likely to throw stones.

INSUFFICIENT JUSTIFICATION

If I offer George $20 to do a boring task, and offer Richard $1 to do the same thing, which one will decide that the assignment was mildly interesting? If I threaten one child with harsh punishment if he does something forbidden, and threaten another child with mild punishment, which one will transgress?

Dissonance theory predicts that when people find themselves doing something and they have neither been rewarded adequately for doing it nor threatened with dire consequences for not doing it, they will find *internal* reasons for their behavior.

Suppose you dislike Woodrow Wilson, and I want you to make a speech in his favor. The most efficient thing I can do is to pay you a lot of money for making the speech, or threaten to kill you if you don't. In either case, you will probably comply with my wish, but you won't change your attitude toward Wilson. If that were my goal, I would have to give you a *minimal* reward or threat. Then, in order not to appear absurd, you would have to seek additional reasons for your speech—this could lead you to find good things about Wilson and hence, to conclude that you really do like Wilson after all.

Lying produces great attitude change only when the liar is undercompensated.

Festinger and J. Merrill Carlsmith asked college students to work on boring and repetitive tasks. Then the experimenters persuaded the students to lie about the work, to tell a fellow student that the task would be interesting and enjoyable. They offered half of their subjects $20 for telling the lie, and they offered the others only $1. Later they asked all subjects how much they had really liked the tasks.

The students who earned $20 for their lies rated the work as deadly dull, which it was. They experienced no dissonance: they lied, but they were well paid for that behavior. By contrast, students who got $1 decided that the tasks were rather enjoyable. The dollar was apparently enough to get them to tell the lie, but not enough to keep them from feeling that lying for so paltry a sum was foolish. To reduce dissonance, they decided that they hadn't lied after all; the task was fun.

Similarly, Carlsmith and I found that mild threats are more effective than harsh threats in changing a child's attitude about a forbidden object, in this case a delightful toy. In the severe-threat condition, children refrained from playing with the toys and had a good reason for refraining—the very severity of the threat provided ample justification for not playing with the toy. In the mild-threat condition, however, the children refrained from playing with the toy but when they asked themselves, "How come I'm not playing with the toy?" they did not have a superabundant justification (because the threat was not terribly severe). Accordingly, they provided additional justification in the form of convincing themselves that the attractive toy was really not very attractive and that they didn't really want to play with it very much in the first place. Jonathan Freedman extended our findings and showed that severe threats do not have a lasting effect on a child's behavior. Mild threats, by contrast, can change behavior for many months.

Perhaps the most extraordinary example of insufficient justification occurred in India, where Jamuna Prasad analyzed the rumors that were circulated after a terrible earthquake in 1950. Prasad found that people in towns that were *not* in immediate danger were spreading rumors of impending doom from floods, cyclones, or unforeseeable calamities. Certainly the rumors could not help people feel more secure; why then perpetrate them? I believe that dissonance helps explain this phenomenon. The people were terribly frightened—after all, the neighboring villages had been destroyed—but they did not have ample excuse for their fear, since the earthquake had missed them. So they invented their own excuse; if a cyclone is on the way, it is reasonable to be afraid. Later, Durganand Sinha studied rumors in a town that had actually been destroyed. The people were scared, but they had good reason to be; they didn't need to seek additional justification for their terror. And their rumors showed no predictions of impending disaster and no serious exaggerations.

THE DECISION TO BE CRUEL

The need for people to believe that they are kind and decent can lead them to say and do unkind and indecent things. After the National Guard killed four students at Kent State, several rumors quickly spread: the slain girls were pregnant, so their deaths spared their families from shame; the students were filthy and had lice on them. These rumors were totally untrue, but the townspeople were eager to believe them. Why? The local people were conservative, and infuriated at the radical behavior of some of the students. Many had hoped that the students would get their comeuppance. But death is an awfully severe penalty. The severity of this penalty outweighs and is dissonant with the "crimes" of the students. In these circumstances, any information that put the victims in a bad light reduces dissonance by implying, in effect, that it was good that the young people died. One high-school teacher even avowed that anyone with "long hair, dirty clothes, or [who goes] barefooted deserves to be shot."

Keith Davis and Edward Jones demonstrated the need to justify cruelty. They persuaded students to help them with an experiment, in the course of which the volunteers had to tell another student that he was a shallow, untrustworthy, and dull person. Volunteers managed to convince themselves that they didn't like the victim of their cruel analysis. They found him less attractive than they did before they had to criticize him.

Similarly, David Glass persuaded a group of subjects to deliver electric shocks to others. The subjects, again, decided that the victim must deserve the cruelty; they rated him as stupid, mean, etc. Then Glass went a step further. He found that a subject with high self-esteem was most likely to derogate the victim. This led Glass to conclude, ironically, that it is precisely because a person thinks he is nice that he decides that the person he has hurt is a rat. "Since nice guys like me don't go around hurting innocent people," Glass's subjects seemed to say, "you must have deserved it." But individuals who have *low* self-esteem do not feel the need to justify their behavior and derogate their victims; it is *consonant* for such persons to believe they have behaved badly. "Worthless people like me do unkind things."

Ellen Berscheid and her colleagues found another factor that limits the need to derogate one's victim: the victim's capacity to retaliate. If the person doing harm feels that the situation is balanced, that his victim will pay him back in coin, he has no need to justify his behavior. In Berscheid's experiment, which involved electric shocks, college students did not derogate or dislike the persons they shocked if they believed the victims could retaliate. Students who were led to believe that the victims would not be able to retaliate *did* derogate them. Her work suggests that soldiers may have a greater need to disparage civilian victims (because they can't retaliate) than military victims. Lt. William L. Calley, who considered the "gooks" at My Lai to be something less than human, would be a case in point.

DISSONANCE AND THE SELF-CONCEPT

On the basis of recent experiments, I have reformulated Festinger's original theory in terms of the self-concept. That is, dissonance is most powerful when self-esteem is threatened. Thus the important aspect of dissonance is not "I said one thing and I believe another," but "I have misled people—and I am a truthful, nice person." Conversely, the cognitions, "I believe the task is dull," and "I told someone the task was interesting," are not dissonant for a psychopathic liar.

David Mettee and I predicted in a recent experiment that persons who had low opinions of themselves would be more likely to cheat than persons with high self-esteem. We assumed that if an average person gets a temporary blow to his self-esteem (by being jilted, say, or not getting a promotion), he will temporarily feel stupid and worthless, and hence do any number of stupid and worthless things—cheat at cards, bungle an assignment, break a valuable vase.

Mettee and I temporarily changed 45 female students' self-esteem. We gave one third of them positive feedback about a personality test they had taken (we said that they were interesting, mature, deep, etc.); we gave one third negative feedback (we said that they were relatively immature, shallow, etc.); and one third of the students got no information at all. Then all the students went on to participate in what they thought was an unrelated experiment, in which they gambled in a competitive game of cards. We arranged the situation so that the students could cheat and thereby win a considerable sum of money, or not cheat, in which case they were sure to lose.

The results showed that the students who had received blows to their self-esteem cheated far more than those who had gotten positive feedback about themselves. It may well be that low self-esteem is a critical antecedent of criminal or cruel behavior.

The theory of cognitive dissonance has proved useful in generating research; it has uncovered a wide range of data. In formal terms, however, it is a very sloppy theory. Its very simplicity provides both its greatest strength and its most serious weakness. That is, while the theory has generated a great deal of data, it has not been easy to define the limits of the theoretical statements, to determine the specific predictions that can be made. All too often re-

searchers have had to resort to the very unscientific rule of thumb, "If you want to be sure, ask Leon."

LOGIC AND PSYCHOLOGIC

Part of the problem is that the theory does not deal with *logical* inconsistency, but *psychological* inconsistency. Festinger maintains that two cognitions are inconsistent if the opposite of one follows from the other. Strictly speaking, the information that smoking causes cancer does not make it illogical to smoke. But these cognitions produce dissonance because they do not make sense psychologically, assuming that the smoker does not want cancer.

One cannot always predict dissonance with accuracy. A man may admire Franklin Roosevelt enormously and discover that throughout his marriage FDR carried out a clandestine affair. If he places a high value on fidelity and he believes that great men are not exempt from this value, then he will experience dissonance. Then I can predict that he will either change his attitudes about Roosevelt or soften his attitudes about fidelity. But, he may believe that marital infidelity and political greatness are totally unrelated; if this were the case, he might simply shrug off these data without modifying his opinions either about Roosevelt or about fidelity.

Because of the sloppiness in the theory several commentators have criticized a great many of the findings first uncovered by dissonance theory. These criticisms have served a useful purpose. Often, they have goaded us to perform more precise research, which in turn has led to a clarification of some of the findings which, ironically enough, has eliminated the alternative explanations proposed by the critics themselves.

For example, Alphonse and Natalia Chapanis argued that the "severe initiation" experiment could have completely different causes. It might be that the young women were not embarrassed at having to read sexual words, but rather were aroused, and their arousal in turn led them to rate the dull discussion group as interesting. Or, to the contrary, the women in the severe-initiation condition could have felt much sexual anxiety, followed by relief that the discussion was so banal. They associated relief with the group, and so rated it favorably.

So Harold Gerard and Grover Mathewson replicated our experiment, using electric shocks in the initiation procedure. Our findings were supported—subjects who underwent severe shocks in order to join a discussion group rated that group more favorably than subjects who had undergone mild shocks. Moreover, Gerard and Mathewson went on to show that merely linking an electric shock with the group discussion (as in a simple conditioning experiment) did not produce greater liking for the group. The increase in liking for the group occurred only when subjects volunteered for the shock *in order to* gain membership in the group—just as dissonance theory would predict.

ROUTES TO CONSONANCE

In the real world there is usually more than one way to squirm out of inconsistency. Laboratory experiments carefully control a person's alternatives, and the conclusions drawn may be misleading if applied to everyday situations. For example, suppose a prestigious university rejects a young Ph.D. for its one available teaching position. If she feels that she is a good scholar, she will experience dissonance. She can then decide that members of that department are narrow-minded and senile, sexist, and wouldn't recognize talent if it sat on their laps. Or she could decide that if they could reject someone as fine and intelligent as she, they must be extraordinarily brilliant. Both techniques will reduce dissonance, but not that they leave this woman with totally opposite opinions about professors at the university.

This is a serious conceptual problem. One solution is to specify the conditions under which a person will take one route to consonance over another. For example if a person struggles to reach a goal and fails, he may decide that the goal wasn't worth it (as Aesop's fox did) or that the effort was justified anyway (the fox got a lot of exercise in jumping for the grapes). My own research suggests that a person will take the first means when he has expended relatively little effort. But when he has put in a great deal of effort, dissonance will take the form of justifying the energy.

This line of work is encouraging. I do not think that it is very fruitful to demand to know what *the* mode of dissonance reduction is; it is more instructive to isolate the various modes that occur, and determine the optimum conditions for each.

IGNORANCE OF ABSURDITY

No dissonance theorist takes issue with the fact that people frequently work to get rewards. In our experiments, however, small rewards tend to be associated with greater attraction and greater attitude change. Is the reverse ever true?

Jonathan Freedman told college students to work on a dull task after first telling them (*a*) their results would be of no use to him, since his experiment was basically over, or (*b*) their results would be of great value to him. Subjects in the first condition were in a state of dissonance, for they had unknowingly agreed to work on a boring chore that apparently had no purpose. They reduced their dissonance by deciding that the task was enjoyable.

Then Freedman ran the same experiment with one change. He waited until the subjects finished the task to tell them whether their work would be important. In this study he found incentive effects: students told that the task was valuable enjoyed it more than those who were told that their work was useless. In short, dissonance theory does not apply when an individual performs an action in good faith without having any way of knowing it was absurd. When we agree to participate in an experiment we naturally assume that it is for a purpose. If we are informed afterward that it *had* no purpose, how were we to have known? In this instance we like the task better if it had an important purpose. But if we agreed to perform it *knowing* that it had no purpose, we try to convince ourselves that it is an attractive task in order to avoid looking absurd.

MAN CANNOT LIVE BY CONSONANCE ALONE

Dissonance reduction is only one of several motives, and other powerful drives can counteract it. If human beings had a pervasive, all-encompassing need to reduce all forms of dissonance, we would not grow, mature, or admit to our mistakes. We would sweep mistakes under the rug, or worse, turn the mistakes into virtues; in neither case would we profit from error.

But obviously people do learn from experience. They often do tolerate dissonance because the dissonant information has great utility. A person cannot ignore forever a leaky roof, even if that flaw is inconsistent with having spent a fortune in the house.

As utility increases, individuals will come to prefer dissonance-arousing but useful information. But as dissonance increases, or when commitment is high, future utility and information tend to be ignored.

It is clear that people will go to extraordinary lengths to justify their actions. They will lie, cheat, live on the San Andreas Fault, accuse innocent bystanders of being vicious provocateurs, ignore information that might save their lives, and generally engage in all manner of absurd postures. Before we write off such behavior as bizarre, crazy, or evil, we would be wise to examine the situations that set up the need to reduce dissonance. Perhaps our awareness of the mechanism that makes us so often irrational will help turn Camus' observation on absurdity into a philosophic curiosity.

11.   ESCAPE FROM REALITY: ILLUSIONS IN EVERYDAY LIFE

Shelley E. Taylor

INTRODUCTION

One of the first things an infant learns is that the self is a separate person. Upon seeing his reflection, the very young baby will pat his image and pat himself in return, knowing that what he is seeing is himself. Much of early knowledge involves distinguishing what is the self from other important people in the environment, especially the mother and father. As a consequence, the self helps to organize thinking around its attributes and its relationships to the social world.[1] Mental health experts suggest that the process by which this differentiation of self occurs should involve the capacity to perceive the self realistically, that is, to acknowledge faithfully both one's strengths and one's weaknesses. This is not, in fact, how the process evolves.

Before the exigencies of the world impinge upon the child's self-concept, the child is his or her own hero. With few exceptions, most children think very well of themselves. They believe they are capable at many tasks and abilities, including those they have never tried. They see themselves as popular. Most kindergartners and first-graders say they are at or near the top of the class. They have great expectations for their future success. Moreover, these grandiose assessments are quite unresponsive to negative feedback, at least until approximately

---

Excerpted from Chapter 1 of *Positive Illusions* by Shelley E. Taylor. Copyright © 1989 by Basic Books, Inc. Reprinted with permission.

age seven. Children see themselves as successful on most tasks, even ones on which they failed. They seem quite cheerfully oblivious to feedback from others that they have not performed as well as they think they have.[2] An architect friend recounts the time he took his five-year-old daughter to work with him. As he finalized some building plans at his drafting table, the child scrupulously mimicked the behavior at a nearby desk. Amused passersby came over to see what the child had accomplished, and one kindly friend remarked, "Someday you'll be an even better architect than your daddy." The child looked up in surprise and responded, "But I already am," and went back to work.

Why do children have such unrealistically positive assessments of their abilities that, moreover, appear to be so unresponsive to feedback? Psychologist Deborah Stipek argues, in part, that children do not necessarily view failure as failure. To a child, the fact that a goal has not been attained does not mean that something bad has occurred or that the experience has any implications for the future. Eventually children learn to judge their performance as a success or failure, but in very young children these concepts have little meaning. Children have fairly short memories and may actually forget how they have done. Children also see ability and effort as very much the same thing, and so they see any activity in pursuit of a goal, whether successful or unsuccessful, as progress. As one child noted, "If you study, it helps the brain and you get smarter."[3] Young children do not differentiate very well between what they wish could be true and what they think is true, and thus they show wishful thinking in their estimations of their abilities.[4]

The view of oneself as a hero who possesses all the qualities necessary to succeed in a world filled with opportunities fades somewhat in late childhood, but it is nonetheless present in adults as well as children. Although mental health experts regard the well-adjusted person as being aware and accepting of negative as well as positive aspects of the self, in fact, most adults hold very positive views of themselves. When asked to describe themselves, most people mention many positive qualities and few, if any, negative ones.[5] Even when people acknowledge that they have faults, they tend to downplay those weaknesses as unimportant or dismiss them as inconsequential.[6]

For those who are mathematically inclined, the world is awash with arithmetic problems waiting to be solved. For those with little talent in that direction, the tasks are best left undone or delegated to a spouse or an accountant. People regard activities that do not hold their interest as less important than things that interest them. To a football fan, football is an important part of life. To those uninterested in football, it is a slow-moving, bizarre contest between surreal giants who could surely think of better ways to spend their time. When people recognize their lack of talent in a particular area, they are likely to see it as a common fault shared by others. Favored abilities, in contrast, are typically regarded as rare and distinctive signs of unusual talent.[7] The child who can hop on one foot is convinced no one else can do it quite as well, while this same child would insistently argue that all her friends eat cereal with their fingers, too. Thus, far from being balanced between positive and negative conceptions, the image that most people hold of themselves is heavily weighted in a positive direction.[8]

But are those self-perceptions actually unrealistic? Is the positive self-image an illusion or a reality? An imbalance in self-perceptions does not in and of itself mean that people's self-perceptions are biased. Most people commit positive actions most of the time, and consequently people's favorable attributes and actions considerably outweigh their negative ones. There is, however, some evidence that adult's positive self-perceptions are unrealistic. Most people, for example, see themselves as better than others and as above average on most of their qualities. When asked to describe themselves and other people, most people provide more positive descriptions of themselves than they do of friends. This tendency to see the self as better than others occurs across a wide variety of tasks and abilities.[9] Because it is logically impossible for most people to be better than everyone else, the positive view that most people have of themselves appears to be, at least to some degree, illusory in nature. Most people even believe that they drive better than others. For example, in one survey, 90 percent of automobile drivers considered themselves better than average drivers. Indeed, these beliefs sometimes show an unresponsiveness to feedback that reminds one of the very young child. When people whose driving had involved them in accidents serious enough to involve hospitalization were interviewed about their driving skills and compared with drivers who had not had accident histories, the two groups gave almost identical descriptions of their driving abilities. Irrespective of their accident records, people judged themselves to be more skillful than average, and this was true even when the drivers involved in accidents had been responsible for them.[10]

The evaluations people offer of themselves are also typically more favorable than judgments made by others about them.[11] For example, when people's descriptions are contrasted with the descriptions of them offered by their friends or acquaintances, the self-descriptions tend to be more positive. Typically, we see ourselves in more flattering terms than we are seen by others. The perception of self that most people hold, then, is not as well balanced as traditional theories of mental health suggest. Rather than being attentive to both the favorable and unfavorable aspects of the self, most people appear to be very cognizant of their strengths and assets and considerably less aware of their weaknesses and faults. Our self-aggrandizing perceptions may result in part from biases in how we remember ourselves and our past actions.

The Self as Personal Historian

Our minds are constructed not only to sift through and digest the information available to us in the present, but to store and make sense of all the information that has been part of the past. In a sense each person acts as a personal historian, recording the events of which he or she has been a part. Rather than acting as a dispassionate recorder of events as they transpire, the self appears to actively fabricate and revise personal history. Moreover, this task is ac-

complished in a way that makes the self an important, central, and positive figure in that history.

In his landmark essay, "The Totalitarian Ego," psychologist Anthony Greenwald argues that "the past is remembered as if it were a drama in which the self is the leading player."[12] In some ways, this fact is a necessity of memory. One can remember only events in which one participated because, by definition, events from which one was absent cannot be remembered, only heard about. Moreover, memory must be limited by our own perceptions of what transpired. We cannot remember other people's interpretations of situations, only our own. We can experience only our own sensations and emotional reactions to situations and not other people's. Since memory is often enriched by the recall of particular feelings or sensations, these details will, of necessity, be egocentric, that is, centered around the self. In recalling a dinner party of the night before, I may remember that I had slightly too much to drink, told an off-color story about a colleague that might best have been censored, and was otherwise fairly outgoing and a little funnier than usual. Were I to share these perceptions with another who had been a guest at the party, they would no doubt bear little resemblance to his recollections. He might dimly remember my off-color story, have no awareness that I had slightly too much to drink, nor be particularly cognizant of the fact that I was entertaining. Rather, his own recollection of the party might involve wondering whether people noticed that he was feeling low and whether they would properly attribute this to problems in his marriage. He might remember several of the stories told, but not necessarily who told which one. He might recall wondering at ten o'clock if the party would ever end, and the relief he felt when at eleven fifteen people finally pushed their chairs away from the table to say good night. The comparison of these experiences suggests that we were at different dinner parties, which indeed is exactly what happened in certain respects. In the absence of any active reconstruction or distortion, memory is egocentric, organized entirely around the experiences of the person constructing the memory.

But memory is egocentric in more important ways as well. Our memories of situations not only bear the traces of egocentric sensations and perspectives, but are also actively organized around our own interests and concerns. Each of us has qualities that we consider to be characteristic of ourselves. One person may think of himself as witty, musical, and hopelessly lacking in athletic ability. Another person may regard herself as kind, overweight, and intelligent. Psychologists call these enduring beliefs that people have about themselves *self-schemas*.[13] Self-schemas are important because they guide the selection and interpretation of information in social situations. The man who thinks of himself as musical will almost certainly remember that a Mozart clarinet concerto played in the background during the dinner party, whereas someone who does not consider himself to be musical might not even be aware that music was playing. The person who thinks of himself as witty is likely to interpret his barbed remark toward another dinner guest as humorous, whereas a person for whom kindness is an important dimension may interpret the same behavior as rude and unkind. The woman who thinks of herself as overweight will almost certainly remember the entire menu, what she ate and what she didn't eat, and the approximate caloric value of each food item.

Self-schemas, then, impose an additional selectivity on the information that people construe from situations and later remember about them. In recalling information that fits self-schemas, those self-schemas are inadvertently reinforced by memory. For example, each situation that a witty person interprets as an example of his own witty banter provides him with additional evidence that he is witty. If he construes three or four remarks that he made as examples of his wit, then his self-perception as a witty person is strengthened by each of these events. Other guests at the party, however, may remember only one or two of the remarks, considering neither especially funny. Self-schemas, then, enable us to take in the information that fits our prior conceptions of what we are like and what interests us and simultaneously helps cement those self-impressions.

Psychologists generally interpret the effects of self-schemas on memory to mean that memory is organized efficiently in a limited number of categories. That is, given that no one can take in all of the available information in a situation, self-schemas provide guidelines for which information should be noticed, thought about, and put away in memory. The fact that these organizing categories are related to the self is in some respects an accident of the fact that the self is taking in the information. If one takes a functional perspective for a moment, however, it is clear that the egocentric organization of information can be very useful. People make a rough cut on information as "relevant to me" or "not relevant to me." Next they interpret exactly how the information is relevant. When that information is later stored egocentrically in memory, it can be applied in extremely useful ways. For example, a woman for whom kindness is important not only uses kindness as a way of sorting people into the categories of kind and unkind, she may also use the information as a basis for her own future social interactions. Having determined that the witty man is unkind, she would be very likely to avoid him in future situations, a highly adaptive maneuver from her standpoint. Clearly, the egocentric organization of memory is useful from an economic standpoint, that is, in reducing information to a manageable load.[14] But beyond this, it may be very adaptive in helping people to construct their future activities.[15]

Most of us think well of ourselves on most attributes, so self-schemas are more likely to be positive than negative. This recognition leads to the realization that memory for past events will likely be recalled in a positive manner, one that reflects well on the self. This logical inference yields a third way in which memory is biased, namely toward positive construals of one's own attributes and roles in events gone by.[16] Indeed, the capacity of memory to recast events in a positive light almost immediately after they have transpired is almost astonishing. People who have just performed poorly on a task such as doing mathematics problems can be asked to recall their performance a scant twenty minutes later, and even in the short interval they misremember their performance as better than it actually was. Within a few days or weeks, the event may be forgotten altogether. If I rush a student in and out of my office in a few minutes, knowing that he has not had a chance to discuss his research with me fully, I may feel guilty shortly thereafter, but will likely have put the event totally out of mind within days. If I later learn that he has told other students that I am too busy to provide useful advice, I might be hurt and amazed by this betrayal, totally forgetting that I once believed it to hold a kernel of truth.

When people are asked to recall their personal qualities, they typically come up with more positive than negative information. Positive information about one's own personality is easily recalled and efficiently processed, whereas negative information about one's personality is poorly processed and difficult to recall.[17] There are, of course, qualifications to this general rule. Most of us know that in making our qualities known to another person, to brag endlessly of our talents without any assessment of our weaknesses would make us appear conceited. In order to achieve the positive picture we wish to construct for others, sometimes we may admit to certain faults. However, even the faults or weaknesses may be carefully chosen to round out a warm, human portrait, rather than one that is balanced between the positive and negative.[18] A woman may be more likely to admit to others that she is hopeless at math than to confess that she sometimes cheats on her husband. Thus, while our characterizations of ourselves to others may incorporate a certain socially desirable modesty, the portraits that we actually believe, when we are given freedom to voice them, are dramatically more positive than reality can sustain. As writer Carlos Fuentes so acutely noted, "Desire will send you back into memory . . . for memory is desire satisfied."[19]

Greenwald's characterization of these memory processes as totalitarian is apt. Unlike the academic historian, who is expected to adhere closely to the facts and insert a personal evaluation only in the interpretation, the personal historian takes unbridled license with the facts themselves, rearranging and distorting them and omitting aspects of history altogether in an effort to create and maintain a positive image of the self. We control the present by using our own interests and attributes as ways of selecting and organizing available information, and then we store it in memory in ways that are both highly positive and consistent with our existing impressions of ourselves. We use the present to construct a benign portrait of the past with ourselves as central actors. In so doing, we pave the way for a similar future.

The Self as Causal Actor

Taking in and recalling information are not the only cognitive tasks that people must perform. Active interpretation of the present is also required. Perceptions of what caused events to happen are among the most important beliefs that people hold about social situations. Here, too, the self is self-serving. A consistent and ubiquitous research finding is that people take credit for good things that happen and deny responsibility for the bad things that happen.[20] This self-serving bias, as it has been called, shows up in a broad array of situations. For example, on the tennis court, after you have soundly beaten an opponent, rarely do you hear the gratifying, "Gee, you're much better than I am, aren't you?" Usually you hear that it was a bad day, your opponent's serve was off, he is still working on his backhand, or the light was in his eyes. On the other hand, when you have just been badly beaten, the smug look and condescending "bad luck" from the opponent are particularly grating because you know that he does not believe it was bad luck for a moment; he simply thinks he is better. Positive outcomes or actions tend to be attributed to one's own personal qualities, whereas negative outcomes are regarded as the result of bad luck or factors beyond one's control.

The following examples from the *San Francisco Chronicle* of drivers' explanations of their accidents to the police reveal how reluctantly people assume blame for negative events.

As I approached an intersection, a sign suddenly appeared in a place where a stop sign had never appeared before. I was unable to stop in time to avoid an accident.

The telephone pole was approaching. I was attempting to swerve out of its way when it struck my front end.[21]

And commenting on students' evaluations of final exams, Greenwald notes:

I have repeatedly found a strong correlation between obtained grade and the belief that the exam was a proper measure. Students who do well are willing to accept credit for success; those who do poorly, however, are unwilling to accept responsibility for failure, instead seeing the exam (or the instructor) as being insensitive to their abilities.[22]

How do people maintain the perception that they cause good things to happen but bear less responsibility for bad outcomes? Is this simply some sleight of mind analogous to the magician's sleight of hand? Or can it be understood as an adaptive cognitive process? Perhaps when people try to understand why an event occurred, they confuse their intentions with their actions.[23] Usually we intend to cause good things and not bad things. When those good things do occur, the tendency to see ourselves as having brought them about may be quite justifiable, given that we did indeed mean to bring the outcome about. However, when our actions produce bad outcomes, we may look for circumstantial explanations precisely because no adverse outcomes were intended. The man who backs out of his driveway and hits a small child may blame the automobile manufacturers for having rear-view mirrors that fail to pick up low objects. Alternatively, he may blame the child's parents for not having trained the child to stay out of the street. He is unlikely to blame himself, because he never intended to hit the child. Whether the confusion of intention and causality underlies the tendency to attribute good outcomes to oneself to a greater degree than bad outcomes remains to be seen. The interpretational bias itself, however, is well established and constitutes yet another way in which the mind actively fosters a positive view of the self.

Self-serving biases in the perception of the causes of events are strengthened by the fact that people typically exaggerate how much of a role they have in any task, particularly one with a good outcome.[24] To take a simple example, when two people have written a book together and are asked to estimate how much of the book they are personally responsible for, the estimates added together will typically exceed 100 percent. The same feature characterizes more mundane tasks. Asked to estimate how much of a contribution they make to housework, adding together husbands' and wives' estimates of their own efforts produces a total that greatly exceeds 100 percent.[25] Even the lore surrounding Nobel Prize winners is filled with such accounts.

In 1923, two Canadians, Banting and Macleod, were awarded the Nobel Prize for their discovery of insulin. Upon receiving the prize, Banting contended that Macleod, who was head of the laboratory, had been more of a hindrance than a help. On the other hand, Macleod managed to omit Banting's name in speeches describing the research leading up to discovery of insulin.[26]

What leads people to overestimate their role in jointly undertaken ventures? Egocentric memory appears once again to be the culprit. We notice our own contributions to a joint task because we are mentally and physically present when making our own contributions. When the other person is contributing his or her share to the joint task, we may not be physically present to observe it or we may be distracted from noticing the other person's effort. When asked to recall who contributed what to the task, it will subsequently be easier to recall one's own contributions, having attended to them better in the first place, than to recall the other person's.[27]

There will also likely be interpretational biases in what constitutes a contribution.[28] A recent tiff between two authors of a book centered on the fact that while one wrote his share of the chapters rather quickly, the other put a great deal more time into preparing his chapters. Because the first writer was more experienced, his chapters needed few revisions; but the second author's chapters required several drafts and received comments from the first author. The first author perceived that he had borne the lion's share of the effort, by both being responsible for his own chapters and critiquing those of his collaborator. The collaborator, in contrast, felt that he had done the most, because his work had taken three times as long as the first author's. Who is right? Clearly it depends on one's perspective, and one can make a case for either position.

The tendency to take more than one's share of credit for a joint outcome would appear to be a maladaptive bias, inasmuch as it creates so many opportunities for misunderstandings. However, the bias may have benefits as well as potential liabilities. By perceiving one's share of a joint product to be larger than it is, people may feel more responsible for the outcome and work harder to make it a positive one. Moreover, the process of contributing to the activity may instill a sense of commitment to the project and to one's collaborators that may undermine, at least temporarily, any feelings of having done more than one's share. The bias, too, may be more one of memory than of active construction during the time that the tasks are being performed. Often, when two people have jointly achieved greatness, the falling out over who was most responsible for the product occurs after the outcome has been achieved, not while the task is going on. Commitment and a sense of responsibility may carry the joint product through completion, but egocentric memory may distort later reconstructions of what actually took place.[29]

At this point, it is useful to take stock and reassess whether normal human self-perception is characterized by realism or not. The evidence from numerous research investigations with both children and adults clearly indicates that people's assessments of their own capabilities are ego-enhancing rather than realistic. The fact that this bias is so clearly prevalent in the normal human mind is surprising. Psychologists have typically interpreted blatant ego enhancement as the resort of weak and insecure people attempting to bolster fragile self-esteem. Weak egos are thought to need narcissism to survive.[30] Alternatively, ego defensiveness has been viewed as a handy refuge for all of us during weak or threatening moments.[31] In this view, we may need the occasional self-serving interpretation to recover from a blow to self-esteem, but not otherwise. The picture furnished by the evidence, however, is quite different and suggests that ego enhancement characterizes most perception most of the time. This fact, in itself, does not make self-enhancement adaptive, but it does make it normal. As such, this picture is in opposition to the portrait of normal functioning painted by many theories of mental health.

THE NEED FOR CONTROL

In 1971, psychologist B. F. Skinner published a book, *Beyond Freedom and Dignity*, that sparked heated debate. Among other points, Skinner argued that freedom and individual will are illusions because behavior is under the control of positive and negative reinforcements provided by the environment. The uproar created by this argument is testimony to the attachment people have to their perceptions of freedom, personal choice, and control. Indeed, Skinner may have gone too far. While there is certainly a basis for contending that freedom, control, and personal will are constructions that people impose on events rather than factors inherent in events themselves, what people construe about their behavior is of great importance. Interpretations enable people to make sense of their experience; moreover, they can have important personal consequences. As psychologist Herbert Lefcourt notes:

To believe that one's freedom is a false myth and that one should submit to wiser or better controls contains the assumption that beliefs or illusions have no immediate consequences. . . . This assumption is specious. Illusions have consequences and . . . the loss of the illusion of freedom may have untoward consequences for the way men live.[32]

Since the days of Aristotle and Plato, philosophers have argued that a sense of personal control is vital to human functioning. Psychologists from many theoretical viewpoints, including social psychologist Fritz Heider, developmental psychologist Robert

White, learning theorist Albert Bandura, and psychoanalytic theorists Alfred Adler and Sandor Fenichel, have maintained that the self-concept cannot mature without a sense of personal control.

The Child's Need for Control

The desire to control and manipulate the world is evident from a remarkably early age. Within weeks after birth, an infant actively explores the environment, responding to a new stimulus, such as a brightly colored rattle, with rapt attention and babbling. Soon, however, when the rattle has been fully explored, the infant shows little response when the rattle is again dangled before her, but may react with the same excitement to a new checkerboard that she has not previously seen. The infant, then, is primed to master new experiences.[33] At first, psychologists observing this behavior tried to identify what reinforcements it might bring for the child. Were the parents more likely to feed or comfort the child when he or she explored and manipulated the environment? What rewards did curiosity evoke that maintained this behavior? Soon it became evident that the child pursued these exploratory activities for their own sake. Exploration and the ability to bring about change in the environment are their own rewards.[34]

As a result of these observations, psychologists believe that even newborn infants have an intrinsic need to understand and manage the environment.[35] Even the youngest children seem to do what is good for them to bring about their own effective learning. They seek out tasks and sources of stimulation that lead to the development of new skills. Children seem to derive pleasure from engaging in this mastery-oriented behavior, and when a child has accomplished some task—that is, when mastery is attained—he or she seems to experience joy and satisfactions. Both pleasure in the activity itself and enjoyment of the sense of mastery promote similar activities in the future.

So evident is this drive toward mastery that psychologists believe the need to master the environment, or at least its basic elements, is wired in via a mastery-motivation system that instigates, maintains, and reinforces activities that lead to the development of new skills. White refers to this as competence motivation, arguing that the process of learning about the environment and gaining mastery over it is actually intrinsic to the child's development and will occur of its own accord unless disrupted by a biological malfunction or an impoverished environment.[36] Daniel Berlyne refers to a curiosity motivation by which the child constantly seeks more and varied objects to manipulate and explore.[37]

Some of the child's exploratory activities involve stretching already evident skills to try something new. For example, the infant who is able to reach and grasp a stationary toy may be stimulated more by a new toy that is moving than by another stationary toy. The moving toy forces her to extend her abilities to track the toy with her eyes and grasp it as it comes into reach. Children seek and produce novel activity and stimulus variability. Moderately new environments that include objects the child has not seen before are far more interesting and stimulating than either radically different environments or environments full of familiar objects.

The child's mastery needs, then, have a certain orderly progression to them that is responsive both to the demands of tasks and to the limits of existing skills.[38] Any parent attempting unrealistically to throw a birthday party for a one-year-old will stumble upon this fact. As each gift is unwrapped, the child reacts not to the contents but to the wrappings, balling up the paper to make a wonderful crumpling noise and waving the brightly colored ribbons overhead. The empty box makes a perfect hat and is far more valued a toy than the train that came in it, which may not be admired and played with for another six or eight months. Children learn and perform new tasks that are just beyond their range of competence. The young child does not try to drive a car. He depresses the accelerator repeatedly. The adolescent, ready for such a challenge, rolls the car down the driveway at night and practices driving while his parents sleep. The very young child's early cooking efforts extend to baking cookies by stirring in the flour and eating too many chocolate bits. The adolescent can cook an entire meal, assuming she can be induced to do so. Mastery skills are used in a discriminating fashion, moving a step or two ahead of the child's current abilities.

By learning to master their own environments, children alter their parents' behaviors dramatically. Parents quickly learn that if they want the infant to reward them with enthusiastic sounds, the best way to achieve this goal is to gradually introduce more and varied novel experiences. Even infants are able to enlist the cooperation of the social environment to their own mastery needs.[39]

The desire to master the environment, then, appears to be a basic drive, perhaps even a fundamental need of the human organism. By learning that he or she can have an impact on the environment, the child acquires the valuable skills, crucial for adult functioning, that enable him or her to actively intervene in the world so as to bring about desired outcomes. The implicit assumption that underlies a functional interpretation of the need to master is that such early experiences provide the child with a realistic sense of self-efficacy, that is, a realization of those things that can be actively changed and controlled in order to realize personal goals. In fact, however, the sense of control that young children develop appears to be exaggerated rather than tempered by realism.

As young children are learning *how* to control the environment, so too are they learning *that* they can control it. Early in development, children gain the sense that they can make things happen.[40] This, too, may be intrinsic to the child's nature, for it can easily be observed in extreme and dramatic form in the young child. In his conversations with children, the esteemed developmental psychologist Jean Piaget discovered that children believe not only that they can master what goes on in the immediate environment but that they control the movements of the sun, moon, and stars as well.[41] The child's sense of omnipotence is so strong that when family crises arise, such as a sibling's illness or parents' divorce, young children may react very strongly, in part be-

cause they believe they brought the tragic events about.[42]

The child's sense of omnipotence extends to schoolwork and other learning tasks. When asked to guess how well they will do on tasks, young children usually substantially overestimate their performance because they believe they can master the tasks easily. Psychologist Carol Dweck and her associates argue that a mastery orientation toward tasks develops and coheres quite early in life.[43] Mastery-oriented children approach new tasks with the question, "How can this best be accomplished and what should I do to solve it correctly?" When they run into trouble on a difficult task, these mastery-oriented children talk to themselves, trying to figure out what is wrong with their performance and developing strategies to change it so they will be more effective. Often they encourage themselves, letting themselves know that they can do the task correctly.

The competence drive that one sees in the infant and young child is remarkably simple, but extraordinary in its effects. On the one hand, it requires no plan or intention. Yet it enables the child to fashion his or her environment in an increasingly complex way, enlisting the cooperation and talents of several powerful adults in the process, and to derive great pleasure and satisfaction from the results, while simultaneously building essential intellectual skills.

Over time, the child's sense of personal control diminishes somewhat, becoming responsive to realistic limits on talents and the limitations inherent in difficult tasks.[44] Despite this movement toward realism, adults not only continue to have a need and desire to control the environment, but also maintain an exaggerated faith in their ability to do so.

The Adult's Need for Control

Most adults believe the world to be inherently controllable. They have faith that a combination of personal effort and advanced technology can solve most of the world's problems. To the extent that we have been unsuccessful in controlling natural forces or, for that matter, the economic, social, and political dilemmas we have ourselves created, we perceive it to be through lack of effort, not ability, that the problems have remained unsolved. We believe that people succeed through their own efforts, and this leads us to impute effort to those who are highly successful and laziness to those who are not.[45] Even if evidence is all around us suggesting that events are less orderly and systematic than we think they are, rarely do we develop a full appreciation of this fact. The failure to recognize the role of random, unsystematic forces in many aspects of life may come, in part, from our need to see the world as a systematic and orderly place. As Ernest Becker noted in his Pulitzer Prize-winning book, *The Denial of Death*, through the imposition of logic and order on the world we spare ourselves the constant realization of the random terror of death.

One source of faith in personal control is that the environment often cooperates in maintaining it. People are typically quite cognizant of the effects of their own actions on the environment, but are considerably less so regarding the effects of the environment on their own actions. We underestimate the degree to which our behavior is determined by social and physical forces that not only are uncontrollable but often escape awareness altogether.[46] One of my colleagues believes, only half in jest, that he can will a parking place in any lot in which he needs to find one. The reason he holds this belief is that apparently most lots into which he drives have one or two spaces left. Until recently, it had escaped his attention that building projects must create an appropriate number of parking spaces. Thus, while he no doubt overestimates the number of times he gets the last spot, it is also the case that getting one of the last spots is a highly probable event, given the small miracle of city planning.

Another source of the belief in control is that people confuse what they want to have happen with what they can actually bring about, and if the desired event occurs, they conclude that they controlled it.[47] I once observed this in a young boy who had been hospitalized for diabetes. Although not confined to bed, he remained in the hospital for observation because his blood sugar level changed er-

ratically and required monitoring. The hospital environment was dull for this youngster, and he soon took to riding the elevators to provide himself with some semblance of stimulation. Deciding that he would become the elevator operator, he positioned himself in front of the control panel, making it impossible for others to press any but the floor numbers. At each floor, the boy would push the "Door Open" button; when the passenger had departed, the boy would push the "Door Close" button. The door obediently opened and shut. The regular passengers tolerated this unusual behavior because they could see that the boy needed to believe that something, however small, was under his personal control. No one had the heart to tell him, and he never figured out on his own, that the elevator was controlled entirely automatically, and that his button presses had no effect whatsoever on its operation. Because the door repeatedly opened and shut when he wanted it to, he mistakenly assumed that his behavior was actually bringing it about.

The process of evaluating whether or not an event is controllable is an example of a broader fallacy of reasoning, namely the search for examples that confirm prior beliefs.[48] To see how this logical fallacy operates, consider the popular belief that people can cure themselves of serious illnesses through positive thinking. Many people believe that illness results primarily from stressful events and that those who are able to maintain a positive attitude can exert control over their bodily processes and drive illness away. What kind of evidence leads people to hold such a belief? Examples of the mental control of illness are readily available. Norman Cousin's book, *Anatomy of an Illness*, describes in warm and humorous detail the methods the author used to treat himself for a disease that is usually fatal. Magazines contain stories of people who have apparently healed themselves of advanced malignancies through positive thinking. Cultural mythology abounds with examples of shamans who cured their sick neighbors through a variety of useless but dramatic ceremonies. These positive examples make compelling reading, but the logical error lies in precisely this point: they are all positive instances.

Suppose one wanted to determine scientifically whether people are able to cure their diseases through positive attitudes. What would one need to know? Most people immediately recognize the need to find examples of people who tried to cure their diseases through positive thinking and were successful. If pushed, one might come up with the observation that it would be useful to find out how many people tried to cure their diseases through positive thinking and failed. What most people miss is that an accurate sense of whether people can cure their illnesses depends on at least two more types of information: the number of people who did not try to cure their incurable illnesses and survived nonetheless, and the number of people who did not make an effort to cure their illnesses and died. In other words, to establish that people can survive a serious illness if they have effectively tried to control it, one needs all four types of information.

Unfortunately, the world of disease is full of people who have tried valiantly to cure themselves of their illnesses and have ultimately failed. Those who have worked extensively with the chronically ill also know that many people survive years longer than expected without having made any effort in their own behalf at all. These people are often just as bewildered as their physicians, family, and friends to find themselves alive some five or ten years after their initial diagnosis, when everyone expected them to die within months.

In short, it is logically incorrect to conclude that people can control their illnesses simply because one can readily find apparent examples. When one is forced to survey all of the evidence—instead of just the positive cases that are so compelling—judgments of control are considerably more muted, and enthusiasm for the initial belief is somewhat diminished.

This is not to say that people are unable to improve their health by maintaining a positive attitude. The jury is still out on this issue. Rather, the point is that people "see" their beliefs confirmed in incomplete evidence that leads them prematurely to desired conclusions. They fail to see that evidence they have ignored is also relevant. Decision theorists despair of ever getting people to avoid this error. Moreover, on this bias, the average person is in good company. The error is virtually irresistible, not only to the general public but to high-level decision makers in government and industry as well. The analysis of numerous policy decisions, such as the disastrous Bay of Pigs invasion in 1961, has implicated as the basis of the failure the tendency to incorporate primarily positive information and to ignore negative information.[49]

The Illusion of Control

As the previous analysis suggests, people not only believe that the world is inherently controllable, they believe that their own ability to personally control events around them is exceptional. Psychologist Ellen Langer argues that most people succumb to an illusion of control, in which they believe they can affect events more than is actually the case. To demonstrate this point, Langer chose gambling.[50]

Gambling is a clear case in which the relative importance of personal control and chance are often confused. Sociologist Erving Goffman, who once took a job as a croupier in Las Vegas, noted that dealers who experienced runs of bad luck, leading the house to lose heavily, ran the risk of losing their jobs, even though the reason for the run of bad luck was ostensibly chance.[51] Experienced dice players engaged in a variety of behaviors suggesting a belief that they could control what numbers the dice turned up. They threw the dice softly if they wanted low numbers to come up and hard if they were trying to get high numbers. Moreover, they believed that effort and concentration were important and often would not roll the dice unless there was silence and they had a few seconds to concentrate on the number they wanted to get.[52] These kinds of behaviors make perfect sense if a game involves skill. They do not make much sense when the outcome is controlled by chance.

Most of us are not heavy gamblers. In an intriguing set of studies, however, Langer was able to demonstrate that virtually all people are subject to the same illusions of control as veteran gamblers.

Beginning with the recognition that people often fail to distinguish between controllable and uncontrollable events, she argued that one reason for this fact is that the cues people use to differentiate situations of luck and skill are often confused. In skill situations, there is a causal link between one's own behavior and likely outcomes. By choosing materials appropriate for a problem, deciding what responses to make, familiarizing oneself with those materials and responses, spending time thinking about the tasks, coming up with strategies that might be used, and exerting effort, people increase their likelihood of succeeding on a skill-based task.[53] On tasks determined by chance, such behaviors have no effect at all.

Langer showed that by introducing skill-related cues into a chance situation, people came to behave as if the situations were under their personal control and not a result of luck at all. Among her observations were the following: If a person had to bet against a suave, confident opponent, he bet less money than if the opponent appeared to be meek and ineffective. When people were able to choose their own lottery card, as opposed to having it chosen for them, they were less likely to turn it in for a new lottery card that offered them a better chance of winning, simply because they felt it was now *their* card and they wanted to hold onto it. The longer a person held on to a lottery card and presumably had time to think about the likelihood of winning and what he would do with all the money, the less likely he was to turn the lottery card in for a ticket in a drawing with better odds. Langer was able to show that perfectly normal people engaged in a wide variety of superstitious and nonsensical behaviors in chance situations, when cues suggesting skill had been subtly introduced.[54]

The significance of Langer's research extends far beyond its curious but rather minor implications regarding gambling. Any situation in which a person confronts options, develops strategies, and devotes thought to a problem is vulnerable to an illusion of control. For several months, I have been plagued with a problem that until recently proved to be intractable, namely the fact that my dogs eat the pansies growing in the backyard. A variety of disciplinary actions as well as the application of foul-smelling but harmless chemicals to the flower beds have proven unsuccessful in keeping them from these meals. Now, however, I have mastered the situation, by planning to plant pansies only in the beds around the front door. In the backyard I will plant marigolds, which are not nearly as appealing to dogs. The successful solution to this problem bolsters my confidence that I am able to handle stressful events. One can legitimately ask, of course, who actually has control in this situation, me or the dogs? While in my weaker moments I acknowledge that one can probably make the stronger case for the dogs, most of the time this does not dampen my self-congratulations at having successfully mastered the problem by choosing an effective solution. The fact that this "choice" was fully constrained by the situation and was the only option remaining, other than eliminating the dogs, is conveniently forgotten.

The illusion of control has powerful effects on the human psyche. Psychologists have demonstrated that people can tolerate extreme distress if they believe they have the ability to control the source of that distress.[55] The following study conducted with college students makes this point. The students were brought into the laboratory for a study of reactions to electric shock. Half of the students were told that once the shock began, they could terminate it simply by pressing a button in front of them. The other half of the students were not given a button to press to terminate the shock. All the students were then exposed to a series of uncomfortable but harmless electric shocks. The shocks were rigged so that both groups of students received exactly the same amount of shock. Despite this fact, those able to terminate the event by pressing the button themselves experienced less psychological distress, fewer symptoms of physiological arousal, and less physical discomfort.[56] This study and ones like it have been carried out many times with different stressful events and, in every known case, those who can exert control over the stressful event experience less distress and arousal than those who cannot. In fact, those able to control the event often show no more psychological distress or physiological arousal than people receiving no aversive experience at all.[57] Clearly it is not the adverse event itself that leads people to feel physically aroused and psychologically distressed, but rather the perception that it cannot be controlled.

Why do we perceive as controllable things that either are not controllable or are much less so than we think they are? We understand control. We know what it means to seek a goal, to develop methods for obtaining it, and then to employ those methods until the goal is obtained. There is an order, logic, and process to control. There is no order or logic to randomness. Perhaps as well we need to see events as controllable and this is why our minds are predisposed to focus in selectively on instances that support our preconceptions. Perhaps it is the false belief in control that makes people persist in pursuing their goals. Would a novelist undertaking her first work want to contemplate other writers who were catapulted into success by their first works, or would she want to focus instead on the far larger group of writers whose first novels never even attracted a publisher? Clearly, the answer is the former. Our need to see things as inherently controllable may well be adaptive, and our tendency to focus on positive cases of the relationships we expect and so badly wish to see may have value, even as it distorts perceptions.

UNREALISTIC OPTIMISM ABOUT THE FUTURE

Most people are oriented toward the future. When asked to describe what occupies their thoughts, people typically mention issues of immediate or future concern.[58] Moreover, optimism pervades thinking about the future. We seem to be optimistic by nature, some of us more than others, but most more than reality can support.[59] Each year, survey researchers query the American public about their current lives and what they think their lives will be like in five years. Most surveys find people reporting that the present is better than the past and that the future will be even better. More than 95 percent of people questioned in these surveys typically believe that the economic picture will be good for everyone and that their personal economic future will be even better than that of others. People are characteristically hopeful and confident that things will improve.[60] Although this warm and generous vision is extended to all people, it is most clearly evident in visions of one's own future. Students asked to envision what their future lives would be like said they were more likely to graduate at the top of the class, get a good job, have a high starting salary, like their first job, receive an award for work, get written up in the paper, and give birth to a gifted child than their classmates. Moreover, they considered themselves far less likely than their classmates to have a drinking problem, to be fired from a job, to get divorced after a few years of marriage, to become depressed, or to have a heart attack or contract cancer.[61]

Unrealistic optimism is not confined to the idealistic young. Older adults also underestimate the likelihood that they will encounter a large number of negative, but unhappily common, events such as having an automobile accident, being a crime victim, having job problems, contracting major diseases, or becoming depressed. Unrealistic optimism appears to be unaffected by age, education, sex, or occupational prestige. The old and young, the well- and the poorly-educated, men and women, and people in all areas of life show unrealistic optimism in their assessments of the future.[62]

When asked to predict the future, most people predict what they would like to see happen, rather than what is objectively likely. Whether it be in a volleyball game, on a driving test, or on a report prepared for one's boss, most people believe that they will do well in the future. People expect to improve their performance over time, and moreover, this optimism typically increases with the importance of the task.[63] People are more unrealistically optimistic about the prospects for their future jobs than about their gardens, for example. People are even unrealistically optimistic about events that are completely determined by chance, such as whether they will win the lottery and whether the weather will be good for a picnic. People seem to be saying, in effect, "The future will be great, especially for me."

One of the more charming optimistic biases that people share is the belief that they can accomplish more in a given period of time than is humanly possible. This bias persists in the face of innumerable contradictions. Perhaps the most poignant example of this unrealistic optimism is the daily to-do list. Each day, the well-organized person makes a list of the tasks to be accomplished and then sets out to get them done. Then the exigencies of the day begin to intrude: phone calls, minor setbacks, a miscalculation of how long a task will take, or a small emergency. The list that began the day crisp and white is now in tatters, with additions, cross-outs and, most significantly, half its items left undone. Yet at the end of the day, the list maker cheerfully makes up another overly optimistic list for the next day, or if much was left undone, simply crosses out the day at the top of the list and writes in the next day. This all-too-familiar pattern is remarkable not only because a to-do list typically includes far more than any person could reasonably expect to accomplish in a given time period, but also because the pattern persists day after day, completely unresponsive to the repeated feedback that it is unrealistic.[64]

Like the overly positive view of the self and the illusion of control, unrealistic optimism develops very early in life. When children are asked how well they will do on a future task, their expectations are typically very high, higher than is realistic. Moreover, unrealistically optimistic assessments of future performance are not very responsive to feedback, such as actual performance, grades in class, comments from teachers, or reactions of parents. By about age seven or eight, children begin to be aware of the meaning of negative feedback. They become more responsive to what their teachers and parents tell them. They also know what objective tests are, and so they are able to use both objective information and feedback from others to evaluate whether or not they have done a good job.[65] In some respects, this intruding realism is a sad aspect of growing older. Stipek notes:

It is perhaps unfortunate that children's naive optimism declines so soon after they enter school. To some degree the development of more realistic expectations is unavoidable and even desirable. However . . . if children were only given tasks on which they could succeed with some effort, continually high expectations for success and the adaptive behaviors that are associated with high expectations might be maintained throughout the school years. Rather than lamenting children's unrealistic judgments about their competencies, perhaps we should try harder to design educational environments that maintain their optimism and eagerness.[66]

But is unrealistic optimism adaptive? Just as ego-enhancing biases have been regarded as defenses against threats to self-esteem, unrealistic optimism has been thought of as a defensive reaction, a distortion of reality designed to reduce anxiety.[67] Consider the following opinions:

Optimism . . . is a mania for maintaining that all is going well when things are going badly. (Voltaire)

Optimism, not religion, is the opiate of the people. (Lionel Tiger)

The place where optimism most flourishes is in the lunatic asylum. (Havelock Ellis)

Two arguments have been made against unrealistic optimism. The first is that optimism about the future is an irrational defense against reality that enables people to ward off the anxiety of threatening events without successfully coming to terms with it. The second is related to the first in maintaining that unrealistic optimism keeps people from perceiving the objective risks of external threats and preparing for them.[68] Several points argue against the appropriateness of these concerns. If unrealistic optimism were merely a defense against anxiety, one would expect that more serious and threatening events would elicit more unrealistic optimism than minor risks. In fact, the evidence does not support this position. The degree of threat posed by a risk is unrelated to the amount of unrealistic optimism people have about their lack of susceptibility to the problem.[69]

Moreover, unrealistic optimism about the future is highly and appropriately responsive to objective qualities of events, including their frequency and whether or not a person has any past experience with that event. People are less unrealistically optimistic about their chances of experiencing common events like divorce or chronic illness than they are about less frequent events, such as being the victim of a flood or fire. Past experience with a threatening event can eliminate unrealistic optimism altogether. Children of divorced parents, for example, regard their own chances of getting divorced as higher than people whose parents were not divorced. People are also more unrealistically optimistic about future events over which they have some control than they are about those that are uncontrollable. For example, although people estimate their chances of winning a lottery to be higher than is objectively likely, they recognize that winning a large amount of money in a lottery is far less likely than having a satisfying job, an event over which they presumably have more direct control. And finally, unrealistic optimism is responsive to information. When people receive objective evidence about the likelihood of risks, they change their estimates accordingly.[70] These qualities most clearly distinguish illusion from delusion. Delusions are false beliefs that persist despite the facts. Illusions accommodate them, though perhaps reluctantly.

Unrealistic optimism, then, is not a Panglossian whitewash that paints all positive events as equally and commonly likely and all negative events as equally and uncommonly unlikely. Rather, unrealistic optimism shows a patterning that corresponds quite well to the objective likelihood of events, to relevant personal experiences with events, and to the degree to which one can actively contribute to bringing events about. Positive events are simply regarded as somewhat more likely and negative events as somewhat less likely to occur than is actually the case.

What accounts for unrealistic optimism? Optimism seems to be intimately bound up with other illusions of life, especially the belief in personal control.[71] Most people think they can con-

trol future events more than is actually the case, and consequently they may underestimate their vulnerability to random events. A driver may perceive the chance of an automobile accident to be low because she believes she is a better than average driver who can avoid such problems. She may conveniently forget the joy-riding teenager or the drunk driver who may cause an accident. People think they can avoid health problems by getting enough sleep or eating well, forgetting that hereditary factors, chance encounters with viruses, or environmental threats of which they may be ignorant can override even the most careful program of health habits. An active homosexual man in the 1970s might have given some thought to the possibility of contracting gonorrhea, but could he possibly have anticipated the horror of AIDS? Could the people attending the American Legion convention in Philadelphia in 1976 have guessed that the air in their hotel held a deadly contaminant, producing what we now call Legionnaires' disease? When people think of the future, they think of events they would like to see happen and the ones they believe they can bring about, rather than the chance events that may disrupt goals and plans.

Reflection suggests that the failure to consider the role of chance is not as surprising as first might appear. What exactly would constitute an effective recognition of chance? Should one begin driving each day with the image of a truck out of control bearing down on one's car? Should one regard every social situation as a potential opportunity for viruses to spread? Should every walk along city streets be considered a potential encounter with a mugger or rapist? While people certainly need to incorporate a certain amount of caution and defensiveness into their daily behavior, to do so by envisioning these potentially tragic but random events is hardly appropriate. Because chance and random factors are precisely that, their importance cannot be assessed in any reasonable way for any given situation. Therefore, people quite properly do not have chance at the forefront of consciousness when they assess their risks.

The belief in personal control may also account for why people see their personal likelihood of experiencing positive events as higher and negative events as lower than those of other people. When people focus on their own behaviors that might enable them to achieve desirable outcomes or avoid bad ones, they may forget that other people have just as many resources in their own lives.[72] People misjudge their risk that negative events can befall them because they have clear-cut stereotypes of the kinds of people who typically succumb to these events.[73] People who foolishly wander down dark streets at night are people who get mugged. Passive, repressed people who do not express their feelings get cancer. With these stereotypes in mind, we are able to comfort ourselves that adverse events will not befall us. The fact that each of us is engaging in this process—that is, imagining how he or she can avoid negative events—appears to escape attention altogether.

Unrealistic optimism may result from more than simple stereotypes about the kinds of people on whom bad outcomes descend. Psychologist Ziva Kunda suggests that people actively construct theories of why positive and negative events occur; in so doing they draw on their own attributes in order to defend against the possibility that the negative events might befall them and to enhance the perceived likelihood that the positive events will happen to them. For example, upon learning that the divorce rate for first marriages is 50 percent, most people predict that they will not be in that 50 percent, but rather will remain married to their spouse throughout their lifetime. They convince themselves that this is the case, Kunda has shown, by highlighting their personal attributes that might be associated with a stable marriage and downplaying the significance of or actively refuting information that might suggest a vulnerability to divorce. Thus, for example, one might point to one's parents' fifty-year marriage, the close family life that existed in one's early childhood, and the fact that one's high school relationship lasted a full four years as evidence to predict a stable marriage. The fact that one's husband has already been divorced once—a factor that predicts a second divorce—might be reinterpreted not only as not leading to divorce in one's own case, but as a protective factor ("He knows he does not want this marriage to fail like the last one, and so he's working especially hard to keep our relationship strong"). The ability to draw seemingly rational relationships between our own assets and good events and to argue away associations between our own attributes and negative events helps to maintain unrealistic optimism.[74]

The Illusion of Progress

The ability to sustain an optimistic view of the future may also come in part from the ability to misconstrue events as progress. There is a well-established bias indicating that people see themselves as having improved even when no actual progress has been made.[75] We all know that people seek out the company of others who are likely to give them positive feedback. It is only reasonable that we should want as friends people who like and value us. There is a corresponding, less obvious tendency to like others whose evaluations of us improve over time. The initially hard to get girlfriend or boyfriend may, for example, be more highly valued than an old faithful partner who was responsive all along. When people's impressions improve over time, rather than staying at a positive level, it simultaneously enhances several other positive beliefs: it encourages a feeling of personal impact, the idea that one can positively affect other people's evaluations. In so doing, it encourages feelings of interpersonal control, the belief that one can bring out in people the kinds of evaluations and judgments of the self that one would like to achieve. And it creates a future as optimistic as the one mentally constructed because just as one fantasizes that progress will occur, progress appears to be made.[76]

This tendency to construct the future so that it will be better than the past is not limited to social interaction. In an intriguing study, Michael Conway and Michael Ross invited college students who were having difficulty studying to enroll in a program designed to show them how to improve their study skills and achieve higher grades.[77] Half of the students who applied to the program were accepted immediately and the other half were put on a waiting list. The first group of students then went through a three-week study skills program. As it happens, most study skills programs are actually quite ineffective in imparting new skills and raising grades,[78] and such was the case with the study skills program initiated by Conway and Ross. The students who took the program did not differ in final grades or study skills from students who had not participated in the program.

Nonetheless, students in the program perceived that they had improved dramatically. They reported better study skills, and they expected better final exam grades. They also distorted retrospectively how bad their study skills had been before going into the program. Moreover, even after final grades had been calculated, the students overestimated their grades for the term. Thus, by revising what they had initially had, the students were able to achieve, at least mentally, what they wanted, namely improvement in their study skills and grades. Failure ("I failed the test") can be reinterpreted as progress ("but I got practice that will help on this kind of test next time"). Through such distortions, several positive biases may be enhanced. One sees oneself in a positive light and as efficacious, and one simultaneously reconstructs the past and future so as to achieve an illusion of progress.

The Effects of Outcomes on Optimism

People are optimistic about the future most of the time, but when something good happens to them, they become even more so.[79] Doing well at work, for example, leads a person to believe that his children will improve their grades in school and that he will win the weekend tennis tournament. Moreover, a good event acts as a generalized opportunity signal, increasing the belief in the likelihood of all kinds of positive events. Happy events are seen as portents of yet more happy things to come. Similarly, when a bad event happens, it increases the perception that other bad events may lie ahead.[80] Getting sick, being burglarized, or failing a test all move beliefs in the direction of pessimism. Even a transitory mood can yield these same effects.[81] on a day when a person feels good for no particular reason, optimism is higher. Likewise, on a day when a person is low for no particular reason, pessimism may set in. The negative event or mood seems to act as a danger signal. Moreover, this danger signal appears to be a general one, in that it sometimes increases the perception that any bad event may follow, even ones having little or nothing to do with the negative event that has already transpired. If a person fails her driving test, she might logically fear that she may do so again, but why should her fear of developing cancer increase? Why should a burglary increase a sense of vulnerability to diabetes? Similarly, why should receiving a raise at work lead to the belief that one can improve one's marriage?

Perhaps when something good happens, it reinforces a person's belief that he or she is an effective, competent person who can make things happen. Since people exaggerate their ability to control events, even those that are determined by chance, any positive outcome may make people think that they can produce other positive outcomes. Similarly, a negative event, such as getting sick, may undermine a person's sense of control and competence by pointing out that one can get in harm's way without much effort. As the person attempts to make sense of the negative event, he or she may become aware of vulnerability in general, increasing the sense that he or she can fall victim to other negative events. Sociologist Kai Erikson describes this feeling from the standpoint of natural disasters:

One of the bargains men make with one another in order to maintain their sanity is to share an illusion that they are safe, even when the physical evidence in the world around them does not seem to warrant that conclusion. The survivors of a disaster, of course, are prone to overestimate the perils of their situation, if only to compensate for the fact that they underestimated those perils once before; but what is worse, far worse, is that they sometimes live in a state of almost constant apprehension because they have lost the human capacity to screen out the signs of danger out of their line of vision.[82]

The generalized danger signal created by negative events lasts only as long as the negative event or bad mood exists. Once these unpleasant experiences pass, unrealistic optimism returns. An obvious and therefore tempting interpretation is that the generalized danger signal has a certain survival value. When the organism is in a weakened state, physically or psychologically, the generalized perception of danger may keep it appropriately timid, modest, and relatively inactive in order that it not overextend its reduced resources. Once the problem passes and physical and psychological resources are replenished, the organism is once again able to assert itself in the world. At this point, unrealistic optimism may return to diminish the sense of threat. Similarly, the generalized opportunity signal created by optimism may lead people to investigate opportunities that they might not otherwise pursue and to pay little heed to information that would suggest more caution. Optimism may, then, be a significant factor in personal progress.[83]

Illusions of the Mind

What we see in the normal human mind does not correspond very well to the predominant view of mental health. Instead of an awareness and acceptance of both the positive and the negative elements of their personalities, most people show a keen awareness of their positive qualities and attributes, an extreme estimation of their ability to master the environment, and a positive assessment of the future. Not only are these assessments positive, they appear to be unrealistically so. It is not just that people believe they are good, but that they think they are better than reality can sustain. Judgments of mastery greatly exceed the actual ability to control many events. Views of the future are so rosy that they would make Pollyanna blush.

Should we say simply that most people are optimists at heart? Are these so-called illusions of everyday life merely a reflection of some underlying optimistic stance, a tendency to look on the good side of things? While there is surely an optimistic core to self-aggrandizing beliefs about the self, the world,

and the future, these illusions also differ in important ways from optimism. One difference is that illusions critically concern the self. While most people are optimistic, the illusions they demonstrate habitually in their thought patterns concern their own attributes, their beliefs in personal mastery, and concerns about their own futures, rather than a positive view of the world more generally. Another difference is that as a general term, *optimism* refers simply to the expectation that things will turn out well, without any consideration of how those beneficial outcomes will be achieved. The illusion of control, a vital part of people's beliefs about their own attributes, is a personal statement about how positive outcomes will be achieved, not merely by wishing and hoping that they will happen, but by making them happen through one's own capabilities. Finally, . . . it is the specific content of illusions, namely beliefs about the self, one's mastery, and the future, that promote psychological adjustment, not simply the underlying optimism reflected in those illusions.

I have repeatedly referred to these beliefs as illusions, and a word must be said about the selection of this term. In some respects, *illusion* is an unfortunate choice, for it evokes images of a conjuror flirting with the border between reality and fantasy. Moreover, when applied to human thought, it suggests a naive blind spot or weakness. Yet *illusion* is appropriate. The terms *error* and *bias*, which one might employ instead, suggest short-term accidental mistakes and distortions, respectively, that might be caused by some careless oversight or other temporary negligence. The term *illusion*, in contrast, reflects a broader and more enduring pattern of beliefs.

Illusion is a perception that represents what is perceived in a way different from the way it is in reality. An illusion is a false mental image or conception which may be a misinterpretation of a real appearance or may be something imagined. It may be pleasing, harmless or even useful.[84]

In this sense, then, illusion captures the essence of these phenomena. People hold mild and benignly positive illusions about themselves, the world, and the future. Moreover, they are linked in mutually reinforcing and thematically consistent ways. While illusion does not characterize everyone's thinking about all issues regarding the self, the world, and the future, these illusions are common, widespread, and easily documented.

The fact that positive illusions are so dramatic in early childhood and lessen over time is especially intriguing. It suggests that they are natural, intrinsic to the cognitive system, and become worn down and tamed through the feedback that life provides. What we see in adults is not a carefully cultivated and crafted positive glow that is provided by years of experience with the adaptiveness of viewing things in a positive light. Rather, we see instead the residual inflated view of oneself and the future that exists in extreme and almost magical form in very young children.

The illusions that adults hold about their attributes, their capacity for control, and the beneficent future are, in fact, quite mild, nowhere near the dillusional distortions that one frequently observes in mental patients, for example. As a consequence, it is tempting to dismiss them as ultimately inconsequential, amusing peccadillos that put a pleasant twist on incoming information without many consequences for important matters. Indeed, one argument for the adaptiveness of positive illusions maintains that these biases are evident primarily when information is inconsequential and not when the stakes are higher. According to this argument, people may hold falsely positive judgments about themselves on unimportant matters that may buffer them in more serious and consequential circumstances when they are forced to become more realistic. In fact, the evidence tends to suggest the opposite conclusion: people's positive distortions often increase, not decrease, as matters become more important and consequential.[85] The more ego-enhancing a situation is, the more likely it is to evoke positive, self-serving interpretations. When outcomes are important, self-enhancing causal attributions are more likely. Positive illusions, then, are pervasive and not confined to the unimportant matters of life.

The fact that positive illusions exist in normal thought raises the larger question of why they exist and whether they serve any useful purpose. Are they simply a surprising and rather charming aspect of human thought, or are they actually adaptive? Trying to understand their prevalence leads one prematurely to suggest why they might be functional, the implicit assumption being that, like other organs, the mind does not evolve in ways that are inherently injurious to its own functioning. Yet these suggestions of adaptiveness have been speculative only, and the next task is to determine whether this is indeed the case.

NOTES

1. Stipek, 1984; Harter, 1981; Greenwald, 1980.

2. See Stipek, 1984; Stipek and MacIver, in press; Harter, 1981, for reviews.

3. Harari and Covington, 1981, p. 25.

4. Stipek, 1984.

5. Alicke, 1985; Brown, 1986; Campbell, 1986; Larwood and Whittaker, 1977; see also Shrauger and Kelly, in press.

6. Campbell, 1986; Marks, 1984; Harackiewicz, Sansone, and Manderlink, 1985; Lewicki, 1984.

7. Campbell, 1986; Marks, 1984.

8. See Greenwald, 1980; Taylor and Brown, 1988, for reviews. One might argue that overly pos-

itive self-descriptions reflect public posturing rather than privately held beliefs. Several factors, however, argue against the plausibility of a strict self-presentational interpretation of this phenomenon. For example, Greenwald and Breckler (1985) reviewed evidence indicating that (a) self-evaluations are at least as favorable under private conditions as they are under public conditions; (b) favorable self-evaluations occur even when strong constraints to be honest are present; (c) favorable self-referent judgments are made very rapidly, suggesting that people are not engaging in deliberate (time-consuming) fabrication; and (d) self-enhancing judgments are acted on. For these as well as other reasons, a consensus is emerging at the theoretical level that individuals offer flattering self-evaluations not merely as a means of managing a public impression of competency but also as a means of managing impressions of themselves for themselves (see Schlenker, 1980; Tesser and Moore, 1986; Tetlock and Manstead, 1985).

9. Brown, 1986; Lewinsohn, Mischel, Chaplin, and Barton, 1980; Forsyth and Schlenker, 1977; Green and Gross, 1979; Mirels, 1980; Schlenker and Miller, 1977; Brown, 1985; Campbell, 1986; Rosenberg, 1979; Sachs, 1982.

10. Svenson, 1981.

11. E.g., Lewinsohn et al., 1980; see Shrauger 1975, 1982, for a review.

12. Greenwald, 1980, p. 64.

13. Markus, 1977.

14. Greenwald, 1980.

15. Markus, 1977.

16. Greenwald, 1980.

17. Kuiper and Derry, 1982; Kuiper and MacDonald, 1982; Kuiper, Olinger, MacDonald, and Shaw, 1985.

18. Schlenker, 1980; Snyder and Wicklund, 1981.

19. Fuentes, 1964, p. 58.

20. See Bradley, 1978; Miller and Ross, 1975; Ross and Fletcher, 1985; Zuckerman, 1979, for reviews.

21. *San Francisco Sunday Examiner and Chronicle.* April 22, 1979, cited in Greenwald, 1980.

22. Greenwald, 1980, p. 605.

23. Miller and Ross, 1975.

24. Ross, 1981; Ross and Sicoly, 1979.

25. Thompson and Kelley, 1981.

26. Harris, 1946, recounted in Ross, 1981.

27. Ross, 1981; Thompson and Kelley, 1981; Ross and Sicoly, 1979.

28. Thompson and Kelley, 1981.

29. See Ross, 1981.

30. Erikson, 1950; Alper, 1952; Sherif and Cantril, 1947.

31. Miller and Ross, 1975; Snyder, Stephan, and Rosenfield, 1978.

32. Lefcourt, 1973, p. 417.

33. White, 1959.

34. Berlyne, 1960; Fowler, 1965; White, 1959.

35. Donaldson, 1978; Harter 1981; White, 1959.

36. White, 1959.

37. Berlyne, 1960.

38. Piaget, 1954; White, 1959.

39. White, 1959.

40. Diener and Dweck, 1978, 1980; Weisz, 1986.

41. Piaget, 1954.

42. E.g., Lindsay and McCarthy, 1974.

43. Diener and Dweck, 1978, 1980.

44. Stipek, 1984.

45. Ryan, 1971.

46. Jones and Davis, 1965; Jones and Harris, 1967.

47. Miller and Ross, 1975.

48. Crocker, 1981; Smedslund, 1963; Ward and Jenkins, 1965; Arkes and Harkness, 1980; Bower, Black, and Turner, 1979; Franks and Bransford, 1971; Owens, Bower, and Black, 1979; Harris, Teske, and Ginns, 1975; Jennings, Amabile, and Ross, 1982.

49. Janis, 1982.

50. Langer, 1975; Langer and Roth, 1975.

51. Goffman, 1967.

52. Henslin, 1967.

53. Langer, 1975; Langer and Roth, 1975; see also Gilovich, 1983.

54. Langer, 1975.

55. See Thompson, 1981; Averill, 1973; Miller, 1979, for reviews.

56. Geer, Davison, and Gatchel, 1970; Geer and Maisel, 1972.

57. Laudenslager, Ryan, Drugan, Hyson, and Maier, 1983; Hanson, Larson, and Snowden, 1976.

58. Gonzales and Zimbardo, 1985. In this study, 57 percent of the people interviewed said that they thought primarily about the present and the future, and another 33 percent were oriented primarily toward the future. Only 1 percent spent most of their time thinking about the past.

59. Tiger, 1979.

60. Free and Cantril, 1968; Brickman, Coates, and Janoff-Bulman, 1978.

61. Markus and Nurius, 1986; Weinstein, 1980, 1982, 1984; see Perloff, 1983, for a review.

62. Crandall, Solomon, and Kelleway, 1955; Irwin, 1944, 1953; Marks, 1951; Robertson, 1977; Perloff and Fetzer, 1986; Weinstein, 1980; Kuiper, MacDonald, and Derry, 1983.

63. Frank, 1953; Pruitt and Hoge, 1965.

64. Hayes-Roth and Hayes-Roth, 1979.

65. Stipek, 1984; Marks, 1951; Irwin, 1953.

66. Stipek, 1984, p. 53.

67. Kirscht, Haefner, Kegeles, and Rosenstock, 1966; Lund, 1975.

68. Weinstein, 1980, 1982.

69. Weinstein, 1980, 1982.

70. Weinstein, 1980, 1982, 1984.

71. Seligman, 1975; Tiger, 1979.

72. Weinstein and Lachendro, 1982.

73. Kunda, 1987.

74. Kunda, 1987.

75. Conway and Ross, 1984.

76. Aronson and Linder, 1965.

77. Conway and Ross, 1984.

78. Gibbs, 1981.

79. Johnson and Tversky, 1983.

80. Kulik and Mahler, 1987.

81. See Clark and Isen, 1982.

82. Erikson, 1976, p. 234.

83. See Tiger, 1979, for a discussion of these issues.

84. *Random House Dictionary, the English Language*, ed. J. Stein, New York: Random House, p. 662.

85. E.g., Nicholls, 1975; Miller, 1976; Snyder et al., 1978; see Greenwald, 1980, for a review and discussion of this issue.

REFERENCES

Alicke, M. D. (1985). Global self-evaluation as determined by the desirability and uncontrollability of trait adjectives. *Journal of Personality and Social Psychology, 49*, 1621–1630.

Alper, T. G. (1952). The interrupted task method in studies of selective recall: A re-evaluation of some recent experiments. *Psychological Review, 59*, 71–88.

Arkes, R. M., & Harkness, A. R. (1980). Effect of making a diagnosis on subsequent recognition of symptoms. *Journal of Experimental Psychology: Human Learning and Memory, 6*, 568–575.

Aronson, E., & Linder, D. (1965). Gain and loss of esteem as determinants of interpersonal attractiveness. *Journal of Experimental Social Psychology, 1*, 156–172.

Averill, J. R. (1973). Personal control over aversive stimuli and its relationship to stress. *Psychological Bulletin, 80*, 286–303.

Berlyne, D. C. (1960). *Conflict, arousal, and curiosity*. New York: McGraw-Hill.

Bower, G. H., Black, J. B., & Turner, T. J. (1979). Scripts in memory for text. *Cognitive Psychology, 11*, 177–220.

Bradley, G. W. (1978). Self-serving biases in the attribution process: A reexamination of the fact or fiction question. *Journal of Personality and Social Psychology, 36*, 56–71.

Brickman, P., Coates, D., & Janoff-Bulman, R. (1978). Lottery winners and accident victims: Is happiness relative? *Journal of Personality and Social Psychology, 35*, 917–927.

Brown, J. D. (1985). *Self-esteem and unrealistic optimism about the future.* Unpublished data, University of California, Los Angeles.

Brown, J. D. (1986). Evaluations of self and others: Self-enhancement biases in social judgments. *Social Cognition, 4*, 353–376.

Campbell, J. D. (1986). Similarity and uniqueness: The effects of attribute type, relevance, and individual differences in self-esteem and depression. *Journal of Personality and Social Psychology, 50*, 281–294.

Clark, M. S., & Isen, A. M. (1982). Toward understanding the relationship between feeling states and social behavior. In A. H. Hastorf & A. M. Isen (Eds.), *Cognitive social psychology* (pp. 73–108). New York: Elsevier.

Conway, M., & Ross, M. (1984). Getting what you want by revising what you had. *Journal of Personality and Social Psychology, 47*, 738–748.

Crandall, V. J., Solomon, D., & Kelleway, R. (1955). Expectancy statements and decision times as functions of objective probabilities and reinforcement values. *Journal of Personality, 24*, 192–203.

Crocker, J. (1981). Judgment of covariation by social perceivers. *Psychological Bulletin, 90*, 272–292.

Diener, C. I., & Dweck, C. S. (1978). An analysis of learned helplessness: Continuous changes in performance, strategy, and achievement cognitions following failure. *Journal of Personality and Social Psychology, 36*, 451–462.

Diener, C. I., & Dweck, C. S. (1980). An analysis of learned helplessness: 2. The processing of success. *Journal of Personality and Social Psychology, 39*, 940–952.

Donaldson, M. (1978) *Children's minds.* New York: Norton.

Erikson, E. H. (1950). *Childhood and society* (2nd ed.). New York: Norton.

Erikson, K. T. (1976). *Everything in its path: Destruction of community in the Buffalo Creek flood.* New York: Simon & Schuster.

Forsyth, D. R., & Schlenker, B. R. (1977). Attributing the causes of group performance: Effects of performance quality, task importance, and future testing. *Journal of Personality, 45*, 220–236.

Fowler, H. (1965). *Curiosity and exploratory behavior.* New York: Macmillan.

Frank, J. D. (1953). Some psychological determinants of the level of aspiration. *American Journal of Psychology, 47*, 285–293.

Franks, J. J., & Bransford, J. D. (1971). Abstraction of visual patterns. *Journal of Experimental Social Psychology, 90*, 65–74.

Free, L. A., & Cantril, H. (1968). *The political beliefs of Americans: A study of public opinion.* New York: Clarion.

Fuentes, C. (1964). *The death of Artemio Cruz*. New York: Farrar Straus Giroux.

Geer, J. H., Davison, G. C., & Gatchel, R. I. (1970). Reduction of stress in humans through non-veridical perceived control of aversive stimulation. *Journal of Personality and Social Psychology, 16*, 731–738.

Geer, J. H., & Maisel, E. (1972). Evaluating the effects of the prediction-control confound. *Journal of Personality and Social Psychology, 23*, 314–319.

Gibbs, G. (1981). *Teaching students to learn*. Milton Keynes, England: Open University Press.

Gilovich, T. (1983). Biased evaluation and persistence in gambling. *Journal of Personality and Social Psychology, 44*, 1110–1126.

Goffman, E. (1967). *Interaction ritual*. Newport Beach, CA: Westcliff.

Gonzales, A., & Zimbardo, P. G. (1985, March). Time in perspective. *Psychology Today*, pp. 21–26.

Green, S. K., & Gross, A. E. (1979). Self-serving biases in implicit evaluations. *Personality and Social Psychology Bulletin, 5*, 214–217.

Greenwald, A. G. (1980). The totalitarian ego: Fabrication and revision of personal history. *American Psychologist, 35*, 603–618.

Greenwald, A. G., & Breckler, S. J. (1985). To whom is the self presented? In B. Schlenker (Ed.), *The self and social life* (pp. 126–145). New York: McGraw-Hill.

Hanson, J. D., Larson, M. C. & Snowden, C. T. (1976). The effects of control over high intensity noise on plasma control in rhesus monkeys. *Behavioral Biology, 16*, 333–334.

Harackiewicz, J. M., Sansone, C., & Manderlink, G. (1985). Competence, achievement orientation, and intrinsic motivation: A process analysis. *Journal of Personality and Social Psychology, 48*, 493–508.

Harari, O., & Covington, M. (1981). Reactions to achievement from a teacher and student perspective: A developmental analysis. *American Educational Research Journal, 18*, 15–28.

Harris, R. J., Teske, R. R., & Ginns, M. J. (1975). Memory for pragmatic implications from courtroom testimony. *Bulletin of the Psychonomic Society, 6*, 494–496.

Harris, S. (1946). *Banting's miracle: The story of the discovery of insulin*. Toronto: J. M. Dent & Sons.

Harter, S. (1981). A model of intrinsic mastery motivation in children: Intrinsic differences and developmental change. In W. A. Collins (Ed.), *Minnesota Symposium on Child Psychology* (Vol. 14, pp. 215–255). Hillsdale, NJ: Erlbaum.

Hayes-Roth, B., & Hayes-Roth, F. (1979). A cognitive model of planning. *Cognitive Science, 3*, 275–310.

Henslin, J. M. (1967). Craps and magic. *American Journal of Sociology, 73*, 316–330.

Irwin, F. W. (1944). The realism of expectations. *Psychological Review, 51*, 120–126.

Irwin, F. W. (1953). Stated expectations as functions of probability and desirability of outcomes. *Journal of Personality, 21*, 329–335.

Janis, I. L. (1982). *Groupthink: Psychological studies of policy decisions and fiascoes* (2nd ed.). Boston: Houghton Mifflin.

Jennings, D., Amabile, T. M., & Ross, L. (1982). Informal covariation assessment: Data-based versus theory-based judgments. In A. Tversky, D. Kahneman, & P. Slovic (Eds.), *Judgment under uncertainty: Heuristics and biases* (pp. 211–230). New York: Cambridge University Press.

Johnson, J. E., & Tversky, A. (1983). Affect generalization and the perception of risk. *Journal of Personality and Social Psychology, 45*, 20–31.

Jones, E. E., & Davis, K. E. (1965). From acts to dispositions: The attribution process in person perception. In L. Berkowitz (Ed.), *Advances in experimental social psychology* (Vol. 2, pp. 219–266). New York: Academic Press.

Jones, E. E., & Harris, V. A. (1967). The attribution of attitudes. *Journal of Experimental Social Psychology, 3*, 1–24.

Kirscht, J. P., Haefner, D. P., Kegeles, F. S., & Rosenstock, I. M. (1966). A national study of health beliefs. *Journal of Health and Human Behavior, 7*, 248–254.

Kuiper, N. A., & Derry, P. A. (1982). Depressed and nondepressed content self-reference in mild depression. *Journal of Personality, 50*, 67–79.

Kuiper, N. A., & MacDonald, M. R. (1982). Self and other perception in mild depressives. *Social Cognition, 1*, 233–239.

Kuiper, N. A., MacDonald, M. R., & Derry, P. A. (1983). Parameters of a depressive self-schema. In J. Suls & A. G. Greenwald (Eds.), *Psychological perspectives on the self* (Vol. 2, pp. 191–217). Hillsdale, NJ: Erlbaum.

Kuiper, N. A., Olinger, L. J., MacDonald, M. R., & Shaw, B. F. (1985). Self-schema processing of depressed and nondepressed content: The effects of vulnerability on depression. *Social Cognition, 3*, 77–93.

Kulik, J. A., & Mahler, I. M. (1987). Health status, perceptions of risk, and prevention interest for health and nonhealth problems. *Health Psychology, 6*, 15–28.

Kunda, Z. (1987). Motivated inference: Self-serving generation and evaluation of causal theories. *Journal of Personality and Social Psychology, 53*, 636–647.

Langer, E. J. (1975). The illusion of control. *Journal of Personality and Social Psychology, 32*, 311–328.

Langer, E. J., & Roth, J. (1975). Heads I win, tails it's chance: The illusion of control as a function of the sequence of outcomes in a purely chance task. *Journal of Personality and Social Psychology, 32*, 951–955.

Larwood, L., & Whittaker, W. (1977). Managerial myopia: Self-serving biases in organizational planning. *Journal of Applied Psychology, 62*, 194–198.

Laudenslager, M. C., Ryan, S. M., Drugan, R. C., Hyson, R. L., & Maier, S. F. (1983). Coping and immunosuppression: Inescapable but not escapable shock suppresses lymphocyte proliferation. *Science, 231*, 568–570.

Lefcourt, H. M. (1973, May). The function of the illusions of control and freedom. *American Psychologist*, pp. 417–425.

Lewicki, P. (1984). Self-schema and social information processing. *Journal of Personality and Social Psychology, 48*, 463–574.

Lewinsohn, P. M., Mischel, W., Chaplin, W., & Barton, R. (1980). Social competence and depression: The role of illusory self-perceptions. *Journal of Abnormal Psychology, 89*, 203–212.

Lindsay, M., & McCarthy, D. (1974). Caring for the brothers and sisters of a dying child. In T. Burton (Ed.), *Care of the child facing death* (pp. 189–206). Boston, MA: Routledge & Kegan Paul.

Lund, F. H. (1975). The psychology of belief: A study of its emotional and volitional determinants. *Journal of Abnormal and Social Psychology, 20*, 63–81.

Marks, G. (1984). Thinking one's abilities are unique and one's opinions are common. *Personality and Social Psychological Bulletin, 10*, 203–208.

Marks, R. W. (1951). The effect of probability, desirability, and "privilege" on the stated expectations of children. *Journal of Personality, 19*, 332–351.

Markus, H. (1977). Self-schemata and processing information about the self. *Journal of Personality and Social Psychology, 35*, 63–78.

Markus, H., & Nurius, P. (1986). Possible selves. *American Psychologist, 41*, 954–969.

Miller, D. T. (1976). Ego involvement and attributions for success and failure. *Journal of Personality and Social Psychology, 34*, 901–906.

Miller, D. T., & Ross, M. (1975). Self-serving biases in attribution of causality: Fact or fiction? *Psychological Bulletin, 82*, 213–225.

Miller, S. M. (1979). Controllability and human stress: Method, evidence and theory. *Behaviour Research and Therapy, 17*, 287–304.

Mirels, H. L. (1980). The avowal of responsibility for good and bad outcomes: The effects of generalized self-serving biases. *Personality and Social Psychology Bulletin, 6*, 299–306.

Nicholls, J. G. (1975). Causal attributions and other achievement-related cognitions: Effects of task outcome, attainment value, and sex. *Journal of Personality and Social Psychology, 31*, 379–389.

Owens, J., Bower, G. H., & Black, J. B. (1979). The "soap-opera" effect in story recall. *Memory and Cognition, 7*, 185–191.

Perloff, L. S. (1983). Perceptions of vulnerability to victimization. *Journal of Social Issues, 39*, 41–61.

Perloff, L. S., & Fetzer, B. K. (1986). Self-other judgments and perceived vulnerability to victimization. *Journal of Personality and Social Psychology, 50*, 502–510.

Piaget, J. (1954). *The construction of reality in the child*. New York: Basic Books.

Pruitt, D. G., & Hoge, R. D. (1965). Strength of the relationship between the value of an event and its subjective probability as a function of method of measurement. *Journal of Experimental Psychology, 5*, 483–489.

Robertson, L. S. (1977). Car crashes: Perceived vulnerability and willingness to pay for crash protection. *Journal of Community Health, 3*, 136–141.

Rosenberg, M. (1979). *Conceiving the self*. New York: Basic Books.

Ross, L. (1981). The "intuitive scientist" formulation and its developmental implications. In J. H. Flavell & L. Ross (Eds.), *Social cognitive development: Frontiers and possible futures* (pp. 1–42). Cambridge: Cambridge University Press.

Ross, M., & Fletcher, G. J. O. (1985). Attribution and social perception. In G. Lindzey & A. Aronson (Eds.), *The handbook of social psychology* (3rd ed., pp. 73–122). Reading, MA: Addison-Wesley.

Ross, M., & Sicoly, F. (1979). Egocentric biases in availability and attribution. *Journal of Personality and Social Psychology, 37,* 322–337.

Ryan, W. (1971). *Blaming the victim.* New York: Vintage Books.

Sachs, P. R. (1982). Avoidance of diagnostic information in self-evaluation of ability. *Personality and Social Psychology Bulletin, 8,* 242–246.

Schlenker, B. R. (1980). *Impression management.* Monterey, CA: Brooks/Cole.

Schlenker, B. R., & Miller, R. S. (1977). Egocentrism in groups: Self-serving biases or logical information processing? *Journal of Personality and Social Psychology, 35,* 755–764.

Seligman, M. E. P. (1975). *Helplessness: On depression, development and death.* San Francisco: Freeman.

Sherif, M., & Cantril, H. (1947). *The psychology of ego-involvements.* New York: Wiley.

Shrauger, J. S. (1975). Responses to evaluation as a function of initial self-perception. *Psychological Bulletin, 82,* 581–596.

Shrauger, J. S. (1982). Selection and processing of self-evaluative information: Experimental evidence and clinical implications. In G. Weary & H. L. Mirels (Eds.), *Integrations of clinical and social psychology* (pp. 128–153). New York: Oxford University Press.

Shrauger, J. S., & Kelley, R. J. (in press). Global self-evaluation and changes in self description as a function of information. *Journal of Personality.*

Smedslund, J. (1963). The concept of correlation in adults. *Scandinavian Journal of Psychology, 4,* 165–173.

Snyder, M. L., Stephan, W. G., & Rosenfield, C. (1978). Attributional egotism. In J. H. Harvey, W. J. Ickes, & R. F. Kidd (Eds.), *New directions in attribution research* (Vol. 2, pp. 91–117). Hillsdale, NJ: Erlbaum.

Snyder, M. L., & Wicklund, R. A. (1981). Attribute ambiguity. In J. H. Harvey, W. Ickes, & R. F. Kidd (Eds.), *New directions in attribution research* (Vol. 3, pp. 197–221). Hillsdale, NJ: Erlbaum.

Stipek, D. J. (1984). Young children's performance expectations: Logical analysis or wishful thinking? In I. Nicholls (Ed.), *Advances in motivation and achievement* (Vol. 3, pp. 33–56). Greenwich, CT: JAI Press.

Stipek, D., & MacIver, D. (in press). Developmental change in children's assessment of intellectual competence. *Child Development.*

Svenson, O. (1981). Are we all less risky and more skillful than our fellow drivers? *Acta Psychologica, 47,* 143–148.

Taylor, S. E., & Brown, J. (1988). Illusion and well-being: A social psychological perspective on mental health. *Psychological Bulletin, 103,* 193–210.

Tesser, A., & Moore, J. (1986). On the convergence of public and private aspects of self. In R. F. Baumeister (Ed.), *Public self and private life* (pp. 99–116). New York: Springer.

Tetlock, P. E., & Manstead, A. S. R. (1985). Impression management versus intrapsychic explanations in social psychology: A useful dichotomy? *Psychological Review, 92,* 59–77.

Thompson, S. C. (1981). Will it hurt less if I can control it? A complex answer to a simple question. *Psychological Bulletin, 90,* 89–101.

Thompson, S. C., & Kelley, J. J. (1981). Judgments of responsibility for activities in close relationships. *Journal of Personality and Social Psychology, 41,* 469–477.

Tiger, L. (1979). *Optimism: The biology of hope.* New York: Simon & Schuster.

Ward, W. D., & Jenkins, H. M. (1965). The display of information and the judgment of contingency. *Canadian Journal of Psychology, 19,* 231–241.

Weinstein, N. D. (1980). Unrealistic optimism about future life events. *Journal of Personality and Social Psychology, 39,* 806–820.

Weinstein, N. D. (1982). Unrealistic optimism about susceptibility to health problems. *Journal of Behavioral Medicine, 5,* 441–460.

Weinstein, N. D. (1984). Why it won't happen to me: Perceptions of risk factors and susceptibility. *Health Psychology, 3,* 431–457.

Weinstein, N. D., & Lachendro, E. (1982). Egocentrism as a source of unrealistic optimism. *Personality and Social Psychology Bulletin, 8,* 195–200.

Weisz, J. R. (1986). Understanding the developing understanding of control. In M. Perlmutter (Ed.), *Minnesota symposia on child psychology: Vol. 18. Cognitive perspectives on children's social and behavioral development* (pp. 219–285). Hillsdale, NJ: Erlbaum.

White, R. W. (1959). Motivation reconsidered: The concept of competence. *Psychological Review, 66,* 297–335.

Zuckerman, M. (1979). Attribution of success and failure revisited, or: The motivational bias is alive and well in attribution theory. *Journal of Personality, 47,* 245–287.

Perceiving Ourselves and the Work Situation

12.   THE SELF-PERCEPTION OF MOTIVATION[1]

Barry M. Staw

Within the area of interpersonal perception, it has been noted (Heider, 1958) that an individual may infer the causes of another's actions to be a function of personal and environmental force:

Action = f (personal force + environmental force)

This is quite close to saying that individuals attempt to determine whether another person is intrinsically motivated to perform an activity (action due to personal force), or extrinsically motivated (action due to environmental force), or both. The extent to which an individual will infer intrinsic motivation on the part of another is predicted to be affected by the clarity and strength of external forces within the situation (Jones & Davis, 1965; Jones & Nisbett, 1971; Kelley 1967). When there are strong forces bearing on the individual to perform an activity, there is little reason to assume that a behavior is self-determined, whereas a high level of intrinsic motivation might be inferred if environ-mental force is minimal. Several studies dealing with interpersonal perception have supported this general conclusion (Jones, Davis, & Gergen, 1961; Jones & Harris, 1967; Strickland, 1958; Thibaut & Riecken, 1955).

Bem (1967a, b) extrapolated this interpersonal theory of causal attribution to the study of self-perception or how one views his *own* behavior within a social context. Bem hypothesized that the extent to which external pressures are sufficiently strong to account for one's behavior will determine the likelihood that a person will attribute his own actions to internal causes. Thus if a person acts under strong external rewards or punishments, he is likely to assume that his behavior is under external control. However, if extrinsic contingencies are not strong or salient, the individual is likely to assume that his behavior is due to his own interest in the activity or that his behavior is intrinsically motivated. De Charms has made a similar point in his discussion of individual's perception of personal causation (1968, p. 328):

As a first approximation, we propose that whenever a person experiences himself to be the locus of causality for his own behavior (to be an Origin), he will consider himself to be intrinsically motivated. Conversely, when a person perceives the locus of causality for his behavior to be external to himself (that he is a Pawn), he will consider himself to be extrinsically motivated.

De Charms emphasized that the individual may attempt psychologically to label his actions on the basis of whether or not he has been instrumental in affecting his own behavior; that is, whether his behavior has been intrinsically or extrinsically motivated.

THE CASE FOR A NEGATIVE RELATIONSHIP BETWEEN INTRINSIC AND EXTRINSIC MOTIVATION

The self-perception approach to intrinsic and extrinsic motivation leads to the conclusion that there may be a negative interrelationship between these two motivational factors. The basis for this prediction stems from the assumption that individuals may work backward from their own actions in inferring sources of causation (Bem, 1967a, b; 1972). For example, if external pressures on an individual are so high that they would ordinarily cause him to perform a given task regardless of the internal characteristics of the activity, then the individual might logically infer that he is extrinsically motivated. In contrast, if external reward contingencies are extremely low or nonsalient, the individual might then infer that his behavior is intrinsically motivated. What is important is the fact that a person, in performing an activity, may *seek out* the probable cause of his own actions. Since behavior has no doubt been caused by something, it makes pragmatic, if not scientific, sense for the person to conclude that the cause is personal (intrinsic) rather than extrinsic if he can find no external reasons for his actions.

Two particular situations provide robust tests of the self-perception prediction. One is a situation in which there is insufficient justification for a person's actions, a situation in which the intrinsic rewards for an activity are very low (e.g., a dull task) and there are no compensating extrinsic rewards (e.g., monetary payment, verbal praise). Although rationally, one ordinarily tries to avoid these situations, there are occasions when one is faced with the difficult question of "why did I do that?" The self-perception theory predicts that in situations of insufficient justification, the individual may cognitively reevaluate the intrinsic characteristics of an activity in order to justify or explain his own behavior. For example, if the individual performed a dull task for no external reward, he may "explain" his behavior by thinking that the task was not really so bad after all.

Sometimes a person may also be fortunate enough to be in a situation in which his behavior is oversufficiently justified. For example, a person may be asked to perform an interesting task and at the same time be lavishly paid for his efforts. In such situations, the self-perception theory predicts that the individual may actually reevaluate the activity in a downward direction. Since the external reward would be sufficient to motivate behavior by itself, the individual may mistakenly infer that he was extrinsically motivated to perform the activity. He may conclude that since he was forced to perform the task by an external reward, the task probably was not terribly satisfying in and of itself.

Figure 12.1 graphically depicts the situations of insufficient and overly sufficient justification. From the figure, we can see that the conceptual framework supporting self-perception theory raises several interesting issues. First, it appears from this analysis that there are only two fully stable attributions of behavior: (1) the perception of extrinsically motivated behavior in which the internal rewards associated with performing an activity are low while external rewards are high; and (2) the perception of intrinsically motivated behavior in which the task is inherently rewarding but external rewards are low. Furthermore, it appears that situations of insufficient justification (where intrinsic and extrinsic rewards are both low) and oversufficient justification (where intrinsic and extrinsic rewards are both high) involve unstable attribution states. As shown in Figure 12.2, individuals apparently resolve this attributional instability by altering their perceptions of intrinsic rewards associated with the task.

An interesting question posed by the self-perception analysis is why individuals are predicted to resolve an unstable attribution state by cognitively reevaluating a task in terms of its intrinsic rewards rather than changing their perceptions of extrinsic factors. The answer to this question may lie in the relative clarity of extrinsic as compared with intrinsic rewards, and the individual's relative ability to distort the two aspects of the situation. Within many settings (and especially within laboratory experiments) extrinsic rewards are generally quite salient and specific, whereas an individual must judge the intrinsic nature of a task for himself. Any shifts in the perception of intrinsic and extrinsic rewards may therefore be more likely to occur in the intrinsic factor. As shown in Figure 12.2 it is these predicted shifts in perceived intrinsic rewards that may theoretically underlie a negative relationship between intrinsic and extrinsic motivation.

Empirical Evidence: Insufficient Justification

Several studies have shown that when an individual is induced to commit an unpleasant act for little or no external justification, he may subsequently conclude that the act was not so unpleasant after all. Actually, the first scientific attempt to account for this phenomenon was the theory of cognitive dissonance (Festinger, 1957). It was predicted by dissonance theorists (Aronson, 1966; Festinger, 1957) that, since performing an unpleasant act for little or no reward would be an inconsistent (and seemingly irrational) thing to do, an individual might subsequently change his attitude toward the action in order to reduce the inconsistency or to appear rational. Bem's self-perception theory yields

the same predictions but does not require one to posit that there is a motivating state such as dissonance reduction or self-rationalization. To Bem, since the individual examines his own behavior in light of the forces around him, he is simply more likely to come to the conclusion that his actions were intrinsically satisfying if they were performed under minimal external force.

In general, two types of experiments have been designed to assess the consequences of insufficient justification. One type of design has involved the performance of a dull task with varied levels of reward (Brehm & Cohen, 1962; Freedman, 1963; Weick, 1964; Weick & Penner, 1965). A second and more popular design has involved some form of counterattitudinal advocacy, either in terms of lying to a fellow subject about the nature of an experiment or writing an essay against one's position on an important issue (Carlsmith, Collins, & Helmreich, 1966; Festinger & Carlsmith, 1959; Linder, Cooper, & Jones, 1967). Fundamentally, the two types of designs are not vastly different. Both require subjects to perform an intrinsically dissatisfying act under varied levels of external inducement, and both predict that, in the low payment condition, the subject will change his attitude to-

| | | Level of Extrinsic Rewards | |
		Low	High
Level of Intrinsic Rewards	Low	Insufficient Justification (unstable perception)	Perception of Extrinsically Motivated Behavior
	High	Perception of Instrinsically Motivated Behavior	Overly Sufficient Justification (unstable perception)

FIGURE 12.1 A Conceptual of Self-Perception Theory.

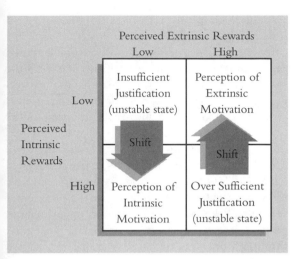

Perceived Extrinsic Rewards

	Low	High
Low	Insufficient Justification (unstable state)	Perception of Extrinsic Motivation
High	Perception of Intrinsic Motivation	Over Sufficient Justification (unstable state)

Perceived Intrinsic Rewards

Shift / Shift

FIGURE 12.2 A Schematic Analysis of the Self-Perception of Intrinsic and Extrinsic Motivation.

ward the activity (i.e., think more favorably of the task or begin to believe the position advocated).

The most well-known experiment designed to test the insufficient justification paradigm was conducted by Festinger and Carlsmith (1959). Subjects participated in a repetitive and dull task (putting spools on trays and turning pegs) and were asked to tell other waiting subjects that the experiment was enjoyable, interesting, and exciting. Half the experimental subjects were paid $1, and half were paid $20 for the counterattitudinal advocacy (and to be "on call" in the future), while control subjects were not paid and did not perform the counterattitudinal act. As predicted, the smaller the reward used to induce subjects to perform the counterattitudinal act, the greater the positive change in their attitudes toward the task. Although the interpretation of the results of this study have been actively debated (e.g., between dissonance and self-perception theorists) the basic findings have been replicated by a number of different researchers. It should be noted, however, that several mediating variables have also been isolated as being necessary for the attainment of this dissonance or self-perception effect: free choice (Linder, Cooper, & Jones, 1967), commitment or ir-

revocability of behavior (Brehm & Cohen, 1962), and substantial adverse consequences (Calder, Ross, & Insko, 1973; Collins & Hoyt, 1972).

Recently, a strong test of the insufficient justification paradigm was also conducted outside the laboratory (Staw, 1974a). A natural field experiment was made possible by the fact that many young men had joined an organization (Army ROTC) in order to avoid being drafted, *and* these same young men subsequently received information (a draft lottery number) that changed the value of this organizational reward. Of particular relevance was the fact that those who joined ROTC did so not because of their intrinsic interest in the activities involved (e.g., drills, classes, and summer camp), but because they anticipated a substantial extrinsic reward (draft avoidance). As a result, those who received draft numbers that exempted them from military service subsequently faced a situation of low extrinsic as well as intrinsic rewards, a situation of insufficient justification. In contrast, persons who received draft numbers that made them vulnerable to military call-up found their participation in ROTC perfectly justified—they were still successfully avoiding the draft by remaining in the organization. To test the insufficient justification effect, both the attitudes and the performance of ROTC cadets were analyzed by draft number before and after the national draft lottery. The results showed that those in the insufficient justification situation enhanced their perception of ROTC and even performed somewhat better in ROTC courses after the lottery. It should be recognized, however, that this task enhancement occurred only under circumstances very similar to those previously found necessary for the dissonance or self-perception effect (i.e., high commitment, free choice, and adverse consequences).

Empirical Evidence: Overly Sufficient Justification

There have been several empirical studies designed to test the self-perception prediction within the context of overly sufficient justification. Generally, a situation in which an extrinsic reward is added to an intrinsically rewarding task has been experimentally contrived for this purpose. Following self-perception theory, it is predicted that an increase in external justification will cause individuals to lose confidence in their intrinsic interest in the experimental task. Since dissonance theory cannot make this prediction (it is neither irrational nor inconsistent to perform an activity for too many rewards), the literature on overly sufficient justification provides the most important data on the self-perception prediction. For this reason, we will examine the experimental evidence in some detail.

In an experiment specifically designed to test the effect of overly sufficient justification on intrinsic motivation, Deci (1971) enlisted a number of college students to participate in a problem-solving study. All the students were asked to work on a series of intrinsically interesting puzzles for three experimental sessions. After the first session, however, half of the students (the experimental group) were told that they would also be given an extrinsic reward (money) for correctly solving the second set of puzzles, while the other students (the control group) were not told anything about the reward. In the third session, neither the experimental nor the control subjects were rewarded. This design is schematically outlined in Table 12.1.

Deci had hypothesized that the payment of money in the second experimental session might decrease subjects' intrinsic motivation to perform the task. That is, the introduction of an external force (money) might cause participants to alter their self-perception about why they are working on the puzzles. Instead of being intrinsically motivated to solve the interesting puzzles, they might find themselves working primarily to get the money provided by the experimenter. Thus Deci's goal in conducting the study was to compare the changes in subjects' intrinsic motivation from the first to third sessions for both the experimental and control groups. If the self-perception hypothesis was correct, the intrinsic motivation of the previously paid experimental subjects would decrease in the third session,

whereas the intrinsic motivation of the unpaid controls should remain unchanged.

As a measure of intrinsic motivation, Deci used the amount of free time participants spent on the puzzle task. To obtain this measure, the experimenter left the room during each session, supposedly to feed some data into the computer. As the experimenter left the room, he told the subjects they could do anything they wanted with their free time. In addition to the puzzles, current issues of *Time, The New Yorker*, and *Playboy* were placed near the subjects. However, while the first experimenter was out of the laboratory, a second experimenter, unknown to the subjects, observed their behavior through a one-way mirror. It was reasoned that if the subject worked on the puzzles during this free time period, he must be intrinsically motivated to perform the task. As shown in Table 12.2, the amount of free time spent on the task decreased for those who were previously paid to perform the activity, while there was a slight increase for the unpaid controls. Although the difference between the experimental and control groups was only marginally significant, the results are suggestive of the fact that an overly sufficient extrinsic reward may decrease one's intrinsic motivation to perform a task.

Lepper, Greene, and Nisbett (1973) also conducted a study that tested the self-perception prediction in a situation of overly sufficient justification. Their study involved having nursery school children perform an interesting activity (playing with Magic Markers) with and without the expectation of an additional extrinsic reward. Some children were induced to draw pictures with the markers by promising them a Good Player Award consisting of a big gold star, a bright red ribbon, and a place to print their name. Other children either performed the activity without any reward or were told about the reward only after completing the activity. Children who participated in these three experimental conditions (expected reward, no reward, unexpected reward) were then covertly observed during the following week in a free-play period. As in the Deci (1971) study, the amount of time children spent on the activity when they could

TABLE 12.1
Basic Design of Deci (1971) Study

	Time 1	Time 2	Time 3
Experimental group	No payment	Payment	No payment
Control group	No payment	No payment	No payment

do other interesting things (i.e., playing with other toys) was taken to be an indicator of intrinsic motivation.

The findings of the Lepper, Greene, and Nisbett study showed that the introduction of an extrinsic reward for performing an already interesting activity caused a significant decrease in intrinsic motivation. Children who played with Magic Markers with the expectation of receiving the external reward did not spend as much subsequent free time on the activity as did the children who were not given a reward or those who were unexpectedly offered the reward. Moreover, the rated quality of drawings made by children with the markers was significantly poorer in the expected-reward group than either the no-reward or unexpected-reward groups.

The results of the Lepper et al. study help to increase our confidence in the findings of the earlier Deci experiment. Not only are the earlier findings replicated with a different task and subject population, but an important methodological problem is minimized. By reexamining Table 12.1, we can see that the second time period in the Deci experiment was the period in which payment was expected by subjects for solving the puzzles. However, we can also see that in time 2 there was a whopping increase in the free time subjects spent on the puzzles. Deci explained this increase as an attempt by subjects to practice puzzle solving to increase their chances of earning money. However, what Deci did not discuss is the possibility that the subsequent decrease in time 3 was due not to the prior administration of rewards but to the effect of satiation or fatigue. One contri-

TABLE 12.2
Mean Number of Seconds Spent Working on the Puzzles during the Free Time Periods

Group	Time 1	Time 2	Time 3	Time 3 Time 1
Experimental ($n = 12$)	248.2	313.9	198.5	−49.7
Control ($n = 12$)	213.9	202.7	241.8	27.9

Source: E. L. Deci, "The Effects of Externally Mediated Rewards as Intrinsic Motivation," *Journal of Personality and Social Psychology* 18 (1971) 105–15. Copyright 1971 by the American Psychological Association. Reprinted by permission.

bution of the Lepper et al. study is that its results are not easily explained by this alternative. In the Lepper et al. experiment, there was over one week's time between the session in which an extrinsic reward was administered and the final observation period.

Although both the Deci and Lepper et al. studies support the notion that the expectation of an extrinsic reward may decrease intrinsic interest in an activity, there is still one important source of ambiguity in both these studies. You may have noticed that the decrease in intrinsic motivation follows not only the prior administration of an extrinsic reward, but also the withdrawal of this reward. For example, in the Deci study, subjects were not paid in the third experimental session in which the decrease in intrinsic motivation was reported. Likewise, subjects were not rewarded when the final observation of intrinsic motivation was taken by Lepper, Greene, and Nisbett. It is therefore difficult to determine whether the decrease in intrinsic interest is due to a change in the self-perception of motivation following the application of an extrinsic reward or merely to frustration following the removal of the reward. An experiment by Kruglanski, Freedman, and Zeevi (1971) helps to resolve this ambiguity.

Kruglanski et al. induced a number of teenagers to volunteer for some creativity and memory tasks. To manipulate extrinsic rewards, the experimenters told half the participants that because they had volunteered for the study, they would be taken on an interesting tour of the psychology laboratory; the other participants were not offered this extrinsic reward. The results showed that teenagers offered the reward were less satisfied with the experimental tasks and were less likely to volunteer for future experiments of a similar nature than were teenagers who were not offered the extrinsic reward. In addition, the extrinsically rewarded group did not perform as well on the experimental task (in terms of recall, creativity, and the Zeigarnik effect) as the nonrewarded group. These findings are similar to those of Deci (1971) and Lepper et al. (1973), but they cannot be as easily explained by a frustration effect. Since in the Kruglanski et al. study the reward was never withdrawn for the experimental

group, the differences between the experimental (reward) and control (no reward) conditions are better explained by a change in self-perception than by a frustration effect.

The designs of the three overly sufficient justification studies described above have varying strengths and weaknesses (Calder & Staw, 1975a), but taken together, their results can be interpreted as supporting the notion that extrinsic rewards added to an already interesting task can decrease intrinsic motivation. This effect, if true, has important ramifications for educational, industrial, and other work settings. There are many situations in which people are offered extrinsic rewards (grades, money, special privileges) for accomplishing a task which may already be intrinsically interesting. The self-perception effect means that, by offering external rewards, we may sometimes be sacrificing an important source of task motivation and not necessarily increasing either the satisfaction or the performance of the participant. Obviously, because the practical implications of the self-perception effect are large, we should proceed with caution. Thus, in addition to scrutinizing the validity of the findings themselves (as we have done above), we should also attempt to determine the exact conditions under which they might be expected to hold.

Earlier, Deci (1971, 1972) had hypothesized that only rewards contingent on a high level of task performance are likely to have an adverse effect on intrinsic motivation. He had reasoned that a reward contingent upon specific behavioral demands is most likely to cause an individual to infer that his behavior is extrinsically rather than intrinsically motivated and that a decrease in intrinsic motivation may result from this change in self-perception. Although this assumption seems reasonable, there is not a great deal of empirical support for it. Certainly in the Kruglanski et al. and Lepper et al. studies all that was necessary to cause a decrease in intrinsic motivation was for rewards to be contingent upon the completion of an activity. In each of these studies what seemed to be important was the cognition that one was performing an activity in order to get an extrinsic reward rather than a prescribed goal for a particular level of output. Thus as long as it is salient, a reward contingency based upon the completion of an activity may decrease intrinsic motivation just like a reward contingency based on the quality or quantity of performance.

Ross (1975) recently conducted two experiments that dealt specifically with the effect of the salience of rewards on changes in intrinsic motivation. In one study, children were asked to play a musical instrument (drums) for either no reward, a nonsalient reward, or a salient reward. The results showed that intrinsic motivation, as measured by the amount of time spent on the drums versus other activities in a free play situation, was lowest for the salient reward condition. Similar results were found in a second study in which some children were asked to think either of the reward (marshmallows) while playing a musical instrument, think of an extraneous object (snow), or not think of anything in particular. The data for this second study showed that intrinsic motivation was lowest when children consciously thought about the reward while performing the task.

In addition to the salience of an external reward, there has been empirical research on one other factor mediating the self-perception effect, the existing norms of the task situation. In examining the prior research using situations of overly sufficient justification, Staw, Calder, and Hess (1976) reasoned that there is one common element which stands out. Always, the extrinsic reward appears to be administered in a situation in which persons are not normally paid or otherwise reimbursed for their actions. For example, students are not normally paid for laboratory participation, but the Deci (1971) and Kruglanski et al. (1971) subjects were. Likewise, nursery school children are not normally enticed by special recognition or rewards to play with an interesting new toy, but both the Lepper et al. (1973) and Ross (1975) subjects were. Thus Staw, Calder, and Hess (1976) manipulated norms for payment as well as the actual payment of money for performing an interesting task. They found an interaction of norms and payment such that the introduction of an extrinsic reward decreased intrinsic interest in a

task only when there existed a situational norm for no payment. From these data and the findings of the Ross study, it thus appears that an extrinsic reward must be both salient and situationally inappropriate for there to be a reduction in intrinsic interest.

Reassessing the Self-Perception Effect

At present there is growing empirical support for the notion that intrinsic and extrinsic motivation *can* be negatively interrelated. The effect of extrinsic rewards on intrinsic motivation has been replicated by several researchers using different classes of subjects (males, females, children, college students) and different activities (puzzles, toys), and the basic results appear to be internally valid. As we have seen, however, the effect of extrinsic rewards is predicated on certain necessary conditions (e.g., situational norms and reward salience), as is often the case with psychological findings subjected to close examination.

To date, the primary data supporting the self-perception prediction have come from situations of insufficient and overly sufficient justification. Empirical findings have shown that individuals may cognitively reevaluate intrinsic rewards in an upward direction when their behavior is insufficiently justified and in a downward direction when there is overly sufficient justification. In general, it can be said that the data of these two situations are consistent with the self-perception hypothesis. Still, theoretically, it is not immediately clear why previous research has been restricted to these two particular contexts. No doubt it is easier to show an increase in intrinsic motivation when intrinsic interest is initially low (as under insufficient justification) or a decrease when intrinsic interest is initially high (as under overly sufficient justification). Nevertheless, the theory should support a negative interrelationship of intrinsic and extrinsic factors at *all levels*, since it makes the rather general prediction that the greater the extrinsic rewards, the less likely is the individual to infer that he is intrinsically motivated.

One recent empirical study has tested the self-perception hypothesis by manipulating *both* intrinsic and extrinsic motivation. Calder and Staw (1975b) experimentally manipulated both the intrinsic characteristics of a task as well as extrinsic rewards in an attempt to examine the interrelationship of these two factors at more than one level. In the study male college students were asked to solve one of two sets of puzzles identical in all respects except the potential for intrinsic interest. One set of puzzles contained an assortment of pictures highly rated by students (chiefly from *Life* magazine but including several *Playboy* centerfolds); another set of puzzles was blank and rated more neutrally. To manipulate extrinsic rewards, half the subjects were promised $1 for their 20 minutes of labor (and the dollar was placed prominently in view), while for half of the subjects, money was neither mentioned nor displayed. After completing the task, subjects were asked to fill out a questionnaire on their reactions to the puzzle-solving activity. The two primary dependent variables included in the questionnaire were a measure of task satisfaction and a measure of subjects' willingness to volunteer for additional puzzle-solving exercises. The latter consisted of a sign-up sheet on which subjects could indicate the amount of time they would be willing to

spend (without pay or additional course credit) in future experiments of a similar nature.

The results of the Calder and Staw experiment showed a significant interaction between task and payment on subjects' satisfaction with the activity and a marginally significant interaction on subjects' willingness to volunteer for additional work without extrinsic reward. These data provided empirical support for the self-perception effect in a situation of overly sufficient justification, but not under other conditions. Specifically, when the task was initially interesting (i.e., using the picture puzzle activity), the introduction of money caused a reduction of task satisfaction and volunteering. However, when the task was initially more neutral (i.e., using the blank puzzle activity), the introduction of money increased satisfaction and subjects' intentions to volunteer for additional work. Thus if we consider Calder and Staw's dependent measures as indicators of intrinsic interest, the first finding is in accord with the self-perception hypothesis, while the latter result is similar to what one might predict from a reinforcement theory. The implications of these data, together with previous findings, are graphically depicted in Figure 12.3

As shown in the figure, self-perception effects have been found *only* at the extremes of insufficient and overly sufficient justification. Thus it may be prudent to withhold judgment on the general hypothesis that there is a uniformly negative relationship between intrinsic and extrinsic motivation. Perhaps we should no longer broadly posit that the greater external rewards and pressures, the weaker the perception of intrinsic interest in an activity; and the lower external pressures, the stronger intrinsic interest. Certainly, under conditions other than insufficient and overly sufficient justification, reinforcement effects of extrinsic rewards on intrinsic task satisfaction have readily been found (Cherrington, 1973; Cherrington, Reitz, & Scott, 1971; Greene, 1974).

At present it appears that only in situations of insufficient or overly sufficient reward will there be attributional instability of such magnitude that shifts will occur in the perception of intrinsic re-

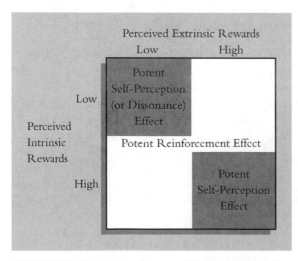

FIGURE 12.3 The Relative Potency of Self-Perception and Reinforcement Mechanisms.

wards. We might therefore speculate that either no attributional instability is evoked in other situations or it is just not strong enough to overcome a countervailing force. This writer would place his confidence in the latter theoretical position. It seems likely that both self-perception *and* reinforcement mechanisms hold true, but that their relative influence over an individual's task attitudes and behavior varies according to the situational context. For example, only in situations with insufficient or overly sufficient justification will the need to resolve attributional instability probably be strong enough for external rewards to produce a decrease in intrinsic motivation. In other situations we might reasonably expect a more positive relationship between intrinsic and extrinsic factors, as predicted by reinforcement theory.

Although this new view of the interrelationship between intrinsic and extrinsic motivation remains speculative, it does seem reasonable in light of recent theoretical and empirical work. Figure 12.4 graphically elaborates this model and shows how the level of intrinsic and extrinsic motivation may depend on the characteristics of the situation. In the figure, secondary reinforcement is depicted to be a general force for producing a positive relationship between intrinsic and extrinsic motivation. However, under situations of insufficient and oversufficient justification, self-perception (and dissonance) effects are shown to provide a second but still potentially effective determinant of a negative interrelationship between intrinsic and extrinsic motivation. Figure 12.4 shows the joint operation of these two theoretical mechanisms and illustrates

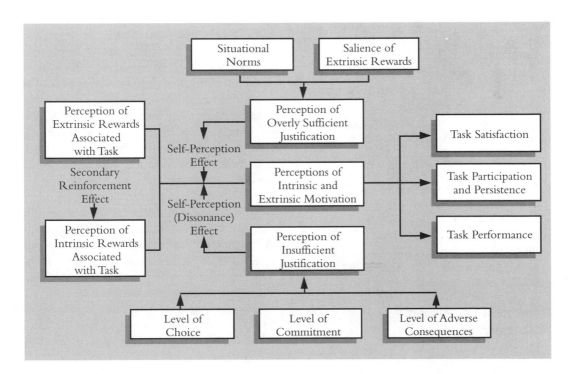

FIGURE 12.4 The Interrelationship of Intrinsic and Extrinsic Motivation as a Function of Situational Characteristics.

their ultimate effect on individuals' satisfaction, persistence, and performance on a task.

IMPLICATIONS OF INTRINSIC AND EXTRINSIC MOTIVATION

In this discussion we have noted that the administration of both intrinsic and extrinsic rewards can have important effects on a person's task attitudes and behavior. Individually, extrinsic rewards may direct and control a person's activity on a task and provide an important source of satisfaction. By themselves, intrinsic rewards can also motivate task-related behavior and bring gratification to the individual. As we have seen, however, the joint effect of intrinsic and extrinsic rewards may be quite complex. Not only may intrinsic and extrinsic factors not be additive in their overall effect on motivation and satisfaction, but the interaction of intrinsic and extrinsic factors may under some conditions be positive and under other conditions negative. As illustrated in Figures 12.3 and 12.4, a potent reinforcement effect will often cause intrinsic and extrinsic motivation to be positively interrelated, although on occasion a self-perception mechanism may be so powerful as to create a negative relationship between these two factors.

The reinforcement predictions of Figures 12.3 and 12.4 are consistent with our common sense. In practice, extrinsic rewards are relied upon heavily to induce desired behaviors, and most allocators of rewards (administrators, teachers, parents) operate on the theory that extrinsic rewards will positively affect an individual's intrinsic interest in a task. We should therefore concentrate on those situations in which our common sense may be in error—those situations in which there may in fact be a negative relationship between intrinsic and extrinsic motivation.

Motivation in Educational Organizations

One of the situations in which intrinsic and extrinsic motivation may be negatively interrelated is our schools. As Lepper and Green (1975) have noted,

many educational tasks are inherently interesting to students and would probably be performed without any external force. However, when grades and other extrinsic inducements are added to the activity, we may, via overly sufficient justification, be converting an interesting activity into work. That is, by inducing students to perform educational tasks with strong extrinsic rewards or by applying external force, we may be converting learning activities into behaviors that will not be performed in the future without some additional outside pressure or extrinsic force.

Within the educational context, a negative relationship between intrinsic and extrinsic motivation poses a serious dilemma for teachers who allocate external rewards. For example, there is no doubt that grades, gold stars, and other such incentives can alter the direction and vigor of specific "in school" behaviors (e.g., getting students to complete assigned exercises by a particular date). But because of their effect on intrinsic motivation, extrinsic rewards may also weaken a student's general interest in learning tasks and decrease voluntary learning behavior that extends beyond the school setting. In essence, then, the extrinsic forces that work so well at motivating and controlling specific task behaviors may actually cause the extinction of these same behaviors within situations devoid of external reinforcers. This is an important consideration for educational organizations, since most of an individual's learning activity will no doubt occur outside the highly regulated and reinforced setting of the classroom.[2]

In order to maintain students' intrinsic motivation in learning activities it is recommended that the use of extrinsic rewards be carefully controlled. As a practical measure, it is recommended that when a learning task is inherently interesting (and would probably be performed without any external force) all external pressures on the individual be minimized. Only when a task is so uninteresting that individuals would not ordinarily perform it should extrinsic rewards be applied. In addition, it is suggested that the student role be both enlarged and enriched to increase rather directly the level of intrinsic motivation. The significance of learning tasks, responsibility for results, feedback, and variety in student activities are all areas of possible improvement.

Motivation in Work Organizations

Voluntary work organizations are very much like educational organizations; their members are often intrinsically motivated to perform certain tasks and extrinsic rewards are generally not necessary to induce the performance of many desired behaviors. Moreover, if for some reason extrinsic rewards were to be offered to voluntary workers for performing their services we would expect to find, as in the educational setting, a decrease in intrinsic motivation. As in the educational context, we would expect an external reward to decrease self-motivated (or voluntary) behavior in settings free from external reinforcement, although the specific behaviors which are reinforced might be increased. As a concrete example, let us imagine a political candidate who decides to "motivate" his volunteer campaign workers by paying them for distributing flyers to prospective voters. In this situation, we might expect that the administration of an extrinsic reward will increase the number of flyers distributed. However, the political workers' subsequent interest in performing other campaign activities *without pay* may subsequently be diminished. Similarly, the volunteer hospital worker who becomes salaried may no longer have the same intrinsic interest in his work. Although the newly professionalized worker may exert a good deal of effort on the job and be relatively satisfied with it, his satisfaction may stem from extrinsic rather than intrinsic sources of reward.

Let us now turn to the implications of intrinsic and extrinsic motivation for nonvoluntary work organizations. Deci (1972), in reviewing his research on intrinsic motivation, cautioned strongly against the use of contingent monetary rewards within industrial organizations. He maintained that paying people contingently upon the performance of specific tasks may reduce intrinsic motivation for these activities, and he recommended noncontingent reinforces in their stead. As we have seen, however, a decrease in intrinsic motivation does not always occur following the administration of extrinsic rewards; certain necessary conditions must be present before there is a negative relationship between intrinsic and extrinsic motivation. Generally, industrial work settings do not meet these necessary conditions.

First, within industrial organizations, a large number of jobs are not inherently interesting enough to foster high intrinsic motivation. Persons would not ordinarily perform many of the tasks of the industrial world (e.g., assembly line work) without extrinsic inducements, and this initial lack of intrinsic interest will probably preclude the effect of overly sufficient justification. Second, even when an industrial job is inherently interesting, there exists a powerful norm for extrinsic payment. Not only do workers specifically join and contribute their labor in exchange for particular inducements, but the instrumental relationship between task behavior and extrinsic rewards is supported by both social and legal standards. Thus the industrial work situation is quite unlike that of either a voluntary organization or an educational system. In the latter cases, participants may be initially interested in performing certain tasks without external force, and the addition of overly sufficient rewards may convey information that the task is not intrinsically interesting. Within industrial organizations, on the other hand, extrinsic reinforcement is the norm, and tasks may often be perceived to be even more interesting when they lead to greater extrinsic rewards.

The very basic distinction between nonvoluntary work situations and other task settings (e.g., schools and voluntary organizations) is that, without extrinsic rewards, nonvoluntary organizations would be largely without participants. The important question for industrial work settings is therefore not one of payment versus nonpayment, but of the recommended degree of contingency between reward and performance. On the basis of current evidence, it would seem prudent to suggest that, within industrial organizations, rewards continue to be made contingent upon behavior. This could be accomplished through performance evaluation, profit sharing, or piece-rate incentive schemes. In addition, intrinsic motivation should be increased directly via the planned alteration of specific job characteristics (e.g., by increasing task variety, complexity, social interaction, task identity, significance, responsibility for results, and knowledge of results).

A FINAL COMMENT

Although the study of the interaction of intrinsic and extrinsic motivation is a relatively young area within psychology, it has been the intent of this paper to outline a theoretical model and provide some practical suggestions based upon the research evidence available to date. As we have seen, the effects of intrinsic and extrinsic motivation are not always simple, and several moderating variables must often be taken into account before specific predictions can be made. Thus in addition to providing "answers" to theoretical and practical problems, this paper may illustrate the complexities involved in drawing conclusions from a limited body of research data. The main caution for the reader is to regard these theoretical propositions and practical recommendations as working statements subject to the influence of future empirical evidence.

NOTES

1. The author wishes to express his gratitude to Bobby J. Calder and Greg R. Oldham for their critical reading of the manuscript, and to the Center for Advanced Study at the University of Illinois for the resources and facilities necessary to complete this work.

2. It is interesting to note that Kazdin and Bootzin (1972) have made a quite similar point in their recent review of research on token economies. They noted that while operant conditioning procedures have been quite effective in altering focal behaviors within a controlled setting, seldom have changes been found to generalize to natural, nonreinforcing environments.

REFERENCES

Aronson, E. "The Psychology of Insufficient Justification: An Analysis of Some Conflicting Data." In *Cognitive Consistency: Motivational Antecedents and Behavior Consequences*, edited by S. Feldman. Academic Press, 1966.

Bem, D. J. "Self-perception: An Alternative Interpretation of Cognitive Dissonance Phenomena." *Psychological Review* 74 (1967): 183–200. (a)

———. "Self-perception: The Dependent Variable of Human Performance." *Organizational Behavior and Human Performance* 2 (1967): 105–21. (b)

———. "Self-perception Theory." In *Advances in Experimental Social Psychology*, vol. 6, edited by L. Berkowitz. New York: Academic Press, 1972.

Brehm, J. W., and Cohen, A. R. *Explorations in Cognitive Dissonance*. New York: Wiley, 1962.

Calder, B. J., Ross, M.; and Insko, C. A. "Attitude Change and Attitude Attribution: Effects of Incentive, Choice, and Consequences." *Journal of Personality and Social Psychology* 25 (1973): 84–100.

————, and Staw, B. M. "The Interaction of Intrinsic and Extrinsic Motivation: Some Methodological Notes." *Journal of Personality and Social Psychology* 31 (1975): 76–80. (a)

————, and Staw, B. M. "Self-perception of Intrinsic and Extrinsic Motivation." *Journal of Personality and Social Psychology* 31 (1975): 599–605. (b)

Carlsmith, J. M.; Collins, B. E.; and Helmreich, R. L. "Studies in Forced Compliance: The Effect of Pressure for Compliance on Attitude Change Produced by Face-to-Face Role Playing and Anonymous Essay Writing." *Journal of Personality and Social Psychology* 4 (1966): 1–13.

Cherrington, D. J. "The Effects of a Central Incentive—Motivational State on Measures of Job Satisfaction." *Organizational Behavior and Human Performance* 10 (1973): 27–89.

————, Reitz, H. J.; and Scott, W. E. "Effects of Reward and Contingent Reinforcement on Satisfaction and Task Performance." *Journal of Applied Psychology* 55 (1971): 531–36.

Collins, B. E., and Hoyt, M. F. "Personal Responsibility-for-Consequences: An Integration and Extension of the Forced Compliance Literature." *Journal of Experimental Social Psychology* 8 (1972): 558–94.

de Charms, R. *Personal Causation: The Internal Affective Determinants of Behavior.* New York: Academic Press, 1968.

Deci, E. L. "The Effects of Externally Mediated Rewards on Intrinsic Motivation." *Journal of Personality and Social Psychology* 18 (1971): 105–15.

————. "The Effects of Contingent and Noncontingent Rewards and Controls on Intrinsic Motivation." *Organizational Behavior and Human Performance* 8 (1972): 217–29.

Festinger, L. *A Theory of Cognitive Dissonance.* Palo Alto: Stanford University Press, 1957.

————, and Carlsmith, J. M. "Cognitive Consequences of Forced Compliance." *Journal of Abnormal and Social Psychology* 58 (1959): 203–10.

Freedman, J. L. "Attitudinal Effects of Inadequate Justification," *Journal of Personality* 31 (1963): 371–85.

Greene, C. N. "Causal Connections Among Manager's Merit Pay, Job Satisfaction, and Performance." *Journal of Applied Psychology* 58 (1974): 95–100.

Heider, F. *The Psychology of Interpersonal Relations.* New York: Wiley, 1958.

Jones, E. E., and Davis, K. E. "From Acts to Dispositions: The Attribution Process in Person Perception." In *Advances in Experimental Psychology,* vol. 2, edited by L. Berkowitz. New York: Academic Press, 1965.

————; Davis, K. E., and Gergen, K. E.; "Role Playing Variations and Their Informational Value for Person Perception." *Journal of Abnormal and Social Psychology* 63 (1961): 302–10.

————, and Harris, V. A. "The Attribution of Attitudes." *Journal of Experimental Social Psychology* 3 (1967): 1–24.

————, and Nisbett, R. E. *The Actor and the Observer: Divergent Perceptions of the Causes of Behavior.* New York: General Learning Press, 1971.

Kazdin, A. E., and Bootzen, R. R. "The Token Economy: An Evaluative Review." *Journal of Applied Behavior Analysis* 5 (1972): 343–72.

Kelley, H. H. "Attribution Theory in Social Psychology." In *Nebraska Symposium on Motivation*, vol. 15, edited by D. Levine. University of Nebraska Press, 1967.

Kruglanski, A. W.; Freedman, I.; and Zeevi, G. "The Effects of Extrinsic Incentives on Some Qualitative Aspects of Task Performance." *Journal of Personality* 39 (1971): 606–17.

Lepper, M. R., and Greene, D. "Turning Play into Work: Effects of Adult Surveillance and Extrinsic Rewards on Children's Intrinsic Motivation." *Journal of Personality and Social Psychology*, in press.

———; Greene, D.; and Nisbett, R. E. "Undermining Children's Intrinsic Interest with Extrinsic Rewards: A Test of the 'Overjustification' Hypothesis." *Journal of Personality and Social Psychology* 28 (1973): 129–37.

Linder, D. E.; Cooper, J.; and Jones, E. E. "Decision Freedom as a Determinant of the Role of Incentive Magnitude in Attitude Change." *Journal of Personality and Social Psychology* 6 (1967): 245–54.

Ross, M. "Salience of Reward and Intrinsic Motivation." *Journal of Personality and Social Psychology* 32 (1975): 245–254.

Staw, B. M. "Attitudinal and Behavioral Consequences of Changing a Major Organizational Reward: A Natural Field Experiment." *Journal of Personality and Social Psychology* 6 (1974): 742–51. (a)

———. "Notes Toward a Theory of Intrinsic and Extrinsic Motivation." Paper presented at Eastern Psychological Association, 1974. (b)

———; Calder, B. J.; and Hess, R. "Intrinsic Motivation and Norms About Payment." Working paper, Northwestern University, 1975.

Strickland, L. H. "Surveillance and Trust." *Journal of Personality* 26 (1958): 200–215.

Thibaut, J. W., and Riecken, H. W. "Some Determinants and Consequences of the Perception of Social Causality." *Journal of Personality* 24 (1955): 113–33.

Weick, K. E. "Reduction of Cognitive Dissonance Through Task Enhancement and Effort Expenditure." *Journal of Abnormal and Social Psychology* 68 (1964): 533–39.

———, and Penner, D. D. "Justification and Productivity." Unpublished manuscript, University of Minnesota, 1965.

13. THE POWER OF SOCIAL INFORMATION IN THE WORKPLACE

Joe G. Thomas and Ricky W. Griffin

After meeting with his district sales managers for the first time, John Rogers, the newly hired vice-president of marketing, reflected on the particularly puzzling conversations he had with two of them—Bill Adams and Dick Woods. Both men had very similar backgrounds and experiences: They had been classmates at a prestigious eastern university and had started employment with the company immediately after college. They had been successful sales representatives and had been promoted to regional sales manager positions after approximately four years with the company. Although they managed different sales areas, both areas appeared equally attractive.

The puzzling part of the conversations with Adams and Woods was their inconsistent views of the organization and their future roles in it. Woods had been particularly positive about the work environment, describing the company as "fair" and the work as "challenging, exciting, and worthwhile." He had praised the company for its excellent reputation with its employees and customers, saying "It's really nice to have a job where you are helping people, where what you do really makes a difference!" Adams, on the other hand, had complained that the company was "ripping off" everybody and that the work was "a real bore." "The customers do not appreciate the quality of service they receive. The employees constantly complain about hours and working conditions. You just cannot keep them happy," he had said. Since both managers were working for the same company and in the same capacity—and

had so much in common—how could they see things so differently?

Most people have been in situations similar to the one experienced by John Rogers—situations in which, from an objective viewpoint, everything seems the same yet the people involved see things quite differently. Even though managers recognize that people's perceptions differ, they tend to assume that all employees evaluate and react to their jobs similarly. That kind of attitude is reflected in the following comment, made by a client in an executive development program: "The job is the same for everybody. There are job descriptions for each job. The employees do exactly what is stated in the job description. We are careful to stick to the job descriptions and not let anyone do more for fear of having problems with the union and EEOC."

The common thread between the experiences of John Rogers and the client in the executive development program is the assumption that employees respond only to the "objective" job. In reality, employees respond to their jobs as they perceive them. Moreover, their perceptions are influenced, at least to some degree, by information they receive from others. Yet much of management research and practice is based on the assumption that managers and employees respond strictly to an objective job.

In their article "A Social Information Processing Approach to Job Attitudes and Task Design" (*Administrative Science Quarterly*, June 1978), Gerald Salancik and Jeffrey Pfeffer reopened the question as to the extent of objectivity in evaluating work

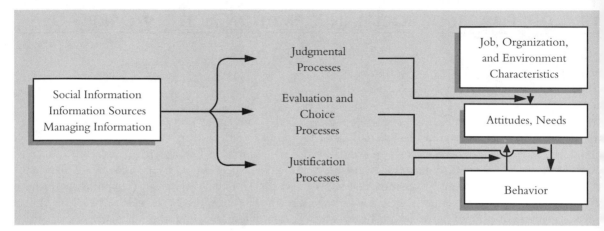

FIGURE 13.1 *Strategic Influence Processes.*

settings. Their theoretical framework, depicted in a simplified form in Figure 13.1, has served as a springboard for various research studies examining employees' reactions to social information. This line of research, commonly referred to as "social information processing," argues that people adopt attitudes, behaviors, and beliefs in light of social information provided by others.

In his book *Organizations and Organization Theory* (Pitman, 1982), Pfeffer notes that "whether one characterizes jobs using dimensions such as variety, autonomy, feedback, and skill required or dimensions such as pay, effort required, and physical surroundings is in part under the control of a social environment in which some dimensions become talked about and other dimensions are ignored and thus are not salient." In one early experiment examining the influence of information from the social environment ("Informational Influence as a Determinant of Perceived Task Characteristics and Job Satisfaction," *Journal of Applied Psychology*, February 1979), Charles O'Reilly and David Caldwell showed that informational cues have a greater impact on reported task characteristics than do the objective task dimensions. In a later study of public health nurses in which objective jobs were identical ("Perceptual Measures of Task Characteristics: The Biasing Effects of Differing

Frames of Reference and Job Attitudes," *Academy of Management Journal*, March 1980), Charles O'Reilly, G. N. Parlette, and J. R. Bloom reported that the perception of task characteristics is influenced by family and professional orientations. In a more recent study of nurses ("Sources of Social Information: A Longitudinal Analysis," *Human Relations*, September 1986), Joe G. Thomas found that information sources perceived as most relevant varied for different aspects of jobs. For example, family members were perceived as important in helping nurses see the significance of their work, but co-workers were perceived as most important in helping nurses develop new job skills.

Social information refers to comments, observations, and similar cues provided by people whose view of the job an employee considers relevant. It may be provided by people directly associated with the job, such as co-workers, supervisors, and customers, or it may be provided by people not employed by the company, such as family members and friends. Although not all aspects of a job are likely to be influenced by cues from others (a hot work environment will be hot despite what anyone tells a worker), it seems realistic to assume that most of an employee's perceptions of job characteristics are subject to influence from information provided by others with whom the employee has contact.

IMPACT OF SOCIAL INFORMATION

Social information can influence an employee's view of the job in several different ways, as shown in Figure 13.1. Social information causes some characteristics of the job to be judged important, and attitudes about these salient characteristics are formed. Once attitudes are formed, social cues offer suggestions in evaluating and choosing appropriate behaviors. Finally, social cues influence the explanations or rationales offered for behavior. To understand and use social information, a manager must first recognize the probable impact of such information on employees and identify sources of information considered relevant.

IDENTIFICATION OF ORGANIZATION AND JOB CHARACTERISTICS

Jobs have many different facets. They allow varying degrees of autonomy, feedback, and job significance. They aid (or inhibit) employees in developing new skills and preparing for advancement. They are performed in a variety of settings, differing in terms of work conditions (such as temperature and noise level), work schedules (such as starting times, break schedules, and time clocks), rewards, and quality of supervision. Organizations differ in terms of attitudes, policies, and treatment of workers. All of these characteristics may influence an employee's feelings about his or her job. However, not all of them are viewed as equally important in each organization.

IMPORTANCE OF CHARACTERISTICS

Social information helps employees identify which characteristics of the job and the organization are considered important by other people. If the temperature in a work area or the requirement of clocking in and out is frequently discussed, those characteristics of the job setting receive increased attention from workers. Frequent discussion of such characteristics increases their perceived importance, and they become more salient.

Rarely discussed job characteristics are less likely to be considered important by job incumbents, although the same job characteristics may be considered essential in another organization. Relatively high noise levels or bureaucratic travel-reimbursement policies, for example, may be major sources of employee concern in one organization, while employees of another organization may dismiss those job characteristics as just a fact of organizational life.

Mining accidents provide an example of job characteristics that may be perceived quite differently by people, depending on their situation. Someone outside the industry may be astonished at a miner's ability to go to work with little apparent fear shortly after a disastrous mining accident at a neighboring mine. Miners *want to believe* information provided by the company and co-workers that there is little probability of an accident happening to them. They perceive occasional industrial accidents as an undesirable but largely unavoidable part of the job. To people outside the industry, however, the danger seems unbelievably high. The different assessments of the danger are at least partly the result of different evaluations of the information provided about the risks of an accident.

EVALUATION OF JOB CHARACTERISTICS

Other people's information about a job reveals their perceptions of the job to employees. All organizations develop cultures that are transmitted to workers. Organizations differ, for example, in terms of the importance attached to customer satisfaction and quality versus quantity of output, employee and subunit autonomy, administrative structures, and attitudes toward risk and diversification. Rituals, stories, symbols, and language are all used to inform employees about the organization and individual jobs.

Military training provides recruits the information they need to evaluate military jobs. That information, much like the information provided to miners, may initially be perceived as inconsistent with the information held by the general public. However, as boot camp continues, the recruits generally become more accepting of authority, place greater importance on military values, and become willing to sacrifice their lives for the good of others. Rituals (such as basic training and mock battles), stories of both successful and unsuccessful missions, symbols (such as the U.S. flag and military heroes), as well as language (such as code words and slang) are used to influence the recruits' perceptions of the organization and their place in it. In effect, social information leads to a reevaluation of the basic meaning of life and its importance to the individual. Orientation programs for new employees are designed to accomplish similar ends, although the change in attitudes may be less marked.

People outside the organization also provide information that is used to evaluate job and organization characteristics. Statements such as "You guys sure have to work some odd hours" or "Isn't that work boring!" provide information about what the speaker considers important as well as the speaker's evaluation of the work situation. A family member who constantly reminds a miner about the dangers of the job will likely increase the attention the miner gives to safety and may force the miner to reassess the risks of the occupation.

JUSTIFICATION OF WORKERS' PERCEPTIONS

Employees who have perceptions of their jobs or behavior that is inconsistent with the social information they receive may attempt to convince the information source of the inaccuracy of the information. Alternately, employees may justify (or rationalize) away the differences, or they may decide to adjust their perceptions to be consistent with the information they receive.

Employees frequently change their perception of a situation to conform with the perception of information sources. In what has become known as the "Asch light experiment," subjects were asked to judge the lengths of lines of light. Less than 1% of the subjects misjudged line length when working individually. However, when co-workers (actually confederates in the experiment) provided incorrect

judgments, more than one-third of the subjects gave an incorrect answer consistent with the incorrect answer provided by their co-workers. (See "Studies of Independence and Conformity: A Minority of One Against a Unanimous Majority" by Solomon E. Asch in *Psychological Monographs,* No. 9, 1956). If people are willing to change their perceptions of objective phenomena such as the length of a line, they probably are even more likely to change their views of the less objective elements of jobs.

SOURCES OF INFORMATION

Employees can receive information from a wide variety of sources, ranging from bathroom graffiti to the evening news. However, the most likely sources of social information are the people employees come into contact with regularly—co-workers, supervisors, friends, family members and, in some cases, customers or clients.

Co-workers

Generally, co-workers are important sources of information for an employee. They not only spend several hours per day with the employee but also are most likely to be familiar with the employee's work. Co-workers' knowledge of a job makes their views of job characteristics, the importance of specific characteristics, and the evaluation of those characteristics particularly credible. Furthermore, the day-to-day contact with co-workers allows frequent discussion of workplace phenomena and thereby reinforces the perceptions co-workers have of a particular job.

To illustrate the latter point, let's return to the story of John Rogers. As John became better acquainted with his new employer and with Adams and Woods, he began to agree with Adams that the work environment was less than ideal. Adams had complained that his job was boring and that he felt unappreciated—relatively mild criticisms compared with the views held by most of the salesforce. Adams and many other employees perceived the company as a place to obtain work experience and a "livable" salary until something better came along. His co-workers explained to John that other companies in the industry offered better benefits, more autonomy, and greater opportunities for advancement. As most employees agreed, promotion out of their adequately paid but dead-end jobs should be a primary career goal.

Supervisors

In many instances, supervisors are also a source of information. They can have a dual impact on worker's job perceptions. Obviously, a supervisor is a representative of higher levels of management and as such has an opportunity to present the organization's view of the job and the characteristics of the job considered important by the organization. For employees seeking rapid upward mobility and other "company" employees, the organization's view of the workplace as presented by the supervisor may be accepted with minimal questioning.

In addition to being "management's representative," a supervisor may function in the capacity of a friend or co-worker. Employees and their supervisors may work as peers to solve particular problems. Similarly, they may interact on an informal basis during breaks, lunch, social functions, and so forth. The supervisor is in a position to comment on various elements of an employee's job during these informal times and may indirectly influence the employee's job perception.

Woods, who had given John a positive view of the job during their conversation, was not particularly influenced by the information provided by his co-workers. Woods had been a personal friend of his division manager before being hired. The division manager continually provided Woods with information from upper management that advancement was almost automatic for employees who remained loyal to the company. Loyalty, seniority, and good performance were the keys to advancement. The division manager had convinced Woods that, although promotions were not as rapid as at other organizations, job pressures were less and job security was better. Woods did not consider himself to be a fast-track employee and preferred the relative safety and low pressure he associated with his current employer.

Friends and Family

Friends and family members provide a perspective on an employee's work situation that is often quite different from the perspective provided by supervisors and co-workers. Friends and family members who are not employed by the company are less subject to its influence and the influence of its employees. Thus they often are in a position to provide a different, and probably more objective, assessment of what a worker should experience on a job. New employees may attach greater validity to information provided by someone from outside the organization, believing that person to be less biased than a co-worker, especially if the person has the added credibility of being a trusted friend or family member. Alternately, some people may discount evaluations made by family members as being uninformed or naive.

Family members and friends also are in a position to provide an external reference point. For example, they can inform a worker about jobs at other organizations. Discussing such jobs allows the employee to compare his or her job with situations elsewhere to determine the relative importance of various job characteristics and the relative merit of the company.

Further, family members and friends often are an especially powerful source of support for new employees and employees who are having problems at work. Discussions with people outside the company allow employees to vent their feelings about their jobs. Family members and friends also provide support for the employee's self-image. They help an employee understand the rationale for particular characteristics of the job. Particularly for new employees, this kind of rationalizing is part of the process whereby a person's perception of what is important is modified to more closely parallel the information provided by others.

In the original example, Wood's family members provided additional information, causing him to be satisfied with the company's slow rate of promotion. John learned that Woods was from a family of blue-collar workers. Woods had been the first family member to earn a college degree and to advance to a management position. Relative to other members of the family, Woods was doing quite well and was earning more than any of them. Besides, a quick promotion would almost certainly mean a transfer from the area, an alternative he did not really want to consider. Therefore, Woods was content to remain in his position and wait for a promotion that did not require a move.

Customers or Clients

In some cases, customers or clients provide workers with job-related information. Especially for employees of service companies, customers provide an evaluation of the company and its products. Such evaluations may not pertain to a specific job, but customers' assessments of the organization become part of its culture. Companies whose products are poorly received by customers are likely to have different expectations for their employees. Pressures to reduce costs, improve product quality, and/or increase quantity of output are usually greater at companies that are performing poorly. On the other hand, contacts with customers and customer treatment may be important considerations for an organization. These customers contacts, for example, often distinguish a self-service discount store from a store providing full service.

Employees may perceive the importance of their work differently if the product is well accepted. Extremely poor customer relations may threaten the survival of the company and increase the attention employees focus on job security. Employees are more likely to feel that their job is secure and that they have career opportunities when a company has good customer relations.

In organizations that encourage full service and personal contact with customers, the customer is likely considered an important source of job-related information. Both the employee and the employer are encouraged to be attentive to the needs and reactions of customers. Organizations with cultures attaching less significance to customer contact and satisfaction would likewise be expected to attribute less validity to information provided by customers. At those organizations, the line "This would not be a bad place to work if it were not for the customers" is too often said with sincerity by employees.

GUIDELINES FOR USING AND MANAGING SOCIAL INFORMATION

Managers often discuss the influence that groups have on the behavior of workers. Yet in planning interactions with employees, managers tend to overlook the social influence on employee behavior. Employee experience is an important factor affecting the ability of social information to influence behavior. Managers should also be sensitive to the impact of different information sources on employee behavior and attitudes. Moreover, they should use caution in attributing the results of various job measures to the "true, objective" job rather than to cues provided by others about the job.

Employee Experience

The length of time an employee has been in a particular position will likely influence the employee's susceptibility to information about the job. Employees who are new to the job, either newly hired workers or those transferred or promoted into a new position, are likely to be more receptive to social information than are employees who have greater seniority in the position. Especially when an employee is new to the job and the organization, a considerable amount of time is spent listening to many employees' views about the company's operations.

The variety of information sources used by an employee decreases with his or her experience in the job, although reliance on a few selected sources may increase. The number of sources used decreases since much of the information provided from some sources is learned quickly. Thus those sources no longer contribute information of significant value to the employee. Other people, however, evolve as credible sources of worthwhile information. The latter will exert increased influence as employees gain work experience.

INFORMATION SOURCE USAGE

There are a vast number of potential sources of job-related information. As discussed above, family members, friends, customers, co-workers, and supervisors often are highly valued sources of information.

During crisis periods of employment, family members and friends can be especially useful sources of information for an employee by helping the employee retain self-confidence. Family members and friends can encourage a new employee to keep trying and promise support if the new job does not work out.

Although there is very little that managers can do to control information obtained from family members and friends, they need to be aware that information from such sources restricts the range of strategies available for responding to employees. Managers also must realize that employees are aware of the things other companies are doing. Depending on their information sources, some employees may know more about other organizations that their supervisors know.

Customers and clients provide information about the value of a company's products relative to a competitor's products. Their evaluations may give employees insight into the probable success (or failure) of the company's product line. Frequent negative criticism of a company's product, for example, tells an employee that the product is inferior in some respect. Continued criticism may cause the employee to question the quality of the product, the quality of the company, and the probability of stable long-term employment. Ultimately, such negative information may provide the incentive for an employee to leave the organization.

As with feedback from the family members and friends, companies have little opportunity to insulate employees from feedback from customers. Instead, they must be sensitive to the feedback employees are receiving. Discussing with employees the information they receive enables management to explain steps the company is taking to correct problems and to assure employees of the company's integrity and stability. It also gives management the opportunity to learn about major developments at other organizations.

Managers may be able to influence the initial image new employees have of the organization by selecting the co-workers to whom they are exposed. Assigning a new employee to a work group supportive of management will likely produce a more favorable initial attitude toward the company than assigning the worker to a more negative work group. However, assignment of coworkers is obviously a temporary control measure. Eventually, the new employee will be exposed to negative views of the company. If the criticisms seem more credible than the positive information provided by the first co-workers, management may be perceived as manipulative. Thus control of co-worker information must be used with discretion.

The social information over which management has the greatest control is information provided by supervisors. Managers often overlook the influence supervisors have on their employees. For many employees, the immediate supervisor *is* the organization. A supervisor's negative attitude about the company or its management can be transmitted to employees, who in turn develop a negative attitude. Employees often know little about top management. Frequent critical remarks by a supervisor, even if the remarks are made in jest, may support negative information from other sources and cause employees to develop critical views of top management as well as the organization.

In his article "Objective and Social Sources of Information in Task Redesign: A Field Experiment" (*Administrative Science Quarterly*, June 1983), Ricky W. Griffin reported that managers could change employees' perceptions of the job and organization *without* changing the job. One group of managers was trained to provide positive social or informational cues to employees. The employees' perceptions of task characteristics such as task variety, autonomy, feedback, and friendship opportunities differed significantly from the perceptions of the control group whose managers had no training in providing positive social or informational cues.

Objective Job Versus Social Information

Managers must be cautious when interpreting data gathered from employees through surveys and interviews. In taking steps to change jobs in response to data collected from employees, managers must be careful to distinguish between responses stemming from the "objective" job and from social information. If the responses are the result of the objective job, changing the objective job likely will change employees' perceptions and attitudes. However, if the responses are the result of information from the social context in which the job is being performed, changing the job will likely have minimal impact on employees' perceptions of and attitudes about the job as long as the social information provided about the job remains unchanged.

SUMMARY

Jobs and the characteristics associated with them rarely are totally objective. Employees' reactions to their jobs are influenced by information provided by co-workers, supervisors, family members, friends, and perhaps customers or clients. New employees are especially likely to use information from external sources to shape their perceptions of the job and the company. Long-term employees also respond to information provided by others. However, they tend to be more selective about their information sources than are new employees.

Recent research suggests that for some aspects of work, social information about the job may be more important to understanding how employees view the job than is the actual "objective" job. Managers frequently overlook the impact that information from various sources may have on employees' perceptions. In fact, changing the job may have little effect on employees' feelings about the job if information provided by others remains unchanged.

SELECTED BIBLIOGRAPHY

The sources of citations in this article are, in order: Gerald R. Salancik and Jeffrey Pfeffer's "A Social Information Processing Approach to Job Attitudes and Task Design" (*Administrative Science Quarterly*, June 1978); Jeffrey Pfeffer's *Organizations and Organization Theory* (Pitman, 1982); Charles O'Reilly and David Caldwell's "Informational Influence as a Determinant of Perceived Task Characteristics and Job Satisfaction" (*Journal of Applied Psychology*, February 1979); Charles O'Reilly, G. N. Parlette, and J. R. Bloom's "Perceptual Measures of Task Characteristics: The Biasing Effects of Differing Frames of Reference and Job Attitudes" (*Academy of Management Journal*, March 1980); Joe G. Thomas' "Sources of Social Information: A Longitudinal Analysis" (*Human Relations*, September 1986); Solomon. E. Asch's "Studies of Independence and Conformity: A Minority of One Against a Unanimous Majority" (*Psychological Monographs*, No. 9, 1956); Ricky W. Griffin's "Objective and Social Sources of Information in Task Redesign: A Field Experiment" (*Administrative Science Quarterly*, June 1983).

The previous citations are intended to provide some insight into the social information processing literature. More extensive reviews of the literature can be found in Gary J. Blau and Ralph Katerburg's "Toward Enhancing Research with the Social Information Processing Approach to Job Design," (*Academy of Management Review*, October 1982); Joe G. Thomas and Ricky W.

Griffin's "The Social Information Processing Model of Task Design: A Review of the Literature" (*Academy of Management Review*, October 1983); and Ricky W. Griffin, Thomas S. Bateman, Sandy J. Wayne, and Thomas C. Head's "Objective and Social Factors as Determinants of Task Perceptions and Responses: An Integrated Perspective and Empirical Investigation" (*Academy of Management Journal*, September 1987).

As is shown in Figure 13.1, the environment in which an employee and organization operate is also subject to social influence. Questions of whether organizations respond to "real" or "constructed" environments is gaining acceptance in the literature on strategic planning. Insight into the social influence processes at a macro-level can be found in Gregory G. Dess and Nancy Origer's "Environment, Structure, and Consensus in Strategy Formulation: A Conceptual Integration" (*Academy of Management Review*, April 1987); Jane Dutton and Susan Jackson's "Categorizing Strategic Issues: Links to Organizational Action" (*Academy of Management Review*, January 1987); Don Hambrick and Phyllis Mason's "Upper Echelons: The Organization as a Reflection of Its Top Managers" (Academy of Management Review, April 1984).

The importance attached to developing a clear mission and the ability to focus an organization's energies on the external, on service, on quality, on people, on informality, and on wanting to be "the best" at something has been effectively presented by Tom Peters and Robert H. Waterman in their book *In Search of Excellence: Lessons from America's Best-Run Companies* (Harper & Row, 1982). According to Peters and Waterman, part of the function of top management is to clarify to employees what the company views as important. The argument, as developed by Linda Smircich and Charles Stubbart in "Strategic Management in an Enacted World" (*Academy of Management Review*, October 1985), is essentially that a company's strategy becomes a reflection of the concerns of top management; it is a reflection of the issues management considers important.

The position that the receptiveness of employees to social cues varies with work experience draws from research on socialization. Two of the most cited books on socialization, John Wanous' *Organizational Entry* (Addison-Wesley, 1980) and Edgar Schein's *Career Dynamics* (Addison-Wesley, 1978), support the view that information source usage becomes more selective and limited as employees become more oriented to their jobs. This view is also supported in Joe G. Thomas' "Sources of Social Information: A Longitudinal Analysis" (*Human Relations*, September 1986).

14.   ORGANIZATIONAL STORIES: MORE VIVID AND PERSUASIVE THAN QUANTITATIVE DATA

Joanne Martin and Melanie E. Powers

Many organizations have become adept at symbolic means of communicating information about their philosophy of management, the culture of their organization, and the humanistic rationale for their policies. Symbolic forms of management include the creation of rituals of initiation and transition, the evolution of shared jargon and special metaphors, and—the focus of this chapter—the telling of organizational sagas, myths, legends, and stories.

COLLECTING HEADS, TAMING WILD DUCKS, AND J.F.K.

One organization that has become known for its attention to symbolic forms of management is I.B.M. Under the guidance of its founder, T. J. Watson, Sr., I.B.M. developed a distinctive culture, a well-articulated philosophy of management, and a strong demand for conformity (cf. Belden & Belden, 1962; Foy, 1975; Malik, 1975). For example the famous I.B.M. dress code required male employees to wear dark suits, crisp white shirts, and narrow black ties. The organizational culture included rules concerning sexual relations between employees (not advisable), the use of coarse language or alcohol during working hours (don't), and the way to make a speech (list key points using simple words on a flip chart). T. J. Watson, Sr., reinforced these forms of organizational control with numerous rituals and ceremonies. For example, until the company became too large, employees lived temporarily in tents on company grounds during the annual picnic. There they sang company songs and listened to speeches given with evangelical fervor.

When T. J. Watson, Jr., took over the leadership of I.B.M. from his father, he wanted to improve the functioning of the corporation and leave his personal mark on its distinctive philosophy of management and culture. One means to these ends was to change the rhetoric, and perhaps the reality, of the corporation's demands for conformity. T. J. Watson, Jr., stated this objective directly in his speeches at company functions: "I just wish somebody would stick his head in my office and say (to me) 'you're wrong.' I would really like to hear that. I don't want yes-men around me" (Malik, 1975, p. 210).

Watson, Jr., justified his encouragement of dissent by citing *The Organization Man*: "When an organization tries to get too close to its people and makes a lot of the team idea, the individual gets swallowed up, loses his identity, and becomes a carbon copy of his fellow employees" (Watson, Jr., 1963, pp. 24–25). He claimed that the company already had in its ranks a number of employees who would dare express dissent:

[Our company] has more than 125,000 employees. A substantial number of them, many of whom I could pick out by name, are highly individualistic men and women. They value their intellectual freedom and I question whether they would surrender it at any price. Admittedly, they may like their jobs and the security and salaries that go along with them. But I know of few who would not put on their hats and slam the door if they felt the organization had intruded

so heavily on them they no longer owned themselves. (Watson, Jr., 1963, pp. 25–26)

Such abstract, direct statements of this change in the demand for the conformity were dismissed as corporate propaganda by many employees: "[Watson, Jr.] says to us to stick our heads into his office and say 'you are wrong'; you should see the collection of heads that he has" (Malik, 1975, p. 210).

Watson, Jr., seemed to recognize the difficulty of convincing I.B.M. employees that this change in policy was truthful, and not corporate propaganda. He repeatedly supplemented abstract, direct statements, such as that quoted above, with stories illustrating his point. His favorite story concerned wild ducks:

The moral is drawn from a story by the Danish philosopher, Soren Kierkegaard. He told of a man on the coast of Zealand who liked to watch the wild ducks fly south in great flocks each fall. Out of charity, he took to putting feed for them in a nearby pond. After a while some of the ducks no longer bothered to fly south; they wintered in Denmark on what he fed them.

In time they flew less and less. When the wild ducks returned, the others would circle up to greet them but then head back to their feeding grounds on the pond. After three or four years they grew so lazy and fat that they found difficulty in flying at all.

Kierkegaard drew his point—you can make wild ducks tame, but you can never make tame ducks wild again. One might also add that the duck who is tamed will never go anywhere anymore.

We are convinced that any business needs its wild ducks. And in I.B.M. we try not to tame them. (Watson, Jr., 1963, pp. 27–28)

This metaphorical story also failed to convince many employees. Indeed, some researchers (cf. Ott, 1979) expressed skepticism about it. One employee put his reaction succinctly: "Even wild ducks fly in formation" (Malik, 1975, p. 210). Watson, Jr., had another story he told which made a similar point. The main characters in this story were I.B.M. employees.

Early in 1961, in talking to our sales force, I attempted to size up the then new Kennedy Administration as I saw it. It was not a political talk. I urged no views on them. It was an optimistic assessment, nothing more. But at the close of the meeting, a number of salesmen came up front. They would listen to what I had to say about business, they said, but they didn't want to hear about the new Administration in a company meeting.

On my return to New York, I found a few letters in the same vein. Lay off, they seemed to say, you're stepping on our toes in something that's none of your business.

At first I was a bit annoyed at having been misunderstood. But when I thought about it, I was pleased, for they had made it quite clear they wore no man's collar and they weren't at all hesitant to tell me so. From what I have read of organization men, that is not the way they are supposed to act. (Watson, Jr., 1963, p. 26)

This last story was more credible than his other statements which encouraged dissent. Even self-appointed critics of I.B.M. do not usually doubt the truthfulness of this particular story (cf. Malik, 1975), although they may continue to be skeptical of the company's actual tolerance of dissent.

This skepticism is not misplaced. Even in public statements, Watson, Jr., betrayed his unchanged desire for conformity:

It's going to be a prodigious job for every one of us to make all of them look and act and have the same basic philosophies in their business lives and their community lives that all of us have . . . I wish I could put it in a page or two and hand it out and say "Give this to every new employee," who will then automatically start to look and act and think as we do. (Belden & Belden, 1962, p. 249)

In this I.B.M. example, Watson, Jr.'s policy change was more rhetoric than reality. Of all the various forms of communicating this purported policy change, the story about organizational employees seemed to arouse the least skepticism. Thus, it was most likely to generate commitment to the policy. Direct statements of the policy in abstract language were apparently less effective.

If organizational stories are a particularly effective means of generating commitment, they are a potentially powerful management tool. From a management point of view, it would be useful to know whether in fact an organizational story is a more effective way to generate commitment than other forms of communicating information. It would also be useful to know the conditions under which an organizational story would lose its impact.

From an employee's point of view, different issues are salient. An employee needs to know whether to believe a given statement is true or whether to dismiss it as corporate propaganda. It is also useful for an employee to know if a particular form of communication, such as a story, is likely to be particularly persuasive. If so, the employee can be wary when information is communicated in this form. These concerns of top management and lower-level employees suggest that symbolic forms of management, such as organizational stories, are an important topic for researchers to investigate.

ORGANIZATIONAL STORIES, MYTHS, LEGENDS, AND SAGAS

Some organizational research indicates that the persuasive power of the story in the I.B.M. example is representative of other organizational settings. This research focuses on organizational stories, myths, sagas, and legends (e.g., Clark, 1970; Meyer & Rowan, 1978; Selznick, 1957). Wilkins and Martin (1979) define an organizational story as an anecdote about an event sequence, apparently drawn from an accurate version of an organization's history. The main characters are organizational participants, usually employees rather than clients.

This research on organizational stories has relied predominantly on qualitative methods (e.g., Clark, 1970; Selznick, 1957). Researchers have found examples of organizational stories in the transcripts of open-ended interviews and in archival material, such as memoranda, brochures, letters, and records of speeches given by company executives.

This organizational research speculates that organizational stories may serve many of the same functions that anthropologists have found myths to serve in tribal societies (e.g., Cohen, 1969; Malinowski, 1948): organizational stories legitimate the power relations within the organization; they rationalize existing practices, traditions, and rituals; and they articulate through exemplars the philosophy of management and the policies which make the organization distinctive. In short, this research suggests the proposition that there is an association between stories and organizational commitment. The next section of this chapter examines this proposition in detail.

STORIES AND COMMITMENT

Alan Wilkins (1978) tested this proposition using a mixture of qualitative and quantitative methods. He obtained transcripts of organizational stories through interviews with employees of two companies, and measured levels of employee commitment with a survey instrument. In the organization in which commitment was stronger, a larger number of stories were told, and their content was more favorable to the organization. Thus Wilkins' research found an association between organizational stories and commitment.

The organizational research discussed above, including Wilkins' work, raises two interesting questions. The first concerns causality. Does the telling of organizational stories increase employee commitment to the organization? Or, is the direction of causality reversed, so that committed employees are more likely to tell favorable stories? Another possibility is that there may not be a causal relationship at all between stories and commitment. The second question concerns the relative impact of stories on commitment, compared to other methods of communicating information about management philosophy or policy. Such other means of communicating information might include abstract policy statements, such as corporate objectives, or a table of statistical data. Are stories a more effective means of generating commitment than these other forms of information? The types of research designs and methodologies used in the organizational research discussed above raised these questions, but did not attempt to provide answers to them (Clark, 1970; Meyer & Rowan, 1978; Selznick, 1957; Wilkins, 1978).

We decided to seek answers to these two questions by using experimental laboratory methods. This methodology is well suited to address these questions. In an experiment it is possible to manipulate the form of information presented to subjects. Potentially confounding variables such as tenure can be controlled by the design of the experimental context and by random assignment of subjects to conditions. Hence a well-designed experiment can provide a context for testing questions of causality and for measuring the comparative strength of various means of communicating information.

We designed experiments to test two propositions based on the organizational research discussed above. We proposed, first, that supporting a management philosophy statement with an organizational story would increase the subjects' commitment to that philosophy. Second, we proposed that stories would produce more commitment than other forms of information.

As considered in more detail elsewhere (Martin, in press), a body of experimental social cognition research is relevant to these propositions. This cognitive research begins with a premise concerning sample size which is familiar to all students of statistical inference: a judgment based on multiple observations should be more reliable than a judgment based on a single observation. Furthermore, if data based on multiple observations is supplemented by an additional observation, then that additional data point should be treated merely as one of the set of observations.

This premise concerning sample size raises some issues about the impact of an organizational story. A story—indeed, any case example—is based on a single observation. Therefore, if the sample size premise is followed, a story should have much less impact than would data based on multiple observations.

Considerable cognitive research suggests that people do not behave in a manner consistent with the sample size premise (Borgida & Nisbett, 1977; McArthur, 1972, 1976; Nisbett & Borgida, 1975; Nisbett & Ross, 1980; Tversky & Kahneman, 1973). Typically in this research, some subjects were randomly selected to receive distributional data about the behavior of a number of other people (consensus information) or the characteristics of a sample (base-rate information). The remaining subjects received the distributional information, plus additional information about a single case example. The dependent variables usually required subjects to make rational cognitive judgments about relatively academic tasks.

The engineers and lawyers problem is representative of these experimental tasks (Kahneman & Tversky, 1973). Subjects were given base-rate data about the percentages of engineers and lawyers in a given sample. Some of the subjects were also given personally descriptive information about a single individual. Subjects were then asked to estimate the probability that this individual was an engineer.

In accord with the sample size premise, subjects exposed only to the distributional data based their cognitive judgments on that data. Subjects exposed both to the distributional data and to the case example, however, weighted the case example much more heavily in their judgments than they should have, had they behaved in accord with sample size considerations.

More recently, researchers have attempted to find the limits of this phenomenon. Some recent research has found that for tasks such as this, the impact of distributional data was equal to or greater than the impact of a single case example (Azjen, 1977; Feldman, Higgins, Karlovac, & Ruble, 1976; Hansen & Donoghue, 1977; Manis, Dovalina, Avis, & Cardoze, 1980; Wells & Harvey, 1977). Even in these studies, though, case examples are usually given weight beyond that dictated by the sample size premise. To summarize, social cognition research provides an experimental paradigm for examining the two hypotheses discussed above. It also provides additional support for the second of the two propositions to be tested: a case example, such as an organizational story, may have strong impact on judgments, stronger than that predicted by sample size considerations alone.

These conclusions, however, assume that the cognitive research results are generalizable to organizational contexts. This assumption may not be warranted, for two reasons. First, the experimental tasks used in the cognitive research require subjects to make rational, usually statistical, judgments. Subjects' knowledge of statistical principles may be sufficient to produce a correct solution to the problem. In organizational contexts, judgments are usually more complex and subjective. Second, the source of the distributional and case example information appears to be objective in the cognitive research. Subjects would have little reason to doubt the truthfulness of this information. In organizational contexts, though, the credibility of the source of information is often questionable. Organizational representatives have been known to distort information about their organizations.

Both of these limitations of the cognitive research suggest the importance of exploring ideas drawn from the cognitive research in contexts which are organizationally relevant. In such contexts, experimental tasks would require complex and subjective solutions, not derivable from statistical principles. The source of the information, whether it is based on single or multiple observations, would be of potentially questionable credibility.

We conducted two experiments with these organizationally relevant characteristics. In each experiment we gave all subjects a statement of an organizational policy, phrased in abstract language. Some subjects also received additional information presented in the form of data (based on multiple observations); others received additional information in the form of an organizational story (based on a single observation). Still others received both the data and the story. Because of the complexity of the information, we were able to incorporate into our questionnaire a broader range of dependent variables than were used in the cognitive research. We included the usual cognitive dependent variables plus accuracy of recall and attitudinal dependent variables such as belief in and commitment to the policy statement. Our two experiments are described below.

SELLING CALIFORNIA WINE WITH A STORY

In the first experiment (Martin & Powers, 1979) M.B.A. students were recruited as subjects for a study of the effectiveness of an advertisement for a winery. An ab-stract policy statement (an advertisement) was read by all subjects. According to this statement, the new Joseph Beaumont Winery used many of the same excellent winemaking techniques as used in the famed Chablis region of France, thus producing California wine as fine as French chablis.

The text of the advertisement contained this policy statement plus some supplemental information. The supplemental information detailed the winemaking procedures used by the Joseph Beaumont winery. Subjects were randomly assigned to receive this information in one of three forms: a story, a table of statistics, or a combination of story plus statistics. Like many organizational stories, the story concerned the founder of a business:

Joseph Beaumont's father spent most of his life growing grapes in Chablis, the famous winemaking area of France. After World War II, Joe's father came to the United States, to live in the Napa area of California. The gravelly soil and cool climate there reminded him of the stony fields and cool nights in Chablis. All the time Joe was growing up, his father would tell him how the wonderful, flinty, dry wines of Chablis were made. Before his father died, Joe promised him that someday he would make a California wine using the traditional winemaking techniques of Chablis.

For ten years, Joe worked at some of the most famous vineyards in the Napa Valley, putting all his savings into a winery and vineyard, which he named Beaumont.

Although money was sometimes scarce, Joe has struggled for the last two years to duplicate the old, but unfortunately expensive, methods of winemaking of Chablis. His Pinot Chardonnay vines were too new; they didn't supply all the grapes he needed and he was forced to buy some inferior grape varieties. He wanted to use glass-lined tanks, like those in Chablis, but could only afford 7 of the 10 he needed, so he had to use a few of the steel tanks usually used in California. In spite of these difficulties, Joe made no other compromises. He ordered special Limosin oak barrels, from the same suppliers used by Chablis winemakers. He filtered his wine using natural methods—egg whites rather than the chemical filters favored by other California wineries. As Joe tasted his first vintage wine he thought, "My father would have been proud of this wine."

In the statistics condition, subjects were given a table summarizing information comparing the winemaking procedures (such as the types of grapes and oak barrels) used at the Joseph Beaumont Winery, at other California wineries, and in Chablis, France. In the story condition, subjects received the story, but no statistical data. In the combination condition, subjects received both the story and the table of statistics. After reading this material, subjects answered a questionnaire about the advertisement which contained the dependent measures of willingness to predict that the organization would behave in accord with the abstract policy statement; willingness to believe the policy statement; ability to recognize its content accurately; and willingness to consider the advertisement a persuasive marketing technique.

Our hypothesis, labeled *the story hypothesis,* predicted the same pattern of results for each of these classes of dependent variables: the story should have the greatest impact, followed by the combination condition, and then the statistics condition. An alternate hypothesis, labeled *the data hypothesis,* predicted the opposite pattern of results: statistics > combination > story.

In contrast to subjects in the other two conditions, subjects who read only the story were slightly more likely to predict that the winery would continue to use the winemaking procedures from France. These subjects were significantly more likely to believe that the advertisement was truthful, to believe that the Beaumont winery actually had used the French winemaking procedures, and to distort their memory of the policy statement, in a direction favorable to the winery. In summary, in accord with the story hypothesis, the story generally had stronger impact than the combination of story plus statistics; and the combination had more impact than did the statistics by themselves.

Interestingly, the subjects were apparently unaware of the strong impact of the story. In accord with the data hypothesis, subjects in the statistics condition rated the advertisement they had read as somewhat more persuasive than did subjects who had read both the story and the statistics. Furthermore, subjects in the statistics condition rated the advertisement as considerably more persuasive than did subjects in the other conditions. Thus the subjects did not realize how powerfully the story had affected their responses. It created a "true believer" reaction even in these quantitatively well-trained M.B.A. students.

GENERATING COMMITMENT TO A POLICY STATEMENT WITH A STORY

In the first experiment the supplemental information supported the policy statement. In this second study (Martin & Powers, 1980), the supplemental information either supported or disconfirmed the policy statement. As in the first study, three forms of that information were used: a story, a table of statistics, or a combination of story plus statistics. Thus in this second study two independent variables were manipulated, creating a two-by-three factorial design.

The M.B.A. subjects all read a policy statement. This policy, based on an actual company policy studied by Wilkins (1978), stated that the company would avoid mass layoffs in times of economic difficulty by asking employees to take a temporary 10% cut in pay. In the story condition, the subjects read about a single employee, Phil Locke. The product which was produced by Phil's division was going to have to be discontinued. According to the story, Phil was worried:

Phil had a wife and two kids. Add to that the usual mortgage payments, car payments, insurance premiums, taxes—you know, he was overextended financially. Well, all that was pretty unsettling for Phil. He's one of those Yankee conservatives who thinks borrowing money is immoral.

Phil knew he was really banking on Electrotec's layoff policy. In fact, that policy was one reason why he had come to Electrotec in the first place. Still, he knew he shouldn't depend totally on the company to protect his career and his family's welfare. He began to look at sales jobs at other firms in the area—just in case. The problem was that none of these jobs fit his training and interests as well as the job he already had, and the market was getting worse.

Phil was in the cafeteria when his secretary came after him with the news that his boss wanted to see him right away.

Phil broke out in a cold sweat as he walked into his boss's office. His boss didn't say much, just something like, "I'm sorry, Phil. I just got the news we've all been dreading; the inertial navigation products are going to be dropped from our line. You and I have been together for a long time, and I will miss you, but . . ."

Two endings for this story were prepared. Subjects in the policy supporting conditions read that:

. . . you'll still have a job with Electrotec. I even think we'll be able to set one up for you in one of the other military hardware divisions. Of course, this means a temporary 10% cut in pay." Not fired! Phil said later he felt as if he had been given a reprieve from a death sentence.

Subjects in the disconfirming conditions read a different ending to the story: "'. . . I have to let you go.' Fired! Phil said later he felt as if he had been given the death sentence."

In the statistics conditions subjects were given numerical data concerning the frequencies of turnover (voluntary and involuntary) and paycuts, both before and after the products were discontinued. In the supporting conditions, the turnover data indicated that no mass layoffs had occurred and that

most employees had taken a 10% cut in pay after the product was discontinued. In the disconfirming conditions, the frequency of turnover implied that a mass layoff had occurred and that pay cuts were rare. In the combination conditions subjects received either the supporting story plus the supporting statistics or the disconfirming story plus the disconfirming statistics.

When the information supported the policy statement, subjects in the story condition, in contrast to subjects in the combination and statistics conditions, were more likely to predict that mass layoffs would be avoided, to believe the policy statement was truthful, and to require a larger salary increase before they would quit for a comparable job at another company. The opposite pattern of effects was found when the information disconfirmed the policy condition. The disconfirming story had an impact equal to or less than the impact of the disconfirming statistics or the combination of disconfirming story plus disconfirming statistics.

In summary, when subjects were given information which supported a policy statement and were then asked to make predictions, to assess their belief in the truthfulness of the policy, or to indicate their commitment to the organization, the supporting story had a stronger impact than the other forms of communication. The power of a story however, is not limitless. When the information disconfirmed the policy statement, the story never had a stronger impact, and frequently had a significantly weaker impact, than the disconfirming statistics and the disconfirming combination of story plus statistics.

CONCLUSIONS

In this final section of the chapter, the theoretical contributions of these experimental results are discussed. The practical implications for organizational employees are outlined and several ethical concerns are raised.

The results of these two studies can be summarized in terms of the two questions raised by the organizational research. First, stories caused commitment. Second, stories caused more commitment than other means of communicating information, such as statistics.

In addition to addressing questions raised by the organizational research, these two experiments extend the results of the cognitive research. A wider range of dependent variables was considered. Whereas previous cognitive research had used dependent measures concerning cognitive judgments, these two experiments also measured belief in the truthfulness of information and commitment to the values underlying the information. The two experiments demonstrated that case examples, such as organizational stories, have strong impact on these attitudes as well as on cognitions.

The second experiment also produced a finding which was not anticipated by previous organizational or cognitive research. It demonstrated a boundary condition or limit to the powerful impact of case examples such as stories. When the content of the information disconfirmed, rather than supported, the policy statement, the story lost its power. Disconfirming statistics had an impact on attitudes and cognitions that was equal to, sometimes even greater than, a disconfirming story. Subjects apparently dismissed the disconfirming story as the single exception to the general rule. The results of the second experiment suggest that if a story is to have strong impact, it must be congruent with prior knowledge.

The results of these two experiments have some clear practical implications. Frequently managers wish to communicate information about a policy change or their philosophy of management. Obviously, they want their messages to be memorable and believable, so that employees will be committed to these ideas. The studies discussed above indicate that the most effective tactic would be to support their points with an organizational story, rather than with statistical information.

Watson, Jr., of I.B.M. was using this tactic when he told the stories about the wild ducks or about the negative reaction to his speech supporting John F. Kennedy. Unfortunately, Watson ran afoul of the boundary condition discovered in the second experiment. He told stories which disconfirmed the employees' prior knowledge about the I.B.M. emphasis on conformity. Consequently, these disconfirming stories were dismissed, by many employees, as corporate propaganda.

The I.B.M. example raises some ethical issues. Employees need to be wary of the potentially powerful impact that a seemingly innocuous story can have. Management, indeed anyone, could use the power of a story to manipulate beliefs about a policy and to generate commitment to an organization when the information is, in fact, corporate propaganda. As this caveat indicates, symbolic forms of management, such as the telling of organizational stories, are powerful and potentially dangerous tools.

REFERENCES

Azjen, I. Intuitive theories of events and the effects of base-rate information on prediction. *Journal of Personality and Social Psychology*, 1977, thirty-five, 303–314.

Belden, T. G., & Belden, M. R. *The lengthening shadow: The life of Thomas J. Watson.* Boston: Little, Brown.

Borgida, E., & Nisbett, R. E. The differential impact of abstract vs. concrete information on decisions. *Journal of Applied Social Psychology*, 1977, seven, 258–271.

Clark, B. *The distinctive college: Antioch, Reed and Swarthmore.* Chicago: Aldine, 1970.

Cohen, P. S. Theories of myth. *Man*, 1969, four, 337–353.

Feldman, N. S., Higins, E. T., Karlovac, M., & Ruble, D. N. Use of consensus information in causal attributions as a function of temporal presentation and availability of direct information. *Journal of Personality and Social Psychology*, 1976, thirty-four, 694–698.

Foy, N. *The sun never sets on IBM*. New York: William Morrow & Company, Inc., 1975.

Hansen, R. D., & Donoghue, J. The power of consensus: Information derived from one's and others' behavior. *Journal of Personality and Social Psychology*, 1977, thirty-five, 294–302.

Kahneman, D., & Tversky, A. On the psychology of prediction. *Psychological Review*, 1973, eighty, 237–251.

Malik, R. *And tomorrow . . . the world? Inside IBM*. London: Millington HD, 1975.

Malinowski, B. Myth in primitive psychology. In *Magic, science, and religion, and other essays*. Boston: Beach Press, 1948.

Manis, M., Dovalina, I., Avis, N., & Cardoze, S. Base rates can affect individual predictions. *Journal of Personality and Social Psychology*, 1980, thirty-eight, 231–248.

Martin, J. Stories and scripts in organizational settings. In A. Hastprf and A. Isen (Eds.), *Cognitive Social Psychology*. New York: Elsevier-North Holland, Inc., In Press.

Martin, J., & Powers, M. E. *If case examples provide no proof, why under-utilize statistical information?* Paper presented at the meetings of the American Psychological Association, New York, September 1979.

Martin, J., & Powers, M. E. *Skepticism and the true believer: The effects of case and/or base rate information on belief and commitment*. Paper presented at the meeting of the Western Psychological Association, Honolulu, May 1980.

McArthur, L. Z. The how and what of why: Some determinants and consequences of causal attribution. *Journal of Personality and Social Psychology*, 1972, twenty-two, 171–193.

McArthur, L. Z. The lesser influence of consensus than distinctiveness information on causal attributions: A test of the person-thing hypothesis. *Journal of Personality and Social Psychology*, 1976, thirty-three, 733–742.

Meyer, J. W., & Rowan, B. Institutionalized organizations: Formal structure as myth and ceremony. In M. M. Meyer & Associates, *Environment and organizations: Theoretical and empirical perspectives*. San Francisco: Jossey-Bass, Inc., 1978, 78–109.

Nisbett, R. E., & Borgida, E. Attribution and the psychology of prediction. *Journal of Personality and Social Psychology*, 1975, thirty-two, 932–943.

Nisbett, R. E., & Ross, L. *Human inference: Strategies and shortcomings of social judgment*. Englewood Cliffs, N.J.: Prentice-Hall, Inc., 1980.

Ott, R. *Are wild ducks really wild: Symbolism and behavior in the corporate environment*. Paper presented at the meeting of the Northeastern Anthropological Association, March 1979.

Selznick, P. *Leadership and administration*. Evanston, Ill.: Row, Peterson, 1957.

Tversky, A., & Kahneman, D. Availability: A heuristic for judging frequency and probability. *Cognitive Psychology*, 1973, five, 207–232.

Watson, Jr., T. J. *A business and its beliefs: The ideas that helped build IBM*. New York: McGraw-Hill Book Company, Inc., 1963.

Wells, G. L., & Harvey, J. H. Do people use consensus information in making causal attributions? *Journal of Personality and Social Psychology*, 1977, thirty-five 279–293.

Wilkins, A. *Organizational stories as an expression of management philosophy: Implications for social control in organizations*. Unpublished doctoral dissertation, Stanford University, 1978.

Wilkins, A., & Martin, J. *Organizational legends* (Research Paper No. 521). Graduate School of Business, Stanford University, 1979.

Making Rational and Irrational Decisions

15. BIASES

Max H. Bazerman

This chapter is written to provide you with the opportunity to audit your own decision making and identify the biases that affect you. A number of problems are presented that allow you to examine your problem solving and learn how your judgments compare to the judgments of others. The quiz items are then used to illustrate 13 predictable biases to which managers are prone, and that frequently lead to judgments that systematically deviate from rationality.

To start out, consider the following two problems:

Problem 1: The following 10 corporations were ranked by *Fortune* magazine to be among the 500 largest United States-based firms according to sales volume for 1987:

Group A: Gillette, Coca-Cola Enterprises, Lever Brothers, Apple Computers, Hershey Foods

Group B: Coastal, Weyerhaeuser, Northrup, CPC International, Champion International

Which group of five organizations listed (A or B) had the larger total sales volume?

Problem 2: (Adapted from Kahneman & Tversky, 1973) The best student in my introductory MBA class this past semester writes poetry and is rather shy and small in stature. What was the student's undergraduate major: (A) Chinese studies or (B) Psychology?

What are your answers? If you answered *A* for each of the two problems, you may gain comfort in knowing that the majority of respondents choose *A*. If you answered *B*, you are part of the minority. In this case, however, the minority represents the correct response. All corporations in group B were

---

Chapter 2 of *Managerial Decision Making* (second edition) by Max H. Bazerman. Copyright © 1990 by John Wiley & Sons, Inc. Reprinted by permission.

ranked in the Fortune 100, while none of the corporations in group A had sales as large. In fact, the total sales for group B was more than double the total sales for group A. In the second problem, the student was actually a psychology major, but more important, selecting psychology as the student's major represents a more rational response given the limited information.

Problem 1 illustrates the availability heuristic. . . . In this problem, group A contains consumer firms, while group B consists of industrial firms and holding companies. Most of us are more familiar with consumer firms than conglomerates and can more easily generate information in our minds

about their size. If we were aware of our bias resulting from the availability heuristic, we would recognize our differential exposure to this information and adjust, or at least question, our judgments accordingly.

Problem 2 illustrates the representativeness heuristic. The reader who responds "Chinese studies" has probably overlooked relevant *baserate* information—namely, the likely ratio of Chinese studies majors to psychology majors within the MBA student population. When asked to reconsider the problem in this context, most people change their response to "psychology" in view of the relative scarcity of Chinese studies majors seeking MBAs.

TABLE 15.1
Chapter Problems

Respond to the following 11 problems before reading the chapter.

Problem 3: Which is risker:

    a. driving a car on a 400-mile trip?
    b. flying on a 400-mile commercial airline flight?

Problem 4: Are there more words in the English language

    a. that start with an *r*?
    b. for which *r* is the third letter?

Problem 5: Mark is finishing his MBA at a prestigious university. He is very interested in the arts and at one time considered a career as a musician. Is Mark more likely to take a job

    a. in the management of the arts?
    b. with a management consulting firm?

Problem 6: In 1986, two research groups sampled consumers on the driving performance of the Dodge Colt versus the Plymouth Champ in a blind road test; that is the consumers did not know when they were driving the Colt or the Champ. As you may know, these cars were identical; only the marketing varied.

One research group (A) sampled 66 consumers each day for 60 days (a large number of days to control for weather and other variables), while the other research group (B) sampled 22 consumers each day for 50 days. Which consumer group observed more days in which 60 percent or more of the consumers tested preferred the Dodge Colt:

    a. Group A?
    b. Group B?

(continued)

TABLE 15.1 (continued)
Chapter Problems

Problem 7: You are about to hire a new central-region sales director for the fifth time this year. You predict that the next director should work out reasonably well, since the last four were "lemons," and the odds favor hiring a least one good sales director in five tries. This thinking is

    a. Correct
    b. Incorrect.

Problem 8: You are sales forecaster for a department store chain with nine locations. The chain depends on you for quality projections of future sales in order to make decisions on staffing, advertising, information system developments, purchasing, renovation, and the like. All stores are similar in size and merchandise selection. The main difference in their sales occurs because of location and random fluctuations. Sales for 1989 were as follows:

Store	1989	1991
1	$12,000,000	$ _____
2	11,500,000	_____
3	11,000,000	_____
4	10,500,000	_____
5	10,000,000	_____
6	9,500,000	_____
7	9,000,000	_____
8	8,500,000	_____
9	8,000,000	_____
TOTAL	$90,000,000	$99,000,000

Your economic forecasting service has convinced you that the best estimate of total sales increases between 1989 and 1991 is 10 percent (to $99,000,000). Your task is to predict 1991 sales for each store. Since your manager belives strongly in the economic forecasting service, it is imperative that your total sales equal $99,000,000.

Problem 9: Linda is 31 years old, single, outspoken, and very bright. She majored in philosophy. As a student, she was deeply concerned with issues of discrimination and social justice, and she participated in antinuclear demonstrations.

Rank order the following eight descriptions in terms of the probability (likelihood) that they describe Linda.

_____ **a.** Linda is a teacher in an elementary school.
_____ **b.** Linda works in a bookstore and takes yoga classes.
_____ **c.** Linda is active in the feminist movement.
_____ **d.** Linda is a psychiatric social worker.
_____ **e.** Linda is a member of the League of Women Voters.
_____ **f.** Linda is a bank teller.
_____ **g.** Linda is an insurance salesperson.
_____ **h.** Linda is a bank teller who is active in the feminist movement.

(continued)

TABLE 15.1 (continued)
Chapter Problems

Problem 10: A newly hired engineer for a computer firm in the Boston metropolitan area has four years of experience and good all-around qualifications. When asked to estimate the starting salary for this employee, my secretary (knowing very little about the profession or the industry) guessed an annual salary of $23,000. What is your estimate?

$ _____ per year.

Problem 11: Which of the following appears most likely?   Which appears second most likely?
   a. Drawing a red marble from a bag containing 50 percent red marbles and 50 percent white marbles.
   b. Drawing a red marble seven times in succession, with replacement (a selected marble is put back in the bag before the next marble is selected), from a bag containing 90 percent red marbles and 10 percent white marbles.
   c. Drawing at least one red marble in seven tries, with replacement, from a bag containing 10 percent red marbles and 90 percent white marbles.

Problem 12: Listed below are 10 uncertain quantities. Do no look up any information on these items. For each, write down your best estimate of the quantity. Next, put a lower and upper bound around your estimate, such that you are 98 percent confident that your range surrounds the actual quantity.

___ **a.** Mobil Oil's sales in 1987
___ **b.** IBM's assets in 1987
___ **c.** Chrysler's profit in 1987
___ **d.** The number of U.S. industrial firms in 1987 with sales greater than those of Conslidated Papers.
___ **e.** The U.S. gross national product in 1945
___ **f.** The amount of taxes collected by the U.S. Internal Revenue Service in 1970
___ **g.** The length (in feet) of the Chesapeake Bay Bridge-Tunnel
___ **h.** The area (in square miles) of Brazil
___ **i.** The size of the black population of San Francisco in 1970
___ **j.** The dollar value of Canadian exports of lumber in 1977

Problem 13: (Adapted from Einhorn & Hogarth, 1978) It is claimed that when a particular analyst predicts a rise in the market, the market always rises. You are to check this claim. Examine the information available about the following four events (cards):

Card 1	Card 2	Card 3	Card 4
Prediction:	Prediction:	Outcome:	Outcome:
Favorable report	Unfavorable report	Risk in the market	Fall in the market

You currently see the predictions (cards 1 and 2) *or* outcomes associated with four events. You are seeing one side of a card. On the other side of cards 1 and 2 is the actual outcome, while on the other side of cards 3 and 4 is the prediction that the analyst made. Evidence about the claim is potentially available by turning over the card(s). Which cards would you turn over for the evidence that you need to check the analyst's claim? (Circle the appropriate cards.)

This example emphasizes that logical base-rate reasoning is often overwhelmed by qualitative judgments drawn from available descriptive information.

The purpose of problems 1 and 2 is to demonstrate how easily faulty conclusions are drawn when we overrely on cognitive heuristics. In the remainder of this chapter, additional problems are presented to further increase your awareness of the impact of heuristics on your decisions and to help you develop an appreciation for the systematic errors that emanate from overdependence on them. The goal of the chapter is to help you "unfreeze" your decision-making patterns and realize how easily heuristics become biases when improperly applied. By working on numerous problems that demonstrate the failures of these heuristics, you will become more aware of the biases in your decision making. By learning to spot these biases, you can improve the quality of your decisions.

Before reading further, please take a few minutes to respond to the problems outlined in Table 15.1. They will be used to illustrate the 13 decision biases presented in the remainder of this chapter.

BIASES EMANATING FROM THE AVAILABILITY HEURISTIC

Bias 1—Ease of Recall (Based Upon Vividness and Recency)

Problem 3: Which is riskier:
a. driving a car on a 400-mile trip?
b. flying on a 400-mile commercial airline flight?

Many people respond that flying in a commercial airliner is far riskier than driving a car. The media's tendency to sensationalize airplane crashes contributes to this perception. In actuality, the safety record for flying is far better than that for driving. Thus, this example demonstrates that a particularly *vivid* event will systematically influence the probability assigned to that type of event by an individ-

ual in the future. This bias occurs because vivid events are more easily remembered and consequently are more available when making judgments.

Consider another example. A buyer of women's wear for a leading department store is assessing her purchasing needs in footwear. To fill the demand for casual shoes, she needs to choose between a proven best-selling brand of running shoes and a newer line of boating shoes. The buyer recalls having seen a number of friends wearing boating shoes at a recent party and concludes that demand for boating shoes is increasing. She decides to order more boating shoes and reduce her order of the historically popular running shoes.

In making this choice, the buyer has biased her ordering decision based upon limited data and the ease with which it came to mind. The buyer judged the demand for boating shoes by the availability of her recollection of a recent party. Under the influence of this bias, she will be consistently less likely to buy popular shoes worn by other groups with whom she tends not to socialize—even though aggregate demand for these alternative styles may be higher.

Tversky and Kahneman (1974) argue that when an individual judges the frequency of an event by the *availability* of its instances, an event whose instances are more easily recalled will appear more numerous than an event of equal frequency whose instances are less easily recalled. They cite evidence of this bias in a lab study in which individuals were read lists of names of well-known personalities of both sexes and asked to determine whether the lists contained the names of more men or women. Different lists were presented to two groups. One group received lists bearing the names of women who were relatively more famous than the listed men, but included more men's names overall. The other group received lists received lists bearing the names of men who were relatively more famous than the listed women, but included more women's names overall. In each case, the subjects incorrectly guessed that the sex that had the more famous personalities was the more numerous.

Many examples of this bias can be observed in the decisions made by managers in the workplace. The following came from the experience of one of my MBA students: As a purchasing agent, he had to select one of several possible suppliers. He chose the firm whose name was the most familiar to him. He later found out that the salience of the name resulted from recent adverse publicity concerning the firm's extortion of funds from client companies!

Managers conducting performance appraisals often fall victim to the availability heuristic. Working from memory, the vivid instances relating to an employee that are more easily recalled from memory (either pro or con) will appear more numerous and will therefore be weighted more heavily in the performance appraisal. Managers also give more weight to performance during the three months prior to the evaluation than to the previous nine months of the evaluation period.

Many consumers are annoyed by repeated exposure to the same advertising message and often wonder why the advertiser doesn't give more useful information, without repeating it so many times. After all, we are smart enough to understand it the first time! Unfortunately, both the frequency and the vividness of the message have been shown to affect our purchasing. This bombardment of repeated, uninformative messages makes the product more easily recalled from memory and is often the best way to get us to buy a product (Alba & Marmorstein, 1987).

Because of our susceptibility to vividness and recency, Kahneman and Tversky suggest that we are particularly prone to overestimating unlikely events. For instance, if we actually witness a burning house, the impact on our assessment of the probability of such accidents is probably greater than the impact of reading about a fire in the local newspaper. The direct observation of such an event makes it more salient to us. Similarly, Slovic and Fischhoff (1977) discuss the implications of the misuse of the availability heuristic on the perceived risks of nuclear power. They point out that any discussion of the potential hazards, regardless of likelihood, will increase the memorability of those hazards and increase their perceived risks.

The stock market provides some telling examples of the tendency to overreact to vivid and recent information in this way. After the April 1986 nuclear accident at Chernobyl in the Soviet Union, U.S. investors sold their nuclear stocks, which caused a dramatic fall in prices. Yet the real safety of the nuclear systems did not change dramatically as a result of the Chernobyl accident. Similarly, the stock of Union Carbide fell 30 percent within three weeks of the December 1984 tragedy at its chemical plant in Bhopal, India. Few investors stopped to realize that Union Carbide might reach an acceptable out-of-court settlement. It was more salient to imagine Union Carbide being hit with a devastating financial penalty. More rational investors who bought the stock at its low point turned a hefty profit—even before the stock moved up higher on an unsuccessful takeover bid (Curran, 1987).

Bias 2—Retrievability (Based Upon Memory Structures)

Problem 4: Are there more words in the English language
a. that start with an *r*?
b. for which *r* is the third letter?

If you responded "start with an *r*," you have joined the majority. Unfortunately, this is again the incorrect answer. Kahneman and Tversky (1973) explain that people typically solve this problem by first recalling words that begin with *r* (like *ran*) and words that have an *r* as the third letter (like *bar*). The relative difficulty of generating words in each of these two categories is then assessed. If we think of our mind as being organized like a dictionary, it is easier to find lots of words that start with an *r*. The dictionary, and our minds, are less efficient at finding words that follow a rule that is inconsistent with the organizing structure—like words that have an *r* as the third letter. Thus, words that start with a particular letter are more available from memory, even though most consonants are more common in the third position than in the first.

Just as our tendency to alphabetize affects our vocabulary-search behavior, organizational modes affect information-search behavior within our work lives. We structure organizations to provide order, but this same structure can lead to confusion if the presumed order is not exactly as suggested. For example, many organizations have a management information systems (MIS) division that has generalized expertise in computer applications. Assume that you are a manager in a product division and need computer expertise. If that expertise exists within MIS, the organizational hierarchy will lead you to the correct resource. If they lack the expertise in a specific application, but it exists elsewhere in the organization, the hierarchy is likely to bias the effectiveness of your search. I am not arguing for the overthrow of organizational hierarchies; I am merely identifying the dysfunctional role of hierarchies in potentially biasing search behavior. If we are aware of the potential bias, we need not be affected by this limitation.

Retail store location is influenced by the way in which consumers search their minds when seeking a particular commodity. Why are multiple gas stations at the same intersection? Why do "upscale" retailers want to be in the same mall? Why are the best bookstores in a city often all located within a couple blocks of each other? An important reason for this pattern is that consumers learn the "location" for a particular type of product or store and organize their minds accordingly. To maximize traffic, the retailer needs to be in the location that consumers associate with this type of product or store.

Bias 3—Presumed Associations

People frequently fall victim to the availability bias in their assessment of the likelihood of two events occurring together. For example, consider the following questions: Is marijuana use related to delinquency? Are couples who get married under the age of 25 more likely to have bigger families? How would you respond if asked these questions? In assessing the marijuana question, most people typically remember several delinquent marijuana

users and assume a correlation or not based upon the availability of this mental data. However, proper analysis would include recalling four groups of observations: marijuana users who are delinquents, marijuana users who are not delinquents, delinquents who do not use marijuana, and nondelinquents who do not use marijuana. The same analysis applies to the marriage question. Proper analysis would include four groups: couples who married young and have large families, couples who married young and have small families, couples who married older and have large families, and couples who married older and have small families. Indeed, there are always at least four separate situations to be considered in assessing the association between two dichotomous events, but our everyday decision making commonly ignores this scientifically valid fact.

Chapman and Chapman (1967) have noted that when we have the probability of two instances in our minds, we usually assign an inappropriately high probability that the two events will co-occur again. Thus, if we know a lot of marijuana users who are delinquents, we assume that marijuana use is related to delinquency. Similarly, if we know of a lot of couples who married young and have had large families, we assume that this trend is more prevalent than it may actually be. In testing for this bias, Chapman and Chapman provided subjects with information about hypothetical psychiatric patients. The information included a written clinical diagnosis of the "patient" and a drawing of a person made by the "patient." The subjects were asked to estimate the frequency with which each diagnosis (for example, suspiciousness or paranoia) was accompanied by various facial and body features in the drawings (for example, peculiar eyes). Throughout the study, subjects markedly overestimated the frequency of pairs commonly associated together by social lore. For example, diagnoses of suspiciousness were overwhelmingly associated with peculiar eyes. In addition, Chapman and Chapman found that conclusions, such as those just noted, were extremely resistant to change, even in the face of contradictory information. Furthermore, the overwhelming impact of this bias toward presumed associations prevented the subjects from detecting other relationships that were, in fact, present.

Summary. A lifetime of experience has led us to believe that, in general, more frequent events are recalled in our minds more easily than less frequent ones, and likely events are easier to recall than unlikely events. In response to this learning, we have developed the availability heuristic for estimating the likelihood of events. In many instances, this simplifying heuristic leads to accurate, efficient judgments. However, as these first three biases (ease or recall, retrievability, and presumed associations) indicate, the misuse of the availability heuristic can lead to systematic errors in managerial judgment. We too easily assume that our available recollections are truly representative of some larger pool of occurrences that exist outside our range of experience.

BIASES EMANATING FROM THE REPRESENTATIVENESS HEURISTIC

Bias 4—Insensitivity to Base Rates

> **Problem 5**: Mark is finishing his MBA at a prestigious university. He is very interested in the arts and at one time considered a career as a musician. Is Mark more likely to take a job
> **a.** in the management of the arts?
> **b.** with a management consulting firm?

How did you decide on your answer? How do most people make this assessment? How *should* people make this assessment? Using the representativeness heuristic . . . most people approach this problem by analyzing the degree to which Mark is representative of their image of individuals who take jobs in each of the two areas. Consequently, they usually conclude "in the management of the arts." However, as we discussed in the first part of this chapter, this response overlooks relevant base-rate information. Reconsider the problem in light of the fact that a much larger number of MBAs take jobs in management consulting than in the management of the

arts—relevant information that should enter into any reasonable prediction of Mark's career path. With this base-rate data, it is only reasonable to predict "management consulting."

Judgmental biases of this type frequently occur when individuals cognitively ask the wrong question. If you answered "in the management of the arts," you were probably thinking in terms of the question "How likely is it that a person working in the management of the arts would fit Mark's description?" However, the problem necessitates the question "How likely is it that someone fitting Mark's description will choose arts management?" By itself, the representativeness heuristic incorrectly leads to a similar answer to both questions, since this heuristic leads individuals to compare the resemblance of the personal description and the career path. However, when base-rate data is considered, it is irrelevant to the first question listed, but it is crucial to a reasonable prediction on the second question. While a large percentage of individuals in arts management may fit Mark's description, there are undoubtedly a larger absolute number of management consultants fitting Mark's description because of the relative preponderance of MBAs in management consulting.

An interesting finding of the research done by Kahneman and Tversky (1972, 1973) is that subjects do use base-rate data correctly when no other information is provided. For example, in the absence of a personal description of Mark in problem 5, people will choose "management consulting" based on the past frequency of this career path for MBAs. Thus, people understand the relevance of base-rate information, but tend to disregard this data when descriptive data is also available.

Bias 5—Insensitivity to Sample Size

> **Problem 6**: In 1986, two research groups sampled consumers on the driving performance of the Dodge Colt versus the Plymouth Champ in a blind road test; that is, the consumers did not know when they were driving the Colt or the Champ. As you may know, these cars were identical; only the marketing varied.

One research group (A) sampled 66 consumers each day for 60 days (a large number of days to control for weather and other variables), while the other research group (B) sampled 22 consumers each day for 50 days. Which consumer group observed more days in which 60 percent or more of the consumers tested preferred the Dodge Colt:

a. group A?
b. group B?

Most individuals expect research group A to provide more 60-percent days for the Dodge Colt, because of the larger number of sample days—in other words, there are 60 chances compared to 50. In contrast, simple statistics tells us that it is much more likely to observe more 60-percent days on daily samples of 22 than on daily samples of 66, and the correct answer is group B. This is because a large sample is far less likely to stray from the expected 50-percent preference split between the Dodge Colt and Plymouth Champ—since the cars are identical. (The interested reader can verify this fact with the use of an introductory statistics book.)

While the importance of sample size is fundamental in statistics, Kahneman and Tversky (1974) note that it "is evidently not part of people's repertoire of intuitions" (p. 1126). Why is this? When responding to problems dealing with sampling, people often use the representativeness heuristic. In their minds, they ask the question, Which group is likely to have more days in which the results are skewed to 60 percent for the Dodge Colt instead of the expected 50 percent? From there, the representative heuristic leads them to focus on the number of days as the pertinent variable for comparison. They then conclude that the group covering the greater number of total days will experience the greater number of total deviations. However, this analogy ignores the issue of sample size—which is critical to an accurate assessment of the problem.

Tversky and Kahneman (1974) first discovered this bias toward ignoring the role of sample size, even when these data were emphasized in the formation of the problem, in testing the following research problem:

A certain town is served by two hospitals. In the larger hospital about 45 babies are born each day, and in the smaller hospital about 15 babies are born each day. As you know, about 50 percent of all babies are boys. However, the exact percentage varies from day to day. Sometimes it may be higher than 50 percent, sometimes lower.

For a period of one year, each hospital recorded the days on which more than 60 percent of the babies born were boys. Which hospital do you think recorded more such days?

The larger hospital? (21)
The smaller hospital? (21)
About the same? (53)
(that is, within 5 percent of each other)

The values in parentheses represent the number of individuals who chose each answer. As explained earlier, sampling theory tells us that the expected number of days on which more than 60 percent of the babies are boys is much greater in the small hospital, since a large sample is less likely to stray from the mean. However, most subjects judged the probability to be the same in each hospital, effectively ignoring sample size.

Consider the implications of this bias in advertising, where people trained in market research understand the need for a sizable sample, but employ this bias to the advantage of their clients. "Four out of five dentists surveyed recommend sugarless gum for their patients who chew gum." There is no mention of the number of dentists involved in the survey and the fact that without these data, the results of the survey are meaningless. If only 5 or 15 dentists were surveyed, the size of the sample would not be generalizable to the overall population of dentists.

Bias 6—Misconceptions of Chance

Problem 7: You are about to hire a new central-region sales director for the fifth time this year. You predict that the next director should work out reasonably well, since the last four were "lemons," and the odds favor hiring at least one good sales director in five tries. This thinking is

a. correct.

b. incorrect.

Most people are comfortable with the foregoing logic, or at least have been guilty of using similar logic in the past. However, the performance of the first four sales directors will not directly affect the performance of the fifth sales director, and the logic in problem 7 is incorrect. Most individuals frequently rely upon their intuition and the representativeness heuristic and incorrectly conclude that a poor performance is unlikely because the probability of getting five "lemons" in a row is extremely low. Unfortunately, this logic ignores the fact that we have already witnessed four "lemons" (an unlikely occurrence), and the performance of the fifth sales director is independent of that of the first four.

This question parallels Kahneman and Tversky's (1972) work in which they show that people expect that a sequence of random events will "look" random. They present evidence of this bias in their finding that subjects routinely judged the sequence of coin flips H-T-H-T-T-H to be more likely than H-H-H-T-T-T, which does not "appear" random, and more likely than the sequence H-H-H-H-T-H, which does not represent the equal likelihood of heads and tails. Simple statistics, of course, tell us that each of these sequences is equally likely because of the independence of multiple random events.

Problem 7 moves beyond dealing with random events in recognizing our inappropriate tendency to assume that random *and* nonrandom events will "balance out." Will the fifth sales director work out well? Maybe. You might spend more time and money on selection, and the randomness of the hiring process may favor you this time. But your earlier failures in hiring sales directors will not directly affect the performance of the new sales director.

The logic concerning misconceptions of chance provides a process explanation of the gambler's fallacy. After holding bad cards on ten hands of poker, the poker player believes that he is due for a good hand. After winning $1,000 in the Pennsylvania State Lottery, a woman changes her regular number—because after all, how likely is it that the same number will come up twice? Tversky and Kahneman (1974) note that "Chance is commonly viewed as a self-correcting process in which a deviation in one direction induces a deviation in the opposite direction to restore the equilibrium. In fact, deviations are not corrected as a chance process unfolds, they are merely diluted."

In each of the preceding examples, individuals expected probabilities to even out. In some situations, our minds misconceptualize chance in exactly the opposite way. In sports (basketball specifically), we often think of a particular player as having a "hot hand" or "being on a good streak." If your favorite player has hit his last four shots, is the probability of his making his next shot higher, lower, or the same as the probability of his making a shot without the preceding four hits? Most sports fans, sports commentators, and players believe that the answer is "higher." In fact, there are many biological, emotional, and physical reasons that this answer could be correct. However, it is wrong! Gilovich, Vallone, and Tversky (1985) did an extensive analysis of the shooting of Philadelphia 76ers and Boston Celtics and found that immediately prior shot performance did not change the likelihood of success on the upcoming shot. Out of all of the findings in this book, this is the effect that my managerial students have had the hardest time believing. The reason is that we can all remember sequences of five hits in a row: streaks are part of our conception of chance in athletic competition. However, our minds do not categorize a string of "four in a row" as being a situation in which "he missed his fifth shot." As a result, we have a misconception of connectedness, when, in fact, chance (or the player's normal probability of success) is really in effect. The belief in the hot hand is especially interesting because of its implication for how players play the game. Passing the ball to the player who is "hot" is commonly endorsed as a good strategy. It can also be expected that the opposing team will concentrate on guarding the hot player. Another player, who is less "hot" but is equally skilled, may have a better chance of scoring. Thus the belief in the "hot hand" is not just erroneous, but could also be costly if you play professional basketball.

Tversky and Kahneman's (1971) work shows that misconceptions of chance are not limited to gamblers, sportsfans, or laypersons. Research psychologists also fall victim to the "law of small numbers." They believe that sample events should be far more representative of the population from which they were drawn than simple statistics would dictate. The researchers put too much faith in the results of initial samples and grossly overestimate the replicability of empirical findings. This suggests that the representativeness heuristic may be so well institutionalized in our decision processes that even scientific training and its emphasis on the proper use of statistics may not effectively eliminate its biasing influence.

Bias 7—Regression to the Mean

Problem 8: You are the sales forecaster for a department store chain with nine locations. The chain depends on you for quality projections of future sales in order to make decisions on staffing, advertising, information system developments, purchasing, renovation, and the like. All stores are similar in size and merchandise selection. The main difference in their sales occurs because of location and random fluctuations. Sales for 1989 were as follows:

Store	1989	1991
1	$12,000,000	$ _____
2	11,500,000	_____
3	11,000,000	_____
4	10,500,000	_____
5	10,000,000	_____
6	9,500,000	_____

Store	1989	1991
7	9,000,000	_____
8	8,500,000	_____
9	8,000,000	_____
TOTAL	$90,000,000	$99,000,000

Your economic forecasting service has convinced you that the best estimate of total sales increases between 1989 and 1991 is 10 percent (to $99,000,000). Your task is to predict 1991 sales for each store. Since your manager believes strongly in the economic forecasting service, it is imperative that your total sales are equal to $99,000,000.

Think about the processes used to answer this problem. Consider the following logical pattern of thought: "The overall increase in sales is predicted to be 10 percent ($99,000,000 – $90,000,000/$90,000,000). Lacking any other specific information on the stores, it makes sense to simply add 10 percent to each 1989 sales figure to predict 1991 sales. This means that I predict sales of $13,2000,000 for store 1, sales of $12,650,000 for store 2, and so on." This logic, in fact, is the most common approach in responding to this item. Unfortunately, this logic is faulty.

Why was the logic presented faulty? Statistical analysis would dictate that we first assess the predicted relationship between 1989 and 1991 sales. This relationship, formally known as a **correlation**, can vary from total independence (that is, 1989 sales do not predict 1991 sales) to perfect correlation (1989 sales are a perfect predictor of 1991 sales). In the former case, the lack of a relationship between 1989 and 1991 sales would mean that 1989 sales would provide absolutely no information about 1991 sales, and your best estimates of 1991 sales would be equal to total sales divided by the number of stores ($99,000,000 divided by 9 equals $11,000,000). However, in the latter case of perfect predictability between 1989 and 1991 sales, our initial logic of simply extrapolating from 1989 performance by adding 10 percent to each store's performance would be completely accurate. Obviously, 1989 sales are most likely to be *partially predictive* of 1991 sales—falling somewhere between independence and perfect correlation. Thus, the best prediction for store 1 should lie between $11,000,000 and $13,200,000 depending upon how predictive you think 1989 sales will be of 1991 sales. The key point is that in virtually all such predictions, you should expect the naive $13,200,000 estimate to regress toward the overall mean ($11,000,000).

In a study of sales forecasting, Cox and Summers (1987) examined the judgments of professional retail buyers. They examined the sales data from 2 department stores for 6 different apparel styles for a total of 12 different sales forecasts over a 2-week period. They found that sales between the 2 weeks regressed to the mean. However, the judgment of all 31 buyers from 5 different department stores failed to reflect the tendency for regression to the mean. As a result, Cox and Summers argued that a sales-forecasting model that considered regression to the mean could outperform the judgments of all 31 professional buyers.

Many effects regress to the mean. Brilliant students frequently have less successful siblings. Short parents tend to have taller children. Great rookies have mediocre second years (the "sophomore jinx"). Firms that have outstanding profits one year tend to have lesser performances the next year. In each case, individuals are often surprised when made aware of these predictable patterns of regression to the mean.

Why is the regression-to-the mean concept, while statistically valid, counterintuitive? Kahneman and Tversky (1973) suggest that the representativeness heuristic accounts for this systematic bias in judgment. They argue that individuals typically assume that future outcomes (for example, 1991 sales) will be maximally representative of past outcomes (1989 sales). Thus, we tend to naively develop predictions that are based upon the assumption of perfect correlation with past data.

In some unusual situations, individuals do intuitively expect a regression-to-the-mean effect. In 1980, when George Brett batted .384, most people

did not expect him to hit .384 the following year. When Wilt Chamberlain scored 100 points in a single game, most people did not expect him to score 100 points in his next game. When a historically 3.0 student got a 4.0 one semester, her friends did not expect a repeat performance the following semester. When a real estate agent sold five houses in one month (an abnormally high performance), his co-agents did not expect similar performance in the following month. Why is regression to the mean more intuitive in these cases? Because the performance is so extreme that we know it cannot last. Thus, under very unusual circumstances, we expect performance to regress. However, we generally do not recognize the regression effect in less extreme cases.

Consider Kahneman and Tversky's (1973) classic example in which the misconceptions surrounding regression led to overestimation of the effectiveness of punishment and the underestimation of the power of reward. Here, in a discussion about flight training, experienced instructors noted that praise for an exceptionally smooth landing was typically followed by a poorer landing on the next try, while harsh criticism after a rough landing was usually followed by an improvement on the next try. The instructors concluded that verbal rewards were detrimental to learning, while verbal punishments were beneficial. Obviously, the tendency of performance to regress to the mean can account for the results; verbal feedback may have had absolutely no effect. However, to the extent that the instructors were prone to biased decision making, they were prone to reach the false conclusion that punishment is more effective than positive reinforcement in shaping behavior.

How do managers respond when they do not acknowledge the regression principle? Consider an employee with very high performance in one performance period. He (and his boss) may inappropriately expect similar performance in the next period. What happens when his performance regresses toward the mean? He (and his boss) begin to make excuses for not meeting expectations. Obviously, they are likely to develop false explanations and may inappropriately plan their future efforts.

Bias 8—The Conjunction Fallacy

Problem 9: Linda is 31 years old, single, outspoken, and very bright. She majored in philosophy. As a student, she was deeply concerned with issues of discrimination and social justice, and she participated in antinuclear demonstrations.

Rank order the following eight descriptions in terms of the probability (likelihood) that they describe Linda:

a. Linda is a teacher in an elementary school.
b. Linda works in a bookstore and takes yoga classes.
c. Linda is active in the feminist movement.
d. Linda is a psychiatric social worker.
e. Linda is a member of the League of Women Voters.
f. Linda is a bank teller.
g. Linda is an insurance salesperson.
h. Linda is a bank teller who is active in the feminist movement.

Examine your rank orderings of descriptions C, F, and H. Most people rank order C as more likely than H and H as more likely than F. The reason for this ordering is that C-H-F is the order of the degree to which the descriptions are *representative* of the short profile of Linda. The description of Linda was constructed by Tversky and Kahneman to be representative of an active feminist and unrepresentative of a bank teller. Recall from the representativeness heuristic that people make judgments according to the degree to which a specific description corresponds to a broader category within their minds. Linda's description is more representative of a feminist than of a feminist bank teller, and is more representative of a feminist bank teller than of a bank teller. Thus, the representativeness heuristic accurately predicts that most individuals will rank order the items C-H-F.

Although the representativeness heuristic accurately predicts how individuals will respond, it also leads to another common, systematic distortion of human judgment—the **conjunction fallacy**

(Tversky & Kahneman, 1983). This is illustrated by a reexamination of the potential descriptions of Linda. One of the simplest and most fundamental qualitative laws of probability is that a subset (for example, being a bank teller and a feminist) cannot be more likely than a larger set that completely includes the subset (e.g., being a bank teller). Statistically speaking, the broad set "Linda is a bank teller" must be rated at least as likely, if not more so, than the description "Linda is a bank teller and a feminist." After all, there is some chance (although it is small) that Linda is a bank teller but not a feminist. Based upon this logic, a rational assessment of the likelihoods of Linda being depicted by the eight descriptions must include a more likely rank for F than H.

While simple statistics can demonstrate that a conjunction (a combination of two or more descriptors) cannot be more probable than any one of its descriptors, the conjunction fallacy predicts and demonstrates that a conjunction will be judged more probable than a single component descriptor when the conjunction appears more representative than the component descriptor. Intuitively, thinking of Linda as a feminist bank teller "feels" more correct than thinking of her as only a bank teller.

The conjunction fallacy can also operate based on greater *availability* of the conjunction than one of the unique descriptors (Yates & Carlson, 1986). That is, if the conjunction creates more intuitive matches with vivid events, acts, or people than a component of the conjunction, the conjunction is likely to be perceived falsely as more probable than the component. For example, Tversky and Kahneman (1983) found experts (in July 1982) to evaluate the probability of

a complete suspension of diplomatic relations between the USA and the Soviet Union, sometime in 1983

as less likely than the probability of

a Russian invasion of Poland, and a complete suspension of diplomatic relations between the USA and the Soviet Union, some time in 1983.

As earlier demonstrated, suspension is necessarily more likely than *invasion and suspension*. However, a

Russian invasion followed by a diplomatic crisis provides a more intuitively viable story than simply a diplomatic crisis. Similarly, in the domain of natural disasters, Kahneman and Tversky's subjects rated

a massive flood somewhere in North America in 1989, in which 1,000 people drown

as less likely than the probability of

an earthquake in California sometime in 1989, causing a flood in which more than 1,000 people drown.

It is obvious that the latter possibility is a subset of the former, and many other events could cause the flood in North America.

Tversky and Kahneman (1983) have shown that the conjunction fallacy is likely to lead to deviations from rationality in the judgments of sporting events, criminal behavior, international relations, and medical judgments. Our obvious concern with biased decision making resulting from the conjunction fallacy is that if we make systematic deviations from rationality in the prediction of future outcomes, we will be less prepared for dealing with future events.

Summary. This discussion concludes our examination of the five biases (insensitivity to base rates, insensitivity to sample size, misconceptions of chance, regression to the mean, and the conjunction fallacy) that emanate from the use of the representativeness heuristic. Experience has taught us that the likelihood of a specific occurrence *is* related to the likelihood of a group of occurrences that that specific occurrence represents. Unfortunately, we tend to overuse this information in making decisions. The five biases we have just explored illustrate the systematic irrationalities that can occur in our judgments when we are not aware of this overreliance.

BIASES EMANATING FROM ANCHORING AND ADJUSTMENT

Bias 9—Insufficient Anchor Adjustment

Problem 10: A newly hired engineer for a computer firm in the Boston metropolitan area

has four years of experience and good all-around qualifications. When asked to estimate the starting salary for this employee, my secretary (knowing very little about the profession or the industry) guessed an annual salary of $23,000. What is your estimate?

$_____ per year.

Was your answer affected by my secretary's response? Most people do not think that my secretary's response affected their response. However, individuals *are* affected by the fairly irrelevant information contained in my secretary's estimate. Reconsider how you would have responded if my secretary had estimated $80,000. On average, individuals give higher salary estimates to the problem when the secretary's estimate is stated as $80,000 than when it is stated as $23,000. Why? Studies have found that people develop estimates by starting from an initial anchor, based upon whatever information is provided, and adjusting from there to yield a final answer. Slovic and Lichtenstein (1971) have provided conclusive evidence that adjustments away from anchors are usually not sufficient to negate the effects of the anchor. In all cases, answers are biased toward the initial anchor, even if it is irrelevant. Different starting points yield different answers. Tversky and Kahneman (1973) named this phenomenon **anchoring and adjustment**.

Tversky and Kahneman (1974) provide systematic, empirical evidence of the anchoring effect. For example, in one study, subjects were asked to estimate the percentage of African countries in the United Nations. For each subject, a *random* number (obtained by an observed spin of a roulette wheel) was given as a starting point. From there, subjects were asked to state whether the actual value of the quantity was higher or lower than this random value and then develop their best estimate for the actual quantity. It was found that the *arbitrary* values from the roulette wheel had a substantial impact on estimates. For example, for groups that received 10 countries and 65 countries as starting points, the median estimates were 25 and 45, respectively. Thus, even though the subjects were aware that the anchor was random and unrelated to the judgment task, the anchor had a dramatic effect on their judgment. Interestingly, paying subjects differentially based upon accuracy did not reduce the magnitude of the anchoring effect.

Salary negotiations represent a very common context for observing anchoring in the managerial world. For example, pay increases often come in the form of a percentage increase. A firm may have an average increase of 8 percent, with increases for specific employees varying from 3 percent to 13 percent. While society has led us to accept such systems as equitable, I believe that such a system falls victim to anchoring and leads to substantial inequities. What happens if an employee has been *substantially* underpaid to begin with? The pay system described does not rectify past inequities, since a pay increase of 11 percent will probably leave that employee still underpaid. Conversely, the system would work in the employee's favor had she been overpaid. It is common for an employer to ask job applicants their current salaries. Why? Employers are searching for a value from which they can anchor an adjustment. If the employee is worth far more than his current salary, the anchoring and adjustment hypothesis predicts that the firm will make an offer below the employee's true value. Does this figure provide fully accurate information about the true worth of the employee? I think not. Thus, the use of such compensation systems accepts past inequities as an anchor and makes inadequate adjustments from that point. Further, these findings suggest that in deciding what offer to make to a potential employee, any anchor that creeps into the discussion is likely to have an inappropriate effect on the eventual offer, even if the anchor is "ignored" as being ridiculous.

There are numerous examples of the anchoring-and-adjustment phenomenon in everyday life.

• In education, children are tracked by a school system that may categorize them into a certain level of performance at an early age. For example, a child who is anchored in the *C* group may meet expectations of mediocre performance. Conversely, a child of similar abilities anchored in the

A track may strive to meet expectations, which will keep him in the *A* track.

• We have all fallen victim to the first-impression syndrome when meeting someone for the first time. We often place so much emphasis on first impressions that we do not adjust our opinion appropriately at a later date.

• Prior to 1973–1974, the speed limit on most interstate highways was 65 miles per hour (mph), with a normal cruising speed in the left-hand lane of 70 to 75 mph. This did not seem to be an extraordinarily unsafe speed to most people. After 1974, the speed limit was reduced to 55 mph. Most people changed their judgments to view a speed of 70 to 75 mph as extremely unsafe— "something only crazy kids would do." Today, the reinstitution of the 65 mph limit on nonurban highways has rejustified the safety of the 70 to 75 mph speed.

In a fascinating study of anchoring and adjustment in the real estate market, Northcraft and Neale (1987) surveyed an association of real estate brokers, who indicated that they believed that they could assess the value of properties to within 5 percent of their true or appraised value. Further, they were unanimous in stating that they did not factor the listing price of the property into their personal estimate of its "true" value. Northcraft and Neale then asked four groups of professional real estate brokers and undergraduate students to estimate the value of a real house. Both brokers and students were randomly assigned to one of four experimental groups. In each group, all participants were given a 10-page packet of information about the house that was being sold. The packet included not only background on the house, but also considerable information about prices and characteristics of other houses in the area that had recently been sold. The only difference in the information given to the four groups was the listing price for the house, which was selected to be +11 percent, +4 percent, −4 percent, and −11 percent of the actual appraised value of the property. After reading the material, all participants toured the house, as well as the surrounding neighborhood. Participants were then asked for their estimate of the house's price. The final results suggested that *both* brokers and students were *significantly* affected by the listing price (the anchor) in determining the value. While the students readily admitted the role that the listing price played in their decision-making process, the brokers flatly denied their use of the listing price as an anchor for their evaluations of the property—despite the evidence to the contrary. This study provides convincing data to indicate that even experts are susceptible to the anchoring bias. Furthermore, experts are less likely to realize their use of this bias in making decisions.

Joyce and Biddle (1981) have also provided empirical support for the anchoring-and-adjustment effect on practicing auditors of Big Eight accounting firms. Specifically, subjects in one condition were asked the following:

It is well known that many cases of management fraud go undetected even when competent annual audits are performed. The reason, of course, is that Generally Accepted Auditing Standards are not designed specifically to detect executive-level management fraud. We are interested in obtaining an estimate from practicing auditors of the prevalence of executive-level management fraud as a first step in ascertaining the scope of the problem.

1. Based on your audit experience, is the incidence of significant executive-level management fraud more than 10 in each 1,000 firms (that is, 1 percent) audited by Big Eight accounting firms?

   a. Yes, more than 10 in each 1,000 Big Eight clients have significant executive-level management fraud.

   b. No, fewer than 10 in each 1,000 Big Eight clients have significant executive-level management fraud.

2. What is your estimate of the number of Big Eight clients per 1,000 that have significant executive-level management fraud? (Fill in the blank below with the appropriate number.)

   _____ in each 1,000 Big Eight clients have significant executive-level management fraud.

The second condition differed only in that subjects were asked whether the fraud incidence was more or less than 200 in each 1,000 audited, rather than 10 in 1,000. Subjects in the former condition estimated a fraud incidence of 16.52 per 1,000 on average, compared with an estimated fraud incidence of 43.11 per 1,000 in the second condition! Here, even professional auditors fell victim to anchoring and adjustment.

The tendency to make insufficient adjustments is a direct result of the anchoring-and-adjustment heuristic.... Interestingly, Nisbett and Ross (1980) present an argument that suggests that the anchoring-and-adjustment bias itself dictates that it will be very difficult to get *you* to change your decision-making strategies as a result of reading this book. They argue that each of the heuristics that we identify are currently serving as your cognitive anchors and are central to your current judgment processes. Thus, any cognitive strategy that I suggest must be presented and understood in a manner that will force you to break your existing cognitive anchors. Based on the evidence in this section, this should be a difficult challenge— but one that is important enough to be worth the effort!

Bias 10—Conjunctive and Disjunctive Events Bias

Problem 11: Which of the following appears most likely? Which appears second most likely?

a. Drawing a red marble from a bag containing 50 percent red marbles and 50 percent white marbles.

b. Drawing a red marble seven times in succession, with replacement (a selected marble is put back in the bag before the next marble is selected), from a bag containing 90 percent red marbles and 10 percent white marbles.

c. Drawing at least one red marble in seven tries, with replacement, from a bag containing 10 percent red marbles and 90 percent white marbles.

The most common answer in ordering the preferences is B-A-C. Interestingly, the correct order of likelihood is C (52 percent), A (50 percent), B (48 percent)—the exact opposite of the most common intuitive pattern! This result illustrates a general bias to overestimate the probability of conjunctive events—events that must occur in conjunction with one another (Bar-Hillel, 1973)—and to underestimate the probability of disjunctive events—events that occur independently (Tversky & Kahneman, 1974). Thus, when multiple events all need to occur (problem B), we overestimate the true likelihood, while if only one of many events needs to occur (problem C), we underestimate the true likelihood.

Kahneman and Tversky (1974) explain these effects in terms of the anchoring-and-adjustment heuristic. They argue that the probability of any one event occurring (for example, drawing one red marble) provides a natural anchor for the judgment of the total probability. Since adjustment from an anchor is typically insufficient, the perceived likelihood of choice B stays inappropriately close to 90 percent, while the perceived probability of choice C stays inappropriately close to 10 percent.

How is each of these biases manifested in an applied context? The overestimation of conjunctive events is a powerful explanation of the timing problems in projects that require multistage planning. Individuals, businesses, and governments frequently fall victim to the conjunction-events bias in terms of timing and budgets. Public works projects seldom finish on time or on budget. New product ventures frequently take longer than expected.

Consider the following:

• You are planning a construction project that consists of five distinct components. Your schedule is tight, and every component must be on time in order to meet a contractual deadline. Will you meet this deadline?

• You are managing a consulting project that consists of six teams, each of which is analyzing a different alternative. The alternatives cannot be compared until all teams complete their portion. Will you meet the deadline?

• After three years of study, doctoral students typically dramatically overestimate the likelihood of completing their dissertations within a year. At this stage, they typically can tell you how long each remaining component will take. Why do they not finish in one year?

The underestimation of disjunctive events explains our surprise when an unlikely event occurs. As Tversky and Kahneman (1974) argue, "A complex system, such as a nuclear reactor or the human body, will malfunction if any of its essential components fails. Even when the likelihood of failure in each component is slight, the probability of an overall failure can be high if many components are involved." In *Normal Accidents*, Perrow (1984) argues against the safety of technologies like nuclear reactors and DNA research. He fears that society significantly underestimates the likelihood of system failure because of our judgmental failure to realize the multitude of things that can go wrong in these incredibly complex and interactive systems.

The understanding of our underestimation of disjunctive events also has its positive side. Consider the following:

It's Monday evening (10:00 P.M.). You get a phone call telling you that you must be at the Chicago office by 9:30 A.M. the next morning. You call all five airlines that have flights that get into Chicago by 9:00 A.M. Each has one flight, and all the flights are booked. When you ask the probability of getting on each of the flights if you show up at the airport in the morning, you are disappointed to hear probabilities of 30 percent, 25 percent, 15 percent, 20 percent, and 25 percent. Consequently, you do not expect to get to Chicago in time.

In this case, the disjunctive bias leads you to expect the worst. In fact, if the probabilities given by the airlines are unbiased and independent there is a 73 percent chance of getting on one of the flights (assuming that you can arrange to be at the right ticket counter at the right time)!

Bias 11—Overconfidence

Problem 12: Listed below are 10 uncertain quantities. Do not look up any information on these items. For each, write down your best estimate of the quantity. Next, put a lower and upper bound around your estimate, such that you are 98 percent confident that your range surrounds the actual quantity.

___ **a**. Mobil Oil's sales in 1987

___ **b**. IBM's assets in 1987

___ **c**. Chrysler's profit in 1987

___ **d**. The number of U.S. industrial firms in 1987 with sales greater than those of Consolidated Papers

___ **e**. The U.S. gross national product in 1945

___ **f**. The amount of taxes collected by the U.S. Internal Revenue Service in 1970

___ **g**. The length (in feet) of the Chesapeake Bay Bridge-Tunnel

___ **h**. The area (in square miles) of Brazil

___ **i**. The size of the black population of San Francisco in 1970

___ **j**. The dollar value of Canadian exports of lumber in 1977

How many of your 10 ranges will actually surround the true quantities? If you set your ranges so that you were 98 percent confident, you should expect to correctly bound approximately 9.8 or 9 to 10 of the 10 quantities. Let's look at the correct answers: (a) $51,223,000,000; (b) $63,688,000,000; (c) $1,289,700,000; (d) 381; (e) $212,300,000,000; (f) $195,722,096,497; (g) 93,203; (h) 3,286,470; (i) 96,078; (j) $2,386,282,000.

How many of your ranges actually surrounded the true quantities? If you surround 9–10, we can conclude that you were appropriately confident in your estimation ability. Most people only surround between 3 (30 percent) and 7 (70 percent), despite claiming a 98 percent confidence that each of the ranges will surround the true value. Why? Most of us are *overconfident* in our estimation abilities and do not acknowledge the actual uncertainty that exists.

In Alpert and Raiffa's (1969) initial demonstration of overconfidence based upon 1,000 observations (100 subjects on 10 items), 42.6 percent of quantities fell outside 90% confidence ranges. Since then, overconfidence has been identified as a common judgmental pattern and demonstrated in a wide variety of settings. For example, Fischhoff, Slovic, and Lichtenstein (1977) found that subjects who assigned odds of 1,000:1 of being correct were correct only 81 to 88 percent of the time. For odds of 1,000,000:1, their answers were correct only 90 to 96 percent of the time! Hazard and Peterson (1973) identified overconfidence among members of the armed forces, while Cambridge and Shreckengost (1980) found extreme overconfidence in CIA agents.

The most well-established finding in the overconfidence literature is the tendency of people to be most overconfident of the correctness of their answers when asked to respond to questions of moderate to extreme difficulty (Fischhoff, Slovic, & Lichtenstein, 1977; Koriat, Lichtenstein, & Fischhoff, 1980; Lichtenstein & Fischhoff, 1977, 1980). That is, as subjects' knowledge of a question decreases, they do not correspondingly decrease their level of confidence (Nickerson & McGoldrick, 1965; Pitz, 1974). However, subjects typically demonstrate no overconfidence, and often some underconfidence, to questions with which they are familiar. Thus we should be most alert to overconfidence in areas outside of our expertise.

There is a large degree of controversy over the explanations of why overconfidence exists (see Lichtenstein, Fischhoff, & Phillips [1982] for an extensive discussion). Tversky and Kahneman (1974) explain overconfidence in terms of anchoring. Specifically, they argue that when individuals are asked to set a confidence range around an answer, their initial estimate serves as an anchor which biases their estimation of confidence intervals in both directions. As explained earlier, adjustments from an anchor are usually insufficient, resulting in an overly narrow confidence band.

In their review of the overconfidence literature, Lichtenstein, Fischhoff, and Phillips (1982) suggest two viable strategies for eliminating overconfidence. First, they have found that giving people feedback about their overconfidence *based on their judgments* has been moderately successful at reducing this bias. Second, Koriat, Lichtenstein, and Fischhoff (1980) found that asking people to explain why their answers might be wrong (or far off the mark) can decrease overconfidence by getting subjects to see contradictions in their judgment.

Why should you be concerned about overconfidence? After all, it has probably given you the courage in the past to attempt endeavors that have stretched your abilities. However, consider the following:

• You are a medical doctor and are considering performing a difficult operation. The patient's family needs to know the likelihood of his surviving the operation. You respond "95 percent." Are you guilty of malpractice if you tend to be overconfident in your projections of survival?

• You work for the Nuclear Regulatory Commission and are 99.9 percent confident that a reactor will not leak. Can we trust your confidence? If not, can we run the enormous risks of overconfidence in this domain?

• Your firm has been threatened with a multimillion dollar law suit. If you lose, your firm is out of business. You are 98 percent confident that the firm will not lose in court. Is this degree of certainty sufficient for you to recommend rejecting an out-of-court settlement? Based on what you know now, are you still comfortable with your 98 percent estimate?

• You have developed a market plan for a new product. You are so confident in your plan that you have not developed any contingencies for early market failure. The plan of attack falls apart. Will your overconfidence wipe out any hope of expediting changes in the marketing strategy?

In each of these examples, we have introduced serious problems that can result from the tendency to be overconfident. Thus, while confidence in your abilities is necessary for achievement in life, and perhaps to inspire confidence in others, you may want to monitor your overconfidence to achieve more effective professional decision making.

Summary. The need for an initial anchor weighs strongly in our decision-making processes when we try to estimate likelihoods (such as the probability of on-time project completion) or establish values (like what salary to offer). Experience has taught us that starting from somewhere is easier than starting from nowhere in determining such figures. However, as the last three biases (insufficient anchor adjustment, conjunctive and disjunctive events bias, and overconfidence) show, we frequently overrely on these anchors and seldom question their validity or appropriateness in a particular situation. As with the other heuristics, we frequently fail even to realize that this heuristic is impacting our judgments.

TWO MORE GENERAL BIASES

Bias 12—The Confirmation Trap

Problem 13: (Adapted from Einhorn and Hogarth, 1978)
It is claimed that when a particular analyst predicts a rise in the market, the market always rises. You are to check this claim. Examine the information available about the following four events (cards):

Card 1 Prediction: Favorable report	Card 2 Prediction: Unfavorable report
Card 3 Outcome: Risk in the market	Card 4 Outcome: Fall in the market

You currently see the predictions (cards 1 and 2) *or* outcomes (cards 3 and 4) associated with four events. You are seeing one side of a card. On the other side of cards 1 and 2 is the actual outcome, while on the other side of cards 3 and 4 is the prediction that the analyst made. Evidence about the claim is potentially available by turning over the card(s). Which cards would you turn over for the evidence that you need to check the analyst's claim? (Circle the appropriate cards.)

Consider the two most common responses: (1) "Card 1 (only)—that is the only card that I know has a favorable report and thus allows me to see whether a favorable report is actually followed by a rise in the market" and (2) "Cards 1 and 3—card 1 serves as a direct test, while card 3 allows me to see whether they made a favorable report when I know the market rose." Logical? Most people think that at least one of these two common responses is logical. However, both strategies demonstrate the tendency to search for confirming, rather than disconfirming, evidence. Einhorn and Hogarth (1978) argue that 1 and 4 is the correct answer to this quiz item. Why? Consider the following logic:

Card 1 allows me to test the claim that a rise in the market will add confirming evidence, while a fall in the market will fully disconfirm the claim, since the claim is that the market will always *rise following a favorable report. Card 2 has no relevant information, since the claim does not address unfavorable reports by the analyst. While card 3 can add confirming evidence to card 1, it provides no unique information, since it cannot disconfirm the claim. That is, if an unfavorable report was made on card 3, then the event is not addressed by the claim. Finally, card 4 is critical. If it says "favorable report" on the other side, the claim is disconfirmed.*

If you chose cards 1 and 3, you may have obtained a wealth of confirmatory information and were likely to inappropriately accept the claim. Only by including card 4 is there potential for disconfirmation of the hypothesis. Why do very few subjects select card 4? *Most of us seek confirmatory evidence and exclude the search for disconfirming information from our*

decision process. However, it is typically not possible to know something to be true without checking for possible disconfirmation.

The initial demonstration of our tendency to ignore disconfirming information was provided in a series of projects by Wason (1960, 1968a, 1968b). In the first study, Wason (1960) presented subjects with the three-number sequence 2–4–6. The subject's task was to discover the numeric rule to which the three numbers conformed. To determine the rule, subjects were allowed to generate other sets of three numbers that the experimenter would classify as either conforming or not conforming to the rule. At any point, subjects could stop when they thought that they had discovered the rule. How would you approach this problem?

Wason's rule was "any three ascending numbers"—a solution which required the accumulation of disconfirming, rather than confirming, evidence. For example, if you thought the rule included "the difference between the first two numbers equaling the difference between the last two numbers" (a common expectation), you must try sequences that do *not* conform to this rule to find the actual rule. Trying the sequences 1–2–3, 10–15–20, 122–126–130, and so on, will only lead you into the confirmation trap. In Wason's (1960) experiment, only 6 out of 29 subjects found the correct rule the first time that they thought they knew the answer. Wason concluded that obtaining the correct solution necessitates "a willingness to attempt to falsify hypotheses, and thus to test those intuitive ideas which so often carry the feeling of certitude" (p. 139).

This result was also observed by Einhorn and Hogarth (1978) with a sample of 23 statisticians. When that group responded to a problem very similar to problem 13, eleven asked for card 1; one asked for card 1 or 3; one asked for any one card; two asked for card 1 or 4; three asked for card 4 alone; and only five trained statisticians asked for cards 1 and 4. Thus, this group tended to realize the worthlessness of card 3 but failed to realize the importance of card 4. This leads to the conclusion that the tendency to exclude disconfirming information in the search process is not eliminated by the for-

TABLE 15.2
Summary of 13 Biases

Bias	Description
Biases Emanating from the Availability Heuristic	
1. Ease of recall	Individuals judge events that are more easily recalled from memory, based upon vividness or recency, to be more numerous than events of equal frequency whose instances are less easily recalled.
2. Retrievability	Individuals are biased in their assessments of the frequency of events based upon how their memory structures affect the search process.
3. Presumed associations	Individuals tend to overestimate the probability of two events co-occurring based upon the number of similar associations that are easily recalled, whether from experience or social influence.
Biases Emanating from the Representativeness Heuristic	
4. Insensitivity to base rates	Individuals tend to ignore base rates in assessing the likelihood of events when any other descriptive information is provided—even if it is irrelevant.
5. Insensitivity to sample size	Individuals frequently fail to appreciate the role of sample size in assessing the reliability of sample information.
6. Misconceptions of chance	Individuals expect that a sequence of data generated by a random process will look "random," even when the sequence is too short for those expectations to be statistically valid.
7. Regression to the mean	Individuals tend to ignore the fact that extreme events tend to regress to the mean on subsequent trials.
8. The conjunction fallacy	Individuals falsely judge that conjunctions (two events co-occurring) are more probable than a global set of occurrences of which the conjunction is a subset.
Biases Emanating from Anchoring and Adjustment	
9. Insufficient anchor adjustment	Individuals make estimates for values based upon an initial value (derived from past events, random assignment, or whatever information is available) and typically make insufficient adjustments from that anchor when establishing a final value.
10. Conjunctive & disjunctive events bias	Individuals exhibit a bias toward overestimating the probability of conjunctive events and underestimating the probability of disjunctive events.
11. Overconfidence	Individuals tend to be overconfident of the infallibility of their judgments when answering moderately to extremely difficult questions.
Two More General Biases	
12. The confirmation trap	Individuals tend to seek confirmatory information for what they think is true and neglect the search for disconfirmatory evidence.
13. Hindsight	After finding out whether or not an event occurred, individuals tend to overestimate the degree to which they would have predicted the correct outcome.

mal scientific training that is expected of statisticians.

It is easy to observe the confirmation trap in your decision-making processes. You make a tentative decision (to buy a new car, to hire a particular employee, to start research and development on a new product line). Do you search for data that support your decision before making the final commitment? Most of us do. However, the existence of the confirmation trap implies that the search for challenging, or disconfirming, evidence will provide the most useful insights. For example, in confirming your decision to hire a particular employee, it is probably easy to find supporting positive information on the individual, but in fact the key issue may be the degree to which negative information on this individual, as well as positive information on another potential applicant, also exists.

Bias 13—Hindsight

Consider the following scenarios:

• You are an avid football fan, and you are watching a critical game in which your team is behind 35–31. With three seconds left, and the ball on the opponent's three-yard line, the quarterback *unsuccessfully* calls a pass play into the corner of the endzone. You immediately respond, "I knew that he shouldn't have called that play."

• You are riding in an unfamiliar area, and your spouse is driving. You approach an unmarked fork in the road, and your spouse decides to go to the right. Four miles and fifteen minutes later, it is clear that you are lost. You blurt out, "I knew that you should have turned left at the fork."

• A manager who works for you hired a new supervisor last year. You were well aware of the choices he had at the time and allowed him to choose the new employee on his own. You have just received production data on every supervisor. The data on the new supervisor are terrible. You call in the manager and claim, "There was plenty of evidence that he (the supervisor) was not the man for the job."

• As director of marketing in a consumer-goods or-

ganization, you have just presented the results of an extensive six-month study on current consumer preferences for the products manufactured by your organization. After the conclusion of your presentation, a senior vice-president responds, "I don't know why we spent so much time and money to collect these data. I could have told you what the results were going to be."

Do you recognize yourself? Do you recognize someone else? Each scenario is representative of a phenomenon that has been named "the Monday morning quarterback syndrome" (Fischhoff, 1975b), "the knew-it-all-along effect" (Wood, 1978), "creeping determinism" (Fischhoff, 1975a, 1975b, 1980), and "the hindsight bias" (Fischhoff, 1975a, 1975b). This body of research demonstrates that people are typically not very good at recalling or reconstructing the way an uncertain situation appeared to them *before* finding out the results of the decision. What play would have you called? Did you *really* know that your spouse should have turned left? Was there *really* evidence that the selected supervisor was not the man for the job? Could the senior vice-president *really* have predicted the results of the survey? Perhaps our intuition is sometimes accurate, but we tend to overestimate what we knew and distort our beliefs about what we knew beforehand based upon what we later found out. The phenomenon occurs when people look back on the judgment of others, as well as of themselves.

Fischhoff has provided substantial evidence of the prevalence of the hindsight effect (1975a, 1975b, 1977; Fischhoff & Beyth, 1975; Slovic & Fischhoff, 1977). For example, Fischhoff (1975a) examined the differences between hindsight and foresight in the context of judging historical events and clinical instances. In one study, subjects were divided into five groups and asked to read a passage about the war between the British and Gurka forces in 1814. One group was not told the result of the war. The remaining four groups of subjects were told either that (1) the British won; (2) the Gurkas won; (3) a military stalemate was reached with no peace settlement; or (4) a military stalemate was reached with a peace settlement.

Obviously, only one group was told the truthful outcome—(1) in this case. Each subject was then asked what his or her subjective assessments of the probability of each of the outcomes would have been without the benefit of knowing the reported outcome. Based upon this and other varied examples, the strong, consistent finding was that knowledge of an outcome increases an individual's belief about the degree to which he or she would have predicted that outcome without the benefit of that knowledge.

A number of explanations of the hindsight effect have been offered. One of the most pervasive is to explain hindsight in terms of the heuristics discussed in this book (Tversky & Kahneman, 1974). Anchoring may contribute to this bias when individuals interpret their prior subjective judgments of probabilities of an event's occurring in reference to the anchor of knowing whether or not that outcome actually occurred. Since adjustments to anchors are known to be inadequate, hindsight knowledge can be expected to bias perceptions of what one thinks one knew in foresight. Further, to the extent that the various pieces of data on the event vary in terms of their support for the actual outcome, evidence that is consistent with the known outcome may become cognitively more salient and thus more *available* in memory (Slovic & Fischhoff, 1977). This will lead an individual to justify a claimed foresight in view of "the facts provided." Finally, the relevance of a particular piece of data may later be judged important to the extent to which it is *representative* of the final observed outcome.

Claiming that what has happened was predictable based on foresight knowledge puts us in a position of using hindsight to criticize another's foresight judgment. In the short run, hindsight has a number of advantages. In particular, it is very flattering to believe that your judgment is far better than it actually is! However, hindsight reduces our ability to learn from the past and to evaluate objectively the decisions of ourselves and others. Leading researchers in performance evaluation (cf. Feldman, 1981) and decision theory (cf. Einhorn & Hogarth, 1981) have argued that, where possible, individuals should be rewarded based on the process and logic of their decisions, not

on the results. A decision maker who makes a high-quality decision that does not work out should be rewarded, not punished. The rationale for this argument is that the results are affected by a variety of factors outside the direct control of the decision maker. However, to the extent that we rely on results and the hindsight corresponding to them, we will inappropriately evaluate the logic used by the decision maker in terms of the outcomes that occurred, not the methods that were employed.

INTEGRATION AND COMMENTARY

Heuristics, or rules of thumb, are the cognitive tools we use to simplify decision making. The preceding pages have described 13 of the most common biases that result when we overrely on these judgmental heuristics. These biases are summarized in Table 15.2, along with their associated heuristics. Again, it should be emphasized that more than one heuristic can be operating on our decision-making processes at any one time. We have attempted to identify only the dominant heuristic affecting each bias. In the last two biases, their effects are so broad that it is difficult to even determine a dominant heuristic.

While the use of quiz items has emphasized the biases that our heuristics create, it should be stressed that, overall, the use of these heuristics results in far more adequate than inadequate decisions. Our minds adopt these heuristics because, on average, any loss in quality of decisions is outweighed by the time saved. However, we argue against blanket acceptance of heuristics based upon this logic. First, as we have demonstrated in this chapter, there are many instances in which the loss in the quality of decisions far outweighs the time saved by the use of the heuristics. Second, the foregoing logic suggests that we have voluntarily accepted tradeoffs associated with the use of heuristics. But in reality, we have not: Most of us are unaware of their existence and their ongoing impact upon our decision making. The difficulty with heuristics is that we typically do not recognize that we are using them, and we consequently fail to distinguish between situations in which their use is more and less appropriate.

REFERENCES

Alba, J. W., and Marmorstein, H. (1987). The effects of frequency knowledge on consumer decision making. *Journal of Consumer Research* 14, 14–25.

Alpert, M., and Raiffa, H. (1969). A progress report on the training of probability assessors. Unpublished manuscript.

Bar-Hillel, M. (1973). On the subjective probability of compound events. *Organizational Behavior and Human Performance* 9, 396–406.

Cambridge, R. M., and Shreckengost, R. C. (1980). Are you sure? The subjective probability assessment test. Unpublished manuscript. Langley, VA: Office of Training, Central Intelligence Agency.

Chapman, L. J., and Chapman, J. P. (1967). Genesis of popular but erroneous diagnostic observations. *Journal of Abnormal Psychology* 72, 193–204.

Cox, A. D., and Summers, J. O. (1987). Heuristics and biases in the intuitive projection of retail sales. *Journal of Marketing Research* 24, 290–297.

Curran, J. J. (1987). Why investors make the wrong choices. *Fortune, 1987 Investor's Guide.*

Einhorn, H. J., and Hogarth, R. M. (1987). Confidence in Judgment: Persistence in the illusion of validity. *Psychological Review* 85, 395–416.

Einhorn, H. J., and Hogarth, R. M. (1981). Behavioral decision theory: Processes of judgment and choice. *Annual Review of Psychology* 32, 53–88.

Feldman, J. M. (1981). Beyond attribution theory: Cognitive processes in performance appraisal. *Journal of Applied Psychology* 66, 127–148.

Fischhoff, B. (1975a). Hindsight = foresight: The effect of outcome knowledge on judgment under uncertainty. *Journal of Experimental Psychology: Human Perception and Performance* 1, 228–299.

Fischhoff, B. (1975b). Hindsight: Thinking backward. *Psychology Today* 8, 71–76.

Fischhoff, B. (1977). Cognitive liabilities and product liability. *Journal of Products Liability* 1, 207–220.

Fischhoff, B. (1980). For those condemned to study the past: Reflections on historical judgment. In R. A. Shweder and D. W. Fiske (Eds.). *New directions for methodology of behavior science: Fallible judgement in behavioral research.* San Francisco: Jossey-Bass.

Fischhoff, B., and Beyth, R. (1975). "I knew it would happen":—Remembered probabilities of once-future things. *Organizational Behavior and Human Performance* 13, 1–16.

Fischhoff, B., Slovic, P., and Lichtenstein, S. (1977). Knowing with certainty: The appropriateness of extreme confidence. *Journal of Experimental Psychology: Human Perception and Performance* 3, 552–564.

Gillovich, T., Vallone, R., and Tversky, A. (1985). The hot hand in basketball: On the misperception of random sequences. *Cognitive Psychology* 17, 295–314.

Hazard, T. H., and Peterson, C. R. (1973). Odds versus probabilities for categorical events (Technical report. 73–2). McLean, VA: Decisions and Designs, Inc.

Joyce, E. J., and Biddle, G. C. (1981). Anchoring and adjustment in probabilistic inference in auditing. *Journal of Accounting Research* 19, 120–145.

Kahneman, D., and Tversky, A. (1972). Subjective probability: A judgement of representativeness. *Cognitive Psychology* 3, 430–454.

Kahneman, D., and Tversky, A. (1973). On the psychology of prediction. *Psychological Review* 80, 237–251.

Koriat, A., Lichtenstein, S., and Fischhoff, B. (1980). Reasons for confidence. *Journal of Experimental Psychology: Human Learning and Memory* 6, 107–118.

Lichtenstein, S. and Fischhoff, B. (1977). Do those who know more also know more about how much they know? The calibration of probability judgments. *Organizational Behavior and Human Performance* 20, 159–183.

Lichtenstein, S., and Fischhoff, B. (1980). Training for calibration. *Organizational Behavior and Human Performance* 26, 149–171.

Lichtenstein, S., Fischhoff, B., and Phillips, L. D. (1982). Calibration of probabilities: State of the art to 1980. In D. Kahneman, P. Slovic, and A. Tversky (Eds.), *Judgment under uncertainty: Heuristics and biases*. New York: Cambridge University Press.

Nickerson, R. S., and McGoldrick, C. C. (1985). Confidence ratings and level of performance on a judgmental task. *Perceptual and Motor Skills* 20, 311–316.

Nisbett, R., and Ross, L. (1980). *Human inference: Strategies and shortcomings of social judgment.* Englewood Cliffs, NJ: Prentice-Hall.

Northcraft, G. B., and Neale, M. A. (1987). Experts, amateurs and real estate: An anchoring-and-adjustment perspective on property pricing decisions. *Organizational Behavior and Human Decision Processes* 39, 84–97.

Perrow, C. (1984). *Normal accidents.* New York: Basic Books.

Pitz, G. F. (1974). Subjective probability distributions for imperfectly known quantities. In L. W. Gregg (Ed.), *Knowledge and cognition* (pp. 29–41). New York: Wiley.

Slovic, P., and Fischhoff, B. (1977). On the psychology of experimental surprises. *Journal of Experimental Psychology: Human Perception and Performance* 3, 544–551.

Slovic, P., and Lichtenstein, S. (1971). Comparison of Bayesian and regression approaches in the study of information processing in judgment. *Organizational Behavior and Human Performance* 6, 649–744.

Slovic, P., Lichtenstein, S., and Fischhoff, B. (1979). Images of disaster: Perception and acceptance of risks from nuclear power. In G. Goodman and W. Rowe (Eds.), *Energy risk management*. London: Academic Press.

Tversky, A., and Kahneman, D. (1971). The belief in the "law of numbers." *Psychological Bulletin* 76, 105–110.

Tversky, A., and Kahneman, D. (1973). Availability: A heuristic for judging frequency and probability. *Cognitive Psychology* 5, 207–232.

Tversky, A., and Kahneman, D. (1974). Judgment under uncertainty: Heuristics and biases. *Science* 185, 1124–1131.

Tversky, A., and Kahneman, D. (1983). Extensional versus intuitive reasoning: The conjunction fallacy in probability judgment. *Psychological Review* 90, 293–315.

Wason, P. C. (1960). On the failure to eliminate the hypotheses in a conceptual task. *Quarterly Journal of Experimental Psychology* 12, 129–140.

Wason, P. C. (1968a). Reason about a rule. *Quarterly Journal of Experimental Psychology* 20, 273–283.

Wason, P. C. (1986b). On the failure to eliminate hypothesis . . . A second look. In P. C. Wason and P. N. Johnson-Laird (Eds.), *Thinking and reasoning*. Harmandsworth: Penguin.

Wood, G. (1978). The knew-it-all-along effect. *Journal of Experimental Psychology: Human Perception and Performance* 4, 345–353.

16.   THE MYTHICAL FIXED-PIE

Max H. Bazerman and Margaret A. Neal

The best negotiations end in a resolution that satisfies all parties. Such agreements are rare. More commonly, successful negotiations end in trade-offs. Where each party gives up something of lesser value to them in return for something of greater. Because people often value the multiple issues in a negotiation differently, trade-offs can speed up and improve a conflict's resolution.

A *distributive* negotiation usually involves a single issue—a "fixed-pie"—in which one person gains at the expense of the other. For example, haggling over the price of a rug in a bazaar is a distributive negotiation. In most conflicts, however, more than one issue is at stake, and each party values the issues differently. The outcomes available are no longer a fixed-pie divided among all parties. An agreement can be found that is better for both parties than what they would have reached through distributive negotiation. This is an *integrative* negotiation.

However, parties in a negotiation often don't find these beneficial trade-offs because each *assumes* its interests *directly* conflict with those of the other party. "What is good for the other side must be bad for us" is a common and unfortunate perspective that most people have. This is the mind-set we call the *mythical* "fixed-pie."

For example, it's Friday evening and you and your spouse are going to dinner and a movie. Unfortunately, you prefer different restaurants and different movies. It's easy to think of the negotiation as purely distributive—your choices are at your spouse's expense—and compromise on both issues. But if you look beyond the fixed-pie and consider how much you value each of your choices, you may

discover that you care more about choosing the restaurant and your spouse cares more about choosing the movie. That way, you can find a restaurant and movie combination that you each value over a compromise. This is an integrative agreement.

Business negotiations also provide opportunities for mutually beneficial trade-offs. Consider the following problem:

A large corporation (CORP) wanted to make a friendly acquisition of one of its suppliers, a privately held company (PRIVATE). Both agreed that PRIVATE would be more valuable as a part of CORP. Despite this agreement, they were unable to complete the acquisition. CORP had offered $14 million for PRIVATE, but PRIVATE had insisted on $16 million. Efforts at a compromise price failed. Neither side found a $15 million price acceptable.

With both sides expecting PRIVATE to be worth more as part of CORP, how could both find the $15 million price unacceptable? The two parties had very different views of the value of a new high-tech, high-risk entrepreneurial division (Venture) of PRIVATE. CORP considered Venture worth only $1 million (of the $14 million offered), while PRIVATE truly believed in the viability of the new products under development and had valued this division at $6 million. When they realized they could trade-off on this underlying issue, they had found their solution. CORP acquired PRIVATE for $12 million, but the owners of PRIVATE retained control of Venture. From CORP's perspective, this agreement was even better than acquiring the entire company for $14 million. From PRIVATE's perspective, this agreement was better than

From *Negotiating Rationally*. New York: The Free Press, 1992, pp.16–22.

he $16 million that they demanded since they still owned Venture, which they valued at $6 million.

Negotiations are more than simply a fight over who gets how much of the pie. While parties often have several interests in a negotiation, they rarely evaluate the relative importance of each. If you clearly identify your priorities before a negotiation, you can find effective trade-offs by conceding less important issues to gain on more important ones.

The fixed-pie assumption leads managers to interpret most competitive situations as win-lose, an orientation that's reinforced in our society by such traditions as athletic competition, admission to academic programs, and corporate promotion systems. People often generalize from these objective win-lose situations to others that are not necessarily win-lose. When both cooperation and competition are required, the competitive outlook dominates, resulting in a fixation on the distributive approach to bargaining. This inhibits the creative problem-solving necessary to develop integrative solutions.

People often fail to solve problems because of the assumptions they place on them.[1] Attempt to draw four (and only four) straight lines that connect all nine dots shown here without lifting your pencil (or pen) from the paper.[2]

People typically try the following solutions.

Most people try to use their logical decision skills on the *perceived* problem: connecting all nine dots without going outside the boundaries they imply. People make an *assumption* that frames the problem,

but keeps them from finding a solution. *This is the most critical barrier to creative problem solving.* People tend to make false assumptions about problems to fit them into their previously established expectations. However, successful *creative* solutions often lie outside these self-imposed assumptions.

For example, once you discard the assumption about the barrier around the nine dots, you should find it fairly easy to come up with a solution similar to this one:

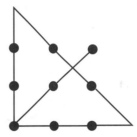

Negotiation is, in some ways, a kind of creative problem solving. To "connect the dots" managers must not assume a mythical fixed-pie, rather, they should look for trade-offs. Finding trade-offs is quite easy if you think to look for them, and quite difficult if you make inappropriate assumptions about the other side's interests.

The pervasiveness and destructiveness of the mythical fixed-pie is captured in the words of South Carolina Congressman Floyd Spence, who said in discussing a proposed SALT treaty: "I have had a philosophy for some time in regard to SALT, and it goes like this: the Russians will not accept a SALT treaty that is not in their best interest, and it seems to me that if it is in their best interest, it can't be in our best interest."[3] The assumption that anything good for the Soviet Union must be bad for the United States is a very clear expression of the mythical fixed-pie. Most political experts, on both sides of the political fence, would agree that the cooperation that has developed between the United States and the Soviet Union over the past few years has been to the benefit of both.

The mythical fixed-pie is a fixation equally prevalent in the business world. In late 1985, the president of Eastern Airlines, Frank Borman (the former astronaut), aware of the company's poor financial condition, presented the airline's three major unions with an ultimatum—if they did not agree to significant wage concessions, he would sell the airline.[4] The unions didn't take him seriously. They had valid contracts for an extended period and did not believe Borman wanted to give up control of the airline. But they became anxious when Borman began discussions with Frank Lorenzo, the most feared executive in the industry. Lorenzo had busted the unions at Continental, and had a general reputation as the most ruthless dictator in the corporate world. The only problem was that Borman had no desire to sell the airline to Lorenzo; it would be a bitter end to his career at Eastern. "What's more," argued Aaron Bernstein of *Business Week*, "if Borman gave up his command of Eastern, it was unlikely that at 57 he'd have anywhere else to go."[5]

Once discussions started, Lorenzo made an offer to the board of directors that forced them to consider selling. The only way to save Eastern was to obtain significant wage cuts from all three unions. While the pilots' and flight attendants' unions agreed to 20 percent wage cuts, the machinists' union, headed by militant Charlie Bryan, would only accept a 15 percent cut. Borman demanded 20 percent. Neither would move. Both argued that the failure of the other side to make a further concession would destroy the airline. They played a game of chicken, and no one chickened out.[6] When the deadline on the Lorenzo offer arrived without any agreement between Borman and the machinists, the board accepted Lorenzo's offer.

The irrationality in this outcome for both Borman and the machinists is evident. Lorenzo forced wage cuts, eliminated jobs, and eventually destroyed the airline.

Why was the airline ever sold to Lorenzo? Largely because Borman and Bryan both assumed mythical fixed-pies in the negotiation. Both negotiated as if the only way to gain was for the other side to lose. They never seriously considered negotiation strategies that would work to the advantage of both sides. They were under incredible pressure, but that simply increases the importance of finding a solution that works to the advantage of both parties. Limited by their assumptions, they ended up with an impasse and never discovered the many integrative trade-offs that would have benefited them both.

People who assume mythical fixed-pies will not find mutually beneficial trade-offs. However, consider what can happen even when both parties have identical preferences on a specific issue. For example, a company wants its workers to be better trained to increase work flexibility, while the workers want to be better trained to increase their employment security. Psychologist Leigh Thompson has found that even when the two sides want the same thing, they often settle for a different outcome because they assume that they must compromise to get agreement.[7] "If I want more training, they must not want me to get more training." This leads to what Thompson calls the "incompatibility bias"—the assumption that one side's interests are incompatible with the other's.

In a negotiation simulation involving eight issues, Thompson included two issues that were compatible—the parties had the same preference. Rationally, there was nothing to negotiate. Yet, 39 percent of the negotiations failed to result in the mutually preferred outcome on at least one of the two compatible issues. Further, even when the two sides reached an optimal agreement, neither realized that the other party had also benefited. Such a misperception in a negotiation can give an executive inflated confidence in his or her persuasive and bargaining abilities.[8]

The mythical fixed-pie also causes managers to "reactively devalue" any concession simply because it's offered by an adversary.[9] Connie Stillinger and her colleagues divided 137 individuals into two groups and asked how favorable an arms reduction proposal would be to the United States and to the U.S.S.R. One group was told (correctly) the proposal came from Mr. Gorbachev. The other group was told that President Reagan (the study was conducted during his presidency) had made the proposal. Fifty-six percent of those who believed the proposal was Gorbachev's thought it dramatically favored the

Russians. Only 16 percent felt that it favored the U.S. The other 28 percent thought that it favored both sides equally. In the group that believed Reagan had initiated the proposal, 45 percent thought it benefited both sides equally, 27 percent thought that it favored the U.S.S.R, and 27 percent thought it favored the United States. Thus, terms that appear beneficial when advanced by one's own side may seem disadvantageous when proposed by the other party, even if the terms are equal. This is consistent with the inherent flaw in the mythical fixed-pie perception— what is good for them must be bad for us.

Managers commonly ask "What should we discuss first in a negotiation?" Some managers believe it is critical to get the most important issue resolved in the beginning as "any other strategy is simply procrastinating." In labor relations, many experienced negotiators recommend "starting with the easy issues first," an institutionalized step in the folklore of labor-management negotiations. Unfortunately, neither view is good advice. Both strategies eliminate possible trade-offs that may create joint benefits. Once resolved, an issue is rarely resurrected to be used in a trade-off.

Advice to solve the easy issues or hard issues first is still taken seriously because of the persistence of the mythical fixed-pie mind-set. But when each side values the issues differently, it is essential to deal with alternative "packages" that allow for the simultaneous discussion of multiple issues. How to build integrative-agreement packages will be discussed later. For now, we simply want you to note the prevalence of the mythical fixed-pie in negotiation decisions.

REFERENCES AND NOTES

1. J. Adams, *Conceptual blockbusting* (San Francisco: San Francisco Book Co., 1979); M. H. Bazerman, *Judgment in managerial decision making*, 2d ed. (New York: John Wiley and Sons, 1990); W. Winklegren, *How to solve problems* (San Francisco: Freeman, 1974).

2. The problem has been used without original reference by many previous authors.

3. We are indebted to C. Stillinger, M. Epelbaum, D. Keltner, and L. Ross, *The 'reactive devaluation' barrier to conflict resolution*, working paper, Stanford University, 1990, for this fascinating quotation.

4. A. Bernstein, *Grounded: Frank Lorenzo and the destruction of Eastern Airlines* (New York: Simon & Schuster, 1990).

5. Ibid., p. 41.

6. The game of chicken is played by two drivers, who drive their trucks toward each other on a one-lane road, each hoping that the other will "chicken" out and veer off first. You win when the other driver chickens out before you. If neither driver chickens out, both lose big.

7. L. Thompson, Information exchange in negotiation, *Journal of Experimental Social Psychology* 27 (1991), 161–79.

8. Ibid; M. A. Neale and M. H. Bazerman, The effects of framing and negotiator overconfidence on bargainer behavior, *Academy of Management Journal* 28 (1985), 34–49.

9. S. Oskamp, Attitudes towards U.S. and Russian actions: A double standard, *Psychological Reports* 16 (1965), 43–46; Stillinger, Epelbaum, Keltner, and Ross, The 'reactive devaluation' barrier to conflict resolution.

17.   UNDERSTANDING BEHAVIOR IN ESCALATION SITUATIONS

Barry M. Staw and Jerry Ross

At an early stage of the Vietnam War, George Ball, then Undersecretary of State, wrote the following memo to Lyndon Johnson, warning him about the likely consequences of making further commitments of men and material:

The decision you face now is crucial. Once large numbers of U.S. troops are committed to direct combat, they will begin to take heavy casualties in a war they are ill-equipped to fight in a noncooperative if not downright hostile countryside. Once we suffer large casualties, we will have started a well-nigh irreversible process. Our involvement will be so great that we cannot—without national humiliation—stop short of achieving our complete objectives. Of the two possibilities I think humiliation will be more likely than the achievement of our objectives—even after we have paid terrible costs [1 July 1965,[1] p. 450].

George Ball's remarks were not only prophetic about the U.S. experience in Vietnam. They also pointed to the more general problem of coping with what are now called "escalation situations." These are situations in which losses have resulted from an original course of action, but where there is the possibility of turning the situation around by investing further time, money, or effort.

The frequency of escalation situations can be depicted by everyday examples. When an individual has a declining investment, a faltering career, or even a troubled marriage, there is often the difficult choice between putting greater effort into the present line of behavior versus seeking a new alternative. At the organizational level, similar dilemmas

occur. Laboratories must make difficult decisions about whether to continue with or withdraw from disappointing research and development (R&D) projects; banks must decide how to manage their involvement in nonperforming loans; and industrial firms often need to determine whether to abandon a questionable venture versus investing further resources. In each of these situations it is frequently observed that individuals as well as organizations can become locked in to the existing course of action, throwing good money or effort after bad. This "decision pathology" has been variously labeled the escalation of commitment,[2] the psychology of entrapment,[3] the sunk cost effect,[4] and the too-much-invested-to-quit syndrome.[5] We will review the state of research on this problem and then provide a summary theoretical model along with some guidelines for future research.

CLASSES OF ESCALATION DETERMINANTS

Much of the early work on the escalation problem focused on psychological factors that lead decision-makers to engage in seemingly irrational acts—that is, behavior not explained by either objective circumstances or standard economic decision-making.[5-7] In response, some researchers have stressed that escalation does involve rational decision-making, because individuals do attend to the economic realities of escalation situations once they are made salient or clear to the person[8]. Alternatively, others

Barry M. Staw and Jerry Ross, "Understanding Behavior in Escalation Situations" from *Science*, Vol. 246, October 1986, pp. 216–220.

have found[9] that escalation behavior can be depicted as a rational calculus, but this requires going beyond the narrow economics of the situation to include many psychological and social costs of withdrawal, such as the personal and public embarrassment of admitting failure.

Debates over the rationality of behavior in escalation or any other situation are not likely to be settled soon. In fact, these arguments may detract attention away from the central phenomenon of interest, which is the tendency of individuals and organizations to persist in failing courses of action. To understand this tendency, one must account for a variety of forces, both behavioral and economic. We will therefore summarize research on four classes of determinants: those associated with objective characteristics of the project as well as psychological, social, and organizational variables.

PROJECT DETERMINANTS

Project variables are the most obvious determinants of persistence in a course of action. Research has shown, for example, that commitment is affected by whether a setback is judged to be due to a permanent or temporary problem,[10] by whether further investment is likely to be efficacious;[11] by how large a goal or payoff may result from continued investment;[7] by future expenditures or costs necessary to achieve a project's payoff;[12] and by the number of times previous commitments have failed to yield returns.[13]

A few project variables are less obvious causes of persistence. Endeavors such as R&D and construction projects often foster commitment because there is a long delay between expenditures and economic benefits. In these cases, shortfalls in revenue or outcomes may not be monitored closely or cause alarm, since losses are (at least initially) expected to occur. In other cases, projects may continue, in part, because they have little salvage value and involve substantial closing costs if terminated in midstream.[8] For example, the World's Fair Expo 86 reached the point late in its construction in which continuation was expected to produce large losses,

but even larger losses would have been sustained if the project had been aborted before its formal opening.[14] In a few cases, projects can become so large that they literally trap the sponsoring organization into continuing the course of action. The Long Island Lighting Company's construction of the Shoreham Nuclear Power Plant is an example of such a no–win situation, in which persistence was seen as costly, yet withdrawal was (until very recently) viewed as bringing even worse economic consequences to the organization.[15]

PSYCHOLOGICAL DETERMINANTS

In addition to the objective properties of a project, several psychological variables can also influence persistence in losing courses of action. Probably the simplest of these determinants are information processing errors on the part of decision-makers.

Although accounting and economics texts routinely state that investments should only be made when marginal (future) revenues exceed marginal costs,[16] people may not actually behave this way. Consider the responses of college students to the following two questions posed by Arkes and Blumer:[4]

Question 3A. *As the president of an airline company, you have invested 10 million dollars of the company's money into a research project. The purpose was to build a plane that would not be detected by conventional radar, in other words, a radar-blank plane. When the project is 90% completed, another firm begins marketing a plane that cannot be detected by radar. Also, it is apparent that their plane is much faster and far more economical than the plane your company is building. The question is: should you invest the last 10% of the research funds to finish your radar-blank plane? Yes, 41; No, 7.*

Question 3B. *As president of an airline company, you have received a suggestion from one of your employees. The suggestion is to use the last 1 million dollars of your research funds to develop a plane that would not be detected by conventional radar, in other words, a radar-blank plane. However, another firm has just begun mar-*

keting a plane that cannot be detected by radar. Also, it is apparent that their plane is much faster and far more economical than the plane your company could build. The question is: should you invest the last million dollars of your research funds to build the radar-blank plane proposed by your employee? Yes, 10; No, 50.

These data clearly indicate that sunk costs (those previously expended but not supposed to affect investment decisions) are not sunk psychologically. They continue to influence subsequent investment decisions.

Not only do escalation situations involve sunk costs in terms of money, time, and effort; they also are framed as losing situations in which new investments hold the promise of turning one's fortunes around. Unfortunately, this is exactly the context in which Kahneman and Tversky[17] and others[18] found individuals to be risk-seeking. People take more risks on investment decisions framed in a negative manner (for example, to recover losses or prevent injuries) than when the same decision is positively framed (to achieve gains).

The miscalculation of sunk costs and negative framing can be characterized as rather "cool" information processing errors, as heuristics (however faulty) called on by individuals to solve escalation problems. Escalation situations can also involve "warmer," more motivated cognitions, however. Self-justification biases[19] have been singled out as a major motivational cause of persistence.

In one of the earliest escalation experiments, Staw[6] hypothesized that people may commit more resources to a losing cause so as to justify or rationalize their previous behavior. He suggested that being personally responsible for losses is an important factor in becoming locked in to a course of action. This hypothesis was first tested in an experimental simulation with business school students. All subjects played the role of a corporate financial officer in allocating R&D funds to the operating divisions of a hypothetical company. Half the subjects allocated R&D funds to one of the divisions, were given feedback on their decisions, and then were asked to make a second allocation of R&D funds.

The other half of the subjects did not make the initial investment decision themselves, but were told that it was made by another financial officer of the firm. Feedback was manipulated so that half the subjects received positive results on their initial decisions, while half received negative results.

Data from Staw's study showed that subjects allocated significantly more money to failing than to successful divisions. It was also found that more money was invested in the chosen division when the participants, rather than another financial officer, were responsible for the earlier funding decision. These results suggest that individuals responsible for previous losses may try to justify (or save) their earlier decisions by committing additional resources to them. Also, because both high-and low-responsibility subjects faced a negative financial scenario (one with previous losses), it can be argued that justification motives may affect commitment above and beyond any sunk cost or framing effects. Several experiments have replicated this self-justification finding with similar responsibility manipulations.[20]

Closely related to the self-justification explanation of persistence are the findings of other motivated biases. Cognitive studies show that people slant data in the direction of their preexisting beliefs and discredit information that conflicts with their opinions.[21] Parallel effects in the escalation area have demonstrated that decision-makers responsible for a failing course of action tend to make greatest use of positive and exonerating information.[22] Thus, it appears that justification motives may not only affect decisions to save a risky course of action, but may also affect the accuracy of data on which such decisions are made.

In addition to efforts to justify behavior, some passive self-inference processes may also affect individuals in escalation situations. Salancik[23] and Kiesler[24] have posited that individuals are likely to become especially bound or committed to a prior behavior when (i) the individual's acts are explicit or unambiguous, (ii) the behavior is irrevocable or not easily undone, (iii) the behavior has been entered into freely or has involved a high degree of volition, (iv) the act has importance for the individual, (v) the act is public or is visible to others, and (vi) the act has been performed a number of times. These six self-inference conditions assume that individuals draw inferences about their own behavior and the context in which it occurs. Though self-inference theories are less motivational than those that use self-justification concepts (no needs for rationalization are implied), the two approaches overlap almost entirely in their empirical predictions.[25]

SOCIAL DETERMINANTS

Although most of the research on escalation has dealt with psychological or project variables, escalation situations are often more complicated social phenomena. For example, administrators may persist in a course of action, not just because they do not want to admit a mistake to themselves, but because they hesitate to expose their errors to others. Fox and Staw[26] tested this notion of external justification in a role-playing experiment. They found that subjects holding administrative roles with low job security and lack of support by management allocated the greatest resources to a losing course of action. Conceptually similar results were reported by Brockner, Rubin, and Lang.[12] They found persistence to be highest under a large audience, high social-anxiety condition and interpreted these results as a face-saving effect. Additional evidence of face-saving can also be found in the bargaining literature,[27] in which it is common to find an escalation of hostilities as both parties refuse to back down from earlier positions. For example, using Shubik's[28] dollar auction game, Tegar[5] found that competitive bidding was influenced first by a simple desire to make money, then as a way to recoup prior losses, and finally, as a means to defeat the other party.

The external binding of people to behavior may also be important in escalation situations. Just as it is possible for individuals to form personal beliefs through a self-inference process,[23,24] observers tend to infer motivation and personal characteristics to ac-

tors after observing their behavior.[29] Thus, people's social identity may become externally bound by their actions with respect to a project. Though no research has specifically tested this idea, one would expect decision-makers to be most closely identified with a project when their advocacy of it has been public, explicit, perceived to be high in volition, and repeated. At the extreme, a project may start to carry the name of its sponsor (for example, "Reaganomics" or "Thatcherism"), increasing the binding of the person to the behavior, thus making withdrawal from the course of action much more difficult.

Although face-saving and external binding can both be viewed as social factors that increase decision-makers' costs of withdrawal, research has also isolated some social rewards for persistence. Staw and Ross[30] had business students study the behavior of managers in a failing situation. Managers were described as either persisting in a losing course of action or switching to another alternative. The descriptions read by subjects also noted that managers' persistence or experimentation led either to further negative results or ultimate success. As predicted, managers were rated highest when they were persistent and successful. Most interestingly, the data also showed a significant interaction of persistence and outcome. This interaction can be interpreted as a "hero effect"—special praise and adoration for managers who "stick to their guns" in the face of opposition and seemingly bleak odds.[31]

ORGANIZATIONAL DETERMINANTS

Since many of the most costly escalation situations involve the persistence of an entire organization (rather than an isolated individual) to a losing course of action, it is important to consider some organizational determinants of persistence. Unfortunately, few organization-level studies have yet been conducted. Therefore, we are forced to rely more on relevant theory than concrete data in outlining likely organizational determinants of escalation.

Probably the simplest organizational determinant is institutional inertia. Just as there is less than full consistency between individual attitudes and behavior,[32] there is also a very loose coupling between organizational goals and action.[33] Organizations have imperfect sensory systems, making them relatively impervious to changes in their environments. And, because of breakdowns in internal communication and difficulties in mobilizing their constituents, organizations are slow to respond. Thus, even when the need for change is recognized, it may not occur. Moreover, if actions require altering long-standing policies, violating rules, or discarding accepted procedures, movement is not likely to happen at all, even though (to an outsider) it may seem obviously useful.

Organizations attempting to withdraw from a losing course of action must also contend with political forces. Not only those who are directly involved with a project will resist its dismantling, but so too will units interdependent or politically aligned with the venture. This can become a special problem when projects are important or central enough to have political support on governing bodies and budget committees charged with their fate. As Pfeffer and Salancik[34] have shown in their research on organizational decision-making, organizational actions may turn as much on politics as on any objective economic criteria.

At times, a project's support can go beyond politics. The project may be tied so integrally to the values and purposes of an organization that it becomes institutionalized,[35] making withdrawal almost an "unthinkable" proposition. Two examples illustrate the problem. The first is Lockheed's L1011 Tri-Star Jet program. Although most outside analysts found the plane unlikely to earn a profit, Lockheed persisted in the venture for more than a decade, accumulating enormous losses.[36] The issue was not ending the project, per se, but in having to reinterpret the company's role in commercial aviation. For Lockheed to drop the L1011 meant having to change its identity from a pioneer in commercial aircraft to that of simply a defense contractor. Pan American Airlines recently faced a similar institutional issue. More than most airlines, Pan Am suffered major losses after deregulation of the industry. However, as losses accumulated, it successively sold off most of its nonairlines assets. First, the Pan Am building was sold to meet debt obligations. Then, as losses continued to mount, the Intercontinental Hotel chain was sold. Finally, Pan Am was forced to sell its valuable Pacific routes to United Airlines. Withdrawing from the real estate and hotel business was probably an easier decision for this organization than ending the more institutionalized airline operations, irrespective of the economics involved.

THE DYNAMICS OF ESCALATION

This review of escalation research has been more illustrative than exhaustive. Yet, it is evident from even this brief summary that studies of escalation behavior have focused primarily on psychological determinants, with social and organizational variables only recently receiving attention. Unfortunately, this difference in research emphasis has had less to do with the relevance of particular determinants of escalation than with the difficulty of operationalizing concepts and conducting empirical studies at more macroscopic levels. Because many of the most disastrous escalation situations involve larger social entities such as governmental and business organizations, further macro-level studies of escalation are therefore needed.

As we have noted, escalation situations are also a forum for a variety of forces, both behavioral and economic. Consequently, an important question for future research is how these various forces combine to affect behavior in escalation contexts. Already some research suggests that escalation behavior may not only be multi-determined, but also temporally dependent. That is, escalation situations may change character over time, such that different determinants of persistence and withdrawal become dominant at separate stages in an escalation cycle. A preliminary model of how the influence of several key variables may unfold over time, based on two field studies of naturally occurring escalation situations,[14,15] is shown in Figure 17.1.

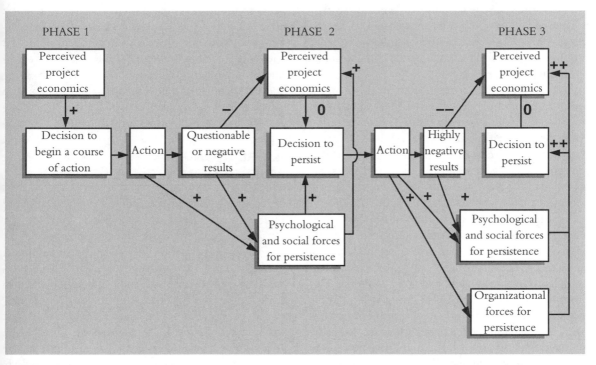

FIGURE 17.1 A three-stage model of the escalation process. The +, –, and 0 show positive, negative, and neutral influences, respectively.

The first phase of escalation is dominated by the economics of a project, with the decision to begin a course of action made largely on the basis of the anticipation of economic benefits. However, when questionable or negative results are received (at Phase 2), the decision to persist is based not just on project economics, but also on psychological and social determinants. Assuming that psychological and social forces are strong enough to outweigh (or bias) any negative economic forecasts, further investment or persistence in the project is likely. If this additional investment does not turn the situation around and further negative results are received (at Stage 3), withdrawal tendencies may be heightened. Unfortunately, at this advanced stage in the escalation cycle any withdrawal tendencies (due to negative project economics) may be counterbalanced and biased by organizational forces for persistence.

Thus, as economic outcomes worsen over time, it is possible for projects to be maintained by the accumulation of psychological, social, and organizational forces, each adding some weight to the decision to persist in a course of action.

At this time, the idea of distinct stages of escalation remains more of a heuristic for understanding the process of persistence than an empirically tested theory. Yet, two in-depth field studies—an analysis of British Columbia's decision to hold Expo 86[14] and an examination of Long Island Lighting's commitment to the Shoreham nuclear power plant[15]— have provided support for a temporally based model. In each situation, economic variables were salient early on and psychological and social variables became important after negative consequences started to accumulate, whereas organizational determinants were manifested rather late in the escalation cycle. Of course, whether these time dependencies are always abrupt enough to constitute distinct stages, or whether in other contexts a more gradual shifting of influence occurs, is still an open question.

No doubt an important step in validating a temporal model of escalation will be the isolation of critical incidents setting off or preconditioning particular determinants of persistence. If these preconditions are found to follow a predictable sequence (that is, arising early or late in the escalation cycle) across a variety of contexts, then a strong case can be made for a temporal model.

In searching for the preconditions of escalation, we would argue that escalation situations typically involve the following sequence of events. First, in launching a new product or project, individual "project champions" will not only work hard to promote the venture but in so doing will probably sow the seeds for subsequent commitment (for example, via self-inference effects). Once questionable or adverse results are received, a negative perceptual frame and sunk costs may then become associated with the project. At this time, those who have had an active hand in developing the project will likely suffer personal embarrassment (or even loss of employment) with the failing situation, leading to self-justification and face-saving effects. And, once the losses associated with the project are fully recognized throughout the organization, external binding of the proponents to the project (for example, "that's Jim's baby") is likely to make withdrawal even more costly to the individuals involved. Finally, assuming that the project does survive several rounds of negative feedback, then more global, organizational processes may start to manifest themselves. Political support may arise as individual careers and whole departments become dependent on the project. And, if the project lasts long enough, withdrawal can become extremely costly not only in terms of the economics involved, but also in terms of the identity of the firm itself.

As elaborated here, the sequence of critical incidents in escalation situations may tend to move from the individual, to the interpersonal environment, and then to the larger organization. We believe this is a natural evolution as project originators (or champions) try to defend a losing course of action, first by themselves (via risk-taking and information biasing) and then by the mobilization of resources involving the larger organization. Additional research on the development of escalation situations is obviously needed to verify these temporal dynamics.

ESCALATION AS A MULTIDETERMINED EVENT

Since several sources of commitment can be triggered by losing courses of action, one might conclude that persistence is an overdetermined variable, an almost inevitable consequence of escalation situations. A contrary view is that escalation is created by a series of small-impact variables, each insufficient by itself to cause one to remain in a losing situation. For example, if economic losses are large and they occur early in a project's life cycle, withdrawal may well be the dominant response. However, if losses do not appear until later in the process (after several behavioral effects have been initiated), then persistence could be the typical response. Thus, the speed and severity of negative economic data could be a crucial element in how relative forces unfold in escalation situations. Though not an explicit test of this hypothesis, an experiment by Golz[37] has shown how sensitive investment decisions are to the pattern of negative consequences. A slow and irregular decline may not only make a line of behavior difficult to extinguish (in the reinforcement theory sense), but may also allow the forces for persistence to grow over time. Adding support to this "unfolding argument" is a study by Brockner and Rubin,[3] in which they found that negative economic data prompted withdrawal when it was introduced early in an escalation situation, but had little influence when introduced after the decision to commit resources had already been made.

CONCLUSION

As shown by our temporal model, escalation situations contain a confluence of forces—some pulling toward withdrawal and others pushing toward persistence—with their relative strengths varying over time. This dynamic view of escalation is consistent with the contextualist perspective[38] in which social reality is seen as dependent on the situation in which it occurs. Contextualist reasoning supports the continued pursuit of case studies on the dynamics of escalation situations and supports efforts to add realism to experimental tests. Greater efforts are needed to capture experimentally the life-span of escalation episodes so that the relative influence of contributing variables can be tracked over time. Only with such temporally based studies, from both the laboratory and the field, are the dynamics of escalation situations likely to be fully understood.

REFERENCES AND NOTES

1. The New York Times (based on the investigative reporting of Neil Sheehan), *The Pentagon Papers* (Bantam Books, New York, 1971).

2. B. M. Staw, *Acad. Manage. Rev. 6*, **577** (1981).

3. J. Brockner and J. Z. Rubin, *Entrapment in Escalating Conflicts* (Springer-Verlag, New York, 1985).

4. H. R. Arkes and C. Blumer, *Organ. Behav. Hum. Decis. Processes* **35**, 124 (1985).

5. A. Tegar. *Too Much Invested To Quit* (Pergamon Press, New York, 1980).

6. For example, B. M. Staw, *Organ. Behav. Hum. Performance* **16**, 27 (1976).

7. J. Z. Rubin and J. Brockner, *J. Pers. Soc. Psychol.* **31**, 1054 (1975).

8. For example, G. B. Northcraft and G. Wolf. *Acad. Manage. Rev.* **9**, 225 (1984).

9. B. M. Staw and J. Ross, in *Research in Organizational Behavior*, L. L. Cummings and B. M. Staw, Eds. (JAI Press, Greenwich, CT, 1987), vol. 9, pp. 39–78.

10. L. Leatherwood and E. Conlon, "The impact of prospectively relevant information and setbacks in persistence in a project following setback" (working paper 85-1, College of Business Administration, University of Iowa, 1985).

11. B. M. Staw and F. V. Fox, *Hum. Relat.* **30**, 431 (1977); T. Bateman, "Resource allocation after success and failure: The roles of attributions of powerful others and probabilities of future success" (Department of Management, Texas A&M, College Station, TX 91983).

12. J. Brockner, J. Z. Rubin, E. Lang, *J. Exp. Soc. Psychol.* **17**, 68 (1981).

13. B. E. McCain, *J. Appl. Psychol.* **71**, 280 (1986).

14. J. Ross and B. Staw, *Adm. Sci. Q.* **31**, 224 (1986).

15. ———, "Escalation and the Long Island Lighting Company: The case of the Shoreham Nuclear Power Plant" (Working paper, Institute Européen d'Administration des Affaires, Fontainebleau, France, 1989).

16. P. A. Samuelson, *Economics* (McGraw-Hill, New York, 1988); C. T. Horngren, *Cost Accounting: A Managerial Emphasis* (Prentice-Hall, Englewood Cliffs, NJ, 1982).

17. D. Kahneman and A. Tversky, *Econometrica* **47**, 263 (1979); D. Kahneman and A. Tversky, *Science* **211**, 453 (1981).

18. M. A. Davis and P. Bobko, *Organ. Behav. Hum. Decis. Processes* **37**, 121 (1986).

19. E. Aronson, *The Social Animal* (Freeman, San Francisco, 1984); L. Festinger, *Theory of Cognitive Dissonance* (Stanford Univ. Press, Stanford, CA, 1970).

20. M. H. Bazerman, R. I. Beekum, F. D. Schoorman, *J. Appl. Psychol.* **67**, 873 (1982); M. H. Bazerman *et al.*, *Organ. Behav. Hum. Performance* **33**, *141* (1984); D. F. Caldwell and C. A. O'Reilly, *Acad. Manage. J.* **25**, 121 (1982).

21. T. Gilovich, *J. Pers. Soc. Psychol.* **44**, 1110 (1983); C. Lord, L. Ross, M. R. Lepper, *ibid.* **37**, 2098 (1979).

22. E. J. Conlon and J. M. Parks, *J. Appl. Psychol.* **72**, 344 (1987).

23. G. R. Salancik, in *New Directions in Organizational Behavior*, B. M. Staw and G. R. Salancik, Eds. (Krieger, Malabar, FL, 1977).

24. C. A. Kiesler, *The Psychology of Commitment* (Academic Press, New York, 1971).

25. P. E. Tetlock and A. Levi, *J. Exp. Soc. Psychol.* **18**, 68 (1982).

26. F. V. Fox and B. M. Staw, *Adm. Sci. Q.* **24**, 449 (1979).

27. H. Raiffa, *The Art and Science of Negotiation* (Harvard Univ. Press, Cambridge, MA 1982).

28. M. Shubik, *J. Conflict Resolut.* **15**, 109 (1971).

29. E. E. Jones and K. E. Davis, in *Advances in Experimental Social Psychology*, L. Berkowitz, Ed. (Academic Press, New York, 1965), vol. 2.

30. B. M. Staw and J. Ross, *J. Appl. Psychol.* **65**, 249 (1980).

31. M. G. Evans and J. W. Medcof, *Can. J. Adm. Sci.* **1**, 383 (1984).

32. M. P. Zanna and R. H. Fazio, in *Consistency in Social Behavior*, M. P. Zanna, E. T. Higgins, C. P. Herman, Eds. (Erlbaum, Hillsdale, NJ, 1982).

33. J. G. March and J. P. Olson, *Ambiguity and Choice in Organizations* (Universitetsforlaget, Bergen, Norway, 1976).

34. J. Pfeffer and G. R. Salancik, *Adm. Sci. Q.* **19**, 135 (1974); G. R. Salancik and J. Pfeffer, *ibid.*, p. 453.

35. P. S. Goodman, M. Bazerman, E. Conlon, in *Research in Organizational Behavior*, B. M. Staw and L. L. Cummings, Eds. (JAI Press, Greenwich, CT, 1980), vol. 2, pp. 215–246; L. G. Zucker in *Research in the Sociology of Organizations*, S. Bacharach, Ed. (JAI Press, Greenwich, CT, 1983).

36. U. E. Reinhardt, *J. Finance* **28**, 821 (1973).

37. S. M. Golz, "A learning-based analysis of escalation of commitment, sunk cost, and entrapment," paper presented at American Psychological Association meeting, Atlanta, GA, August 1988.

38. W. J. McGuire, in *Advances in Experimental Social Psychology*, L. Berkowitz, Ed. (Academic Press, New York, 1984).

39. Supported by the Institute of Industrial Relations, University of California, Berkeley.

Making Ethical and Unethical Decisions

18. BUSINESS ETHICS: FOUR SPHERES OF EXECUTIVE RESPONSIBILITY

Joseph L. Badaracco, Jr.

In *The Functions of the Executive*, his landmark book on managers and organizations, Chester Barnard wrote: "It seems to me inevitable that the struggle to maintain cooperation among men should as surely destroy some men morally as battle destroys some physically."[1] This is a grim observation. It flies in the face of our widespread celebration of business leadership, entrepreneurial achievement, and the triumphal march of capitalism into Asia and now Eastern Europe. Barnard's view also seem unrealistic. Management life is surely not, after all, a series of anguishing moral dilemmas. And when ethical issues do arise, the right answer, morally and legally, is often clear. The typical challenge is finding practical ways to do the right thing, not discerning what is right. The investment bankers who met in dark garages to exchange inside information for suitcases of cash were not struggling on the horn of moral dilemmas but were breaking the law and violating their clients' trust.

Yet in other cases, the central challenge is deciding what is right. In 1988, for example, the executives of Roussel UCLAF, a French pharmaceutical company, had to decide whether to market a new drug called RU 486. Early tests had shown that the drug was 90 to 95% effective in causing a miscarriage during the first five weeks of a pregnancy. A scientific and medical breakthrough, RU 486 was an alternative to surgical abortions, and its creators believed it could ultimately help hundreds of thousands of women avoid injury and death from botched abortions. As researchers and business managers, many Roussel UCLAF executives had been personally committed to developing RU 486. They faced the question, however, of whether to introduce the drug and how to do so. Protests against Roussel and debates within the company were already diverting a great deal of management time and sapping employee morale. Some of the countries that faced severe population problems and wanted access to RU 486—such as China—did not have the medical infrastructure to use the drug safely. Anti-abortion groups were threatening an international boycott of the products made by Roussel UCLAF and Hoechst, the German chemical giant that was Roussel UCLAF's largest shareholder. Indeed, the costs of the boycott seemed likely to outstrip the profits from selling RU 486.

From: *California Management Review*, Vol. 34, No. 3, Spring 1992, pp. 64–79.

Moreover, Hoechst's corporate credo emphasized support for life, a reaction to its collaboration with the Nazi death camps during the 1940s.

What were the moral responsibilities of Roussel's executives? How should they have balanced their ethical obligations to the company's shareholders, to their employees, to the women who might use RU 486, and to the medical, and scientific, governmental, and political groups their decisions would effect? What did they owe to their own consciences? In such situations, executives face morally treacherous problems. These are not issues of right versus wrong; they involve conflicts of right versus right, of responsibility versus responsibility. In such cases, managers cannot avoid getting their hands dirty: in meeting some responsibilities, they will fail to meet others, and so they face the anguishing struggle that Barnard described.

The problem of dirty hands is the lot of men and women with power and complex responsibilities. In a play by Jean-Paul Sartre, a young idealist accuses a veteran Communist leader of having sold out to the Nazi occupation. The older man replies:

How you cling to your purity, young man! How afraid you are to soil your hands! All right, stay pure! What good will it do? Why did you join us? Purity is an idea for a yogi or a monk. . . . To do nothing, to remain motionless, arms at your sides, wearing kid gloves. Well I have dirty hands. Right up to the elbows. I've plunged them in filth and blood. But what do you hope? Do you think you can govern innocently?[2]

Yet hard moral choices are at times the inescapable lot of men and women in positions of power. How do you fire a friend, someone you have worked with for years? When is it right to violate an employee's privacy—someone with a drinking problem, for example—to get him help he badly needs? Can you have a clear conscience when your company's product will be misused by some customers and hurt innocent people? When can an executive wreak havoc on a workforce and a local community by moving an operation to a low-cost, overseas site? Is it sometimes right to pay a bribe to win a contract and protect jobs?

Some people believe there are fundamentally simple approaches to such situations: let the market decide, search one's heart and be true to one's values, do what is best for the shareholders, take care of the people in the company "family," do what is right for all of a company's stakeholders. These ways of resolving the moral dilemmas of management are beguilingly clear, simple, praiseworthy—and misleading. The search for a grand, unifying principle of management morality leads to frustration and often cynicism. The moral dilemmas of management are, at bottom, clashes among different, conflicting moralities, among very different spheres of responsibility. Each sphere is, in many ways, a nearly complete moral universe—its own world of commitments, human relationships, strong duties, norms of behavior, personal aspirations, and choices that bring happiness and suffering to others.[3] When the claims of these different spheres of commitment pull in different directions, managers face the hazards of which Chester Barnard warned.

FOUR SPHERES OF MORALITY

The Commitments of Private Life

The first of these moral worlds is the sphere of private life. In part, this realm consists of duties and obligations which are usually stated as abstract, universal principles: tell the truth, keep promises, and avoid injuring others. Individuals disagree about the origins of these duties and the priorities among them, but most people believe that certain fairly clear obligations are binding on everyone. Such principles, however, offer only an abstract, attenuated view—a philosopher's x-ray—of the complex morality of individuals' commitments, ideals, and aspirations.

Consider, for example, the case of a young woman who worked as an associate at a New York investment banking firm. She had contributed significantly to a successful assignment, and the client invited the project team to a celebratory luncheon. The young woman was eager to attend, but the luncheon would be held at a small men's club that required women to enter through a side door. As she struggled with this issue, the young woman did not find herself consulting a universal, prioritized list of abstract, ethical duties. She did spend a great deal of time thinking about her family, her experiences in college, her grandmother's decision not to pursue a career with an established law firm because she would have to learn typing and shorthand to get the job, the experiences of other women at her investment bank, and about her hopes for her career.

In short, her "analysis" was refracted through the personal realities of her life and past experience. Moreover, her decision was not simply a choice but an act of self-definition or self-creation: it would partially define the person she would become, someone who had gone through the side door or someone who had done something else. The poet Adrienne Rich observed that "the story of our life becomes our life," and this young woman was about to write—or live out—an important chapter of her personal narrative.

There was no single, universal, "right" decision in this case. The morality of private life differs from person to person, reflecting factors that are individual and often highly particular. Some people are deeply committed to their families, others to their work, or political reform, or strong friendships. For many, the sphere of private morality is suffused with religious belief, while others find ideals and aspirations elsewhere—in their parents' example, in philosophy, literature, the lives of people they admire, or convictions born of their own lives and reflection. Personal morality is usually embedded in the unexamined norms and assumptions, the slowly evolving commitments and responsibilities, and the enveloping ways of life of families, friends, and communities.

Much of the morality of private life is implicit and intuitive, and it appears clearest in retrospect, in the patterns underlying one's past actions. Few people have the skills and the inclinations—so highly prized in academia—to state their implicit morality in clear, precise, systematic terms. For some people, rational articulation is a betrayal, a denial of Pascal's observation that the heart has its reasons that reason

does not know. Individuals often do not fully understand how or why they made a particular decision. After long reflection, something simply seems right.

Integrity and character play important roles in the morality of private life. From time to time, most people wonder about questions that ancient philosophers first articulated: What distinguishes a good person from a bad one? What ways of living, what guidelines, what virtues make for a good person and a good life? What do I want my life to add up to? What abiding aspirations and commitments will give my life purpose and a sense of wholeness, coherence, and integrity? In the Western world, such questions have defined the morality of private life ever since Socrates, Plato, and Aristotle asked them 2500 years ago.

This sphere of morality seems to be primary, to be morality in its truest and deepest sense. It seems clear, after all, that people are first and foremost individual moral agents and only later take on social roles as executives, attorneys, or physicians. But this is not the whole story. The men and women who become business executives, like others who hold positions of power in society, shoulder the weight of other moral responsibilities. The British historian R.H. Tawney wrote: "To argue, in the manner of Machiavelli, that there is one rule for business and another for private life, is to open the door to an orgy of unscrupulousness before which the mind recoils. To argue that there is no difference at all is to lay down a principle which few men who have faced the difficulty in practice will be prepared to endorse."[4] Like Chester Barnard, Tawney acknowledges a struggle: between the "rule for business" and the moral claims of private life. But what is this "rule for business?"

The answer, in short, is that certain moral responsibilities come with certain social roles. The job of being a military officer, a nurse, or an attorney brings particular obligations, as does the job of running a business. The chairman of Roussel UCLAF, Edouard Sakiz, decided at one point to overrule his strong, personal convictions and oppose the marketing of RU 486. Sakiz feared that protests and boycotts by anti-abortion groups would do too much damage to Roussel and Hoechst, saying "We have a responsibility in managing a company. But if I were a lone scientist, I would have acted differently."

Why couldn't Sakiz act on the basis of his personal values and commitments in life? The reason is that, as a business executive, Sakiz had to take account of other compelling responsibilities.

The Commitments of Economic Agents

Some of these responsibilities arose from a second sphere of moral claims, which derived from Sakiz's role as an economic agent. These obligations are familiar territory for American managers. Their job, as economists, corporate attorneys, and their superiors often remind them, is to serve the interests of shareholders. What is realized less often is that this is not just a legal and practical obligation but also the most visible and familiar element in a sphere of responsibilities that are deeply moral in character.

The ties between the owners of a company and the managers who act as their agents are inescapably moral. Shareholders entrust their assets to managers, and managers promise, implicitly or explicitly, to work for the shareholders' interests. Like any promise, this relationship of trust carries strong moral weight. Moreover, this obligation is reenforced by the duty that all citizens have to obey the law. In an overview of executives' legal obligations, Robert Clark, the Dean of the Harvard Law School, wrote: "Case law on managers' fiduciary duty of care can fairly be read to say that the manager has an affirmative, open-ended duty to maximize the beneficiaries' wealth, regardless of whether this is specified in any actual contract."[5] Of course, this obligation does not always trump all other moral claims, and difficulties arises when fiduciary obligations clash with other moral interests. Nevertheless, the laws obligating managers to serve shareholders' interests are woven deeply into the legal fabric of commercial life in the United States and many other countries. These laws reflect the preferences and considered judgments of societies;

they have been enacted by legitimate government bodies; hence, they create strong moral claims on business executives.

The economic responsibilities of executives do not arise solely from duties to keep promises and obey the law. Consequences also matter. Society benefits when managers and companies compete vigorously to serve owners' interests. Much of the wealth flowing from the capitalist cornucopia directly alleviates human suffering and provides pleasure, security, health, and prosperity for many members of society. These consequences are a moral achievement, not simply a material or economic one. The British philosopher John Stuart Mill concluded that good actions—that is, *morally* good actions—are those that bring the greatest happiness to the greatest number. Indeed, Mill asked what else morality could be about, if it were not fundamentally a matter of promoting happiness and alleviating suffering. Does capitalism accomplish this? The economist Joseph Schumpeter gave this answer: "Verification is easy. There are no doubt some things available to the modern workman that Louis XIV himself would have been delighted to have— modern dentistry for instance . . . the capitalist process, not by coincidence but by virtue of its mechanism, progressively raises the standard of life of the masses."[6] Capitalism, in short, provides the material base for the lives, happiness, and welfare of many people.

Market systems, moreover, achieve these moral ends in moral ways. Individuals choose the work they wish to do, the products and services they wish to buy, and the ways they invest their savings. Vigorous competition expands the range of choices in the markets for labor, capital, and goods. When people make these choices, they are exercising their rights as autonomous individuals. Market transactions are, in Robert Nozick's phrase, "capitalist acts between consenting adults."[7] Of course, actual capitalist systems fall far short of these ideals—because of class interests, power politics, disparities in income and wealth, and the political influence of corporations and other groups. Nevertheless, market systems rest upon bedrock moral beliefs about the autonomy of individuals, the value of freedom and consent, and the centuries-long struggle to free individuals from the power of the state and the church. The Boston Tea Party was at once a commercial and a political act, and it is no accident that the nations of Eastern Europe are simultaneously embracing capitalism and democracy. To be sure, serious problems co-exist with market systems and are often exacerbated by them, and the failures and limits of capitalist economies have been well chronicled. But to acknowledge that markets fail is not to deny their basic moral traits: providing the material base for the happiness of many people and widening the range of ways of choices open to them.

It would be natural to think that the moral dilemmas of management arise when economic duties conflict with executives' personal values and convictions. But two other spheres of responsibility also make strong claims on managers and make these dilemmas even more complex. Both of these other spheres share the same origin: the fact that modern economies do not fit the Adam Smith picture of tiny economic units banging against each other like billiard balls in competitive markets. This view presupposes that firms and their managers have little power, a condition that holds mainly in theory. Under conditions of pure competition, firms are price-takers, and when a company innovates and earns exceptional profits, competitors rush in, drive prices down, and take from the innovator the market power that its breakthrough gave it. In actuality, however, firms and their managers often wield enormous economic, political, and social power. With this power, come other responsibilities.

Commitments as Company Leaders

Another sphere of responsibility exists because employees and managers are members of semi-permanent human communities, conventionally called companies. This new form of social organization emerged roughly a hundred years ago, when the entrepreneurial capitalism of small-scale business gave way in many industries to managerial capitalism. This was a development that the classical economists had not thought about or perhaps even imagined. In the 600 pages of *The Wealth of Nations*, Adam Smith treats firms only in a few passing references to tiny operations like apothecaries, collieries, and farms. However, within a century of Smith's death, giant firms, exploiting economies of scale and scope, came to dominate much of the economic landscape. They employed thousands or tens of thousands of people, as workers and managers, on a long-term basis. Some were larger than countries. In the mid-1960s, for example, General Motors' sales exceeded the gross national products of all but four countries, and despite its recent woes, General Motors has now survived longer than the Soviet Union.

A Japanese scholar has described firms in his own country as "capsules." Such firms are semi-closed societies, communal groups that enlist the loyalty and trust of employees and envelop much of their lives.[8] Indeed, the word "employee" is misleading. People become *members* of these business organizations, they devote much of their life's energy to their work, and their lives and livelihoods are deeply bound up in the firms' activities. This phenomenon, of course, is hardly unique to Japan. Consider an episode at Levi Strauss, a leading apparel maker, just a few years ago. The company had made substantial efforts to protect the rights of people with HIV and AIDS and help them continue working when they were ill. One man with AIDS said, "It was so important for me to come to work and get away from all the pain—the company was the environment that helped me keep my self-respect." Later, when this man died, one of his co-workers said "I shed tears for him and for the great friend I had lost."

What does this vignette suggest? First, that work is a powerful source of meaning and value—in this case, self-respect—in individuals' lives. Many people realize some of their deepest aspirations—for security, for a sense of belonging, contribution, and achievement—on the job. The co-worker's comment also reminds us how workplaces can nurture deep loyalties, strong friendships, and abiding ties among individuals. People live much of their lives at work, rather than in neighborhoods, religious and political groups, or even at home with families. Finally, the episode reveals managers' power: as business executives lead, guide, and shape these large, semi-permanent social and economic communities, they exert enormous power over the lives and welfare of many other human beings.

The power that executives exercise over the lives of others leads to two strong moral claims. The first is the obligation not to abuse this power. Consider, for a moment, how great the force of authority can be. In the early 1960s, a psychologist at Yale University performed a famous experiment in which volunteers from all walks of life were asked to help a researcher learn about the effects of punishment on memory. The learner, who was actually an accomplice of the experimenter, was strapped into a chair. The volunteers were told to give electrical shocks to the learner, depending on whether or not his answers were correct. (In actuality, no shocks were given—the subject was just acting.) Approximately 60% of the volunteers were extraordinarily obedient to authority: when the learner erred, the volunteers followed the directions of the experimenter and administered the highest levels of shock, even though the learner shouted, screamed, pleaded, and eventually fell silent.[9]

In some respects, situations in companies differ from this experiment. People often have time to reflect before acting, and they can talk about hard choices with friends, peers, and family members. Yet the "tools of management"—measurement and reward systems, culture, and the examples of peers and bosses—exert enormous, cumulative pressures on employees and managers. People often give in to organizational pressure to act unethically, or they stand on the sidelines while others do so. Responsibilities in organizations are often shared so no one feels personally and directly accountable. People say to themselves "It's not part of my job," or "It's the CEO's call and he runs the place," or "I have to pick my battles and this isn't the right one." The great twentieth century theologian Reinhold Niebuhr believed that individuals tended to behave less morally in groups than in their own private lives. Niebuhr wrote: "In every human group, there is less reason to guide and check impulses, less capacity for self-transcendence, less ability to comprehend the needs of others and therefore more unrestrained egoism than the individuals, who compose the group, reveal in their personal relationships."[10]

Power begets responsibility. Hence, business executives must exercise their stewardship over company communities in ways that meet a basic threshold of decency and respect for the rights and dignity of employees and managers. But this duty merely sets a base level of responsibility: it says only "do no harm" and ignores the enduring commitments that motivate executives' work. For these men and women, work is the stage upon which they live out many of their hopes and fears, seek identity and purpose, and gain the sense of achievement and self-worth that undergirds their lives. Their ideals and aspirations take different forms but nearly all are variations on the same themes: many executives want to build companies that are independent, strong, growing, and vital; that attract and keep top-quality talent; that are challenging and rewarding places to work; that provide opportunities for employees to grow and develop; that will survive hostile, uncertain competitive environments, and will endure and prosper for decades. Some executives have even broader aspirations. Steve Job's mission for Apple Computer was "to make a contribution to this world by making tools for the mind that advance humankind." Merck's corporate purpose is "preserving and improving human life."

Many men and women commit much of their lives and energy to creating such companies. And while companies must serve shareholders' interests, neither their executives nor their employees leap from bed in the morning in order to maximize the risk-adjusted present value of streams of future cash flows. The animating, creative forces of great human institutions originate elsewhere. The men and women who build and guide enduring, productive, and challenging human communities are engaged in efforts which are not simply financial and administrative, but social, political, and moral. The political scientist James MacGregor Burns concluded that moral leadership arises when leaders and followers share needs, aspirations, and values. This is an aspect of successful companies that the widely touted notions of "family" and "team" try to capture. Not all companies and managers think in these terms; many, indeed, seem to subscribe to Woody Allen's observation that most of getting ahead in life is just showing up. But the many managers who are committed to higher aims are working within a distinctive, compelling sphere of moral responsibility.

Responsibilities Beyond Firm's Boundaries

It is natural to think that executives' responsibilities stop at their firms' boundaries. This supposes that companies are, in the words of one economist, islands of managerial coordination in a sea of market relations.[11] But this picture of the world is inaccurate and misleading. Many companies have complex relationships with government agencies, labor unions, or—through strategic alliances—with customers, suppliers, and even competitors. These firms resemble global networks and their boundaries are blurred.

This organizational reality creates a new and enormously complex sphere of responsibilities for managers. Again, the central issue is power. Just as business executives have enormous influence over the people "inside" their companies, they also have power over people and organizations that are "outside," but with which their operations and sometimes their destinies are intertwined. In Japan, West Germany, and other countries, groups of large and small firms are clustered in the form of cartels, keiretsu, and other confederations. America, despite its ideological preference for the Adam Smith model of small-firm competition, is home to many of the largest firms in the world, and they, too, are surrounded by vast cadres of suppliers and customers and often have close relationships with many government agencies.

Even when it is not part of a network of alliances, a firm's power extends beyond its boundaries. Through its products, the jobs it provides, the taxes it pays, and the business a firm gives its suppliers, a company influences, sometimes profoundly, the lives of many people. RU 486 provides a dramatic example. Its developers believed the drug could ultimately save tens of thousands of lives by providing another alternative to "coat hanger" abortions. Critics of RU 486 argued it would make abortion much easier, leading to more deaths of unborn children. RU 486 also seemed likely to change the politics of abortion: fewer abortions would take place in clinics, which were ready targets for protest, and abortions at the very start of a pregnancy seemed less likely to arouse political passions. In many other cases—less dramatic, but more commonplace than RU 486—a company's power and

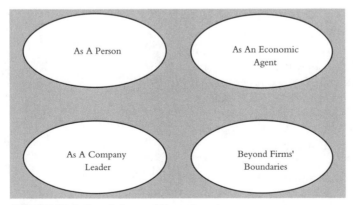

FIGURE 18.1 Four Spheres of Commitments

influence, and hence the responsibilities of its managers, also extend beyond the traditional boundaries of the firm. Pollution, unsafe products, and unfair competitive practices all injure other parties. And, when a company fails and shutters its factories, employees, their families, schools, local governments, and sometimes entire communities pay a price.

Obviously, managers cannot be held responsible for everything. Other groups in society—government bodies, labor unions, and consumers—have significant responsibilities as well. In the case of RU 486, for example, government bodies were responsible for decisions on whether abortions were legal and whether particular drugs were safe and effective while physicians and women made choices among medical procedures. Sometimes, the law or widely accepted practices provide answers that are clear and morally sound, but in many cases the situation is more complex. Roussel UCLAF, for example, had to decide whether to make RU 486 available to the Chinese government. China wanted the drug for its population control program. The country's population was already 1.1 billion, and demographers had described the early 1990s as "the Himalayas of population growth" because 150 million Chinese women would soon reach their prime child-bearing years, and the government's decade-old "one couple, one child" policy seemed to have failed.

RU 486 might have helped China manage its population growth, but Roussel UCLAF had to consider how the drug might be used. In particular, would it be given to women under the strict medical supervision planned for France? Might women be forced to take RU 486, violating the "right to choose" that many company officials believed in? Given these uncertainties, how far did the company's responsibility extend? One could argue that they stopped at the "point of sale," that Chinese physicians and public officials then became accountable for the use or misuse of the drug. This viewpoint avoids the taint of cultural imperialism by respecting the rights and competence of the Chinese government. But suppose RU 486 was given improperly (too late in a pregnancy, for example) at several rural clinics in China and some

women died, others were permanently injured, and some gave birth to handicapped children. Would the "point of sale" argument enable company executives to wash their hands of responsibility? Would this way of thinking allay the guilt they might feel? And would the publicity and fear resulting from these tragedies impede the use of the drug in other countries, even under careful medical supervision? Company responsibilities do not cease at the point when a customer exchanges cash for goods. But where does the buck stop in a web of interdependent actors and shared responsibility?

FOUR ENDURING QUESTIONS

Moral claims arising from different spheres of responsibility often collide with each other, creating difficult, sometimes anguishing dilemmas for business executives. There is, unfortunately, no final, supreme principle for resolving conflicts of responsibility—not in the Bible or the Koran, nor in philosophy or theology books, not in the law, nor deep in the human heart, nor anywhere else. There is instead a long tradition of serious thought about power and responsibility that can help executives deal with conflicts among commitments and mitigate the problem of dirty hands. This tradition of thought is not a progression of ideas, culminating in some final conclusion, but a long, reflective conversation—spanning many generations, varied cultures, different social, political, and economic conditions, and the experiences and insights of many individuals.

Four questions represent important voices in this long conversation. Each encapsulates a fundamental idea about the responsibilities of men and women in positions of power. Moreover, each is closely associated with a handful of thinkers who used the question to crystal-lize the moral issues that confronted their societies at crucial moments in human history. Used together, the four questions provide a basic framework for assessing possible ways of resolving a difficult dilemma. The four questions are:

• Which course of action will do the most good and the least harm?

- Which alternative best serves others' rights, including shareholders' rights?
- What plan can I live with, which is consistent with the basic values and commitments of my company?
- Which course of action is feasible in the world as it is?

The first question—what will do the most good and the least harm—focuses on the morality of consequences. It is, in rough terms, John Stuart Mill's question. His basic view, called utilitarianism, is that morally good actions bring the best consequences for everyone they affect and do so with the least cost, risk, and harm. In the case of RU 486, the consequences were enormous: the survival of the Roussel UCLAF, the health and safety of millions of women who might use RU 486, the health of people with diseases the drug could treat, and the morality, politics, and regulation of abortion around the world.

Mill's question asks managers to examine the full range of consequences that will result from different ways of resolving a dilemma. The basic question must be broken into sub-questions: Which groups and individuals will benefit from different ways of resolving a dilemma? How greatly? Who will be put at risk or suffer? How severe will the suffering be? Can the risk and harm be alleviated? These questions, inevitably, serve as starting points of a process of fact-gathering and analysis; they are not a formula for reaching conclusions. There are no universal definitions of good or harm, nor are there any hard and fast ways of measuring and trading off harms and benefits against each other. Much depends upon particular circumstances, institutions, and legal and social arrangements. But the basic guiding question remains: Which course of action is likely to do the most good and the least harm?

The second question focuses on the morality of rights, an idea that crystallized in the seventeenth and eighteenth centuries. For Americans, the question is Thomas Jefferson's. His draft of the *Declaration of Independence* stated bluntly that human beings had inalienable rights to life, liberty, and the pursuit of happiness. We accept similar ideas in everyday life, believing that we and others have rights to be treated with respect, to have promises kept, to be told the truth, and to be spared unnecessary injury. Others have duties to respect these rights, particularly powerful individuals such as business executives. Hence, when executives consider various ways of resolving some dilemma, they must ask what rights are at stake. In the case of RU 486, this meant asking about the rights of women to have access to safer methods of abortion, about rights to safe medical procedures in countries with less developed medical infrastructures, and about the rights of the unborn.

Like the question of consequences, the question of rights does not draw sharp boundaries around companies or around managers' responsibilities. The question asks about the rights of everyone affected by a decision. Both questions are the ethical counterparts of what many management analysts now call the borderless world: they look beyond the familiar boundaries of firm and nations, acknowledging Dr. Martin Luther King's insight that all people are bound together in a "seamless web of mutuality."

The third great force in moral thinking is captured in the third question. It asks: What course of action can I live with? What best serves my commitments and aspirations in life? And, for a business executive, this perspective asks: What course of action is most consistent with the kind of human community we are seeking to create? The roots of these questions lie in Aristotle's philosophy and in many religions. They ask executives who face difficult decisions to search their consciences, to regard their lives and aspirations as a whole, to ask, in effect, what they want to appear in their obituaries. This perspective also asks managers to think hard about what kind of human community their company is, and about the values that guide it and the purposes it solves. Inevitably, executives in wrenching situations, like that faced by the executives at Roussel UCLAF, will ask themselves—as they should—what course of action they can live with, as individuals and as leaders of a particular company.

The fourth question is Machiavelli's. It asks, purely pragmatically, what will work in the world as it is? In any situation, there may be several options that could, in theory, reconcile the competing claims. The crucial question then becomes: What is actually feasible—in view of a manager's actual power in an organization, a company's competitive, financial, and political strength, the likely costs and risks of various plans of action, and the time available for action?

For some people, this question is amoral or worse. It focuses on the means, not the ends, and it fails to examine the morality of the means. Moreover, Nicolo Machiavelli, the fifteenth-century Italian statesman and political philosopher, is widely considered an apologist for unscrupulous opportunism. But Machiavelli would not be remembered today for simply having argued the obvious: that unscrupulous people often get ahead. Machiavelli was a realist, preoccupied with "the necessities of power," with what leaders must do so their organizations can at least survive and perhaps prosper in the world that one finds, not the world one hopes for. Hence, morality must be practical. For people with real responsibility, meaning well is

not good enough. A plan of action, however high-minded it may be, usually accomplishes little if it does not work. Moreover, Machiavelli's question was not a request for the cautious, satisficing action plans of the "organization man." He asked what will work if a leader is resourceful, persistent, imaginative, bold, and does not shun risk.

The four questions must be asked and answered together because, in crucial ways, they balance and correct each other. Enshrining any of them as "the answer" is dangerous. Machiavelli's question is a strong pull towards practicality, but as a sole perspective on difficult decisions it risks sleazy opportunism and needs to be balanced by the explicitly ethical concerns of the other three questions. Aristotle's question tries to root decisions in the abiding values of particular individuals and institutions; but this approach, by itself, can open the door to prejudiced, self-interested judgments.

In short, the moral dilemmas of management must be resolved through balancing acts—through decisions and actions that meet, as best they can, the conflicting claims of different spheres of responsibility. Edouard Sakiz's decision on RU 486 provides an instructive example. As mentioned earlier, Sakiz

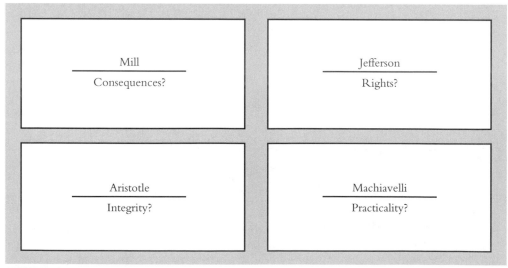

FIGURE 18.2 Four Questions.

voted to suspend distribution of the drug. Five days later, Roussel UCLAF announced to the public that "pressure from anti-abortion groups" had led to this decision. The result was a firestorm of criticism—from women's groups, family planning organizations, and physicians in Europe and the United States. A few days later, the French Minister of Health told Roussel UCLAF that he would use his legal authority to transfer the RU 486 patent to another firm unless the company changed its decision. Roussel UCLAF quickly agreed to market the drug in France. After the Minister's decision, the company's vice-chairman said: "We are now relieved of the moral burden weighing on our company."

How successfully did Roussel and its managers meet their conflicting responsibilities? Sakiz and his fellow executives met their personal aspirations, as scientists and medical researchers, to introduce an alternative to surgical abortions, one that might someday reduce the number of women who would suffer and die from abortions, especially in poor countries. Their decision respected the rights of women, guaranteed by French law, to decide whether to seek an abortion, and it also acknowledged the right of the French government to play a role in a decision with potentially vast moral, social, and medical consequences. The rights of shareholders were served because a promising new product was brought to market, but in a fashion that might have diverted protests and boycotts away from Roussel UCLAF and its parent since the French government made the final decision on marketing RU 486. Finally, the company sought to achieve important consequences—principally re-

ducing suffering and death—while seeking to minimize the negative repercussions for the firm, its executives, and Roussel UCLAF employees.

Yet this decision was an anguishing one for Sakiz and had the marks of a "dirty hands" dilemma. Roussel UCLAF would not be spared protests and boycotts; threats of violence would continue. Its executives were accused of shirking their responsibilities by letting the government make the final decision: a prominent scientist who contributed greatly to the development of RU 486 called the company's initial decision against distribution a "moral scandal." Some people even accused Sakiz of Machiavellian maneuvering, alleging that he and the Minister of Health had orchestrated the whole series of decisions about RU 486. Opponents of abortions, in Europe and the United States, continued to criticize Roussel UCLAF and its executives for killing unborn children.

In some situations, there is no win-win solution. Life does not come with a guarantee that good intentions, hard work, imagination, and far-sightedness will turn all moral dilemmas into happy outcomes that satisfy the moral claims of all parties. The "best" way of resolving a dilemma may inevitably involve some violation of people's rights, it may bring harmful consequences, or it may severely test an executive's sense of integrity. Responsible, thoughtful, practical-minded people will often disagree on what is right in a particular situation. The four enduring questions posed above are not a formula for replacing judgment and are no guarantee against "dirty hands." They are, at best, an aid to judgment and a way to keep one's hands as clean as possible in the world as it is.

REFERENCES

1. Chester Barnard, *The Functions of the Executive* (Cambridge, MA: Harvard University Press, 1982), p. 278.

2. Jean-Paul Sartre, *Dirty Hands*, in *No Exit and Three Other Plays*, translated by Lionel Abel (New York, NY: Vintage International, 1989), p. 218. The specific problem Sartre poses, the prob-

lem of "dirty hands" in public life, is analyzed in Michael Walzer, "Political Action: The Problem of Dirty Hands," *Philosophy and Public Affairs* (Winter 1973), pp. 160–180.

3.   I am using the notion of spheres in a way that is roughly analogous to that developed by the political philosopher Michael Walzer. His analysis of distributive justice is based upon a division of social life into different spheres of activities—each centered upon different goods—such as health or education. Walzer argues that the moral standards governing the distribution of each of these goods derive not from some grand, over-arching theory of justice but rather from the particular meanings associated with a good in a particular community with a particular history. See Michael Walzer, *Spheres of Justice* (New York, NY: Basic Books, 1983), pp. 3–30.

4.   Richard H. Tawney, *Religion and the Rise of Capitalism* (New York, NY: Harcourt, Brace and Company, 1926), p. 184.

5.   Robert C. Clark, "Agency Costs Versus Fiduciary Duties," in John W. Pratt and Richard J. Zeckhauser, eds., *Principals and Agents: The Structure of Business*, (Boston, MA: Harvard Business School, 1985), pp. 71–79.

6.   Joseph Schumpeter, *Capitalism, Socialism, and Democracy*, 3rd edition (New York, NY: Harper Colophon/Harper & Row, 1975), pp. 67–68, 83.

7.   Robert Nozick, *Anarchy, State and Utopia* (New York, NY: Basic Books, Inc., 1974), p. 163.

8.   See Moriaki Tsuchiya, "The Japanese Firm as a Capsule," *Japanese Economic Studies* (Fall 1984), pp. 8–41.

9.   See Stanley Milgram, *Obedience to Authority* (New York, NY: Harper and Row, 1974).

10.   Reinhold Niebuhr, *Moral Man and Immoral Society: A Study in Ethics and Politics* (New York, NY: C. Scribner's Sons, 1932), p. xi.

11.   G.B. Richardson, "The Organization of Industry," *Economic Journal* (October 1972), p. 883.

19. THE GLOBALIZATION OF BUSINESS ETHICS: WHY AMERICA REMAINS DISTINCTIVE

David Vogel

In a number of important respects, the increased globalization of the economies of the United States, Western Europe, and Japan is making business practices more uniform. The structure and organization of firms, manufacturing technologies, the social organization of production, customer relations, product development, and marketing—are all becoming increasingly similar throughout the advanced industrial economies. One might logically think that a similar trend would be taking place with respect to the principles and practices of business ethics.

This is occurring, but only very slowly. Business ethics has not yet globalized; the norms of ethical behavior continue to vary widely in different capitalist nations. During the last decade, highly publicized incidents of misconduct on the part of business managers have occurred in virtually every major industrial economy. These scandals have played an important role in increasing public, business, and academic awareness of issues of business ethics in the United States, Western Europe, and Japan. Yet the extent of both public and academic interest in business ethics remains substantially greater in the United States than in other advanced capitalist nations. While interest in business ethics has substantially increased in a number of countries in Europe, and to a lesser extent in Japan, no other capitalist nation approaches the United States in the persistence and intensity of public concern with the morality of business conduct.

The unusual visibility of issues of business ethics in the United States lies in the distinctive institutional, legal, social, and cultural context of the American business system. Moreover the American approach to business ethics is also unique: it is more individualistic, legalistic, and universalistic than in other capitalist societies.

RECENT BUSINESS SCANDALS

Much of the current surge in public, business, and academic interest in business ethics in the United States can be traced to the scandals associated with Wall Street during the 1980s. Characterized by one journalist as "the most serious corporate crime wave since the foreign bribery cases of the mid-1970s," these abuses began with money-laundering by the Bank of Boston in 1986 and check-kiting by E. F. Hutton in 1987. They went on to include: violations of insider-trading regulations by Paul Thayer, who received a five-year jail term; Dennis Levine and the so-called "yuppie Five"; and Ivan Boesky, who was fined $100 million and sentenced to prison for three years. Half of all the cases brought by the SEC alleging illegal use of stock market information since 1949 were filed during a five-year period in the middle of the 1980s.

In 1988, "junk-bond king" Michael Milken and his firm, Drexel Burnham, were indicted for violat-

From: *California Management Review* Reprint Series © 1992 by The Regents of the University of California *CMR*, Volume 35, Number 1, Fall 1992

ing federal securities laws and regulations. Both subsequently paid large fines and Milken was sentenced to prison for ten years, subsequently reduced to two. At about the same time, the public became aware of widespread evidence of fraud in the savings and loan industry. A number of bankers were indicted and convicted, including Charles Keating Jr., head of one of the nation's largest savings and loan associations. In 1991, Salomon Brothers admitted that it had committed, "irregularities and rule violations in connection with its submission of bids in certain auctions of Treasury securities."[1] Two managing directors were suspended and the investment bank's Chairman and Chief Executive, John Gutfreund, was forced to resign after admitting that he had known of the firm's misconduct, but had neglected to report it.

Much of the recent increase in interest in business ethics outside the United States can also be attributed to various business scandals that came to light in Europe and Japan during roughly the same time-period. In 1982, an American company that had acquired a leading British member of Lloyd's found "undisclosed financial commitments and funds missing from the firm's reinsurance subsidiaries."[2] In 1985, another major scandal struck London's insurance market: 450 individual members of Lloyd's lost $180 million underwriting policies organized by agents who were alleged to have stolen some of the funds. At about the same time in London, "a wave of suspicious price movements in advance of takeover bids . . . prompted concern that insider trading is spreading."[3] In 1987, Geoffrey Collier, a top trader at Morgan Grenfell Group PLC, was indicted for illegally earning more than $20,000 on two mergers involving his prestigious investment banking firm.

The same year, Ernest Saunders, the chief executive of Guinness, a major British-based alcohol beverages company, was accused of attempting to illegally prop up the price of his company's shares in order to help support its bid for the Distillers beverages group. Saunders was arrested and spent a night in jail. He was subsequently forced to sell many of his possessions, including his spacious home in Buckinghamshire, to meet legal costs, and all of his remaining assets were frozen. Saunders' trial did not begin for another three and half years, making the "Guinness Affair," the most prolonged financial scandal in the history of the City of London. In 1990, Saunders was found guilty of having helped engineer the stock's "fortuitous rise" and was sentenced to five years in prison. Three other prominent executives were also found guilty in what has been described as the "financial trial of the century."[4] The Guardian noted, "The six-month trial has lifted the lid on the seamy side of the City, exposing a sordid story of greed, manipulation and total disregard for takeover regulations."[5]

In 1991, another prominent British businessmen, Robert Maxwell, was implicated in a number of wide-ranging abuses, including the looting of a large pension fund and deceptive record-keeping designed to conceal the insolvency of various firms that he controlled. Maxwell died under mysterious circumstances shortly before his "massive international confidence game"—involving large numbers of respectable British and American banks and accounting firms—became public.[6] It was subsequently revealed that Maxwell had plundered a total of £450 million from various pension funds he controlled.

In the fall of 1991, the Irish press reported that "four times in the [space of] 16 months, major Irish companies have been hit by crises over secret deals, alleged cover-ups and hidden conflicts of interest."[7] These "crises" included the falsification of company records by Aer Lingus Holidays and Goodman International, the purchase by Irish Sugar of a firm in which the company's chief executive was a part owner, and the "questionable purchase" of a piece of property by Telecom Eireann which had been previously owned by the firm's chairman, Michael Smurfit. Smurfit, the wealthiest businessmen in Ireland, was forced to resign his position following press disclosure of this apparent conflict of interest.

In 1989, the French stock market experienced two "blockbuster scandals" that "hinted of insider trading before takeovers."[8] In the most celebrated case, investors in France, Luxembourg and Switzerland bought more than 200,000 shares in the Triangle Corporation, shortly before the firm was acquired by Pechiney, the state-owned aluminum company. The stock purchases had been made in the United States and had been brought to the French Governments' attention by the Securities and Exchange Commission. While the accusations were "modest by American standards," they "ballooned into a huge scandal" that dominated the front pages of the French press for more than a week.[9]

In 1990, an official at Deutsche Bank, Germany's largest commercial bank and a major participant in Frankfurt's bank-dominated securities market, was implicated in tax evasion linked to insider trading.[10] By the summer of 1991, "the number of people under investigation in Germany for insider trading and/or related tax evasion [had] . . . risen to 25."[11] The following year, billionaire financier Carlo De Beneditti, Olivetti's Chief Executive Officer, was sentenced to six years in prison for having been an accessory to the 1982 collapse of Banco Ambrosiano. Thirty-two co-defendants were also convicted.[12]

Japan, too, has recently experienced a considerable number of business-related scandals. In the spring of 1987, one of the subsidiaries of the Toshiba Corporation was discovered to have sold advanced milling equipment to the Soviet navy to be used for making submarine propellers, in violation of both Japanese law and an international treaty restricting the export of military-related technology to Communist-bloc countries. Both the Chairman and President of the company were forced to resign. Shortly thereafter numerous cases of influence-peddling by the Recruit Company become public: a press report revealed that the firm had given shares at below-market prices to a number of prominent politicians in the ruling Liberal Democratic Party in exchange for various political favors. A number of politicians were forced to resign and the chairman of Recruit, Hisashi Shinto, along with several of his fellow executives, were indicted on bribery charges. On October 9, 1990,

Shinto was convicted: he was fined $170,000 and given a two-year prison term, which was suspended due to his age.

In 1991, another major scandal surfaced in Japan. Nomura Securities and Nikko Securities, two of Japan's major brokerage firms, admitted to having lent more than $250 million to a well-known underworld organization. Tax authorities revealed that the same two firms had been secretly reimbursing large clients for stock market loses; other firms were subsequently implicated in this practice as well. In addition, the Sumitomo Bank, Japan's second largest, had lent more than $1 billion to an Osaka trading company headed by a former official of the bank, who then squandered nearly $2 billion in "shady deals." In another major banking scandal, a number of Japan's most prestigious financial institutions, including the Industrial Bank of Japan Ltd., were linked to a scheme involving $2.5 billion in fraudulently obtained loans. In the Spring of 1992, former Chisan Co. Chairman Hirotomo Takai was sentenced to four years in prison and fined $3.8 million dollars for evading $25.6 million in taxes, "the largest-ever tax fraud by an individual."[13] And in 1992, Sagawa Kyubin, a mob-related company, was revealed to have donated more than $17 million to a number of prominent Japanese politicians, including three former prime ministers and two current cabinet members.

Three important business-related scandals have also occurred in Australia. In July 1989, five prominent businessmen, including Ian Johns, the former managing director of an Australian merchant bank, were arrested and charged with insider trading. The following month, Laurie Connell, a prominent Perth financier, was charged with making statements in the annual report of Rothwells, the merchant bank that collapsed in 1988. In 1990, George Herscu, the bankrupt Australian property magnate, was sentenced to five years in jail for bribing a state government minister. Two years later, Alan Bond, one of Australia's most successful entrepreneurs—his fortune is estimated at $7.6 billion—was sentenced to two and one-half years in prison for fraud.

THE RESPONSE

As a response, in part, to these numerous cases of business misconduct, the level of public, business, and academic interest in issues of business ethics increased throughout much of the industrialized world. While interest in this subject was largely confined to the United States during the 1970s, during the 1980s it spread to a number of other capitalist nations as well. In 1983, the first chair in business ethics was established in Europe at the Netherlands School of Business; a second was established at another Dutch university three years later and four more have been founded subsequently in other European countries. In 1986, the Lord Mayor of London organized a formal conference on company philosophy and codes of business ethics for 100 representatives from industry and the professions. The following year, a group of 75 European business managers and academics established the European Business Ethics Network (EBEN); its first conference was held in 1987, and four more have been held since, most recently in Paris in 1992. In 1987, the first European business ethics journal, *Ethica Degli Affari*, was published, in Italy.

Since the mid-1980s, two ethics research centers have been established in Great Britain, in addition to one each in Belgium, Spain, Germany, and Switzerland. A survey of developments in European business ethics published in 1990 reported that, "since three or four years ago the stream of publications (on business ethics) has been rapidly growing," with a disproportionate amount coming from Great Britain, Germany, Austria, and Switzerland.[14] In addition to the EBEN, business ethics networks have been established and national conferences held in Italy (1988), France (1989), and the Netherlands (1990).

Three leading European business schools—INSEAD in France, the London Business School, and Italy's Bocconni—have established elective courses in business ethics and several others have held public conferences on this topic; some have also begun to include sessions on ethics in their executive educational programs. The first European business ethics casebook was published in 1991 and the first issue of a management-oriented publication, *Business Ethics: A European Review*, appeared in the winter of 1992.[15] Interest in business ethics is also increasing in Japan, though on a much smaller scale. In 1989 and 1991, the Institute of Moralogy sponsored international ethics conferences in Kashiwa City, Chiba Ken, Japan.

THE "ETHICS GAP"

Notwithstanding these initiatives, the "ethics gap," between the United States and the rest of the developed world remains substantial. By any available measure, the level of public, business, and academic interest in issues of business ethics in the United States far exceeds that in any other capitalist country. Nor does this gap show any sign of diminishing: while interest in the subject in Europe has increased in recent years, its visibility in America has increased even more.

In America, each new disclosure of business misconduct prompts a new wave of public indignation, accompanied by numerous articles in the business and popular press which bemoan the general decline in the ethical conduct of managers and seek to explain "what went wrong" in the most recent case. This is frequently followed by Congressional hearings featuring politicians demanding more vigilant prosecution of white-collar criminals; shortly thereafter, regulatory standards are tightened, penalties are increased, and enforcement efforts are strengthened. Executives, in turn, make speeches emphasizing the importance of good ethical behavior for business success, using the most recent round of indictments and associated business failures to demonstrate the "wages of sin." Business educators then re-emphasize the need for additional instruction in ethics, often receiving substantial sums of money from various businessmen to support new educational programs. The most recent scandal then becomes the subject of a case, to be taught in an ever increasing number of business ethics courses designed to assist the next generation of managers in avoiding the pitfalls of their predecessors. When a new scandal occurs—as it invariably does—the cycle begins anew.

No comparable dynamic has occurred in other capitalist nations, where public interest in business ethics tends to be episodic rather than cumulative: thus, only in America are the 1980s referred to as a "decade of greed." As the *Financial Times* noted in the summer of 1992, "Despite the all-pervasive scandals of the 1980s, there is a tendency in Europe to regard the study of business ethics as faddish."[16] To be sure, the level of public concern with the mortality of business does vary in other capitalist nations. For example, it has been much higher in Great Britain and the Netherlands than in Japan. But no other nation has approached the United States in the intensity and duration of public interest in business misconduct. Why? Why are Americans so outraged? How can one account for the distinctive importance of issues of business ethics in American society?

The most obvious explanation is that the conduct of American business has in fact been less ethical. Thus, Americans may be more preoccupied with the ethics of business because there is more misconduct to worry about. Not surprisingly, this explanation is favored by many European managers. However it is not persuasive. Certainly Japan has experienced at least as many major business scandals, and yet there is less interest in business ethics in Japan than in any other major capitalist nation. Moreover, when one compares the relative size of the American economy to that of other capitalist nations, it is not true that either more, or more important, cases of misconduct by businessmen have surfaced in the United States during the last decade.

Rather the importance of issues of business ethics in the United States lies in the distinctive institutional, legal, social, and cultural context of the American business system. In brief, Americans are more concerned with the ethics of business because they have higher expectations of business conduct. Not only is more business conduct considered unethical in the United States, but unethical behavior is more likely to be exposed, punished, and therefore become a "scandal" in America than in other capitalist nations.

MORE REGULATION

The most important reason why there appears to be so much more white-collar crime in the United States is that there are so many more laws regulating business in the United States to be broken. Moreover, regulations governing business tend to be more strictly enforced in the United States than in other capitalist nations. In addition, thanks to more aggressive journalism, as well as to government disclosure requirements, business misdeeds are more likely to be exposed in the United States.

One British journalist commented following the "Maxwell mess," that, "unlike in America, there is no vigorous probing process that names and uncovers embarrassments. Regulators here are invariably shy about using their powers and often are unable to do so."[17] The situation in Britain is in striking contrast to the resources the American federal government devoted to investigating and prosecuting Michael Milken. Moreover, British libel laws also make it more difficult for journalists to disclose the abuses they do uncover. Some observers have suggested that the French insider-trading scandal of 1989 would have been buried, "as previous French governments . . . have buried previous scandals, were it not for the SEC's involvement."[18] One Japanese journalist recently observed, "In Japan today, if you have the word 'Inc.' attached to your name, you can commit crimes with little risk and only minor penalties."[19] In fact, the only reason why the "dubious behavior" of Japan's brokerage firms in reimbursing clients for losses became a major financial scandal in 1991 was due to the involvement of organized crime; otherwise the government would have been unlikely to investigate.

By contrast, with the active help of an unrestricted and uninhibited media that places a high priority on investigative reporting, Congressional committees with substantial resources to conduct investigations, and ninety-five entrepreneurial United States Attorneys, America appears to have developed a "great . . . scandal machine [that is] running with ferocious momentum."[20] The chances that business misdeeds will escape exposure and prosecution are fewer in the United States than in any other capitalist nation.

Moreover, many activities for which American managers and corporations have pleaded guilty or have been convicted—most notably making campaign contributions from company funds and providing gifts to foreign government officials to secure contracts—are not illegal in other capitalist nations. This is also the case with respect to the violations of American securities laws to which Michael Milken pleaded guilty, as well as for Salomon Brothers' violations of the Treasury Department's bond trading rules (in fact, the rule that Salomon broke only came into existence in the United States some months earlier). With the exception of France, insider trading was legal throughout Europe until the early 1980s. It is still not against the law in Germany—although there is a voluntary code prohibiting it—and was only banned in Japan in 1989.

The issue of sexual harassment also illustrates of the contrast between the standards of business conduct in America and other capitalist nations. Americans in general and American women in particular have higher standards for the conduct of male managers and more reason to expect that their complaints will be taken seriously by both the press and by government officials than in most other capitalist nations. While sexual harassment has been considered a form of sex discrimination in the United States since 1979, it only became illegal in France in 1992, while the concept itself was translated into Japanese for the first time in 1989. The first successful legal action against sexual harassment in Japan took place in April 1992. Moreover, American laws and regulations governing workplace discrimination on the basis of sex are both stricter—and better enforced—than in most other capitalist nations.

LEGAL VULNERABILITY

Another distinctive feature of the contemporary legal environment of business in the United States is the relatively large exposure of both individual executives and corporations to legal prosecution. As recently as two decades ago, the prosecution of individuals for white-collar crime in the United States was relatively rare. On occasion, high-status individuals were sentenced to prison; for example, in 1938, Richard Whitney, who had been president of the New York Stock Exchange, was found guilty of embezzlement and sentenced to five years in federal prison. In the early 1960s, a handful of senior managers from General Electric and Westinghouse received light prison sentences after they were found guilty of price-fixing.

However, this began to change in the early 1970s when, in connection with Watergate, a number of high-status individuals were sentenced to prison. By the end of the decade, what began as a trickle had become a flood: "Businessmen spent more time in jail for price-fixing in 1978 than in all the 89 years since the passage of the Sherman Antitrust Act."[21] Sixty-five percent of the individuals convicted of security law violations during the 1980s received jail sentences.

While the Federal Corrupt Practices Act made senior managers personally liable for monitoring its enforcement, the most important increase in the exposure of individual managers for corporate compliance took place in the area of environmental law. As recently as 1983, "jail sentences for polluters were unheard of."[22] In 1984, Federal courts handed out prison terms totaling two years and individual fines totaling $198,000. But five years later they handed out prison terms totaling 37 years and fines totaling $11.1 million. The number of individuals indicted increased from 40 in 1983 to 134 in 1990. Between 1986 and 1991, a total of 90 individuals were jailed for Federal environmental crimes. Of those sentenced to prison for environmental violations through 1988, one-third were corporate presidents while less than one-quarter were workers who had actually released the pollution.

During the 1980s Congress added tougher criminal penalties to a number of environmental statutes while Federal sentencing guidelines issued in 1987 increased penalties for a number of environmental violations, putting them on a par with drug-related felonies. "As a result, jail has become much more likely for defendants in environmental cases, even for first-time offenders."[23] The Clean Air Act Amendments of 1990 not only expanded the number of violations that can be treated as criminal, but subjected to criminal prosecution any executive who had knowledge that a particular violation had taken place. According to a government official, now senior executives "realize that there is a real risk" of a prison term when environmental damage can be traced specifically to a company's acts. He added, "the word has really gotten out because of the increased level of enforcement." A corporate lawyer commented, "[Prosecutors] don't have much flexibility. If [the company] make[s] a mistake, the guy's going to jail."[24]

The *Economist* observed, "Polluters . . . have replaced drug-money launderers as the favorite target of government prosecutors out to make a name for themselves.[25] The number of lawyers employed by the environmental crimes section of the Justice Department increased from 3 in 1982 to 25 in 1991, while the criminal enforcement program of the Environmental Protection Agency grew from 23 investigators in 1982 to 60 in 1991. Similar expansions took place in a number of states.

A growing number of executives also have been indicted on criminal charges for violations of workplace health and safety regulations. In one "landmark" case, Film Recovery Inc., three corporate officials were, for the first time in American history, found guilty of murder in connection with the death of an employee. The owner and executives were jailed for 25 years each and fined for murder, involuntary manslaughter, and reckless conduct for knowingly exposing their employees to workplace hazards. Nearly one-half of American states now have legislation providing for corporate criminal liability for the death of employees. "Los Angeles County law-enforcement officers have been requested to treat every workplace fatality as a potential homicide."[26]

Not only has there been a steady increase in the number of corporate law violations classified as criminal, but the federal government also has become much more aggressive in seeking large financial penalties against corporations. The average corporate fine increased eight-fold between 1988 and 1990. Prominent corporations fined substantial sums from the mid-1980s to 1992 include the Bank of Boston ($500,000 for violating the Bank Secrecy Act of 1970); Exxon ($100 million for the Exxon Valdez disaster); Chrysler ($7.5 million for rolling back odometers in more than 60,000 vehicles); General Electric ($10 million for overbilling the government for computers); Northrop ($17 million for weapons test fraud); Salomon Inc. ($200 million in penalities); and Drexel Burnham ($650 million in fines and restitution for violations of federal securities laws). The penality imposed on Drexel was the largest in the history of capitalism and helped force the firm into bankruptcy—a fate that has not befallen any large firm subject to government prosecution in either Europe or Japan.

One important reason why so many American corporations have established ethics codes and training programs has to do with federal sentencing guidelines that went in effect on November 1, 1991, but which had been made public much earlier. These guidelines not only double the median fine for corporations found guilty of crimes such as fraud, but state that companies convicted of various crimes will receive more lenient treatment if they have previously demonstrated good faith efforts to "be a good corporate citizen." For example, "a fine of $1 million to $2 million could be knocked down to as low as $50,000 for a company with a comprehensive program, including a code of conduct, an ombudsman, a hotline, and mandatory training programs for executives."[27]

ENFORCEMENT IN EUROPE AND JAPAN

It is true that regulation has been strengthened and penalties increased in other capitalist nations as well. For example, in response to the deregulation of London's capital markets that took place in the mid-1980s, the British Government moved to better protect the interest of investors. Britain now has unlimited fines and up to two years of imprisonment for insider-trading violations. However, the British have emphasized the streamlining of industry self-regulation, not the establishment of a government oversight body similar to the American Securities and Exchange Commission. Notwithstanding the Saunders case, enforcement, while it has increased, still "remains infrequent" in Britain.[28]

In response to the insider-trading scandals that occurred in France during the late 1980s, the French Government expanded the size and power of the Commission des Operations de Bourse, its principal stock market oversight agency. Previously known as a "small and toothless watchdog," its budget was increased fourfold and its staff size doubled—making it comparable in resources to the S.E.C.[29] It also was empowered to impose fines of up to 10 million francs (approximately $2 million) or up to ten times the illegal profits in cases involving insider trading. Insider trading in France is also punishable by up to two years in prison. However, France's regulatory agency has yet to use its new authority to impose civil fines for insider trading, although through the summer of 1991, it had conducted 79 investigations and turned 15 of them over to prosecutors.

Following a highly publicized number of financial scandals in Japan, four prominent businessmen—the president and chairman of Nomura, the chairman of Sumitomo Bank, and the president of Nikko Securities—were forced to resign in the fall of 1991. But only one individual was arrested. The Ministry of Finance subsequently imposed suspensions of up to six weeks on Japan's four leading stockbrokers. Although this represented "some of the stiffest sentences ever meted out by ministerial order," unlike in the case of Drexel, the penalty did not affect the four companies' dominance of Japanese stock trading. Nor has the Ministry of Finance made a serious effort to strengthen its regulation of Japan's financial markets. The maximum fine for violating the recently enacted ban on brokers for paying compensation for losses is only ¥500,000 (approximately $3,760). There has been only one prosecution for insider trading, and only one for share-price manipulation, "even though market professionals consider this to be a chronic problem."[30]

The prosecution of violators of environmental regulations has increased in a number European countries. For example, the German penal code was recently amended to provide for the increased use of criminal penalties. "The German criminal law system is considered to be one of the best legal systems for the protection of the environment."[31] The number of criminal proceedings nearly doubled between 1980 and 1985, while the rate of conviction is among the highest in Europe.

Criminal law has also begun to be used to enforce environmental regulations in Spain, Sweden, Holland, and Finland. However, criminal penalties are still not imposed on polluters in France, Italy, and Britain. Historically, the British have been reluctant to impose any form of judicial penalties against violators of environmental regulations. This has recently begun to change; for example, the number of successful civil prosecutions against companies and individuals initiated by the newly established National Rivers Authority increased from 334 in 1989 to 574 in 1990. But fines remain modest: only two have been for more than £200,000, with the average less than £10,000. Moreover, the individuals who have been prosecuted have been small businessmen and farmers, not corporate executives. Even in Germany, it remains highly unusual for senior managers to be held personally responsible for environmental violations committed by their subordinates.

On balance during the last 15 years, more corporate officers and prominent businessmen have been jailed or fined in the United States than in all other capitalist nations combined. Likewise, the fines imposed on corporations in the United States have been substantially greater than in other capitalist nations. While the penalties for white-collar crime also have increased outside the United States, over the last decade the magnitude of the difference between the legal vulnerability of corporations and individual managers in the United States and those in other capitalist nations has increased. This development both reflects the high standards that exist for corporate conduct in the United States and also serves to re-enforce the perception that business misconduct is more pervasive in the United States.

PUBLIC EXPECTATIONS

The high expectations of business conduct in the United States are not confined to the legal system. They also are reflected in the way many Americans invest and consume. For example, "ethical investment" funds in the United States enable individuals and institutions to make their investment strategy consistent with their political/ social values either by avoiding investments in firms they judge to be behaving irresponsibly or by increasing their holdings of the stocks and bonds of firms that are acting "socially responsibly." While such funds exist in a number of European countries—including Britain and the Netherlands—they both originated and remain much larger in the United States. The same is true of the use of various social criteria to screen investments by institutional investors. For example, in no other capitalist nation have so many institutional investors divested themselves of shares of firms with investments in South Africa.

The American penchant for evaluating and comparing corporate social and ethical performance extends beyond capital markets; it also informs consumer judgments of business. Various private non-profit organizations in America regularly "rank" corporations in terms of their behavior on such dimensions as women and minority employment, military contracting, concern about the environment, and animal testing; one such guide, published by the Council on Economic Priorities, has sold more than 350,000 copies.[32] Such rankings are virtually unknown outside the United States, as are awards for "excellence in ethics." The Japanese may be obsessed with ranking corporations, but they appear to have overlooked this particular dimension of corporate performance.

Similarly, the number of companies that have been subject to consumer boycotts on the basis of their social policies has increased substantially in the United States in recent years. By contrast, consumer boycotts are much less common in Europe and virtually unknown in Japan (the most recent took place in the early 1970s and it involved the prices of televisions). A number of consumer boycotts have taken place in Great Britain, but far fewer than in the United States—even after taking into account the relative sizes of the two economies.

Once again, the contrast in public expectations of business behavior in the United States and other capitalist nations is marked: relatively few consumers or investors outside the United States appear to pay much attention to the political and social behavior of the firms whose products they consume or whose stocks and bonds they purchase. Indeed, what is striking is how little writing on business ethics in continental Europe actually mentions individual corporations at all; rather it tends to focus on more abstract concerns having to do with the relationship between ethics and economics. This is also true of the numerous statements of the Papacy on the "moral philosophy of business," which focus on the justice or lack thereof of the economic system, not on the ethics of particular corporations.[33] More generally, the debate over the role of business in Europe has focused on how to organize the economy, while in the United States it has emphasized standards of conduct for companies whose private ownership is assumed.

This is in turn may be due to another distinctive characteristic of American society, namely, the considerable emphasis that has historically been placed on the social obligations of business. Because business corporations played a critical role in the development of cities and the shaping of communities in the United States, they have long been perceived as social institutions with substantial responsibility for the moral and physical character of the communities in which they have invested. Both the doctrine of corporate social responsibility and the practice of corporate philanthropy date back more than a century in the United States. By contrast, in both Europe and Japan, the responsibility of business has historically been defined more narrowly. Since all these economies, with the exception of Britain, industrialized latter, it was government rather than corporations that both set the terms of economic development and assumed responsibility for various civic functions. Even today, corporate philanthropy remains primarily an American phenomenon.

BUSINESS VALUES

Ironically, it may be precisely because the values of "business civilization" are so deeply ingrained in American society that Americans tend to become so upset when the institutions and individuals whom they have looked up to—and whose values and success they have identified with—betray their trust. More generally: "In the United States . . . the single all-pervasive 'ought' rampages widely beyond the control of the 'is.' The result is a unique and ever-present challenge . . . posed by the gap between the ideals by which the society lives and the institutions by which it functions."[34] Because the public's expectations of business conduct are so high, the invariable result is a consistently high level of public dissatisfaction with the actual ethical performance of business.

An important key to understanding the unique interest of Americans in the subject of business ethics lies in America's Protestant heritage: "The United States is the only country in the world in which a majority of the population has belonged to dissenting Protestant sects."[35] This has important implications for the way in which Americans approach the subject of business ethics. By arguing that one can and should do "God's work" by creating wealth, Protestantism raised the public's expectations of the moral behavior of business managers. Thus, thanks in part to the role played by Reformed Protestantism in defining American values, America remains a highly moralistic society. Compared to the citizens of other capitalist nations, Americans are more likely to believe that business and morality are, and should be, related to each other, that good ethics is good business, and that business activity both can and should be consistent with high personal moral values.

While the high expectations of business conduct shared by Americans has a strong populist dimension, this particular understanding of the proper relationship between business and morality is not in any sense anti-business. It is also shared by much of the American business community. Indeed, the latter appear as concerned about the ethical lapses of their colleagues as is the American public. A survey of key business leaders conducted by Touche Ross in 1987 reported that more than two-thirds believe "that the issue of ethics in business has not been overblown in the current public debate."[36] Admittedly, some of these expressions of concern about business ethics amount to little more than public relations. But it is impossible to read through the reports on business ethics in the United States issued by such organizations as the Business Roundtable, Touche Ross, or the Conference Board without being struck by the sincerity of the concerns of the executives whose views they report.

Where else but in the United States would a group of nationally prominent executives establish and fund an organization such as the Business Enterprise Trust in order to offer annual awards for outstanding ethical behavior by corporations and individual managers?[37] While the belief that good ethics and high profits go hand in hand is certainly not confined to American businessmen, they seem to articulate it more frequently than do their counterparts in other capitalist nations. One senses that many of the latter are a bit more cynical about this relationship. For example, in Germany, "Insider trading doesn't have much of a stigma. Tax evasion is a gentleman's sport."[38]

Because the moral status of capitalism in Europe has traditionally been problematic, there appears to be much more cynicism about the ethics of business in Europe and Japan. Europeans, in part due to the legacy of aristocratic and pre-capitalist values, have always tended to view the pursuit of profit and wealth as somewhat morally dubious, making them less likely to be surprised—let alone outraged—when companies and managers are discovered to have been "greedy." For their part, the "Japanese seem almost inured to the kind of under-the-table favors whose disclosure sparked the [1991] scandal." As one Japanese investor put it, "It's so much a part of Japanese culture and tradition that the people don't think they're doing anything wrong."[39]

One Japanese political consultant recently mused: "I wonder sometimes when the Japanese people will rise up and say, 'We've had enough'" But the only answer I can give for sure is 'Not in this century, at least.'"[40]

Not surprisingly, many Europeans regard the current level of interest of Americans in the ethics and morality of business conduct—to say nothing of other aspects of American society—as somewhat excessive. Corporate codes of conduct, ethics training programs, lists of "ethical" and "unethical" firms—are all seen as signs of an "unusually moralizing society," one that "people in old and cynical Europe often find difficult to take . . . seriously."[41] The extent of moral scrutiny and self-criticism that pervades contemporary American society prompted the *Economist* to publish an editorial entitled, "Hey, America, Lighten Up A Little."[42]

KEY DIFFERENCES IN BUSINESS ETHICS

The United States is distinctive not only in the intensity of public concern with the ethical behavior of business, but also in the way in which business ethics are defined. Americans tend to emphasize the role of the individual as the most critical source of ethical values, while in other capitalist nations relatively more emphasis is placed on the corporation as the locus of ethical guidance. Second, business ethics tends to be much more legalistic and rule-oriented in the United States. Finally, Americans are more likely to consider their own ethical rules and standards to be universally applicable.

Business ethics in the United States has been strongly affected by the "tradition of liberal individualism that . . . is typical of American culture."[43] Not surprisingly, a frequent characteristics of business ethics cases developed in the United States is that they require the individual to decide what is right on the basis of his or her own values. While the company's goals and objectives or the views of the individual's fellow employees are not irrelevant,

in the final analysis they are not intended to be decisive. Indeed, they may often be in conflict.

By contrast, "in European circumstances it is not at all evident that managers, when facing a moral dilemma, will navigate first and foremost on their personal moral compass."[44] Rather managers are more likely to make decisions based on their shared understanding of the nature and scope of the company's responsibilities. The legitimate moral expectations of a company are shaped by the norms of the community, not the personal values or reflections of the individual. The latter has been labeled "communicative" or "consensual" business ethics."[45]

One possible outcome of the tension between the interests and values of the company and those of the individual employee is whistle-blowing. Critics of business in the United States have urged increased legal protection for whistle-blowers— and, in fact, some regulatory statutes in the United States explicitly protect those who publicly expose violations of various company policies.

By contrast, the idea that there could even be such a tension between the individual and the organization is thoroughly alien to Japanese business culture, where whistle-blowers would be regarded more as traitors than heroes. Only a handful of European countries have laws protecting whistle-blowers. And few non-American firms have established formal mechanisms, such as the appointment of ombudsmen, to enable employees to voice their moral concerns about particular corporate policies. Workers in many other capitalist nations may well feel a greater sense of loyalty toward the firms for which they work, and a greater respect for those in authority.

A second critical difference between business ethics in America and other capitalist countries has to do with the role of law and formal rules. Notwithstanding—or perhaps because of—its traditions of individualism, Americans tend to define business ethics in terms of rules; the writing on business ethics by Americans is replete with checklists, principles, and guidelines for individual managers to follow in distinguishing right from wrong.

Americans' tendency to think of ethics in terms of rules is reflected in the widespread use of corporate codes among U.S.-based companies. Such codes are much less common in Europe, although their use has recently increased in Britain. One French observer notes:

The popularity of codes of ethics in the United States meets with little response in Europe, America's individualism does not correspond to the social traditions of Europe. These large differences make fruitless all desire to imitate the other's steps.[46]

One French manager, whose firm had recently been acquired by an American company, stated:

I resent having notions of right and wrong boiled down to a checklist. I come from a nation whose ethical traditions date back hundreds of years. Its values have been transmitted to me by my church and through my family. I don't need to be told by some American lawyers how I should conduct myself in my business activities.[47]

Henri-Claude de Bettignies, who teaches business ethics at INSEAD, adds:

Some European leaders perceive corporate codes of conduct as a device which deresponsibilizes the individual, i.e., he does not have to think for himself, he just needs to apply the codes of conduct which he has learnt and which—through training—have programmed him to respond in a certain "corporate" way.[48]

By contrast, European firms appear to place greater emphasis on informal mechanisms of social control within the firm. Indeed, European managers frequently profess astonishment at the apparent belief of many American executives, as well as government officials, that a company's adoption of a code can actually alter the behavior of its employees.

There is a third critical difference between business ethics in the United States and other capitalist nations. Americans not only tend to define business ethics in terms of rules and procedures; they also tend to believe that American rules and procedures should be applied universally. For example, no other nation requires the foreign subsidiaries of its multinational corporations to follow the laws of their home country as frequently as does the United

States. Thus the United States is the only nation that restricts its firms from making payments to secure contracts or other benefits outside its borders. A survey of European executives reported that, "nearly 40 percent would never complain about bribery by a business rival—or answer charges of bribery against themselves."[49] Similarly, in no other nation have corporations been so frequently criticized for exporting products that do not conform to the health and safety standards of their "home" country.

Universalism also has a second dimension having to do with the importance of the distinction between "us" and "them." American business culture—and American society—attaches considerable importance to treating everyone in the same arm's-length manner. By contrast, the Japanese—and, to a lesser extent, the citizens of Latin Europe—define their responsibilities in more particularistic terms: managers, as well as government officials, in these countries place less value on treating everyone equally and attach much more importance to fulfilling their obligations to those individuals and institutions with whom they have developed long-standing and long-term relationships. (Significantly, it is very difficult to translate the phrases "equal opportunity" and "level playing field" into Japanese.) On this dimension, Britain and much of northern Europe is much closer to the United States.

All these dimensions are, in fact, inter-related. To summarize the American approach: business ethics is about individuals making moral judgments based on general rules that treat everyone the same. By contrast, business ethics in Europe and Japan has more to do with managers arriving at decisions based on shared values, often rooted in a particular corporate culture, applied according to specific circumstances and strongly affected by the nature of one's social ties and obligations.

CONCLUSION

Regulatory rules and standards, especially within the European Community and between the United

States and Western Europe, are certainly becoming more similar. For example, a strengthening of environmental regulation has occurred in virtually all capitalist nations, while legal restrictions on insider trading—a decade ago, largely confined to the United States—are now the norm in Europe. Similarly, a number of European nations have recently enacted legislation banning sexual harassment. The prosecution of white-collar criminals has also recently increased in Europe. In 1989, the first Swede to be found guilty of insider trading was sentenced to five years in prison. Not only are many American legal norms and standards of corporate conduct being adopted in other capitalist nations, but as globalization proceeds and world commerce is increasingly driven by multinational firms, these firms may well come to adopt common ethical standards. These developments are important. But they continue to be overshadowed by the persistence of fundamental national differences in the ways in which business ethics is defined, debated, and judged.

While much has been written on differences in the laws and business norms of developed and less-developed nations, the equally important contrasts in the way in which ethical issues are discussed and defined *among* the developed nations has been all but ignored.[50] Significantly, among the hundreds of ethics cases developed for use in management education in the United States and Europe, only *one*—Toshiba Machine Company—contrasts differences in ethical norms between two advanced industrial nations.[51] We need a better appreciation of the differences in the legal and cultural context of business ethics between the United States and other capitalist nations, and between Western and Asian economies as well, if managers are to work effectively in an increasingly integrated global economy.

REFERENCES

1. "The Salomon Shocker: How Bad Will It Get?" *Business Week*, August 26, 1991, p. 36.

2. Barnaby Feder, "Overseeing Insurance Reform at London's Venerable Mart," *New York Times*, January 8, 1984, p. 6.

3. Gary Putka, "British Face Finance-Industry Scandals Just as They Move to Deregulate Markets," *Wall Street Journal*, August 12, 1985, p. 20.

4. Robert Rice and Richard Waters, "Fraud Office Drops Charges in Third Guinness Case," *Financial Times*, February 9, 1992, p. 1.

5. *The Guardian*, August 28, 1990, p. 1.

6. "An Honor System Without Honor," *Economist*, December 14, 1991, p. 81.

7. Mike Milotte and David Nally, "A Season of Scandals," *The Sunday Tribune*, September 22, 1991, p. 6; see also Peter Clarke and Elizabeth Tierney, "Business Troubles in the Republic of Ireland," *Business Ethics; A European Review* (April 1992), pp. 134–138.

8. Steven Greenhouse, "An Old Club Transformed," *New York Times*, July 23, 1991, p. C6.

9. Steven Greenhouse, "Modest Insider-Trading Stir Is a Huge Scandal in France," *New York Times*, January 30, 1989, p. D1.

10. Ferdinand Protzman, "Insider Trading Scandal Grows," *New York Times*, July 23, 1991, p. C6.

11. "Sweeping out the Stables," *Economist*, August 31, 1991, p. 15.

12. Alan Riding, "Olivetti's Chairman Is Convicted in Bank Fraud that Shocks Italy," *New York Times*, April 17, 1992.

13. "Top Tax-Evader Gets Four-Year Sentence," *Japan Times Weekly International Edition*, May 11–17, 1992, p. 2.

14. Henk J. L. van Luijk, "Recent Developments in European Business Ethics," *Journal of Business Ethics*, 9: 538.

15. John Donaldson, *Ethics in European Business—A Casebook* (London: Academic Press Ltd., 1991).

16. "Ethics and Worse," *Financial Times*, July 3, 1992, p. 12.

17. Paul Farhi and Glenn Frankel, "Pardon Me, Old Bean, But Aren't Your Pants on Fire?" *Washington Post National Weekly Edition*, December 23–29, 1991, p. 20.

18. Greenhouse (1989), op. cit., p. D9.

19. James Sterngold, "Japan's Rigged Casino," *New York Times Magazine*, April 26, 1992, p. 48.

20. The quotation is from *Scandal* by Suzanne Garment. Quoted in Jonathan Yardley, "The Truly Corrupt Vs. the Merely Sleazy," *Washington Post National Weekly Edition*, October 7–23, 1991, p. 35. While Garment's book is about political scandals, her analysis can be applied to scandals involving the private sector as well.

21. Nick Galluccio, "The Boss in the Slammer," *Forbes*, February 5, 1979, p. 61.

22. Steven Ferrey, "Hard Time," *The Amicus Journal* (Fall 1988), p. 12.

23. Allen Gold, "Increasingly, A Prison Term Is the Price Paid by Polluters," *New York Times*, February 15, 1991, p. B10.

24. Ibid.

25. "Dishing the Dirt," *Economist*, February 9, 1991, p. 70.

26. Joseph Kahn, "When Bad Management Becomes Criminal," *INC.* (March 1987), p. 48.

27. Ibid.

28. "Investors Beware: Stock Market Rules Vary Considerably," *New York Times*, July 23, 1991, p. C7.

29. Greenhouse (1991), op. cit., p. C9.

30. James Sterngold, "Informal Code Rules Markets," *New York Times*, July 23, 1991, C6.

31. Antonio Vercher, "The Use of Criminal Law for the Protection of the Environment in Europe: Council of Europe Resolution (77)28," *Northwestern Journal of International Law and Business*, 10 (1990), p. 448.

32. Ben Corson, et al., *Shopping for A Better World* (New York, NY: Ballantine Books, 1989).

33. Philippe de Woot, "The Ethical Challenge To The Corporations: Meaningful Progress and Individual Development," in George Enderle et al., eds., *People In Corporations*, (Boston, MA: Kluwer Academic Publishers, 1990), p. 79.

34. Samuel P. Huntington, *American Politics: The Promise of Disharmony* (Cambridge, MA: Harvard University Press, 1981), p. 60.

35. Ibid, p. 15.

36. *Ethics in American Business*, Touche Ross, December 1987, p. 2.

37. See James O'Toole "Doing Good By Doing Well," *California Management Review*, 33/3 (Spring 1991): 9–24.

38. "The Insider-Trading Dragnet Is Stretching Across the Globe," *Business Week*, March 23, 1987, p. 51.

39. "Hidden Japan," *Business Week*, August 26, 1991, p. 18.

40. T. R. Reid, "In Japan, Too, Money Is The Mother's Milk of Politics," *Washington Post National Weekly Edition*, September 14–29, 1991, p. 18.

41. Ibid.

42. "Hey, America, Lighten Up A Little," *Economist*, July 28, 1990.

43. van Luijk, op. cit., p. 542.

44. Ibid.

45. Ibid., pp. 543–544.

46. Antoine Kerhuel, "De Part et D'Autre De L'Atlantique" [David Vogel translation].

47. This statement was made at an executive training session at IMD in the fall of 1991 that the author taught.

48. Henri-Claude de Bettignies, "Ethics and International Business: A European Perspective," paper presented at the Tokyo Conference on the Ethics of Business in a Global Economy, Kashiwashi, Japan, September 10–12, 1991, p. 11.

49. Paul Lewis, "European Businessmen Don't Take Their Morality So Seriously," *New York Times*, March 3, 1978, Section 4, p. 2.

50. The handful of exceptions includes: Catherine Langlois and Bodo Schegelmilch, "Do Corporate Codes of Ethics Reflect National Character? Evidence from Europe and the United States," *Journal of International Business Studies* (Fourth Quarter 1990), pp. 519–539; van Luijk, op. cit., pp. 537–544; Ernest Gundling, "Ethics and Working with the Japanese: The Entrepreneur and the 'Elite Course,'" *California Management Review*, 33/3 (Spring 1991): 25–39; Joanne Ciulla, "Why Is Business Talking about Ethics?" *California Management Review*, 34/1 (Fall 1991): 67–86.

51. Toshiba Machine Company, Harvard Business School #388-197.

INTERACTING WITH OTHERS: SOCIAL AND GROUP PROCESS

Foundations of Conformity and Obedience

20.   OPINIONS AND SOCIAL PRESSURE

Solomon E. Asch

That social influences shape every person's practices, judgments and beliefs is a truism to which anyone will readily assent. A child masters his "native" dialect down to the finest nuances; a member of a tribe of cannibals accepts cannibalism as altogether fitting and proper. All the social sciences take their departure from the observation of the profound effects that groups exert on their members. For psychologists, group pressure upon the minds of individuals raises a host of questions they would like to investigate in detail.

How, and to what extent, do social forces constrain people's opinions and attitudes? This question is especially pertinent in our day. The same epoch that has witnessed the unprecedented technical extension of communication has also brought into existence the deliberate manipulation of opinion and the "engineering of consent." There are many good reasons why, as citizens and as scientists, we should be concerned with studying the ways in which human beings form their opinions and the role that social conditions play.

Studies of these questions began with the interest in hypnosis aroused by the French physician Jean Martin Charcot (a teacher of Sigmund Freud) toward the end of the nineteenth century. Charcot believed that only hysterical patients could be fully hypnotized, but this view was soon challenged by two other physicians, Hyppolyte Bernheim and A. A. Liébault, who demonstrated that they could put most people under the hypnotic spell. Bernheim proposed that hypnosis was but an extreme form of a normal psychological process which became known as "suggestibility." It was shown that monotonous reiteration of instructions could induce in normal persons in the waking state involuntary bodily changes such as swaying or rigidity of the arms, and sensations such as warmth and odor.

It was not long before social thinkers seized upon these discoveries as a basis for explaining numerous social phenomena, from the spread of opinion to the formation of crowds and the following of leaders. The sociologist Gabriel Tarde summed it all up in the aphorism: "Social man is a somnambulist."

When the new discipline of social psychology was born at the beginning of this century, its first experiments were essentially adaptations of the suggestion demonstration. The technique generally followed a simple plan. The subjects, usually college students, were asked to give their opinions or preferences concerning various matters; some time later they were again asked to state their choices, but now they were also informed of the opinions held by authorities or large groups of their peers on the same matters. (Often the alleged consensus was fictitious.) Most of these studies had substantially the same result: confronted with opinions contrary to their own, many subjects apparently shifted their judgments in the direction of the views of the majorities or the experts. The late psychologist Edward L. Thorndike reported that he had succeeded in modifying the esthetic preferences of adults by this procedure. Other psychologists reported that people's evaluations of the merit of a literary passage could be raised or lowered by ascribing the passage to different authors. Apparently the sheer weight of numbers or authority sufficed to change opinions, even when no arguments for the opinions themselves were provided.

Now the very ease of success in these experiments arouses suspicion. Did the subjects actually change their opinions, or were the experimental victories scored only on paper? On grounds of common sense, one must question whether opinions are generally as watery as these studies indicate. There is some reason to wonder whether it was not the investigators who, in their enthusiasm for a theory, were suggestible, and whether the ostensibly gullible subjects were not providing answers which they thought good subjects were expected to give.

The investigations were guided by certain underlying assumptions, which today are common currency and account for much that is thought and said about the operations of propaganda and public opinion. The assumptions are that people submit uncritically and painlessly to external manipulation by suggestion or prestige, and that any given idea or value can be "sold" or "unsold" without reference to its merits. We should be skeptical, however, of the supposition that the power of social pressure necessarily implies uncritical submission to it: independence and the capacity to rise above group passion are also open to human beings. Further, one may question on psychological grounds whether it is possible as a rule to change a person's judgment of a situation or an object without first changing his knowledge or assumptions about it.

In what follows I shall describe some experiments in an investigation of the effects of group

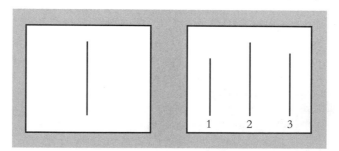

FIGURE 20.1 Subjects were shown two cards. One bore a standard line. The other bore three lines, one of which was the same length as the standard. The subjects were asked to choose this line.

pressure which was carried out recently with the help of a number of my associates. The tests not only demonstrate the operations of group pressure upon individuals but also illustrate a new kind of attack on the problem and some of the more subtle questions that it raises.

A group of seven to nine young men, all college students, are assembled in a classroom for a "psychological experiment" in visual judgment. The experimenter informs them that they will be comparing the lengths of lines. He shows two large white cards. On one is a single vertical black line—the standard whose length is to be matched. On the other card are three vertical lines of various lengths. The subjects are to choose the one that is of the same length as the line on the other card. One of the three actually is of the same length; the other two are substantially different, the difference ranging from three quarters of an inch to an inch and three quarters.

The experiment opens uneventfully. The subjects announce their answers in the order in which they have been seated in the room, and on the first round every person chooses the same matching line. Then a second set of cards is exposed; again the group is unanimous. The members appear ready to endure politely another boring experiment. On the third trial there is an unexpected disturbance. One person near the end of the group disagrees with all the others in his selection of the matching line. He looks surprised, indeed incredulous, about the disagreement. On the following trial he disagrees again, while the others remain unanimous in their choice. The dissenter becomes more and more worried and hesitant as the disagreement continues in succeeding trials; he may pause before announcing his answer and speak in a low voice, or he may smile in an embarrassed way.

What the dissenter does not know is that all the other members of the group were instructed by the experimenter beforehand to give incorrect answers in unanimity at certain points. The single individual who is not a party to this prearrangement is the focal subject of our experiment. He is placed in a position in which, while he is actually giving the correct answers, he finds himself unexpectedly in a minority of one, opposed by a unanimous and arbitrary majority with respect to a clear and simple fact. Upon him we have brought to bear two opposed forces: the evidence of his senses and the unanimous opinion of a group of his peers. Also, he must declare his judgments in public, before a majority which has also stated its position publicly.

The instructed majority occasionally reports correctly in order to reduce the possibility that the naive subject will suspect collusion against him. (In only a few cases did the subject actually show suspicion; when this happened, the experiment was stopped and the results were not counted. There are 18 trials in each series, and on 12 of these the majority responds erroneously. How do people respond to group pressure in this situation? I shall report first the statistical results of a series in which a total of 123 subjects from three institutions of higher learning (not including my own, Swarthmore College) were placed in the minority situation described above.

Two alternatives were open to the subject: he could act independently, repudiating the majority, or he could go along with the majority, repudiating the evidence of his senses. Of the 123 put to the test, a considerable percentage yielded to the majority. Whereas in ordinary circumstances individuals matching the lines will make mistakes less than 1 percent of the time, under group pressure the minority subjects swung to acceptance of the misleading majority's wrong judgments in 36.8 percent of the selections.

Of course individuals differed in response. At one extreme, about one quarter of the subjects were completely independent and never agreed with the erroneous judgments of the majority. At the other extreme, some individuals went with the majority nearly all the time. The performances of individuals in this experiment tend to be highly consistent. Those who strike out on the path of independence do not, as a rule, succumb to the majority even over an extended series of trials, while those who choose the path of compliance are unable to free themselves as the ordeal is prolonged.

The reasons for the startling individual differences have not yet been investigated in detail. At this point we can only report some tentative generalizations from talks with the subjects, each of whom was interviewed at the end of the experiment. Among the independent individuals were many who held fast because of staunch confidence in their own judgment. The most significant fact about them was not absence of responsiveness to the majority but a capacity to recover from doubt and to reestablish their equilibrium. Others who acted independently came to believe that the majority was correct in its answers, but they continued their dissent on the simple ground that it was their obligation to call the play as they saw it.

Among the extremely yielding persons we found a group who quickly reached the conclusion: "I am wrong, they are right." Others yielded in order "not to spoil your results." Many of the individuals who went along suspected that the majority were "sheep" following the first responder, or that the majority were victims of an optical illusion; nevertheless, these suspicions failed to free them at the moment of decision. More disquieting were the reactions of subjects who construed their difference from the majority as a sign of some general deficiency in themselves, which at all costs they must hide. On this basis they desperately tried to merge with the majority, not realizing the longer-range consequences to themselves. All the yielding subjects underestimated the frequency with which they conformed.

Which aspect of the influence of a majority is more important—the size of the majority or its unanimity? The experiment was modified to examine this question. In one series the size of the opposition was varied from one to fifteen persons. The results showed a clear trend. When a subject was confronted with only a single individual who contradicted his answers, he was swayed little: he

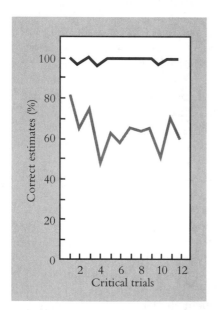

FIGURE 20.2 Error of 123 subjects, each of whom compared lines in the presence of six to eight opponents, is plotted in the gray curve. The accuracy of judgment not under pressure is indicated in black.

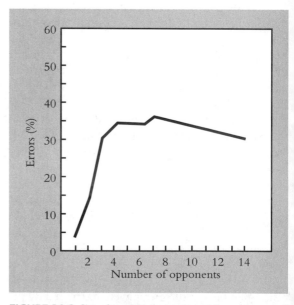

FIGURE 20.3 Size of majority that opposed them have an effect on the subjects. With a single opponent, the subject erred only 3.6 percent of the time; with two opponents he erred 13.6 percent; with three, 31.8 percent; with four, 35.1 percent; with six, 35.2 percent; with seven, 37.1 percent; with nine, 35.1 percent; with fifteen, 31.2 percent.

continued to answer independently and correctly in nearly all trials. When the opposition was increased to two, the pressure became substantial: minority subjects now accepted the wrong answer 13.6 percent of the time. Under the pressure of a majority of three, the subjects' errors jumped to 31.8 percent. But further increases in the size of the majority apparently did not increase the weight of the pressure substantially. Clearly the size of the opposition is important only up to a point.

Disturbance of the majority's unanimity had a striking effect. In this experiment the subject was given the support of a truthful partner—either another individual who did not know of the prearranged agreement among the rest of the group, or a person who was instructed to give correct answers throughout.

The presence of a supporting partner depleted the majority of much of its power. Its pressure on the dissenting individual was reduced to one-fourth: that is, subjects answered incorrectly only one-fourth as often as under the pressure of a unanimous majority (Figure 20.4). The weakest persons did not yield as readily. Most interesting were the reactions to the partner. Generally the feeling toward him was one of warmth and closeness; he was credited with inspiring confidence. However, the subjects repudiated the suggestion that the partner decided them to be independent.

Was the partner's effect a consequence of his dissent, or was it related to his accuracy? We now introduced into the experimental group a person who was instructed to dissent from the majority but also to disagree with the subject. In some experiments the majority was always to choose the worst of the comparison lines and the instructed dissenter to pick the line that was closer to the length of the standard one; in others the majority was consistently intermediate and the dissenter most in error. In this manner we were able to study the relative influence of "compromising" and "extremist" dissenters.

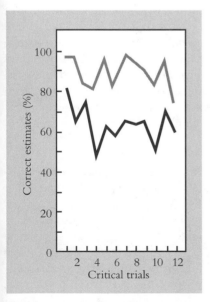

FIGURE 20.4 Two subjects supporting each other against a majority made fewer errors (gray curve) than one subject did against a majority (black curve).

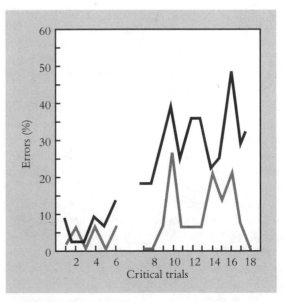

FIGURE 20.5 Partner left subject after six trials in a single experiment. The gray curve shows the error of the subject when the partner "deserted" to the majority. The black curve shows error when the partner merely left the room.

Again the results are clear. When a moderate dissenter is present, the effect of the majority on the subject decreases by approximately one-third, and extremes of yielding disappear. Moreover, most of the errors the subjects do make are moderate, rather than flagrant. In short, the dissenter largely controls the choice of errors. To this extent the subjects broke away from the majority even while bending to it.

On the other hand, when the dissenter always chose the line that was more flagrantly different from the standard, the results were of quite a different kind. The extremist dissenter produced a remarkable freeing of the subjects; their errors dropped to only 9 percent. Furthermore, all the errors were of the moderate variety. We were able to conclude that dissent *per se* increased independence and moderated the errors that occurred, and that the direction of dissent exerted consistent effects.

In all the foregoing experiments each subject was observed only in a single setting. We now turned to studying the effects upon a given individual of a change in the situation to which he was exposed. The first experiment examined the consequences of losing or gaining a partner. The instructed partner began by answering correctly on the first six trials. With his support the subject usually resisted pressure from the majority: eighteen of twenty-seven subjects were completely independent. But after six trials the partner joined the majority. As soon as he did so, there was an abrupt rise in the subjects' errors. Their submission to the majority was just about as frequent as when the minority subject was opposed by a unanimous majority throughout.

It was surprising to find that the experience of having had a partner and of having braved the majority opposition with him had failed to strengthen the individuals' independence. Questioning at the conclusion of the experiment suggested that we had overlooked an important circumstance; namely, the strong specific effect of "desertion" by the partner to the other side. We therefore changed the conditions so that the partner would simply leave the group at the proper point. (To allay suspicion it was announced in advance that he had an appointment with the dean.) In this form of the experiment, the partner's effect outlasted his presence. The errors increased after his departure, but less markedly than after a partner switched to the majority.

In a variant of this procedure the trials began with the majority unanimously giving correct answers. Then they gradually broke away until on the sixth trial the naive subject was alone and the group unanimously against him. As long as the subject had anyone on his side, he was almost invariably independent, but as soon as he found himself alone, the tendency to conform to the majority rose abruptly.

As might be expected, an individual's resistance to group pressure in these experiments depends to a considerable degree on how wrong the majority is. We varied the discrepancy between the standard line and the other lines systematically, with the hope of reaching a point where the error of the majority would be so glaring that every subject would repudiate it and choose independently. In this we regretfully did not succeed. Even when the difference between the lines was seven inches, there were still some who yielded to the error of the majority.

The study provides clear answers to a few relatively simple questions, and it raises many others that await investigation. We would like to know the degree of consistency of persons in situations which differ in content and structure. If consistency of independence or conformity in behavior is shown to be a fact, how is it functionally related to qualities of character and personality? In what ways is independence related to sociological or cultural conditions? Are leaders more independent than other people, or are they adept at following their followers? These and many other questions may perhaps be answerable by investigations of the type described here.

Life in society requires consensus as an indispensable condition. But consensus, to be productive, requires that each individual contribute independently out of his experience and insight. When consensus comes under the dominance of conformity, the social process is polluted and the individual at the same time surrenders the powers on which his functioning as a feeling and thinking being depends. That we have found the tendency to conformity in our society so strong that reasonably intelligent and well-meaning young people are willing to call white black is a matter of concern. It raises questions about our ways of education and about the values that guide our conduct.

Yet anyone inclined to draw too pessimistic conclusions from this report would do well to remind himself that the capacities for independence are not to be underestimated. He may also draw some consolation from a further observation: those who participated in this challenging experiment agreed nearly without exception that independence was preferable to conformity.

REFERENCES

Asch, S. E. Effects of group pressure upon the modification and distortion of judgments. *Groups, leadership, and men*, Harold Guetzdow (ed.). Carnegie Press, 1951.

Asch, S. E. *Social psychology*. Prentice-Hall, Inc., 1952.

Miller, N. E., and Dollard, J. *Social learning and imitation*. Yale University Press, 1941.

21. BEHAVIORAL STUDY OF OBEDIENCE

Stanley Milgram

Obedience is as basic an element in the structure of social life as one can point to. Some system of authority is a requirement of all communal living, and it is only the man dwelling in isolation who is not forced to respond, through defiance or submission, to the commands of others. Obedience, as a determinant of behavior, is of particular relevance to our time. It has been reliably established that from 1933–1945 millions of innocent persons were systematically slaughtered on command. Gas chambers were built, death camps were guarded, daily quotas of corpses were produced with the same efficiency as the manufacture of appliances. These inhumane policies may have originated in the mind of a single person, but they could only be carried out on a massive scale if a very large number of persons obeyed orders.

Obedience is the psychological mechanism that links individual action to political purpose. It is the dispositional cement that binds men to systems of

Reprinted with permission from the author and *The Journal of Abnormal and Social Psychology*, Vol. 67, No. 4, 1963. Copyright 1963 by the American Psychological Association.

This research was supported by a grant (NSF G-17916) from the National Science Foundation. Exploratory studies conducted in 1960 were supported by a grant from the Higgins Fund at Yale University. The research assistance of Alan E. Elms and Jon Wayland is gratefully acknowledged.

authority. Facts of recent history and observation in daily life suggest that for many persons obedience may be a deeply ingrained behavior tendency, indeed, a prepotent impulse overriding training in ethics, sympathy, and moral conduct. C. P. Snow (1961) points to its importance when he writes:

When you think of the long and gloomy history of man, you will find more hideous crimes have been committed in the name of obedience than have ever been committed in the name of rebellion. If you doubt that, read William Shirer's "Rise and Fall of the Third Reich." The German Officer Corps were brought up in the most rigorous code of obedience . . . in the name of obedience they were party to, and assisted in, the most wicked large scale actions in the history of the world [p. 24].

While the particular form of obedience dealt with in the present study has its antecedents in these episodes, it must not be thought all o0bedience entails acts of aggression against others. Obedience serves numerous productive functions. Indeed, the very life of society is predicated on its existence. Obedience may be ennobling and educative and refer to acts of charity and kindness, as well as to destruction.

General Procedure

A procedure was devised which seems useful as a tool for studying obedience (Milgram, 1961). It consists of ordering a naive subject to administer electric shock to a victim. A simulated shock generator is used, with 30 clearly marked voltage levels that range from 15 to 450 volts. The instrument bears verbal designations that range from Slight Shock to Danger: Severe Shock. The responses of the victim, who is a trained confederate of the experimenter, are standardized. The orders to administer shocks are given to the naive subject in the context of a "learning experiment" ostensibly set up to study the effects of punishment on memory. As the experiment proceeds the naive subject is commanded to administer increasingly more intense shocks to the victim, even to the point of reaching the level marked Danger: Severe Shock.

Internal resistances become stronger, and at a certain point the subject refuses to go on with the experiment. Behavior prior to this rupture is considered "obedience," in that the subject complies with the commands of the experimenter. The point of rupture is the act of disobedience. A quantitative value is assigned to the subject's performance based on the maximum intensity shock he is willing to administer before he refuses to participate further. Thus for any particular subject and for any particular experimental condition the degree of obedience may be specified with a numerical value. The crux of the study is to systematically vary the factors believed to alter the degree of obedience to the experimental commands.

The technique allows important variables to be manipulated at several points in the experiment. One may vary aspects of the source of command, content and form of command, instrumentalities for its execution, target object, general social setting, etc. The problem, therefore, is not one of designing increasingly more numerous experimental conditions, but of selecting those that best illuminate the *process* of obedience from the sociopsychological standpoint.

Related Studies

The inquiry bears an important relation to philosophic analyses of obedience and authority (Arendt, 1958; Friedrich, 1958; Weber, 1947), an early experimental study of obedience by Frank (1944), studies in "authoritarianism" (Adorno, Frenkel-Brunswik, Levinson, and Sanford, 1950; Rokeach, 1961), and a recent series of analytic and empirical studies in social power (Cartwright, 1959). It owes much to the long concern with *suggestion* in social psychology, both in its normal forms (e.g., Binet, 1900) and in its clinical manifestations (Charcot, 1881). But it derives, in the first instance, from direct observation of a social fact; the individual who is commanded by a legitimate authority ordinarily obeys. Obedience comes easily and often. It is a ubiquitous and indispensable feature of social life.

TABLE 21.1
Distribution of Age and Occupational Types in the Experiment

Occupations	20–29 years n	30–39 years n	40–50 years n	Percentage of total (occupations)
Workers, skilled and unskilled	4	5	6	37.5
Sales, business, and white-collar	3	6	7	40.0
Professional	1	5	3	22.5
Percentage of total (age)	20	40	40	

METHOD

Subjects

The subjects were 40 males between the ages of 20 and 50, drawn from New Haven and the surrounding communities. Subjects were obtained by a newspaper advertisement and direct mail solicitation. Those who responded to the appeal believed they were to participate in a study of memory and learning at Yale University. A wide range of occupations is represented in the sample. Typical subjects were postal clerks, high school teachers, salesmen, engineers, and laborers. Subjects ranged in educational level from one who had not finished elementary school, to those who had doctorate and other professional degrees. They were paid $4.50 for their participation in the experiment. However, subjects were told that payment was simply for coming to the laboratory, and that the money was theirs no matter what happened after they arrived. Table 21.1 shows the proportion of age and occupational types assigned to the experimental condition.

Personnel and Locale

The experiment was conducted on the grounds of Yale University in the elegant interaction laboratory. (This detail is relevant to the perceived legitimacy of the experiment. In further variations, the experiment was dissociated from the university, with consequences for performance.) The role of experimenter was played by a 31-year-old high school teacher of biology. His manner was impassive, and his appearance somewhat stern throughout the experiment. He was dressed in a gray technician's coat. The victim was played by a 47-year-old accountant, trained for the role; he was of Irish-American stock, whom most observers found mild-mannered and likable.

Procedure

One naive subject and one victim (an accomplice) performed in each experiment. A pretext had to be devised that would justify the administration of electric shock by the naive subject. This was effectively accomplished by the cover story. After a general introduction on the presumed relation between punishment and learning, subjects were told:

But actually, we know very little *about the effect of punishment on learning, because almost no truly scientific studies have been made of it in human beings.*

For instance, we don't know how much *punishment is best for learning—and we don't know how much difference it makes as to who is giving the punishment, whether an adult learns best from a younger or an older person than himself—or many things of that sort.*

So in this study we are bringing together a number of adults of different occupations and ages. And we're asking some of them to be teachers and some of them to be learners.

We want to find out just what effect different people have on each other as teachers and learners, and also what effect punishment will have on learning in this situation.

Therefore, I'm going to ask one of you to be the teacher here tonight and the other one to be the learner.

Does either of you have a preference?

Subjects then drew slips of paper from a hat to determine who would be the teacher and who would be the learner in the experiment. The drawing was rigged so that the naive subject was always the teacher and the accomplice always the learner. (Both slips contained the word "Teacher.") Immediately after the drawing the teacher and learner were taken to an adjacent room and the learner was strapped into an "electric chair" apparatus.

The experimenter explained that the straps were to prevent excessive movement while the learner was being shocked. The effect was to make it impossible for him to escape from the situation. An electrode was attached to the learner's wrist, and electrode paste was applied "to avoid blisters and burns." Subjects were told that the electrode was attached to the shock generator in the adjoining room.

In order to improve credibility the experimenter declared, in response to a question by the learner: "Although the shocks can be extremely painful, they cause no permanent tissue damage."

Learning Task. The lesson administered by the subject was a paired-associate learning task. The subject read a series of word pairs to the learner, and then read the first word of the pair along with four terms. The learner was to indicate which of the four terms had originally been paired with the first word. He communicated his answer by pressing one of four switches in front of him, which in turn lit up one of four numbered quadrants in an answer-box located atop the shock generator.

Shock Generator. The instrument panel consists of 30 lever switches set in a horizontal line. Each switch is clearly labeled with a voltage designation that ranges from 15 to 450 volts. There is a 15-volt increment from one switch to the next going from left to right. In addition, the following verbal designations are clearly indicated for groups of four switches going from left to right: Slight Shock, Moderate Shock, Strong Shock, Very Strong Shock, Intense Shock, Extreme Intensity Shock, Danger: Severe Shock. (Two switches after this last designation are simply marked XXX.)

Upon depressing a switch: a pilot light corresponding to each switch is illuminated in bright red; an electric buzzing is heard; an electric blue light, labeled "voltage energizer," flashes; the dial on the voltage meter swings to the right; various relay clicks are sounded.

The upper left-hand corner of the generator is labeled Shock Generator, Type ZLB, Dyson Instrument Company, Waltham, Mass. Output 15 Volts—450 Volts.

Details of the instrument were carefully handled to insure an appearance of authenticity. The panel was engraved by precision industrial engravers, and all components were of high quality. No subject in the experiment suspected that the instrument was merely a simulated shock generator.[1]

Sample Shock. Each naive subject is given a sample shock on the shock generator, prior to beginning his run as teacher. This shock is always 45 volts, and is applied by pressing the third switch of the generator. The shock is applied to the wrist of the naive subject, and has its source in a 45-volt battery wired into the generator. This further convinces the subject of the authenticity of the generator.

Shock Instructions. The subject is told to administer a shock to the learner each time he gives a wrong response. Moreover—and this is the key command— the subject is instructed to "move one lever higher on the shock generator each time the learner flashes a wrong answer." He is also instructed to announce the voltage level before administering a shock. This serves to continually remind subjects of the increasing intensity of shocks administered to the learner.

Preliminary and Regular Run. Pretests revealed that the procedure of reading words and administering shocks requires some practice before it can be handled smoothly. Therefore, immediately preceding the regular run, the teacher is given a preliminary series of 10 words to read to the learner. There are 3 neutral words in the practice series (i.e., words that the learner answers correctly), so that shocks are administered for 7 of the words, with the maximum shock at 105 volts (moderate shock). Almost all subjects master the procedure by the time the preliminary run is over.

Subjects are then presented with a second list, and are told that the procedure is the same as for the first list; the experimenter adds, however:

When you get to the bottom of the list, repeat it over again, and continue giving shocks, until the learner has learned all the pairs correctly.

The experimenter instructs the subject to

start from 15 volts and increase the shock level one step each time the learner gives a wrong answer.

Feedback from the Victim. In all conditions the learner gives a predetermined set of responses to the word pair test, based on a schedule of approximately three wrong answers to one correct answer. In the present experimental condition no vocal response or other sign of protest is heard from the learner until Shock Level 300 is reached. When the 300-volt shock is administered, the learner pounds on the wall of the room in which he is bound to the electric chair. The pounding can be heard by the subject. From this point on, the learner's answers no longer appear on the four-way panel.

At this juncture, subjects ordinarily turn to the experimenter for guidance. The experimenter instructs the subject to treat the absence of a response as a wrong answer, and to shock the subject according to the usual schedule. He advises the subjects to allow 5–10 seconds before considering no

response as a wrong answer, and to increase the shock level one step each time the learner fails to respond correctly. The learner's pounding is repeated after the 315-volt shock is administered; afterwards he is not heard from, nor do his answers reappear on the four-way signal box.

Experimenter Feedback. At various points in the experiment the subject may turn to the experimenter for advice on whether he should continue to administer shocks. Or he may indicate that he does not wish to go on. It was important to standardize the experimenter's responses to these inquiries and reactions.

If the subject indicated his unwillingness to go on, the experimenter responded with a sequence of "prods," using as many as necessary to bring the subject into line.

> *Prod 1: Please continue.* or *Please go on.*
> *Prod 2: The experiment requires that you continue.*
> *Prod 3: It is absolutely essential that you continue.*
> *Prod 4: You have no other choice, you* must *go on.*

The prods were always made in sequence: Only if Prod 1 had been unsuccessful, could Prod 2 be used. If the subject refused to obey the experimenter after Prod 4, the experiment was terminated. The experimenter's tone of voice was at all times firm, but not impolite. The sequence was begun anew on each occasion that the subject balked or showed reluctance to follow orders.

Special prods. If the subject asked if the learner was liable to suffer permanent physical injury, the experimenter said:

Although the shocks may be painful, there is no permanent tissue damage, so please go on. [Followed by Prods 2, 3, and 4 if necessary.]

If the subject said that the learner did not want to go on, the experimenter replied:

Whether the learner likes it or not, you must go on until he has learned all the word pairs correctly. So please go on. [Followed by Prods 2, 3, and 4 if necessary.]

Dependent Measures

The primary dependent measure for any subject is the maximum shock he administers before he refuses to go any further. In principle this may vary from 0 (for a subject who refuses to administer even the first shock) to 30 (for a subject who administers the highest shock on the generator). A subject who breaks off the experiment at any point prior to administering the thirtieth shock level is termed a *defiant* subject. One who complies with experimental commands fully, and proceeds to administer all shock levels commanded, is termed an *obedient* subject.

Further Records. With few exceptions, experimental sessions were recorded on magnetic tape. Occasional photographs were taken through one-way mirrors. Notes were kept on any unusual behavior occurring during the course of the experiments. On occasion, additional observers were directed to write objective descriptions of the subjects' behavior. The latency and duration of shocks were measured by accurate timing devices.

Interview and Dehoax. Following the experiment, subjects were interviewed; open-ended questions, projective measures, and attitude scales were employed. After the interview, procedures were undertaken to assure that the subject would leave the laboratory in a state of well being. A friendly reconciliation was arranged between the subject and the victim, and an effort was made to reduce any tensions that arose as a result of the experiment.

RESULTS

Preliminary Notions

Before giving an account of the experimental results, it is instructive to consider how persons predict others will perform when commanded to administer powerful shocks to another person. Fourteen Yale seniors, all psychology majors, were provided with a detailed description of the experimental situation. They were asked to reflect carefully on it, and to predict the behavior of 100 hypothetical subjects. More specifically, they were instructed to plot the distribution of obedience of "100 Americans of diverse occupations, and ranging in age from 20 to 50 years," who were placed in the experimental situation.

There was considerable agreement among the respondents on the expected behavior of hypothetical subjects. All respondents predicted that only an insignificant minority would go through to the end of the shock series. (The estimates ranged from 0 to 3 percent; i.e., the most "pessimistic" member of the class predicted that of 100 persons, 3 would continue through to the most potent shock available on the shock generator— 450 volts.) The class mean was 1.2 percent. The question was also posed informally to colleagues of the author, and the most general feeling was that few if any subjects would go beyond the designation Very Strong Shock.

Result of Experiment I

Subjects Accept Situation. With few exceptions subjects were convinced of the reality of the experimental situation, that they were administering shocks to another person, and the most potent shocks were extremely painful. In the post-experimental interview subjects were asked: "How painful to the learner were the last few shocks that you administered to him?" Subjects were instructed to indicate their answers on a printed 14-point scale ranging from "Not at all painful" to "Extremely painful." The modal response was 14 (Extremely painful) with the mean at 13.42.

Signs of Extreme Tension. Many subjects showed signs of nervousness in the experimental situation, and especially upon administering the more powerful shocks. In a large number of cases the degree of tension reached extremes that are rarely seen in sociopsychological laboratory studies. Subjects were observed to sweat, tremble, stutter, bite their lips, groan, and dig their fingernails into their flesh. These were characteristic rather than exceptional responses to the experiment.

One sign of tension was the regular occurrence of nervous laughing fits. Fourteen of the 40 sub-jects showed definite signs of nervous laughter and smiling. The laughter seemed entirely out of place, even bizarre. Full-blown, uncontrollable seizures were observed for 3 subjects. On one occasion we

TABLE 21.2
Distribution of Breakoff Points

Verbal Designation and Voltage Indication	Number of Subjects for Whom This Was Maximum Shock
Slight Shock	
15	0
30	0
45	0
60	0
Moderate Shock	
75	0
90	0
105	0
120	0
Strong Shock	
135	0
150	0
165	0
180	0
Very Strong Shock	
195	0
210	0
225	0
240	0
Intense Shock	
255	0
270	0
285	0
300	5
Extreme Intensity Shock	
315	4
330	2
345	1
360	1
Danger: Severe Shock	
375	1
390	0
405	0
420	0
XXX	
435	0
450	26

observed a seizure so violently convulsive that it was necessary to call a halt to the experiment. The subject, a 46-year-old encyclopedia salesman, was seriously embarrassed by his untoward and uncontrollable behavior. In the post-experimental interviews subjects took pains to point out that they were not sadistic types, and that the laughter did not mean they enjoyed shocking the victim.

Distribution of Scores. It had been conjectured that persons would not, in general, agree to administer shocks beyond the level designated as Very Strong Shock. The distribution of maximum shocks for this experiment is shown in Table 21.2. The obtained distribution of scores deviates radically from the prediction.

Upon command of the experimenter, each of the 40 subjects went beyond the expected breakoff point. No subject stopped prior to administering Shock Level 20. (At this level—300 volts—the victim kicks on the wall and no longer provides answers to the teacher's multiple-choice questions.)

Of the 40 subjects, 5 refused to obey the experimental commands beyond the 300-volt level. Four more subjects administered one further shock, and then refused to go on. Two broke off at the 330-volt level, and 1 each at 345, 360, and 375 volts. Thus a total of 14 subjects defied the experimenter. It is instructive to reprint their remarks at the point of defiance, as transcribed from the tape recordings:

[0124] I think he's trying to communicate, he's knocking . . . Well it's not fair to shock the guy . . . these are terrific volts. I don't think this is very humane . . . Oh, I can't go on with this; no, this isn't right. It's a hell of an experiment. The guy is suffering in there. No, I don't want to go on. This is crazy. [Subject refused to administer more shocks.]

[0123] He's banging in there. I'm gonna chicken out. I'd like to continue, but I can't do that to a man . . . I'm sorry I can't do that to a man. I'll hurt his heart. You take your check . . . No really, I couldn't do it.

These subjects were frequently in a highly agitated and even angered state. Sometimes, verbal protest was at a minimum, and the subject simply got up from his chair in front of the shock generator, and indicated that he wished to leave the laboratory.

Of the 40 subjects, 26 obeyed the orders of the experimenter to the end, proceeding to punish the victim until they reached the most potent shock available on the shock generator. At that point, the experimenter called a halt to the session. (The maximum shock is labeled 450 volts, and is two steps beyond the designation: Danger: Severe Shock.) Although obedient subjects continued to administer shocks, they often did so under extreme stress. Some expressed reluctance to administer shocks beyond the 300-volt level, and displayed fears similar to those who defied the experimenter; yet they obeyed.

After the maximum shocks had been delivered, and the experimenter called a halt to the proceedings, many obedient subjects heaved sighs of relief, mopped their brows, rubbed their fingers over their eyes, or nervously fumbled cigarettes. Some shook their heads, apparently in regret. Some subjects had remained calm throughout the experiment, and displayed only minimal signs of tension from beginning to end.

DISCUSSION

The experiment yielded two findings that were surprising. The first finding concerns the sheer strength of obedient tendencies manifested in this situation. Subjects have learned from childhood that it is a fundamental breach of moral conduct to hurt another person against his will. Yet, 26 subjects abandon this tenet in following the instructions of an authority who has no special powers to enforce his commands. To disobey would bring no material loss to the subject; no punishment would ensue. It is clear from the remarks and outward behavior of many participants that in punishing the victim they are often acting against their own values. Subjects often expressed deep disapproval of shocking a man in the face of his objections, and other denounced it as stupid and senseless. Yet the majority complied with the experimental comnands. This outcome was surprising from two perspectives: first, from the standpoint of predictions made in the questionnaire described earlier. (Here, however, it is possible that the remoteness of the respondents from the actual situation, and the difficulty of conveying to them the concrete details of the experiment, could account for the serious underestimation of obedience.)

But the results were also unexpected to persons who observed the experiment in progress, through one-way mirrors. Observers often uttered expressions of disbelief upon seeing a subject administer more powerful shocks to the victim. These persons had a full acquaintance with the details of the situation, and yet systematically underestimated the amount of obedience that subjects would display.

The second unanticipated effect was the extraordinary tension generated by the procedures. One might suppose that a subject would simply break off or continue as his conscience dictated. Yet, this is very far from what happened. There were striking reactions of tension and emotional strain. One observer related:

I observed a mature and initially poised businessman enter the laboratory smiling and confident. Within 20 minutes he was reduced to a twitching, stuttering wreck, who was rapidly approaching a point of nervous collapse. He constantly pulled on his earlobe, and twisted his hands. At one point he pushed his fist into his forehead and muttered: "Oh God, let's stop it." And yet he continued to respond to every word of the experimenter, and obeyed to the end.

Any understanding of the phenomenon of obedience must rest on an analysis of the particular conditions in which it occurs. The following features of the experiment go some distance in explaining the high amount of obedience observed in the situation.

1. The experiment is sponsored by and takes place on the grounds of an institution of unimpeachable reputation, Yale University. It may be reasonably presumed that the personnel are competent and reputable. The importance of this background authority is now being studied by conducting a series of experiments outside of New Haven, and without any visible ties to the university.

2. The experiment is, on the face of it, designed to attain a worthy purpose—advancement of knowledge about learning and memory. Obedience occurs not as an end in itself, but as an instrumental element in a situation that the subject construes as significant, and meaningful. He may not be able to see its full significance, but he may properly assume that the experimenter does.

3. The subject perceives that the victim has voluntarily submitted to the authority system of the experimenter. He is not (at first) an unwilling captive impressed for involuntary service. He has taken the trouble to come to the laboratory presumably to aid the experimental research. That he later becomes an involuntary subject does not alter the fact that, initially, he consented to participate without qualification. Thus he has in some degree incurred an obligation toward the experimenter.

4. The subject, too, has entered the experiment voluntarily, and perceives himself under obligation to aid the experimenter. He has made a commitment, and to disrupt the experiment is a repudiation of this initial promise of aid.

5. Certain features of the procedure strengthen the subject's sense of obligation to the experimenter. For one, he has been paid for coming to the laboratory. In part this is canceled out by the experimenter's statement that:

Of course, as in all experiments, the money is yours simply for coming to the laboratory. From this point on, no matter what happens, the money is yours.[2]

6. From the subject's standpoint, the fact that he is the teacher and the other man the learner is purely a chance consequence (it is determined by drawing lots) and he, the subject, ran the same risk as the other man in being assigned the role of learner. Since the assignment of positions in the experiment was achieved by fair means, the learner is deprived of any basis of complaint on this count. (A similar situation obtains in Army units, in which—in the absence of volunteers—a particularly dangerous mission may be assigned by drawing lots, and the unlucky soldier is expected to bear his misfortune with sportsmanship.)

7. There is, at best, ambiguity with regard to the prerogatives of a psychologist and the corresponding rights of his subject. There is a vagueness of expectation concerning what a psychologist may require of his subject, and when he is overstepping acceptable limits. Moreover, the experiment occurs in a closed setting, and thus provides no opportunity for the subject to remove these ambiguities by discussion with others. There are few standards that seem directly applicable to the situation, which is a novel one for most subjects.

8. The subjects are assured that the shocks administered to the subject are "painful but not dangerous." Thus they assume that the discomfort caused the victim is momentary, while the scientific gains resulting from the experiment are enduring.

9. Through Shock Level 20 the victim continues to provide answers on the signal box. The subject may construe this as a sign that the victim is still willing to "play the game." It is only after Shock Level 20 that the victim repudiates the rules completely, refusing to answer further.

These features help to explain the high amount of obedience obtained in this experiment. Many of the arguments raised need not remain matters of speculation, but can be reduced to testable propositions to be confirmed or disproved by further experiments.[3]

The following features of the experiment concern the nature of the conflict which the subject faces.

10. The subject is placed in a position in which he must respond to the competing demands of two persons: the experimenter and the victim. The conflict must be resolved by meeting the demands of one or the other; satisfaction of the victim and the experimenter are mutually exclusive. Moreover, the resolution must take the form of a highly visible action, that of continuing to shock the victim or breaking off the experiment. Thus the subject is forced into a public conflict that does not permit any completely satisfactory solution.

11. While the demands of the experimenter carry the weight of scientific authority, the demands of the victim spring from his personal experience of pain and suffering. The two claims need not be regarded as equally pressing and legitimate. The experimenter seeks an abstract scientific datum; the victim cries out for relief from physical suffering caused by the subject's actions.

12. The experiment gives the subject little time for reflection. The conflict comes on rapidly. It is only minutes after the subject has been seated before the shock generator that the victim begins his protests. Moreover, the subject perceives that he has gone through but two-thirds of the shock levels at the time the subject's first protests are heard. Thus he understands that the conflict will have a persistent aspect to it, and may well become more intense as increasingly more powerful shocks are required. The rapidity with which the conflict descends on the subject, and his realization that it is predictably recurrent may well be sources of tension to him.

13. At a more general level, the conflict stems from the opposition of two deeply ingrained behavior dispositions: first, the disposition not to harm other people, and second, the tendency to obey those whom we perceive to be legitimate authorities.

REFERENCES

Adorno, T., Frenkel-Brunswik, Else, Levinson, D. J., and Sanford, R. N. *The authoritarian personality*. New York: Harper, 1950.

Arendt, H. What was authority? In C. J. Friedrich (ed.), *Authority*. Cambridge: Harvard Univer. Press, 1958. Pp. 81–112.

Binet, A. *La suggestibilité*. Paris: Schleicher, 1900.

Buss, A. H. *The psychology of aggression*. New York: Wiley, 1961.

Cartwright, S. (ed.) *Studies in social power*. Ann Arbor: University of Michigan Institute for Social Research, 1959.

Charcot, J. M. *Oeuvres complètes*. Paris: Bureaux du Progrès Médical, 1881.

Frank, J. D. Experimental studies of personal pressure and resistance. *J. gen. Psychol.*, 1944, *30*, 23–64.

Friedrich, C. J. (ed.) *Authority*. Cambridge: Harvard Univer. Press, 1958.

Milgram, S. Dynamics of obedience. Washington: National Science Foundation, 25 January 1961. (Mimeo)

Milgram, S. Some conditions of obedience and disobedience to authority. *Hum. Relat.*, 1965, *18*, 57–76.

Rokeach, M. Authority, authoritarianism, and conformity. In I. A. Berg and B. M. Bass (eds.), *Conformity and deviation*. New York: Harper, 1961. Pp. 230–257.

Snow, C. P. Either-or. *Progressive*, 1961 (Feb.), 24.

Weber, M. *The theory of social and economic organization*. Oxford: Oxford Univer. Press, 1947.

NOTES

1. A related technique, making use of a shock generator, was reported by Buss (1961) for the study of aggression in the laboratory. Despite the considerable similarity of technical detail in the experimental procedures, each investigator proceeded in ignorance of the other's work. Milgram provided plans and photographs of his shock generator, experimental procedure, and first results in a report to the National Science Foundation in January 1961. This report received only limited circulation. Buss reported his procedure six months later, but to a wider audience. Subsequently, technical information and reports were exchanged. The present article was first received in the editor's office on December 27, 1961; it was resubmitted with deletions on July 27, 1962.

2. Forty-three subjects, undergraduates at Yale University, were run in the experiment without payment. The results are very similar to those obtained with paid subjects.

3. A series of recently completed experiments employing the obedience paradigm is reported in Milgram (1965).

Organizational Socialization and Commitment

22. COMMITMENT AND THE CONTROL OF ORGANIZATIONAL BEHAVIOR AND BELIEF

Gerald R. Salancik

Most articles on organizational commitment extol the virtues of commitment. In them, you will find that the committed employee is the happy employee, the success of the organization is a matter of its members sacrificing their time and effort, and commitment to the values of the organization gives meaning to a person's life. In them commitment enhances productivity, assures quality in the final product, and guarantees the flow of adaptive innovation. In them, you will find, in short, a lot of nonsense mixed with a lot of common sense. But from them your understanding of commitment may not be enhanced. . . .

The view of commitment we present in this paper is one which is grounded in behavior and the implications of behavior in one situation for behavior in another. The view derives primarily from the model of commitment developed by Kiesler (1971), with intellectual roots going back to Festinger (1957, 1964) and Lewin (1947). We borrow considerably from Keisler's work, and deviate in significant ways. As a working definition, "commitment is the binding of the individual to behavioral acts" (Kiesler & Sakumura, 1966). The important words are "binding" and "acts."

To act is to commit oneself. A person may talk about how important it is to keep the population growth rate down, but to be sterilized is to give eloquent, unshakeable force to the statement. An adulterer may proclaim unrelenting devotion to a lover, but to give up children, home, and joint bank accounts is to put meaning into the proclamation. Thus, at a minimum, a concept of commitment implies that behavior, or action, be a central focus.

DETERMINANTS OF COMMITMENT

While action is a necessary ingredient in commitment, all behaviors are not equally committing.

There are degrees of commitment. A statement of a belief or attitude is a less committing action than the signing of a petition in favor of the belief, which in turn is less committing than actively advocating the belief to a hostile or skeptical audience.

The degree of commitment derives from the extent to which a person's behaviors are binding. Four characteristics of behavioral acts make them binding, and hence determine the extent of commitment: explicitness; revocability; volition; and publicity. The first is the *explicitness* or deniability of the act, and concerns the extent to which an action can be said to have taken place. Two contributors to explicitness are the observability of the act and the unequivocality of the act. Some acts are not observable and we may know them only by inference from assumed consequences. You leave a dollar bill on a checkout counter, turn away for a moment, then find it missing. The consequence is obvious, but do you know if the customer next to you took it or if it was carried away by a draft from the open door? Acts themselves can be equivocal, forgotten, or otherwise intractable. A person who says, "I sometimes think . . ." is behaving more equivocally than one who says, "I think. . . ."

A second characteristic of behavior affecting commitment is the *revocability* or reversibility of the action. Some actions are like trials. We try them out, see how they fit with us, and if they don't suit us we change our minds and do something else. Few actions are really irreversible. Even a vasectomy can be undone. Promises can be made and broken. Jobs can be quit. Marriages can be dissolved; engagements, broken. Contracts can be torn up. On the other hand, some actions are permanent and having occurred, they cannot be undone. They are committing. Slapping someone in the face can be excused, forgiven, forgotten or reciprocated, but it cannot be taken back. Consumption of food or drink may be regretted but not reversed. Pulling the trigger of a loaded gun pointed at a friend commits all to its gross reality.

The explicitness and irrevocability of an act link action to an indelible reality. *Volition*, a third characteristic of committing behaviors, links action to the individual. This is one of the more difficult characteristics of human action to define precisely, and is frequently associated with such concepts as freedom and personal responsibility. What makes definition difficult is that all human action is both free and constrained, being done under one's own volition and in response to contingencies. Even the most seemingly free and personal action can be perceived as constrained. Artists and writers, such as Dostoevski and George Bernard Shaw, describe their acts of creation as the result of compulsions and external forces. And even the most seemingly constrained acts can be considered free. A person with a gun to his head ultimately is free to choose, whether to comply or accept the consequences of noncompliance. The perception of volition, moreover, can vary with the consequences that follow acts. A manager who takes a decision which turns out to be a disaster for his firm may make every effort to divest himself of responsibility. And one can observe in the annual reports of most corporations the following simple relationship. When sales increase from the previous year, the annual report points out how management's ingenious investments and development programs are paying off; when, the next year, sales decrease, an astounding downturn in the economy is lugubriously noted.

Despite difficulties in developing a precise concept of volition, volition wields powerful influences on the attitudes and behaviors of people, at least in Western culture. Some major characteristics found to relate to the degree of perceived volition of action are: (1) choice; (2) the presence of external demands for action; (3) the presence of extrinsic bases for action; and (4) the presence of other contributors to action. Thus a person who works hard in order to make a lot of money is not perceived as having as much volition as a person who works hard for nothing. A person who works hard because his superior stands over him constantly is not perceived as having as much volition as one who does as much on his own. With regard to choice, a person who buys a Ford because that is the only car available for sale is not perceived as having as much volition as one who passes over a hundred other models to make the same purchase. . . .

A fourth characteristic of action affecting commitment is the *publicity* or publicness of the act. This characteristic links the action into a social context. While all action and behavior is by definition observable, publicity refers to the extent to which others know of the action and the kinds of persons who know of it. Some audiences are unimportant to us, as are their observations of our behavior. One of the simplest ways to commit yourself to a course of action is to go around telling all your friends that you are definitely going to do something. You will find yourself bound by your own statements. The same commitment will not develop from proclamations to strangers you meet on trains. The publicity of one's action places the action in a social context which is more or less binding and, as we shall describe, contributes to directing the effect of those behaviors on subsequent behaviors. . . .

COMMITMENT TO ORGANIZATIONS

A careless interpretation of the consistency assumption might lead one to infer that having chosen to join an organization or to do a job, individuals will be willing to stay with it and be quite satisfied. After all, one implication of taking a job is that the person likes it. Choice, however, is not enough. The choice itself must be committing. The person must be bound to this choice. . . .

Sacrifice and Initiation Rites

Some organizations prefer not to leave a member's commitment to the happenstance of his own decision process. Corporations frequently publicize the decisions of their new managers. The *Wall Street Journal* is crammed with advertisements by companies announcing that a particular individual has joined their firm, an act giving instant status to the manager's new role. Friends and past associates call in their congratulations and set into motion a climate of expectation that he is part of that firm. In recent years, insurance companies have been taking full spreads in such magazines as *Time* and *Newsweek* to publish the pictures of their sales personnel.

Western Electric has done the same with television scans of their employees working on the job. For a few hundred dollars, an individual is identified with the organization. Next-door neighbors rush to ask, "Say, is this you?" One implication of the advertisement to both the employee and his friends is that the company really cares about its employees, and as a consequence it becomes more and more difficult to complain about it to friends. Harvard Business School uses a particularly effective method of maintaining long-term commitment from its graduates. Entering MBAs are immediately assigned to a group of classmates. This class does everything together from then on. They live in the same dormitories, hear the same lectures, and take the same exams. Virtually everything is scheduled for the class as a whole. Within each class, individuals are identified by namecards so that everyone knows the name of everyone else and is referred to by name in classroom discussions. Twenty years later, when the individuals have long departed the ivy-draped halls, the social network created there continues to operate. One of the things it is used for is to drum donations to the "B School," as it is fondly called.

In addition to advertising a person's commitment, some organizations take pains to make sure the individual is aware he has made a decision. Like the experiments with a well-constructed social psychological choice manipulation, the new employer commits the beginner: "Now, we want to be sure you're taking this job because you want to. We know you've given up a lot to come here and we're grateful. You left your home, your old friends. It must have been very difficult for you. And the salary we're offering, while more than you were making, is never enough to compensate for that."

The idea of giving up something to join the organization is one exploited in many ways. A common form is the initiation rites which still persist in college fraternities and sororities, fraternal clubs like the Masons or Elks, prisons, military organizations, revolutionary cadres, communal living experiments, police academies and religious organizations, orders and cults. An important part of the initiation process is the forcing of a sacrifice, in which members are asked to give up something as a price of membership (Karter, 1968). College fraternities require pledges to do hours of push-ups, to take verbal abuse, to have their privileges restricted, to accept subservient roles; in the end, those who endure love it. The effect is obvious. The individual in order to give meaning to his sacrifices is left to conclude they were made because of his devotion to the organization, a conclusion made more likely by his public pledge to enter the organization out of his own choosing. Other organizations have less colorful forms of sacrifice. Exclusive country clubs require their new members to make large initial donations in addition to yearly fees. The donations themselves provide for no services, and members pay for almost all services. But having given up an initial thousand, or a few thousand dollars, members feel a certain compulsion to spend $3.00 for a martini at the club's bar rather than half that at a public lounge.

Investments and Tenure

Many organizations do not exploit the idea of sacrifice as a price of membership. Instead they emphasize the instrumental or exchange bases for participation. Members are hired rather than invited into the organization. Commitment under such circumstances will obviously be more difficult.

Studies on commitment to organizations that emphasize the instrumental bases for membership—work organizations—have consistently found two factors as most reliably related to commitment. The two factors are position in the organization and tenure with the organization. Study after study on the issue comes down to: People with good jobs are willing to stay in them, and, the longer a person has been with an organization, the more he wants to stay. Unfortunately, most of the studies were done in such ways that it is difficult, and in many cases impossible, to interpret the meaning of the findings.

The relationship of tenure to organizational commitment is predictable from the model of commitment presented in this chapter and has been discussed in a related manner. Howard Becker (1960) suggested that individuals build up commitment over time through certain "sidebets" they make in the organization. One obvious form of accumulation investments in an organization is the build-up of pension benefits and credits over the course of a lifetime. Until recently, such employee benefits, often called the "golden padlock," were not transferable from one organization to another. If an individual terminated in one organization he lost some of his future wealth or security and had to begin accumulating it again in another organization. The costs of leaving the organization thus increase the longer one's involvement and one becomes more and more likely to continue where one is.

Regardless of financial investments, mobility also declines with tenure in an organization. As time goes by, one becomes less employable. And one's expertise becomes increasingly specific to one's current organization. Some organizations purposely manipulate the costs of leaving for some individuals. Universities will promote some of their assistant professors at rapid rates, making it more costly for other organizations to entice them away. Some business organizations will give young managers attractive positions unusual for their age, knowing it would be difficult for them to obtain equivalent offers elsewhere and also knowing it is cheaper to buy their commitment at an early age than it would be when they become industry hot-shots. . . .

WORK ENVIRONMENTS AND ORGANIZATIONAL COMMITMENT

Thus far we have discussed commitment to the organization as the result of the constraints on an individual's ability to leave the organization, and the extent to which the individual himself has made a definite and committing choice. In reading this over, one gets the feeling that commitment to an organization is an entrapment: an individual is either cut off from other alternatives because no one else wants him or because his own situation doesn't allow him to change it. Thus, individuals rarely make job changes involving moves when their children are entrenched in a school. In all, it is a rather negative view of commitment. You are committed because the facts of your life have bound you.

What about more positive features? Do people become committed to their jobs because they are attracted to them and find then enjoyable? The research on this issue is unimpressive. Much is based on termination interviews which find that workers who quit say they quit because they didn't like the job or the pay. Having taken so decisive a step, it would be rather amusing to find them saying that they loved the job. Studies attempting to predict employee turnover or absenteeism from prior reports of job satisfaction have been notoriously unsuccessful from a practical point of view; that is, the studies report statistically reliable relationships of so low a magnitude that they predict little about behavior. Even superior measurement techniques do poorly (Newman, 1974).

The typical relationship found between job attitudes and turnover or absenteeism is clouded by other factors. We have already discussed that one of these factors is the tenure of the employee. Job satisfaction increases with age and tenure, as does commitment to the organization (see Grupp & Richards, 1975; Organ & Greene, 1974; Gow, Clark, & Dossett, 1974 for illustrative studies). Where investigators have bothered to make the necessary causal analyses, they have found that the change is a "real" one and not simply a function of changes in position, jobs, or salary (Stagner, 1975). As a person becomes more able to cope with the negative and positive features of his job. . . .

Commitment and Job Features

Despite the rather unpredictable relationship between job attitudes, absenteeism, turmoil, and turnover, the model of commitment presented here does suggest that certain features of a person's job situation will affect his commitment. In general, any characteristic of a person's job situation which reduces his felt responsibility will reduce his commitment. As for the relationship between commitment and satisfaction, our own view is that enjoyment is more likely to follow commitment than the reverse.

Many characteristics of job situations can affect a person's perception of responsibility. Some positions simply carry more responsibility, and persons in higher positions tend to be more committed. Similarly, some jobs offer more discretion and self-determination to their occupants, and it has been found that employees in autonomous positions generally have more favorable attitudes than those with little freedom to decide how to do their jobs (Hackman & Lawler, 1971; Hackman & Oldham, 1974).

In addition to the job and the freedom it permits, the manner by which the job is supervised or monitored can affect perceptions of responsibility. The supervisor who stands over a subordinate provides an excuse for the subordinate's behavior. When unpleasant aspects of the job become apparent, rather than coping with them, and finding some joy in the job, the subordinate can attribute his endurance to the supervisor's tenacious pressure. Lepper and Greene (1975) found that surveillance deteriorates interest in a task. Zanna (1970) found that when students are led to believe they worked very hard for a nasty supervisor, they enjoyed the task more than when they worked very hard for a nice supervisor. When they work for a nice person they attribute their effort to their liking for him, not the job. This would be an unrealistic attribution to a nasty boss, so they like the job more.

If a supervisor merely stands by without taking an active part in determining the subordinate's behavior, his presence may serve to reinforce the subordinate's felt responsibility. Maguire and Ouchi (1975) found that close output supervision improves employee satisfaction but that close behavioral supervision does not. Monitoring and providing an individual with feedback about his work performance can increase a person's felt responsibility. The person, knowing his outcomes and knowing his outcomes are known by others, may become more aware that the outcomes are his responsibility. Hackman and Oldham (1974) found worker's perception of responsibility was in part a function of feedback about their performance. While the precise effects of various supervisory conditions on commitment have not been well studied, we would expect that high output monitoring coupled with low behavioral control would lead to the greatest felt responsibility on the part of the worker. Whether or not these conditions will lead to greater satisfaction, would depend on whether or not the worker can handle the task. Maguire and Ouchi (1975) found more satisfaction among monitored workers who could do their jobs without depending on others (i.e., low interdependence), than those who could not.

Commitment also derives from the relation of an employee's job to those of others in the organization. Some jobs are rather isolated and can be done independently of other jobs in the organization. It has been found that jobs which are not integrated with the work activities of others tend to be associated with less favorable attitudes (Sheperd, 1973). Gow, Clark and Dossett (1974), for instance, find that telephone operators who quit tend to be those who are not integrated into the work group. Work integration can affect commitment by the fact that integrated jobs are likely to be associated with salient demands from others in the organization. If a person has a job which affects the work of others in the organization, it is likely that those others will communicate their expectations for performance of that job. Such expectations can be committing in that the other people implicitly or explicitly hold the person accountable for what he does. Earlier we mentioned that when individuals did not know what was expected of them they tended to be less committed to the organization.

One reason an individual will not know what is expected is because no one is telling him. In general, we would expect that anything which contributes to creating definite expectations for a person's behavior would enhance his felt responsibility, and hence commitment. Integration may be one such contributor.

Perhaps the most pervasive condition of a job which affects commitment is its instrumentality, the fact that work is a means to some other end. While all jobs in industrial and commercial organizations are done in exchange for salary, there are perhaps great variations in the extent to which the instrumental basis for the work is salient or not. In general, we would expect that when the instrumental basis for work is salient it will reduce a person's felt responsibility. The attribution, "I am doing this job only for the money," should inhibit commitment. A similar point was raised by Ingham (1970), who analyzed absenteeism and turnover in light engineering firms in Bradford, England. Observing that larger organizations had more absenteeism (but lower turnover), he argued that workers were attracted to large firms because of the higher pay offered, but that this instrumental orientation led to little personal involvement with the organization. . . .

There is far too little empirical work on the nature of commitment to jobs, and how features of the work situation lead to or detract from feelings of personal responsibility for work. Much more detailed accountings of the particulars of job situations need to be made.

REFERENCES

Becker, H. S. Notes on the concept of commitment. *American Journal of Sociology*, 1960, 66, 32–40.

Festinger, L. *A theory of cognitive dissonance*. Stanford, Calif.: Stanford University Press, 1957.

Festinger, *Conflict, decision, and dissonance*. Stanford, Calif.: Stanford University Press, 1964.

Gow, J. S., Clark, A. W., & Dossett, G. S. A path analysis of variables influencing labour turnover. *Human Relations*. 1974, 27, 703–19.

Hackman, J. R., & Lawler, E. E. Employee reactions to job characteristics. *Journal of Applied Psychology*, 1971, 55, 259–86.

Hackman, J. R., & Oldham, G. R. Motivation through the design of work: Test of a theory. Technical Report no. 6, Administrative Sciences, Yale University, 1974.

Ingham, G. K. *Size of industrial organizations and worker behavior.* Cambridge: Cambridge University Press, 1970.

Kanter, R. M. Commitment and social organizations. *American Sociological Review.* 1968.

Kiesler, C. A. *The psychology of commitment: Experiments linking behavior to belief.* New York: Academic Press, 1971.

Kiesler, C. A., & Sakumura, J. A test of a model for commitment. *Journal of Personality and Social Psychology*, 1966, 3 349–53.

Lepper, M. R., Greene, D., & Nisbett, R. E. Undermining children's intrinsic interest with extrinsic rewards: A test of the "overjustification" hypothesis. *Journal of Personality and Social Psychology*, 1973, 28, 129–37.

Lewin, K. Group decision and social change. In T. M. Newcomb and E. L. Hartley (Eds.), *Readings in social psychology.* New York: Holt, Reinhart & Winston, 1947, pp. 330–44.

Maguire, M. A., & Ouchi, W. Organizational control and work satisfaction. Research Paper no. 278, Graduate School of Business, Stanford University, 1975.

Newman, J. E. Predicting absenteeism and turnover: A field comparison of Fishbein's model and traditional job attitude measures. *Journal of Applied Psychology*, 1975, 17, 69–78.

Organ, D. W., & Greene, N. The perceived purposefulness of job behavior: Antecedents and consequences. *Academy of Management Journal*, 1974, 17, 69–78.

Stagner, R. Boredom on the assembly line: Age and personality variables. *Industrial Gerontology*, 1975, 21, 23–44.

Zanna, M. P. Attitude inference in a low choice setting. Ph. D. dissertation, Yale University, 1970.

23. THE SMILE FACTORY: WORK AT DISNEYLAND

John Van Maanen

Part of Walt Disney Enterprises includes the theme park Disneyland. In its pioneering form in Anaheim, California, this amusement center has been a consistent money maker since the gates were first opened in 1955. Apart from its sociological charm, it has, of late, become something of an exemplar for culture vultures and has been held up for public acclaim in several best-selling publications as one of America's top companies, most notably by Peters and Waterman (1982). To out-

From: Peter J. Frost, Larry F. Moore, Meryl Reis Lois, Craig C. Lundberg, and Joanne Martin (Eds.). *Reframing Organizational Culture.* Newbury Park, CA: Sage Publications, pp. 58–76.

Author's Note: This paper has been cobbled together using three-penny nails of other writings. Parts come from a paper presented to the American Anthropological Association Annual Meetings in Washington D.C. on November 16, 1989, called "Whistle While You Work." Other parts come from Van Maanen and Kunda (1989). In coming to this version, I've had a good deal of help from my friends Steve Barley, Nicloe Biggart, Michael Owen Jones, Rosanna Hertz, Gideon Kunda, Joanne Martin, Maria Lydia Spinelli, Bob Sutton, and Bob Thomas.

siders, the cheerful demeanor of its employees, the seemingly inexhaustible repeat business it generates from its customers, the immaculate condition of park grounds, and, more generally, the intricate physical and social order of the business itself appear wondrous.

Disneyland as the self-proclaimed "Happiest Place on Earth" certainly occupies an enviable position in the amusement and entertainment worlds as well as the commercial world in general. Its product, it seems, is emotion—"laughter and well-being." Insiders are not bashful about promoting the product. Bill Ross, a Disneyland executive, summarizes the corporate position nicely by noting that "although we focus our attention on profit and loss, day-in and day-out we can not lose sight of the fact that this is a feeling business and we make our profits from that."[1]

The "feeling business" does not operate, however, by management decree alone. Whatever services Disneyland executives believe they are providing to the 60 to 70 thousand visitors per day that flow through the park during its peak summer season, employees at the bottom of the organization are the ones who most provide them. The work-a-day practices that employees adopt to amplify or dampen customer spirits are therefore a core concern of this feeling business. The happiness trade is an interactional one. It rests partly on the symbolic resources put into place by history and park design but it also rests on an animated workforce that is more or less eager to greet the guests, pack the trams, push the buttons, deliver the food, dump the garbage, clean the streets, and, in general, marshal the will to meet and perhaps exceed customer expectations. False moves, rude words, careless disregard, detected insincerity, or a sleepy and bored presence can all undermine the enterprise and ruin a sale. The smile factory has its rules.

IT'S A SMALL WORLD

The writing that follows[2] represents Disneyland as a workplace. It is organized roughly as an old-fashioned realist ethnography that tells of a culture in native categories (Van Maanen, 1988). The culture of interest is the Disneyland culture but it is not necessarily the same one invented, authorized, codified, or otherwise approved by park management. Thus the culture I portray here is more of an occupational than a strictly organizational one (Van Maanen & Barley, 1985).

This rendition is of course abbreviated and selective. I focus primarily on such matters as the stock appearance (vanilla), status order (rigid), and social life (full), and swiftly learned codes of conduct (formal and informal) that are associated with Disneyland ride operators. These employees comprise the largest category of hourly workers on the payroll. During the summer months, they number close to four thousand and run the 60-odd rides and attractions in the park.

They are also a well-screened bunch. There is—among insiders and outsiders alike—a rather fixed view about the social attributes carried by the standard-make Disneyland ride operator. Single, white males and females in their early twenties, without facial blemish, of above average height and below average weight, with straight teeth, conservative grooming standards, and a chin-up, shoulder-back posture radiating the sort of good health suggestive of a recent history in sports are typical of these social identifiers. There are representative minorities on the payroll but because ethnic displays are sternly discouraged by management, minority employees are rather close copies of the standard model Disneylander, albeit in different colors.

This Disneyland look is often a source of some amusement to employees who delight in pointing out that even the patron saint, Walt himself, could not be hired today without shaving off his trademark pencil-thin mustache. But, to get a job in Disneyland and keep it means conforming to a rather exacting set of appearance rules. These rules are put forth in a handbook on the Disney image in which readers learn, for example, that facial hair or long hair is banned for men as are aviator glasses and earrings and that women must not tease their hair, wear fancy jewelry, or apply more than a modest dab of makeup. Both men and women are to look neat and prim, keep their uniforms fresh, polish their shoes, and maintain an upbeat countenance and light dignity to complement their appearance—no low spirits or cornball raffishness at Disneyland.

The legendary "people skills" of park employees, so often mentioned in Disneyland publicity and training materials, do not amount to very much according to ride operators. Most tasks require little interaction with customers and are physically designed to practically insure that is the case. The contact that does occur typically is fleeting and swift, a matter usually of only a few seconds. In the rare event sustained interaction with customers might be required, employees are taught to deflect potential exchanges to area supervisors or security. A Training Manual offers the proper procedure: "On misunderstandings, guests should be told to call City Hall . . . In everything from damaged cameras to physical injuries, don't discuss anything with guests . . . there will always be one of us nearby." Employees learn quickly that security is hidden but everywhere. On Main Street, security cops are Keystone Kops; in Frontierland, they are Town Marshalls; on Tom Sawyer's Island, they are Cavalry Officers, and so on.

Occasionally, what employees call "line talk" or "crowd control" is required of them to explain delays, answer direct questions, or provide directions that go beyond the endless stream of recorded messages coming from virtually every nook and cranny of the park. Because such tasks are so simple, consisting of little more than keeping the crowd informed and moving, it is perhaps obvious why management considers the sharp appearance and wide smile of employees so vital to park operations. There is little more they could ask of ride operators whose main interactive tasks with visitors consist of being, in their own terms, "information booths," "line signs," "pretty props," "shepherds," and "talking statues."

A few employees do go out of their way to initiate contact with Disneyland customers but, as a rule, most do not and consider those who do to be a bit odd. In general, one need do little more than exercise common courtesy while looking reasonably alert and pleasant. Interactive skills that are advanced by the job have less to do with making customers feel warm and welcome than they do with keeping each other amused and happy. This is, of course, a more complex matter.

Employees bring to the job personal badges of status that are of more than passing interest to peers. In rough order, these include: good looks, college affiliation, career aspirations, past achievements, age (directly related to status up to about age 23 or 24 and inversely related thereafter), and assorted other idiosyncratic matters. Nested closely alongside these imported status badges are organizational ones that are also of concern and value to employees.

Where one works in the park carries much social weight. Postings are consequential because the ride and area a person is assigned provide rewards and benefits beyond those of wages. In-the-park stature for ride operators turns partly on whether or not unique skills are required. Disneyland neatly complements labor market theorizing on this dimension because employees with the most differentiated skills find themselves at the top of the internal status ladder, thus making their loyalties to the organization more predictable.

Ride operators, as a large but distinctly middle-class group of hourly employees on the floor of the organization, compete for status not only with each other but also with other employee groupings whose members are hired for the season from the same applicant pool. A loose approximation of the rank ordering among these groups can be constructed as follows:

1. The upper-class prestigious Disneyland Ambassadors and Tour Guides (bilingual young women in charge of ushering—some say rushing—little bands of tourists through the park);

2. Ride operators performing coveting "skilled work" such as live narrations or tricky transportation tasks like those who symbolically control customer access to the park and drive, the costly entry vehicles such as the antique trains, horse-drawn carriages, and Monorail);

3. All other ride operators;

4. The proletarian Sweepers (keepers of the concrete grounds);

5. The sub-prole or peasant status Food and Concession workers (whose park sobriquets reflect their lowly social worth—"pancake ladies," "peanut pushers," "coke blokes," "suds divers," and the seemingly irreplaceable "soda jerks").

Pay differentials are slight among these employee groups. The collective status adheres, as it does internally for ride operators, to assignment or functional distinctions. As the rank order suggests, most employee status goes to those who work jobs that require higher degrees of special skill, relative freedom from constant and direct supervision, and provide the opportunity to organize and direct customer desires and behavior rather than to merely respond to them as spontaneously expressed.

The basis for sorting individuals into these various broad bands of job categories is often unknown to employees—a sort of deep, dark secret of the casting directors in personnel. When prospective employees are interviewed, they interview for "a job at Disneyland," not a specific one. Personnel decides what particular job they will eventually occupy. Personal contacts are considered by employees as crucial in this job-assignment process as they are in the hiring decision. Some employees, especially those who wind up in the lower ranking jobs, are quite disappointed with their assignments as is the case when, for example, a would-be Adventureland guide is posted to a New Orleans Square restaurant as a pot scrubber. Although many of the outside acquaintances of our pot scrubber may know only that he works at Disneyland, rest assured, insiders will know immediately where he works and judge him accordingly.

Uniforms are crucial in this regard for they provide instant communication about the social merits or demerits of the wearer within the little world of Disneyland workers. Uniforms also correspond to a wider status ranking that casts a significant shadow on employees of all types. Male ride operators on the Autopia wear, for example, untailored jumpsuits similar to pit mechanics and consequently generate about as much respect from peers as the grease-stained outfits worn by pump jockeys generate from real motorists in gas stations. The ill-fitting and homogeneous "whites" worn by Sweepers signify lowly institutional work tinged, perhaps, with a reminder of hospital orderlies rather than street cleanup crews. On the other hand, for males, the crisp, officer-like Monorail operator stands alongside the swashbuckling Pirate of the Caribbean, the casual cowpoke of Big Thunder Mountain, or the smartly vested Riverboat pilot as carriers of valued symbols in and outside the park. Employees lust for these higher status positions and the rights to small advantages such uniforms provide. A lively internal labor market exists wherein there is much scheming for the more prestigious assignments.

For women, a similar market exists although the perceived "sexiness" of uniforms, rather than social rank, seems to play a larger role. To wit, the rather heated antagonisms that developed years ago when the ride "It's a Small World" first opened and began outfitting the ride operators with what were felt to be the shortest skirts and most revealing blouses in the park. Tour Guides, who traditionally headed the fashion vanguard at Disneyland in their above-the-knee kilts, knee socks, tailored vests, black English hats, and smart riding crops were apparently appalled at being upstaged by their social inferiors and lobbied actively (and, judging by the results, successfully) to lower the skirts, raise the necklines, and generally remake their Small World rivals.

Important, also, to ride operators are the break schedules followed on the various rides. The more the better. Work teams develop inventive ways to increase the number of "time-outs" they take during the work day. Most rides are organized on a rotational basis (e.g., the operator moving from a break, to queue monitor, to turnstile overseer, to unit loader, to traffic controller, to driver, and, again, to a break). The number of break men or women on a rotation (or ride) varies by the number of employees on duty and by the number of units on line. Supervisors, foremen, and operators also vary as to what they regard as appropriate break standards (and, more importantly, as to the value of the many situational factors that can enter the calculation of break rituals—crowd size, condition of ride, accidents, breakdowns, heat, operator absences, special occasions, and so forth). Self-monitoring teams with sleepy supervisors and lax (or savvy) foremen can sometimes manage a shift comprised of 15 minutes on and 45 minutes off each hour. They are envied by others and rides that have such a potential are eyed hungrily by others who feel trapped by their more rigid (and observed) circumstances.

Movement across jobs is not encouraged by park management but some does occur (mostly within an area and job category). Employees claim that a sort of "once a sweeper, always a sweeper" rule obtains but all know of at least a few exceptions to prove the rule. The exceptions offer some (not much) hope for those working at the social margins of the park and perhaps keep them on the job longer than might otherwise be expected. Dishwashers can dream of becoming Pirates, and with persistence and a little help from their friends, such dreams just might come true next season (or the next).

These examples are precious, perhaps, but they are also important. There is an intricate pecking order among very similar categories of employees. Attributes of reward and status tend to cluster, and there is intense concern about the cluster to which one belongs (or would like to belong). To a degree, form follows function in Disneyland because the jobs requiring the most abilities and offering the most interest also offer the most status and social reward. Interaction patterns reflect and sustain this order. Few Ambassadors or Tour Guides, for instance, will stoop to speak at length with Sweepers who speak mostly among themselves or to Food workers. Ride operators, between the poles, line up in ways referred to above with only ride proximity (i.e., sharing a break area) representing a potentially significant intervening variable in the interaction calculation.

These patterns are of more than slight concern because Disneyland, especially in the summer, can be compared quite usefully to a college mixer

where across-sex pairing is of great concern (Schwartz & Lever, 1976). More to the point, what Waller (1937) so accurately called the "rating and dating complex" is in full bloom among park employees. The various modern forms of mating games are valued pastimes among Disneyland employees and are often played with corporate status markers in mind. Thus, when Yvone, the reigning Alice in Wonderland, moved in one summer with Ted, a lowly Sweeper, heads were scratched in puzzlement even though most knew that Yvone was, in her other life, a local junior college student and Ted was in premed at USC. The more general point is that romance flourishes in the park and, at least, if folklore is our guide, marriages made in Disneyland are not uncommon.

Even when not devoted strictly to pairing-off objectives, employee pastimes usually involve other employees. Disneyland's softball and volleyball leagues, its official picnics, canoe races, employee nights at the park, beach parties, and so on provide a busy little social scene for those interested. Areas and rides, too, offer social excitement and bonuses such as when kegs of beer are rolled out at an off-site party after work crews break turnstile records ("We put 33,147 on the mountain today"). During the summer, some night crews routinely party in the early morning while day shift crews party at night. Sleep is not a commodity greatly valued by many employees caught up in a valued social whirl.

The so-called youth culture is indeed celebrated in and out of the park. Many employees, for example, live together in the large and cheap (by Los Angeles standards) apartment complexes that surround Disneyland. Employees sometimes refer to these sprawling, pastel, and slightly seedy structures as "the projects" or "worker housing." Yet, the spirited attractiveness of the collective, low-rent lifestyle for those living it is easily grasped by a few landlords in the area who flatly refuse to rent to Disneyland employees during the summer as a matter of principle and, maybe, sorry experience because these short-term rentals serve as amusement parks for off-duty Disneylanders who, as they say, "know how to party."

A fusion of work and play is notable, however, even when play seems to be the order of the occasion. Certainly no Disneyland get-together would be complete without ride operators launching into their special spiel practiced (or heard continuously on tape) at work:

Welcome aboard the African Queen, folks. My name is John and I'll be your guide and skipper for our trip down these rivers of adventure. As we pull away from the loading dock, turn around and take a last look at the people standing there, it may be the last time you ever see them . . . Please keep your hands inside the boat as we go past these hungry alligators, they're always looking for a handout . . . And now we return to civilization and the greatest danger of all, the California freeways.

The figurative parallel of this party is, of course, the atmosphere of a most collegial college. It has a literal parallel as well.

Paid employment at Disneyland begins with the much renowned University of Disneyland whose faculty runs a day-long orientation program (Traditions I) as part of a 40-hour apprenticeship program, most of which takes place on the rides. In the classroom, however, newly hired ride operators are given a very thorough introduction to matters of managerial concern and are tested on their absorption of famous Disneyland fact, lore, and procedure. Employee demeanor is governed, for example, by three rules:

First, we practice the friendly smile.
Second, we use only friendly and courteous phrases.
Third, we are not stuffy—the only Misters in Disneyland are Mr. Toad and Mr. Smee.

Employees learn too that the Disneyland culture is officially defined. The employee handbook put it in this format:

Dis-ney Cor-po-rate Cul-ture (diz'ne kor'pr'it kul'cher) n 1. Of or pertaining to the Disney organization, as a: the philosophy underlying all business decisions; b: the commitment of top leadership and management to that philosophy; c: the actions taken by individual cast members that reinforce the image.

Language is also a central feature of university life and new employees are schooled in its proper use. Customers at Disneyland are, for instance, never referred to as such, they are "guests." There are no rides at Disneyland, only "attractions." Disneyland itself is a "Park," not an amusement center, and it is divided into "back-stage," "on-stage," and "staging" regions. Law enforcement personnel hired by the park are not policemen, but "security hosts." Employees do not wear uniforms but check out fresh "costumes" each working day from "wardrobe." And, of course, there are no accidents at Disneyland, only "incidents."

So successful is such training that Smith and Eisenberg (1987) report that not a single Disneyland employee uttered the taboo and dread words "uniform," "customer," or "amusement park" during the 35 half-hour interviews they conducted as part of a study on organizational communication. The *Los Angeles Times* (July 28, 1988) also gives evidence on this matter, quoting a tour guide's reaction to the employee's annual canoe races. "It's a good release," she says, "it helps you see the other cast members (park employees) go through the same thing you do." Whether or not employees keep to such disciplined talk with one another is, of course, a moot point because the corporate manual is concerned only with how employees talk to customers or outsiders.

The university curriculum also anticipates probable questions ride operators may someday face from customers and they are taught the approved public response. A sample:

Question (posed by trainer): What do you tell a guest who requests a rain check?

Answer (in three parts): We don't offer rain checks at Disneyland because (1) the main attractions are all indoors; (2) we would go broke if we offered passes; and (3) sunny days would be too crowded if we gave passes.

Shrewd trainees readily note that such an answer blissfully disregards the fact that waiting areas of Disneyland are mostly outdoors and that there are no subways in the park to carry guests from land to land. Nor do they miss the economic assumption concerning the apparent frequency of Southern California rains. They discuss such matters together, of course, but rarely raise them in the training classroom. In most respects, these are recruits who easily take the role of good student.

Classes are organized and designed by professional Disneyland trainers who also instruct a well-screened group of representative hourly employees straight from park operations on the approved newcomer training methods and materials. New-hires seldom see professional trainers in class but are brought on board by enthusiastic peers who concentrate on those aspects of park procedure thought highly general matters to be learned by all employees. Particular skill training (and "reality shock") is reserved for the second wave of socialization occurring on the rides themselves as operators are taught, for example, how and when to send a mock bobsled caroming down the track or, more delicately, the proper ways to stuff an obese adult customer into the midst of children riding the Monkey car on the Casey Jones Circus Train or, most problematically, what exactly to tell an irate customer standing in the rain who, in no uncertain terms, wants his or her money back and wants it back now.

During orientation, considerable concern is placed on particular values the Disney organization considers central to its operations. These values range from the "customer is king" verities to the more or less unique kind, of which "everyone is a child at heart when at Disneyland" is a decent example. This latter piety is one few employees fail to recognize as also attaching to everyone's mind as well after a few months of work experience. Elaborate checklists of appearance standards are learned and gone over in the classroom and great efforts are spent trying to bring employee emotional responses in line with such standards. Employees are told repeatedly that if they are happy and cheerful at work, so, too, will the guests at play. Inspirational films, hearty pep talks, family imagery, and exemplars of corporate performance are all representative of the strong symbolic stuff of these training rites.

Another example, perhaps extreme, concerns the symbolic role of the canonized founder in the corporate mythology. When Walt Disney was alive, newcomers and veterans alike were told how much he enjoyed coming to the park and just how exacting he was about the conditions he observed. For employees, the cautionary whoop, "Walt's in the park," could often bring forth additional energy and care for one's part in the production. Upon his death, trainers at the University were said to be telling recruits to mind their manners because, "Walt's in the park all the time now."

Yet, like employees everywhere, there is a limit to which such overt company propaganda can be effective. Students and trainers both seem to agree on where the line is drawn for there is much satirical banter, mischievous winking, and playful exaggeration in the classroom. As young seasonal employees note, it is difficult to take seriously an organization that provides its retirees "Golden Ears" instead of gold watches after 20 or more years of service. All newcomers are aware that the label "Disneyland" has both an unserious and artificial connotation and that a full embrace of the Disneyland role would be as deviant as its full rejection. It does seem, however, because of the corporate imagery, the recruiting and selection devices, the goodwill trainees hold toward the organization at entry, the peer-based employment context, and the smooth fit with real student calendars, the job is considered by most ride operators to be a good one. The University of Disneyland, it appears, graduates students with a modest amount of pride and a considerable amount of fact and faith firmly ingrained as important things to know (if not always accept).

Matters become more interesting as new hires move into the various realms of Disneyland enterprise. There are real customers "out there" and employees soon learn that these good folks do not always measure up to the typically well mannered and grateful guest of the training classroom. Moreover, ride operators may find it difficult to utter the prescribed "Welcome Voyager" (or its equivalent) when it is to be given to the 20-thousandth human being passing through the Space Mountain turnstile on a crowded day in July. Other difficulties present themselves as well, but operators learn that there are others on-stage to assist or thwart them.

Employees learn quickly that supervisors and, to a lesser degree, foremen are not only on the premises to help them, but also to catch them when they slip over or brazenly violate set procedures or park policies. Because most rides are tightly designed to eliminate human judgment and minimize operational disasters, much of the supervisory monitoring is directed at activities ride operators consider trivial: taking too long a break; not wearing parts of one's official uniform such as a hat, standard-issue belt, or correct shoes; rushing the ride (although more frequent violations seem to be detected for the provision of longer-than-usual rides for lucky customers); fraternizing with guests beyond the call of duty; talking back to quarrelsome or sometimes merely querisome customers; and so forth. All are matters covered quite explicitly in the codebooks ride operators are to be familiar with, and violations of such codes are often subject to instant and harsh discipline. The firing of what to supervisors are "malcontents," "trouble-makers," "bumblers," "attitude problems," or simply "jerks" is a frequent occasion at Disneyland, and among part-timers, who are most subject to degradation and being fired, the threat is omnipresent. There are few workers who have not witnessed firsthand the rapid disappearance of a co-worker for offenses they would regard as "Mickey Mouse." Moreover, there are few employees who themselves have not violated a good number of operational and demeanor standards and anticipate, with just cause, the violation of more in the future.[3]

In part, because of the punitive and what are widely held to be capricious supervisory practices in the park, foremen and ride operators are usually drawn close and shield one another from suspicious area supervisors. Throughout the year, each land is assigned a number of area supervisors who, dressed alike in short-sleeved white shirts and ties with walkie-talkies hitched to their belts, wander about their territories on the lookout for deviations from park procedures (and other signs of disorder). Occasionally, higher level supervisors pose in "plainclothes" and ghost-ride the various attractions just to be sure everything is up to snuff. Some area supervisors are well-known among park employees for the variety of surreptitious techniques they employ when going about their monitoring duties. Blind observation posts are legendary, almost sacred, sites within the park ("This is where Old Man Weston hangs out. He can see Dumbo, Storybook, the Carousel, and the Tea Cups from here"). Supervisors in Tomorrowland are, for example, famous for their penchant of hiding in the bushes above the submarine caves, timing the arrivals and departures of the supposedly fully loaded boats making the 8½ minute cruise under the polar icecaps. That they might also catch a submarine captain furtively enjoying a cigarette (or worse) while inside the conning tower (his upper body out of view of the crowd on the vessel) might just make a supervisor's day—and unmake the employee's. In short, supervisors, if not foremen, are regarded by ride operators as sneaks and tricksters out to get them and representative of the dark side of park life. Their presence is, of course, an orchestrated one and does more than merely watch over the ride operators. It also draws operators together as cohesive little units who must look out for one another while they work (and shirk).

Supervisors are not the only villains who appear in the park. The treachery of co-workers, while rare, has its moments. Pointing out the code violations of colleagues to foremen and supervisors—usually in secret—provides one avenue of collegial duplicity. Finks, of all sorts, can be found among the peer ranks at Disneyland, and although their dirty deeds are uncommon, work teams on all rides go to some effort to determine just who they might be and, if possible, drive them from their midst. Although there is little overt hazing or playing of pranks on newcomers, they are nonetheless carefully scrutinized on matters of team (and ride) loyalty, and those who fail the test of "member in good standing" are subject to some very uncomfortable treatment. Innuendo and gossip are the primary tools in this regard, with ridicule and ostracism (the good old silent treatment) providing the backup. Since perhaps the greatest rewards working at Disneyland offers its ride operator personnel are those that come from belonging to a tight little network of like-minded and sociable peers where off-duty interaction is at least as vital and pleasurable as the on-duty sort, such mechanisms are quite effective. Here is where some of the most powerful and focused emotion work in the park is found, and those subject to negative sanction, rightly or wrongly, will grieve, but grieve alone.

Employees are also subject to what might be regarded as remote controls. These stem not from supervisors or peers but from thousands of paying guests who parade daily through the park. The public, for the most part, wants Disneyland employees to play only the roles for which they are hired and costumed. If, for instance, Judy of the Jets is feeling tired, grouchy, or bored, few customers want to know about it. Disneyland employees are expected to be sunny and helpful; and the job, with its limited opportunities for sustained interaction, is designed to support such a stance. Thus, if a ride operator's behavior drifts noticeably away from the norm, customers are sure to point it out—"Why aren't you smiling?" "What's wrong with you?" "Having a bad day?" "Did Goofy step on your foot?" Ride operators learn swiftly from the constant hints, glances, glares, and tactful (and tactless) cues sent by their audience what their role in the park is to be, and as long as they keep to it, there will be no objections from those passing by.

I can remember being out on the river looking at the people on the Mark Twain looking down on the people in the Keel Boats who are looking up at them. I'd come by on my raft and they'd all turn and stare at me. If I gave them a little wave and a grin, they'd all wave back and smile; all ten thousand of them. I always wondered what would happen if I gave them the finger? (Ex-ride operator, 1988)

Ride operators also learn how different categories of customers respond to them and the parts they are playing on-stage. For example, infants and small children are generally timid, if not frightened, in their presence. School-age children are somewhat curious, aware that the operator is at work playing a role but sometimes in awe of the role itself. Nonetheless, these children can be quite critical of any flaw in the operator's performance. Teenagers, especially males in groups, present problems because they sometimes go to great lengths to embarrass, challenge, ridicule, or outwit an operator. Adults are generally appreciative and approving of an operator's conduct provided it meets their rather minimal standards, but they sometimes overreact to the part an operator is playing (positively) if accompanied by small children. A recent study of the Easter Bunny points out a similar sort of response on the part of adults to fantasy (Hickey, Thompson, & Foster, 1988). It is worth noting too that adults outnumber children in the park by a wide margin. One count reports an adult-to-children ratio of four-to-one (King, 1981).

The point here is that ride operators learn what the public (or, at least, their idealized version of the public) expects of their role and find it easier to conform to such expectations than not. Moreover, they discover that when they are bright and lively others respond to them in like ways. This Goffmanesque balancing of the emotional exchange is such that ride operators come to expect good treatment. They assume, with good cause, that most people will react to their little waves and smiles with some affection and perhaps joy. When they do not, it can ruin a ride operator's day.

With this interaction formula in mind, it is perhaps less difficult to see why ride operators detest and scorn the ill-mannered or unruly guest. At times, these grumpy, careless, or otherwise unresponsive characters insult the very role the operators play and have come to appreciate—"You can't treat the Captain of the USS Nautilus like that!" Such out-of-line visitors offer breaks from routine, some amusement, consternation, or the occasional job challenge that occurs when remedies are deemed necessary to restore employee and role dignity.

By and large, however, the people-processing tasks of ride operators pass good naturedly and smoothly, with operators hardly noticing much more than the bodies passing in front of view (special bodies, however, merit special attention as when crew members on the subs gather to assist a young lady in a revealing outfit on board and then linger over the hatch to admire the view as she descends the steep steps to take her seat on the boat). Yet, sometimes, more than a body becomes visible, as happens when customers overstep their roles and challenge employee authority, insult an operator, or otherwise disrupt the routines of the job. In the process, guests become "dufusses," "ducks," and "assholes" (just three of many derisive terms used by ride operators to label those customers they believe to have gone beyond the pale). Normally, these characters are brought to the attention of park security officers, ride foremen, or area supervisors who, in turn, decide how they are to be disciplined (usually expulsion from the park).

Occasionally, however, the alleged slight is too personal or simply too extraordinary for a ride operator to let it pass unnoticed or merely inform others and allow them to decide what, if anything, is to be done. Restoration of one's respect is called for and routine practices have been developed for these circumstances. For example, common remedies include: the "seatbelt squeeze," a small token of appreciation given to a deviant customer consisting of the rapid cinching-up of a required seatbelt such that the passenger is doubled-over at the point of departure and left gasping for the duration of the trip; the "break-toss," an acrobatic gesture of the Autopia trade whereby operators jump on the outside of a norm violator's car, stealthily unhitching the safety belt, then slamming on the brakes, bringing the car to an almost instant stop while the driver flies on the hood of the car (or beyond); the "seatbelt slap," an equally distinguished (if primitive) gesture by which an offending customer receives a sharp, quick snap of a hard plastic belt across the face (or other parts of the body) when entering or exiting a seat-belted ride; the "break-up-the-party" gambit, a queuing device put to use in officious fashion whereby bothersome pairs are separated at the last minute into different units, thus forcing on them the pain of strange companions for the duration of a ride through the Haunted Mansion or a ramble on Mr. Toad's Wild Ride; the "hatch-cover ploy," a much beloved practice of Submarine pilots who, in collusion with mates on the loading dock, are able to drench offensive guests with water as their units pass under a waterfall; and, lastly, the rather ignoble variants of the "Sorry-I-didn't-see-your-hand" tactic, a savage move designed to crunch a particularly irksome customer's hand (foot, finger, arm, leg, etc.) by bringing a piece of Disneyland property to bear on the appendage, such as the door of a Thunder Mountain railroad car or the starboard side of a Jungle Cruise boat. This latter remedy is, most often, a "near miss" designed to startle the little criminals of Disneyland.

All of these unofficial procedures (and many more) are learned on the job. Although they are used sparingly, they are used. Occasions of use provide a continual stream of sweet revenge talk to enliven and enrich colleague conversation at break time or after work. Too much, of course, can be made of these subversive practices and the rhetoric that surrounds their use. Ride operators are quite aware that there are limits beyond which they dare not pass. If they are caught, they know that restoration of corporate pride will be swift and clean.

In general, Disneyland employees are remarkable for their forbearance and polite good manners even under trying conditions. They are taught, and some come to believe, for a while at least, that they are really "on-stage" at work. And, as noted, surveillance by supervisory personnel certainly fades in light of the unceasing glances an employee receives from the paying guests who tromp daily through the park in the summer. Disneyland employees know well that they are part of the product being sold and learn to check their more discriminating manners in favor of the generalized countenance of a cheerful lad or lassie whose enthusiasm and dedication is obvious to all.

At times, the emotional resources of employees appear awesome. When the going gets tough and the park is jammed, the nerves of all employees are frayed and sorely tested by the crowd, din, sweltering sun, and eye-burning smog. Customers wait in what employees call "bullpens" (and park officials call "reception areas") for up to several hours for a 3½ minute ride that operators are sometimes hell-bent on cutting to 2½ minutes. Surely a monument to the human ability to suppress feelings has been created when both users and providers alike can maintain their composure and seeming regard for one another when in such a fix.

It is in this domain where corporate culture and the order it helps to sustain must be given its due. Perhaps the depth of a culture is visible only when its members are under the gun. The orderliness—a good part of the Disney formula for financial success—is an accomplishment based not only on physical design and elaborate procedures, but also on the low-level, part-time employees who, in the final analysis, must be willing, even eager, to keep the show afloat. The ease with which employees glide into their kindly and smiling roles is, in large measure, a feat of social engineering. Disneyland does not pay well; its supervision is arbitrary and skin-close; its working conditions are chaotic; its jobs require minimal amounts of intelligence or judgment; and asks a kind of sacrifice and loyalty of its employees that is almost fanatical. Yet, it attracts a particularly able workforce whose personal backgrounds suggest abilities far exceeding those required of a Disneyland traffic cop, people stuffer, queue or line manager, and button pusher. As I have suggested, not all of Disneyland is covered by the culture put forth by management. There are numerous pockets of resistance and various degrees of autonomy maintained by employees. Nonetheless, adherence and support for the organization are remarkable. And, like swallows returning to Capistrano, many part-timers look forward to their migration back to the park for several seasons.

THE DISNEY WAY

Four features alluded to in this unofficial guide to Disneyland seem to account for a good deal of the social order that obtains within the park. First, socialization, although costly, is of a most selective, col-lective, intensive, serial, sequential, and closed sort.[4] These tactics are notable for their penetration into the private spheres of individual thought and feeling (Van Maanen & Schein, 1979). Incoming identities are not so much dismantled as they are set aside as employees are schooled in the use of new identities of the situational sort. Many of these are symbolically powerful and, for some, laden with social approval. It is hardly surprising that some of the more problematic positions in terms of turnover during the summer occur in the food and concession domains where employees apparently find little to identify with on the job. Cowpokes on Big Thunder Mountain, Jet Pilots, Storybook Princesses, Tour Guides, Space Cadets, Jungle Boat Skippers, or Southern Belles of New Orleans Square have less difficulty on this score. Disneyland, by design, bestows identity through a process carefully set up to strip away the job relevance of other sources of identity and learned response and replace them with others of organizational relevance. It works.

Second, this is a work culture whose designers have left little room for individual experimentation. Supervisors, as apparent in their focused wandering and attentive looks, keep very close tabs on what is going on at any moment in all the lands. Every bush, rock, and tree in Disneyland is numbered and checked continually as to the part it is playing in the park. So too are employees. Discretion of a personal sort is quite limited while employees are "on-stage." Even "back-stage" and certain "off-stage" domains have their corporate monitors. Employees are indeed aware that their "off-stage" life beyond the picnics, parties, and softball games is subject to some scrutiny for police checks are made on potential and current employees. Nor do all employees discount the rumors that park officials make periodic inquiries on their own as to a person's habits concerning sex and drugs. Moreover, the sheer number of rules and regulations is striking, thus making the grounds for dismissal a matter of multiple choice for supervisors who discover a target for the use of such grounds. The feeling of being watched is, unsurprisingly, a rather prevalent complaint among

Disneyland people and it is one that employees must live with if they are to remain at Disneyland.

Third, emotional management occurs in the park in a number of quite distinct ways. From the instructors at the university who beseech recruits to "wish every guest a pleasant good day," to the foremen who plead with their charges to, "say thank you when you herd them through the gate," to the impish customer who seductively licks her lips and asks, "what does Tom Sawyer want for Christmas?" appearance, demeanor, and etiquette have special meanings at Disneyland. Because these are prized personal attributes over which we normally feel in control, making them commodities can be unnerving. Much self-monitoring is involved, of course, but even here self-management has an organizational side. Consider ride operators who may complain of being "too tired to smile" but, at the same time, feel a little guilty for uttering such a confession. Ride operators who have worked an early morning shift on the Matterhorn (or other popular rides) tell of a queasy feeling they get when the park is opened for business and they suddenly feel the ground begin to shake under their feet and hear the low thunder of the hordes of customers coming at them, oblivious of civil restraint and the small children who might be among them. Consider, too, the discomforting pressures of being "on-stage" all day and the cumulative annoyance of having adults ask permission to leave a line to go to the bathroom, whether the water in the lagoon is real, where the well-marked entrances might be, where Walt Disney's cryogenic tomb is to be found,[5] or—the real clincher—whether or not one is "really real."

The mere fact that so much operator discourse concerns the handling of bothersome guests suggests that these little emotional disturbances have costs. There are, for instance, times in all employee careers when they put themselves on "automatic pilot," "go robot," "can't feel a thing," "lapse into a dream," "go into a trance," or otherwise "check out" while still on duty. Despite a crafty supervisor's (or curious visitor's) attempt to measure the glimmer in an employee's eye, this sort of willed emotional numbness is common to many of the "on-stage" Disneyland personnel. Much of this numbness is, of course, beyond the knowledge of supervisors and guests because most employees have little trouble appearing as if they are present even when they are not. It is, in a sense, a passive form of resistance that suggests there still is a sacred preserve of individuality left among employees in the park.

Finally, taking these three points together, it seems that even when people are trained, paid, and told to be nice, it is hard for them to do so all of the time. But, when efforts to be nice have succeeded to the degree that is true of Disneyland, it appears as a rather towering (if not always admirable) achievement. It works at the collective level by virtue of elaborate direction. Employees—at all ranks—are stage-managed by higher ranking employees who, having come through themselves, hire, train, and closely supervise those who have replaced them below. Expression rules are laid out in corporate manuals. Employee time-outs intensify work experience. Social exchanges are forced into narrow bands of interacting groups. Training and retraining programs are continual. Hiding places are few. Although little sore spots and irritations remain for each individual, it is difficult to imagine work roles being more defined (and accepted) than those at Disneyland. Here, it seems, is a work culture worthy of the name.

NOTES

1. The quote is drawn from a transcript of a speech made to senior managers of Hurrah's Club by Bill Ross, Vice President for Human Relations at Disneyland, in January 1988. Elsewhere in this account I draw on other in-house publications to document my tale. Of use in this regard are: "Your Role in the Show" (1982), "Disneyland: The First Thirty Years" (1985), "The Disney Approach to Management" (1986), and Steven Birnbaum's semi-official travel guide to

Disneyland (1988). The best tourist guide to the park I've read is Sehlinger's (1987) adamantly independent *The Unofficial Guide to Disneyland*.

2. This account is drawn primarily on my three-year work experience as a "permanent part-time" ride operator at Disneyland during the late 1960s. Sporadic contacts have been maintained with a few park employees and periodic visits, even with children in tow, have proved instructive. Also, lengthy, repeated beach interviews of a most informal sort have been conducted over the past few summers with ride operators (then) employed at the park. There is a good deal written about Disneyland, and I have drawn from these materials as indicated in the text. I must note finally that this is an unsponsored and unauthorized treatment of the Disneyland culture and is at odds on several points with the views set forth by management.

3. The author serves as a case in point for I was fired from Disneyland for what I still consider a Mickey Mouse offense. The specific violation—one of many possible—involved hair growing over my ears, an offense I had been warned about more than once before the final cut was made. The form my dismissal took, however, deserves comment for it is easy to recall and followed a format familiar to an uncountable number of ex-Disneylanders. Dismissal began by being pulled off the ride after my work shift had begun by an area supervisor in full view of my cohorts. A forced march to the administration building followed where my employee card was turned over and a short statement read to me by a personnel officer as to the formal cause of termination. Security officers then walked me to the employee locker room where my work uniforms and equipment were collected and my personal belongings returned to me while an inspection of my locker was made. The next stop was the time shed where my employee's time card was removed from its slot, marked "terminated" across the top in red ink, and replaced in its customary position (presumably for Disneylanders to see when clocking on or off the job over the next few days). As now an ex-ride operator, I was escorted to the parking lot where two security officers scraped off the employee parking sticker attached to my car. All these little steps of status degradation in the Magic Kingdom were quite public and, as the reader might guess, the process still irks. This may provide the reader with an account for the tone of this narrative, although it shouldn't since I would also claim I was ready to quit anyway since I had been there far too long. At any rate, it may just be possible that I now derive as much a part of my identity from being fired from Disneyland as I gained from being employed there in the first place.

4. These tactics are covered in some depth in Van Maanen (1976, 1977) and Van Maanen and Schein (1979). When pulled together and used simultaneously, a people processing system of some force is created that tends to produce a good deal of conformity among recruits who, regardless of background, come to share very similar occupational identities, including just how they think and feel on the job. Such socialization practices are common whenever recruits are bunched together and processed as a batch and when role innovation is distinctly unwanted on the part of the agents of such socialization.

5. The unofficial answer to this little gem of a question is: "Under Sleeping Beauty's castle." Nobody knows for sure since the immediate circumstances surrounding Walt Disney's death are vague—even in the most careful accounts (Mosley, 1983; Schickel, 1985). Officially, his ashes are said to be peacefully at rest in Forest Lawn. But the deep freeze myth is too good to let go of because it so neatly complements all those fairy tales Disney expropriated and popularized when alive. What could be more appropriate than thinking of Walt on ice, waiting for technology's kiss to restore him to life in a hidden vault under his own castle in the Magic Kingdom?

24. EMPLOYEE WORK ATTITUDES AND MANAGEMENT PRACTICE IN THE U.S. AND JAPAN: EVIDENCE FROM A LARGE COMPARATIVE SURVEY

James R. Lincoln

What do we really know about the work motivation of the Japanese and the role of Japanese management practice in shaping it? How deeply rooted in the culture of Japan and the psyches of the Japanese people is the legendary commitment and discipline of the Japanese labor force? How important are Japanese work patterns and the internal management of the Japanese firm for explaining the Japanese economic miracle, as compared with the macro forces of state guidance, *keiretsu* enterprise groupings, corporate strategy, and low-cost capital? If Japanese management practice does provide part of the explanation for the cooperation and productivity of the Japanese, does it only work with Japanese employees? That is to say, how transportable is Japanese management style: do overseas Japanese firms produce similar results with foreign workers? Do American and European firms that organize in "Japanese" fashion achieve the labor discipline, cooperation, and commitment that seem to characterize Japan?

Attempts to answer these and similar questions have filled the pages of the business press as well as scholarly journals in the nearly 8 years since the publication of *Theory Z* and *The Art of Japanese Management* marked the onset of the Japanese management boom.[1] The quality of these accounts has ranged widely. Too many are ill-informed and opportunistic efforts to capitalize on the explosive demand for information on Japan and Japanese business. Others are thoughtful, incisive discussions by expert journalists, scholars, and consultants able to bring to bear on the issue rich experience from studying, living, and working in Japan. Notably absent until quite recently is much prominent commentary by the Japanese themselves, who, to a surprising extent, have followed the lead and absorbed the claims of Western observers of the Japanese management scene.[2]

Even the recent expert testimony of writers like Abegglen, Dore, and Vogel on Japanese organization and its lessons for the West is based much more on long personal experience, intuitive understanding, and generally "soft" journalistic research.[3] What does quantitative social science have to say about the contrasts in work motivation and worker productivity between Japan and the U.S.? Though the United States arguably has the world's largest, best-funded, and technically most sophisticated behavioral science community, surprisingly little of this research expertise has been aimed at a problem of critical contemporary importance to Americans: the nature, scope, and origins of the Japanese labor productivity advantage in manufacturing.

This article reviews a large survey research investigation of 106 factories in the U.S. (central Indiana) and Japan (Kanagawa Prefecture) and 8,302 of their employees. Between 1981 and 1983, my colleagues and I interviewed factory executives about the management style and organization of the plant and distributed questionnaires to representative samples of employees. To the best of our knowledge, the resulting data set is the largest and

James R. Lincoln, "Employee Work Attitudes and Management Practice in the U.S. and Japan: Evidence from a Large Comparative Survey" from *California Management Review*, Fall 1989, vol. 32, No. 1, pp. 89–106.

most detailed body of survey information on American and Japanese factory workers and their employing organizations.

ARE WORK ATTITUDES DIFFERENT IN JAPAN AND THE U.S.?

The Japanese Are Less Satisfied ...

A twofold question motivated our research: how do the work attitudes of Japanese manufacturing employees differ between Japan and the U.S.; and do those differences depend on the management and organization of the factory? Let's take the question of work attitudes first. We sought to measure through questionnaire items two attitude dimensions: job satisfaction and commitment to the company. Many would expect Japanese workers to score higher than Americans on both. The long hours, low absenteeism and turnover, the productivity and esprit de corps, the careers spent within a single company, the reluctance even to take time off for vacation—these are all well-documented patterns of Japanese worker behavior. Surely they suggest that job satisfaction and commitment to a particular company are extraordinarily high in Japan.

As Table 24.1 shows, however, what we initially found was quite different. If our survey data are to be believed, it appears that commitment to the company is essentially the same in our American and Japanese employee samples. The specific questionnaire items in the six-item factor-weighted scale likewise either show no difference or the Americans appear to give the "more committed" response. Is the much-touted loyalty of the Japanese employee, then, a myth? Does the stability and discipline of Japanese labor have no basis in the attitudes and values of Japanese workers? These results seemed so at odds with expectations and the impressions of previous scholars that we were quite taken aback.

On the other hand, Table 24.1 *does* show large country differences in the job satisfaction items, but the direction is *contrary* to expectations. American employees seem much more satisfied with their jobs than do the Japanese. We were not, in fact, sur-

prised by this finding. Every prior survey contrasting Japanese and Western work attitudes has likewise found work satisfaction to be lowest among the Japanese.[4]

How are we to interpret these results? Any first-year MBA student knows that high job satisfaction does not spell high work motivation.[5] As Ronald Dore suggests, low job satisfaction in Japan may imply a restless striving for perfection, an ongoing quest for fulfillment of lofty work values and company goals.[6] By the same token, American observers have cautioned that the high percentages of the U.S. workforce routinely reporting satisfaction with their jobs may be more cause for concern than complacency.[7] It may signal low expectations and aspirations, a willingness to settle for meager job rewards, and a preoccupation with leisure-time pursuits.[8]

Another possibility, of course, is that the Japan-U.S. differences in work attitudes we found are due, not to real cultural contrasts in work motives and values, but to measurement biases.[9] Many would argue that a distinctly American impulse is to put the best face on things, to be upbeat and cheerful, to appear in control and successful even when uncertainty is high and the future looks bleak. The Japanese, it appears, bias their assessments in the opposite direction. From the Japanese mother who turns aside praise of her child's piano playing with: *"ie, mada heta desu!"* (no, it is still bad) to the Japanese politicians who, despite Japan's booming economy, persist in protesting the country's weak and dependent posture in world affairs—the Japanese seem to color their evaluations of nearly everything with a large dose of pessimism, humility, and understatement.

... But More Committed

In order to better understand the country differences in our sample's work attitudes, we estimated a statistical simultaneous equations model which assumed that satisfaction and commitment are each caused by the other (and by other variables as well). The results

TABLE 24.1
Descriptive Statistics for Measures of Organizational Commitment and Job Satisfaction

	U.S. Mean (SD)	Japan Mean (SD)
Organizational Commitment Scale[a] (alpha = .75, U.S.; .79, Japan)	2.13(.469)	2.04(.503)[b]
"I am willing to work harder than I have to in order to help this company succeed." (1 = strongly disagree, 5 = strongly agree)	3.91(.895)	3.44(.983)[b]
"I would take any job in order to continue working for this company." (same codes)	3.12(1.14)	3.07(1.13)
"My values and the values of this company are quite similar."	3.15(1.06)	2.68(.949)[b]
"I am proud to work for this company." (same codes)	3.70(.943)	3.51(1.02)[b]
"I would turn down another job for more pay in order to stay with this company." (same codes)	2.71(1.17)	2.68(1.08)
"I feel very little loyalty to this company." (1 = strongly agree, 5 = strongly disagree)	3.45(1.13)	3.40(1.03)
Job Satisfaction Scale (alpha = .78, U.S.; .65, Japan)	1.54(.449)	.962(.350)[b]
"All in all, how satisfied would you say you are with your job?" (0 = not at all, 4 = very)	2.95(1.12)	2.12(1.06)[b]
"If a good friend of yours told you that he or she was interested in working at a job like yours at this company, what would you say?" (0 = would advise against it, 1 = would have second thoughts, 2 = would recommend it)	1.52(.690)	.909(.673)[b]
"Knowing what you know now, if you had to decide all over again whether to take the job you now have, what would you decide?" (0 = would not take job again, 1 = would have some second thoughts, 2 = would take job again)	1.61(.630)	.837(.776)[b]
"How much does your job measure up to the kind of job you wanted when you first took it?" (0 = not what I wanted, 1 = somewhat, 2 = what I wanted)	1.20(.662)	.427(.591)[b]

[a]Factor-weighted composite of commitment (satisfactory) items. "Alpha" is Cronbach's measure of internal consistency reliability.

[b]Difference in means between countries significant at p<.001.

showed that commitment to the company is strongly determined by job satisfaction but the reverse relation is weak to nonexistent.[10] Moreover, with the causal reciprocity thus statistically controlled, we found satisfaction still lower in Japan but commitment to the company proved substantially higher. Our initial impression of no commitment difference, it appeared, was due to our earlier failure to adjust for the very large gap in reported job satisfaction. The resulting picture of Japanese work attitudes as combining low job satisfaction and high organizational commitment is not inconsistent with what some theories hold to be a state of strong work motivation. We thus took this evidence as support for our hypothesis that the discipline of the Japanese workforce does have some basis in the work attitudes of Japanese employees.

WORK ATTITUDES AND JAPANESE-STYLE ORGANIZATION

What then about the other questions we raised—particularly the extent to which management and organization have something to do with Japan-U.S. differences in work attitudes? Much has been written on the distinctiveness of Japanese management and its power to motivate work effort and loyalty among employees. While our survey could not address all the ways the Japanese firm is thought to be successful at mobilizing its human assets, we were nonetheless able to examine several such hypotheses.

Seniority Systems Breed Workforce Commitment

First, consider the age and seniority of the worker. The pervasive age and seniority-grading (nenko) of Japanese organizations is a much discussed and documented phenomenon.[11] Once maligned as arational and feudalistic, more and more economic and organizational theory has come to recognize the inner logic to seniority systems, particularly in work settings

where skills are hard to measure and are peculiar to the firm.[12] Moreover, part of the motivational logic to an employment system that couples permanent employment with seniority compensation is that it builds loyalty and identification with the company's goals. With time spent in the organization individuals accumulate investments and incur opportunity costs. To realize a fair return on these investments they must stick with the company and work to maximize its success. Moreover, the psychological phenomenon of cognitive dissonance—the need to seek congruence or equilibrium between one's acts and one's cognitions—leads people to justify to themselves their past organizational investments by embracing the company's values and goals as their own.

Our survey found, as previous studies had, that age and seniority are strong predictors of company commitment and job satisfaction. Moreover, we found pervasive evidence that these and other work attitudes were more age-dependent in Japan. Part of the reason, it appears, is that rewards and opportunities are more likely to be explicitly tied to age and seniority than in the American workplace. Another reason has less to do with age or seniority per se than with differences among generations. Given Japan's rapid postwar social change, older Japanese are apt to have the scarcity- and production-mentality typical of populations in the early stages of economic development. Younger Japanese are much more likely to share American-style values of leisure, consumption, and affluence. The latter fact evokes endless fretting by Japanese elders over the erosion of traditional values and its dire implications for Japan's future productivity and economic growth.

Strong Social Bonds Foster Positive Work Attitudes

One of the very distinctive features of Japanese work organization is the cohesiveness of work groups and the strong social bonds that develop between superiors and subordinates.[13] Our survey findings underscore these patterns. The Japanese employees in our sample reported an average of more than two close friends on the job, while the Americans' averaged fewer than one. Moreover, the much-noted Japanese practice of *tsukiai* (work group socializing over food and drink) appears in our finding that Japanese employees were far more likely than Americans to get together after hours with workmates and supervisors. Our study found that employees enmeshed in such networks of coworker relationships, whether Japanese or American, had more positive attitudes toward the company and the job. The clear implication is that a rise in the cohesion of the U.S. workplace to the level typical of Japanese firms would help to narrow the U.S. "commitment gap" with Japan.

There is still the question of whether work group cohesion in the Japanese company is an outcome of rational management efforts at job and organizational design. The alternative interpretation is that Japanese people are simply culturally inclined to cluster into tight-knit cliques.[14] The cultural explanation has many advocates, and certainly a strong case can be made that Japanese values motivate people to bind themselves to groups. On the other side is all the evidence that the Japanese workplace is organized in ways that seem consciously aimed at fostering enterprise community.

AUTHORITY AND STATUS HIERARCHIES

Are Japanese Hierarchies "Flat?"

A number of observers have pointed to the shape of the management pyramid in Japanese companies as an example of organizational architecture whose logic is that of fostering commitment to the firm. While American executives and consultants commonly allude (often as a rationale for middle-management reductions at home) to the lean and flat hierarchies of Japanese firms,[15] most scholars generally agree that finely graded hierarchies and narrow spans of control are typical of Japanese organization.[16]

Japanese companies are on the average smaller, more specialized to particular industries, and less likely to use the decentralized, multidivisional structures typical of large, diversified U.S. firms.[17] These traits imply smaller corporate staffs and economies in the deployment of middle-level functional managers. But within a particular plant or business unit, one tends to find levels proliferating, as well as status rankings (based largely on seniority) which bear little direct relation to decision making and responsibility.

Does the shape of Japanese managerial hierarchies play a role in promoting workforce discipline, integration, and commitment? A number of thoughtful observers believe that they do. A finely layered management pyramid implies opportunities for steady progression up long career paths, a critical factor in motivation when employees expect to spend their working lives within a single firm. Status differentiation also works to avert the polarization and alienation, common in U.S. and British manufacturing, when a rigid class division is drawn between homogeneous "management" and "labor" groups. Japanese hierarchies incorporate many small steps which break up this homogeneity and serve as career ladders. Yet the inequality in status and reward between peak management and production rank-and-file is typically much smaller than in comparably-sized U.S. firms.[18] To many observers, this kind of structure figures importantly in the company-wide community and commitment for which the Japanese company is renowned.

Our survey of 51 Japanese factories and 55 American plants showed the Japanese organizations, despite their smaller mean size (461 vs. 571 employees), averaging 5.5 management levels compared with 4.9 for the American plants. The samples did not differ in average first-line supervisor's span of control, but we did find some evidence in the Japanese plants of more organizational subunits for the same number of employees; a pattern indicative of smaller spans of control.

Do Flat Hierarchies Produce Positive Work Attitudes?

Japanese plants may have taller hierarchies, but *in both countries* plants with more levels proved to have less committed and satisfied employees.[19] This was the only instance where an organizational design feature typical of U.S. manufacturing appeared to have the motivational advantage. And even here there were some indications that the Japanese approach had merit. We found clear and consistent evidence across a large number of indicators that work attitudes, behaviors, and relations were far less determined by the employee's status position than in the U.S. As we argued above, this is part of the motivational logic of a finely graded hierarchy—to blur the boundaries and reduce the distance between echelons and hence the potential for conflict.

Do Narrow Spans of Control Mean Domineering Supervisors?

Another highly distinctive feature of Japanese authority hierarchies is the nature of supervision and the quality of the superior-subordinate relationship. Rather than bosses exercising direct authority and issuing commands to subordinate employees, Japanese supervisors seem to function as counselor and confidante to their work groups, building communication and cohesion with a minimum of direct, authoritarian control.[20] In sharp contrast to American workers who generally favor an arm's-length, strictly business, low-intensity relationship with their supervisors, workforce surveys in Japan regularly turn up evidence that Japanese employees prefer a paternalistic, diffuse, and personal supervisory style.[21]

Our study revealed a number of differences in Japanese and U.S. patterns of supervision.[22] The Japanese were much more likely to get together socially with supervisors outside of work. This, of course, is part of *tsukiai*, the Japanese practice of after hours socializing with workgroups. The Japanese were also much less likely than the American respondents to report that their supervisors: *"let them alone unless they asked for help."*[23] Moreover, such contact with supervisors raised the morale of the Japanese employees but lowered that of the Americans. Finally, we found clear evidence in the American sample that narrow supervisory spans of control reduced commitment and satisfaction. This was not the case in

Japan. It appears that narrow spans in the American workplace have a connotation, absent in Japan, of "close and domineering supervision."

These findings paint a consistent picture: frequent supervisor-subordinate interactions have a positive quality in Japanese work settings which is missing in the U.S. While American manufacturing employees keep their distance from supervisors, Japanese employees seek such contact and through it develop stronger bonds to the work group and the organization as a whole.

DECISION-MAKING STRUCTURES

Japanese Organizations Are Centralized But Participatory ...

Japanese decision-making styles are commonly characterized as participatory, consensus-seeking, and "bottom-up."[24] At the management level, they involve less formal delegation of authority to individual managers and more informal networking *(nemawashi)* to draw people into the decision process. The ironic result is that the formal structure of Japanese decision making appears quite centralized. High-level executives bear at least symbolic responsibility for many decisions which, in U.S. firms, are typically delegated.[25]

The *ringi* system exemplifies this pattern. A middle-level manager drafts a document proposing a course of action *(ringi-sho)*. It then circulates up through the hierarchy, acquiring the "chops" (personal stamps) of other managers symbolizing their participation in the decision and willingness to commit to it.

At the shop- or office-floor level, participation operates through small group activities such as quality circles, production teams, and high-responsibility systems that hold workers accountable for quality, minor maintenance, and clean-up in the conduct of their tasks.[26]

We measured decision making in our Japanese and U.S. plants in three ways. First, we used a modification of the standard Aston scale of centralization.[27] For each of 37 standard decision-items, the chief executive of the plant was asked to report the hierarchical level where: the formal authority for the decision was located; and where, in practice, the decision was usually made. Averaged over the 37 decisions, we found strong evidence that, compared with U.S. plants, authority was more centralized in the Japanese plants but there was also more *de facto* participation by lower ranks.

Secondly, in the Japanese plants, we measured the prevalence of *ringi* by asking whether, for each of 37 decisions, the *ringi* system was used. Averaged across the 51 Japanese plants, our informants reported that the *ringi* method was applied to approximately one-third of this set of decisions.

Finally, we measured quality circle participation from our questionnaire survey of employees. We found that 81% of the Japanese plants had quality circle programs in which 94% percent of the employees of those plants participated; 62% of the U.S. plants had circles and 44% of their employees were members.

Our survey results are thus consistent with the impressions of more casual observers: Japanese organizations centralize authority but decentralize participation in decision. The *ringi* system is used to a substantial degree in decision making in Japanese factories. And quality circle participation is close to universal in Japanese plants, though it is reasonably widespread in American plants as well.[28]

… A Pattern Which Produces Positive Work Attitudes in Both Countries

The question then becomes: do Japanese decision-making practices help shape the work attitudes of Japanese employees? As with work group cohesion, the motivational payoff to participation has been a central theme in management theory, at least since the Hawthorne studies. We found *in both countries* that organizations which in Japanese fashion coupled formal centralization with de facto participation had more committed and satisfied employees.

Why? This outcome fits the general proposition that Japanese-style management works in the U.S. as well as in Japan. But it is not obvious why this particular configuration should have greater motivational value than one in which formal and *de facto* authority are aligned and both decentralized. Our reasoning is that formal decentralization (as the Aston scale measures it) taps delegation of specialized decision-making roles to lower management positions. First- and second-line supervisors in American manufacturing commonly enjoy a good deal of power over narrow jurisdictional areas. Yet that kind of delegation opens up few opportunities for participation either by the rank-and-file *or* by supervisors in other areas.

When formal authority stays high in the organization but widespread participation occurs, the power of lower management is reduced and decision making becomes the diffuse, participatory kind typical of Japanese organization, not the individualistic, compartmentalized delegation found in American firms. Clark has argued that Japanese middle managers are delegated so little formal authority that they have no choice but to negotiate with their employees in order to get things done.[29] In his view, the networking and consensus-seeking found in Japanese organizations are a direct response to their centralized authority structures.

Ringi and Quality Circles Also Produce Positive Work Attitudes

What about the specific participatory practices of *ringi* and quality circles? Do they also foster job satisfaction and commitment to a company? Our data suggest that they do. In the sample of Japanese plants, we found a statistically significant positive association between a plant's use of the *ringi* system and the employee's commitment to the firm. This was a noteworthy finding, for the majority of our employee sample were rank-and-file people who would not ordinarily be involved in the *ringi* process. The use of *ringi* is probably symptomatic of a generally participatory decision-making climate which has motivational value for workers and managers alike.

There are good reasons to suppose that quality circle programs are quite different in the U.S. and Japan. Owing in large part to the centralized oversight of the Japan Union of Scientists and Engineers, quality circle programs in Japanese industry generally comprise a much more uniform set of practices than in the United States. They require a high level of technical training on the part of production workers and a substantial commitment of resources on the part of the firm. American quality circle programs, with much less centralized guidance form professional and managerial bodies, are generally a hodgepodge. Few such programs exhibit the rigor and structure of Japanese practice.

Yet quality circle participation proved to be positively associated with job satisfaction and organizational commitment in both the U.S. and Japan. Moreover, the effect was stronger in the U.S. sample. The reason may in part lie in the later inception of American quality circles which give them a novelty value that has worn off the more established Japanese programs. Recent observers of Japanese quality circle programs have commented on growing problems of maintaining worker interest and motivation.[30]

In summary, our evidence, with rather remarkable consistency, suggests that Japanese-style decision-making arrangements (quality circles, *ringi*, centralized authority combined with dispersed participation) have positive effects on the work attitudes of Japanese and American employees alike. The fact that such arrangements are much more prevalent in Japanese industry suggest a partial explanation for the Japanese edge in labor discipline and commitment.

COMPANY-SPONSORED EMPLOYEE SERVICES

Yet another distinctive feature of the Japanese employment system is the large bundle of services, programs, and social activities that Japanese firms sponsor and provide for their employees. Such services figure significantly in the traditional portrait of Japanese "paternalism" in industry.[31] The array of programs, activities, classes, ceremonies, peptalks, calisthenics, songs, and other practices that Japanese firms employ in the quest of building community and commitment among the workforce is downright dizzying.[32]

How effective are such programs as motivational devices? Would more ceremonies, company picnics, sports teams, newsletters, and the like create a stronger bond between the U.S. manufacturing worker and the firm? Or, as many Western observers seem to think, are individualistic British and American workers likely to be contemptuous of overt management gestures at creating a happy corporate family?[33] Once again, a case can be made that employee services in Japan are a reflection, not a cause, of Japanese work values and attitudes. Cultural and historical forces have bred within companies an inclusive enterprise community one sign of which is a profusion of company-planned activities and services.

Still, there are some indications in the historical record that Japanese employers set upon welfarism (along with permanent employment and other labor practices) as a rational instrument for curbing labor militancy and creating, in a time of labor shortage, a more docile and dependent workforce.[34] Its timing coincided with the era of "welfare capitalism" in the United States (the 1920s), which large firms ushered in for similar purposes of managing an unruly labor force and appeasing the growing ranks of muckrakers and progressivist reformers. Why welfarism seemed to "stick" in Japan but faded in the U.S., at least until the postwar period, may be due to several forces: the milder impact on Japan of the Great Depression (which in the U.S. led many firms to jettison expensive welfare programs); the heightened stress on industrial discipline produced by militarist and imperialist policies; and, for cultural reasons, the greater receptivity of Japanese workers to corporate paternalism and the principle of an enterprise family.[35]

Employee Services Are More Abundant in Japan ...

Our strategy for measuring the level of welfare, social, and ceremonial activity was a relatively simple one. We inquired of our informants in each plant whether a list of nine company-sponsored activities/services were present. The list included: outside training, in-house training, an employee newsletter, company ceremonies, company-sponsored sports and recreation programs, new employee orientation programs, an employee handbook, regular plant-wide information-sharing/"pep-talk" sessions, and a morning calisthenics program.

Our hypothesis was that such programs are more prevalent in Japanese firms. That proved to be the case for most of them, specifically: in-house training (by a small margin), formal ceremonies (present in all Japanese plants), sports and recreational activities, formal orientation programs, peptalks, and morning exercise sessions (nonexistent in the U.S. plants we studied). On the other hand, the American plants were more likely to encourage and support enrollment in high school and college coursework (by a large margin) and (by a small one) to provide employees with a company handbook. We found no difference between Japanese and U.S. plants in the likelihood of publishing a company newspaper. The indices proposed by summing these items had acceptable internal consistency reliability levels of .60 in the Japanese sample and .62 in the U.S. sample, indicating that these services tended to cluster in the same firms.

... But Raise Commitment and Satisfaction in Both Countries

When we estimated the effect of the services index on employee commitment to the company and satisfaction with the job, we found almost identical positive associations in the two countries. Individualistic or not, the Americans in our sample appeared to react every bit as favorably as the Japanese to company-sponsored employee-oriented services. Once again the lesson seems clear: were such services in American industry to rise to the level typical of Japanese manu-facturers, we should witness a corresponding shrinkage in the Japan-U.S. commitment gap.

ENTERPRISE UNIONS

Finally we consider the structure of unions and their implication for employee work attitudes. A legacy of the postwar Occupation reforms, Japanese unions are organized on a per-enterprise basis, concentrated in the largest firms, and combined into weak federations at higher levels.[36] They organize all regular (blue- and white-collar) employees, up to second-line supervision. Much debate has centered on whether Japanese enterprise unions are truly independent labor organizations in the Western sense. Some writers see them as highly dependent upon and easily coopted by the company, avoiding confrontations to advance their members' interests and working to build commitment to the firm. Hanami expresses this view well:

There exists a climate of collusion ... between the employers and the union representing the majority of employees ... Basically the relationship is one of patronage and dependence, though the unions frequently put on an outward show of radical militancy in their utterances and behavior. [Moreover] the president of an enterprise union is in effect the company's senior executive in charge of labor relations.[37]

Yet other observers argue that, despite the constraints posed by dependence on a single firm, Japanese unions bargain hard on wage and benefit issues and have effectively coordinated their militancy in the annual Spring offensives *(shunto)* which present groups of employers with a set of unified wage demands.[38] A study by Koshiro concludes that union militancy has been an important factor behind rising aggregate wage levels in the postwar Japanese economy.[39]

U.S. Unions Foster Negative Work Attitudes, Japanese Unions Do Not

What, however, about the impact of unionism on employee work attitudes? Much survey research shows that U.S. union members report *lower* job satisfaction than do nonunion employees.[40] This pattern seems consistent with the goals of American union strategy: to aggregate grievances, foster an adversarial industrial relations climate, and drive a wedge between the worker and the firm.

Yet unionized workers are less likely to quit their jobs than nonunion employees.[41] One interpretation is that "true" dissatisfaction is probably no higher among union members but that the union politicizes the employment relation and encourages workers to inflate and publicize their grievances. In the nonunion workplace, by contrast, workers have no such vehicle for airing dissatisfactions and therefore act on them by simply terminating their relationship with the firm. This view, grounded in Albert Hirschman's "exit-voice-loyalty" model,[42] is also supported by evidence that grievance rates are higher in union shops even when objective working conditions are no worse.[43]

We would not anticipate finding similar union effects on the work attitudes of Japanese unionists. Indeed, a reasonable argument can be made for the opposite prediction: that enterprise unions build support for and loyalty to the company—that they are, in effect, one more Japanese management device for building motivation and commitment.

Our data do not show that. We find no statistically significant effect of union membership on job satisfaction, although we do find a slight tendency for company commitment to be lower in union plants. Thus, it does not appear that Japanese unions are in some sense instruments of a proactive policy of building discipline and dedication in the workforce. On the other hand, what we find in the U.S. still poses a decisive contrast with the Japan case. Consistent with other research, our survey produced strong and clear evidence that unions in U.S. factories give rise to sharply more negative employee work attitudes. Holding constant a large number of variables pertaining to the pay, status, job, skills, and gender of the worker, plus the size, age, and technology of the plant, company commitment and job satisfaction in our Indiana sample were markedly lower among the unionized plants.

The implications appear to be as follows. Japanese unions are not the agents of management that some critics hold them to be. But neither do they present the challenge to harmonious labor-management relations or high workforce morale that U.S. unions historically have posed. Since enterprise-specific unions are generally absent from the U.S. economy, we have no evidence on how they might perform in an American setting.

Some circumstantial evidence from the New United Motors Manufacturing, Inc. (NUMMI) plant in Fremont, California (the Toyota-GM joint venture), suggests, however, that U.S. workers may react very well to Japanese-style collective bargaining.[44] The union at NUMMI is a local of the United Auto Workers, but it made a number of concessions to the company in the area of work rules and job classifications. In turn, the company provides the union with space in the plant, shares information extensively, and enlists the cooperation of the union in enforcing policy with respect to absenteeism, quality, safety, and other issues. Though a small dissident movement has been formed, the level of labor-management cooperation and the productivity and discipline of the workforce at NUMMI has few parallels in the American auto industry. The special relationship between the company and the UAW local, reminiscent of the interdependence between enterprise unions and firms in Japan, is clearly part of the reason.

DISCUSSION

What conclusions can be drawn from our survey evidence on Japanese and U.S. work attitudes and the role of plant organization and management practice in shaping them? First, though a preliminary reading of the data sends mixed signals, the Japanese employee's combination of high commitment coupled with low satisfaction is in line with the hypothesis of a highly motivated Japanese workforce. Second, we found quite con-

TABLE 24.2
Do "Japanese"-Style Management Practices Produce Company Commitment and Job Satisfaction in Japan and in the United States?

"Japanese" Management/Employment Practice	Impact on Work Attitudes
long-term employment and age/seniority grading	positive in both countries[a]
cohesive work groups	positive in both countries
dense supervision; close supervisor–subordinate contact	positive in Japan; negative in U.S.
"tall," finely layered hierarchies	negative in both countries; but contributes to management-labor consensus in Japan
formal centralization/de facto decentralization of decision-making	positive in both countries
ringi system	positive in Japan[b]
quality circle participation	positive in both countries
welfare services	positive in both countries
unions (enterprise-specific in Japan; industry/occupation-specific in the U.S.)	weak negative to null in Japan; strongly negative in U.S.

[a]In the sense that psychological attachment to the firm is found in both countries to rise with age and seniority.

[b]No comparable measure from the U.S. survey.

sistent evidence that "Japanese-style" management and employment methods, whether practiced by Japanese or U.S. plants, produce very similar gains in employee work attitudes (see the summary of findings in Table 24.2). These include cohesive work groups, quality circles, participatory (but not delegated) decision making, and company-sponsored services. The fact that such practices are more widely deployed in Japanese than in U.S. industry does suggest they may provide part (though we would hardly argue all) of the reason for the Japan-U.S. "commitment gap" in manufacturing.

Other management and employment practices we examined are not directly comparable across countries and our results cannot therefore be interpreted in this way. They nonetheless testify that tangible differences in Japanese and U.S. management translate into competitive advantages for Japanese firms in the area of employee motivation and cooperative industrial relations. In both coun-

tries, rising age and seniority engender increasingly positive work attitudes. As career employment and seniority promotion and compensation are more central to Japanese than U.S. employment practice, Japanese companies are better able to capitalize on these motivational returns. The Japanese system of enterprise unions offers collective bargaining in an atmosphere of mutual dependence and cooperation, and, in sharp contrast to U.S. unions, does little to foster tension between the worker and the firm.

Our findings seem to contradict the argument that Japanese management styles are only effective with employees who hold Japanese-type work values. The credibility of this view, which has much face validity, is also undercut by the apparent success of Japanese manufacturing firms in managing their U.S. operations and their American employees. Japanese management is no panacea, and mindless attempts to copy from the Japanese are doubtless doomed to failure. Still, our study strongly suggests that Japanese management practices are in part responsible for the work motivation of Japanese employees and that similar practices in the American workplace yield similar returns. Careful attempts on the part of U.S. managers to move in the direction of Japanese organizational design and human resource management may well yield some long-run competitive payoffs for American manufacturing.

REFERENCES

1. William G. Ouchi, *Theory Z: How American Business Can Meet the Japanese Challenge* (Reading, MA: Addison-Wesley, 1981); Richard Tanner Pascale and Anthony G. Athos, *The Art of Japanese Management: Applications for American Managers* (New York, NY: Simon and Schuster, 1981).

2. But see, Masahiko Aoki, "Risk Sharing in the Corporate Group," in Masahiko Aoki, ed., *The Economic Analysis of the Japanese Firm* (Amsterdam: North-Holland, 1984), pp. 259–264; Taishiro Shirai, ed., *Contemporary Industrial Relations in Japan* (Madison, WI: University of Wisconsin Press, 1983).

3. James C. Abegglen and George Stalk, Jr., *Kaisha: The Japanese Corporation* (New York, NY: Basic Books, 1985); Ronald Dore, *Flexible Rigidities* (Stanford, CA: Stanford University Press, 1987); Ronald Dore, *Taking Japan Seriously* (Stanford, CA: Stanford University Press, 1987); Ezra F. Vogel, *Comeback* (New York, NY: Simon and Schuster, 1985).

4. See the review in James R. Lincoln and Kerry McBride, "Japanese Industrial Organization in Comparative Perspective," *Annual Review of Sociology*, 13(1987): 289–312.

5. See, for example, Charles Perrow, *Complex Organizations: A Critical Essay*, 3rd edition (Glenview, IL: Scott, Foresman, 1986).

6. Ronald Dore, *British Factory, Japanese Factory: The Origins of Diversity in Industrial Relations* (Berkeley, CA: University of California Press, 1973).

7. Robert Blauner, "Work Satisfaction and Industrial Trends in Modern Society," in Walter Galenson and Seymour Martin Lipset, eds., *Labor and Trade Unionism* (New York, NY: John Wiley, 1960), pp. 339–360; HEW Report, *Work in America* (Cambridge, MA: MIT Press, 1973).

8. John H. Goldthorpe, David Lockwood, F. Bechhofer, and J. Platt, *The Affluent Worker: Industrial Attitudes and Behavior* (London: Cambridge University Press, 1968).

9. Dore, 1973, op. cit.

10. James R. Lincoln and Arne L. Kalleberg, "Work Organization and Workforce Commitment: A Study of Plants and Employees in the U.S. and Japan," *American Sociological Review*, 50 (1985): 738–760; James R. Lincoln and Arne L. Kalleberg, *Culture, Control, and Commitment: A Study of Work Organization and Work Attitudes in the U.S. and Japan* (Cambridge: Cambridge University Press, 1989).

11. Kazuo Koike, "Internal Labor Markets: Workers in Large Firms," in Taishiro Shirai, ed., op. cit., pp. 29–62.

12. Edward Lazear, "Why Is There Mandatory Retirement?" *Journal of Political Economy*, 87(1979): 1261–1284.

13. Robert E. Cole, "Permanent Employment in Japan: Facts and Fantasies," *Industrial and Labor Relations Review*, 26 (1972): 612–630; Thomas P. Rohlen, *For Harmony and Strength* (Berkeley, CA: University of California Press, 1974).

14. See, for example, Chie Nakane, *Japanese Society* (Berkeley, CA: University of California Press, 1970).

15. Thomas J. Peters and Robert H. Waterman, Jr., *In Search of Excellence: Lessons from America's Best-Run Companies* (New York, NY: Harper and Row, 1982).

16. Michael Y. Yoshino, *Japan's Managerial System: Tradition and Innovation* (Cambridge, MA: MIT Press, 1968); Dore, 1973, op. cit.; Richard Tanner Pascale, "Zen and the Art of Management," *Harvard Business Review*, 56 (1978): 153–162.

17. Rodney C. Clark, *The Japanese Company* (New Haven, CT: Yale, 1979).

18. Abegglen and Stalk, op. cit.

19. Lincoln and Kalleberg, 1985, op. cit.

20. Dore, 1973, op. cit.; Cole, 1972, op. cit.

ORGANIZATIONAL CULTURE

25. CORPORATIONS, CULTURE, AND COMMITMENT: MOTIVATION AND SOCIAL CONTROL IN ORGANIZATIONS

Charles O'Reilly

Corporate culture is receiving much attention in the business press. A recent article in *Fortune* describes how the CEO at Black & Decker "transformed an entire corporate *culture*, replacing a complacent manufacturing mentality with an almost manic, market-driven way of doing things."[1] Similarly, the success of Food Lion (a $3 billion food-market chain that has grown at an annual rate of 37% over the past 20 years with annual returns on equity of 24%) is attributed to a culture which emphasizes "hard work, simplicity, and frugality."[2] Other well-known firms such as 3M, Johnson & Johnson, Apple, and Kimberly-Clark have been routinely praised for their innovative cultures.[3] Even the success of Japanese firms in the U.S. has been partly attributed to their ability to change the traditional culture developed under American managers. Peters and Waterman report how a U.S. television manufacturing plant, under Japanese management, reduced its defect rate from 140 to 6, its complaint rate from 70% to 7%, and the turnover rate among employees from 30% to 1%, all due to a changed management philosophy and culture.[4]

Even more dramatic is the turnaround at the New United Motors Manufacturing Incorporated (NUMMI) plant in Fremont, California. When General Motors closed this facility in 1982, it was one of the worst plants in the GM assembly division with an 18 percent daily absenteeism rate and a long history of conflict in its labor relations. The plant reopened as a joint venture between Toyota and GM in 1983. Over 85 percent of the original labor force was rehired, and workers are still represented by the UAW. Although the technology used is vintage 1970s and the plant is not as automated as many others within GM and Toyota, productivity is almost double what GM gets in other facilities. In 1987, it took an estimated 20.8 hours to produce a car at NUMMI versus 40.7 in other GM plants and 18.0 at Toyota. Quality of the NUMMI automobiles is the highest in the GM system, based on both internal audits and owner surveys, and absenteeism

Charles O'Reilly, "Corporations, Culture and Commitment: Motivation and Social Control in Organizations" from *California Management Review*, Summer 1989, Vol. 31, No. 4, pp. 9–25.

is at 2 percent compared to 8 percent at other GM facilities. What accounts for this remarkable success? According to one account, "At the system's core is a *culture* in which the assembly line workers maintain their machines, ensure the quality of their work, and improve the production process."[5]

But a culture is not always a positive force. It has also been implicated when firms run into difficulties. The CEO of financially troubled Computerland, William Tauscher, has attempted to restructure the firm, noting that "a low-cost culture is a must."[6] Henry Wendt, CEO of SmithKline Beckman, has attributed his firm's current difficulties to complacency. "We've been victims of our own success. . . . I want to create a new culture."[7] Corporate culture has also been implicated in problems faced by Sears, Caterpillar, Bank of America, Polaroid, General Motors, and others. Even difficulties in mergers and acquisitions are sometimes attributed to cultural conflicts which make integration of separate units difficult. Failure to merge two cultures can lead to debilitating conflict, a loss of talent, and an inability to reap the benefits of synergy.

But what is really meant when one refers to a firm's "culture"? Do all organizations have them? Are they always important? Even if we can identify cultures, do we know enough about how they work to manage them? Four major questions need to be answered:

• What is culture?
• From a manager's perspective, when is culture important?
• What is the process through which cultures are developed and maintained?
• How can cultures be managed?

WHAT IS CULTURE?

If culture is to be analyzed and managed, it is important that we be clear about what is meant by the term. Failure to clearly specify what "culture" is can result in confusion, misunderstanding, and conflict about its basic function and importance.

Culture as Control

Clearly, little would get done by or in organizations if some control systems were not in place to direct and coordinate activities. In fact, organizations are often seen to be efficient and effective solely because control systems operate.[8]

But what is a "control system"? A generic definition might be that a control system is "the knowledge that someone who knows and cares is paying close attention to what we do and can tell us when deviations are occurring." Although broad, this definition encompasses traditional formal control systems ranging from planning and budgeting systems to performance appraisals. According to this definition, control systems work when those who are monitored are aware that someone who matters, such as a boss or staff department, is paying attention and is likely to care when things aren't going according to plan.

Several years ago a large toy manufacturer installed, at considerable expense, a management-by-objectives (MBO) performance appraisal system. After a year or so, top management became aware that the system was working well in one part of the organization but not another. They conducted an investigation and discovered the reason for the failure. In the part of the organization where MBO was working well, senior management was enthusiastic and committed. They saw real benefits and conveyed their belief up and down the chain of command. In the part of the organization where the system had failed, senior management saw MBO as another bureaucratic exercise to be endured. Subordinate managers quickly learned to complete the paperwork but ignore the purpose. The lesson here was that a control system, no matter how carefully designed, works only when those being monitored believe that people who matter care about the results and are paying close attention. When Jan Carlzon became head of SAS Airline, he was concerned about the poor on-time record. To correct this, he personally requested a daily accounting of the on-time status of all flights. In the space of two years, SAS on-time record went from 83% to 97%.[9]

In designing formal control systems, we typically attempt to measure either outcomes or behaviors. For example, in hospitals it makes no sense to evaluate the nursing staff on whether patients get well. Instead, control systems rely on assessing behaviors. Are specified medical procedures followed? Are checks made at appropriate times? In other settings, behavior may not be observable. Whenever possible, we then attempt to measure outcomes. Sales people, for instance, are usually measured on their productivity, since the nature of their job often precludes any effective monitoring of their behavior. In other situations, control systems can be designed that monitor both behaviors and outcomes. For example, for some retail sales jobs both behaviors (how the customer is addressed, how quickly the order is taken, whether the sales floor is kept stocked) and outcomes (sales volume) can be measured.

However, it is often the case that neither behavior nor outcomes can be adequately monitored.[10] These are the activities that are non-routine and unpredictable, situations that require initiative, flexibility, and innovation. These can be dealt with only by developing social control systems in which common agreements exist among people about what constitutes appropriate attitudes and behavior.

Culture may be thought of as a potential social control system. Unlike formal control systems that typically assess outcomes or behaviors only intermittently, social control systems can be much more finely tuned. When we care about those with whom we work and have a common set of expectations, we are "under control" whenever we are in their presence. If we want to be accepted, we try to live up to their expectations. In this sense, social control systems can operate more extensively than most formal systems. Interestingly, our response to being monitored by formal and social control systems may also differ. With formal systems people often have a sense of external constraint which is binding and unsatisfying. With social controls, we often feel as though we have great autonomy, even though paradoxically we are conforming much more.

Thus, from a management perspective, culture in the form of shared expectations may be thought of as a social control system. Howard Schwartz and Stan Davis offer a practical definition of culture as "a pattern of beliefs and expectations shared by the organization's members. These beliefs and expectations produce norms that powerfully shape the behavior of individuals and groups."[11]

Culture as Normative Order

What Schwartz and Davis are referring to as culture are the central norms that may characterize an organization. Norms are expectations about what are appropriate or inappropriate attitudes and behaviors. They are socially created standards that help us interpret and evaluate events. Although their content may vary, they exist in all societies and, while often unnoticed, they are pervasive. For instance, in our society we have rather explicit norms about eye-contact. We may get uncomfortable when these are violated. Consider what happens when someone doesn't look at you while speaking or who continues to look without pause. In organizations we often find peripheral or unimportant norms around issues such as dress or forms of address. In the old railroads, for example, hats were a must for all managers, while everyone addressed each other with a formal "mister."

More important norms often exist around issues such as quality, performance, flexibility, or how to deal with conflict. In many organizations, it is impolite to disagree publicly with others. Instead, much behind-the-scenes interaction takes place to anticipate or resolve disputes. In other organizations, there may be norms that legitimate and encourage the public airing of disputes. Intel Corporation has an explicit policy of "constructive confrontation" that encourages employees to deal with disagreements in an immediate and direct manner.

In this view, the central values and styles that characterize a firm, perhaps not even written down, can form the basis for the development of norms that attach approval or disapproval to holding certain attitudes or beliefs and to acting in certain ways. For instance, the fundamental value of aggressiveness or competition may, if widely held and supported, be expressed as a norm that encourages organizational participants to stress winning competition. Pepsico encourages competition and punishes failure to compete.[12] Service is a pivotal norm at IBM; innovation is recognized as central at 3M. It is through norms—the expectations shared by group members and the approval or disapproval attached to these expectations—that culture is developed and maintained.

However, there is an important difference between the guiding beliefs or vision held by top management and the daily beliefs or norms held by those at lower levels in the unit or organization. The former reflect top managements' beliefs about how things ought to be. The latter define how things actually are. Simply because top management is in agreement about how they would like the organization to function is no guarantee that these beliefs will be held by others. One CEO spoke at some length about the glowing corporate philosophy that he believed in and felt characterized his firm's culture. After spending some time talking to mid-level managers in the organization, a very different picture emerged. A central norm shared by many of these managers was "Good people don't stay here." It is a common occurrence to find a noble sounding statement of corporate values framed on the wall and a very different and cynical interpretation of this creed held by people who have been around long enough to realize what is really important.

Moreover, norms can vary on two dimensions: the intensity or amount of approval/disapproval attached to an expectation; and the crystallization or degree of consensus or consistency with which a norm is shared. For instance, when analyzing an organization's culture it may be that for certain values there can be wide consensus but no intensity. Everyone understands what top management values, but there is no strong approval or disapproval attached to these beliefs or behaviors. Or, a given norm, such as innovation, can be positively valued in one group (e.g., marketing or R&D) and negatively valued in another (manufacturing or personnel). There is intensity but no crystallization.

It is only when there exist both intensity and consensus that strong cultures exist. This is why it is difficult to develop or change culture. Organizational members must come to know and share a common set of expectations. These must, in turn, be consistently valued and reinforced across divisions and management levels.[13] Only when this is done will there be both intensity and consensus. Similarly, a failure to share the central norms or to consistently reinforce them may lead to vacuous norms, conflicting interpretations, or to microcultures that exist only within subunits.

To have a strong culture, an organization does not have to have very many strongly held values. Only a few core values characterize strong culture firms such as Mars, Marriott, Hewlett-Packard, and Walmart. What is critical is that these beliefs be widely shared and strongly held; that is, people throughout the organization must be willing to tell one another when a core belief is not being lived up to.

The Role of Culture in Promoting Innovation

How is it that firms such as Intel, Hewlett-Packard, Cray Research, 3M, and Johnson & Johnson successfully develop both new products and new ways of doing things? How can culture help or hinder this process? The answer lies in those norms that, if they were widely shared and strongly held by members of the organization, would actively promote the generation of new ideas and would help in the implementation of new approaches.

What are these norms? This question was put to over 500 managers in firms as diverse as pharmaceuticals, consumer products, computers and semiconductors, and manufacturing. Table 25.1 contains a list of the norms that were most frequently cited. Several things are notable about this list. First, regardless of the industry or technology, managers identified virtually the same sets of norms as important. While the progress of innovation varies widely across efforts to discover new drugs, improve oil exploration, build new electronic devices, or develop a new toilet bowl

TABLE 25.1
Norms That Promote Innovation

A. Norms to Promote Creativity	B. Norms to Promote Implementation
1) Risk Taking • freedom to try things and fail • acceptance of mistakes • allow discussion of "dumb" ideas • no punishments for failure • challenge the status quo • forget the past • willingness *not* to focus on the short term • expectation that innovation is part of your job • positive attitudes about change • drive to improve	1) Common Goals • sense of pride in the organization • teamwork • willingness to share the credit • flexibility in jobs, budgets, functional areas • sense of ownership • eliminate mixed messages • manage interdependencies • shared visions and a common direction • build consensus • mutual respect and trust • concern for the whole organization

2) Rewards for Change
• ideas are valued
• respect for beginning ideas
• build into the structure:
  • budgets • opportunities
  • resources • tools
  • time • promotions
• top management attention and support
• celebration of accomplishments
• suggestions are implemented
• encouragement
	2) Autonomy
	• decision-making responsibility at lower levels
	• decentralized procedures
	• freedom to act
	• expectation of action
	• belief that *you* can have an impact
	• delegation
	• quick, flexible decision making
	• minimize the bureaucracy

3) Openness • open communication and share information • listen better • open access • bright people, strong egos • scanning, broad thinking • force exposure outside the company • move people around • encourage lateral thinking • adopt the customer's perspective • accept criticism • don't be too sensitive • continuous training • intellectual honesty • expect and accept conflict • willing to consult others	3) Belief in Action • don't be obsessed with precision • emphasis on results • meet your commitments • anxiety about timeliness • value getting things done • hard work is expected and appreciated • empower people • emphasis on quality • eagerness to get things done • cut through the bureaucracy

cleaner, the norms that facilitate these efforts are remarkably consistent. Second, these norms all function to facilitate the process of introducing new ways of doing things and to help people implement them. For example, when people share the expectation that it is not only permissible but also desirable to challenge the status quo, the likelihood of innovation is increased.

At Cray Research, a prime example of a firm whose success depends on its ability to innovate, creativity and diversity are seen as virtues. Similarly, at Intel Corporation, a company whose strategy has long been to be a first-mover and innovator, all employees are told to expect conflict and to deal with it directly. To resolve conflicts, employees are trained in a process called "constructive confrontation," which helps them deal with the conflict in productive rather than destructive ways. At Johnson & Johnson a similar belief is referred to as "creative conflict."

To appreciate how critical the norms shown in Table 25.1 can be to innovation, envision an organization that is characterized by norms the opposite of those listed. Imagine an organization where failure is punished severely, where no recognition or rewards are provided for those doing things differently, where the past is venerated and only ideas generated internally are considered worthwhile, where "dumb" ideas are ridiculed and people are never encouraged to take risks, and where there is no drive to change or improve things. In this environment, one would be amazed to see any change. Contrast this with an organization such as 3M in which a basic financial goal is to have 25 percent of annual sales come from products developed over the last five years. Allen Jacobsen, 3M's CEO, says, "People ask me how do you get people to be innovative. It's simple. You give them responsibility for their own destinies and encourage them to take risks."[14] The secret to 3M's success isn't in Mr. Jacobsen's words but in the norms that form 3M's culture. These norms are widely shared and strongly held because management up and down the line provides the resources and encouragement to sustain them. It is the expectations held by people throughout the company, not just in R&D, that makes 3M and similar firms so innovative.

There is nothing magical or elusive about corporate culture. One has only to be clear about the specific attitudes and behaviors that are desired, and then to identify the norms or expectations that promote or impede them.

WHY CULTURE IS IMPORTANT

There are two reasons why a strong culture is valuable:

• the fit of culture and strategy, and
• the increased commitment by employees to the firm.

Both these factors provide a competitive edge, giving a strong culture firm an advantage over its competitors.[15]

Strategy and Corporate Culture

Every firm has, implicitly or explicitly, a competitive strategy which dictates how it attempts to position itself with respect to its competitors. Once established, a firm's strategy dictates a set of critical tasks or objectives that must be accomplished through a congruence among the elements of people, structure, and culture. For example, a decision to compete on innovation rather than price requires an appropriate formal structure and control system which then indicates the types of people required to accomplish the objectives and to fit the structure. The choice of a strategy also has significant implications for the informal organization or culture; that is, the norms of the organization must help execute the strategy.

An illustration of the importance of fit between strategy, people, structure, and culture can be seen in the history of the three major Silicon Valley firms that manufacture integrated circuits. Although operating in the same product market, Intel, National Semiconductor, and Advanced Micro Devices have each pursued a different strategy that is reflected in their people, structures, and cultures. National

Semiconductor has chosen to compete largely as a low-cost manufacturer. To do this, it emphasizes strict cost control, a functional organizational structure, and a culture emphasizing numbers, a lack of frills, and a certain ruthlessness that has earned its people the sobriquet of "animals of the valley." Intel, however, has chosen to compete on product innovation. It has a looser formal organization with a culture valuing collegial interaction and the development of new technologies and products. Advanced Micro Devices has chosen a marketing strategy offering very high quality products, often as second source. Its strength has been in its marketing, and its culture reflects the value placed on selling, service, and quality.

For a strategy to be successfully implemented, it requires an appropriate culture. When firms change strategies, and often structures, they sometimes fail because the underlying shared values do not support the new approach. For example, a large, integrated electronics firm with a very strong culture based on technical excellence decided to enter the word processing market. Although they already made equipment that could easily be used as a basis for a word processor, the culture that made them successful in the design and manufacture of satellites and other sophisticated equipment ultimately sabotaged their efforts to design a word processor. The firm's engineers had a strong ethic of "getting it right" and would not release the machine. The window of opportunity for entry into the market passed, leaving the firm with a $40 million write-off of their investment. The point is both simple and important. As firms grow and strategies change, the culture or social control system also needs to be realigned to reflect the new direction.

Culture and Commitment

Culture is critical in developing and maintaining levels of intensity and dedication among employees that often characterizes successful firms. This strong attachment is particularly valuable when the employees have knowledge that is instrumental to the success of the organization or when very high levels of motivation are required. When IBM bought ROLM, the critical resource was not the existing product line but the design and engineering expertise of ROLM's staff. A failure to gain the commitment of employees during mergers and acquisitions can diminish or destroy the value of the venture. In contrast, a highly dedicated work-force represents a significant competitive advantage. Under turbulent or changing conditions, relying on employees who wait to be told exactly what to do can be a liability.

How, then, do strong culture organizations develop intensity and commitment? A 20-year veteran of IBM was quoted in a *Wall Street Journal* article as saying, "I don't know what a cult is and what it is those bleary-eyed kids selling poppies really do, but I'm probably that deeply committed to the IBM company."[16] To understand this process, we need to consider what commitment is and how it is developed. By understanding the underlying psychology of commitment, we can then think about how to design systems to develop such an attachment among employees.

Organizational Commitment. What is meant by the term "organizational commitment"? It is typically conceived of as an individual's psychological bond to the organization, including a sense of job involvement, loyalty, and a belief in the values of the organization. There are three processes or stages of commitment: *compliance, identification*, and *internalization*.[17] In the first stage, *compliance*, a person accepts the influence of others mainly to obtain something from others, such as pay. The second stage is *identification* in which the individual accepts influence in order to maintain a satisfying, self-defining relationship. People feel pride in belonging to the firm. The final stage of commitment is *internalization* in which the individual finds the values of the organization to be intrinsically rewarding and congruent with personal values.

Conceiving of commitment as developing in this manner allows us to understand how a variety of organizations—ranging from cults to strong culture corporations—generate commitment among their members. In fact, these organizations can be categorized based on the type of commitment displayed by their members. Cults and religious organizations, for example, typically have members who have internalized the values of the organization and who become "deployable agents," or individuals who can be relied upon to go forth and proselytize.[18] Japanese organizations, Theory Z, and strong culture firms are characterized by members who have a strong identification with the organization. These employees identify with the firm because it stands for something they value. In typical corporations, members comply with directions but may have little involvement with the firm beyond self-interest; that is, there is no commitment with the firm beyond that of a fair exchange of effort for money and, perhaps, status.

HOW CULTURE IS DEVELOPED

How do people become committed to organization? Why, for example, would someone choose to join a cult? How do firms such as NUMMI get the incredible levels of productivity from their employees (as one team member said, "I like the new system so much it scares me. I'm scared because it took me 18 years to realize that I blew it at GM. Now we have a chance to do things a different way.")? The answer to this puzzle is simultaneously simple and nonobvious. As Jerry Salancik has noted, "commitment is too easy," yet it relies on an understanding of human motivation that is counter-intuitive.[19]

Constructing Social Realities

Most discussions of motivation assume a stable set of individual needs and values.[20] These are seen as shaping expectations, goals, and attitudes. In turn, these are presumed to guide behavior and people's responses to situations. In Maslow's theory, for instance, people are assumed to have a hierarchy of needs.[21] The managerial consequence of this view can be seen in our theories of job design in which jobs are supposed to be designed to take advantage

of the desire of people to grow and self-actualize.[22] But are such theories correct? The empirical evidence is weak at best.[23] In spite of numerous efforts to demonstrate the effect of needs and personality, there is little support for the power of individual differences to predict behavior.

Consider the results of two experiments. In the first, Christian seminary students were approached and given one of two requests. Both asked them to extemporaneously address a visiting class in a discussion of the parable of the Good Samaritan. They were told to walk over to a classroom building to do this. In one condition they were informed that the class was already there and that they should hurry. In the other condition they were told that the class would arrive in several minutes. As they walked to the classroom, all subjects passed an old man (the "victim") dressed in shabby clothes and in obvious need of help. The experimenters were interested in what proportion of Christian seminarians thinking of the Good Samaritan would stop and help this person. Surprisingly, in the condition in which the subjects were told to hurry, only 30 percent paid any attention. Think about this. Seventy percent of a group of individuals with religious values who were training to be ministers failed to stop. Ninety-five percent of those who were not in a hurry stopped to help.

In another experiment, researchers observed when students using a campus restroom washed their hands. They discovered that when another person was visible in the restroom, 90 percent washed their hands. When no other person was visible, less than 20 percent did so.

What explains these and other findings? What often seems to account for behavior are the expectations of others. As individuals, we are very susceptible to the informational and normative influence of others. We pay attention to the actions of others and learn from them. "In actuality, virtually all learning phenomena resulting from direct experience occur on a vicarious basis by observing other people's behavior and its consequences for them." We watch others and form expectations about how and when we should act.[24]

Yet, we are not sensitive to how much of our world is really a social construction—one that rests on shared agreements. We often tend to underestimate the degree to which situations and the expectations of others can constrain and shape behavior. Strong situations—ones in which there are very clear incentives and expectations about what constitutes appropriate attitudes and behavior—can be very powerful. When we care what others think, the power of these norms or social expectations can be heightened.

Mechanisms for Developing Culture

How can cultures be developed and managed in organizations? All organizations—from cults to strong culture corporations—draw on the same underlying psychology and create situations characterized by strong norms that focus people's attention, provide clear guidance about what is important, and provide for group reinforcement of appropriate attitudes and behavior. Four common mechanisms are used to accomplish this. What varies across these organizations is not what is done but only the degree to which these mechanisms are used.

Participation. The first mechanism that is critical in developing or changing a culture are systems that provide for participation. These systems encourage people to be involved and send signals to the individual that he or she is valued. These may range from formal efforts such as quality circles and advisory boards to less formal efforts such as suggestion systems and opportunities to meet with top managers and informal social gatherings. What is important about these processes is that people are encouraged to make incremental choices and develop a sense of responsibility for their actions. In some cases, such as work design, the specific choices made may be less important for future success than the fact that people had the chance to make them.

From a psychological perspective, choice is often associated with commitment. When we choose of our own volition to do something, we often feel responsible.[25] When the choice is voli-

tional, explicit, public, and irrevocable, the commitment is even more binding. For instance, direct sales companies have learned that by getting the customer to fill out the order sheet, they can cut cancellations dramatically. A large number of psychological experiments have convincingly shown that participation can lead to both commitment and enjoyment, even when people are induced to engage in physically and emotionally stressful activities such as eating earthworms and becoming bone marrow donors.[26]

How do organizations use participation? Marc Galanter has documented how members of the Unification Church use processes of incremental commitment to recruit cult members.[27] Individuals are invited to dinner, convinced to spend the weekend for a seminar, and in some cases, induced to remain permanently with their new found "friends." Interestingly, there is no evidence that people who join cults under these circumstances are suffering from any psychopathology. Religious organizations often use elaborate systems of incremental choice and participation leading to greater and greater involvement. Japanese-managed automobile companies in the U.S. also have elaborate systems of selection and orientation that rely heavily on these approaches, as do American "strong culture" firms.

Management as Symbolic Action. The second mechanism commonly seen in strong culture organizations is that of clear, visible actions on the part of management in support of the cultural values.[28] In organizations, participants typically want to know what is important. One way we gain this information is to carefully watch and listen to those above us. We look for consistent patterns. When top management not only says that something is important but also consistently behaves in ways that support the message, we begin to believe what is said. When the CEO of Xerox, David Kearns, began his quest for improved quality, there was some initial uncertainty about whether he meant it. Over time, as the message was repeated again and again, and as resources continued to be devoted to the quality effort, norms developed setting expectations about the role and importance of quality throughout the corporation.[29]

An important function of management is to provide interpretations of events for the organization's members. Without a shared meaning, confusion and conflict can result. Managers need to be sensitive to how their actions are viewed. Interpreting (or reinterpreting) history, telling stories, the use of vivid language, spending time, and being seen as visible in support of certain positions are all potential ways of shaping the organization's culture. This does not mean that managers need to be charismatic. However, managers need to engage in acts of "mundane symbolism." By this they can insure that important issues get suitable amounts of time, that questions are continually asked about important topics, and that the subject gets on the agenda and it is followed up.

The appropriate use of symbols and ceremonies is also important. When Jerry Sanders, CEO of Advanced Micro Devices, decided to shift the firm's strategy toward innovation, he not only made substantive changes in budget, positions, and organizational structure, he also used a symbol. As a part of the many talks he had with employees describing the need to change, Sanders would also describe how important it was to invest in areas that others could not easily duplicate—such as investing in proprietary products. He would describe how a poor farmer would always need a cash crop at the end of the year if he was to survive. But if he began to prosper, a smart farmer would begin to plant crops that others might not be able to afford—crops, for example, that took more than a year to come to fruition; crops like asparagus. The notion of asparagus became a visible and important symbol for change within AMD, even to the point where managers begin referring to revenues from new proprietary products as "being measured on asparagus."

Symbols are not a substitute for substance, and ceremonies cannot replace content. Rather, many of the substantive changes that occur in organizations, such as promotions or reorganizations have multiple meanings and interpretations. Over time, people may lose a clear sense for what the superordinate goals are and why their jobs are important. In strong culture organizations, managers frequently and consistently send signals helping to renew these understandings. They do this by continually calling attention to what is important, in word and in action.

Information from Others. While clear messages from management are an important determinant of a culture, so too are consistent messages from coworkers. If control comes from the knowledge that someone who matters is paying attention, then the degree to which we care about our coworkers also gives them a certain control over us. Years ago, several researchers conducted an experiment in which subjects were placed in a room to complete a questionnaire. While they were doing this, smoke began to flow from an air vent. While 75% of the subjects who were alone responded by notifying the experimenter of a possible fire, only 38% did so when in the company of two other subjects. When these other two were confederates of the experimenter and deliberately said nothing, only 10% of the subjects responded. One conclusion from this and other similar experiments is that we often take our cue from others when we are uncertain what to do.

In organizations, during periods of crisis or when people are new to the situation, they often look to others for explanations of what to do and how to interpret events. Strong cultures are typically characterized by consensus about three questions. In these settings there are often attempts made to insure a consistency of understanding and to minimize any us–them attitudes between parts of the organization. For instance, strong culture firms often pride themselves on the equality of treatment of all employees. At Mars, all employees punch a time clock and no one has a private secretary. At Gore-Tex, WalMart, Disney, and others there are no employees or managers, only associates, team members, and hosts. At NUMMI, Honda, and Nissan there are no private dining rooms for managers and both managers and workers often wear uniforms. In the Rajneesh Commune, everyone wore clothes with the color magenta.

The goal here is to create a strong social construction of reality by minimizing contradictory interpretations. In cults, this is often done by isolating the members from family and friends. Some religious organizations do this by encouraging extensive involvement in a variety of church activities and meetings. Japanese firms expect after work socializing. At NUMMI, for instance, each work team is given a semiannual budget to be spent only on team-sponsored activities where the entire team participates. In corporations, 60 hour work weeks can also isolate people from competing interpretations. Some electronics firms in Silicon Valley have provided employee T-shirts with slogans such as "Working 80 hours a week and loving it." With this commitment of time, workers may be as isolated as if they had joined a cult.

Comprehensive Reward Systems. A final mechanism for promoting and shaping culture is the reward system, but not simply monetary rewards. Rather, these systems focus on rewards such as recognition and approval which can be given more frequently than money. These rewards also focus on the intrinsic aspects of the job and a sense of belonging to the organization. Recognition by your boss or coworkers for doing the right thing can be more potent in shaping behavior than an annual bonus. In the words of a popular management book, the trick is to catch someone doing something right and to reward it on the spot. While tokens such as scrolls or badges can be meaningless, under the right circumstances they can also be highly valued.

It is easy to desire one type of behavior while rewarding another. Often management professes a concern for quality while systematically rewarding only those who meet their goals, regardless of the quality. Innovation may be espoused but even the slightest failure is punished. At its simplest, people usually do what they are rewarded for and don't do what they're punished for. If this is true and to be taken seriously, then a simple analysis of what gets management's attention should give us a sense for

what the culture supports. Who gets promoted? At 3M, one important aspect of success is to be associated with a new product introduction. If innovation is espoused, but doing things by-the-book is what is rewarded, it doesn't take a psychologist to figure out what the firm actually values. In fact, if there are inconsistencies between what top management says and what is actually rewarded, the likely outcome will be confusion and cynicism.

MANAGING CULTURE

Each of these can affect the development of a shared set of expectations. As shown in Figure 25.1, the process begins with words and actions on the part of the group's leaders. Even if no explicit statements are made, subordinates will attempt to infer a pattern. If management is credible and communicates consistently, members of the group may begin to develop consistent expectations about what is important. When this consensus is also rewarded, clear norms can then emerge.

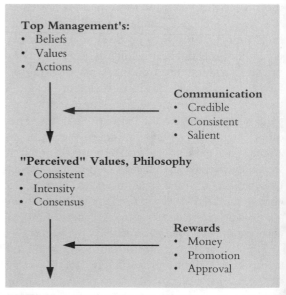

FIGURE 25.1 Employees' beliefs, attitudes, and behaviors expressed as norms.

Whether or not these norms constitute a desirable culture depends on the critical tasks to be accomplished and whether the formal control system provides sufficient leverage to attain these. If culture *is* important, four steps can help a manager understand how to manage it.

• Identify the strategic objectives of the unit. Once identified, specify the short-term objectives and critical actions that need to be accomplished if the strategic objectives are to be accomplished.

• Analyze the existing values and norms that characterize the organization. This can be done by focusing on what people in the unit feel is expected of them by their peers and bosses and what is actually rewarded. What does it take to get ahead? What stories are routinely told? Who are the people who exemplify the group? Look for norms that are widely shared and strongly felt.

• Once these are identified, look for norms that may hinder the accomplishment of critical tasks; norms that would help but are not currently present; and conflicts between what is needed and what is currently rewarded.

• Once these are identified, programs can be designed to begin to shape or develop the desired norms. These can draw upon the psychological mechanisms discussed previously.

The logic here is straightforward and links culture to those activities critical for the implementation of strategy and for generating widespread understanding and commitment among the organization's members. Obviously, these actions take time and management resources to accomplish. However, to ignore them is to ignore a social control system that may already be operating in the organization. The issue is whether this system is helping or hindering. Managers need to be sensitive to what the central organizational norms are and how they can affect them. To not be sensitive to these issues is to ignore the advice of a CEO who said, "We will either be a victim or a successful result of our culture."

REFERENCES

1. *Fortune*, January 2, 1989.

2. *Fortune*, August 15, 1988.

3. *Fortune*, June 6, 1988.

4. T. Peters and R. H. Waterman, *In Search of Excellence: Lessons From America's Best-Run Companies* (New York, NY: Harper & Row, 1982), p. 32.

5. *Fortune*, January 30, 1989.

6. *Business Week*, October 10, 1988.

7. *Business Week*, October 10, 1988.

8. A. Wilkins and W. Ouchi, "Efficient Cultures: Exploring the Relationship between Culture and Organizational Performance." *Administrative Science Quarterly*, 28 (1983): 468–481: O. Williamson, *Markets and Hierarchies* (New York, NY: The Free Press, 1975).

9. J. Carlzon, *Moments of Truth* (Cambridge, MA: Ballinger, 1987).

10. S. Dornbusch and W. R. Scott, *Evaluation and the Exercise of Authority* (San Francisco, CA: Jossey-Bass, 1975).

11. H. Schwartz and S. Davis, "Matching Corporate Culture and Business Strategy," *Organizational Dynamics* (1981), pp. 30–48.

12. *Fortune,* April 10, 1989.

13. D. Feldman, "The Development and Enforcement of Group Norms," *Academy of Management Review,* 9 (1984): 47–53.

14. Fortune, June 6, 1988.

15. For example, see S. Davis, *Managing Corporate Culture* (Cambridge, MA: Ballinger, 1984); T. Deal and A. Kennedy, *Corporate Cultures* (Reading, MA: Addison-Wesley, 1982); Peters and Waterman, op. cit.

16. *Wall Street Journal,* April 7, 1986.

17. C. O'Reilly and J. Chatman, "Organizational Commitment and Psychological Attachment: The Effects of Compliance, Identification and Internalization on Prosocial Behavior," *Journal of Applied Psychology,* 71 (1986): 492–499.

18. W. Appel, *Cults in America* (New York, NY: Holt, Rinehart and Winston, 1983); D. Gerstel, *Paradise Incorporated: Synanon* (San Francisco, CA: Presidio Press, 1982).

19. G. Salancik, "Commitment Is Too Easy!" *Organizational Dynamics* (Summer 1977), pp. 62–80.

20. For example, see F. Herzberg, B. Mausner, and B. Snyderman, *The Motivation to Work* (New York, NY: John Wiley, 1959); A. Maslow, *Motivation and Personality* (New York, NY: Harper & Row, 1970).

21. Maslow, op. cit.

22. For example, see J. R. Hackman and G. Oldham, *Work Redesign* (Reading, MA: Addison-Wesley, 1980).

23. For example, see G. Salancik and J. Pfeffer, "A Social Information Processing Approach to Job Attitudes and Task Design," *Administrative Science Quarterly,* 23 (1978): 224–253.

24. For example, see S. Milgram, *Obedience to Authority* (New York, NY: Harper & Row, 1969); A. Bandura, *Social Learning Theory* (Englewood Cliffs, NJ: Prentice-Hall, 1977).

25. Salancik, op. cit.

26. For example, see I. Janis and L. Mann, *Decision Making: A Psychological Analysis of Conflict, Choice, and Commitment* (New York, NY: Free Press, 1977).

27. M. Galanter, "Psychological Induction into the Large Group: Findings from a Modern Religious Sect." *American Journal of Psychiatry,* 137 (1980): 1574–1579.

28. J. Pfeffer, "Management as Symbolic Action: The Creation and Maintenance of Organizational Paradigms," in L. Cummings and B. Staw, eds., *Research in Organizational Behavior,* Volume 3 (Greenwich, CT: JAI Press, 1981).

29. G. Jacobsen and J. Hillkirk, *Xerox: American Samurai* (New York, NY: Collier Books, 1986).

26. THE ROLE OF THE FOUNDER IN CREATING ORGANIZATIONAL CULTURE

Edgar H. Schein

How do the entrepreneur/founders of organizations create organizational cultures? And how can such cultures be analyzed? These questions are central to this article. First I will examine what organizational culture is, how the founder creates and embeds cultural elements, why it is likely that first-generation companies develop distinctive cultures, and what the implications are in making the transition from founders or owning families to "professional" managers.

The level of confusion over the term *organizational culture* requires some definitions of terms at the outset. An organizational culture depends for its existence on a definable organization, in the sense of a number of people interacting with each other for the purpose of accomplishing some goal in their defined environment. An organization's founder simultaneously creates such a group and, by force of his or her personality, begins to shape the group's culture. But that new group's culture does not develop until it has overcome various329 crises of growth and survival, and has worked out solutions for coping with its external problems of adaptation and its internal problems of creating a workable set of relationship rules.

Organizational culture, then, is the pattern of basic assumptions that a given group has invented, discovered, or developed in learning to cope with its problems of external adaptation and internal integration—a pattern of assumptions that has worked well enough to be considered valid and, therefore, to be taught to new members as the correct way to perceive, think, and feel in relation to those problems.

In terms of external survival problems, for example, I have heard these kinds of assumptions in first-generation companies:

The way to decide on what products we will build is to see whether we ourselves like the product; if we like it, our customers will like it.

The only way to build a successful business is to invest no more than 5 percent of your own money in it.

The customer is the key to our success, so we must be totally dedicated to total customer service.

In terms of problems of internal integration the following examples apply:

Ideas can come from anywhere in this organization, so we must maintain a climate of total openness.

The only way to manage a growing business is to supervise every detail on a daily basis.

The only way to manage a growing business is to hire good people, give them clear responsibility, tell them how they will be measured, and then leave them alone.

Several points should be noted about the definition and the examples. First, culture is not the overt behavior or visible artifacts one might observe on a visit to the company. It is not even the philosophy or value system that the founder may articulate or write down in various "charters." Rather, it is the assumptions that underlie the values and determine not only behavior patterns, but also such visible artifacts as architecture, office layout, dress codes, and so on. This distinction is important because founders bring many of these assumptions with them when the organization begins; their problem is how to articulate, teach, embed, and in other ways get their own assumptions across and working in the system.

Founders often start with a theory of how to succeed; they have a cultural paradigm in their heads, based on their experience in the culture in which they grew up. In the case of a founding *group*, the theory and paradigm arise from the way that group reaches consensus on their assumptions about how to view things. Here, the evolution of the culture is a multi-stage process reflecting the several stages of group formation. The ultimate organizational culture will always reflect the complex interaction between (1) the assumptions and theories that founders bring to the group initially and (2) what the group learns subsequently from its own experiences.

TABLE 26.1
External and Internal Problems

Problems of External Adaptation and Survival

1. Developing consensus on the *primary task, core mission, or manifest and latent functions of the group*–for example, strategy.
2. Consensus on *goals*, such being the concrete reflection of the core mission.
3. Developing consensus on the *means to be used* in accomplishing the goals—for example, division of labor, organization structure, reward system, and so forth.
4. Developing consensus on the *criteria to be used in measuring how well the group is doing against its goals and targets*—for example, information and control systems.
5. Developing consensus on *remedial or repair strategies* as needed when the group is not accomplishing its goals.

Problems of Internal Integration

1. *Common language and conceptual categories*. If members cannot communicate with and understand each other, a group is impossible by definition.
2. Consensus on *group boundaries and criteria for inclusion and exclusion*. One of the most important areas of culture is the shared consensus on who is in, who is out, and by what criteria one determines membership.
3. Consensus on *criteria for the allocation of power and status*. Every organization must work out its pecking order and its rules for how one gets, maintains, and loses power. This area of consensus is crucial in helping members manage their own feelings of aggression.
4. Consensus on *criteria for intimacy, friendship, and love*. Every organization must work out its own rules of the game for peer relationships, for relationships between the sexes, and for the manner in which openness and intimacy are to be handled in the context of managing the organization's tasks.
5. Consensus on *criteria for allocation of rewards and punishments*. Every group must know what its heroic and sinful behaviors are: what gets rewarded with property, status, and power; and what gets punished through the withdrawal of rewards and, ultimately, excommunication.
6. Consensus on *ideology and "religion."* Every organization, like every society, faces unexplainable events that must be meaning so that members can respond to them and avoid the anxiety of dealing with the unexplainable and uncontrollable.

WHAT IS ORGANIZATIONAL CULTURE ABOUT?

Any new group has the problem of developing shared assumptions about the nature of the world in which it exists, how to survive in it, and how to manage and integrate internal relationships so that it can operate effectively and make life livable and comfortable for its members. These external and internal problems can be categorized as shown in Table 26.1.

The external and internal problems are always intertwined and acting simultaneously. A group cannot solve its external survival problem without being integrated to some degree to permit concerted action, and it cannot integrate itself without some successful task accomplishment vis-à-vis its survival problem or primary task.

The model of organizational culture that then emerges is one of shared solutions to problems which work well enough to begin to be taken for granted—to the point where they drop out of awareness, become unconscious assumptions, and are taught to new members as a reality and as the correct way to view things. If one wants to identify the elements of a given culture, one can go down the list of issues and ask how the group views itself in relation to each of them: What does it see to be its core mission, its goals, the way to accomplish those goals, the measurement systems and procedures it uses, the way it remedies actions, its particular jargon and meaning system, the authority system, peer system, reward system, and ideology? One will find, when one does this, that there is in most cultures a deeper level of assumptions which ties together the various solutions to the various problems, and this deeper level deals with more ultimate questions. The real cultural essence, then, is what members of the organization assume about the issues shown in Table 26.2.

In a fairly "mature" culture—that is, in a group that has a long and rich history—one will find that

TABLE 26.2
Basic Underlying Assumptions around which Paradigms Form

1. *The organization's relationship to its environment.* Reflecting even more basic assumptions about the relationship of humanity to nature, one can assess whether the key members of the organization view the relationship as one of dominance, submission, harmonizing, finding an approppriate niche, and so on.

2. *The nature of reality and truth.* Here are the linguistic and behavioral rules that define what is real and what is not, what is a "fact," how truth is ultimately to be determined, and whether truth is "revealed" or "discovered"; basic concepts of time as linear or cyclical, monochronic or individual; and so forth.

3. *The nature of human nature.* What does it mean to be "human," and what attributes are considered intrinsic or ultimate? Is human nature good, evil, or neutral? Are human beings perfectible or not? Which is better, Theory X or Theory Y?

4. *The nature of human activity.* What is the "right" thing for human beings to do, on the basis of the above presumptions about reality, the environment, and human nature; to be active, passive, self-developmental, fatalistic, or what? What is work and what is play?

5. *The nature of human relationships.* What is considered to be the "right" way for people to relate to each other, to distribute power and love? Is life cooperative or competitive; individualistic, group collaborative, or communal; based on traditional lineal authority, law, or charisma, or what?

these assumptions are patterned and interrelated into a "cultural paradigm" that is the key to understanding how members of the group view the world. In an organization that is in the process of formation, the paradigm is more likely to be found only in the founder's head, but it is important to try to decipher it in order to understand the biases or directions in which the founder "pushes" or "pulls" the organization.

HOW DO ORGANIZATIONAL CULTURES BEGIN?

The Role of the Founder

Groups and organizations do not form accidentally or spontaneously. They are usually created because someone takes a leadership role in seeing how the concerted action of a number of people could accomplish something that would be impossible through individual action alone. In the case of social movements or new religions, we have prophets, messiahs, and other kinds of charismatic leaders. Political groups or movements are started by leaders who sell new visions and new solutions. Firms are created by entrepreneurs who have a vision of how a concerted effort could create a new product or service in the marketplace. The process of culture formation in the organization begins with the founding of the group. How does this happen?

In any given firm the history will be somewhat different, but the essential steps are functionally equivalent:

1. A single person (founder) has an idea for a new enterprise.

2. A founding group is created on the basis of initial consensus that the idea is a good one: workable and worth running some risks for.

3. The founding group begins to act in concert to create the organization by raising funds, obtaining patents, incorporating, and so forth.

4. Others are brought into the group according to what the founder or founding group considers necessary, and the group begins to function, developing its own history.

In this process the founder will have a major impact on how the group solves its external survival and internal integration problem. Because the founder had the original idea, he or she will typically have biases on how to get the idea fulfilled—biases based on previous cultural experiences and personality traits. In my observation, entrepreneurs are very strong-minded about what to do and how to do it. Typically they already have strong assumptions about the nature of the world, the role their organization will play in that world, the nature of human nature, truth, relationships, time, and space.

Three Examples

Founder A, who built a large chain of supermarkets and department stores, was the dominant ideological force in the company until he died in his seventies. He assumed that his organization could be dominant in the market and that his primary mission was to supply his customers with a quality, reliable product. When A was operating only a corner store with his wife, he built customer relations through a credit policy that displayed trust in the customer, and he always took products back if the customer was not satisfied. Further, he assumed that stores had to be attractive and spotless, and that the only way to ensure this was by close personal supervision. He would frequently show up at all his stores to check into small details. Since he assumed that only close supervision would teach subordinates the right skills, he expected all his store managers to be very visible and very much on top of their jobs.

A's theory about how to grow and win against his competition was to be innovative, so he encouraged his managers to try new approaches, to bring in consulting help, to engage in extensive training, and to feel free to experiment with new technologies. His view of truth and reality was to find it wherever one could and, therefore, to be open to one's environment and never take it for granted that had all the answers. If new things worked, A encouraged their adoption.

Measuring results and fixing problems was, for A, an intensely personal matter. In addition to using traditional business measures, he went to the stores and, if he saw things not to his liking, immediately insisted that they be corrected. He trusted managers who operated on the basis of similar kinds of assumptions and clearly had favorites to whom he delegated more.

Authority in this organization remained very centralized; the ultimate source of power, the voting shares of stock, remained entirely in the family. A was interested in developing good managers throughout the organization, but he never assumed that sharing ownership through some kind of stock option plan would help in that process. In fact, he did not even share ownership with several key "lieutenants" who had been with the company through most of its life but were not in the family. They were well paid, but received no stock. As a result, peer relationships were officially defined as competitive. A liked managers to compete for slots and felt free to get rid of "losers."

A also introduced into the firm a number of family members who received favored treatment in the form of good developmental jobs that would test them for ultimate management potential. As the firm diversified, family members were made division heads even though they often had relatively little general management experience. Thus peer relationships were highly politicized. One had to know how to stay in favor, how to deal with family members, and how to maintain trust with nonfamily peers in the highly competitive environment.

A wanted open communication and high trust levels, but his own assumptions about the role of the family, the effect of ownership, and the correct way to manage were, to some degree, in conflict with each other, leading many of the members of the organization to deal with the conflicting signals by banding together to form a kind of counter-culture within the founding culture. They were more loyal to each other than to the company.

Without going into further detail. I want to note several points about the "formation" of this organization and its emerging culture. By definition, something can become part of the culture only if it works. A's theory and assumptions about how things "should be" worked, since his company grew and prospered. He personally received a great deal of reinforcement for his own assumptions, which undoubtedly gave him increased confidence that he had a correct view of the world. Throughout his lifetime he steadfastly adhered to the principles with which he started, and did everything in his power to get others to accept them as well. At the same time, however, A had to share concepts and assumptions with a great many other people. So as his company grew and learned from its own experience, A's assumptions gradually had to be modified, or A had to withdraw from certain areas of running the business. For example, in their diversification efforts, the management bought several production units that would permit backward integration in a number of areas—but, because they recognized that they knew little about running factories, they brought in fairly strong, autonomous managers and left them alone.

A also had to learn that his assumption did not always lead to clear signals. He thought he was adequately rewarding his best young general managers, but could not see that for some of them the political climate, the absence of stock options, and the arbitrary rewarding of family members made their own career progress too uncertain. Consequently, some of his best people left the company—a phenomenon that left A perplexed but unwilling to change his own assumptions in this area. As the company matured, many of these conflicts remained and many sub-cultures formed around groups of younger managers who were functionally or geographically insulated from the founder.

Founder B built a chain of financial service organizations using sophisticated financial analysis techniques in an urban area where insurance companies, mutual funds, and banks were only beginning to use these techniques. He was the conceptualizer and the salesman in putting together the ideas for these new organizations, but he put only a small percentage of the money up himself, working from a theory that if he could not convince investors that there was a market, then the idea was not sound. His initial assumption was that he did not know enough about the market to gamble with his own money—an assumption based on experience, according to a story he told about the one enterprise in which he had failed miserably. With this enterprise, he had trusted his own judgment on what customers would want, only to be proven totally wrong the hard way.

B did not want to invest himself heavily in his organizations, either financially or personally. Once he had put together a package, he tried to find people whom he trusted to administer it. There were usually people who, like himself, were fairly open in their approach to business and not too hung up on previous assumptions about how things should be done. One can infer that B's assumptions about concrete goals, the means to be used to achieve them, measurement criteria, and repair strategies were pragmatic: Have a clear concept of the mission, test it by selling it to investors, bring in good people who understand what the mission is, and then leave them alone to implement and run the organization, using only ultimate financial performance as a criterion.

B's assumptions about how to integrate a group were, in a sense, irrelevant since he did not inject himself very much into any of his enterprises. To determine the cultures of those enterprises, one had to study the managers put into key positions by B—matters that varied dramatically from one enterprise to the next. This short example illustrates that there is nothing automatic about an entrepreneur's process of inserting personal vision or style into his or her organization. The process depends very much on whether and how much that person wants to impose himself or herself.

Founder C, like A, was a much more dominant personality with a clear idea of how things should be. He and four others founded a manufacturing concern several years ago, one based on the founder's product idea along with a strong intuition that the market was ready for such a product. In this case, the founding group got together because they shared a concept of the core mission, but they found after a few years that the different members held very different assumptions about how to build an organization. These differences were sufficient to split the group apart and leave C in control of the young, rapidly growing company.

C held strong assumptions about the nature of the world—how one discovers truth and solves problems—and they were reflected in his management style. He believed that good ideas could come from any source; in particular, he believed that he himself was not wise enough to know what was true and right, but that if he heard an intelligent group of people debate an idea and examine it from all sides, he could judge accurately whether it was sound or not. He also knew that he could solve problems best in a group where many ideas were batted around and where there was a high level of mutual confrontation around those ideas. Ideas came from individuals, but the testing of ideas had to be done in a group.

C also believed very strongly that even if he knew what the correct course of action was, unless the parties whose support was critical to implementation were completely sold on the idea, they would either misunderstand or unwittingly sabotage the idea. Therefore, on any important decision, C insisted on wide debate, many group meetings, and selling the idea down and laterally in the organization; only when it appeared that everyone understood and was committed would he agree to going ahead. C felt so strongly about this that he often held up important decisions even when he personally was already convinced of the course of action to take. He said that he did not want to be out there leading all by himself if he could not count on support from the troops; he cited past cases in which, thinking he had group support, he made a decision and, when it failed, found his key subordinates claiming that he had been alone in the decision. These experiences, he said, taught him to ensure commitment before going ahead on anything, even if doing so was time-consuming and frustrating.

While C's assumptions about how to make decisions led to a very group-oriented organization, his theory about how to manage led to a strong individuation process. C was convinced that the only way to manage was to give clear and simple individual responsibility and then to measure the person strictly on those responsibilities. Groups could help make decisions and obtain commitment, but they could not under any circumstance be responsible or accountable. So once a decision was made, it had to be carried out by individuals. If the decision was complex, involving a reorganization of functions, C always insisted that the new organization had to be clear and simple enough to permit the assignment of individual accountabilities.

C believed completely in a proactive model of man and in man's capacity to master nature; hence he expected of his subordinates that they would always be on top of their jobs. If a budget had been negotiated for a year, and if after three months the subordinate recognized that he would overrun the budget, C insisted that the subordinate make a clear decision either to find a way to stay within the budget or to renegotiate a larger budget. It was not acceptable to allow the overrun to occur without informing others and renegotiating, and it was not acceptable to be ignorant of the likelihood that there would be an overrun. The correct way to behave was always to know what was happening, always to be responsible for what was happening, and always to feel free to renegotiate previous agreements if they no longer made sense. C believed completely in open communications and the ability of people to reach reasonable decisions and compromises if they confronted their problems, figured out what they wanted to do, were willing to marshal arguments for their solution, and scrupulously honored any commitments they made.

On the interpersonal level, C assumed "constructive intent" on the part of all members of the organization, a kind of rational loyalty to organizational goals and to shared commitments. This did not prevent people from competitively trying to get ahead—but playing politics, hiding information, blaming others, or failing to cooperate on agreed-upon plans were defined as sins. However, C's assumptions about the nature of truth and the need for every individual to keep thinking out what he or she thought was the correct thing to do in any given situation led to frequent interpersonal tension. In other words, the rule of honoring commitments and following through on consensually reached decision was superseded by the rule of doing only what you believed sincerely to be the best thing to do in any given situation. Ideally, there would be time to challenge the original decision and renegotiate, but in practice time pressure was such that the subordinate, in doing what was believed to be best, often had to be insubordinate. Thus people in the organization frequently complained that decisions did not "stick," yet had to acknowledge that the reason they did not stick was that the assumption that one had to do the correct thing was even more important. Subordinates learned that insubordination was much less likely to be punished than doing something that the person knew to be wrong or stupid.

C clearly believed in the necessity of organization and hierarchy, but he did not trust the authority of position nearly so much as the authority of reason. Hence bosses were granted authority only to the extent that they could sell their decisions; as indicated above, insubordination was not only tolerated, but actively rewarded if it led to better outcomes. One could infer from watching this organization that it thrived on intelligent, assertive, individualistic people—and, indeed, the hiring policies reflected this bias.

So, over the years, the organization C headed had a tendency to hire and keep the people who fit into the kind of management system I am describing. And those people who fit the founder's assumptions found themselves feeling increasingly like family members in that strong bonds of mutual support grew up among them, with C functioning symbolically as a kind of benign but demanding father figure. These familial feelings were very important, though quite implicit, because they gave subordinates a feeling of security that was needed to challenge each other and C when a course of action did not make sense.

The architecture and office layout in C's company reflected his assumptions about problem solving and human relationships. He insisted on open office landscaping; minimum status differentiation in terms of office size, location, and furnishings (in fact, people were free to decorate their offices any way they liked); open cafeterias instead of executive dining rooms; informal dress codes; first-come, first-serve systems for getting parking spaces; many conference rooms with attached kitchens to facilitate meetings and to keep people interacting with each other instead of going off for meals; and so forth.

In summary, C represents a case of an entrepreneur with a clear set of assumptions about how things should be, both in terms of the formal business arrangements and in terms of internal relationships in the organization—and these assumptions still reflect themselves clearly in the organization some years later.

Let us turn next to the question of how a strong founder goes about embedding his assumptions in the organization.

HOW ARE CULTURAL ELEMENTS EMBEDDED?

The basic process of embedding a cultural element—a given belief or assumption—is a "teaching" process, but not necessarily an explicit one. The basic model of cultural formation, it will be remembered, is that someone must propose a solution to a problem the group faces. Only if the group shares the perception that the solution is working will that element be adopted, and only if it continues to work will it come to be taken for granted and taught to newcomers. It goes without saying, therefore, that only elements that solve group problems will survive, but the previous issue of "embedding" is how a founder or leader gets the group to do things in a certain way in the first place, so that the question of whether it will work can be settled. In other words, embedding a cultural element in this context means only that the founder/leader has ways of getting the group to try out certain responses. There is no guarantee that those responses will, in fact, succeed in solving the group's ultimate problem. How do founder/leaders do this? I will describe a number of mechanisms ranging from very explicit teaching to very implicit messages of which even the founder may be unaware. These mechanisms are shown in Table 26.3.

As the above case examples tried to show, the initial thrust of the messages sent is very much a function of the personality of the founder; some founders deliberately choose to build an organization that reflects their own personal biases while others create the basic organization but then turn it over to subordinates as soon as it has a life of its own. In both cases, the process of culture formation is complicated by the possibility that the founder is "conflicted," in the sense of having in his or her own personality several mutually contradictory assumptions.

The commonest case is probably that of the founder who states a philosophy of delegation but who retains tight control by feeling free to intervene, even in the smallest and most trivial decisions, as A did. Because the owner is granted the "right" to run his or her own company, subordinates will tolerate this kind of contradictory behavior and the organization's culture will develop complex assumptions about how one runs the organization "in spite of" or "around" the founder. If the founder's conflicts are severe to the point of interfering with the running of the organization, buffering layers of management may be built in or, in the extreme, the board of directors may have to find a way to move the founder out altogether.

The mechanisms listed in Table 26.3 are not equally potent in practice, but they can reinforce each other to make the total message more potent than individual components. In my observation the most important or potent messages are role modeling by leaders (item 3), what leaders pay attention to (item 6), and leader reactions to critical events (item 7). Only if we observe these leader actions can we begin to decipher how members of the organization "learned" the right and proper things to do, and what model of reality they were to adopt.

TABLE 26.3
How Is Culture Embedded and Transmitted?

Each of the mechanisms listed below is used by founders and key leaders to embed a value or assumption they hold, though the message may be very implicit in the sense that the leader is not aware of sending it. Leaders also may be conflicted, which leads to conflicting messages. A given mechanism may convey the message very explicitly, ambiguously, or totally implicitly. The mechanisms are listed below from more or less explicit to more or less implicit ones.

1. *Formal statements of organizational philosophy, charters, creeds, materials used for recruitment and selection, and socialization.*
2. *Design of physical spaces, facades, buildings.*
3. *Deliberate role modeling, teaching, and coaching by leaders.*
4. *Explicit reward and status system, promotion criteria.*
5. *Stories, legends, myths, and parables about key people and events.*
6. *What leaders pay attention to, measure, and control.*
7. *Leader reactions to critical incidents and organizational crises* (times when organizational survival is threatened, norms are unclear or challenged, insubordination occurs, threatening or meaningless events occur, and so forth).
8. *How the organization is designed and structured.* (The design of work, who reports to whom, degree or decentralization, functional or other criteria for differentiation, and mechanisms used for integration carry implicit messages of what leaders assume and value.)
9. *Organizational systems and procedures.* (The types of information, control, and decision support systems in terms of categories of information, and when and how performance appraisal and other review processes are conducted carry implicit messages of what leaders assume and value.)
10. *Criteria used for recruitment, selection, promotion, leveling off, retirement, and "excommunication" of people.* (The implicit and possibly unconscious criteria that leaders use to determine who "fits" and who doesn't "fit" membership roles and key slots in the organization.)

To give a few examples, A demonstrated his need to be involved in everything at a detailed level by frequent visits to stores and detailed inspections of what was going on in them. When he went on vacation, he called the office every single day at a set time and wanted to know in great detail what was going on. This behavior persisted into his period of semi-retirement, when he would still call *daily* from his retirement home, where he spent three winter months.

A's loyalty to his family was quite evident: He ignored bad business results if a family member was responsible, yet punished a non-family member involved in such results. If the family member was seriously damaging the business, A put a competent manager in under him, but did not always give that manager credit for subsequent good results. If things continued to go badly, A would finally remove the family member, but always with elaborate rationalizations to protect the family image. If challenged on this kind of blind loyalty, A would assert that owners had certain rights that could not be challenged. Insubordination from a family member was tolerated and excused, but the same kind of insubordination from a non-family member was severely punished.

In complete contrast, B tried to find competent general managers and turn a business over to them as quickly as he could. He involved himself only if he absolutely had to in order to save the business, and he pulled out of businesses as soon as they were stable and successful. B separated his family life completely from his business and had no assumptions about the rights of a family in a business. He wanted a good financial return so that he could make his family economically secure, but he seemed not to want his family involved in the businesses.

C, like B, was not interested in building the business on behalf of the family; his preoccupation with making sound decisions overrode all other concerns. Hence C set out to find the right kinds of managers and then "trained" them through the manner in which he reacted to situations. If managers displayed ignorance or lack of control of an area for which they were responsible, C would get publicly angry at them and accuse them of incompetence. If managers overran a budget or had too much inventory and did not inform C when this was first noticed, they would be publicly chided, whatever the reason was for the condition. If the manager tried to defend the situation by noting that it developed because of actions in another part of the same company, actions which C and others had agreed to, C would point out strongly that the manager should have brought that issue up much earlier and forced a rethinking or renegotiation right away. Thus C made it clear through his reactions that poor ultimate results could be excused, but not being on top of one's situation could never be excused.

C taught subordinates his theory about building commitment to a decision by systematically refusing to go along with something until he felt the commitment was there, and by punishing managers who acted impulsively or prematurely in areas where the support of others was critical. He thus set up a very complex situation for his subordinates by demanding on the one hand a strong individualistic orientation (embodied in official company creeds and public relations literature) and, on the other, strong rules of consensus and mutual commitment (embodied in organizational stories, the organization's design, and many of its systems and procedures).

The above examples highlighted the differences among the three founders to show the biases and unique features of the culture in their respective companies, but there were some common elements as well that need to be mentioned. All three founders assumed that the success of their business(es) hinged on meeting customer needs: their most severe outbursts at subordinates occurred when they learned that a customer had not been well treated. All of the official message highlighted customer concern, and the reward and control systems focused heavily on such concerns. In the case of A, customer needs were even put ahead of the needs of the family; one way a family member could really get into trouble was to mess up a customer relationship.

All three founders, obsessed with product quality, had a hard time seeing how some of their own managerial demands could undermine quality by forcing compromises. This point is important because in all the official messages, commitment to customers and product quality were uniformly emphasized—making one assume that this value was a clear priority. It was only when one looked at the inner workings of A's and C's organizations that one could see that other assumptions which they held created internal conflicts that were difficult to overcome—conflicts that introduced new cultural themes into the organizations.

In C's organization, for example, there was simultaneously a concern for customers and an arrogance toward customers. Many of the engineers involved in the original product designs had been successful in estimating what customers would really want—a success leading to their assumption that they understood customers well enough to continue to make product designs without having to pay too much attention to what sales and marketing were trying to tell them. C officially supported marketing as a concept, but his underlying assumption was similar to that of his engineers, that he really understood what his customers wanted; this led to a systematic ignoring of some inputs from sales and marketing.

As the company's operating environment changed, old assumptions about the company's role in that environment were no longer working. But neither C nor many of his original group had a paradigm that was clearly workable in the new situation, so a period of painful conflict and new learning arose. More and more customers and marketing people began to complain, yet some parts of the organization literally could not hear or deal with these complaints because of their belief in the superiority of their products and their own previous assumptions that they knew what customers wanted.

In summary, the mechanisms shown in Table 26.3 represent *all* of the possible ways in which founder messages get communicated and embedded, but they vary in potency. Indeed, they may often be found to conflict with each other—either because the founder is internally conflicted or because the environment is forcing changes in the original paradigm that lead different parts of the organization to have different assumptions about how to view things. Such conflicts often result because new, strong managers who are not part of the founding group begin to impose their own assumptions and theories. Let us look next at how these people may differ and the implications of such differences.

FOUNDER/OWNERS VS. "PROFESSIONAL MANAGERS"

Distinctive characteristics or "biases" introduced by the founder's assumptions are found in first-generation firms that are still heavily influenced by founders and in companies that continue to be run by family members. As noted above, such biases give the first-generation firm its distinctive character, and such biases are usually highly valued by first-generation employees because they are associated with the success of the enterprise. As the organization grows, as family members or non-family managers begin to introduce new assumptions, as environmental changes force new responses from the organization, the original assumptions begin to be strained. Employees begin to express concern that some of their "key" values will be lost or that the characteristics that made the company an exciting place to work are gradually disappearing.

Clear distinctions begin to be drawn between the founding family and the "professional" managers who begin to be brought into key positions. Such "professional" managers are usually identified as non-family and as non-owners and, therefore, as less "invested" in the company. Often they have been specifically educated to be managers rather than experts in whatever is the company's particular product or market. They are perceived, by virtue of these facts, as being less loyal to the original values and assumptions that guided the company, and as being more concerned with short-run financial performance. They are typically welcomed for bringing in much needed organizational and functional skills, but they are often mistrusted because they are not loyal to the founding assumptions.

Though these perceptions have strong stereotypic components, it's possible to see that much of the stereotype is firmly based in reality if one examines a number of first-generation and family-owned companies. Founders and owners do have distinctive characteristics that derive partly from their personalities and partly from their structural position as owners. It is important to understand these characteristics if one is to explain how strongly held many of the values and assumptions of first-generation or family-owned companies are. Table 26.4 examines the "stereotype" by polarizing the founder/owner and "professional" manager along a number of motivational, analytical, interpersonal, and structural dimensions.

The main thrust of the differences noted is that the founder/owner is seen as being more self-oriented, more willing to take risks and pursue non-economic objectives and, by virtue of being the founder/owner, more *able* to take risks and to pursue such objectives. Founder/owners, are more often intuitive and holistic in their thinking, and they are able to take a long-range point of view because they are building their own identities through

TABLE 26.4
How Do Founder/Owners Differ from Professional Managers?

Motivation and Emotional Orientation	
Entrepreneurs / founders / owners are...	*Professional managers are...*
Oriented toward creating, building.	Oriented towardconsolidating, surviving, growing.
Achievement-oriented.	Power-and influence-oriented.
Self-oriented, worried about own image; needs for "glory" high	Organization-oriented, worried about company image.
Jealous of own perogatives, needs for autonomy high.	Interested in developing the organization and subordinates.
Loyal to own company, "local".	Loyal to profession of management, "cosmopolitan".
Willing and able to take moderate risks on own authority.	Able to take risks, but more cautious and in need of support.
Analytical Orientation	
Primarily intuitive, trusting of own intuitions	Primarily analytical, more cautious about intuitions.
Long-range time horizon.	Short-range time horizon.
Holistic; able to see total picture, patterns.	Specific; able to see details and their sequences.
Interpersonal Orientation	
"Particularistic," in the sense of seeing individuals as individuals.	"Universalistic," in the sense of seeing individuals as members of categories like employees, customers, suppliers, and so on.
Personal, political, involved.	Impersonal, rational, univolved.
Centralist, autocratic.	Participative, delegation-oriented.
Family ties count.	Family ties are irrelevant.
Emotional, impatient, easily bored.	Unemotional, patient, persistent.
Structural/Positional Differences	
Have the privileges and risks of owership.	Have minimal ownership; hence fewer privileges and risks.
Have secure position by virtue of ownership.	Have less secure position, must constantly prove themselves.
Are enerally highly visible and get close attention.	Are often invisible and do not get much attention.
Have the support of family members in the business.	Function alone or with the support of non-family members.
Have the obligation of dealing with family members and deciding on the priorities family issues should have relative to company issues.	Do not have to worry about family issues at all, which are by definition irrelevant.
Have weak bosses, Boards that are under their own control.	Have strong bosses, Boards that are not under their own control.

their enterprises. They are often more particularistic in their orientation, a characteristic that results in the building of more of a community in the early organizational stages. That is, the initial founding group and the first generation of employees will know each other well and will operate more on personal acquaintance and trust than on formal principles, job descriptions, and rules.

The environment will often be more political than bureaucratic, and founder-value biases will be staunchly defended because they will form the basis for the group's initial identity. New members who don't fit this set of assumptions and values are likely to leave because they will be uncomfortable, or they will be ejected because their failure to confirm accepted patterns is seen as disruptive.

Founder/owners, by virtue of their position and personality, also tend to fulfill some *unique functions* in the early history of their organizations:

1. *Containing and absorbing anxiety and risk.* Because they are positionally more secure and personally more confident, owners more than managers absorb and contain the anxieties and risks that are inherent in creating, developing, and enlarging an organization. Thus in time of stress, owners play a special role in reassuring the organization that it will survive. They are the stakeholders; hence they do have the ultimate risk.

2. *Embedding non-economic assumptions and values.* Because of their willingness to absorb risk and their position as primary stakeholders, founder/owners are in a position to insist on doing things which may not be optimally efficient from a short-run point of view, but which reflect their own values and biases on how to build an effective organization and/or how to maximize the benefits to themselves and their families. Thus founder/owners often start with humanistic and social concerns that become reflected in organizational structure and process. Even when "participation," or "no layoffs," or other personnel practices such as putting marginally competent family members into key slots are "inefficient," owners can in-

sist that this is the only way to run the business and make that decision stick in ways that professional managers cannot.

3. *Stimulating innovation.* Because of their personal orientation and their secure position, owners are uniquely willing and able to try new innovations that are risky, often with no more than an intuition that things will improve. Because managers must document, justify, and plan much more carefully, they have less freedom to innovate.

As the organization ages and the founder becomes less of a personal force, there is a trend away from this community feeling toward more of a rational, bureaucratic type of organization dominated by general managers who may care less about the original assumptions and values, and who are not in a position to fulfill the unique functions mentioned above. This trend is often feared and lamented by first- and second-generation employees. If the founder introduces his or her own family into the organization, and if the family assumptions and values perpetuate those of the founder, the original community feeling may be successfully perpetuated. The original culture may then survive. But at some point there will be a complete transition to general management, and at that point it is not clear whether the founding assumptions survive, are metamorphosed into a new hybrid, or are displaced entirely by other assumptions more congruent with what general managers as an occupational group bring with them.

4. *Originating evolution through hybridization.* The founder is able to impose his or her assumptions on the first-generation employees, but these employees will, as they move up in the organization and become experienced managers, develop a range of new assumptions based on their own experience. These new assumptions will be congruent with some of the core assumptions of the original cultural paradigm, but will add new elements learned from experience. Some of these new elements or new assumptions will solve problems better than the original ones because

external and internal problems will have changed as the organization matured and grew. The founder often recognizes that these new assumptions are better solutions, and will delegate increasing amounts of authority to those managers who are the best "hybrids": those who maintain key old assumptions yet add relevant new ones.

The best example of such hybrid evolution comes from a company that was founded by a very freewheeling, intuitive, pragmatic entrepreneur: "D" who, like C in the example above, believed strongly in individual creativity, a high degree of decentralization, high autonomy for each organizational unit, high internal competition for resources, and self-control mechanisms rather than tight, centralized organizational controls. As this company grew and prospered, coordinating so many autonomous units became increasingly difficult, and the frustration that resulted from internal competition made it increasingly expensive to maintain this form of organization.

Some managers in this company, notably those coming out of manufacturing, had always operated in a more disciplined, centralized manner—without, however, disagreeing with core assumptions about the need to maximize individual autonomy. But they had learned that in order to do certain kinds of manufacturing tasks, one had to impose some discipline and tight controls. As the price of autonomy and decentralization increased, D began to look increasingly to these manufacturing managers as potential occupants of key general management positions. Whether he was conscious of it or not, what he needed was senior general managers who still believed in the old system but who had, in addition, a new set of assumptions about how to run things that were more in line with what the organization now needed. Some of the first-generation managers were quite nervous at seeing what they considered to be their "hardnosed" colleagues groomed as heirs apparent. Yet they were relieved that these potential successors were part of the original group rather than complete outsiders.

From a theoretical standpoint, evolution through hybrids is probably the only model of culture change that can work, because the original culture is based so heavily on community assumptions and values. Outsiders coming into such a community with new assumptions are likely to find the culture too strong to budge, so they either give up in frustration or find themselves ejected by the organization as being too foreign in orientation. What makes this scenario especially likely is the fact that the *distinctive* parts of the founding culture are often based on biases that are not economically justifiable in the short run.

As noted earlier, founders are especially likely to introduce humanistic, social service, and other non-economic assumptions into their paradigm of how an organization should look, and the general manager who is introduced from the outside often finds these assumptions to be the very thing that he or she wants to change in the attempt to "rationalize" the organization and make it more efficient. Indeed, that is often the reason the outsider is brought in. But if the current owners do not recognize the positive functions their culture plays, they run the risk of throwing out the baby with the bath water or, if the culture is strong, wasting their time because the outsider will not be able to change things anyway.

The ultimate dilemma for the first-generation organization with a strong founder-generated culture is how to make the transition to subsequent generations in such a manner that the organization remains adaptive to its changing external environment without destroying cultural elements that have given it its uniqueness, and that have made life fulfilling in the internal environment. Such a transition cannot be made effectively if the succession problem is seen only in power or political terms. The thrust of this analysis is that the *culture* must be analyzed and understood, and that the founder/owners must have sufficient insight into their own culture to make an intelligent transition process possible.

ACKNOWLEDGMENTS AND SELECTED BIBLIOGRAPHY

The research on which this paper is based was partly sponsored by the Project on the Family Firm, Sloan School of Management, M.I.T., and by the Office of Naval Research, Organizational Effectiveness Research Programs, under Contract No. N00014-80-C-0905, NR 170-911.

The ideas explored here have been especially influenced by my colleague Richard Beckhard and by the various entrepreneurs with whom I have worked for many years in a consulting relationship. Their observations of themselves and their colleagues have proved to be an invaluable source of ideas and insights.

Earlier work along these lines has been incorporated, into my book *Career Dynamics* (Addison-Wesley, 1978). Further explication of the ideas of an organizational culture can be found in Andrew M. Pettigrew's article "On Studying Organizational Cultures" (*Administrative Science Quarterly*, December 1979), Meryl Louis's article "A Cultural Perspective on Organizations" (*Human Systems Management*, 1981, 2, 246–258), and in H. Schwartz and S. M. Davis's "Matching Corporate Culture and Business Strategy" (*Organizational Dynamics*, Summer 1981).

The specific model of culture that I use was first published in my article "Does Japanese Management Style Have a Message for American Managers?" (*Sloan Management Review*, Fall 1981) and is currently being elaborated into a book on organizational culture.

Power, Influence, and Interpersonal Attraction

27. WHO GETS POWER—AND HOW THEY HOLD ON TO IT: A STRATEGIC-CONTINGENCY MODEL OF POWER

Gerald R. Salancik and Jeffrey Pfeffer

Power is held by many people to be a dirty word or, as Warren Bennis has said, "It is the organization's last dirty secret."

This article will argue that traditional "political" power, far from being a dirty business, is, in its most naked form, one of the few mechanisms available for aligning an organization with its own reality. However, institutionalized forms of power—what we prefer to call the cleaner forms of power: authority, legitimization, centralized control, regulations, and the more modern "management information systems"—tend to buffer the organization from reality and obscure the demands of its environment. Most great states and institutions declined, not because they played politics, but because they failed to accommodate to the political realities they faced. Political processes, rather than being mechanisms for unfair and unjust allocations and appointments, tend toward the realistic resolution of conflicts among interests. And power, while it eludes defini-

tion, is easy enough to recognize by its consequences—the ability of those who possess power to bring about the outcomes they desire.

The model of power we advance is an elaboration of what has been called strategic-contingency theory, a view that sees power as something that accrues to organizational subunits (individuals, departments) that cope with critical organizational problems. Power is used by subunits, indeed, used by all who have it, to enhance their own survival through control of scarce critical resources, through the placement of allies in key positions, and through the definition of organizational problems and policies. Because of the processes by which power develops and is used, organizations become both more aligned and more misaligned with their environments. This contradiction is the most interesting aspect of organizational power and one that makes administration one of the most precarious of occupations.

WHAT IS ORGANIZATIONAL POWER?

You can walk into most organizations and ask without fear of being misunderstood, "Which are the powerful groups of people in this organization?" Although many organizational informants may be *unwilling* to tell you, it is unlikely they will be *unable* to tell you. Most people do not require explicit definitions to know what power is.

Power is simply the ability to get things done the way one wants them to be done. For a manager who wants an increased budget to launch a project that he thinks is important, his power is measured by his ability to get that budget. For an executive vice president who wants to be chairman, his power is evidenced by his advancement toward his goal.

People in organizations not only know what you are talking about when you ask who is influential but they are likely to agree with one another to an amazing extent. Recently, we had a chance to observe this in a regional office of an insurance company. The office had 21 department managers; we asked 10 of these managers to rank all 21 according to the influence each one had in the organization. Despite the fact that ranking 21 things is a difficult task, the managers sat down and began arranging the names of their colleagues and themselves in a column. Only one person bothered to ask, "What do you mean by influence?" When told "power," he responded, "Oh," and went on. We compared the rankings of all ten managers and found virtually no disagreement among them in the managers ranked among the top five or the bottom five. Differences in the rankings came from department heads claiming more influence for themselves than their colleagues attributed to them.

Such agreement on those who have influence, and those who do not, was not unique to this insurance company. So far we have studied over 20 very different organizations—universities, research firms, factories, banks, retailers, to name a few. In each one we found individuals able to rate themselves and their peers on a scale of influence or power. We have done this both for specific decisions and for general impact on organizational policies.

Their agreement was unusually high, which suggests that distributions of influence exist well enough in everyone's mind to be referred to with ease—and we assume with accuracy.

WHERE DOES ORGANIZATIONAL POWER COME FROM?

Earlier we stated that power helps organizations become aligned with their realities. This hopeful prospect follows from what we have dubbed the strategic-contingencies theory of organizational power. Briefly, those subunits most able to cope with the organization's critical problems and uncertainties acquire power. In its simplest form, the strategic-contingencies theory implies that when an organization faces a number of lawsuits that threaten its existence the legal department will gain power and influence over organizational decisions. Somehow other organizational interest groups will recognize its critical importance and confer upon it a status and power never before enjoyed. This influence may extend beyond handling legal matters and into decisions about product design, advertising production, and so on. Such extensions undoubtedly would be accompanied by appropriate, or acceptable, verbal justifications. In time, the head of the legal department may become the head of the corporation, just as in times past the vice president for marketing had become the president when market shares were a worrisome problem and, before him, the chief engineer, who had made the production line run as smooth as silk.

Stated in this way, the strategic-contingencies theory of power paints an appealing picture of power. To the extent that power is determined by the critical uncertainties and problems facing the organization and, in turn, influences decisions in the organization, the organization is aligned with the realities it faces. In short, power facilitates the organization's adaptation to its environment—or its problems.

We can cite many illustrations of how influence derives from a subunit's ability to deal with critical contingencies. Michael Crozier described a French cigarette factory in which the maintenance engineers had a considerable say in the plant-wide operation. After some probing he discovered that the group possessed the solution to one of the major problems faced by the company, that of trouble-shooting the elaborate, expensive, and irascible automated machines that kept breaking down and dumbfounding everyone else. It was the one problem that the plant manager could in no way control.

The production workers, while troublesome from time to time, created no insurmountable problems; the manager could reasonably predict their absenteeism or replace them when necessary. Production scheduling was something he could deal with since, by watching inventories and sales, the demand for cigarettes was known long in advance. Changes in demand could be accommodated by slowing down or speeding up the line. Supplies of tobacco and paper were also easily dealt with through stockpiles and advance orders.

The one thing that management could neither control nor accommodate to, however, was the seemingly happenstance breakdowns. And the foremen couldn't instruct the workers what to do when emergencies developed since the maintenance department kept its records or problems and solutions locked up in a cabinet or in its members' heads. The breakdowns were, in truth, a critical source of uncertainty for the organization, and the maintenance engineers were the only ones who could cope with the problem.

The engineers' strategic role in coping with breakdowns afforded them a considerable say on plant decisions. Schedules and production quotas were set in consultation with them. And the plant manager, while formally their boss, accepted their decisions about personnel in their operation. His submission was to his credit, for without their co-operation he would have had an even more difficult time in running the plant.

Ignoring Critical Consequences

In this cigarette factory, sharing influence with the maintenance workers reflected the plant manager's awareness of the critical contingencies. However, when organizational members are not aware of the critical contingencies they face and do not share influence accordingly, the failure to do so can create havoc. In one case, an insurance company's regional office was having problems with the performance of one of its departments, the coding department. From the outside, the department looked like a disaster area. The clerks who worked in it were somewhat dissatisfied; their supervisor paid little attention to them, and they resented the hard work. Several other departments were critical of this manager, claiming that she was inconsistent in meeting deadlines. The person most critical was the claims manager. He resented having to wait for work that was handled by her department, claiming that it held up his claims adjusters. Having heard the rumors about dissatisfaction among her subordinates, he attributed the situation to poor supervision. He was second in command in the office and therefore took up the issue with her immediate boss, the head of administrative services. They consulted with the personnel manager, and the three of them concluded that the manager needed leadership training to improve her relations with her subordinates. The coding manager objected, saying it was a waste of time, but agreed to go along with the training and also agreed to give more priority to the claims department's work. Within a week after the training, the results showed that her workers were happier but that the performance of her department had decreased, save for the people serving the claims department.

About this time, we began, quite independently, a study of influence in this organization. We asked the administrative services director to draw up flow charts of how the work of one department moved onto the next department. In the course of the interview, we noticed that the coding department began or interceded in the work flow of most of the other departments and casually mentioned to him, "The coding manager must be very influential." He said, "No, not really. Why would you think so?" Before we could reply, he recounted the story of her leadership training and the fact that things were worse. We then told him that it seemed obvious that the coding department would be influential from the fact that all the other departments depended on it. It was also clear why productivity had fallen. The coding manager took the training seriously and began spending more time raising her workers' spirits than she did worrying about the problems of all the departments that depended on her. Giving priority to the claims area only exaggerated the problem, for their work was getting done at the expense of the work of the other departments. Eventually the company hired a few more clerks to relieve the pressure in the coding department and performance returned to a more satisfactory level.

Originally we got involved with this insurance company to examine how the influence of each manager evolved from his or her department's handling of critical organizational contingencies. We reasoned that one of the most important contingencies faced by all profit-making organizations was that of generating income. Thus we expected managers would be influential to the extent to which they contributed to this function. Such was the case. The underwriting managers, who wrote the policies that committed the premiums, were the most influential; the claims managers, who kept a lid on the funds flowing out, were a close second. Least influential were the managers of functions unrelated to revenue, such as mailroom and payroll managers. And contrary to what the administrative services manager believed, the third most powerful department head (out of 21) was the woman in charge of the coding function, which consisted of rating, recording, and keeping track of the codes of all policy applications and contracts. Her peers attributed more influence to her than could have been inferred from her place on the organization chart. And it was not surprising, since they all depended on her department. The coding department's records, their accuracy, and the speed with which they could be retrieved, affected virtually every other operating department in the insurance office. The underwriters depended on them in getting the contracts straight; the typing department depended on them in preparing the formal contract document; the claims department depended on them in adjusting claims; and accounting depended on them for billing. Unfortunately, the "bosses" were not aware of these dependences, for unlike the cigarette factory, there were no massive breakdowns that made them obvious, while the coding manager, who was a hardworking but quiet person, did little to announce her importance.

The cases of this plant and office illustrate nicely a basic point about the source of power in organizations. The basis for power in an organization derives from the ability of a person or subunit to take or not take actions that are desired by others. The coding manager was seen as influential by those who depended on her department, but not by the people at the top. The engineers were influential because of their role in keeping the plant operating. The two cases differ in these respects: The coding supervisor's source of power was not as widely recognized as that of the maintenance engineers, and she did not use her source of power to influence decisions; the maintenance engineers did. Whether power is used to influence anything is a separate issue. We should not confuse this issue with the fact that power derives from a social situation in which one person has a capacity to do something and another person does not but wants it done.

POWER SHARING IN ORGANIZATIONS

Power is shared in organizations; and it is shared out of necessity more than out of concern for principles of organizational development or participatory democracy. Power is shared because no one person controls all the desired activities in the organization. While the factory owner may hire people to operate his noisy machines, once hired they have some control over the use of the machinery. And thus they have power over him in the same way he has power over them. Who has more power over whom is a mooter point than that of recognizing the inherent nature of organizing as a sharing of power.

Let's expand on the concept that power derives from the activities desired in an organization. A major way of managing influence in organizations is through the designation of activities. In a bank we studied, we saw this principle in action. This bank was planning to install a computer system for routine credit evaluation. The bank, rather progressive-minded, was concerned that the change would have adverse effects on employees and therefore surveyed their attitudes.

The principal opposition to the new system came, interestingly, not from the employees who performed the routine credit checks, some of whom would be relocated because of the change, but from the manager of the credit department. His reason was quite simple. The manager's primary function was to give official approval to the applications, catch any employee mistakes before giving approval, and arbitrate any difficulties the clerks had in deciding what to do. As a consequence of his role, others in the organization, including his superiors, subordinates, and colleagues, attributed considerable importance to him. He, in turn, for example, could point to the low proportion of credit approvals, compared with other financial institutions, that resulted in bad debts. Now, to his mind, a wretched machine threatened to transfer his role to a computer programmer, a man who knew nothing of finance and who, in addition, had ten years less seniority. The credit manager eventually quit for a position at a smaller firm with lower pay, but one in which he would have more influence than his redefined job would have left him with.

Because power derives from activities rather than individuals, an individual's or subgroup's power is never absolute and derives ultimately from the context of the situation. The amount of power an individual has at any one time depends, not only on the activities he or she controls, but also on the existence of other persons or means by which the activities can be achieved and on those who determine what ends are desired and, hence, on what activities are desired and critical for the organization. One's own power always depends on other people for these two reasons. Other people, or groups or organizations, can determine the definition of what is a critical contingency for the organization and can also undercut the uniqueness of the individual's personal contribution to the critical contingencies of the organization.

Perhaps one can best appreciate how situationally dependent power is by examining how it is distributed. In most societies, power organizes around scarce and critical resources. In the United States, a person doesn't become powerful because he or she can drive a car. There are simply too many others who can drive with equal facility. In certain villages in Mexico, on the other hand, a person with a car is accredited with enormous social status and plays a key role in the community. In addition to scarcity, power is also limited by the need for one's capacities in a social system. While a racer's ability to drive a car around a 90° turn at 80 mph may be sparsely distributed in a society, it is not likely to lend the driver much power in the society. The ability simply does not play a central role in the activities of the society.

The fact that power revolves around scarce and critical activities, of course, makes the control and organization of those activities a major battleground in struggles for power. Even relatively abundant or trivial resources can become the bases for power if one can organize and control their allocation and the definition of what is critical. Many occupational and professional groups attempt to do just this in modern economies. Lawyers organize themselves into associations, regulate the entrance requirements for novitiates, and then get laws passed specifying situations that require the services of an attorney. Workers had little power in the conduct of industrial affairs until they organized themselves into closed and controlled systems. In recent years, women and blacks have tried to define themselves as important and critical to the social system, using law to reify their status.

In organizations there are obviously opportunities for defining certain activities as more critical than others. Indeed, the growth of managerial thinking to include defining organizational objectives and goals has done much to foster these opportunities. One sure way to liquidate the power of groups in the organization is to define the need for their services out of existence. David Halberstam presents a description of how just such a thing happened to the group of correspondents that evolved around Edward R. Murrow, the brilliant journalist, interviewer, and war correspondent of CBS News. A close friend of CBS chairman and controlling stockholder William S. Paley, Murrow, and the news department he directed, were endowed with freedom to do what they felt was right. He used it to create some of the best documentaries and commentaries ever seen on television. Unfortunately, television became too large, too powerful, and too suspect in the eyes of the federal government that licensed it. It thus became, or at least the top executives believed it had become, too dangerous to have in-depth, probing commentary on the news. Crisp, dry, uneditorializing headliners were considered safer. Murrow was out and Walter Cronkite was in.

The power to define what is critical in an organization is no small power. Moreover, it is the key to understanding why organizations are either aligned with their environments or misaligned. If an organization defines certain activities as critical when in fact they are not critical, given the flow of resources coming into the organization, it is not likely to survive, at least in its present form.

Most organizations manage to evolve a distribution of power and influence that is aligned with the critical realities they face in the environment. The environment, in turn, includes both the internal environment, the shifting situational contexts in which particular decisions are made, and the external environment that it can hope to influence but is unlikely to control.

THE CRITICAL CONTINGENCIES

The critical contingencies facing most organizations derive from the environmental context within which they operate. This determines the available needed resources and thus determines the problems to be dealt with. That power organizes around handling these problems suggests an important mechanism by which organizations keep in turn with their external environments. The strategic-contingencies model implies that subunits that contribute

to the critical resources of the organization will gain influence in the organization. Their influence presumably is then used to bend the organization's activities to the contingencies that determine its resources. This idea may strike one as obvious. But its obviousness in no way diminishes its importance. Indeed, despite its obviousness, it escapes the notice of many organizational analysts and managers, who all too frequently think of the organization in terms of a descending pyramid, in which all the departments in one tier hold equal power and status. This presumption denies the reality that departments differ in the contributions they are believed to make to the overall organization's resources, as well as to the fact that some are more equal than others.

Because of the importance of this idea to organizational effectiveness, we decided to examine it carefully in a large midwestern university. A university offers an excellent site for studying power. It is composed of departments with nominally equal power and is administered by a central executive structure much like other bureaucracies. However, at the same time it is a situation in which the departments have clearly defined identities and face diverse external environments. Each department has its own bodies of knowledge, its own institutions, its own sources of prestige and resources. Because the departments operate in different external environments, they are likely to contribute differentially to the resources of the overall organization. Thus a physics department with close ties to NASA may contribute substantially to the funds of the university; and a history department with a renowned historian in residence may contribute to the intellectual credibility or prestige of the whole university. Such variations permit one to examine how these various contributions lead to obtaining power within the university.

We analyzed the influence of 29 university departments throughout an 18-month period in their history. Our chief interest was to determine whether departments that brought more critical resources to the university would be more powerful than departments that contributed fewer or less critical resources.

To identify the critical resources each department contributed, the heads of all departments were interviewed about the importance of seven different resources to the university's success. The seven included undergraduate students (the factor determining size of the state allocations by the university), national prestige, administrative expertise, and so on. The most critical resource was found to be contract and grant monies received by a department's faculty for research or consulting services. At this university, contract and grants contributed somewhat less than 50 percent of the overall budget, with the remainder primarily coming from state appropriations. The importance attributed to contract and grant monies, and the rather minor importance of undergraduate students, was not surprising for this particular university. The university was a major center for graduate education; many of its departments ranked in the top ten of their respective fields. Grant and contract monies were the primary source of discretionary funding available for maintaining these programs of graduate education, and hence for maintaining the university's prestige. The prestige of the university itself was critical both in recruiting able students and attracting top-notch faculty.

From university records it was determined what relative contributions each of the 29 departments made to the various needs of the university (national prestige, outside grants, teaching). Thus, for instance, one department may have contributed to the university by teaching 7 percent of the instructional units, bringing in 2 percent of the outside contracts and grants, and having a national ranking of 20. Another department, on the other hand, may have taught one percent of the instructional units, contributed 12 percent to the grants, and be ranked the third best department in its field within the country.

The question was: Do these different contributions determine the relative power of the departments within the university? Power was measured in several ways; but regardless of how measured, the answer was "Yes." Those three resources together accounted for about 70 percent of the variance in subunit power in the university.

But the most important predictor of departmental power was the department's contribution to the contracts and grants of the university. Sixty percent of the variance in power was due to this one factor, suggesting that the power of departments derived primarily from the dollars they provided for graduate education, the activity believed to be the most important for the organization.

THE IMPACT OF ORGANIZATIONAL POWER ON DECISION MAKING

The measure of power we used in studying this university was an analysis of the responses of the department heads we interviewed. While such perceptions of power might be of interest in their own right, they contribute little to our understanding of how the distribution of power might serve to align an organization with its critical realities. For this we must look to how power actually influences the decisions and policies of organizations.

While it is perhaps not absolutely valid, we can generally gauge the relative importance of a department of an organization by the size of the budget allocated to it relative to other departments. Clearly it is of importance to the administrators of those departments whether they are squeezed in a budget crunch or are given more funds to strike out after new opportunities. And it should also be clear that when those decisions are made and one department can go ahead and try new approaches while another must cut back on the old, then the deployment of the resources of the organization in meeting its problems is most directly affected.

Thus our study of the university led us to ask the following question: Does power lead to influence in the organization? To answer this question, we found it useful first to ask another one, namely: Why should department heads try to influence organization decisions to favor their own departments to the exclusion of other departments? While this second question may seem a bit naive to anyone who has witnessed the political realities of organizations, we posed it in a context of research on organizations that sees power as an illegitimate threat to the neater rational authority of modern bureaucracies. In this context, decisions are not believed to be made because of the dirty business of politics but because of the overall goals and purposes of the organization. In a university, one reasonable basis for decision making is the teaching workload of departments and the demands that follow from that workload. We would expect, therefore, that departments with heavy student demands for courses would be able to obtain funds for teaching. Another reasonable basis for decision making is quality. We would expect, for that reason, that departments with esteemed reputations would be able to obtain funds both because their quality suggests they might use such funds effectively and because such funds would allow them to maintain their quality. A rational model of bureaucracy intimates, then, that the organizational decisions taken would favor those who perform the stated purposes of the organization—teaching undergraduates and training professional and scientific talent—well.

The problem with rational models of decision making, however, is that what is rational to one person may strike another as irrational. For most departments, resources are a question of survival. While teaching undergraduates may seem to be a major goal for some members of the university, developing knowledge may seem so to others; and to still others, advising governments and other institutions about policies may seem to be the crucial business. Everyone has his own idea of the proper priorities in a just world. Thus goals rather than being clearly defined and universally agreed upon are blurred and contested throughout the organization. If such is the case, then the decisions taken on behalf of the organization as a whole are likely to reflect the goals of those who prevail in political contests, namely, those with power in the organization.

Will organizational decisions always reflect the distribution of power in the organization? Probably not. Using power for influence requires a certain expenditure of effort, time, and resources. Prudent and judicious persons are not likely to use their power needlessly or wastefully. And it is likely that power will be used to influence organizational de-

cisions primarily under circumstances that both require and favor its use. We have examined three conditions that are likely to effect the use of power in organizations: scarcity, criticality, and uncertainty. The first suggests that subunits will try to exert influence when the resources of the organization are scarce. If there is an abundance of resources, then a particular department or a particular individual has little need to attempt influence. With little effort, he can get all he wants anyway.

The second condition, criticality, suggests that a subunit will attempt to influence decisions to obtain resources that are critical to its own survival and activities. Criticality implies that one would not waste effort, or risk being labeled obstinate, by fighting over trivial decisions affecting one's operations.

An office manager would probably balk less about a threatened cutback in copying machine usage than about a reduction in typing staff. An advertising department head would probably worry less about losing his lettering artist than his illustrator. Criticality is difficult to define because what is critical depends on people's beliefs about what is critical. Such beliefs may or may not be based on experience and knowledge and may or may not be agreed upon by all. Scarcity, for instance, may itself affect conceptions of criticality. When slack resources drop off, cutbacks have to be made—those "hard decisions," as congressmen and resplendent administrators like to call them. Managers then find themselves scrapping projects they once held dear.

The third condition that we believe affects the use of power is uncertainty: When individuals do not agree about what the organization should do or how to do it, power and other social processes will affect decisions. The reason for this is simply that, if there are no clear-cut criteria available for resolving conflict of interest, then the only means for resolution is some form of social process, including power, status, social ties, or some arbitrary process like flipping a coin or drawing straws. Under conditions of uncertainty, the powerful manager can argue his case on any grounds and usually win it. Since there is no real consensus, other contestants are not likely to develop counterarguments or amass sufficient opposition. Moreover, because of his power and their need for access to the resources he controls, they are more likely to defer to his arguments.

Although the evidence is slight, we have found that power will influence the allocations of scarce and critical resources. In the analysis of power in the university, for instance, one of the most critical resources needed by departments is the general budget. First granted by the state legislature, the general budget is later allocated to individual departments by the university administration in response to requests from the department heads. Our analysis of the factors that contribute to a department getting more or less of this budget indicated that subunit power was the major predictor, overriding such factors as student demand for courses, national reputations of departments, or even the size of a department's faculty. Moreover, other research has shown that when the general budget has been cut back or held below previous uninflated levels, leading to monies becoming more scarce, budget allocations mirror departmental powers even more closely.

Student enrollment and faculty size, of course, do themselves relate to budget allocations, as we would expect since they determine a department's need for resources, or at least offer visible testimony of needs. But departments are not always able to get what they need by the mere fact of needing them. In one analysis it was found that high-power departments were able to obtain budget without regard to their teaching loads and, in some cases, actually in inverse relation to their teaching loads. In contrast, low-power departments could get increases in budget only when they could justify the increases by a recent growth in teaching load, and then only when it was far in excess of norms for other departments.

General budget is only one form of resource that is allocated to departments. There are others such as special grants for student fellowships or faculty research. These are critical to departments because they affect the ability to attract other resources, such as outstanding faculty or students. We examined how power influenced the allocations of four re-

sources department heads had described as critical and scarce.

When the four resources were arrayed from the most to the least critical and scarce, we found that departmental power best predicated the allocations of the most critical and scarce resources. In other words, the analysis of how power influences organizational allocations leads to this conclusion: Those subunits most likely to survive in times of strife are those that are more critical to the organization. Their importance to the organization gives them power to influence resource allocations that enhance their own survival.

HOW EXTERNAL ENVIRONMENT IMPACTS EXECUTIVE SELECTION

Power not only influences the survival of key groups in an organization, it also influences the selection of individuals to key leadership positions, and by such a process further aligns the organization with its environmental context.

We can illustrate this with a recent study of the selection and tenure of chief administrators in 57 hospitals in Illinois. We assumed that since the critical problems facing the organization would enhance the power of certain groups at the expense of others, then the leaders to emerge should be those most relevant to the context of the hospitals. To assess this we asked each chief administrator about his professional background and how long he had been in office. The replies were then related to the hospitals' funding, ownership, and competitive conditions for patients and staff.

One aspect of a hospital's context is the source of its budget. Some hospitals, for instance, are run much like other businesses. They sell bed space, patient care, and treatment services. They charge fees sufficient both to cover their costs and to provide capital for expansion. The main source of both their operating and capital funds is patient billings. Increasingly, patient billings are paid for, not by patients, but by private insurance companies. Insurers like Blue Cross dominate and represent a potent interest group outside a hospital's control but critical to its income. The insurance companies, in order to limit their own costs, attempt to hold down the fees allowable to hospitals, which they do effectively from their positions on state rate boards. The squeeze on hospitals that results from fees increasing slowly while costs climb rapidly more and more demands the talents of cost accountants or people trained in the technical expertise of hospital administration.

By contrast, other hospitals operate more like social service institutions, either as government healthcare units (Bellevue Hospital in New York City and Cook County Hospital in Chicago, for example) or as charitable institutions. These hospitals obtain a large proportion of their operating and capital funds, not from privately insured patients, but from government subsidies or private donations. Such institutions rather than requiring the talents of a technically efficient administrator are likely to require the savvy of someone who is well integrated into the social and political power structure of the community.

Not surprisingly, the characteristics of administrators predictably reflect the funding context of the hospitals with which they are associated. Those hospitals with larger proportions of their budget obtained from private insurance companies were most likely to have administrators with backgrounds in accounting and least likely to have administrators whose professions were business or medicine. In contrast, those hospitals with larger proportions of their budget derived from private donations and local governments were most likely to have administrators with business or professional backgrounds and least likely to have accountants. The same held for formal training in hospital management. Professional hospital administrators could easily be found in hospitals drawing their incomes from private insurance and rarely in hospitals dependent on donations or legislative appropriations.

As with the selection of administrators, the context of organizations has also been found to affect the removal of executives. The environment, as a source of organizational problems, can make it more or less difficult for executives to demonstrate their value to the organization. In the hospitals we studied, long-term administrators came from hospitals with few problems. They enjoyed amicable and stable relations with their local business and social communities and suffered little competition for funding and staff. The small city hospital director who attended civic and Elks meetings while running the only hospital within a 100-mile radius, for example, had little difficulty holding on to his job. Turnover was highest in hospitals with the most problems, a phenomenon similar to that observed in a study of industrial organizations in which turnover was highest among executives in industries with competitive environments and unstable market conditions. The interesting thing is that instability characterized the industries rather than the individual firms in them. The troublesome conditions in the individual firms were attributed, or rather misattributed, to the executives themselves.

It takes more than problems, however, to terminate a manager's leadership. The problems themselves must be relevant and critical. This is clear from the way in which an administrator's tenure is affected by the status of the hospital's operating budget. Naively we might assume that all administrators would need to show a surplus. Not necessarily so. Again, we must distinguish between those hospitals that depend on private donations for funds and those that do not. Whether an endowed budget shows a surplus or deficit is less important than the hospital's relations with benefactors. On the other hand, with a budget dependent on patient billing, a surplus is almost essential; monies for new equipment or expansion must be drawn from it, and without them quality care becomes more difficult and patients scarcer. An administrator's tenure reflected just these considerations. For those hospitals dependent upon private donations, the length of an administrator's term depended not at all on the status of the operating budget but was fairly predictable from the hospital's relations with the business community. On the other hand, in hospitals dependent on the operating budget for capital financing, the greater the deficit the shorter was the tenure of the hospital's principal administrators.

CHANGING CONTINGENCIES AND ERODING POWER BASES

The critical contingencies facing the organization may change. When they do, it is reasonable to expect that the power of individuals and subgroups will change in turn. At times the shift can be swift and shattering, as it was recently for powerholders in New York City. A few years ago it was believed that David Rockefeller was one of the ten most powerful people in the city, as tallied by *New York* magazine, which annually sniffs out power for the delectation of its readers. But that was before it was revealed that the city was in financial trouble, before Rockefeller's Chase Manhattan Bank lost some of its own financial luster, and before brother Nelson lost some of his political influence in Washington. Obviously David Rockefeller was no longer as well positioned to help bail the city out. Another loser was an attorney with considerable personal connections to the political and religious leaders of the city. His talents were no longer in much demand. The persons with more influence were the bankers and union pension fund executors who fed money to the city; community leaders who represent blacks and Spanish-Americans, in contrast, witnessed the erosion of their power bases.

One implication of the idea that power shifts with changes in organizational environments is that the dominant coalition will tend to be that group that is most appropriate for the organization's environment, as also will the leaders of an organization. One can observe this historically in the top executives of industrial firms in the United States. Up until the early 1950s, many top corporations were headed by former production line managers or engineers who gained prominence because of their abilities to cope with the problems of production. Their success, however, only spelled their demise. As production became routinized and mechanized, the problem of most firms became one of selling all those goods they so efficiently produced. Marketing executives were more frequently found in corporate boardrooms. Success outdid itself again, for keeping markets and production steady

and stable requires the kind of control that can only come from acquiring competitors and suppliers or the invention of more and more appealing products—ventures that typically require enormous amounts of capital. During the 1960s, financial executives assumed the seats of power. And they, too, will give way to others. Edging over the horizon are legal experts, as regulation and antitrust suits are becoming more and more frequent in the 1970s, suits that had their beginnings in the success of the expansion generated by prior executives. The more distant future, which is likely to be dominated by multinational corporations, may see former secretaries of state and their minions increasingly serving as corporate figureheads.

THE NONADAPTIVE CONSEQUENCES OF ADAPTATION

From what we have said thus far about power aligning the organization with its own realities, an intelligent person might react with a resounding ho-hum, for it all seems to obvious: Those with the ability to get the job done are given the job to do.

However, there are two aspects of power that make it more useful for understanding organization and their effectiveness. First, the "job" to be done has a way of expanding itself until it becomes less and less clear what the job is. Napoleon began by doing a job for France in the war with Austria and ended up Emperor, convincing many that only he could keep the peace. Hitler began by promising an end to Germany's troubling postwar depression and ended up convincing more people than is comfortable to remember that he was destined to be the savior of the world. In short, power is a capacity for influence that extends far beyond the original bases that created it. Second, power tends to take on institutionalized forms that enable it to endure well beyond its usefulness to an organization.

There is an important contradiction in what we have observed about organizational power. On the one hand we have said that power derives from the contingencies facing an organization and that when those contingencies change so do the bases for power. On the other hand we have asserted that subunits will tend to use their power to influence organizational decisions in their own favor, particularly when their own survival is threatened by the scarcity of critical resources. The first statement implies that an organization will tend to be aligned with its environment since power will tend to bring to key positions those with capabilities relevant to the context. The second implies that those in power will not give up their positions so easily; they will pursue policies that guarantee their continued domination. In short, change and stability operate through the same mechanism, and as a result, the organization will never be completely in phase with its environment or its needs.

The study of hospital administrators illustrates how leadership can be out of phase with reality. We argued that privately funded hospitals needed trained technical administrators more so than did hospitals funded by donations. The need as we perceived it was matched in most hospitals, but by no means in all. Some organizations did not conform with our predictions. These deviations imply that some administrators were able to maintain their positions independent of their suitability for those positions. By dividing administrators into those with long and short terms of office, one finds that the characteristics of longer-termed administrators were virtually unrelated to the hospital's content. The shorter-termed chiefs on the other hand had characteristics more appropriate for the hospital's problems. For a hospital to have a recently appointed head implies that the previous administrator had been unable to endure by institutionalizing himself.

One obvious feature of hospitals that allowed some administrators to enjoy a long tenure was a hospital's ownership. Administrators were less entrenched when their hospitals were affiliated with and depended upon larger organizations, such as governments or churches. Private hospitals offered more secure positions for administrators. Like private corporations, they tend to have more diffused ownership, leaving the administrator unopposed as he institutionalizes his reign. Thus he endures,

sometimes at the expense of the performance of the organization. Other research has demonstrated that corporations with diffuse ownership have poorer earnings than those in which the control of the manager is checked by a dominant shareholder. Firms that overload their boardrooms with more insiders than are appropriate for their context have also been found to be less profitable.

A word of caution is required about our judgment of "appropriateness." When we argue some capabilities are more appropriate for one context than another, we do so from the perspective of an outsider and on the basis of reasonable assumptions as to the problems the organization will face and the capabilities they will need. The fact that we have been able to predict the distribution of influence and the characteristics of leaders suggests that our reasoning is not incorrect. However, we do not think that all organizations follow the same pattern. The fact that we have not been able to predict outcomes with 100 percent accuracy indicates they do not.

MISTAKING CRITICAL CONTINGENCIES

One thing that allows subunits to retain their power is their ability to name their functions as critical to the organization when they may not be. Consider again our discussion of power in the university. One might wonder why the most critical tasks were defined as graduate education and scholarly research, the effect of which was to lend power to those who brought in grants and contracts. Why not something else? The reason is that the more powerful departments argued for those criteria and won their case, partly because they were more powerful.

In another analysis of this university, we found that all departments advocate self-serving criteria for budget allocation. Thus a department with large undergraduate enrollments argued that enrollments should determine budget allocations, a department with a strong national reputation saw prestige as the most reasonable basis for distributing funds, and so on. We further found that advocating such self-serving criteria actually benefited a department's budget allotments but, also, it paid off more for departments that were already powerful.

Organizational needs are consistent with a current distribution of power also because of a human tendency to categorize problems in familiar ways. An accountant sees problems with organizational performances as cost accountancy problems or inventory flow problems. A sales manager sees them as problems with markets, promotional strategies, or just unaggressive salespeople. But what is the truth? Since it does not automatically announce itself, it is likely that those with prior credibility, or those with power, will be favored as the enlightened. This bias, while not intentionally self-serving, further concentrates power among those who already possess it, independent of changes in the organization's content.

INSTITUTIONALIZING POWER

A third reason for expecting organizational contingencies to be defined in familiar ways is that the current holders of power can structure the organization in ways that institutionalize themselves. By institutionalization we mean the establishment of relatively permanent structures and policies that favor the influence of a particular subunit. While in power, dominant coalition has the ability to institute constitutions, rules, procedures, and information systems that limit the potential power of others while continuing their own.

The key to institutionalizing power always is to create a device that legitimates one's own authority and diminishes the legitimacy of others. When the "Divine Right of Kings" was envisioned centuries ago it was to provide an unquestionable foundation for the supremacy of royal authority. There is generally a need to root the exercise of authority in some higher power. Modern leaders are no less affected by this need. Richard Nixon, with the aid of John Dean, reified the concept of executive privilege, which meant in effect that what the President wished not to be discussed need not be discussed.

In its simpler form, institutionalization is achieved by designating positions or roles for organizational activities. The creation of a new post legitimizes a function and forces organization members to orient to it. By designating how this new post relates to older, more established posts, moreover, one can structure an organization to enhance the importance of the function in the organization. Equally, one can diminish the importance of traditional functions. This is what happened in the end with the insurance company we mentioned that was having trouble with its coding department. As the situation unfolded, the claims director continued to feel dissatisfied about the dependency of his functions on the coding manager. Thus he instituted a reorganization that resulted in two coding departments. In so doing, of course, he placed activities that affected his department under his direct control, presumably to make the operation more effective. Similarly, consumer-product firms enhance the power of marketing by setting up a coordinating role to interface production and marketing functions and then appoint a marketing manager to fill the role.

The structures created by dominant powers sooner or later become fixed and unquestioned features of the organization. Eventually, this can be devastating: It is said that the battle of Jena in 1806 was lost by Frederick the Great, who died in 1786. Though the great Prussian leader had no direct hand in the disaster, his imprint on the army was so thorough, so embedded in its skeletal underpinnings, that the organization was inappropriate for others to lead in different times.

Another important source of institutionalized power lies in the ability to structure information systems. Setting up committees to investigate particular organizational issues and having them report only to particular individuals or groups facilitates their awareness of problems by members of those groups while limiting the awareness of problems by the members of other groups. Obviously, those who have information are in a better position to interpret the problems of an organization, regardless of how realistically they may, in fact, do so.

Still another way to institutionalize power is to distribute rewards and resources. The dominant group may quiet competing interest groups with small favors and rewards. The credit for this artful form of co-optation belongs to Louis XIV. To avoid usurpation of his power by the nobles of France and the Fronde that had so troubled his father's reign, he built the palace at Versailles to occupy them with hunting and gossip. Awed, the courtiers basked in the reflected glories of the "Sun King" and the overwhelming setting he had created for his court.

At this point, we have not systematically studied the institutionalization of power. But we suspect it is an important condition that mediates between the environment of the organization and the capabilities of the organization for dealing with that environment. The more institutionalized power is within an organization, the more likely an organization will be out of phase with the realities it faces. President Richard Nixon's structuring of his White House is one of the better documented illustrations. If we go back to newspaper and magazine descriptions of how he organized his office from the beginning in 1968, most of what occurred subsequently follows almost as an afterthought. Decisions flowed through virtually only the small White House staff; rewards, small presidential favors of recognition, and perquisites were distributed by this staff to the loyal; and information from the outside world—the press, Congress, the people on the streets—was filtered by the staff and passed along only if initiated "bh." Thus it was not surprising that when Nixon met war protestors in the early dawn, the only thing he could think to talk about was the latest football game, so insulated had he become from their grief and anger.

One of the more interesting implications of institutionalized power is that executive turnover among the executives who have structured the organization is likely to be a rare event that occurs only under the most pressing crisis. If a dominant coalition is able to structure the organization and interpret the meaning of ambiguous events like declining sales and profits or lawsuits, then the "real" problems to emerge will easily be incorporated into traditional molds of thinking and acting. If opposition is designed out of the organization, the interpretations will go unquestioned. Conditions will remain stable until a crisis develops, so overwhelming and visible that even the most adroit rhetorician would be silenced.

IMPLICATIONS FOR THE MANAGEMENT OF POWER IN ORGANIZATIONS

While we could derive numerous implications from this discussion of power, our selection would have to depend largely on whether one wanted to increase one's power, decrease the power of others, or merely maintain one's position. More important, the real implications depend on the particulars of an organizational situation. To understand power in an organization one must begin by looking outside it—into the environment—for those groups that mediate the organization's outcomes but are not themselves within its control.

Instead of ending with homilies, we will end with a reversal of where we began. Power, rather than being the dirty business it is often made out to be, is probably one of the few mechanisms for reality testing in organizations. And the cleaner forms of power, the institutional forms, rather than having the virtues they are often credited with, can lead the organization to become out of touch. The real trick to managing power in organizations is to ensure somehow that leaders cannot be unaware of the realities of their environments and cannot avoid changing to deal with those realities. That, however, would be like designing the "self-liquidating organization," an unlikely event since anyone capable of designing such an instrument would be obviously in control of the liquidations.

Management would do well to devote more attention to determining the critical contingencies of their environments. For if you conclude, as we do, that the environment sets most of the structure influencing organizational outcomes and problems, and that power derives from the organization's activities that deal with those contingencies, then it is the environment that needs managing, not power. The first step is to construct an accurate model of the environment, a process that is quite difficult for most organizations. We have recently started a project to aid administrators in systematically understanding their environments. From this, experience, we have learned that the most critical blockage to perceiving an organization's reality accurately is a failure to incorporate those with the relevant expertise into the process. Most organizations have the requisite experts on hand but they are positioned so that they can be comfortably ignored.

One conclusion you can, and probably should, derive from our discussion is that power—because of the way it develops and the way it is used—will always result in the organization suboptimizing its performance. However, to this grim absolute, we add a comforting caveat: If any criteria other than power were the basis for determining an organization's decisions, the results would be even worse.

SELECTED BIBLIOGRAPHY

The literature on power is at once both voluminous and frequently empty of content. Some is philosophical musing about the concept of power, while other writing contains popularized palliatives for acquiring and exercising influence. Machiavelli's *The Prince*, if read carefully, remains the single best perspective treatment of power and its use. Most social scientists have approached power descriptively, attempting to understand how it is acquired, how it is used, and what its effects are. Mayer Zald's edited collection *Power in Organizations* (Vanderbilt University Press, 1970) is one of the more useful sets of thoughts about power from a sociological perspective, while James Tedeschi's edited book, *The Social Influence Processes* (Aldine-Atherton, 1972) represents the social psychological approach to understanding power and influence. The strategic contingencies's approach, with its emphasis on the importance of uncertainty for understanding power in organizations, is described by David Hickson and his colleagues in "A Strategic Contingencies Theory of Intraorganizational Power" (*Administrative Science Quarterly*, December 1971, pp. 216–29).

Unfortunately, while many have written about power theoretically, there have been few empirical examinations of power and its use. Most of the work has taken the form of case studies. Michel Crozier's *The Bureaucratic Phenomenon* (University of Chicago Press, 1964) is important because it describes a group's source of power as control over critical activities and illustrates how power is not strictly derived from hierarchical position. J. Victor Baldridge's *Power and Conflict in the University* (John Wiley & Sons, 1971) and Andrew Pettigrew's study of computer purchase decisions in one English firm (*Politics of Organizational Decision Making*, Tavistock, 1973) both present insights into the acquisition and use of power in specific instances. Our work has been more empirical and comparative, testing more explicitly the ideas presented in this article. The study of university decision making is reported in articles in the June 1974, pp. 135–51, and December 1974, pp. 453–73, issues of the *Administrative Science Quarterly*, the insurance firm study in J. G. Hunt and L. L. Larson's collection, *Leadership Frontiers* (Kent State University Press, 1975), and the study of hospital administrator succession appeared in 1977 in the *Academy of Management Journal*.

28. INFLUENCE WITHOUT AUTHORITY: THE USE OF ALLIANCES, RECIPROCITY, AND EXCHANGE TO ACCOMPLISH WORK

Allan R. Cohen and David L. Bradford

Bill Heatton is the director of research at a $250 million division of a large West Coast company. The division manufactures exotic telecommunications components and has many technical advancements to its credit. During the past several years, however, the division's performance has been spotty at best; multimillion dollar losses have been experienced in some years despite many efforts to make the division more profitable. Several large contracts have resulted in major financial losses, and in each instance the various parts of the division blamed the others for the problems. Listen to Bill's frustration as he talks about his efforts to influence Ted, a colleague who is marketing director, and Roland, the program manager who reports to Ted.

Another program is about to come through. Roland is a nice guy, but he knows nothing and never will. He was responsible for our last big loss, and now he's in charge of this one. I've tried to convince Ted, his boss, to get Roland off the program, but I get nowhere. Although Ted doesn't argue that Roland is capable, he doesn't act to find someone else. Instead, he comes to me with worries about my area.

I decided to respond by changing my staffing plan, assigning to Roland's program the people they wanted. I had to override my staff's best judgment about who should be assigned. Yet I'm not getting needed progress reports from Roland, and he's never available for planning. I get little argument from him, but there's no action to correct the problem. That's bad because I'm responding but not getting any response.

There's no way to resolve this. If they disagree, that's it. I could go to a tit-for-tat strategy, saying that if they don't do what I want, we'll get even with them next time. But I don't know how to do that without hurting the organization, which would feel worse than getting even!

Ted, Roland's boss, is so much better than his predecessor that I hate to ask that he be removed. We could go together to our boss, the general manager, but I'm very reluctant to do that. You've failed in a matrix organization if you have to go to your boss. I have to try hard because I'd look bad if I had to throw it in his lap.

Meanwhile, I'm being forceful, but I'm afraid it's in a destructive way. I don't want to wait until the program has failed to be told it was all my fault.

Bill is clearly angry and frustrated, leading him to behave in ways that he does not feel good about. Like other managers who very much want to influence an uncooperative co-worker whom they cannot control, Bill has begun to think of the intransigent employee as the enemy. Bill's anger is narrowing his sense of what is possible; he fantasizes revenge but is too dedicated to the organization to actually harm it. He is genuinely stuck.

Organizational members who want to make things happen often find themselves in this position. Irrespective of whether they are staff or line employees, professionals or managers, they find it increasingly necessary to influence colleagues and superiors. These critical others control needed resources, possess required information, set priorities on important activities, and have to agree and cooperate if

Allan R. Cohen and David L. Bradford, "Influence Without Authority: the Use of Alliances, Reciprocity, and Exchange to Accomplish Work" from *Organizational Dynamics*, Winter 1989.

plans are to be implemented. They cannot be ordered around because they are under another area's control and can legitimately say no because they have many other valid priorities. They respond only when they choose to. Despite the clear need and appropriateness of what is being asked for (certainly as seen by the person who is making the request), compliance may not be forthcoming.

All of this places a large burden on organizational members, who are expected not only to take initiatives but also to respond intelligently to requests made of them by others. Judgment is needed to sort out the value of the many requests made of anyone who has valuable resources to contribute. As Robert Kaplan argued in his article "Trade Routes: The Manager's Network of Relationships" (*Organizational Dynamics*, Spring 1984), managers must now develop the organizational equivalent of "trade routes" to get things done. Informal networks of mutual influence are needed. In her book *The Change Masters* (Simon & Schuster, 1983) Rosabeth Moss Kanter showed that developing and implementing all kinds of innovations requires coalitions to be built to shape and support new ways of doing business.

A key current problem, then, is finding ways to develop mutual influence without the formal authority to command. A peer cannot "order" a colleague to change priorities, modify an approach, or implement a grand new idea. A staff member cannot "command" his or her supervisor to back a proposal, fight top management for greater resources, or allow more autonomy. Even Bill Heatton, in dealing with Roland (who was a level below him in the hierarchy but in another department), could not dictate that Roland provide the progress reports that Bill so desperately wanted.

EXCHANGE AND THE LAW OF RECIPROCITY

The way influence is acquired without formal authority is through the "law of reciprocity"—the almost universal belief that people should be paid back for what they do, that one good (or bad) deed deserves another. This belief is held by people in primitive and not-so-primitive societies all around the world, and it serves as the grease that allows the organizational wheels to turn smoothly. Because people expect that their actions will be paid back in one form or another, influence is possible.

In the case of Bill Heatton, his inability to get what he wanted from Roland and Ted stemmed from his failure to understand fully how reciprocity works in organizations. He therefore was unable to set up mutually beneficial exchanges. Bill believed that he had gone out of his way to help the marketing department by changing his staffing patterns, and he expected Roland to reciprocate by providing regular progress reports. When Roland failed to provide the reports, Bill believed that Ted was obligated to remove Roland from the project. When Ted did not respond, Bill became angry and wanted to retaliate. Thus Bill recognized the appropriateness of exchange in making organizations work. However, he did not understand how exchange operates.

Before exploring in detail how exchange can work in dealing with colleagues and superiors, it is important to recognize that reciprocity is the basic principle behind all organizational transactions. For example, the basic employment contract is an exchange ("an honest day's work for an honest day's pay"). Even work that is above and beyond what is formally required involves exchange. The person who helps out may not necessarily get (or expect) immediate payment for the extra effort requested, but some eventual compensation is expected.

Think of the likely irritation an employee would feel if his or her boss asked him or her to work through several weekends, never so much as said thanks, and then claimed credit for the extra work. The employee might not say anything the first time this happened, expecting or hoping that the boss would make it up somehow. However, if the effort were never acknowledged in any way, the employee, like most people, would feel that something important had been violated.

The expectation of reciprocal exchanges occurs between an employee and his or her supervisor, among peers, with higher-level managers in other parts of the organization, or all of the above. The exchange can be of tangible goods, such as a budget increase, new equipment, or more personnel; of tangible services, such as a faster response time, more information, or public support; or of sentiments, such as gratitude, admiration, or praise. Whatever form exchanges take, unless they are roughly equivalent over time, hard feelings will result.

Exchanges enable people to handle the give-and-take of working together without strong feelings of injustice arising. They are especially important during periods of rapid change because the number of requests that go far beyond the routine tends to escalate. In those situations, exchanges become less predictable, more free-floating and spontaneous. Nevertheless, people still expect that somehow or other, sooner or later, they will be (roughly) equally compensated for the acts they do above and beyond those that are covered by the formal exchange agreements in their job. Consequently, some kind of "currency" equivalent needs to be worked out, implicitly if not explicitly, to keep the parties in the exchange feeling fairly treated.

CURRENCIES: THE SOURCE OF INFLUENCE

If the basis of organizational influence depends on mutually satisfactory exchanges, then people are influential only insofar as they can offer something that others need. Thus power comes from the ability to meet others' needs.

A useful way to think of how the process of exchange actually works in organizations is to use the metaphor of "currencies." This metaphor provides a powerful way to conceptualize what is important to the influencer and the person to be influenced. Just as many types of currencies are traded in the world financial market, many types are "traded" in organizational life. Too often people think only of money or promotion and status. Those "curren-

cies," however, usually are available only to a manager in dealing with his or her employees. Peers who want to influence colleagues or employees who want to influence their supervisors often feel helpless. They need to recognize that many types of payments exist, broadening the range of what can be exchanged.

Some major currencies that are commonly valued and traded in organizations are listed in Table 28.1. Although not exhaustive, the list makes evident that a person does not have to be at the top of an organization or have hands on the formal levers of power to command multiple resources that other may value.

Part of the usefulness of currencies comes from their flexibility. For example, there are many ways to express gratitude and to give assistance. A manager who most values the currency of appreciation could be paid through verbal thanks, praise, a public statement at a meeting, informal comments to his peers, and/or a note to her boss. However, the same note of thanks seen by one person as a sign of appreciation may be seen by another person as an attempt to brownnose or by a third person as a cheap way to try to repay extensive favors and service. Thus currencies have value not in some abstract sense but as defined by the receiver.

Although we have stressed the interactive nature of exchange, "payments" do not always have to be made by the other person. They can be self-generated to fit beliefs about being virtuous, benevolent, or committed to the organization's welfare. Someone may respond to another person's request because it reinforces cherished values, a sense of identity, or feelings of self-worth. The exchange is interpersonally stimulated because the one who wants influence has set up conditions that allow this kind of self-payment to occur by asking for cooperation to accomplish organizational goals. However, the person who responds because "it is the right thing to do" and who feels good about being the "kind of person who does not act out of narrow self-interest" is printing currency (virtue) that is self-satisfying.

Of course, the five categories of currencies listed in Table 28.1 are not mutually exclusive. When the demand from the other person is high, people are likely to pay in several currencies across several categories. They may, for example stress the organizational value of their request, promise to return the favor at a later time, imply that it will increase the other's prestige in the organization, and express their appreciation.

ESTABLISHING EXCHANGE RATES

What does it take to pay back in a currency that the other party in an exchange will perceive as equiva-

TABLE 28.1
Commonly Traded Organizational Currencies

Inspiration-Related Currencies	
Vision	Being involved in a task that has larger significance for the unit, organization, customers, or society.
Excellence	Having a chance to do important things really well.
Moral/Ethical Correctness	Doing what is "right" by a higher standard than efficiency.
Task-Related Currencies	
Resources	Lending or giving money, budget increases, personnel, space, and so forth.
Assistance	Helping with existing projects or undertaking unwanted tasks.
Cooperation	Giving task support, providing quicker response time, approving a project, or aiding implementation.
Information	Providing organizational as well as technical knowledge.
Position-Related Currencies	
Advancement	Giving a task or assignment that can aid in promotion.
Recognition	Acknowledging effort, accomplishment, or abilities.
Visibility	Providing chance to be known by higher-ups or significant others in the organization.
Reputation	Enhancing the way a person is seen.
Importance/Insiderness	Offering a sense of importance, of "belonging."
Network/Contacts	Providing opportunities for linking with others.
Relationship-Related Currencies	
Acceptance/Inclusion	Providing closeness and friendship.
Personal Support	Giving personal and emotional backing.
Understanding	Listening to others' concerns and issues.
Personal-Related Currencies	
Self-Concept	Affirming one's values, self-esteem, and identity.
Challenge/Learning	Sharing tasks that increase skills and abilities.
Ownership/Involvement	Letting others have ownership and influence.
Gratitude	Expressing appreciation or indebtedness.

lent? In impersonal markets, because everything is translated into a common monetary currency, it generally is easy to say what a fair payment is. Does a ton of steel equal a case of golfclubs? By translating both into dollar equivalents, a satisfactory deal can be worked out.

In interpersonal exchanges, however, the process becomes a bit more complicated. Just how does someone repay another person's willingness to help finish a report? Is a simple thank-you enough? Does it also require the recipient to say something nice about the helper to his or her boss? Whose standard of fairness should be used? What if one person's idea of fair repayment is very different from the other's?

Because of the natural differences in the way two parties can interpret the same activity, establishing exchanges that both parties will perceive as equitable can be problematic. Thus it is critical to understand what is important to the person to be influenced. Without a clear understanding of what that person experiences and values, it will be extremely difficult for anyone to thread a path through the minefield of creating mutually satisfactory exchanges.

Fortunately, the calibration of equivalent exchanges in the interpersonal and organizational worlds is facilitated by the fact that approximations will do in most cases. Occasionally, organizational members know exactly what they want in return for favors or help, but more often they will settle for very rough equivalents (providing that there is reasonable goodwill).

THE PROCESS OF EXCHANGE

To make the exchange process effective, the influencer needs to (1) think about the person to be influenced as a potential ally, not an adversary; (2) know the world of the potential ally, including the pressures as well as the person's needs and goals; (3) be aware of key goals and available resources that may be valued by the potential ally; and (4) understand the exchange transaction itself so that win-win outcomes are achieved. Each of these factors is discussed below.

Potential Ally, Not Adversary

A key to influence is thinking of the other person as a potential ally. Just as many contemporary organizations have discovered the importance of creating strategic alliances with suppliers and customers, employees who want influence within the organization need to create internal allies. Even though each party in an alliance continues to have freedom to pursue its own interests, the goal is to find areas of mutual benefit and develop trusting, sustainable relationships. Similarly, each person whose cooperation is needed inside the organization is a potential ally. Each still has self-interests to pursue, but those self-interests do not preclude searching for and building areas of mutual benefit.

Seeing other organizational members as potential allies decreases the chance that adversarial relationships will develop—an all-too-frequent result (as in the case of Bill Heatton) when the eager influencer does not quickly get the assistance or cooperation needed. Assuming that even a difficult person is a potential ally makes it easier to understand that person's world and thereby discover what that person values and needs.

The Potential Ally's World

We have stressed the importance of knowing the world of the potential ally. Without awareness of what the ally needs (what currencies are valued), attempts to influence that person can only be haphazard. Although this conclusion may seem self-evident, it is remarkable how often people attempt to influence without adequate information about what is important to the potential ally. Instead, they are driven by their own definition of "what should be" and "what is right" when they should be seeing the world from the other person's perspective.

For example, Bill Heatton never thought about the costs to Ted of removing Roland from the project. Did Ted believe he could coach Roland to perform better on this project? Did Ted even agree that Roland had done a poor job on the previous project, or did Ted think Roland had been hampered by other departments' shortcomings? Bill just did not know.

Several factors can keep the influencer from seeing the potential ally clearly. As with Bill Heatton, the frustration of meeting resistance from a potential ally can get in the way of really understanding the other person's world. The desire to influence is so strong that only the need for cooperation is visible to the influencer. As a result of not being understood, the potential ally digs in, making the influencer repeat an inappropriate strategy or back off in frustration.

When a potential ally's behavior is not understandable ("Why won't Roland send the needed progress report?"), the influencer tends to stereotype that person. If early attempts to influence do not work, the influencer is tempted to write the person off as negative, stubborn, selfish, or "just another bean counter/whiz kid/sales-type" or whatever pejorative label is used in that organizational culture to dismiss those organizational members who are different.

Although some stereotypes may have a grain of truth, they generally conceal more than they reveal. The actuary who understands that judgment, not just numbers, is needed to make decisions disappears as an individual when the stereotype of "impersonal, detached number machine" is the filter through which he or she is seen. Once the stereotype is applied, the frustrated influencer is no longer likely to see what currencies that particular potential ally actually values.

Sometimes, the lack of clear understanding about a potential ally stems from the influencer's failure to appreciate the organizational forces acting on the potential ally. To a great extent, a person's behavior is a result of the situation in which that person works (and not just his or her personality). Potential allies are embedded in an organizational culture that shapes their interests and responses. For example, one of the key determinants of anyone's behavior is likely to be the way the person's performance is measured and rewarded. In many instances, what is mistaken for personal orneriness is merely the result of the person's doing something that will be seen as good performance in his or her function.

The salesperson who is furious because the plant manager resists changing priorities for a rush order may not realize that part of the plant manager's bonus depends on holding unit costs down—a task made easier with long production runs. The plant manager's resistance does not necessarily reflect his or her inability to be flexible or lack of concern about pleasing customers or about the company's overall success.

Other organizational forces that can affect the potential ally's behavior include the daily time demands on that person's position; the amount of contact the person has with customers, suppliers, and other outsiders, the organization's information flow (or lack of it); the style of the potential ally's boss; the belief and assumptions held by that person's co-workers; and so forth. Although some of these factors cannot be changed by the influencer, understanding them can be useful in figuring out how to frame and time requests. It also helps the influencer resist the temptation to stereotype the noncooperator.

Self-Awareness of the Influencer

Unfortunately, people desiring influence are not always aware of precisely what they want. Often their requests contain a cluster of needs (a certain product, arranged in a certain way, delivered at a specified time). They fail to think through which aspects are more important and which can be jettisoned if necessary. Did Bill Heatton want Roland removed, or did he want the project effectively managed? Did he want overt concessions from Ted, or did he want better progress reports?

Further, there is a tendency to confuse and intermingle the desired end goal with the means of accomplishing it, leading to too many battles over the wrong things. In *The Change Masters*, Kanter reported that successful influencers in organizations were those who never lost sight of the ultimate objective but were willing to be flexible about means.

Sometimes influencers underestimate the range of currencies available for use. They may assume, for example, that just because they are low in the organization they have nothing that others want.

Employees who want to influence their boss are especially likely not to realize all of the supervisor's needs that they can fulfill. They become so caught up with their feelings of powerlessness that they fail to see the many ways they can generate valuable currencies.

In other instances, influencers fail to be aware of their preferred style of interaction and its fit with the potential ally's preferred style. Everyone has a way of relating to others to get work done. However, like the fish who is unaware of the water, many people are oblivious of their own style of interaction or see it as the only way to be. Yet interaction style can cause problems with potential allies who are different.

For example, does the influencer tend to socialize first and work later? If so, that style of interaction will distress a potential ally who likes to dig right in to solve the problem at hand and only afterward chat about sports, family, or office politics. Does the potential ally want to be approached with answers, not problems? If so, a tendency to start influence attempts with open-ended, exploratory problem solving can lead to rejection despite good intentions.

Nature of the Exchange Transaction

Many of the problems that occur in the actual exchange negotiation have their roots in the failure to deal adequately with the first three factors outlined above. Failure to treat other people as potential allies, to understand a potential ally's world, and to be self-aware are all factors that interfere with successful exchange. In addition, some special problems commonly arise when both parties are in the process of working out a mutually satisfactory exchange agreement.

Not Knowing How to Use Reciprocity. Using reciprocity requires stating needs clearly without "crying wolf," being aware of the needs of an ally without being manipulative, and seeking mutual gain rather than playing "winner takes all." One trap that Bill Heatton fell into was not being able to

"close on the exchange." That is, he assumed that if he acted in good faith and did his part, others would automatically reciprocate. Part of his failure was not understanding the other party's world; another part was not being able to negotiate cleanly with Ted about what each of them wanted. It is not even clear that Ted realized Bill was altering his organization as per Ted's requests, that Ted got what he wanted, or that Ted knew Bill intended an exchange of responses.

Preferring to Be Right Rather than Effective. This problem is especially endemic to professionals of all kinds. Because of their dedication to the "truth" (as their profession defines it), they stubbornly stick to their one right way when trying to line up potential allies instead of thinking about what will work given the audience and conditions. Organizational members with strong technical backgrounds often chorus the equivalent of "I'll be damned if I'm going to sell out and become a phony salesman, trying to get by on a shoe-shine and smile." The failure to accommodate to the potential ally's needs and desires often kills otherwise sound ideas.

Overusing What Has Been Successful. When people find that a certain approach is effective in many situations, they often begin to use it in places where it does not fit. By overusing the approach, they block more appropriate methods. Just as a weight lifter becomes muscle-bound from overdeveloping particular muscles at the expense of others, people who have been reasonably successful at influencing other people can diminish that ability by overusing the same technique.

For example, John Brucker, the human resources director at a medium-size company, often cultivated support for new programs by taking people out to fancy restaurants for an evening of fine food and wine. He genuinely derived pleasure from entertaining, but at the same time he created subtle obligations. One time, a new program he wanted to introduce required the agreement of William Adams, head of engineering. Adams, an old-timer, perceived Brucker's proposal as an unnecessary frill, mainly because he did not perceive the real benefits to the overall organization. Brucker responded to Adam's negative comments as he always did in such cases—by becoming more friendly and insisting that they get together for dinner soon. After several of these invitations, Adams became furious. Insulted by what he considered to be Brucker's attempts to buy him off, he fought even harder to kill the proposal. Not only did the program die, but Brucker lost all possibility of influencing Adams in the future. Adams saw Brucker's attempts at socializing as a sleazy and crude way of trying to soften him up. For his part, Brucker was totally puzzled by Adams's frostiness and assumed that he was against all progress. He never realized that Adams had a deep sense of integrity and a real commitment to the good of the organization. Thus Brucker lost his opportunity to sell a program that, ironically, Adams would have found valuable had it been implemented.

As the case above illustrates, a broad repertoire of influence approaches is needed in modern organizations. Johnny-one-notes soon fall flat.

THE ROLE OF RELATIONSHIPS

All of the preceding discussion needs to be conditioned by one important variable: the nature of the relationship between both parties. The greater the extent to which the influencer has worked with the potential ally and created trust, the easier the exchange process will be. Each party will know the other's desired currencies and situational pressures, and each will have developed a mutually productive interaction style. With trust, less energy will be spent on figuring out the intentions of the ally, and there will be less suspicion about when and how the payback will occur.

A poor relationship (based on previous interactions, on the reputation each party has in the organization, and/or on stereotypes and animosities between the functions or departments that each party represents) will impede an otherwise easy exchange. Distrust of the goodwill, veracity, or reliability of the influencer can lead to the demand for

"no credit; cash up front," which constrains the flexibility of both parties.

The nature of the interaction during the influencer process also affects the nature of the relationship between the influencer and the other party. The way that John Brucker attempted to relate to William Adams not only did not work but also irreparably damaged any future exchanges between them.

Few transactions within organizations are one-time deals. (Who knows when the other person may be needed again or even who may be working for him or her in the future?) Thus in most exchange situations two outcomes matter: success in achieving task goals and success in improving the relationship so that the next interaction will be even more productive. Too often, people who want to be influential focus only on the task and act as if there is no tomorrow. Although both task accomplishment and an improved relationship cannot always be realized at the same time, on some occasions the latter can be more important than the former. Winning the battle but losing the war is an expensive outcome.

INCONVERTIBLE CURRENCIES

We have spelled out ways organizational members operate to gain influence for achieving organizational goals. By effectively using exchange, organizational members can achieve their goals and at the same time help others achieve theirs. Exchange permits organizational members to be assertive without being antagonistic by keeping mutual benefit a central outcome.

In many cases, organizational members fail to acquire desired influence because they do not use all of their potential power. However, they sometimes fail because not all situations are amenable to even the best efforts at influencing. Not everything can be translated into compatible currencies. If there are fundamental differences in what is valued by two parties, it may not be possible to find common ground, as illustrated in the example below.

The founder and chairman of a high-technology company and the president he had hired five years previously were constantly displeased with one another. The president was committed to creating maximum shareholder value, the currency he valued most as a result of his M.B.A. training, his position, and his temperament. Accordingly, he had concluded that the company was in a perfect position to cash in by squeezing expenses to maximize profits and going public. He could see that the company's product line of exotic components was within a few years of saturating its market and would require massive, risky investment to move to sophisticated end-user products.

The president could not influence the chairman to adopt this direction, however, because the chairman valued a totally different currency, the fun of technological challenge. An independently wealthy man, the chairman had no interest in realizing the $10 million or so he would get if the company maximized profits by cutting research and selling out. He wanted a place to test his intuitive, creative research hunches, not a source of income.

Thus the president's and chairman's currencies were not convertible into one another at an acceptable exchange rate. After they explored various possibilities but failed to find common ground, they mutually agreed that the president should leave— on good terms and only after a more compatible replacement could be found. Although this example acknowledges that influence through alliance, currency conversion, and exchange is not always possible, it is hard to be certain that any situation is hopeless until the person desiring influence has fully applied all of the diagnostic and interpersonal skills we have described.

Influence is enhanced by using the model of strategic alliances to engage in mutually beneficial exchanges with potential allies. Even though it is not always possible to be successful, the chances of achieving success can be greatly increased. In a period of rapid competitive, technological, regulative, and consumer change, individuals and their organizations need all the help they can get.

SELECTED BIBLIOGRAPHY

Some of the classic work on exchange as a process of influence was done by Peter Blau. His book *The Dynamics of Bureaucracy* (University of Chicago Press, 1963) was a landmark study of how tax assessors traded gratitude for expert assistance. When exchange is added to notions about the universality of reciprocity, as outlined by Alvin Gouldner in his pioneering article "The Norm of Reciprocity: A Preliminary Statement" (*American Sociological Review*, 25, 1960), a powerful way of thinking about influence is created.

David Berlew picked up on these ideas and wrote an interesting piece addressed to people who want more influence: "What You Can Do When Persuasion Doesn't Work" (*NTL Connection*, 1986). He discussed three types of exchange that can be used by those attempting to get things done.

The case for managers needing to build alliances in order to accomplish work was made by Robert Kaplan in his article "Trade Routes: The Manager's Network of Relationships" (*Organization Dynamics*, 1984). John Kotter found in his study of successful general managers (*The General Managers*, Free Press, 1982) that they had wide networks of contacts in their organizations, which helped them find the right person(s) when trying to make things happen. Rosabeth Moss Kanter's *The Change Masters* (Simon & Schuster, 1983) is the best examination of the ways organization members go about achieving major innovations through alliances. It shows the steps that innovative members go through, including the many ways they use influence to build coalitions and overcome resistance. We have built on her work by looking with a microscope at the mechanisms behind the processes she describes.

Other researchers have explored influence processes from many angles. David Kipnis and his collaborators found that they can categorize influence styles along seven dimensions. In "Patterns of Managerial Influence: Shotgun Managers, Tacticians, and Bystanders" (*Organizational Dynamics*, 1984), they identify the problem of managers who lack organizational power (and by implication what to do about it) and therefore give up attempting to influence. John Kotter addressed ways of increasing influence in *Power in Management: How to Understand, Acquire and Use It* (AMACOM, 1979). He shows the advantages and disadvantages of different methods.

Our own book *Managing for Excellence: The Guide to High Performance in Contemporary Organizations* (John Wiley & Sons, 1984) addresses influence downward by arguing that shared responsibility is needed with subordinates in order to get the best from them and that treating them as full partners in the unit's management is necessary even though formal authority rests with the manager. We also show that mutual influence is needed to allow both parties to use their full strength. These ideas translate directly into lessons for influence when formal authority is lacking.

Finally, the literature of negotiations has many applications for using exchange for influence. Although there are popular books on negotiating that overlook important issues of trust when relationships are ongoing within the same organization, there is much to be learned from applying negotiating insights. Roger Fisher's and William Ury's book *Getting to Yes* (Houghton Mifflin, 1981) is helpful on ways to approach someone to look for common interests despite having differing specific objectives. An excellent overview of the issues involved in any kind of negotiation can be found in Roy Lewicki and Joseph Litterer's test *Negotiation* (R.D. Irwin, 1985). Their discussion of exchange and equity is particularly relevant to influence as we have described it. In addition, Roy Lewicki's comments on an earlier draft of this article were particularly helpful, and we are grateful for his wisdom and generosity.

29. MANAGING ATTRACTION AND INTIMACY AT WORK

Marcy Crary

In recent years the number of women in management and professional positions has increased, so men and women are working together more frequently than ever before. As a result, we now have a relatively new and unstudied phenomenon in organizations: attraction and intimacy at work.

A large part of the writing to date on this topic has dealt with the "office romance," the ways in which managers can deal with these romances, and the problems these relationships create for others in the organization. However, little attention has been devoted to the two people actually involved in a relationship (whether sexual, nonsexual, or assumed by others to be sexual) and to understanding what it is like to be attracted to a co-worker of the opposite sex. There has been little discussion of the ways in which people deal with these feelings and the intense emotional responses that frequently can accompany them.

The label of "office romance" often trivializes the range and complexity of the issues faced by people in a close relationship at work. Outsiders' views of the attraction between two people typically oversimplify the experiences those individuals may be struggling with. These views may also be distorted by the viewer's projection of his or her own concerns into the situation.

Whether one is the person who feels attracted, the one who is the object of attraction, or the manager who is faced with the situation, all three individuals can profit from a better understanding of attractions and close relationships between men and women in organizations. Furthermore, this understanding should emerge from the perspective of the individual involved.

The observations in this article are drawn from the author's research on individuals' experiences of attraction and closeness in the workplace. This work has involved conversations with professional men and women whose workplaces include financial services companies, consulting groups, mental health clinics, state agencies, hospitals, and universities. These people have primarily been individuals in their thirties or forties, married or single, in either the early or the middle stages of their careers. The issues covered include (1) what "intimacy" at work means to different people, (2) what it is like to feel attracted to someone at work, (3) the choice between closeness and distance in female–male work relationships, and (4) the tensions and dilemmas of being in an "intimate" relationship at work (see Table 29.1). The final section of this article discusses the broader implications of these data for people and their organizations.

DIFFERENT MEANINGS OF ATTRACTION AND INTIMACY AT WORK

Part of the complexity of male-female relationships in the workplace is that individuals may experience the phenomena of attraction and intimacy in very different ways. (The discussions in this article can apply to same-gender work relationships in which there is a conscious component of sexuality present. There are obviously further complexities in people's experiences with homosexual relationships, given the organizational and cultural taboos against homosexuality.) Being "attracted" to or feeling "intimate" with a member of the opposite sex at work can have a variety of meanings. Attraction is not

Marcy Crary, "Managing Attraction and Intimacy at Work" from *Organizational Dynamics*, Spring 1987.

TABLE 29.1
Questionnaire on Attraction and Intimacy at Work

Think of a time when you felt attracted to someone of the opposite sex at work . . .

What did you do with these feelings?
a. I ignored them, hoping they would go away.
b. I talked about them with someone else.
c. I talked about them with the person to whom I was attracted.

How did you behave with the person?
a. I avoided him/her.
b. I continued to work with him/her, but I stayed distant emotionally.
c. I tried to get to know him/her better personally.
d. I sought out more opportunities to work with him/her.

Think of a close relationship you have with a colleague of the opposite sex . . .

How would you define/describe the closeness of the relationship?
a. Purely professional.
b. Emotional.
c. Spiritual.
d. Sexual.
e. None of the above.
f. Some of the above.
g. All of the above.
h. Other.

What tensions or dilemmas have you had about this relationship at work?
a. I felt vulnerable around him/her.
b. I worried about what other people would be thinking.
c. I worried about what would happen if something/someone came between us.
d. It was hard to balance work and personal time.
e. All of the above.
f. Some of the above.

What effect did the relationship have upon your work?
a. I felt more productive.
b. It interfered with my work.
c. It had no impact on my work.

The questions reflect a sampling of the issues encountered by people who are attracted to or have close relationships with work colleagues of the opposite sex. Deciding how to manage one's own feelings and behavior in these situations is not often easy, and the norms of most workplaces do not make it any easier.

always based on physical attractiveness; it can be based upon any number of factors, including one's attraction to the other's competence, power, values and beliefs, and so forth.

Similarly, "intimacy" at work can refer to relationships that are close but not necessarily sexual. If people's experiences are to be guides in our thinking about male-female relationships at work, intimacy and sexuality need to be treated as separate dimensions of such relationships.

What then do people mean by "intimacy" at work? The individuals who were interviewed gave a wide range of comments:

It's being able to exchange honest, straightforward, constructive feedback on our work.

We have very creative, free exchanges of ideas about the things we are working on.

I can share any or all of the 'backstage' thoughts and feelings that come up for me in this place or in my life outside work.

I have the feeling that she is always looking out for me, always ready to help me out or make suggestions.

Some people describe intimate work relationships that are or have been sexual, but the experience of intimacy at work is not as automatically associated with sexuality as one might think.

In brief, the experience of "intimacy" at work varies from person to person, and ranges in the depth of self shared, the degree to which it involves the task at hand, and the extent to which a sexual relationship is involved. These variations undoubtedly reflect the differences in the needs and interests that people bring to cross-gender relationships at work, the nature of their work and the degree of interaction it requires, their position in the organization, and the organization's norms about closeness at work.

DEALING WITH ATTRACTIONS AT WORK

Individuals have different ways of managing their feelings of attraction and closeness to the opposite sex; the interview data bear this out. Some of the aspects involved are the degree of awareness of the attraction, feelings about attraction, and problems with expressing attraction.

The Degree of Awareness of One's Attractions

There are significant differences in people's ability to observe and talk about their experiences of attraction (often the first stage in the development of a close relationship). Some people seem very aware of their feelings when they are drawn to another person. For example, one woman who was interviewed about her experiences of attraction was able to describe 11 different steps in her typical attraction experience (see Table 29.2). Her response shows a strong familiarity with the experience of attraction to others in her work setting, as well as an unusual ability to describe her own experience in the process. Most people find it difficult to step back and make such observations about their own experiences. The people who have a greater awareness of these feelings are probably also more skilled in discussing and managing their feelings of attraction.

Feelings About Attraction: Positive or Negative?

Feeling attracted to a member of the opposite sex at work can be very stimulating and productive for some people. However, attraction is also associated with a range of negative feelings. A number of people talked about feeling intensely distracted by their feelings of attraction, to the point where they were unable to attend to their work. In some cases such a feeling leads to uncertainty, confusion, and frustrations. For example, one woman said, "For me, attraction equals tension. I don't know what he is thinking or feeling—it makes me feel *really* insecure. I hope I look okay, I can't be casual with him or around him. I'm on eggshells!"

One male professor described the difficulties he experienced when he felt attracted to one of his students:

I had a young woman in two of my classes this semester who was strikingly beautiful and, I thought, quite sexy. I

TABLE 29.2

One Woman's Description of the Process of "Getting Attracted" to Someone in the Workplace

1. I'm first attracted to the person-as-a-person—noticing his intelligence, the way he talks, etc. I'll find myself noticing something about his physical appearance (clothes, jewelry, hair) in the midst of a conversation.

2. Apart from his physical self, I may find myself remembering or ruminating over some personal data about him. I find myself thinking about something that is interesting about him, something that has piqued my curiosity.

3. The person may appear in my dreams. (This is an indication to me that I'm using him psychically, as a symbol of some thing in myself; he is becoming a source of my own growth.)

4. At this point I start really to pay attention to him. I'm interested in him on a psychic level, interested in him as a person; I want to relate to him apart from the work context. I've moved into a more active process at this point.

5. I begin to ask him questions about himself, watching how he is with other people, perhaps getting into conversations with friends at work about who's cute or not and thinking of him. This kind of talk with others helps to crystallize my feelings, making me aware of my own internal "ranking" of this person. The opinion of others also affects my interest in the other, perhaps magnifying my attraction.

6. I am consciously paying attention to his clothing, watching how he moves, perhaps giggling at his jokes more. I noticed what I like about his personality and his abilities.

7. I'll initiate more conversations with him. At meetings that he attends, I find myself stretching the "inclusion stage," the initial warm-up time in the meeting, by asking questions about his weekend, seeking more personal data.

8. At this point, if I'm really interested in him, I may covertly pass on information about my availability by not mentioning that I was with another person when I went to the movie over the weekend. I notice whom he mentions and whom he doesn't mention in his discussions of his weekend.

9. I move into a more personal state. I seek contact with him outside the workplace, or we might celebrate a work event by going somewhere outside the workplace.

10. Another signal of the intensifying of the relationship is his frequent appearance in my dreams. I may also be physically turned on by something he tells me about himself.

11. At this point, I'm usually clear that I want to develop a friendship with this person. I may or may not seek a sexual relationship with him. I can nurse such attractions and not act on them, but just enjoy them as they unfold.

---

found I noticed her more than others in the classroom. As a result, I also felt more uptight when I was around her. In some way I felt disempowered by her, or maybe it was that I was empowering her. It felt like our relationship was cluttered by my sexual fantasies. Some of my uptightness was in response to my assumption that I was not equally attractive to her. Plus, I assumed she could see my interest in her given how strongly I felt attracted to her. My vul- *nerability in this situation is that if she knows I'm attracted to her, she can somehow use that against me.*

Attraction can also be associated with fear, or even with resentment or anger. Obvious difficulties can arise when a person feels attraction but also resents these very feelings (and the person who evokes them) because of the internal tensions they generate. One organizational consultant who was interviewed said, "If you show me some avoidance or punitive behavior between a man and a woman in a workplace that needs to be addressed or resolved—and that is not tied to some specific incident—my bet is that they have some attraction to each other that they can't deal with." His observation was confirmed by other comments by a number of the people interviewed. Feelings of attraction can, ironically, be a reason for distancing oneself from a colleague at work.

Problems with Expressing One's Attraction

Many people struggle with the question of whether to discuss an attraction with the other person. The difficulty with *not* discussing the attraction is that one can end up with pent-up energy, which can in turn lead to a preoccupation with the attraction and sometimes even to counterproductive behavior. (Some people seek the aid of a close but neutral party to help them sort out their feelings and gain some perspective on their attraction—particularly when the costs of directly expressing that attraction to the person seem too high.)

Often, people are afraid that discussing the attraction will propel them into acting on it, thus causing them to lose control of the situation. They worry that revealing their feelings will galvanize the relationship with the other person, making the situation even more difficult to manage because they then have the other person's feelings to deal with as well as their own.

There are also fears that their intentions will be misunderstood by the other individual. One woman consultant said:

I chose to tell him that I was attracted to him but that for a number of reasons I was not going to act on it. This was in response to his telling me that he found me very attractive. Well, it turned out that in telling him I was attracted to him I had made the situation much worse. He continued to pursue the issue, so much so that it almost felt like sexual harassment. I then chose to back off from working with him because he was making it so difficult.

This woman went on to talk about how painful she found the issue of managing attraction. All of her experiences to date had been very difficult, and none of them had had happy endings. She now feels scared when she feels attracted to a man at work.

The decision of whether to express one's attraction to the other person can have ramifications far beyond the literal act of self-expression. There are often other "publics" to keep in mind. The complexity of this decision making can be seen in one man's description of the process he goes through before deciding whether to be open about his feelings.

I may have the feeling of "Wow, that person excites me." Depending on the environment, I am cautious about acting on the excitement…. If there is enough energy so that the attraction is not just fleeting, and I think about it beyond our last face-to-face contact … I start wondering if I should make the statement publicly or privately to her. The more I feel at risk, the more likely I am to make the statement publicly. It gives it less power, diffuses it.

The risk here is that if I make the statement to a woman who is part of a minority in the organization, she may feel undermined. If you make a public statement that demonstrates affection or intimacy, it can be undermining because it may be seen as turfstaking, a signal of ownership, thus decreasing her power and influence among men in the room. My own risk is that if we don't have enough of a relationship to support my statement, she may misconstrue it and use it against me. By making the statement publicly, I make sure that there are other versions of it available.

For this man, managing the internal tension is closely linked to his concerns about the interpersonal, group, and organizational "fallout" concerning the expression of his attraction. He was particularly aware of the political implications of his behavior and had many different ways of managing his feelings in relation to others' needs and behaviors. For others, less skilled in managing their own attractions, however, the question of how, when, where, and if to express their attraction becomes an emotional maze. The effective resolution of the "attraction question" between two people can make a noticeable contribution to the development of a more productive work relationship. However, the way to achieve this resolution is not always readily apparent to those involved.

THE CHOICE OF "GETTING CLOSER" VS. "KEEPING ONE'S DISTANCE"

Whether there is initial attraction or not, and whether this attraction is sexual or not, people differ in terms of the amount of distance they consider appropriate in their relationships with the opposite sex at work. Degrees of closeness versus distance in work relationships can generally be seen in (1) the amount and quality of self-disclosure shared with the other person, (2) the kinds of shared activities and interactions on and off the job, and (3) the extent to which these interactions are solely work-role related. But how and why individuals choose to shape the distance between themselves and their colleagues of the opposite sex varies a great deal from person to person.

Crane, one of the bank managers interviewed, was a strong believer in the "keep your distance" orientation. He described his own attitudes and behaviors toward women in his work setting as follows:

I can see nothing more damaging than getting involved with someone at work. I don't do it, ever. It can demoralize staff and add complications to your personal life.

I have no attractions. I keep myself as tightly controlled as I possibly can. My eyes don't rove.

It's a litigious society. Other's perceptions rule. I'd rather err on the side of being fearful of others' perceptions than be overly supportive to my women subordinates.

To Crane, keeping distance between himself and other employees at work meant, among other things, never discussing his personal life with anyone. He took pride in the fact that his boss did not know where he lived. For a number of different reasons, Crane also felt it particularly appropriate to keep women apart from his personal self at work. While he might have lunch or play squash with a male colleague, he would avoid such situations with women colleagues. He characterized women in their twenties and thirties as "seething with emotion"—emotions that in turn might affect him. He

expressed a preference for working with older women whose emotions had "cooled off with age" and were therefore more stable to work with. By choosing to keep a distance between himself and his female colleagues, he hoped to preclude the dangers of attractions at work.

Ben provides a sharp contrast to Crane's orientation toward women at work. Ben, a psychologist, described his relationships with women with whom he has worked in this way:

In every job I've had, I have always been attracted to one woman in a "monogamous," sexually tinged, intense, emotionally seductive relationship. We usually show a lot of physical attention and give a lot of emotional support to each other.

The intimacy Ben developed in a number of his cross-gender work relationships was very functional to the work he did. These pairings provided an important emotional and political base of operations within the highly charged situations in which he worked. Ben indicated that none of these relationships were physically sexual ones; the "monogamy" he refers to evolved from his tendency to pair with one woman in the organization with whom he could share emotional, professional, and organizational secrets. (Their pairing was often thought to be sexual by others, given the frequency with which they met and the intensity of their emotional connectedness.)

These two cases provide very different examples of how people resolve the dilemma of whether to be close to fellow workers or to keep them at a distance. Most people's work relationships with the opposite sex are variations on the patterns found in the experiences of these two men.

People seem to have different reasons for seeking closeness or keeping distance in these relationships. These differences may partly stem from different levels of the need for intimacy. In his book *Power, Intimacy and the Life Story* (Dorsey Press, 1985), D.P. McAdams found that "individuals high on intimacy motivation have been shown to spend more time thinking about relationships with others, to engage in more conversations with others, and to experience more positive effects when interacting with others than individuals scoring low on intimacy motivation."

Issues of power and/or sexuality are also likely to influence peoples' orientations toward closeness or distance at work. For some, having power may enable them to create close relationships and not have to worry about the ramifications; for others, having power may lead them to avoid closeness with work colleagues. On the other hand, people may seek distance to avoid dealing with issues of sexuality. As one woman put it,

I find it difficult to deal with intimacy and professionalism together because I link intimacy and sexuality. I can't separate the two. I am more likely to choose distance in most situations because of this.

For whatever reasons, each of us makes choices about this fundamental question—to be close or to be distant—whether we are conscious of it or not.

BEING IN AN INTIMATE RELATIONSHIP AT WORK

Many of the close relationships described by the individuals interviewed were obviously of enormous importance to them—whether it be to their personal, social, professional, or physical well-being. Descriptions of the positive side of these relationships include the following:

I delight in our ability to think together; we have "sophisticated" communication between us. We shoot meta-level analyses of what is going on in the work situation back and forth at each other in meetings. We're both good at systems thinking.

When I'm with him I feel centered, fully alive, more resourceful. I feel more generous to the world. I am the "better half" of myself.

When we work together I feel effective, centered—almost like I'm "tripping out" on myself and on him.

At the same time many of the professionals interviewed were explicit about the personal difficulties they experience when they are in an "intimate" relationship (whether sexual or nonsexual) with an-

other person at work. Four different categories of problems can be isolated in these people's experiences: (1) the tension of balancing intimacy with work, (2) the feeling of increased vulnerability both inside and outside the relationship, (3) dealing with outsiders' views and feelings about the relationship, and (4) dealing with ongoing changes in the definition of the relationship.

Balancing Intimacy and Work with the Same Person

Most of us have been socialized into thinking of intimacy and work as two separate compartments in our lives; intimacy takes place at home and work takes place at our place of employment. But for many people the realities of day-to-day experiences at work belie these rational arrangements of our worlds. Working closely together can create a sense of intimacy between people, or the creation of intimate relationships may be essential to performing the task itself. One woman's success as a consultant depended on establishing good relationships with the line managers she worked with; she saw these close connections as essential to the quality of their mutual effort, stating that "our intimacy makes for a better business relationship."

But the combination of intimacy and work is not an easy blend for many people; it presents significant emotional challenges. Romantic relationships at work require balancing the roles of boyfriend/girlfriend with one's organizational responsibilities. For some, the conflicting demands are too much, while for others the challenge is stimulating.

Allen, who worked in a financial services firm, talked about a romantic relationship he developed with one of his female co-workers. Having his girlfriend in his work group became problematic over time:

She walks into my office unannounced, and I don't have the time to be with her. When I'm in the office I'm always very short with people—and I was with her on a number of occasions as well. I also felt that I couldn't comfortably talk about what we were going to do that night.

This was interfering with my performance at work. I felt I should spend time with her and I couldn't; she didn't like that.

For Allen, the experience of having a girlfriend in his workplace felt too complicated and jeopardized the quality of his work. He expressed a strong preference, after having had this experience, for keeping his personal and professional lives separate. Putting them together created too many emotional and psychological stresses for him. According to his theory, keeping them separate would allow him to express his "work self" at work and his intimate self at home. These two selves seemed incompatible in a single setting.

A contrasting example came from David, who stated that he had little difficulty in having a romantic relationship in his company. He talked about his decision to start up a sexual relationship with a younger woman in his own company. Both of them kept this secret. His initial attraction to the woman had in fact distracted him from work, but once he developed an intimate, sexual relationship with her, he reported little difficulty in keeping his attention on his work. (However, he did not rule out possible difficulties in the future if others found out about the relationship.)

Part of the relative ease he experienced, in contrast to Allen, may have come from his position as president of the company and his years of experience on the job. His external power and established expertise may have minimized the internal anxieties that are usually associated with such a relationship at work.

The tensions of people caught in the dilemmas of balancing an intimate relationship with a working relationship may stem partly from their difficulties in sorting out their own needs as they relate to the other person. The difficulties seemed particularly great when people's work attitudes and behaviors were significantly different from the kinds of attitudes and behaviors they exhibited when they were with that other person. In effect, the work self collided with the intimate self. Putting their two different "selves" together in the same physical space was

dysfunctional for them, for the relationship, and in some cases for the organization. There are other people, however, for whom the intimate and work selves are in less intense conflict; for these individuals, managing intimacy at work may be less difficult.

Increased Vulnerability Within and Outside of the Relationship

Maintaining a close relationship at work makes some people feel more vulnerable both to the other person involved and to others in the work environment. Things shared within the relationship can be misused by that other person. This kind of vulnerability may be illustrated by an incident involving one man's interaction with a female employee to whom he had felt quite close. They shared a common outlook on many different issues, worked very well together, and shared a lot of personal feelings. One day he walked past her as she was talking with some of his other employees. As he passed by, she remarked, "You look like a sad little boy." Although he kept walking and did not respond, a number of strong feelings welled up in him. He said, "She was exactly right. She cut me to the quick with her remark. I was surprised; I didn't know I was so accessible to others. I felt really exposed." He felt she had misused knowledge she had gained through their friendship to embarrass him in front of his other employees. She had made a public observation about what he felt was a private part of himself. This was double vulnerability, both inside and outside of the relationship.

Dealing with Outsiders' Views of the Relationship

An increased vulnerability to outsiders' attitudes often accompanies an intimate relationship at work. Everyone is aware of the taboo against sexual intimacy at work; indeed, many people have their own rules about not having a sexual relationship with colleagues or clients. But an obvious closeness to a colleague of the opposite sex invites outsiders to make their own interpretations about the nature of the relationship. They will usually suspect that the relationship is sexual, whether or not this is actually true.

Some of the women interviewed talked about their fears of being disempowered by outsiders' perceptions (or misperceptions) of their closeness to a male colleague or client. They feared the classic accusation that associates a woman's rise in an organization with her sexual activity rather than with her competence. As a result these women have learned to be very discreet in managing their close relationships, whether these relationships are sexual or not. They also feel that they must always be aware of how others perceive their relationships. One single female consultant stated that she wished she were married, if only to be rid of other people's constant assumptions that her relationships with male clients were sexual. (Interestingly enough, very few of the people interviewed mentioned concerns about their being unfair or unobjective as a result of their close relationships. Ironically, these are the concerns expressed most often by outsiders.)

Dealing with Changes in the Relationship

The development and maintenance of any close relationship involves various changes in the relationship over time. The degrees of involvement in, commitment to, and dependence on the relationship are significant dimensions that are subject to change. Many of the difficulties reported by people in close relationships at work involve coping with the ongoing issues raised by such changes. Because these relationships develop in a work setting, the changes in them are apt to have organizational as well as personal implications.

In ongoing intimate relationships, many women and men struggle with the issue of sexual involvement. When there is a lack of reciprocal interest in exploring such involvement, it can be very difficult for one of the pair to respond to this issue and not hurt the other's feelings, the quality of the relationship, or the quality of their work together.

One woman commented, "If you pay attention to men at certain levels emotionally and develop a close relationship, they often sexualize it. I have to be careful about this." Her statement was based on the experience she had had with a male manager in her organization who was her boss's peer. They had built a relationship based on their conversations about company management styles and a variety of outside interests that they shared. She had sometimes gone to his office to chat with him. Finally one day he told her that if they wanted to have a personal relationship they should have it outside work, or people might talk. She knew that this statement was also an invitation. She was surprised by his comment because she had never wanted to develop a personal relationship with him outside the company. She cut down on the amount of contact they had in order to keep their relationship on a more professional basis. As a result of this experience, she became more careful of her interactions with men in the work environment.

A male manager reported a similar experience in which his female boss thought he wanted to begin a more personal and potentially sexual relationship. He did not share her needs and interests, and he had to communicate this to her very delicately in order to maintain both their professional relationship and his career.

Another difficulty with work relationships is the question of how deeply the intimacy should be carried into the individuals' projects. One woman reported an incident in which she worked closely with a man she was employing as a consultant on her art project. They had been working intensely together for a number of months and had achieved a special intimacy from their similar spiritual and aesthetic orientations. They were agonizing over a particularly difficult decision when the man drew back and said, "Well, it's your project, you decide." At that moment, the woman felt confronted with the deep division between their respective personal investments in the project. The limits to their intimacy were exposed to her in a very abrupt, raw fashion.

Subtle shifts in interest and investment in a relationship may seem relatively unimportant to outsiders. For the people in the relationship, however, these changes can have a substantial impact.

CONCLUSION

The data presented in this paper have implications not only for individual employees, but for the organizations in which they work as well.

Issues for Employees

Figure 29.1 lists some common questions a person may have as he or she deals with the issues of attraction and intimacy at work. How one deals with these questions will have an obvious impact on the kinds of experiences a person will encounter. Negative and positive responses lead one in different directions.

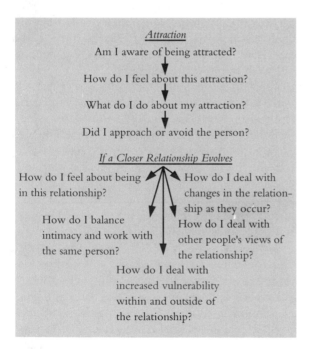

Attraction

Am I aware of being attracted?

How do I feel about this attraction?

What do I do about my attraction?

Did I approach or avoid the person?

If a Closer Relationship Evolves

How do I feel about being in this relationship?

How do I deal with changes in the relationship as they occur?

How do I balance intimacy and work with the same person?

How do I deal with other people's views of the relationship?

How do I deal with increased vulnerability within and outside of the relationship?

FIGURE 29–1 *Attraction and Intimacy Questions for the Employee*

For example, people who always respond negatively to the question will probably not experience the problems that arise from attempting to get closer to another person. Being unaware of one's feelings, having negative reactions to one's feeling of attraction, and avoiding the person to whom one is attracted can distance one from the emotional complexity of managing closeness in a work relationship. To these people, such distance from one's feelings and from colleagues of the opposite sex seems safer. In remaining distant, one avoids potential misunderstandings that may lead to charges of sexual harassment or other volatile outcomes. But there are potential costs to the choice of distance from one's feelings and one's colleagues. These costs are highlighted in a 1981 *Wall Street Journal* article that quoted a female manager for AT&T who was 29 years old and single:

I build an iron fence around myself for twelve hours a day. That isn't really me, but I feel it's a responsibility I have to take as a woman, to make clear I'm not available. I'm sociable; lunch or a drink after work is fine because it's work related. But if I find myself attracted to a colleague, I just don't allow it to go anywhere, and I don't let myself get into a situation with that person in which it might be hard to control my feelings.

Though no more detail is given about this woman and her life apart from her career, one must wonder about the potential costs of her choice of behavior: (1) Might she be keeping herself from forming interpersonal friendships that could contribute to her own personal development? (2) Might she be keeping herself from opportunities to form close relationships with male colleagues, connections that might help to advance her career? (3) Might she be keeping herself from experiencing and expressing her own emotional needs? Several women interviewed mentioned their experience of feeling neutered in their workplace. This may work insofar as suppressing one's sexuality is one way of resolving the problem of attractions at work—but again, at what cost?

Choosing closeness in a cross-gender work relationship, however, leads a person into a challenging set of personal and interpersonal issues. One must manage a more complex set of needs and concerns in relation to both one's self and the other person. One risks feelings of increased vulnerability; one must manage outsiders' interpretations of the relationship; one has to meet the changing needs and concerns of both people involved. But if the result of one's efforts is a good working relationship with a colleague of the opposite sex, one has a precious commodity.

Issues for Organizations

What is the significance of employee attraction and intimacy for organizations and their managers? Experiences in these areas involve strong feelings; for better or for worse, these feelings affect people's behavior and performance on the job. Because there is such variation in the way people deal with these issues, managers need a better understanding of how people experience these situations and how their behavior is affected by them. Managers also need to become more aware of their own attitudes on these issues.

Managers themselves face a number of risks in assuming that all people's experiences are similar, or in not understanding how those involved in the situation actually feel. If they don't understand differences between people, or if they have a simplistic or negative view of intimacy at work, they will often react negatively to such intimate relationships, including some in which intimacy could be very productive both for the involved individuals and the organization.

These negative reactions can also make managers avoid relationships in which they themselves anticipate "intimacy problems." In this case, these people may miss out on the potential growth that develops out of working through complex issues with close colleagues. Moreover, the organization risks losing the potential synergy and creativity that these relationships may bring to the work environment.

Organizations as a whole need to develop constructive standards about close male-female relationships. As Edgar H. Schein has pointed out in his article "Coming to a New Awareness of Organizational Culture" (*Sloan Management Review*, Winter 1984), one of the major issues of internal integration within an organization's culture is the problem of intimacy, friendship, and love. Organizations need to develop a consensus regarding closeness among their members. But if the consensus-building process (and the rules that result from it) are to be effective as a cultural "solution" for the organization, they must include the perceptions, thoughts, and feelings of that organization's members. Managers cannot merely legislate "solutions" to attraction and intimacy by making rules that prohibit romantic involvements. Such formal rules and sanctions only drive emotions underground, thus preventing people from dealing more constructively with the issues involved.

A consensus-building process requires open conversation and active participation. Companies can make it easier for people to learn about and manage issues of attraction and intimacy at work by making conversations about these issues easier. Internal training programs can make employees more sensitive to differences in people's experiences in these areas, as well as to the tensions and dilemmas associated with close male-female relationships at work. Skill-building sessions can help people assess the costs and benefits of their own ways of managing these issues (both for themselves and for others in the organization), and they can teach people alternative strategies. Role models of close, effective male-female relationships in management can have an obvious impact on people's hopes and fears concerning attraction and intimacy at work. With a more open climate in which to approach these issues, men and women should be freer to create high-quality working relationships that contribute to both their personal and professional development. Organizations will be rewarded in turn with the energy and creativity these relationships may contribute to the resolution of organizational problems.

ACKNOWLEDGMENT

I would like to thank Fernando Bartolomé, Tim Hall, Meryl Louis, Carolyn Lukensmeyer, Asya Pazy, Duncan Spelman, and Peter Vaill for their feedback on earlier versions of this paper. I am especially indebted to the people who were willing to talk with me about their own experiences with attraction and intimacy at work.

SELECTED BIBLIOGRAPHY

Issues of attraction and intimacy at work must be understood in terms of the development of working relationships. For an excellent overview of the literature on this subject, see John J. Gabarro's chapter on "The Development of Working Relationships" in *The Handbook of Organizational Behavior*, edited by Jay W. Lorsch (Prentice-Hall, 1986). Kathy E. Kram's *Mentoring at Work* (Scott Foresman, 1985) provides a very thorough discussion of the complexities of close working relationships.

A knowledge of the role of intimacy in adult development contributes a very different perspective to the issues of intimacy at work. Capacities for understanding and managing intimacy can be linked to stages of adult development. Robert Kegan describes different stages in the evolution of one's understanding of the self and one's relations to others in *The Evolving Self* (Harvard University Press, 1982). *Communication, Intimacy, and Close Relationships* (Academic Press, 1984), edited by Valerian J. Derlega, presents a rich compilation of theories and research on intimate relationships. The chapter by Dan McAdams, "Human Motives and Personal Relationships," explores the roles of power and intimacy in close relationships.

For a discussion of intimacy and its relation to organizational culture, see Edgar H. Schein's article, "Coming to a New Awareness of Organizational Culture" (*Sloan Management Review*, Winter 1984).

An excellent general reference for issues relating to sexuality in the workplace is *Sexuality in Organizations*, edited by Dale A. Neugarten and Jay M. Shafritz (Moore, 1980). This book addresses the overall complexity of managing attraction in hierarchical structures. Of particular interest are the articles "The Executive Man and Woman: The Issue of Sexuality" by David L. Bradford, Alice G. Sargent, and Melinda Sprague, and "Coping with Cupid: The Formation, Impact and Management of Romantic Relationships in Organizations" by Robert E. Quinn. Bradford et al. examine how the issues of sexuality *per se* influence male-female working relationships. Quinn's article presents his research on the effects of office affairs on superiors', co-workers', and other employees' attitudes and behaviors. A more recent treatment of sexual politics at work is Robert E. Quinn and Patricia L. Lees' article "Attraction and Harassment: Dynamics of Sexual Politics in the Workplace" (*Organizational Dynamics*, Autumn 1984).

A number of interesting articles have been written on managing attraction in the workplace. An article by Lynn R. Cohen, "Minimizing Communication Breakdowns Between Male and Female Managers" (*Personnel Administrator*, 1982) offers an explanation of nonverbal cues that create sexual tension in the office. James G. Clawson and Kathy E. Kram examine the dilemmas of intimacy versus distance in male-female developmental work relationships in their article "Managing Cross-Gender Mentoring" (*Business Horizons*, May/June 1984). In the *Harvard Business Review* (September/October 1983), Eliza G. C. Collins examines the impact of love relationships between top executives in a company and explores the options of dealing with them in ways to maintain organizational stability. In the article "Sexual Relationships at Work: Attraction, Transference, Coercion or Strategy" (*Personnel Administrator*, March 1982), Natasha Josefowitz describes the stages of attraction and the different reasons why people have sexual relationships at work. In the article "Managing Sexual Attraction in the Workplace" (*Personnel Administrator*, August 1983), Kaleel Jamison makes suggestions about what the manager can do to deal with incidents of sexual attraction in his or her company. Duncan Spelman, Marcy Crary, Kathy Kram, and James Clawson discuss the range of forces within the individual, work group, and organization that influence the development and management of attractions at work in their chapter "Sexual

Attractions at Work: Managing the Heart" in *Not As Far As You Think* (Lexington Books, 1986), edited by Lynda L. Moore.

For a fascinating discussion of managing emotional expression on the job and its effects on the individual, see Arlene R. Hochschild's *The Managed Heart* (University of California Press, 1983).

Group Processes

30. SUPPOSE WE TOOK GROUPS SERIOUSLY . . .

Harold J. Leavitt

INTRODUCTION

This chapter is mostly a fantasy, but not a utopian fantasy. As the title suggests, it tries to spin out some of the things that might happen if we really took small groups seriously; if, that is, we really used groups, rather than individuals, as the basic building blocks for an organization.

This seems an appropriate forum for such a fantasy. It was fifty years ago, at Hawthorne, that the informal face-to-face work group was discovered. Since then groups have been studied inside and out; they have been experimented with, observed, built, and taken apart. Small groups have become the major tool of the applied behavioral scientist. Organizational development methods are group methods. Almost all of what is called participative management is essentially based on group techniques.

So the idea of using groups as organizational mechanisms is by no means new or fantastic. The fantasy comes in proposing to start with groups, not add them in; to design organizations from scratch around small groups, rather than around individuals.

But right from the start, talk like that appears to violate a deep and important value, individualism. But, this fantasy will not really turn out to be anti-individualistic in the end.

The rest of this chapter will briefly address the following questions: (1) Is it fair to say that groups have not been taken very seriously in organizational design? (2) Why are groups even worth thinking about as organizational building materials? What are the characteristics of groups that might make them interesting enough to be worth serious attention? (3) What would it mean "to take groups seriously?" Just what kinds of things would have to be done differently? (4) What compensatory changes would probably be needed in other aspects of the organization, to have groups as the basic unit? And finally, (5) is the idea of designing the organization around small face-to-face groups a very radical idea, or is it just an extension of a direction in which we are already going?

HAVEN'T GROUPS BEEN TAKEN SERIOUSLY ENOUGH ALREADY?

The argument that groups have not been taken "seriously" doesn't seem a hard one to make. The contemporary ideas about groups didn't really come along until the 30s and 40s. By that time a logical, rationalistic tradition for the construction of organizations already existed. That tradition was very heavily based on the notion that the individual was the construction unit. The logic moved from the projected task backward. Determine the task, the goal, then find an appropriate structure and technology, and last of all fit individual human beings into predefined man-sized pieces of the action. That was, for instance, what industrial psychology was all about during its development between the two world wars. It was concerned almost entirely with individual differences and worked in the service of structuralists, fitting square human pegs to predesigned square holes. The role of the psychologist was thus ancillary to the role of the designers of the whole organization. It was a backup, supportive role that followed more than it led design.

It was not just the logic of classical organizational theory that concentrated on the individual. The whole entrepreneurial tradition of American society supported it. Individuals, at least male individuals, were taught achievement motivation. They were taught to seek individual evaluation, to compete, to see the world, organizational or otherwise, as a place in which to strive for individual accomplishment and satisfaction.

In those respects the classical design of organizations was consonant with the then existent cultural landscape. Individualized organizational structures blended with the environment of individualism. All the accessories fell into place: individual incentive schemes for hourly workers, individual merit rating and assessment schemes, tests for selection of individuals.

The unique characteristic of the organization was that it was not simply a racetrack within which individuals could compete, but a system in which somehow the competitive behavior of individuals could be coordinated, harnessed and controlled in the interest of the common tasks. Of course one residual of all that was a continuing tension between individual and organization, with the organization seeking to control and coordinate the individual's activities at the same time that it tried to motivate him, while the competitive individual insisted on reaching well beyond the constraints imposed upon him by the organization. One product of this tension became the informal organization discovered here at Western; typically an informal coalition designed to fight the system.

Then it was discovered that groups could be exploited for what management saw as positive purposes, *toward* productivity instead of away from it. There followed the era of experimentation with small face-to-face groups. We learned to patch them on to existing organizations as bandaids to relieve tensions between individual and organization. We promoted coordination through group methods. We leaned that groups were useful to discipline and control recalcitrant individuals.

Groups were fitted onto organizations. The group skills of individual members improved so that they could coordinate their efforts more effectively, control deviants more effectively and gain more commitment from subordinate individuals. But groups were seen primarily as tools to be tacked on and utilized in the preexisting individualized organizational system. With a few notable exceptions, like Renis Likert (1961), most did not design organizations around groups. On the contrary, as some of the ideas about small groups began to be tacked onto existing organizational models, they generated new tensions and conflicts of their own. Managers complained not only that groups were slow, but that they diffused responsibility, vitiated the power of the hierarchy because they were too "democratic and created small in-groups empires which were very hard for others to penetrate." There was the period, for example, of the great gap between T-group training (which had to be conducted on "cultural islands") and the organization back home. The T-groups therefore talked a lot about the "reentry problem," which meant in part the problem of movement from a new culture (the T-group culture) designed around groups back into the organizational culture designed around individuals.

But of course groups didn't die despite their difficulties. How could they die? They had always been there, though not always in the service of the organization. They turned out to be useful, indeed necessary, though often unrecognized tools. For organizations were growing, and professionalizing, and the need for better coordination grew even as the humanistic expectations of individuals also grew. So "acknowledged" groups (as distinct from "natural," informal groups) became fairly firmly attached even to conservative organizations, but largely as compensating addenda very often reluctantly backed into by organizational managers.

Groups have never been given a chance. It is as though someone had insisted that automobiles be designed to fit the existing terrain rather than build roads to adapt to automobiles.

ARE GROUPS WORTH CONSIDERING AS FUNDAMENTAL BUILDING BLOCKS?

Why would groups be more interesting than individuals as basic design units around which to build organizations? What are the prominent characteristics of small groups? Why are they interesting? Here are several answers:

First, small groups seem to be good for people. They can satisfy important membership needs. They can provide a moderately wide range of activities for individual members. They can provide support in times of stress and crisis. They are settings in which people can learn not only cognitively but empirically to be reasonably trusting and helpful to one another. Second, groups seem to be good problem finding tools. They seem to be useful in promoting innovation and creativity. Third, in a wide variety of decision situations, they make better de-

cisions than individuals do. Fourth, they are great tools for implementation. They gain commitment from their members so that group decisions are likely to be willingly carried out. Fifth, they can control and discipline individual members in ways that are often extremely difficult through more impersonal quasi-legal disciplinary systems. Sixth; as organizations grow large, small groups appear to be useful mechanisms for fending off many of the negative effects of large size. They help to prevent communication lines from growing too long, the hierarchy from growing too steep, and the individual from getting lost in the crowd.

There is a seventh, but altogether different kind of argument for taking groups seriously. Thus far the designer of organizations seemed to have a choice. He could build an individualized *or* a groupy organization. A groupy organization will, de facto, have to deal with individuals; but what was learned here so long ago is that individual organizations, must, de facto, deal with groups. Groups are natural phenomena, and facts of organizational life. They can be created but their spontaneous development cannot be prevented. The problem is not shall groups exist or not, but shall groups be planned or not? If not, the individualized organizational garden will sprout groupy weeds all over the place. By defining them as weeds instead of flowers, they shall continue, as in earlier days, to be treated as pests, forever fouling up the beauty of rationally designed individualized organizations, forever forming informally (and irrationally) to harass and outgame the planners.

It is likely that the reverse could also be true, that if groups are defined as the flowers and individuals as the weeds, new problems will crop up. Surely they will, but that discussion can be delayed for at least a little while.

WHO USES GROUPS BEST?

So groups look like interesting organizational building blocks. But before going on to consider the implications of designing organizations around groups, one useful heuristic might be to look around the existing world at those places in which groups seem to have been treated somewhat more seriously.

One place groups have become big is in Japanese organizations (Johnson & Ouchi, 1974). The Japanese seem to be very groupy, and much less concerned than Americans about issues like individual accountability. Japanese organizations, of course, are thus consonant with Japanese culture, where notions of individual aggressiveness and competitiveness are deemphasized in favor of self-effacement and group loyalty. But Japanese organizations seem to get a lot done, despite the relative suppression of the individual in favor of the group. It also appears that the advantages of the groupy Japanese style have really come to the fore in large technologically complex organizations.

Another place to look is at American conglomerates. They go to the opposite extreme, dealing with very large units. They buy large organizational units and sell units. They evaluate units. In effect they promote units by offering them extra resources as rewards for good performance. In that sense conglomerates, one might argue, are designed around groups, but the groups in question are often themselves large organizational chunks.

GROUPS IN AN INDIVIDUALISTIC CULTURE

An architect can design a beautiful building which either blends smoothly with its environment or contrasts starkly with it. But organization designers may not have the same choice. If we design an organization which is structurally dissonant with its environment, it is conceivable that the environment will change to adjust to the organization. It seems much more likely, however, that the environment will reject the organization. If designing organizations around groups represents a sharp counterpoint to environmental trends, maybe we should abort the idea.

Our environment, one can argue, is certainly highly individualized. But one can also make a less solid argument in the other direction; an argument that American society is going groupy rather than individual this year. Or at least that it is going groupy as well as individual. The evidence is sloppy at best. One can reinterpret the student revolution and the growth of anti-establishment feelings at least in part as a reaction to the decline of those institutions that most satisfied social membership needs. One can argue that the decline of the Church, of the village and of the extended family is leaving behind a vacuum of unsatisfied membership and belongingness motives. Certainly popular critics of American society have laid a great deal of emphasis on the loneliness and anomie that seem to have resulted not only from materialism but from the emphasis on individualism. It seems possible to argue that, insofar as there has been any significant change in the work ethic in America, the change has been toward a desire for work which is socially as well as egoistically fulfilling, and which satisfies human needs for belongingness and affiliation as well as needs for achievement.

In effect, the usual interpretation of Abraham Maslow's need hierarchy may be wrong. Usually the esteem and self-actualization levels of motivation are emphasized. Perhaps the level that is becoming operant most rapidly is neither of those, but the social-love-membership level.

The rising role of women in American society also has implications for the groupiness of organizations. There is a moderate amount of evidence that American women have been socialized more strongly into affiliative and relational sorts of attitudes than men. They probably can, in general, more comfortably work in direct achievement roles in group settings, where there are strong relational bonds among members, than in competitive, individualistic settings. Moreover it is reasonable to assume that as women take a more important place in American society, some of their values and attitudes will spill over to the male side.

Although the notion of designing organizations around groups in America in 1974 may be a little premature, it is consonant with cultural trends that may make the idea much more appropriate ten years from now.

But groups are becoming more relevant for organizational as well as cultural reasons. Groups seem to be particularly useful as coordinating and integrating mechanisms for dealing with complex tasks that require the inputs of many kinds of specialized knowledge. In fact the development of matrix-type organizations is high technology industry is perhaps one effort to modify individually designed organizations toward a more groupy direction; not for humanistic reasons but as a consequence of tremendous increase in the informational complexity of the jobs that need to be done.

WHAT MIGHT A SERIOUSLY GROUPY ORGANIZATION LOOK LIKE?

Just what does it mean to design organizations around groups? Operationally how is that different from designing organizations around individuals? One approach to an answer is simply to take the things organizations do with individuals and try them out with groups. The idea is to raise the level from the atom to the molecule, and *select* groups rather than individuals; *train* groups rather than individuals, *pay* groups rather than individuals, *promote* groups rather than individuals, *design jobs* for groups rather than for individuals, *fire* groups rather than individuals, and so on down the list of activities which organizations have traditionally carried on in order to use human beings in their organizations.

Some of the items on that list seem easy to handle at the group level. For example, it doesn't seem terribly hard to design jobs for groups. In effect that is what top management already does for itself to a great extent. It gives specific jobs to committees, and often runs itself as a group. The problem seems to be a manageable one: designing job sets which are both big enough to require a small number of persons and also small enough to require only a small number of persons. Big enough in this context means not only jobs that would occupy the hands of group members but that would provide opportunities for learning and expansion.

Ideas like evaluating, promoting, and paying groups raise many more difficult but interesting problems. Maybe the best that can be said for such ideas is that they provide opportunities for thinking creatively about pay and evaluation. Suppose, for example, that as a reward for good work the group gets a larger salary budget than it got last year. Suppose the allocation for increases within the group is left to the group members. Certainly one can think up all sorts of difficulties that might arise. But are the potential problems necessarily any more difficult than those now generated by individual merit raises? Is there any company in America that is satisfied with its existing individual performance appraisal and salary allocation schemes? At least the issues of distributive justice within small groups would presumably be open to internal discussion and debate. One might even permit the group to allocate payments to individuals differentially at different times, in accordance with some criteria of current contribution that they might establish.

As far as performance evaluation is concerned, it is probably easier for people up the hierarchy to assess the performance of total groups than it is to assess the performance of individual members well down the hierarchy. Top managers of decentralized organizations do it all the time, except that they usually reward the formal leader of the decentralized unit rather than the whole unit.

The notion of promoting groups raises another variety of difficulties. One thinks of physically transferring a whole group, for example, and of the costs associated with training a whole group to do a new job, especially if there are no bridging individuals. But there may be large advantages too. If a group moves, its members already know how to work with one another. Families may be less disrupted by movement if several move at the same time.

There is the problem of selection. Does it make sense to select groups? Initially, why not? Can't means be found for selecting not only for appropriate knowledge and skill but also for potential ability to work together? There is plenty of groundwork in the literature already.

After the initial phase, there will of course be problems of adding or subtracting individuals from existing groups. We already know a good deal about how to help new members get integrated into old groups. Incidentally, I was told recently by a plant manager in the midwest about an oddity he had encountered: the phenomenon of groups applying for work. Groups of three or four people have been coming to his plant seeking employment together. They wanted to work together and stay together.

COSTS AND DANGER POINTS

To play this game of designing organizations around groups, what might be some important danger points? In general, a group-type organization is somewhat more like a free market than present organizations. More decisions would have to be worked out ad hoc, in a continually changing way. So one would need to schedule more negotiation time both within and between groups.

One would encounter more issues of justice, for the individual vis-à-vis the group and for groups vis-à-vis one another. More and better arbitration mechanisms would probably be needed along with highly flexible and rapidly adaptive record keeping. But modern record-keeping technology is, potentially, both highly flexible and rapidly adaptive.

Another specific issue is the provision of escape hatches for individuals. Groups have been know to be cruel and unjust to their deviant members. One existing escape route for the individual would of course continue to exist: departure from the organization. Another might be easy means of transfer to another group.

Another related danger of a strong group emphasis might be a tendency to drive away highly individualistic, nongroup people. But the tight organizational constraints now imposed do the same thing. Indeed might not groups protect their individualists better than the impersonal rules of present-day large organizations?

Another obvious problem: If groups are emphasized by rewarding them, paying them, promoting them, and so on, groups may begin to perceive themselves as power centers, in competitive conflict with other groups. Intergroup hostilities are likely to be exacerbated unless we can design some new coping mechanisms into the organization. Likert's proposal for solving that sort of problem (and others) is the linking pin concept. The notion is that individuals serve as members of more than one group, both up and down the hierarchy and horizontally. But Likert's scheme seems to me to assume fundamentally individualized organizations in the sense that it is still individuals who get paid, promoted and so on. In a more groupy organization, the linking pin concept has to be modified so that an individual might be a part-time member of more than one group, but still a real member. That is, for example, a portion of an individual's pay might come from each group in accordance with that group's perception of his contribution.

Certainly much more talk, both within and between groups, would be a necessary accompaniment of group emphasis; though we might argue about whether more talk should be classified as a cost or a benefit. In any case careful design of escape hatches for individuals and connections among groups would be as important in this kind of organization as would stairways between floors in the design of a private home.

There is also a danger of overdesigning groups. All groups in the organization need not look alike. Quite to the contrary. Task and technology should have significant effects on the shapes and sizes of different subgroups within the large organization. Just as individuals end up adjusting the edges of their jobs to themselves and themselves to their jobs, we should expect flexibility within groups, allowing them to adapt and modify themselves to whatever the task and technology demand.

Another initially scary problem associated with groups is the potential loss of clear formal individual leadership. Without formal leaders how will we motivate people? Without leaders how will we control and discipline people? Without leaders how will we pinpoint responsibility? Even as I write those questions I cannot help but feel that they are archaic. They are questions which are themselves a product of the basic individual building block design of old organizations. The problem is not leaders so much as the performance of leadership functions. Surely groups will find leaders, but they will emerge from the bottom up. Given a fairly clear job description, some groups, in some settings, will set up more or less permanent leadership roles. Others may let leadership vary as the situation demands, or as a function of the power that individuals within any group may possess relative to the group's needs at that time. A reasonable amount of process time can be built in to enable groups to work on the leadership problem, but the problem will have to be resolved within each group. On the advantage side of the ledger, this may even get rid of a few hierarchical levels. There should be far less need for individuals who are chiefly supervisors of other individuals' work. Groups can serve as hierarchical leaders of other groups.

Two other potential costs: With an organization of groups, there may be a great deal of infighting, and power and conflict issues will come even more to the fore than they do now. Organizations of groups may become highly political, with coalitions lining up against one another on various issues. If so, the rest of the organizational system will have to take those political problems into account, both by setting up sensible systems of intercommunications among groups, and by allocating larger amounts of time and expertise to problems of conflict resolution.

But this is not a new problem unique to groupy organizations. Conflict among groups is prevalent in large organizations which are political systems now. But because these issues have not often been foreseen and planned for, the mechanisms for dealing with them are largely ad hoc. As a result, conflict is often dealt with in extremely irrational ways.

But there is another kind of intergroup power problem that may become extremely important and difficult in groupy organizations. There is a real danger that relatively autonomous and cohesive groups may be closed, not only to other groups but more importantly to staff advice or to new technological inputs.

These problems exist at present, of course, but they may be exacerbated by group structure. I cannot see any perfect way to handle those problems. One possibility may be to make individual members of staff groups part-time members of line groups. Another is to work harder to educate line groups to potential staff contributions. Of course the reward system, the old market system, will probably be the strongest force for keeping groups from staying old-fashioned in a world of new technologies and ideas.

But the nature and degree of many of the second order spinoff effects are not fully knowable at the design stage. We need to build more complete working models and pilot plants. In any case it does not seem obvious that slowdowns, either at the work place or in decision-making processes, would necessarily accompany group based organizational designs.

SOME POSSIBLE ADVANTAGES TO THE ORGANIZATION

Finally, from an organizational perspective, what are the potential advantages to be gained from a group-based organization? The first might be a sharp reduction in the number of units that need to be controlled. Control would not have to be carried all the way down to the individual level. If the average group size is five, the number of blocks that management has to worry about is cut to 20 percent of what it was. Such a design would also probably cut the number of operational levels in the organization. In effect, levels which are now primarily supervisory would be incorporated into the groups that they supervise.

By this means many of the advantages of the small individualized organization could be brought back. These advantages would occur within groups simply because there would be a small number of blocks, albeit larger blocks, with which to build and rebuild the organization.

But most of all, and this is still uncertain, despite the extent to which we behavioral scientists have been enamoured of groups, there would be increased human advantages of cohesiveness, motivation, and commitment, and via that route, both increased productivity, stronger social glue within the organization, and a wider interaction between organization and environment.

SUMMARY

Far and away the most powerful and beloved tool of applied behavioral scientists is the small face-to-face group. Since the Western Electric researches, behavioral scientists have been learning to understand, exploit and love groups. Groups attracted interest initially as devices for improving the implementation of decisions and to increase human commitment and motivation. They are not loved because they are also creative and innovative, they often make better quality decisions than individuals, and because they make organizational life more livable for people. One can't hire an applied behavioral scientist into an organization who within ten minutes will not want to call a group meeting and talk things over. The group meeting is his primary technology, his primary tool.

But groups in organizations are not an invention of behavioral types. They are a natural phenomenon of organizations. Organizations develop informal groups, like it or not. It is both possible and sensible to describe most large organizations as collections of groups in interaction with one another; bargaining with one another, forming coalitions with one another, cooperating and competing with one another. It is possible and sensible, too, to treat the decisions that emerge from large organizations as a resultant of the interplay of forces among groups within the organization, and not just the resultant of rational analysis.

On the down side, small face-to-face groups are great tools for disciplining and controlling their members. Contemporary China, for example, has just a fraction of the number of lawyers in the United States. Partially this is a result of the lesser complexity of Chinese society and lower levels of education. But a large part of it, surprisingly enough, seems to derive from the fact that modern China is designed around small groups. Since small groups take responsibility for the discipline and control of their members, many deviant acts which would be considered illegal in the United States never enter the formal legal system in China. The law controls individual deviation less, the group controls it more (Li, 1971).

Control of individual behavior is also a major problem of large complex western organizations. This problem has driven many organizations into elaborate bureaucratic quasi-legal sets of rules, ranging from job evaluation schemes to performance evaluations to incentive systems; all individually based, all terribly complex, all creating problems of distributive justice. Any organizational design that might eliminate much of the legalistic superstructure therefore begins to look highly desirable.

Management should consider building organizations using a material now understood very well and with properties that look very promising, the small group. Until recently, at least, the human group has primarily been used for patching and mending organizations that were originally built of other materials.

The major unanswered questions in my mind are not in the understanding of groups, not in the potential utility of the group as a building block. The more difficult answered question is whether or not the approaching era is one in which Americans would willingly work in such apparently contra-individualistic units. I think we are.

REFERENCES

Johnson, Richard T., and Ouchi, William G. "Made in America (under Japanese Management)." *Harvard Business Review*, September-October 1974.

Li, Victor. "The Development of the Chinese Legal System" *China: The Management of a Revolutionary Society*, edited by John Lindbeck. Seattle: University of Washington Press, 1971.

Likert, Rensis. *New Patterns of Management*, New York: McGraw-Hill, 1961.

The U.S. road to disaster—in Vietnam, the Bay of Pigs, Korea, and Pearl Harbor—is paved with

31. GROUPTHINK

Irving L. Janis

The U.S. road to disaster—in Vietnam, the Bay of Pigs, Korea, and Pearl Harbor—is paved with —*the desperate drive for consensus at any cost that suppresses dissent among the mighty in the corridors of power.*

"How could we have been so stupid?" President John F. Kennedy asked after he and a close group of advisers had blundered into the Bay of Pigs invasion. For the last two years I have been studying that question, as it applies not only to the Bay of Pigs decision makers but also to those who led the United States into such other major fiascos as the failure to be prepared for the attack on Pearl Harbor, the Korean War stalemate, and the escalation of The Vietnam War.

Stupidity certainly is not the explanation. The men who participated in making the Bay of Pigs decision, for instance, comprised one of the greatest arrays of intellectual talent in the history of American Government—Dean Rusk, Robert McNamara, Douglas Dillon, Robert Kennedy, McGeorge Bundy, Arthur Schlesinger Jr., Allen Dulles, and others.

It also seemed to me that explanations were incomplete if they concentrated only on disturbances in the behavior of each individual within a decision-making body: temporary emotional states of elation, fear, or anger that reduce a man's mental efficiency, for example, or chronic blind spots arising from a man's social prejudices or idiosyncratic biases.

I preferred to broaden the picture by looking at the fiascos from the standpoint of group dynamics as it has been explored over the past three decades, first by the great social psychologist Kurt Lewin and later in many experimental situations by myself and other behavioral scientists. My conclusion after poring over hundreds of relevant documents—historical reports about formal group meetings and informal conversations among the members—is that the groups that committed the fiascos were victims of what I call "groupthink."

"GROUPY"

In each case study, I was surprised to discover the extent to which each group displayed the typical phenomena of social conformity that are regularly encountered in studies of group dynamics among ordinary citizens. For example, some of the phenomena appear to be completely in line with findings from social-psychological experiments showing that powerful social pressures are brought to bear by the members of a cohesive group whenever a dissident begins to voice his objections to a group consensus. Other phenomena are reminiscent of the shared illusions observed in encounter groups and friendship cliques when the members simultaneously reach a peak of "groupy" feelings.

Above all, there are numerous indications pointing to the development of group norms that bolster morale at the expense of critical thinking. One of the most common norms appears to be that of remaining loyal to the group by sticking with the policies to which the group has already committed itself, even when those policies are obviously working out badly and have unintended consequences that disturb the conscience of each member. This is one of the key characteristics of groupthink.

1984

I use the term *groupthink* as a quick and easy way to refer to the mode of thinking that persons engage in when *concurrence seeking* becomes so dominant in

a cohesive ingroup that it tends to override realistic appraisal of alternative course of action. Groupthink is a term of the same order as the words in the newspeak vocabulary George Orwell used in his dismaying world of *1984*. In that context, groupthink takes on an invidious connotation. Exactly such a connotation is intended, since the term refers to a deterioration in mental efficiency, reality testing, and moral judgments as a result of group pressures.

The symptoms of groupthink arise when the members of decision-making groups become motivated to avoid being too harsh in their judgments of their leaders' or their colleagues' ideas. They adopt a soft line of criticism, even in their own thinking. At their meetings, all the members are amiable and seek complete concurrence on every important issue, with no bickering or conflict to spoil the cozy, "we-feeling" atmosphere.

KILL

Paradoxically, soft-headed groups are often hard-hearted when it comes to dealing with outgroups or enemies. They find it relatively easy to resort to dehumanizing solutions—they will readily authorize bombing attacks that kill large numbers of civilians in the name of the noble cause of persuading an unfriendly government to negotiate at the peace table. They are unlikely to pursue the more difficult and controversial issues that arise when alternatives to a harsh military solution come up for discussion. Nor are they inclined to raise ethical issues that carry the implication that *this fine group of ours, with its humanitarianism and its high-minded principles, might be capable of adopting a course of action that is inhumane and immoral.*

NORMS

There is evidence from a number of social-psychological studies that as the members of a group feel more accepted by the others, which is a central feature of increased group cohesiveness, they display less overt conformity to group norms. Thus we would expect that the more cohesive a group becomes, the less the members will feel constrained to censor what they say out of fear of being socially punished for antagonizing the leader or any of their fellow members.

In contrast, the groupthink type of conformity tends to increase as group cohesiveness increases. Groupthink involves nondeliberate suppression of critical thoughts as a result of internalization of the group's norms, which is quite different from deliberate suppression on the basis of external threats of social punishment. The more cohesive the group, the greater the inner compulsion on the part of each member to avoid creating disunity, which inclines him to believe in the soundness of whatever proposals are promoted by the leader or by a majority of the group's members.

In a cohesive group, the danger is not so much that each individual will fail to reveal his objections to what the others propose but that he will think the proposal is a good one, without attempting to carry out a careful, critical scrutiny of the pros and cons of the alternatives. When groupthink becomes dominant, there also is considerable suppression of deviant thoughts, but it takes the form of each person's deciding that his misgivings are not relevant and should be set aside, that the benefit of the doubt regarding any lingering uncertainties should be given to the group consensus.

STRESS

I do not mean to imply that all cohesive groups necessarily suffer from groupthink. All ingroups may have a mild tendency toward groupthink, displaying one or another of the symptoms from time to time, but it need not be so dominant as to influence the quality of the group's final decision. Neither do I mean to imply that there is anything necessarily inefficient or harmful about group decisions in general. On the contrary, a group whose members have properly defined roles, with traditions concerning the procedures to follow in pur-

suing a critical inquiry, probably is capable of making better decisions than any individual group member working alone.

The problem is that the advantages of having decisions made by groups are often lost because of powerful psychological pressures that arise when the members work closely together, share the same set of values, and, above all, face a crisis situation that puts everyone under intense stress.

The main principle of groupthink, which I offer in the spirit of Parkinson's Law, is this: *The more amiability and esprit de corps there is among the members of a policy-making ingroup, the greater the danger that independent critical thinking well be replaced by groupthink, which is likely to result in irrational and dehumanizing actions directed against outgroups.*

SYMPTOMS

In my studies of high-level governmental decision makers, both civilian and military, I have found eight main symptoms of groupthink.

1. Invulnerabilty

Most or all of the members of the ingroup share an *illusion* of invulnerability that provides for them some degree of reassurance about obvious dangers and leads them to become overoptimistic and willing to take extraordinary risks. It also causes them to fail to respond to clear warnings of danger.

The Kennedy ingroup, which uncritically accepted the Central Intelligence Agency's disastrous Bay of Pigs plan, operated on the false assumption at they could keep secret the fact that the United States was responsible for the invasion of Cuba. Even after news of the plan began to leak out, their belief remained unshaken. They failed even to consider the danger that awaited them: a worldwide revulsion against the U.S.

A similar attitude appeared among the members of President Lyndon B. Johnson's ingroup, the "Tuesday Cabinet," which kept escalating the Vietnam War despite repeated setbacks and failures. "There was a belief," Bill Moyers commented after he resigned, "that if we indicated a willingness to use our power, they [the North Vietnamese] would get the message and back away from an all-out confrontation. . . . There was a confidence—it was never bragged about, it was just there—that when the chips were really down, the other people would fold."

A most poignant example of an illusion of invulnerability involves the ingroup around Admiral H. E. Kimmel, which failed to prepare for the possibility of a Japanese attack on Pearl Harbor despite repeated warnings. Informed by his intelligence chief that radio contact with Japanese aircraft carriers had been lost, Kimmel joked about it: "What, you don't know where the carriers are? Do you mean to say that they could be rounding Diamond Head (at Honolulu) and you wouldn't know it?" The carriers were in fact moving full-steam toward Kimmel's command post at the time. Laughing together about a danger signal, which labels it as a purely laughing matter, is a characteristic manifestation of groupthink.

2. Rationale

As we see, victims of groupthink ignore warnings; they also collectively construct rationalizations in order to discount warnings and other forms of negative feedback that, taken seriously, might lead the group members to reconsider their assumptions each time they recommit themselves to past decisions. Why did the Johnson ingroup avoid reconsidering its escalation policy when time and again the expectations on which they based their decisions turned out to be wrong? James C. Thompson Jr., a Harvard historian who spent five years as an observing participant in both the State Department and the White House, tells us that the policymakers avoided critical discussion of their prior decisions and continually invented new rationalizations so that they could sincerely recommit themselves to defeating the North Vietnamese.

In the fall of 1964, before the bombing of North Vietnam began, some of the policymakers predicted that six weeks of air strikes would induce the North

Vietnamese to seek peace talks. When someone asked, "What if they don't?" the answer was that another four weeks certainly would do the trick.

Later, after each setback, the ingroup agreed that by investing just a bit more effort (by stepping up the bomb tonnage a bit, for instance), their course of action would prove to be right. *The Pentagon Papers* bear out these observations.

In *The Limits of Intervention*, Townsend Hoopes, who was acting Secretary of the Air Force under Johnson, says that Walt W. Rostow in particular showed a remarkable capacity for what has been called "instant rationalization." According to Hoopes, Rostow buttressed the group's optimism about being on the road to victory by culling selected scraps of evidence from news reports or, if necessary, by inventing "plausible" forecasts that had no basis in evidence at all.

Admiral Kimmel's group rationalized away their warnings, too. Right up to December 7, 1941, they convinced themselves that the Japanese would never dare attempt a full-scale surprise assault against Hawaii because Japan's leaders would realize that it would precipitate an all-out war which the United States would surely win. They made no attempt to look at the situation through the eyes of the Japanese leaders—another manifestation of groupthink.

3. Morality

Victims of groupthink believe unquestioningly in the inherent morality of their ingroup; this belief inclines the members to ignore the ethical or moral consequences of their decisions.

Evidence that this symptom is at work usually is of a negative kind—the things that are left unsaid in group meetings. At least two influential persons had doubts about the morality of the Bay of Pigs adventure. One of them, Arthur Schlesinger, Jr., presented his strong objections in a memorandum to President Kennedy and Secretary of State Rusk but suppressed them when he attended meetings of the Kennedy team. The other, Senator J. William Fulbright, was not a member of the group, but the President invited him to express his misgivings in a speech to the policymakers. However, when Fulbright finished speaking the President moved on to other agenda items without asking for reactions of the group.

David Kraslow and Stuart H. Loory, in the *The Secret Search for Peace in Vietnam*, report that during 1966 President Johnson's ingroup was concerned primarily with selecting bomb targets in North Vietnam. They based their selections on four factors—the military advantage, the risk to American aircraft and pilots, the danger of forcing other countries into the fighting, and the danger of heavy civilian casualties. At their regular Tuesday luncheons, they weighed these factors the way school teachers grade examination papers, averaging them out. Though evidence on this point is scant, I suspect that the group's ritualistic adherence to a standardized procedure induced the members to feel morally justified in their destructive way of dealing with the Vietnamese people—after all, the danger of heavy civilian casualties from U.S. air strikes was taken into account on their checklists.

4. Stereotypes

Victims of groupthink hold stereotyped views of the leaders of enemy groups; they are so evil that genuine attempts at negotiating differences with them are unwarranted, or they are too weak or too stupid to deal effectively with whatever attempts the ingroup makes to defeat their purposes, no matter how risky the attempts are.

Kennedy's groupthinkers believed that Premier Fidel Castro's air force was so ineffectual that obsolete B-26s could knock it out completely in a surprise attack before the invasion began. They also believed that Castro's army was so weak that a small Cuban-exile brigade could establish a well-protected beachhead at the Bay of Pigs. In addition, they believed that Castro was not smart enough to put down any possible internal uprisings in support of the exiles. They were wrong on all three assumptions. Though much of the blame was attributable to faulty intelligence, the point is that none of Kennedy's advisers even questioned the CIA planners about these assumptions.

The Johnson advisers' sloganistic thinking about "the Communist apparatus" that was "working all around the world" (as Dean Rusk put it) led them to overlook the powerful nationalistic strivings of the North Vietnamese government and its efforts to ward off Chinese domination. The crudest of all stereotypes used by Johnson's inner circle to justify their policies was the domino theory ("If we don't stop the Reds in South Vietnam, tomorrow they will be in Hawaii and next week they will be in San Francisco," Johnson once said.) The group so firmly accepted this stereotype that it became almost impossible for any adviser to introduce a more sophisticated viewpoint.

In the documents on Pearl Harbor, it is clear to see that the Navy commanders stationed in Hawaii had a naive image of Japan as a midget that would not dare to strike a blow against a powerful giant.

5. Pressure

Victims of groupthink apply direct pressure to any individual who momentarily expresses doubts about any of the group's shared illusions or who questions the validity of the arguments supporting a policy alternative favored by the majority. This gambit reinforces the concurrence-seeking norm that loyal members are expected to maintain.

President Kennedy probably was more active than anyone else in raising skeptical questions during the Bay of Pigs meetings, and yet he seems to have encouraged the group's docile, uncritical acceptance of defective arguments in favor of the CIA's plan. At every meeting, he allowed the CIA representatives to dominate the discussion. He permitted them to give their immediate refutations in response to each tentative doubt that one of the others expressed, instead of asking whether anyone shared the doubt or wanted to pursue the implications of the new worrisome issue that had just been raised. And at the most crucial meeting, when he was calling on each member to give his vote for or against the plan, he did not call on Arthur Schlesinger, the one man there who was known by the President to have serious misgivings.

Historian Thompson informs us that whenever a member of Johnson's ingroup began to express doubts, the group used subtle social pressures to "domesticate" him. To start with, the dissenter was made to feel at home, provided that he lived up to two restrictions: (1) that he did not voice his doubts to outsiders, which would play into the hands of the opposition; and (2) that he kept his criticisms within the bounds of acceptable deviation, which meant not challenging any of the fundamental assumptions that went into the group's prior commitments. One such "domesticated dissenter" was Bill Moyers. When Moyers arrived at a meeting, Thompson tells us, the President greeted him with, "Well, here comes Mr. Stop-the-Bombing."

6. Self-Censorship

Victims of groupthink avoid deviating from what appears to be group consensus; they keep silent about their misgivings and even minimize to themselves the importance of their doubts.

As we have seen, Schlesinger was not at all hesitant about presenting his strong objections to the Bay of Pigs plan in a memorandum to the President and the Secretary of State. But he became keenly aware of his tendency to suppress objections at the White House meetings. "In the months after the Bay of Pigs I bitterly reproached myself for having kept so silent during those crucial discussions in the cabinet room," Schlesinger writes in *A Thousand Days*. "I can only explain my failure to do more than raise a few timid questions by reporting that one's impulse to blow the whistle on this nonsense was simply undone by the circumstances of the discussion."

7. Unanimity

Victims of groupthink share an *illusion* of unanimity within the group concerning almost all judgments expressed by members who speak in favor of the majority view. This symptom results partly from the preceding one, whose effects are augmented by the false assumption that any individual who remains silent during any part of the discussion is in full accord with what the others are saying.

When a group of persons who respect each other's opinions arrives at a unanimous view, each member is likely to feel that the belief must be true. This reliance on consensual validation within the group tends to replace individual critical thinking and reality testing, unless there are clear-cut disagreements among the members. In contemplating a course of action such as the invasion of Cuba, it is painful for the members to confront disagreements within their group, particularly it it becomes apparent that there are widely divergent views about whether the preferred course of action is too risky to undertake at all. Such disagreements are likely to arouse anxieties about making a serious error. Once the sense of unanimity is shattered, the members no longer can feel complacently confident about the decision they are inclined to make. Each man must then face the annoying realization that there are troublesome uncertainties and he must diligently seek out the best information he can get in order to decide for himself exactly how serious the risks might be. This is one of the unpleasant consequences of being in a group of hardheaded, critical thinkers.

To avoid such an unpleasant state, the members often become inclined, without quite realizing it, to prevent latent disagreements from surfacing when they are about to initiate a risky course of action. The group leader and the members support each other in playing up the areas of convergence in their thinking, at the expense of fully exploring divergencies that might reveal unsettled issues.

"Our meetings took place in a curious atmosphere of assumed consensus," Schlesinger writes. His additional comments clearly show that, curiously, the consensus was an illusion—an illusion that could be maintained only because the major participants did not reveal their own reasoning or discuss their idiosyncratic assumptions and vague reservations. Evidence from several sources makes it clear that even the three principals—President Kennedy, Rusk and McNamara—had widely differing assumptions about the invasion plan.

8. Mindguards

Victims of groupthink sometimes appoint themselves as mindguards to protect the leader and fellow members from adverse information that might break the complacency they shared about the effectiveness and morality of past decisions. At a large birthday party for his wife, Attorney General Robert F. Kennedy, who had been constantly informed about the Cuban invasion plan, took Schlesinger aside and asked him why he was opposed. Kennedy listened coldly and said, "You may be right or you may be wrong, but the President has made his mind up. Don't push it any further. Now is the time for everyone to help him all they can."

Rusk also functioned as a highly effective mindguard by failing to transmit to the group the strong objections of three "outsiders" who had learned of the invasion plan—Undersecretary of State Chester Bowles, USIA Director Edward R. Murrow, and Rusk's intelligence chief, Roger Hilsman. Had Rusk done so, their warnings might have reinforced Schlesinger's memorandum and jolted some of Kennedy's ingroup, if not the President himself, into reconsidering the decision.

PRODUCTS

When a group of executives frequently displays most or all of these interrelated symptoms, a detailed study of their deliberations is likely to reveal a number of immediate consequences. These consequences are, in effect, products of poor decision-making practices because they lead to inadequate solutions to the problems under discussion.

First, the group limits its discussions to a few alternative courses of action (often only two) without an initial survey of all the alternative that might be worthy of consideration.

Second, the group fails to reexamine the course of action initially preferred by the majority after they learn of risks and drawbacks they had not considered originally.

Third, the members spend little or no time discussing whether there are nonobvious gains they may have overlooked or ways of reducing the seemingly prohibitive costs that made rejected alternatives appear undesirable to them.

Fourth, members make little or no attempt to obtain information from experts within their own organizations who might be able to supply more precise estimates of potential losses and gains.

Fifth, members show positive interest in facts and opinions that support their preferred policy; they tend to ignore facts and opinions that do not.

Sixth, members spend little time deliberating about how the chosen policy might be hindered by bureaucratic inertia, sabotaged by political opponents, or temporarily derailed by common accidents. Consequently, they fail to work out contingency plans to cope with foreseeable setbacks that could endanger the overall success of their chosen course.

SUPPORT

The search for an explanation of why groupthink occurs had led me through a quagmire of complicated theoretical issues in the murky area of human motivation. My belief, based on recent social psychological research, is that we can best understand the various symptoms of groupthink as a mutual effort among the group members to maintain self-esteem and emotional equanimity by providing social support to each other, especially at times when they share responsibility for making vital decisions.

Even when no important decision is pending, the typical administrator will begin to doubt the wisdom and morality of his past decisions each time he receives information about setbacks, particularly if the information is accompanied by negative feedback from prominent men who originally had been his supporters. It should not be surprising, therefore, to find that individual members strive to develop unanimity and esprit de corps that will help bolster each other's morale, to create an optimistic outlook about the success of pending decisions, and to reaffirm the positive value of past policies to which all of them are committed.

PRIDE

Shared illusions of invulnerability, for example, can reduce anxiety about taking risks. Rationalizations help members believe that the risks are really not so bad after all. The assumption of inherent morality helps the members to avoid feelings of shame or guilt. Negative stereotypes function as stress-reducing devices to enhance a sense of moral righteousness as well as pride in a lofty mission.

The mutual enhancement of self-esteem and morale may have functional value in enabling the members to maintain their capacity to take action, but it has maladaptive consequences insofar as concurrence-seeking tendencies interfere with critical, rational capacities and lead to serious errors of judgment.

While I have limited my study to decision-making bodies in government, groupthink symptoms appear in business, industry and any other field where small, cohesive groups make the decisions. It is vital, then, for all sorts of people—and especially group leaders—to know what steps they can take to prevent groupthink.

REMEDIES

To counterpoint my case studies of the major fiascos, I have also investigated two highly successful group enterprises, the formulation of the Marshall Plan in the Truman Administration and the handling of the Cuban missile crisis by President Kennedy and his advisers. I have found it instructive to examine the steps Kennedy took to change his group's decision-making processes. These changes ensured that the mistakes made by his Bay of Pigs ingroup were not repeated by the missile-crisis ingroup, even though the membership of both groups was essentially the same.

The following recommendations for preventing groupthink incorporate many of the good practices I discovered to be characteristic of the Marshall Plan and missile-crisis groups:

1. The leader of a policy-forming group should assign the role of critical evaluation to each member, encouraging the group to give high priority to open airing of objections and doubts. This practice needs to be reinforced by the leader's acceptance of criticism of his own judgments in order to discourage members from soft-pedaling their disagreements and from allowing their striving for concurrence to inhibit critical thinking.

2. When the key members of a hierarchy assign a policy-planning mission to any group within their organization, they should adopt an impartial stance instead of stating preferences and expectations at the beginning. This will encourage open inquiry and impartial probing of a wide range of policy alternatives.

3. The organization routinely should set up several outside policy-planning and evaluation groups to work on the same policy question, each deliberating under a different leader. This can prevent the insulation of an ingroup.

4. At intervals before the group reaches a final consensus, the leader should require each member to discuss the group's deliberations with associates in his own unit of the organization—assuming that those associates can be trusted to adhere to the same security regulations that govern the policy-makers—and then to report back their reactions to the group.

5. The group should invite one or more outside experts to each meeting on a staggered basis and encourage the experts to challenge the views of the core members.

6. At every general meeting of the group, whenever the agenda calls for an evaluation of policy alternatives, at least one member should play devil's advocate, functioning as a good lawyer in challenging the testimony of those who advocate the majority position.

7. Whenever the policy issue involves relations with a rival nation or organization, the group should devote a sizable block of time, perhaps an entire session, to a survey of all warning signals from the rivals and should write alternative scenarios on the rivals' intentions.

8. When the group is surveying policy alternatives for feasibility and effectiveness, it should from time to time divide into two or more subgroups to meet separately, under different chairmen, and then come back together to hammer out differences.

9. After reaching a preliminary consensus about what seems to be the best policy, the group should hold a "second-chance" meeting at which every member expresses as vividly as he can all his residual doubts, and rethinks the entire issue before making a definitive choice.

HOW

These recommendations have their disadvantages. To encourage the open airing of objections, for instance, might lead to prolonged and costly debates when a rapidly growing crisis requires immediate solution. It also could cause rejection, depression and anger. A leader's failure to set a norm might create cleavage between leader and members that could develop into a disruptive power struggle if the leader looks on the emerging consensus as anathema. Setting up outside evaluation groups might increase the risk of security leakage. Still, inventive executives who know their way around the organizational maze probably can figure out how to apply one or another of the prescriptions successfully, without harmful side effects.

They also could benefit from the advice of outside experts in the administrative and behavioral sciences. Though these experts have much to offer, they have had few chances to work on policy-making machinery within large organizations. As matters now stand, executives innovate only when they need new procedures to avoid repeating serious errors that have deflated their self-images.

In this era of atomic warheads, urban disorganization and ecocatastrophes, it seems to me that policymakers should collaborate with behavioral scientists and give top priority to preventing groupthink and its attendant fiascos.

32. THE DESIGN OF WORK TEAMS

J. Richard Hackman

In an essay written to commemorate the fiftieth anniversary of the well-known Hawthorne studies at Western Electric Corporation, Harold Leavitt (1975,76) observed:

Far and away the most powerful and beloved tool of applied behavioral scientists is the small face-to-face group. Since the Western Electric research, behavioral scientists have been learning to understand, exploit and love groups. Groups attracted interest initially as devices for improving the implementation of decisions and to increase human commitment and motivation. They are now loved because they are also creative and innovative, they often make better quality decisions than individuals, and because they make organizational life more livable for people. One can't hire an applied behavioral scientist into an organization who within ten minutes will not want to call a group meeting and talk things over.

"The Design of Work Teams" in *Handbook of Organizational Behavior*, *J. W. Lorsch, ed. (1987) © 1987, pp. 315, 322, 323–331, 332, 338, 339. Reprinted by permission of Prentice-Hall Inc., Englewood Cliffs, New Jersey.

Leavitt's paper, entitled "Suppose We Took Groups Seriously. . . ," raises the possibility that both people and organizations would be better off if groups, rather than individuals, were the basic building blocks in the design and management of organizations. Recent trends in organizational practice—such as the increasing use of quality circles, autonomous work groups, project teams, and management task forces—suggest that groups are indeed becoming a popular way to get things done in organizations.

While groups can yield the kinds of benefits Leavitt discusses, they also have a shady side, at least as they typically are designed and managed in contemporary organizations. They can, for example, waste the time and energy of members, rather than use them well. They can enforce norms of low rather than high productivity (Whyte 1955). They sometimes make notoriously bad decisions (Janis 1982). Patterns of destructive conflict can arise, both within and between groups (Alderfer 1977). And groups can exploit, stress, and frustrate their members—sometimes all at the same time (Hackman 1976).

Clearly, if Leavitt's vision is to be realized, we must expand what we know about how to design, manage, and consult to work groups in organizations. There is currently no well-tested and accepted body of research and theory to guide practitioners in using groups to do work, nor do we have a documented record of success in using behavioral-science techniques to help groups become more effective.

This chapter . . . provides a conceptual model for integrating and extending that knowledge, and offers some action guidelines for structuring, supporting, and managing groups in contemporary organizations.

A NORMATIVE MODEL OF GROUP EFFECTIVENESS

The model of work-group effectiveness described in this section is an attempt to bridge between *understanding group behavior* and *doing something to improve it* (the topic of the final section of this chapter).[1] The intent of the normative model is to identify the factors that most powerfully enhance or depress the task effectiveness of a group and to do so in a way that increases the possibility that change can occur. This requires that the variables used in the model be powerful (i.e., they make nontrivial differences in how a group performs), potentially manipulable (i.e., it is feasible to change them in an organization), and accessible (i.e., people can understand them and use them). Moreover, they must be arranged sensibly: the model is not a naturalistic chronological description of what leads to what as a group goes about its work; yet if it is to be useful, it must be plausible.

That is a reasonably tall order, and if we are to have a chance of filling it, we must be very clear about both the kinds of groups to which the model applies and what we mean by "group effectiveness."

SCOPE OF THE MODEL

Domain

The normative model focuses exclusively on *work groups in organizations*. This means that the model applies only to (1) real groups (that is, intact social systems complete with boundaries and differentiated roles among members); (2) groups that have one or more *tasks* to perform, resulting in discernible and potentially measurable group products; and (3) groups that operate within an *organizational context*.

This turns out to be a fairly inclusive statement. The model would apply, for example, to a group of executives charged with deciding where to locate a new plant, a team of rank-and-file workers assembling a product, a group of students writing a case assigned by their instructor, a health-care team tending to the needs of a group of patients, and a group of economists analyzing the budgetary implications of a proposed new public policy.

Nonetheless, many sets of people commonly referred to as "groups" are excluded. Social groups are out (no task), as are reference groups (not an intact social system), coacting groups (i.e., people who may report to the same manager but who have their own, individual tasks to perform—no *group* task), and free-standing groups (no organizational context).

This statement of domain may seem relatively straightforward, but it often is difficult to determine what is a "real" group, a "group task," and an "organizational context." For a detailed and more formal discussion of these issues, see Hackman (1983).

GROUP EFFECTIVENESS DEFINED

In conducting experiments on group performance, researchers try to select tasks for which it is relatively easy to tell how well a group has performed: one can count the number of right answers, or measure how long it takes the group to finish, or see if the group solved the problem correctly. For teams in organizations, effectiveness criteria are more complex. Most organizational tasks do not have clear right-or-wrong answers, for example, nor do they lend themselves to quantitative measures that validly indicate how well a group has done its work. Moreover, one needs to be concerned about more than raw productivity or decision quality when assessing groups in organizations. Unlike participants in laboratory experiments (who come in, do the task, and go home), members of work groups and committees usually continue to relate to one another long after the group task is completed; what happens in the work group can substantially affect their willingness (and their ability) to do so.

For these reasons, we use three criteria to assess team effectiveness. The first deals with the actual output of the group, the second with the state of the group as a performing unit, and the third with the impact of the group experience on individual members.

1. *The productive output of the work group should meet or exceed the performance standards of the people who receive and/or review the output.* If a group's output is not acceptable to its "clients" and/or to managers charged with evaluating its performance, then it cannot be considered effective. An effectiveness criterion that relies explicitly on assessments made by organization members or clients (rather than on "objective" indexes of performance) was chosen for two reasons. First, reliable and valid objective criteria are available for only a small proportion of work teams in organizations; to deal only with those teams would restrict radically the domain of the model. In addition, what *happens* to a group and its members usually depends far more on others' assessments of the group's output than on any objective performance index (even though such assessments may be based, in part, on whatever objective measures happen to be available).[2]

2. *The social processes used in carrying out the work should maintain or enhance the capability of members to work together on subsequent team tasks.* Some groups operate in such a way that the integrity of the group as a performing unit is destroyed; the group "burns itself up" in the process of performing the task. Even if the product of such a group is acceptable, it would be difficult to argue that the group has been a fully effective performing unit.

3. *The group experience should, on balance, satisfy rather than frustrate the personal needs of group members.* If the primary effect of group membership is to keep individuals from doing what they want and need to do, or if members' predominant reactions to the group experience are disgust and disillusionment, then the costs of generating the group product, at least those borne by individual members, are probably too high.

The inclusion of social and personal criteria in a definition of effectiveness is a departure from tradition—as is the use of system-defined (rather than researcher-defined) assessments of a group's output. Yet the criteria themselves require neither extraordinary accomplishment nor exemplary social processes. All that is necessary is output judged acceptable by those who receive it, a team that winds up its work at least as healthy as when it started, and members who are at least as satisfied as they are frustrated by what has transpired. The challenge for researchers and practitioners is to develop ways of understanding, designing, and managing groups that help them meet or exceed these modest standards of team effectiveness.

The Basic Proposition

The normative model presented in the pages that follow rests on the validity of one key proposition. If this proposition is valid (and if its implications are appropriately developed), it should be possible to explain why some groups perform better than others, to assess the strengths and weaknesses of specific groups in organizations, and to determine what needs to be done to help a group become more effective.

Specifically, it is proposed that the overall effectiveness of work groups in organizations is a joint function of

• The level of *effort* group members collectively expend carrying out task work,

• The amount of *knowledge and skill* members bring to bear on the group task, and

• The appropriateness to the task of the *performance* strategies used by the group in its work.[3]

We will refer to effort, knowledge and skill, and performance strategies as *process criteria of effectiveness*. They are the hurdles a group must surmount to be effective. To assess the adequacy of a group's task processes, then, we might ask: Is the group working hard enough to get the task done well and on time? Do members have the expertise required to accomplish the task, and are they using their knowledge and skill efficiently? Has the group developed an approach to the work that is fully ap-

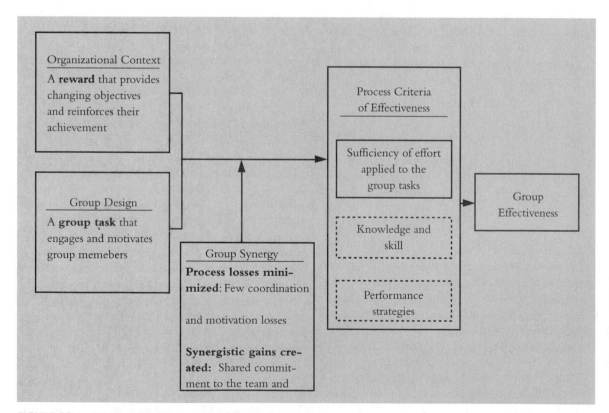

FIGURE 32.1   *Conditions That Foster Hard Work on a Group Task.*

propriate for the task being performed, and are they implementing that strategy well?

Answers to these questions provide diagnostic data about a group's strengths and weaknesses as a performing unit, and they should enable us to predict with some confidence a group's eventual performance effectiveness. But, as strongly implied by research on interventions that focus exclusively on improving group processes, direct attempts to *manipulate* a group's standing on the process criteria (e.g., by exhortation or instruction) are likely to fail.

A more promising approach is to design and manage a group so that task-effective group processes emerge naturally. Several features of the group and its context can potentially lead to improvements in a group's level of effort, its application of member knowledge and skill, and the appropriateness of its task performance strategies. In particular, we will examine the impact of the following three classes of variables on each of the process criteria:[4]

- The *design of the group* as a performing unit: the structure of the group task, the composition of the group, and group norms that regulate member behavior
- The *organizational context* of the group: the reward, education, and information systems that influence the group, and the material resources that are put at the group's disposal.
- *Group synergy* resulting from members' interactions as they carry out the task[5]

Throughout, we will emphasize aspects of group design, context, and synergy that foster both high-quality task behavior and eventual team effectiveness. After completing this analysis, we will explore ways of assessing the standing of a group on the variables in the normative model, and speculate about the implications of the model for the creation and management of work teams in organizations.[6]

CONDITIONS THAT SUPPORT EFFORT

Group members are most likely to work hard on their task if (1) the task itself is motivationally engaging, (2) the organizational reward system provides challenging performance objectives and reinforces their achievement, and (3) interaction among members minimizes "social loafing" and instead promotes a shared commitment among members to the team and its work. These factors are illustrated in Figure 32.1 and discussed below.

Design of the Group

We would expect a group to work especially hard on its tasks when the following conditions are met:

- The group task requires members to use a variety of relatively high-level skills.
- The group task is a whole and meaningful piece of work, with a visible outcome.
- The outcomes of the group's work on the task have significant consequences for other people (e.g., other organization members or external clients).
- The task provides group members with substantial autonomy for deciding about how they do the work—in effect, the group "owns" the task and is responsible for the work outcomes.
- Work on the task generates regular, trustworthy feedback about how well the group is performing.

If a group task meets these criteria, it is likely that members will experience their work as meaningful, they will feel collectively responsible for the products they create, and they will know, on a more or less continuous basis, how they are doing. And, extrapolating from Hackman and Oldham's (1980, chap. 4), model of individual task motivation, a group task with these properties should result in high built-in motivation for a group to try hard to do well (see, for example, Wall and Clegg 1981).

This emphasis on the group task runs counter to traditional wisdom about motivated work behavior. One often hears managers report that some group is "filled with lazy [or hard-working] people," or that group members "have a norm of not working very hard [or of always giving their best]." It is true that people have different chronic energy levels, but there is not much one can do about that. And while norms do emerge in groups that encourage especially high or low effort, such norms usually develop as a reaction to how things are set up, as a means of coping with the group task and work situation.

Thus, if a group's work is routine and unchallenging, of dubious importance, and wholly preprogrammed with no opportunity for feedback, members are likely to develop antiproductivity norms. But if a group task is challenging, important to the organization or its clients, "owned" by the group, and consequential for group members, then a norm encouraging high effort on the task is likely to emerge. Improving the design of a group's work is usually a better way to foster high collective effort than directly addressing group norms about productivity.

Organizational Context

A supportive organizational reward system can reinforce the motivational benefits of a well-designed team task, and a poorly structured reward system can undermine and erode those benefits. Reward systems that support high effort by work teams tend to have the following three features:

Challenging, Specific Performance Objectives. There is a great deal of research evidence that goal-directed effort is greater when a group accepts moderately difficult performance objectives and receives feedback about its progress in attaining those objectives (Zander 1971, 1980). When the organization specifies a challenging performance target (e.g., a date by which the work must be done, the number of items to be produced, a quality level to be achieved), mem-

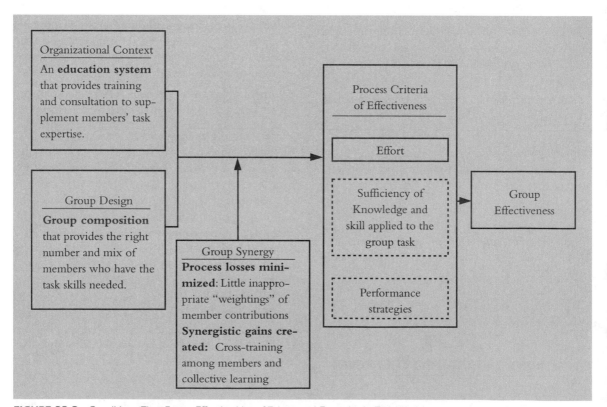

FIGURE 32.2. Conditions That Foster Effective Use of Talent and Expertise in Task Work.

bers often mobilize their efforts to achieve that target. Objectives, however, should supplement rather than replace task-based motivation. A group is unlikely to persist in working toward challenging objectives if its task is inherently frustrating and alienating.

Positive Consequences for Excellent Performance. A reward system that recognizes and reinforces excellent group performance can complement and amplify the motivational incentives of a well-designed group task. People tend to engage in behaviors that are rewarded, and people in groups are no exception (Glaser and Klaus 1966). Which specific kinds of rewards will work best, of course, depends on what group members value. Sometimes simple recognition of excellence will suffice; in other cases, more tangible rewards will be required. But whatever the content of the consequences, their impact on team effort will be greater if members understand that they are contingent on performance—that is, that the group will receive them only if it earns them by performing well.

Rewards and Objectives that Focus on Group, Not Individual, Behavior. . When rewards are given to individuals on the basis of managers' judgments about who has contributed most to a group product, dissension and conflict often develop within the group. This is the dilemma of the athletic coach, who must try to motivate the team as a whole while simultaneously cultivating and reinforcing individual performance. And it is a problem routinely faced by managers of work teams in organizations where the reward system has traditionally focused on the identification and recognition of excellent *individual* performers.

The destructive effects of rewarding individual contributions rather than team performance can be considerable. Therefore, if it is not feasible to provide performance-contingent rewards to the group as a unit, it may be better to base rewards on the performance of even larger groups (such as a department or division) or not to use contingent rewards at all, than to invite the divisiveness that can develop when members of a team are put into competition with one another for scarce and valued rewards (Lawler 1981).

Group Synergy

Group synergy can contribute to effective task behavior in two ways. First, group members can find innovative ways to avoid "process losses," and thereby minimize waste and misuse of members' time, energy, and talent. Second, members can interact synergistically to create *new* internal resources that can be used in their work—capabilities that did not exist before the group created them. Process losses and synergistic gains that affect how much effort a group applies to its task are discussed below.

Minimizing Coordination and Motivation Losses. There are always some "overhead costs" to be paid when groups perform tasks. The need to coordinate member activities, for example, takes time and energy away from productive work, resulting in a level of actual productivity that is less than what theoretically would be possible with optimum use of member resources (Steiner 1972). In addition, group productivity often is compromised by what Steiner terms "motivation decrements" and what Latané (e.g., Latané, Williams, and Harkins 1979) has called "social loafing." As groups get larger, the amount of effort *each member* contributes to the group task decreases—perhaps because each individual feels less responsible for the outcome than would be the case in a smaller group or if one person were doing the task alone.

Some groups suffer much greater coordination and motivation losses than others. And group members can cultivate process skills that help them behave in ways that minimize such losses. But if the group is large or if the task is ill defined or alienating, it may be impossible for the group to avoid serious coordination and motivation losses.

Creating Shared Commitment to the Team and Its Work. Some groups show great "spirit": everyone is committed to the team, proud of it, and willing to work hard to make it one of the best. When individuals value their membership in the group and find it rewarding to work collaboratively with their teammates, they may work considerably harder than they would otherwise. Managers often engage in group-building activities (such as encouraging members of an ongoing team to give the group a name, to decorate their work area, or to participate in an athletic league as a team) in the hope of increasing members' commitment to the group and their willingness to work especially hard on the group task.[7]

Commitment to a team sometimes can result in high effort on the group task even when objective performance conditions are highly unfavorable (e.g., a team that develops a "can do" attitude and comes to view each new adversity as yet another challenge to be met). It is questionable, however, whether such commitment is sustainable if performance conditions remain poor (e.g., a frustrating or alienating group task, or a reward system that does not recognize excellence).

CONDITIONS THAT SUPPORT KNOWLEDGE AND SKILL

A group is most likely to bring sufficient talent and expertise to bear on its task when (1) the group has an appropriate number of members with a good mix of skills, (2) the education system of the organization offers training or consultation as needed to supplement members' existing knowledge, and (3) group interaction avoids inappropriate "weighting" of members' contributions and instead fosters sharing of expertise and collective learning. These factors are illustrated in Figure 32.2 and discussed below.

Design of the Group

A group's composition is the most important condition affecting the amount of knowledge and skill members apply to their tasks. Well-composed groups have the following four characteristics:

Individual Members Have High Task-Relevant Expertise. The most efficient way to make sure a group has the expertise it needs for its work is simply to assign talented individuals to it. This seemingly obvious principle, however, is not always straightforward in practice. Even when people with ample task-relevant knowledge and skill are available, they may be overlooked—for example, when groups are composed with only political considerations in mind. This can result in a team whose members cover all the right bases, but one that is not capable of carrying out well the work it was created to do.

The Group Is Just Large Enough to Do the Work. If a task required four sets of hands, then there should be four people in the group—but no more than that. The research literature offers abundant evidence documenting the dysfunctions that occur in large groups (see Steiner 1972, chap. 4 for a review) and establishing the advantages of groups that are slightly *smaller* than the task technically requires (Wicker et al. 1976). Yet large work groups (especially decision-making committees) are widely used in organizations. Often the decision to put additional people in a group allows managers to avoid difficult personnel choices or sensitive political issues (e.g., how to involve a department in the work of a task force on which it has no representatives), but the cost may be losses in the quality of the group product and the efficiency with which it is produced.

Members Have Interpersonal as Well as Task Skills. If a group task is well designed (i.e., it provides the group considerable autonomy in managing a challenging piece of work), then at least moderate interpersonal skills are required to bring the *task* skills of members to bear on the group's work—especially if members are diverse (i.e., they come from different demographic groups, represent different organizational units, or have divergent personal views on the matter at hand). Some individuals have little competence in working collaboratively with other people, especially if those people differ from themselves in important ways. Even one or two such individuals can significantly impede the ability of a group to bring members' expertise effectively to bear on the group task.

Membership Is Moderately Diverse. Members of an excessively homogeneous group may get along well together but lack the resources needed to perform the task because the members essentially replicate one another. An excessively heterogeneous group, on the other hand, may have a rich complement of talent within the group but be unable to use that talent well because members are so diverse in values or perspective that they cannot work together effectively. The aspiration in composing a group is to strike just the right balance between homogeneity and heterogeneity: members should have a variety of talents and perspective, yet be similar enough that they can understand and coordinate with one another.[8]

Organizational Context

Sometimes a group has within its bounds all the knowledge and skill needed for optimum task performance. More commonly there are aspects of the work for which additional talent or expertise would be helpful. The educational system of the organization can play a useful role in helping the group obtain the outside expertise it needs for its work.

For this potential to be realized, two conditions must be met. First, relevant educational resources (which can include technical consultation as well as training) must exist somewhere in the organization. Second, some sort of "delivery system" must be in place to make those resources accessible to the group. This may not be a simple matter for rank-and-file teams in organizations where employees have never had the right to call on staff resources.

The particular kind of assistance required will, of course, depend on both the task requirements and the specific needs of the group. And the appropriate form of assistance will vary as well. Sometimes a one-shot technical consultation will suffice; sometimes a continuing consulting relationship will be needed; and sometimes a training program for group members will be more appropriate, to build the relevant expertise into the group itself. Whatever the content of the assistance and the vehicle used to provide it, the role of the educational system is the same: to help groups obtain the full complement of knowledge and skill required for excellent task performance.

Group Synergy

Minimizing Inappropriate Weighting of Member Contributions. The knowledge and skill of group members can be wasted if the group solicits and weights contributions in a way that is incongruent with members' expertise—as when the credence given a member's idea depends on such task-irrelevant considerations as his or her demographic attributes (e.g., gender, ethnicity, or age) or behavioral style (e.g., talkativeness or verbal dominance). This process loss has been well documented in the research literature (e.g., Johnson and Torcivia 1967; Thomas and Fink 1961; Torrance 1954). Groups often have trouble assessing which members have the special expertise needed for the task, and they appear to have even more difficulty explicitly acknowledging these differences and weighting members' contributions in accord with them. To the extent a group is able to minimize this problem, it will take better advantage of the expertise that was put in the group when it was composed.

Fostering Collective Learning. When members of a group interact in ways that help them learn from one another, they can increase the total pool of talent available for task work—a synergistic gain from group interaction. The practice of "cross-training," often encouraged in autonomous work groups in industry, is an example of such behavior, as are more informal activities that involve the sharing of knowledge, expertise, and experience among members. A group that orients itself to collective learning and whose members share what is learned with each other should be far better able to exploit the educational resources of an organization than a group that takes a laissez-faire stance toward the development of its internal talent.

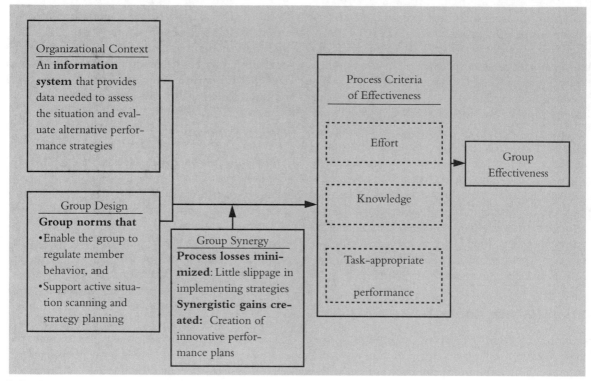

FIGURE 32.3. Conditions that Encourage the Use of Task-appropriate Performance Strategies.

CONDITIONS THAT SUPPORT APPROPRIATE PERFORMANCE STRATEGIES

The likelihood that the group will employ a task-appropriate performance strategy increases when (1) group norms support explicit assessment of the performance situation and active consideration of alternative ways of proceeding with the work; (2) the information system of the organization provides members with the data they need to assess the situation and evaluate alternative strategies; and (3) group interaction results in little "slippage" when performance plans are executed and instead prompts creative new ideas about ways to proceed with the work. These factors are illustrated in Figure 32.3 and discussed below.

Design of Group

Group members typically reach agreement on how they will go about performing their task relatively early in their time together. Indeed, for familiar tasks, members may not talk about their strategy at all, because it is obvious to everyone how the task should be done. Once a strategy is agreed to, whether implicitly or explicitly, members tend to behave in accord with it and enforce adherence to it (March and Simon 1958, chap. 6). Performance strategies thus become part of the fabric of the group, a "given" that is no more open to question than the task of the group or who is in the group.

The specific strategies that will be most appropriate for a given group depend both on the task to be done and on the imperatives and resources in the performance situation. No "one best strategy" can be specified in advance for most task-performing groups in organizations. It is possible, however, to build group norms that increase the likelihood that members will develop task-appropriate performance strategies and execute them well. Such norms have two properties, the first being a prerequisite for the second.[9]

Group Norms Support Self-Regulation. Behavior in some groups is so chaotic and subject to individual whim as to approach anarchy. Such groups are unlikely to be able to execute any performance strategy in an orderly fashion, even one that has been specified in detail by management. Thus, a normative structure that enables a group to regulate member behavior is essential to the efficient execution of performance strategies. This requires that behavioral norms be sufficiently crystallized (i.e., members have consensus about them) and intense (i.e., compliance results in substantial approval or avoidance of substantial disapproval by other members) that individuals will wish to behave in accord with them (Jackson 1965).

Group Norms Support Situation Scanning and Strategy Planning. Groups that actively assess the demands and opportunities in the performance situation and that consider several alternative ways of proceeding with the work tend to develop more appropriate performance strategies than groups that do not (Hackman, Brousseau, and Weiss 1976; Maier 1963). Yet such activities tend not to take place spontaneously. Instead, it appears that the general disinclination of group members to "talk about process" extends even to discussions about how the work of the group will be carried out.[10]

For this reason, it is necessary somehow to prompt or encourage group members to engage in situation scanning and strategy planning activities. Group norms provide an efficient and powerful way to accomplish this. Such norms focus attention on opportunities and constraints that might otherwise be overlooked and make it difficult for members to fall into familiar or habitual patterns of behavior that may be inappropriate for the particular task at hand.[11]

Group norms governing performance processes can be established when a group is first formed or can be introduced during a hiatus in the work, when members are ready to reconsider how they operate as a team. Regardless of how and when they are developed, the norms that guide a group's performance processes are an important structural feature of the group—an aspect of group design that often has been overlooked by both scholars and managers interested in work-team effectiveness.

Organizational Context

The information system of an organization is critical to a group's ability to plan and execute a task-appropriate performance strategy. If a group cannot obtain clear information about its performance situation, or if it does not have access to data about the likely outcomes of alternative approaches to the task, it may develop a way of proceeding that seems reasonable to group members but that turns out, when executed, to be grossly inappropriate.

Clarity About the Parameters of the Performance Situation. To develop a task-appropriate performance strategy, a group needs a relatively clear map of the performance situation. Of special importance is information about (1) task requirements and constraints that may limit strategic options, (2) the material resources available for use, and (3) the people who will receive, review, and/or use the group product, and the standards they are likely to employ in assessing its adequacy.

Access to Data About Likely Consequences of Alternative Strategies. The information system also should make available to a group the data and analytic tools members need to compare and evaluate the probable consequences of alternative performance strategies. Consider, for example, a manufacturing team that is attempting to decide how to approach a complex assembly task. One possibility might be a cyclic strategy, in which all members build components for a period of time, then assemble final products (producing a relative flood of output), followed by another component-building period, and so on. How would this strategy compare to one in which some members build components continuously while others are dedicated to final assembly? To choose between these strategies, the group needs information about the timing of demand for their product, the availability of space for storing components and completed products, and the cost of obtaining and holding parts for use in batch-component production. It would be quite risky for a group to choose a strategy without data about such matters.

How much information a group needs depends in part on how much latitude it has to manage its own affairs. Groups that have the authority to invent their own strategies and manage their own performance processes will need relatively complete data on both the parameters of the performance situation and the likely consequences of alternative ways of proceeding. Groups with less authority for setting their own directions will have less need for such data.

Managers who control access to performance-relevant information must make sure that data needed by a team are realistically available to it. This is not always easy: the relevant data may not exist, they may be costly to obtain, or the manager may be unable to convince his or her colleagues that it is appropriate to share with the group politically or competitively sensitive information. In such circumstances, the group needs to know *that*—that it will have to make do with imperfect or incomplete data.[12] Care also must be taken not to flood the group with excess or

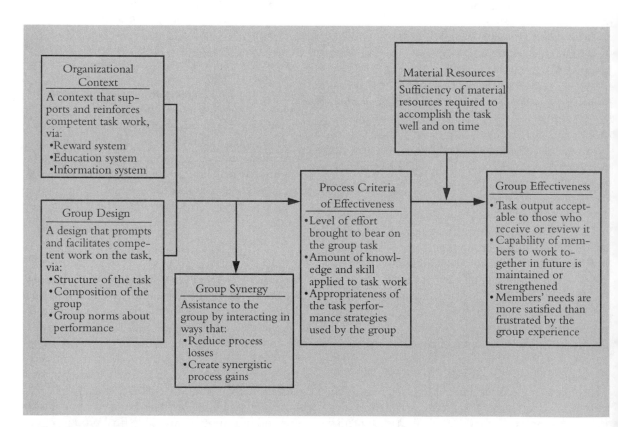

FIGURE 32.4. An Overview of the Normative Model of Group Effectiveness.

irrelevant information, data that members must process but for which they have no present use. Some organizations minimize this risk by initially providing teams only with basic data about the parameters of the performance situation and a guide to other information available. The group has the responsibility for deciding what additional data it requires and for determining when and how to obtain it.

Group Synergy

Minimizing Slippage in Strategy Implementation. Plans are never perfectly implemented—there is always a slip or two, something that wastes or misdirects the time and energy of group members, compromising even well-conceived plans. To the extent a group minimizes this process loss, the opportunities provided by norms that foster strategy planning and by a supportive information system can be well used. But if slippage is high, the group may fail to exploit even a highly favorable performance situation.[13]

Creating Innovative Strategic Plans. On the positive side, groups can develop ways of interacting that occasionally result in truly original or insightful ways of proceeding with the work. For example, a group might find a way to exploit some resources that everyone else has overlooked; it might invent a way to get around a seemingly insurmountable performance obstacle; or it might come up with a novel way to generate ideas for solving a difficult problem. When group members get in the habit of thinking creatively about how they will do their work, interesting and useful ideas can emerge—ideas that did not exist before the group invented them.

OVERVIEW AND SUMMARY

An overview of the normative model is presented in Figure 32.4. It shows three major points of leverage for fostering group effectiveness: (1) the design of the group as a performing unit, (2) the supports provided by the organizational context in which the group operates, and (3) the synergistic outcomes of the interaction among group members.

The contributions of each of these classes of variables are summarized next in brief.

Design

The design of a group—task structure, group composition, and group norms—should promote effective task behavior and lessen the chances that members will encounter built-in obstacles to good performance. While a good group design cannot guarantee competent group behavior, it does create conditions that make it easier and more natural for task-effective behaviors to emerge and persist.

Context

The organizational context of a group—the reward, education, and information systems of the organization—should support and reinforce the design features. A supportive organizational context gives a group what it needs to exploit the potential of a good basic design (although it probably cannot compensate for a fundamentally flawed design). An unsupportive organizational context can easily undermine the positive features of even a well-designed team. Excellent group performance requires *both* a good design for the team and a supportive organizational context.

Figure 32.4 shows one important contextual feature not previously discussed—the *material resources* required to do the work. If a group lacks the tools, equipment, space, raw materials, money, or human resources it needs, its performance surely will suffer—even if it stands high on the process criteria of effectiveness. A talented, well-motivated production team, for example, will not perform well if the raw materials it needs to make its products are not available, or if production tools are unsatisfactory. Similarly, a committee formed to select a new agency manager cannot be successful if there are no qualified candidates available. And a group that provides human services to clients may have performance problems if members' work stations are so spread about that they cannot coordinate their activities, or if money is so scarce that needed support staff cannot be obtained.[14]

Synergy

Group synergy "tunes" the impact of design and contextual factors. Positive synergy—that is, when the synergistic gains from group interaction exceed group process losses—can help a group overcome the limitations of a poor performance situation (e.g., a badly designed group task or an unsupportive reward system). And if performance conditions are favorable, positive synergy can help a group exploit the opportunities those conditions provide. Negative synergy, when process losses exceed synergistic gains, has opposite effects. It can amplify the negative impact of a poor performance situation, and it can prevent a group from taking advantage of favorable circumstances. The relationship between performance conditions (i.e., the group design and the organizational context) and group synergy are illustrated in Figure 32.5.[15]

IMPLICATIONS FOR THE MANAGEMENT OF TEAMS

Because this chapter represents a departure from traditional thinking about group performance, it may be appropriate to conclude by briefly highlighting some of the broader management implications of what has been proposed.

On Leadership

The research literature is rich with studies of leadership in groups (for reviews, see Hare 1976, chap. 13, and Stogdill 1974). Most of this research assesses what leaders do *within* groups or tests propositions about what leader traits and styles are most effective under what circumstances. Such questions are derivative in the approach taken here, because leaders are viewed as exercising influence primarily through the decisions they make about how to frame the group task, how to structure the group and its context, and how to help the group get started up well and headed in an appropriate direction.

Indeed, we have not even discussed whether an internal group leader should be named—let alone how he or she should behave. It often does make sense to have such a role, especially when substantial coordination among members is required, when there is lots of information to be processed (Maier 1967), or when it is advisable to have one

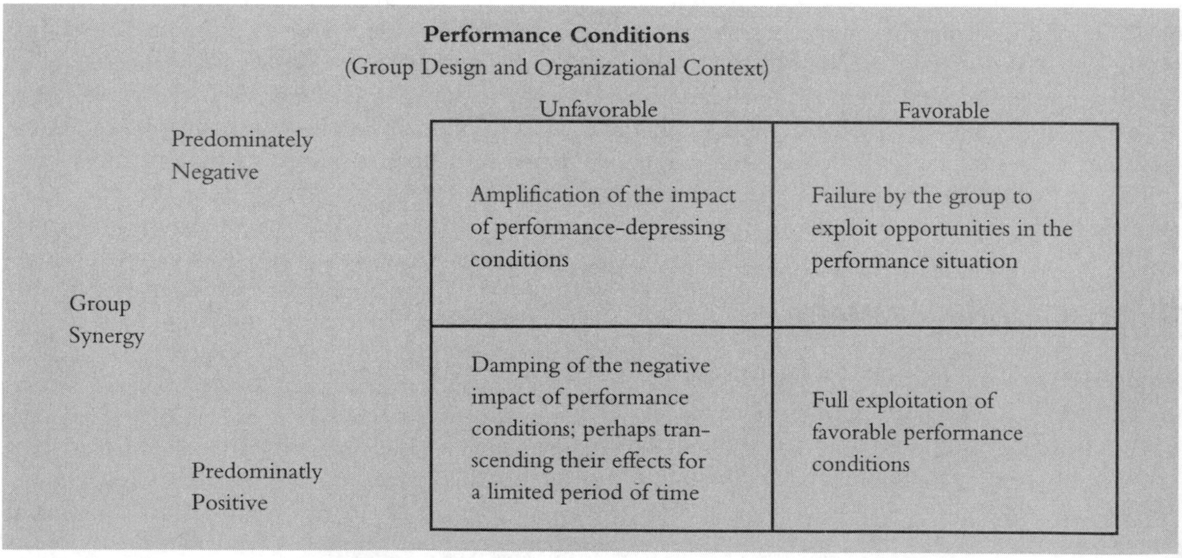

		Performance Conditions (Group Design and Organizational Context)	
		Unfavorable	Favorable
Group Synergy	Predominately Negative	Amplification of the impact of performance-depressing conditions	Failure by the group to exploit opportunities in the performance situation
	Predominatly Positive	Damping of the negative impact of performance conditions; perhaps transcending their effects for a limited period of time	Full exploitation of favorable performance conditions

FIGURE 32.5. Consequences for Task Behavior of the Interaction Between Performance Conditions and Group Synergy.

person be the liaison with other groups or with higher management. Yet it is rarely a good idea to decide in advance about the leadership structure of a work group. If a group has been designed well and helped to begin exploring the group norms and member roles it wishes to have, questions of internal leadership should appear naturally. And while there invariably will be a good deal of stress and strain in the group as leadership issues are dealt with, when a resolution comes it will have the considerable advantage of being the group's own.

The manager's role, then, is to make sure a group confronts the leadership issue directly (even if members would prefer to deal with it implicitly or avoid it entirely), not to resolve it for the group. To do the latter is to short-circuit an important developmental task in the life of a team and to rob the group of a significant opportunity to organize and develop its own internal resources.

On Creating Redundant Conditions

There are many ways for a group to be effective in performing a task, and even more ways for it to be ineffective. Moreover, different task and organizational circumstances involve vastly different demands and opportunities. Thus it is impossible to specify in detail what specific behaviors managers should adopt to help groups perform effectively. There are simply too many ways a group can operate and still wind up with the same outcome.[16] Attempts to specify contingencies for managerial behavior do not help much, in that they usually result in prescriptions too complex for anyone to follow (Hackman 1984).

Thus, while many models of leadership call for the active manipulation of "causes" that are assumed to be tightly linked to "effects," our view of group behavior suggests that the key to effective group management may be to create redundant conditions that support good performance, leaving groups ample room to develop and enact their own ways of operating within those conditions.

A manager interested in encouraging a group to work hard, for example, would try to make the group task more motivationally engaging. *And* he

or she would try to provide more (or more potent) positive consequences contingent on hard, effective work. *And* he or she would work with the group members to improve the efficiency of their internal processes and to build a positive team spirit. And if there were other steps that could be taken to create conditions supportive of high effort, these would be attempted as well.

Group performance does not have clean, unitary causes. To help a group improve its effectiveness involves doing whatever is possible to create multiple, redundant conditions that together may nudge the group toward more competent task behavior and, eventually, better performance.[17]

On Managerial Authority

The approach taken in this chapter clearly favors the creation of conditions that empower groups, that increase their authority to manage their own work. While this does not imply a diminution of managerial authority, it does suggest that it be redirected.

One critical use of authority, already discussed at some length, is in creating organizational conditions that foster and support effective group behavior. Managers must not view design and contextual features as "givens" over which they have little control. Instead, influence must be wielded upward and outward in the organization to make organizational structures and systems as supportive of team effectiveness as possible. If a manager does not have the authority to initiate discussions about making such changes, he or she should consider trying to get it, because it will be hard to be a good team manager without it.

Managerial authority also should be used to establish and enforce standards of group behavior and acceptable performance. When a manager defines a piece of work to be done, sets performance standards, and is clear about the bounds of acceptable group behavior, he or she is exercising managerial authority—and concurrently empowering the group that will do the work. To be vague about what is required and expected can be just as debilitating to a group as traditional, hands-on supervision. To enable groups to use their authority well, managers must not be afraid to exercise their own.

On Knowing Some Things

The management behaviors implied by the model of team effectiveness explored in this chapter will seem unfamiliar and awkward to some managers, and may be hard for them to perform well. But any new endeavor can be difficult. Trying to make sense of a balance sheet, for example, or figuring out a good design for a production process can feel just as awkward and be just as hard for an unpracticed manager to do well. Yet for some reason we are far more willing to acknowledge the need for training and experience in these areas than we are in aspects of managerial work related to the effective use of human resources.

Managing work groups is every bit as tough as figuring out what to do about the numbers on a balance sheet. To manage teams well, one needs to know some things, have some skills, and have opportunities to practice. The sooner those requirements are acknowledged, the sooner we will be able to develop a cadre of managers who are expert in creating work teams, developing them, and harvesting the considerable contributions they have to make to organizational effectiveness.

REFERENCES

1. The work of Cummings (e.g., 1978, 1981) on the design and management of work groups from a sociotechnical-systems perspective has much in common with what is presented here, although it comes from a rather different intellectual tradition. For an overview of that tradition, see Trist (1981).

2. There are, however, occasions when it may not be sensible to rely on client assessments of a group's output. Consider, for example, a situation in which the legitimate clients of the group are seriously disturbed, ethnocentric, or competitive with the group. The very meaning of "good performance" under these circumstances is problematic.

3. For example, a group might decide to divide itself into two sub-groups, each of which would do part of the overall task, with the final product to be assembled later. Or it might choose to free associate about task solutions in the first meeting, reflect for a week about the ideas that came up, and then meet to draft the product. Or it might decide to spend considerable time checking and rechecking for errors after learning that its client cares a great deal about product quality. All of these are choices about task performance strategy.

4. For simplicity, feedback loops among classes of variables in the framework (e.g., how the organizational context may change in response to a team's level of effectiveness) are not shown or discussed here.

5. As applied to group behavior in this chapter, "synergy" refers to group-level phenomena that (1) emerge from the interaction among members, and (2) affect how well a group is able to deal with the demands and opportunities in its performance situation.

6. Some of the material that follows is adapted from Hackman and Oldham (1980), chaps. 7–8.

7. Such activities are not risk free. "Team spirit" can evolve into group ethnocentrism and can prompt dysfunctional competition and conflict between groups.

8. A number of scholars have examined the impact of member compatibility on task behavior and performance. See, for example, Belbin (1981); Hewett, O'Brien, and Hornik (1974); and Schutz (1958, 1961).

9. Following Jackson (1965), norms are conceptualized as structural features of a group that summarize members' shared approval (or disapproval) of various behaviors. Norms simplify group influence processes because they make it possible for members to count on certain things being done and other things not being done. For more detailed discussion of how norms structure and channel behavior in a group, see Hackman (1976).

10. Spontaneous strategy planning does, of course, occur if a task is so novel that members are at a loss about how to proceed with it, and is generally more likely when the task is unfamiliar.

11. This analysis presumes that a team has at least some latitude for planning its own strategy. Usually this is the case. In some groups, however, behavior is so completely preprogrammed or closely supervised that members have essentially no strategy choices to make. For such groups, there is little need for a norm supporting scanning and planning, because those activities are someone else's responsibility. All that is needed is the orderly execution of the strategy that has been supplied. The implications of giving a team the authority to devise its own strategies (rather than reserving that authority for management) are explored later in this chapter.

12. Particularly unfortunate are occasions when a manager deliberately withholds performance-relevant information from a group, to make sure the group remains dependent on him or her. While this may preserve a manager's feelings of personal power, it can result in inappropriate performance strategies and needlessly poor team performance.

13. One particularly virulent form of this process loss bears special mention. Members of some groups collude with each other in a way that makes it impossible ever to implement performance plans. Such a group may have ample information about the performance situation and may develop a fully task-appropriate performance strategy. But once the plans are complete they are ignored. When members reconvene, they develop new plans and a new resolve, and the cycle repeats itself. The group acts as if a good strategy is all that is needed for team effectiveness, and its inevitable failures are always well-wrapped in new and better plans for the future. This kind of synergy often is driven by unconscious forces, it is not uncommon in groups that have high-pressure work environments, and it can be lethal to team effectiveness.

14. The importance of mundane aspects of the performance situation such as these are increasingly being recognized as critical to effective work performance (see, for example, Peters and O'Connor 1980, and Peters, O'Connor, and Rudolf 1980). To overlook them is to jeopardize the effort expended to design a team well and provide it with appropriate contextual supports.

15. Although performance conditions and group synergy are placed on separate axes in the figure, they are not independent: positive synergy is more likely under favorable conditions, and negative synergy is more likely under unfavorable conditions. Thus performance spirals can develop. For example, good group performance can lead to management decisions that improve the group's performance situation, which promotes positive synergy, which results in even better performance, and so on. Equally plausible is a negative spiral, in which poor performance begets organizational "tightening up," resulting in negative synergy, and so on.

16. Systems theorists call this aspect of organized endeavor "equifinality" (Katz and Kahn 1978, 30). According to this principle, a social system can reach the same outcome from a variety of initial conditions and by a variety of methods.

17. We see here a key difference between descriptive and action models of behavior in organization. A descriptive model parcels up the world for conceptual clarity: in contrast, a good action

model parcels up the world to increase the chances that something can be created or changed. Rather than seek to isolate unitary causes, an action model attempts to identify clusters of co-varying factors that can serve as useful levers for change. For related views, see Hackman (1984), Mohr (1982), and Weick (1977).

ADDITIONAL READINGS

C. P. Alderfer (1977) "Group and Intergroup Relations" in J. R. Hackman and J. L. Suttle, eds., *Improving Life at Work*. Santa Monica, Calif.: Goodyear.

C. Argyris (1969) "The Incompleteness of Social Psychological Theory: Examples from Small Group, Cognitive Consistency, and Attribution Research." *American Psychologist*, 24, pp. 893–908.

————. (1980) *The Inner Contradictions of Rigorous Research*. New York: Academic Press.

————. (1983) "Action Science and Intervention." *Journal of Applied Behavioral Science*, 19, pp. 115–35.

R. F. Bales (1950) *Interaction Process Analysis: A Method for the Study of Small Groups*. Cambridge, Mass.: Addison-Wesley.

————. (1970) *Personality and Interpersonal Behavior*. New York: Holt, Rinehart and Winston.

R. F. Bales and S. P. Cohen (1979) *SYMLOG: A System for the Multiple Level Observation of Groups*. New York: Free Press.

M. Beer (1976) "The Technology of Organization Development" in M. D. Dunnette, ed., *Handbook of Industrial and Organizational Psychology*. Chicago: Rand McNally.

R. M. Belbin (1981) *Management Teams: Why They Succeed or Fail*. London: Heinemann.

H. J. Bertcher and F. F. Maple (1977) *Creating Groups*. Beverly Hills, Calif.: Sage.

R. R. Blake and J. S. Mouton (1969) *Building a Dynamic Corporation Through Grid Organization Development*. Reading, Mass.: Addison-Wesley.

A. D. Colman, and W. H. Bexton (1975) *Group Relations Reader*. Sausalito, Calif.: GREX.

C. L. Cooper, (1975), ed., *Theories of Group Processes*. London: Wiley.

T. G. Cummings (July 1978) "Self-Regulating Work Groups: A Socio-Technical Synthesis." *Academy of Management Review*, 2, no. 3, pp. 625–34.

————. (1981) "Designing Effective Work Groups" in P. C. Nystrom and W. H. Starbuck, eds., *Handbook of Organizational Design*, vol. 2. London: Oxford University Press.

N. C. Dalkey (1967) *Delphi*. Santa Monica, Calif.: Rand.

J. H. Davis (1973) "Group Decision and Social Interaction: A Theory of Social Decision Schemes." *Psychological Review*, 80, pp. 97–125.

J. H. Davis and V. B. Hinsz (1982) "Current Research Problems in Group Performance and Group Dynamics" in H. Brandstätter, J. H. Davis, and G. Stocker-Kreichgauer, eds., *Group Decision Making*. London: Academic Press.

A. L. Delbecq, A. H. Van de Ven, and D. H. Gustafson (1975) *Group Techniques for Program Planning*. Glenview, Ill.: Scott, Foresman.

M. D. Dunnette, J. Campbell, and K. Jaastad (1963) "The Effect of Group Participation on Brainstorming Effectiveness for Two Industrial Samples." *Journal of Applied Psychology*, 47, pp. 30–37.

W. G. Dyer (1977) *Team Building: Issues and Alternatives.* Reading, Mass.: Addison-Wesley.

F. Friedlander and L. D. Brown (1974) "Organization Development" in M. R. Rosenzweig and L. W. Porter, eds., *Annual Review of Psychology*, vol. 25. Palo Alto, Calif.: Annual Reviews.

C. J. G. Gersick (1983) "Life Cycles of *Ad Hoc* Groups." Technical report no. 3, Group Effectiveness Research Project, School of Organization and Management, Yale University.

R. Glaser and D. J. Klaus (1966) "A Reinforcement Analysis of Group Performance." *Psychological Monographs*, 80, whole no. 621, pp. 1–23.

P. Goodman, R. Atkin, and E. Ravlin (1982) "Some Observations on Specifying Models of Group Performance." Paper delivered at a symposium on Productive Work Teams and Groups, American Psychological Association Convention, Washington, D. C.

T. B. Green (1975) "An Empirical Analysis of Nominal and Interacting Groups." *Academy of Management Journal*, 18, pp. 63–73.

J. R. Hackman (1969) "Toward Understanding the Role of Tasks in Behavioral Research." *Acta Psychologica* 31, pp. 97–128.

———. (1976) "Group Influences on Individuals" in M. D. Dunnette, ed., *Handbook of Industrial and Organizational Psychology*. Chicago: Rand McNally.

———. (1982) "A Set of Methods for Research on Work Teams." Technical report no. 1, Group Effectiveness Research Project, School of Organization and Management, Yale University.

———. (1983) "A Normative Model of Work Team Effectiveness." Technical report no. 2, Group Effectiveness Research Project, School of Organization and Management, Yale University.

———. (1984) "Psychological Contributions to Organizational Productivity: A Commentary" in A. P. Brief, ed., *Productivity Research in the Behavioral and Social Sciences*. New York: Praeger.

J. R. Hackman, K. R. Brousseau, and J. A. Weiss (1976) "The Interaction of Task Design and Group Performance Strategies in Determining Group Effectiveness." *Organizational Behavior and Human Performance*, 16, pp. 350–65.

J. R. Hackman and C. G. Morris (1975) "Group Tasks, Group Interaction Process, and Group Performance Effectiveness: A Review and Proposed Integration" in L. Berkowitz, ed., *Advances in Experimental Social Psychology*. New York: Academic Press.

J. R. Hackman and G. R. Oldham (1980) *Work Redesign*. Reading, Mass.: Addison-Wesley.

A. P. Hare (1976) *Handbook of Small Group Research*. 2d ed. New York: Free Press.

———. (1982) *Creativity in Small Groups*. Beverly Hills, Calif.: Sage.

J. S. Heinen and E. Jacobson (1976) "A Model of Task Group Development in Complex Organizations and a Strategy of Implementation." *Academy of Management Review*, 1, pp. 98–111.

D. M. Herold (1978) "Improving the Performance Effectiveness of Groups Through a Task-Contingent Selection of Intervention Strategies." *Academy of Management Review*, 3, pp. 315–25.

T. T. Hewett, G. E. O'Brien, and J. Hornik (1974) "The Effects of Work Organization, Leadership Style, and Member Compatibility Upon the Productivity of Small Groups Working on a Manipulative Task." *Organizational Behavior and Human Performance*, 11, pp. 283–301.

L. R. Hoffman (1979a) "Applying Experimental Research on Group Problem Solving to Organizations." *Journal of Applied Behavioral Science*, 15, pp. 375–91.

———. (1979b), ed., *The Group Problem Solving Process: Studies of a Valence Model*. New York: Praeger.

J. Jackson (1965) "Structural Characteristics of Norms" in I. D. Steiner and M. Fishbein, eds., *Current Studies in Social Psychology*. New York: Holt, Rinehart and Winston.

I. L. Janis (1982) *Groupthink*. 2d ed. Boston: Houghton Mifflin.

H. H. Johnson and J. M. Torcivia (1967) "Group and Individual Performance on a Single-Stage Task as a Function of Distribution of Individual Performance." *Journal of Personality and Social Psychology*, 3, pp. 266–73.

R. E. Kaplan (1979) "The Conspicuous Absence of Evidence that Process Consultation Enhances Task Performance." *Journal of Applied Behavioral Science*, 15, pp. 346–60.

D. Katz and R. L. Kahn (1978) *The Social Psychology of Organizations*. 2d ed. New York: Wiley.

R. Katz (1982) "The Effects of Group Longevity on Project Communication and Performance." *Administrative Science Quarterly*, 27, pp. 81–104.

B. Latané, K. Williams, and S. Harkins (1979) "Many Hands Make Light the Work: The Causes and Consequences of Social Loafing." *Journal of Personality and Social Psychology*, 37, pp. 822–32.

E. E. Lawler (1981) *Pay and Organization Development*. Reading, Mass.: Addison-Wesley.

H. J. Leavitt (1975) "Suppose We Took Groups Seriously . . ." in E. L. Cass and F. G. Zimmer, eds., *Man and Work in Society*. New York: Van Nostrand Reinhold.

N. R. F. Maier (1963) *Problem Solving Discussions and Conferences: Leadership Methods and Skills*. New York: McGraw-Hill.

———. (1967) "Assets and Liabilities in Group Problem Solving: The Need for an Integrative Function." *Psychological Review*, 74, pp. 239–49.

J. G. March and H. A. Simon (1958) *Organizations*. New York: Wiley.

J. E. McGrath (1964) *Social Psychology: A Brief Introduction*. New York: Holt, Rinehart and Winston.

———. (1984) *Groups: Interaction and Performance*. Englewood Cliffs, N.J.: Prentice-Hall.

J. E. McGrath and I. Altman (1966) *Small Group Research: A Synthesis and Critique of the Field*. New York: Holt, Rinehart and Winston.

J. E. McGrath and D. A. Kravitz (1982) "Group Research." *Annual Review of Psychology*, 33, pp. 195–230.

U. Merry and M. E. Allerhand (1977) *Developing Teams and Organizations*. Reading, Mass.: Addison-Wesley.

L. B. Mohr (1982) *Explaining Organizational Behavior*. San Francisco: Jossey-Bass.

D. C. Myers and H. Lamm (1976) "The Group Polarization Phenomenon." *Psychological Bulletin*, 83, pp. 602–27.

D. H. Nagao, D. A. Vollrath, and J. H. Davis (1978) "Group Decision Making: Origins and Current Status" in H. Brandstätter, J. H. Davis, and H. C. Schuler, eds., *Dynamics of Group Decisions*. Beverly Hills, Calif.: Sage.

A. F. Osborn (1957) *Applied Imagination*. Rev. ed. New York: Scribner's.

R. Payne and C. L. Cooper, eds. (1981) *Groups at Work*. Chichester, England: Wiley.

L. H. Peters and E. J. O'Connor (1980) "Situational Constraints and Work Outcomes: The Influences of a Frequently Overlooked Construct." *Academy of Management Review*, 5, pp. 391–97.

L. H. Peters, E. J. O'Connor, and C. J. Rudolf (1980) "The Behavioral and Affective Consequences of Performance-Relevant Situational Variables." *Organizational Behavior and Human Performance*, 25, pp. 79–96.

E. J. Poza and M. L. Marcus (1980) "Success Story: The Team Approach to Work Restructuring." *Organizational Dynamics*, Winter, pp. 3–25.

T. B. Roby and J. T. Lanzetta (1958) "Considerations in the Analysis of Group Tasks." *Psychological Bulletin*, 55, pp. 88–101.

I. M. Rubin, M. S. Plovnick, and R. E. Fry (1977) *Task-Oriented Team Development*. New York: McGraw-Hill.

P. J. Runkel and J. E. McGrath (1972) *Research on Human Behavior*. New York: Holt, Rinehart and Winston.

E. H. Schein (1969) *Process Consultation*. Reading, Mass.: Addison-Wesley.

W. C. Schutz (1958) *FIRO: A Three-Dimensional Theory of Interpersonal Behavior*. New York: Holt, Rinehart and Winston.

———. (1961) "On Group Composition." *Journal of Abnormal and Social Psychology*, 62, pp. 275–81.

G. Stasser and J. H. Davis (1981) "Group Decision Making and Social Influence: A Social Interaction Sequence Model." *Psychological Review*, 88, pp. 523–51.

M. I. Stein (1975) *Stimulating Creativity*, Vol. 2. New York: Academic Press.

I. D. Steiner (1972) *Group Process and Productivity*. New York: Academic Press.

R. M. Stogdill (1974) *Handbook of Leadership*. New York: Free Press.

S. A. Stumpf, D. E. Zand, and R. D. Freedman (1979) "Designing Groups for Judgmental Decisions." *Academy of Management Review*, 4, pp. 589–600.

E. J. Thomas and C. F. Fink (1961) "Models of Group Problem Solving." *Journal of Abnormal and Social Psychology*, 63, pp. 53–63.

———. (1963) "Effects of Group Size." *Psychological Bulletin*, 60, pp. 371–84.

E. P. Torrance (1954) "Some Consequences of Power Differences on Decision Making in Permanent and Temporary Three-Man Groups." *Research Studies, State College of Washington*, 22, pp. 130–40.

E. L. Trist (1981) "The Evolution of Sociotechnical Systems as a Conceptual Framework and as an Action Research Program" in A. H. Van de Ven and W. F. Joyce, eds., *Perspectives on Organization Design and Behavior*. New York: Wiley.

B. W. Tuckman (1965) "Developmental Sequence in Small Groups." *Psychological Bulletin*, 63, pp. 384–99.

N. Vidmar and J. R. Hackman (1971) "Interlaboratory Generalizability of Small Group Research: An Experimental Study." *Journal of Social Psychology*, 83, pp. 129–39.

T. D. Wall and C. W. Clegg (1981) "A Longitudinal Field Study of Group Work Design." *Journal of Occupational Behavior*, 2, pp. 31–49.

R. E. Walton and L. S. Schlesinger (1979) "Do Supervisors Thrive in Participative Work Systems?" *Organizational Dynamics*, Winter, pp. 24–38.

K. E. Weick (1965) "Laboratory Experimentation with Organizations" in J. G. March, ed., *Handbook of Organizations*. Chicago: Rand McNally.

―――. (1977) "Organization Design: Organizations as Self-Designing Systems." *Organizational Dynamics*, Autumn, pp. 31–46.

W. F. Whyte (1955) *Money and Motivation: An Analysis of Incentives in Industry*. New York: Harper.

A. Wicker, S. L. Kirmeyer, L. Hanson, and D. Alexander (1976) "Effects of Manning Levels on Subjective Experiences, Performance, and Verbal Interaction in Groups." *Organizational Behavior and Human Performance*, 17, pp. 251–74.

R. W. Woodman and J. J. Sherwood (1980) "The Role of Team Development in Organizational Effectiveness: A Critical Review." *Psychological Bulletin*, 88, pp. 166–86.

A. Zander (1971) *Motives and Goals in Groups*. New York: Academic Press.

―――. (1980) "The Origins and Consequences of Group Goals" in L. Festinger, ed., *Retrospections on Social Psychology*. New York: Oxford University Press.

FACING THE FUTURE: CREATIVITY, INNOVATION, AND ORGANIZATIONAL LEADERSHIP

Foundations of Individual Creativity

33. WITHIN YOU, WITHOUT YOU: THE SOCIAL PSYCHOLOGY OF CREATIVITY, AND BEYOND

Teresa M. Amabile

I study creativity because I'm still trying to figure out something that happened in kindergarten. That's when I first heard the word *creativity*. My teacher had come to our home for the end-of-the-year conference with my mother. While eavesdropping, I heard Mrs. Bollier say, "I think Teresa shows a lot of potential for artistic creativity, and I hope that's something she really develops over the years." I remember feeling thrilled but, sadly, my pride was premature. I haven't done anything even vaguely artistic in the years since; I still draw the way I did in kindergarten. I'd really like to know why.

There are at least two obvious explanations. Mrs. Bollier might have been wrong; maybe I had no particular talent for artwork. I, however, prefer the alternative explanation: I *did* have the beginnings of artistic talent, but my later experiences with art squelched its development. In kindergarten, we had plenty of free access to art materials—easels, paper, lots of paint, clay, and crayons—and plenty of encouragement to experiment with them. The following year, I entered a strict, traditional parochial school where experience with art was limited to an hour every Friday afternoon when, I think, the nuns were too tired to do anything else with us.

Week after week, we were given the same task. Each child would receive a small index-card-sized copy of one of the great masterworks in painting. In second grade, one week, we had Da Vinci's *Adoration of the Magi*. From third grade I remember Chagall's *I and the Village*. Rather than discussing these paintings and artists with us, our teachers instead told us to *copy* them. Given our limited skill development, and our limited materials (loose-leaf paper and a few broken crayons), "art" became an experience in frustration. I couldn't even get all those horses and angels to fit on the page! But, worse than that, we were strictly graded on our monstrosities. I felt my interest in artwork waning, and I no longer pestered my mother to let me draw and color when I was at home.

Only once in those school years did I hear the word *creative*. Inexplicably one day, our teacher told us to take out our art materials and do whatever we wanted. Eager as a prisoner set free, I began drawing a brightly colored abstract mosaic. Sister Carmelita, pacing the aisles, stopped by my desk, lowered her head, and said, "I think maybe we're being a little *too* creative!"

I wondered often what happened to my promised artistic creativity, but my interest in the problem stayed underground for many years. Meanwhile, I was experiencing frustration of a different sort. I had been interested in science throughout high school, but had no idea *which* science to major in once I entered college. I chose chemistry because it looked the hardest. Although I did well, earning A's in my chemistry, physics, and calculus courses, it all left me cold. I worked as a research assistant during the summers, which gave me ample opportunity to observe what I lacked. Each day, our small band of professors and research assistants would troop off to lunch in the cafeteria and seat ourselves around a large table. Each day, the professors could talk of little else but their work—what was going nicely, what had taken a bad turn, what new ideas they had. They spoke with passion and excitement, and by the time we left the table each day, it was strewn with napkins showing hastily sketched equations and models. That passion was what I lacked, and I knew I'd never have it for chemistry; I never found myself wanting to think about my research outside of the laboratory.

I did discover that passion when I took my first psychology course as an elective in college. *Here* was a science I could care about—an exciting science of people, not a boring science of molecules. I had found my true interest, and everything else began to fall into place.

One important piece fell into place when I started the graduate program in psychology at Stanford and learned about Mark Lepper's work on intrinsic motivation. Lepper defined *intrinsic motivation* as the motivation to do an activity for its own sake, because it was intrinsically interesting, enjoyable or satisfying. In contrast, extrinsic motivation was defined as the motivation to do an activity primarily in order to achieve some extrinsic goal, such as a reward. Lepper and his colleagues had investigated the phenomenon they called the "overjustification effect": If an individual who is initially intrinsically interested in an activity engages in that activity in order to meet some extrinsic goal, that individual's intrinsic motivation to engage in that activity in the future will be undermined (e.g. Deci, 1971; Lepper, Greene, & Nisbett, 1973). That certainly sounded like what had happened to me and my artistic potential. Could it be that intrinsic motivation is necessary for creativity?

The overjustification research, however, had not examined creativity or other aspects of performance. It had focused on subsequent interest to engage in an activity. To clarify my hypotheses about the impact of intrinsic/extrinsic motivation on creativity, and to renew my old curiosity about creativity, I began to read the creativity literature—both psychological theory and research, and the self-report writings of individuals recognized for their creativity.

In the psychological literature, I found that little attention had been paid to motivation. Instead, research (most of it done after 1950) had focused on personality characteristics of outstanding creative individuals (e.g., Baron, 1955; Helson, 1965 MacKinnon, 1962), cognitive abilities involved in creative achievement (e.g., Guilford, 1956), the development of creativity tests (e.g., Torrance, 1966) or methods for training creativity skills (e.g. Gordon, 1961; Parnes, 1967; Stein, 1974).

However, there was some psychological literature outside of the "creativity camp" that provided strong suggestive evidence of a link between intrinsic motivation and creativity. Crutchfield's (1955, 1959, 1962) work on conformity found that individuals who had been identified as highly creative were much less likely to conform in the Asch situation than were those identified as less creative.

According to Crutchfield, conformity pressures can lead to extrinsic, "ego-involved" motivation, in which finding a solution is simply a means to an ulterior end. This contrasts sharply with intrinsic, "task-involved" motivation, in which the creative act is an end in itself.

McGraw (1978) reviewed a vast literature on problem solving and concluded that reward (an extrinsic motivator) has very different effects on performance, depending on the type of task. *Algorithmic* tasks are those having a clear, straightforward path to solution. *Heuristic* tasks are those with no such clear, straightforward path; some exploration is required. McGraw concluded that performance on algorithmic tasks should be enhanced by increases in extrinsic motivation, but performance on heuristic tasks should be adversely affected. McGraw's descriptions of heuristic tasks clearly included tasks that require creativity.

In his pioneering work on enjoyment, Csikszentmihályi (1975) studied people who were deeply intrinsically involved in activities ranging from chess to musical composition to rock climbing to dancing to surgery. He described the *flow experience* in such individuals, the experience of being totally involved in the activity, where one action flows smoothly into the next and extrinsic concerns disappear.

Csikszentmihályi's description of the flow experience, along with McGraw's assertions about the effect of extrinsic motivation on heuristic tasks, and Crutchfield's discussion of ego-involved and task-involved motivation all fit remarkably well with first-person descriptions of the creative process by widely recognized creative individuals. In reading the autobiographies, letters, and journals of people such as Albert Einstein and Sylvia Plath, I discovered a recurring theme: They felt most inhibited in their creative work when focusing on extrinsic concerns such as expected evaluation, surveillance, or promised reward. They did their most creative work when they experienced the "flow" of deep intrinsic motivation. Using this support from the psychological literature, the phenomenological literature, and my own (limited) experience, I formulated what I then called the

intrinsic motivation hypothesis of creativity: intrinsic motivation is conducive to creativity, and extrinsic motivation is detrimental. I planned to test this hypothesis by having subjects do creativity tasks in the presence or absence of extrinsic constraints—clearly, a social-psychological paradigm.

When I told my graduate advisers that I wanted to do research in the social psychology of creativity, they informed me that there was no such thing. But, just weeks after that conversation, I opened the new *Journal of Personality and Social Psychology* to find an article by Dean Simonton (1975) with the phrase "social psychology of creativity" splashed boldly about. That was all the encouragement I needed.

ASSUMPTIONS, DEFINITIONS, AND ASSESSMENTS

Before beginning any creativity experiments, of course, I had to figure out what I was studying and how I was going to measure it. I venture to say that this is the single most difficult problem shared by all creativity researchers. A perusal of previous research revealed that the majority of creativity studies relied on some sort of standardized tests, such as the Torrance Tests of Creative Thinking. Apart from reservations I had about calling performance on these tests "creativity," I was concerned that these tests had all been formulated to pinpoint individual differences in creative ability. To the extent that they were indeed sensitive to such individual differences, these tests were quite appropriate for personality studies of creativity, but quite inappropriate for social-psychological studies of creativity. In my planned studies, I intended to identify social factors that could undermine *any* person's creativity, no matter what that person's baseline level of skill in creative activity. In such studies, individual differences would be error variance, and measures sensitive to such differences would contribute to error.

I decided, instead of using creativity tests for my studies, to simply have subjects make products in response to clearly defined tasks; the tasks would be designed so as not to depend heavily on special skills in drawing, verbal fluency, mathematical ability, or the like. Some such tasks that my students and I have used include making paper collages and writing haiku poems. Once these products have been made in the context of our studies, we have them rated on creativity and other dimensions by experts—people who are familiar with the domain; for example, we ask studio artists to rate the paper collages. This approach to creativity assessment was used by a few previous researchers (e.g., Getzels & Csikszentmihályi, 1976; Kruglanski, Friedman, & Zeevi, 1971), with apparent success. We call it the consensual assessment technique.

The consensual assessment technique for creativity is based on this operational definition: *A product or response is creative to the extent that appropriate observers independently agree it is creative. Appropriate observers are those familiar with the domain in which the product was created or the response articulated* (Amabile, 1982b). Interjudge agreement, clearly, is the most important requirement of this technique. But mere statistical agreement would be suspect without certain precautions: We do not train the judges in any way; we ask them to use their own subjective definitions of creativity; and we ensure that they work independently. Repeatedly, in dozens of studies with small groups of judges, we have found interjudge reliabilities ranging above .70, and often above .80. Moreover, we have found that creativity ratings are statistically separable from other rated product dimensions, such as technical quality or aesthetic appeal.

Although it may be necessary to specify an operational definition of creativity that relies solely on subjective criteria, such a definition is not, by itself, sufficient for a comprehensive theory of creativity—or even for a social psychology of creativity. Any theoretical formulation must make guesses about what judges are responding to when they rate products as more or less creative. For this reason, we have been guided by a conceptual definition of creativity that is closely aligned with many previous definitions (e.g., Barron, 1955; MacKinnon, 1975; Stein, 1974): A product or response will be judged as creative to the

extent that (a) it is both a novel and appropriate, useful, correct, or valuable response to the task at hand, and (b) the task is heuristic rather than algorithmic (Amabile, 1983b).

Our approach to creativity definition and measurement rests on several assumptions about key creativity issues. Indeed, either implicitly or explicitly, all creativity researchers must make assumptions about these issues. I defend mine only by saying that I have not seen persuasive evidence to the contrary. These are the issues: Can creativity be recognized as a quality of products? I believe that the assessment of creativity is much like the judgment of attitude statements on degrees of favorability (Thurstone & Chave, 1929) or the identification of individuals as physically attractive (Walster, Aronson, Abrahams, & Rottman, 1966). Although creativity may be very difficult for judges to define (I have asked them!), it is something they can recognize when they see it. Moreover, experts can agree on the extent to which a given product is creative. And not only can judges recognize creativity in products; I believe they can also recognize it in persons and processes. However, a focus on the *product* seems to me the most straightforward and scientifically conservative; products are the most easily observed discrete units and probably the least subject to disagreement.

Certainly, this approach cannot be used for assessing creativity in products that may be at the frontiers of a domain, where there is bound to be great disagreement as to whether a new idea is highly creative or simply bizarre. But then, *no* approach to creativity assessment will work at those levels. Only the passage of time, and an eventual social consensus, can yield a proper assessment.

Is creativity a continuous or discontinuous quality? I believe that the highest levels of creativity that we see in the world—the greatest scientific advances, the most startling artistic achievements—lie on the high end of the same continuum on which we see everyday "garden variety" creativity—ideas and responses that are more modestly novel and less earth-shattering. I do not believe that there is a discontinuous break in the abilities or thought processes behind differing levels of creativity. The difference seems to lie instead in vastly differing abilities, cognitive styles, motivational levels, and circumstances. The difference in *kind*. Thus I believe it is appropriate to ask expert judges to rate degrees of creativity in products. And I also believe it is justifiable to say that experiments using "ordinary" subjects doing relatively low-level tasks are informative even about Einstein's creativity.

Is the creative process different in different domains? I believe that it is basically the same—that a scientist attempting to develop a new process in her laboratory is going through essentially the same process as an artist in his studio or a poet at her desk. Certainly, different cognitive processes will be differentially important in the various domains. However, in general, the creative process will depend on the same components and be affected by the same social factors. Thus it is appropriate to use tasks from a variety of domains in establishing a social psychology of creativity, or any psychology of creativity.

EVIDENCE ON THE INTRINSIC MOTIVATION PRINCIPLE OF CREATIVITY

Using the consensual technique for creativity assessment, my students and I have conducted dozens of studies over the past 12 years to test the intrinsic motivation hypothesis of creativity. We find our results sufficiently compelling that we now refer to the intrinsic motivation *principle* of creativity: Intrinsic motivation is conducive to creativity, but extrinsic motivation is detrimental. In other words, people will be most creative when they feel motivated primarily by the interest, enjoyment, satisfaction, and challenge of the work itself—and not by external pressures.

The Phenomenology of Creativity

The first source of evidence on the intrinsic motivation principle is rather a source of hypotheses about specific social factors that may lead to decrements in intrinsic motivation and creativity: the first-person account. We have studied a great many autobiographies, personal journals, letters, biographies, and interviews of widely of recognized creative individuals in a variety of fields. These include writers T. S. Eliot, Anne Sexton, Sylvia Plath, Thomas Wolfe, Fyodor Dostoyevski, D. H. Lawrence, Joyce Carol Oates, Charles Dickens, Gertrude Stein, George Eliot, Isaac Asimov, and John Irving; scientists Albert Einstein, Marie Curie, and James Watson; musician/composers W. A. Mozart and Pablo Casals; artists Pablo Picasso and Ansel Adams; social scientist Margaret Mead; and filmmaker Woody Allen.

Richly complex as they are, these sources strongly suggest the validity of the intrinsic motivation principle in two ways. First, repeatedly, these individuals express high levels of intrinsic motivation for doing their work. The novelist John Irving *(The World According to Garp)* is just one of many examples:

The unspoken factor here is love. The reason I can work so hard at my writing is that it's not work to me. Or, as I said before, my work is pleasure to me. (Amabile, in press)

In addition, these creative individuals report numerous incidents in which their intrinsic motivation and creativity were undermined by salient extrinsic constraints. The constraints cited include expected evaluation, strictly regimented educational methods, surveillance, competition, reward, restricted choice, and deadlines. The poet Sylvia Plath provides perhaps the clearest lay-person's statement of the intrinsic motivation principle of creativity in action:

Editors and publishers and critics and the world ... I want acceptance there, to feel my work good and well-taken. Which ironically freezes me at my work, corrupts my nunnish labor of work-for-itself-as-its-own-reward. (Hughes & McCullough, 1982, p. 305)

Experimental Evidence

The second and most important source of evidence on the intrinsic motivation principle is the laboratory experiment. My students and I have used the basic overjustification paradigm in our research: subjects work on an interesting creativity task either in the presence or in the absence of a specific extrinsic constraint. Subsequently, their products are rated on creativity by several independent experts. We have carried out such experiments with a wide range of independent variables (extrinsic constraints), subject groups ranging in age from preschool children to working adults, and a variety of artistic, verbal and problem-solving creativity tasks. Though they are not without their complexities, our results reveal consistent patterns in strong support of the intrinsic motivation hypothesis:

Evaluation. Expected evaluation has a detrimental effect on creativity (Amabile, 1979; Amabile, Goldfarb, & Brackfield, in press; Hennessey, 1989). Actual prior positive evaluation has a detrimental effect on subsequent creativity (Berglas, Amabile, & Handel, 1979).

Surveillance. Being watched while working has a detrimental effect on creativity (Amabile, Goldfarb, & Brackfield, in press).

Reward. Contracted-for reward has a detrimental effect on creativity (Amabile, Hennessey, & Grossman, 1986; Hennessey, 1989). "Bonus" reward (not contracted for) has a positive effect on creativity (Amabile, Hennessey, & Grossman, 1986).

Competition. Competing for prizes has a detrimental effect on creativity (Amabile, 1982a, 1987).

Restricted choice. Restricted choice in how to do an activity has a detrimental effect on creativity (Amabile & Gitomer, 1984; Hennessey, 1989).

Each of the social-environmental factors shown in our research to negatively affect creativity has also been shown, in overjustification research, to negatively affect intrinsic motivation. In an effort to provide a more direct link between intrinsic motivation and creativity within the same study, we attempted a motivational induction with creative

writers. I will describe the study in some detail as a way of illustrating our basic paradigm.

This study (Amabile, 1985) was designed to directly create an extrinsic motivational state in some subjects without going through the intermediate step of first imposing an extrinsic constraint. And the same method was used to directly create an intrinsically motivated state in other subjects. For this purpose, we borrowed a technique from Salancik (1975). We asked subjects to complete a questionnaire about their attitudes toward the target creativity task (writing). Some were given an intrinsic questionnaire, on which all of the items dealt with the intrinsically interesting aspects of the activity. Other subjects completed an extrinsic questionnaire, which dealt with only extrinsic reasons for doing the activity. The purpose of the questionnaire was simply to lead subjects to think about the activity in intrinsic terms or in extrinsic terms. Then, immediate effects of this intrinsic or extrinsic orientation could be directly observed.

It was important in this study to find subjects who were already involved in this type of creative activity on a regular basis so that we might temporarily influence their orientation toward that activity. To this end, we recruited creative writers, using advertisements such as this: "Writers: If you are involved in writing, especially poetry, fiction, or drama, you can make three dollars for about an hour of your time. We are studying people's reasons for writing."

Most of those who responded to the advertisements were undergraduates or graduate students in English or creative writing at Brandeis University or Boston University, although a few were not affiliated with any university. The most important characteristic of these participants, for our purposes, is that they identified themselves as *writers*—they came to us with a high level of involvement in writing. On a prescreening questionnaire, we discovered that they spent an average of 6.3 hours of their own time per week writing poetry, fiction, or drama; the range was 3 to 18 hours.

Upon arrival at our laboratory, each writer completed a questionnaire on "reasons for writing"—

reasons for being involved in writing. (Some subjects, in a control condition, did not complete any questionnaire.) On the intrinsic questionnaire, subjects were asked to rank-order (in terms of importance to them personally) seven reasons for writing; all of these reasons had been consistently rated as intrinsic on a pretest. Two of the intrinsic items were these: "You get a lot of pleasure out of reading something good that you have written"; and "You like to play with words." By contrast, the extrinsic questionnaire asked subjects to rank-order seven reasons that had pretested as strongly extrinsic, such as "You have heard of cases where one bestselling novel or collection of poems has made the author financially secure"; and "You enjoy public recognition of your work." After completing the questionnaire, the writers were asked to write a short haiku-style poem. (Those in the control group were simply asked to write the poem.)

After the study was completed, we asked several poets to judge the poems, using the consensual assessment technique. The results were quite dramatic. As might be expected, the writers in the control group wrote poems that were judged fairly high on creativity; these were, after all, creative writers. The writers in the intrinsic group wrote poems that were judged as somewhat higher in creativity than those in the control group, but the difference was not large. The most important result comes from the extrinsic group. Those writers produced poems that were judged as significantly lower in creativity than the poems produced by either of the other groups.

Consider the implications of this study for "real-world" work environments. These writers entered our laboratory with an intrinsic motivational orientation toward writing. Apparently, we were not able to increase that intrinsic orientation much; the creativity of the intrinsic group isn't notably higher than the creativity of the control group. On the other hand, with a terribly brief and simple manipulation, we significantly reduced the creativity of writers in the extrinsic group. People who had been writing creatively for years, who had long-standing interests in creative writing, suddenly found their creativity

blocked after spending barely five minutes thinking about the extrinsic reasons for doing what they do. (A note about the ethics of this experiment: We fully debriefed all of our participants before they left the lab, and we had all of the extrinsic subjects fill out the intrinsic questionnaire at the end of their experimental sessions.)

In this study, a brief and subtle written manipulation had a significant impact on the creativity of highly motivated individuals. Consider, then, the potential effects of extrinsic constraints in everyday work environments on the creativity of people who work in those environments every day.

Observational Data

It is one thing to assume that the social-environmental factors we manipulate in the laboratory play an important role in real-world creativity. It is another thing to actually find out. In an attempt to do so, I worked with colleagues at the Center for Creative Leadership to interview a large number of research and development scientists about creative and noncreative events in their work experience (Amabile & Gryskiewicz, 1988). We asked the participants, who were 120 R&D scientists from over 20 corporations, to tell us about an example of high creativity and an example of low creativity from their work experience (defining creativity as they saw fit). We told them that we were particularly interested in anything about the events that stood out in their minds—anything about the person or persons involved and anything about the work environment. We felt that, by using this critical incident technique, we would be more likely to avoid the interjection of personal beliefs about creativity than if we simply asked interviewees what they thought was important for supporting or undermining creativity in organizations.

In our search for information about the major influences on creativity and innovation, we did a detailed content analysis of verbatim transcripts of these tape-recorded interviews. The types of things our interviewees talked about fell into four major categories. Rank-ordered by frequency, they are as follows: (a) qualities of environments that promote creativity, (b) qualities of environments that inhibit creativity, (c) qualities of problem-solvers that promote creativity, and (d) qualities of problem-solvers that inhibit creativity. In our system, "qualities of environments" are any factors outside of the problem-solvers themselves (including other people) that appeared to consistently influence creativity positively, as in the high-creativity stories, or negatively, as in the low-creativity stories. "Qualities of problem-solvers" are any factors of ability, personality, or mood within the problem-solvers themselves that seemed to consistently influence creativity either positively or negatively. We found that environmental factors were mentioned much more frequently than personal qualities. Because this finding appeared in both the high- and low-creativity stories, and because a large percentage of the stories did not involve the interviewee as a central character (problem-solver), we feel that this preponderance of environmental factors cannot be dismissed as a simple attributional bias.

The prominence of the environment in these interviews is an important finding for the social psychology of creativity. It suggests that our laboratory research on the effects of social constraints has produced not only statistically significant findings but ecologically significant ones as well. The *environment* was a much more salient factor than the *individual* for these R&D scientists in their experience of specific creative and uncreative events. Does this mean that, in an absolute sense, environmental factors account for more of the variance in creative output than individual difference factors? Does this mean that the forces *within you* are less significant than the forces *without you* in determining the creativity of your behavior? Not necessarily, and not even probably. Certainly, at a macroscopic level, personal factors such as general intelligence, experience in the field, and ability to think creatively are the major influences on output of creative ideas by R&D scientists. But, assuming that hiring practices at major corporations select individuals who exhibit relatively high levels of these personal qualities, the variance above this baseline may well be accounted for primarily by factors in the work environment.

Social factors may be responsible for only a small part of the total variance in creative behavior, but they may account for the lion's share of the variance that anyone can do anything about! It is almost always easier to change the social environment (or one's perception of it) than to change traits and abilities.

Our detailed content analysis of the interviews, done by independent coders, revealed several environmental factors that inhibit creativity. Among these are many that we had already studied in experimental paradigms: constrained choice, an overemphasis on tangible reward, evaluation expectation, and competition. There were other inhibiting factors, however, that remain for future experimental investigation: perceived apathy toward the target project, unclear goals, distraction, insufficient resources, overemphasis on the status quo, and time pressure.

BEYOND THE INTRINSIC MOTIVATION PRINCIPLE

Clearly, there's much more to the social psychology of creativity than just the intrinsic motivation principle. While I have worked within mainstream social-psychological paradigms to study the effects of specific social constraints on the immediate creative performance of ordinary individuals, Dean Simonton has used pioneering historiometric techniques to study the effects of complex social phenomena (such as cultural diversity, warfare, and zeitgeist) on historically recognized creative achievements (see Simonton, 1984, in press). A comprehensive social psychology of creativity must include this work, as well as the work of others who have studied social influences at the macroscopic level (e.g., Albert, 1980; Andrews, 1975).

The data from the R&D interview study suggest a number of environmental variables that may *enhance* creativity. In our previous devotion to the overjustification paradigm and the intrinsic motivation hypothesis, we *de facto* eliminated an investigation of such variables. It may, in fact, be true that undermining creativity is much easier than stimulating it. But that's no reason not to try.

Recently, our own experimental research has begun moving beyond the simplicity of the intrinsic motivation principle. Nearly all of our previous experiments assumed *a hydraulic* relationship between intrinsic and extrinsic motivation: As extrinsic motivation increases, intrinsic motivation (and creativity) must decrease. However, it seems clear from anecdotal evidence that extrinsic motivators such as reward and competition need not undermine creativity. In fact, for some people, there seems to be an *additive* relationship: not only does their intrinsic motivation remain high, but their creativity may actually be enhanced in the face of extrinsic motivators.

For example, the filmmaker Woody Allen seems to have managed to maintain both a high level of intrinsic motivation and a high level of creativity in an extremely extrinsically oriented profession. He more or less ignores both the awards and the critics, continuing to innovate with new styles and themes. As another example, the scientists Watson and Crick clearly felt strong competitive pressure in their race to discover the structure of DNA (Watson, 1968). Yet, at the moments that they made their greatest breakthroughs, they were so single-mindedly focused on the puzzle before them that they temporarily forgot not only about their competitors and the prizes awaiting the victors but also about the time of day and their own need for food. In another feat of cognitive distancing, the poet Anne Sexton told her agent that, although she would love to make a great deal of money from her books, she knew that she had to forget all about that while actually writing her poems.

Two of our recent studies provide some exciting evidence suggestive of an additive effect of intrinsic and extrinsic motivators. In one study (Hennessey, Amabile, & Martinage, in press), we set out to determine if it would be possible to immunize people against the negative effects of con-

1 Domain-relevant Skills	2 Creativity-relevant Skills	3 Task Motivation

Includes:
−Knowledge about the domain
−Technical skills required
−Special domain-relevant
  "talent"
Depends on:
−Innate cognitive abilities
−Innate perceptual and
  motor skills
−Formal and informal
  education
	Includes:
	−Appropriate cognitive style
	−Implicit or explicit knowledge
	  of heuristics for generating
	  novel ideas
	−Conducive work style
	Depends on:
	−Training
	−Experience in idea generation
	−Personality characteristics
		Includes:
		−Attitudes toward the task
		−Perceptions of own motivation
		  for undertaking the task
		Depends on:
		−Initial level of intrinsic
		  motivation toward the task
		−Presence or absence of
		  salient extrinsic constraints
		  in the social environment
		−Individual ability to
		  cognitively minimize
		  extrinsic constraints

FIGURE 33.1 Components of Creative Performance.

Source: From Amabile, T. M. Social psychology of creativity: A componential conceptualization. *Journal of Personality and Social Psychology* 45(1983): 357–77.

straint on intrinsic motivation and creativity by training them to think of intrinsic and extrinsic motivation in the way that Allen, Watson, Crick, and Sexton seemed to: I am well aware of my strong intrinsic interest in my work, and that can't be easily shaken; I certainly enjoy the benefits of wealth, fame, and critical acclaim, but I place all that secondary to my own passion for what I do.

Planning to do this training study with children, we made a set of videotapes in which two attractive children answered an adult's questions about their work. The script was written so as to portray these children as models of intrinsic motivation. They spoke excitedly about different aspects of their schoolwork that interested them, and, while acknowledging the importance of good grades and praise from parents, they firmly stated that "those are not what's really important." After the children watched these videotapes, the experimenter led the children to discuss what had been said, and to describe their own intrinsic interests or ways of dealing with constraint. In later testing sessions with a different experimenter, we found that children who had watched the intrinsic motivation training tapes scored higher on a measure of intrinsic motivation (Harter, 1981) than children who had watched tapes on other topics. In addition, although the control-group children exhibited lower creativity when offered a reward, the trained children showed no such decrement. This was what we had predicted. But we got more than we'd bargained for. The trained children produced *higher* levels of creativity under contracted-for reward—a clearly additive effect.

Another, earlier study of ours may provide a clue about the mechanism at work in this surprising additive effect (surprising, at least, to those of us who expected only hydraulic effects). With both adults and children, we found (as expected) that contracted-for reward leads to lower levels of creativity (Amabile, Hennessey, & Grossman, 1986). The design was a basic 2×2 factorial, where reward was crossed with choice. Thus, subjects in the choice-reward condition had previously chosen to do the activity in order to obtain

a reward. Subjects in the no-choice/reward condition, however, were simply given the reward as something that went along with the activity. They were given no choice in the matter; they made no contract with the experimenter. We expected that subjects in this condition would show no decrement in creativity, because they should not have had the self-perception of working on the activity in order to gain the reward (extrinsic motivation). Not only did we find no decrement, we found an *increment*: Subjects in this "bonus" reward condition showed higher levels of creativity than in any of the other three conditions.

We speculate that perhaps the bonus reward enhances *positive affect*, which may simply add on to the conductive effect of intrinsic motivation on creativity. Not only did subjects in this condition *not* have their intrinsic motivation undermined, they were led to feel even better about what they were doing because of the unexpected bonus. Indeed, a postexperimental questionnaire assessing affect lends some support to this speculation.

So it may be that the children in the training study's intrinsic motivation condition learned to interpret extrinsic constraints such as reward in a way that did not detract from intrinsic motivation but instead added to positive affect about task engagement. This possibility seems likely when we consider the kind of statements that appeared in the intrinsic motivation training videotape:

Adult: *It sounds like both of you do the work in school because you like it, but what about getting good grades from your teacher or presents from your parents for doing well? Do you think about those things?*

Tommy: *Well, I like to get good grades, and when I bring home a good report card, my parents always give me money. But that's not what's really important. I like to learn a lot. There are a lot of things that interest me, and I want to learn about them, so I work hard because I enjoy it.*

It appears, then, that the intrinsic motivation principle of creativity, in its simple form, is incomplete. It implies that extrinsic constraints will always undermine creativity. But both observational evidence and experimental evidence suggest that this isn't so. Individual differences in people's *interpretation* of the constraints can significantly affect the outcomes on creativity, whether those individual differences arise through explicit training (as in our study) or occur naturally as personality characteristics.

BEYOND THE SOCIAL PSYCHOLOGY OF CREATIVITY: WITHIN YOU AND WITHOUT YOU

The intense study of social-environmental influences on creativity, which has flourished over the

past dozen years, was a necessary correction to the almost exclusive focus on creative *persons* in preceding decades. Clearly, however, in any comprehensive psychology of creativity, both person influences and environment influences must appear prominently. Even in our own research on the social psychology of creativity, we have repeatedly been led to consider the influence of personality, ability, and experience. The R&D scientists we interviewed (Amabile & Gryskiewicz, 1988) may have mentioned work environment factors more frequently than person factors in their stories of high and low creativity, but person factors certainly did appear prominently. Positive personal factors mentioned frequently in the high-creativity stories included personality traits such as persistence, cu-

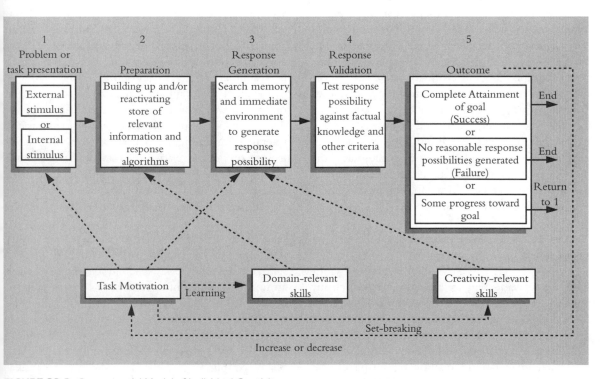

FIGURE 33.2 Componential Model of Individual Creativity.

Source: From Amabile, T. M. Social psychology of creativity: A componential conceptualization. *Journal of Personality and Social Psychology* 45 (1983): 357–77.

Note: Broken lines indicate the typical sequence of steps in the process. Only direct and primary influences are depicted here.

riosity, energy, and intellectual honesty; self-motivation, the intrinsic motivation of being excited by the work itself; special cognitive abilities; risk orientation; expertise in the area; diverse experience; social skill; and brilliance. Negative personal factors mentioned frequently in the low-creativity stories included being unmotivated, unskilled, inflexible, externally motivated, or socially unskilled.

Earlier, I argued: "Social factors may be responsible for only a small part of the total variance in creative behavior, but they may account for the lion's share of the variance that anyone can do anything about!" I believe this is true and vitally important for anyone wishing to enhance creativity in practice. However, for purposes of theory building, we must pay heed to all factors contributing significantly to the *total variance* in creative behavior.

The componential model of creativity, which we have been using as a theoretical guide in our research, attempts to include all such factors. The model is described in more detail elsewhere (Amabile, 1983a, 1983b, 1988a, 1988b). Figure 33.1 outlines the three major components of creativity included in the model. It is not surprising that intrinsic task motivation is featured as one prominent component, but the factors of talent, personality, and cognitive style that have been so extensively investigated by other researchers are also included. As a way of illustrating the components and their role in the creative process, let me describe the hypothetical (and highly simplified) case of an artist creating a sculpture.

Domain-Relevant Skills

Domain-relevant skills are the basis from which any performance must proceed. They include memory for factual knowledge, technical proficiency, and special talents in the domain in question. A sculptor's domain-relevant skills include her innate talent for visual imagery and realistic rendering of that imagery, her factual knowledge of art history and the properties of the clay she has chosen, her familiarity with the subject she wishes to depict, and the technical skill she has acquired in her craft.

This component can be viewed as the set of cognitive pathways that may be followed to solve a given problem or do a given task. As Newell and Simon (1972, p. 82) poetically describe it, this component can be considered the problem-solver's "network of possible wanderings."

Creativity-Relevant Skills

Herein lies the "something extra" of creative performance. Assuming that an individual has some incentive to perform an activity, performance will be "technically good" or "adequate" or "acceptable" if the requisite domain-relevant skills are there. However, even with these skills at an extraordinarily high level, an individual will not produce creative work if creativity-relevant skills are lacking. Creativity-relevant skills include a cognitive style favorable to taking new perspectives on problems, an application of heuristics for the exploration of new cognitive pathways, and a working style conducive to persistent, energetic pursuit of one's work.

Creativity-relevant skills, depend to some extent on personality characteristics related to independence, self-discipline, orientation toward risk taking, tolerance for ambiguity, perseverance in the face of frustration, and a relative unconcern for social approval (Barron, 1955; Feldman, 1980; Golann, 1963; Hogarth, 1980; MacKinnon, 1962; Stein, 1974).

Our sculptor's arsenal of creativity skills might include her ability to break perceptual set when observing physical objects, her tolerance for ambiguity in the process of deciding on a theme and how to render it, her ability to suspend judgment as she plays around with different approaches, and her ability to break out of strict algorithms for sculpting. She might also have learned to employ some of the creativity heuristics described by theorists: "When all else fails, try something counterintuitive" (Newell, Shaw, & Simon, 1962); or "Make the familiar strange" (Gordon, 1961). Finally, if she is productively creative, her work style is probably marked by an ability to concentrate effort for long periods of time (Campbell, 1960; Hogarth, 1980) and an ability to abandon unproductive strategies, temporarily putting aside stubborn problems (Simon, 1966).

Intrinsic Task Motivation

A person can have no motivation for doing a task, a primarily intrinsic motivation, or a primarily extrinsic motivation; obviously, intrinsic and extrinsic motivation for the same task may coexist. However, one is likely to be primary. As I have argued on the basis of our empirical results, a primarily intrinsic motivation will be more conducive to creativity than a primarily extrinsic motivation. For practical purposes, there are two ways in which motivation can be considered the most important of the three creativity components. First, as I've noted, it may be the easiest to affect in a straightforward way because intrinsic/extrinsic motivation is strongly subject to even subtle social influences. Second, no amount of skill in the domain or in methods of creative thinking can compensate for a lack of intrinsic motivation to perform an activity. Without intrinsic motivation, an individual either will not perform the activity at all or will do it in a way that simply satisfies the extrinsic goals. But, to some extent, a high degree of intrinsic motivation *can* make up for a deficiency of domain-relevant skills or creativity-relevant skills. A highly intrinsically motivated individual is likely to draw skills from other domains or apply great effort to acquire necessary skills in the target domain.

Task motivation makes the difference between what our sculptor *can* do and what she *will* do. The former depends on her levels of domain-relevant skills and creativity-relevant skills. But it is her task motivation that determines the extent to which she will fully engage her domain-relevant skills and creativity-relevant skills in the service of creative performance.

Within the componential model, task motivation includes two elements: the individual's baseline attitude toward the task and the individual's perceptions of his or her reasons for undertaking the task in a given instance. For example, the sculptor approaches each task with a baseline level of interest—probably

quite high for most sculpture tasks but perhaps quite low for print-making. For any given sculpture task, however, her interest will vary from the baseline as a function of any extrinsic constraints imposed on her (such as competition) *and* her own strategies for dealing with those constraints.

Stages of the Creative Process

The three components of domain-relevant skills, creativity-relevant skills, and task motivation are the building blocks for the componential model of creativity. The model is, conceptually, a multiplicative one: Each of the components is necessary for some level of creativity to be produced; the higher the level of each of the three components, the higher the overall level of creativity should be.

The three components appear to operate at different levels of specificity. Creativity-relevant skills operate at the most general level; they may influence responses in any content domain. Thus, if the sculptor has a rich store of creativity-relevant skills, she may indeed appear to be a creative "type," in the sense that she produces unusual responses in many domains of behavior. Domain-relevant skills operate at an intermediate level of specificity. This component includes all skills relevant to a general domain, such as sculpture, rather than skills relevant to only a specific task within a domain, such as sculpting a clay bust of Beethoven. Obviously, within a particular domain, skills relevant to any given specific task will overlap with skills relevant to any other task. Finally, task motivation operates at the most specific level. In terms of impact on creativity, motivation may be very specific to particular tasks within domains, and may even vary over time for a particular task. Our artist may be highly intrinsically motivated to sculpt a friend's head, but she may be singularly uninterested in a commissioned job to sculpt the head of the city's mayor.

How do these building blocks figure into the overall process of individual creativity? Figure 33.2 presents a schematic representation of the componential model of the creative process (Amabile, 1983a, 1983b). This model describes the way in which an individual (such as the sculptor) might assemble and use information in attempting to arrive at a solution, response, or product. In information-processing terms, task motivation is responsible for initiating and sustaining the process; it determines whether the artist even undertakes the task, and it also determines some aspects of her response generation. Domain-relevant skills are the raw materials that feed the process. They determine what approaches the sculptor will take initially and what criteria she will use to assess the response possibilities that are generated. Creativity-relevant skills act as an executive controller; they can influence the way in which the artist searches for possibilities.

The process outlined in Figure 33.2 applies to both high and low levels of creativity; the level of creativity of a product or response varies as a function of the levels of each of the three components. This model resembles previous theories of creativity in the specification of the stages of problem presentation, preparation, response generation, and response validation (e.g., Hogarth, 1980; Nystrom, 1979; Wallas, 1926)—although there are a number of variations in the exact number and naming of stages in the sequence. This model is more detailed than previous ones, however, in its inclusion of the impact of each of the three components of creativity at each stage in the process. (Note that only direct and primary influences are depicted in the figure.)

The initial step in this sequence is the presentation of the task or the problem. Task motivation has an important influence at this stage. If the sculptor has a high level of intrinsic interest in the task, this interest will often be sufficient to begin the creative process. Under these circumstances, in essence, she poses the problem to herself. For example, she may decide that she wishes to sculpt the head of a friend. In other situations, however, the problem is presented by someone else. The problem might, of course, be intrinsically interesting under these circumstances as well. If that friend came up with the idea and asked the artist to sculpt his head, she might still be intrinsically interested in the task. However, in general, an externally posed problem is less likely to be intrinsically interesting than an internally generated one.

The second stage is preparatory to the actual generation of responses or solutions. At this point, the sculptor builds up or reactivates her store of information about the task, including her knowledge of response algorithms for doing tasks like this. If her domain-relevant skills are rather impoverished at the outset, this stage may be quite a long one during which a great deal of learning takes place. On the other hand, if her domain-relevant skills are already sufficiently rich to afford an ample set of possibilities to explore, the reactivation of this already stored set of information and algorithms may be almost instantaneous.

Note one important implication of this model: Contrary to popular belief, it is not possible to have *too much* knowledge about a task domain. According to this belief, people who have the smallest knowledge base in a domain are able to produce the most creative ideas. Certainly, people who are new to a field often do exhibit a higher level of creativity than those who have a longer work history. But it is clear from empirical research (e.g., Findlay & Lumsden, 1988) that the important distinction is not the *amount* of knowledge but the way in which that knowledge is stored and the ease with which it can be accessed. If the artist stores her information and techniques according to rigid algorithms (which may be more likely for an old-timer than a new arrival), creativity is less probable. But if she stores information in wide categories with easy access of association, increased information should only lead to increased creativity. It is not possible to have too much knowledge; it *is* possible to have algorithms that are applied too inflexibly.

The novelty of the product or response is determined in the third stage. Here, the individual generates response possibilities by searching through the available pathways and exploring features of the environment that are relevant to the task at hand. Both creativity-relevant skills and task motivation play an important role at this stage. The sculptor's existing repertoire of creativity-relevant skills determines her flexibility in exploring cognitive pathways, the attention she gives to particular aspects of the task, and the extent to which she follows a particular pathway in pursuit of a product. In addition, creativity-relevant skills can influence the sub-goals of the response-generation stage by determining whether she will generate a large number of response possibilities through a temporary suspension of judgment. Finally, and most important, if the artist's task motivation is intrinsic rather than extrinsic, it can add to her existing repertoire of creativity-relevant skills a willingness to take risks with this particular task and to notice aspects of the task that might not be obviously relevant to creating the final product.

Domain-relevant skills again figure prominently in the fourth stage–the validation of the response possibility that has been chosen on a particular trial. Using her knowledge of the domain, the artist tests the response possibility for correctness or appropriateness, given her particular set of goals. Thus it is this stage that determines whether the product or response will be appropriate, useful, correct, or valuable—the second response characteristic that, together with novelty, is essential for the product to be considered creative according to the conceptual definition of creativity.

The fifth stage represents the decision making that must be carried out on the basis of the test performed in stage four. If the artist feels that this test has been passed—if she believes she has attained her goal—the process terminates. If she sees complete failure—if no reasonable response possibility has been generated—the process will also terminate. If she senses some progress toward the goal—if at least a reasonable response possibility has been generated (or if, in Simon's 1978, terms, there is some evidence of "getting warmer")—the process returns to the first stage, where the problem is once again posed. In any case, information gained from the trial is added to the artist's existing repertoire of domain-relevant skills. If her intrinsic task motivation remains sufficiently high, she will try again, perhaps with information gained from the previous trial being used to pose the problem in a some-what different form. If, however, her task motivation drops below some critical minimum, she will give up.

For complex tasks, the application of this model to the production of creative responses also becomes complex. Work on any given task or problem may involve a long series of loops through the process until success in a final product is achieved. Indeed, work on what seems to be one task may actually involve a series of rather different subtasks, each with its own separate solution. And, of course, the sequence represented in Figure 33.2 is an idealized one. In actuality, for example, the sculptor may attempt to generate ideas on how to render her subject, have difficulty, go immediately back to the preparation stage to gather more information or learn new techniques, and then continue on with idea generation.

The Feedback Cycle

The outcome of one cycle of the creative process can directly influence task motivation, thereby setting up a feedback cycle through which future engagement in the same or similar tasks can be affected. If the sculptor has been completely successful, in her view, she will have no motivation to undertake exactly the same task again, because that task has truly been completed. However, with success, her intrinsic motivation for similar sculpting tasks should increase. If complete failure has occurred—if no reasonable response were generated—her intrinsic motivation for the task should decrease. If partial success has been met, intrinsic motivation will increase if she has the sense of getting warmer in approaching her goal. However, it will decrease when she finds herself essentially no closer to the goal than at the outset.

Harter's theory of "effectance motivation" (1978) suggests this influence of process outcome on task motivation. Harter built on White's (1959) definition of the "urge toward competence," a definition proposing a motivational construct that "impels the organism toward competence and is satisfied by a feeling of efficacy" (Harter, 1978, p. 34). According to Harter's theory, failure at mastery attempts eventually leads to decreases in intrinsic motivation striving for competence. However, success (which will be more probable the higher the level of skills) leads to intrinsic gratification, feelings of efficacy, and increases in intrinsic motivation, which, in turn, lead to more mastery attempts. In essential agreement with Harter, a number of social-psychological theorists (e.g., Deci & Ryan, 1985) have proposed that success (confirmation of competence) leads to increased intrinsic motivation.

Through its influence on task motivation, outcome assessment can also indirectly affect domain-relevant and creativity-relevant skills. If the sculptor ends up with a higher level of intrinsic task motivation, set-breaking and cognitive risk taking may become more habitual with her, thereby increasing her permanent repertoire of creativity skills. Also, a higher level of motivation may motivate learning about the task and related subjects, thereby increasing her domain-relevant skills.

A MAP FOR THE FUTURE

In nearly all of my previous research, I have focused on establishing one link in the model depicted in Figure 33.2: the influence of intrinsic/extrinsic task motivation on response generation. Now, with a bit more information and a great deal less hubris, my students, colleagues, and I are moving beyond the simple establishment of the intrinsic motivation principle of creativity to a broader examination of the social psychology of creativity. At the same time, we are moving beyond the social psychology of creativity toward a more integrated social-personality-cognitive psychology of creativity.

A More Inclusive Social Psychology of Creativity

Within the social psychology of creativity, we are attempting a more macroscopic look at social influences—both negative *and* positive. For example, we are beginning to think of ways in which intrinsic motivation training may be incorporated into school curricula (Hennessey & Amabile, 1987).

In addition, building on the results of the R&D interview study, we have developed an instrument called the Work Environment Inventory

(WEI). Designed to assess the presence of factors in the work environment that inhibit or stimulate individual creativity, the WEI is being tested with data collected in dozens of different organizations. As a guide in this work, I have articulated a preliminary model of organizational innovation that incorporates and builds on the componential model of individual creativity depicted in Figure 33.2 (Amabile, 1988a, 1988b). The ultimate goal is to develop and test a comprehensive model of organizational innovation that meets four criteria. First, the entire process of individual creativity must be considered as a crucial element in the process of organizational innovation. Second, the model must attempt to incorporate all aspects of organizations that influence innovation, with innovation being defined as *the successful implementation of creative ideas within an organization.* Third, the model must show the major stages of the organizational innovation process. Fourth, it must describe the influence of organizational factors on individual creativity.

While we are expanding our social-psychological perspective at macroscopic levels above the intrinsic motivation phenomenon, we are also beginning to take a more microscopic look within that phenomenon to discover mechanisms by which it occurs. Specifically, we are addressing three questions: How does motivational state (intrinsic versus extrinsic) influence creative thinking? What is the role of affect? What is the role of individual differences?

How Motivation Influences Creative Thinking

In his classic paper on creative thinking, Campbell (1960) describes the process as involving a consideration of widely varying, blindly generated ideas, followed by a selective retention of those ideas that best fit some criteria. Simonton (1988) suggests much the same process in his "chance-configuration" theory of creativity. And, in his analysis of motivation and cognition, Simon (1967) asserts that the most important function of motivation is the control of attention.

We have used these theories to suggest a model of the way in which motivational orientation might influence creativity. The metaphor for this model is a maze with several exits; performing a task is represented as attempting to find a way out of the maze. The task can be done by rote, using familiar algorithms, and resulting in an uncreative solution; in the maze metaphor, the individual can take the straight, well-worn, familiar pathway out of the maze. This is the route most likely to be taken by extrinsically motivated individuals (those motivated primarily by factors outside of the task itself, outside of the maze). Because they view the task as merely a means to an end, their attention has been narrowed to doing the minimum necessary to meet the extrinsic constraint (see Kruglanski, Stein, & Riter, 1977). However, finding a creative solution requires exploration through the maze, a more heuristic approach to the task. Individuals will only be likely to take this more creative approach if they are initially intrinsically interested in the activity itself *and* if their social environment does not demand a narrowing of behavior into the familiar algorithm.

This model leads to several specific predictions about differences in the ways intrinsically and extrinsically motivated individuals will process tasks, leading ultimately to the more creative outcomes under intrinsic motivation. (Notice, however, that the model would predict no decrements in the more algorithmic *technical quality* of work under extrinsic motivation.) Compared with extrinsically motivated individuals, intrinsically motivated persons should generate and examine a larger number of ideas and possibilities while engaged in the task; make associations and juxtapositions that are more unusual; spend a longer period of time on the activity; become more deeply involved cognitively in the activity, as evidenced by several attention measures; experience more positive affect when *anticipating* working on the task, as well as when actually working on it; depart more frequently from familiar algorithms for task engagement; spend more time thinking about the task after they have finished it; and produce more creative end products. Some previous studies with various cognitive tasks

offer suggestive evidence (e.g., Kruglanski, Stein & Riter, 1977; McGraw & Fiala, 1982; Pittman, Emery, & Boggiano, 1982). We have planned a series of studies to examine these predictions directly.

The Role of Affect

We will also be investigating the role of affect in the motivation-creativity link. Several theorists (e.g., Csikszentmihályi, 1975; Deci & Ryan, 1985; Izard, 1977) have suggested that intrinsic motivation involves positive affective experience, and extrinsic motivation involves negative affect. There is considerable empirical support for this suggestion (e.g., Pretty & Seligman, 1983; Reeve, Cole, & Olsen, 1986; Ryan, 1982). As I described earlier, we have suggested affect as a possible explanation for the unexpectedly high creativity of subjects in the "bonus" reward condition of our choice-reward study (Amabile, Hennessey, & Grossman, 1986).

Isen and her colleagues have demonstrated that induced positive affect increases the probability of unusual associations, set-breaking responses, heuristic problem-solving strategies, and inclusive categorization of stimuli (e.g., Isen, Daubman, & Nowicki, 1987; Isen, Johnson, Mertz, & Robinson, 1985; Isen, Means, Patrick, & Nowicki, 1982). We have planned a series of studies to examine affect as a possible mediator of the effects of motivational orientation on creativity. Do differences in motivational orientation correspond to differences in affect? Are motivational orientation differences causally prior to affective differences? Are the effective differences necessary to produce differences in creativity? Is there a difference between trait (chronic) and state (temporary) motivation, and between chronic and situation-specific affective states in these effects?

We predict a link between intrinsic motivation, positive affect, and high creativity, but we will attempt to determine the causal direction of this link and whether this link might be found only for state intrinsic motivation. It may be that the more enduring trait intrinsic motivation of individuals actively committed to a creative pursuit in their daily lives is not marked by the kind of positive affect studied by Isen but by a more "sober" positive affect—a sense of intimate involvement with and dedication to the work.

Toward a Comprehensive Psychology of Creativity

In beginning to examine specific mechanisms and subtle interactions within the intrinsic motivation phenomenon, we have, of necessity, moved beyond the social psychology of creativity toward a broader view of the creative process. We will be looking at reaction times, attentional measures, memory tests, and the use of algorithms, all taken from cognitive psychology. We are beginning to inform our work with concepts from personality psychology as well. We recognize the significant roles of both situation-induced *and* chronic affective states. We realize that intrinsic/extrinsic motivational orientation is not only a state that can be influenced by the presence or absence of extrinsic social constraints. It is also a *trait*, an enduring attitude that an individual has toward tasks within a domain. We have even developed a questionnaire (the Work Preference Inventory, or WPI) designed to assess individual differences in adults' motivational orientation. Our preliminary results are most encouraging.

This, I believe, is what all of us creativity researchers must do in mapping our future courses. In delving more deeply into the details of the phenomena that interest us, we must constantly attempt to integrate our own perspectives with those offered by others. A comprehensive psychology of creativity *is* within our grasp.

In moving toward that comprehensive understanding, I would still like, somehow, someday, to study the impact of telling subjects that they are "maybe being a little too creative." Then I would like to track down Sister Carmelita and thank her for getting me involved in all of this.

REFERENCES

Albert, R. S. (1980). Family positions and the attainment of eminence: A study of special family experiences. *Gifted Child Quarterly, 24*, 87–95.

Amabile, T. M. (1979). Effects of external evaluation on artistic creativity. *Journal of Personality and Social Psychology, 37*, 221–223.

Amabile, T. M. (1982a). Children's artistic creativity: Detrimental effects of competition in a field setting. *Personality and Social Psychology Bulletin, 8*, 573–578.

Amabile, T. M. (1982b). Social psychology of creativity: A consensual assessment technique. *Journal of Personality and Social Psychology, 43*, 997–1013.

Amabile, T. M. (1983a). *The social psychology of creativity*. New York: Springer-Verlag.

Amabile, T. M. (1983b). Social psychology of creativity: A componential conceptualization. *Journal of Personality and Social Psychology, 45*, 357–377.

Amabile, T. M. (1985). Motivation and creativity: Effects of motivational orientation on creative writers. *Journal of Personality and Social Psychology, 48*, 393–399.

Amabile, T. M. (1987). The motivation to be creative. In S. Isaksen (Ed.), *Frontiers in creativity: Beyond the basics*, Buffalo, NY: Bearly Limited.

Amabile, T. M. (1988a). From individual creativity to organizational innovation. In K. Gronhaug & G. Kaufman (Eds.), *Achievement and motivation: A social-developmental perspective.* New York: Cambridge University Press.

Amabile, T. M. (1988b). A model of organizational innovation. In B. M. Staw & L. L. Cummings (Eds.), *Research in organizational behavior* (Vol. 10). Greenwich, CT: JAI.

Amabile, T. M. (in press). *Growing up creative.* New York: Crown.

Amabile, T. M., & Gitomer, J. (1984). Children's artistic creativity: Effects of choice in task materials. *Personality and Social Psychology Bulletin, 10,* 209–215.

Amabile, T. M., Goldfarb, P., & Brackfield, S. (in press). Social influences on creativity: Evaluation, coaction, and surveillance. *Creativity Research Journal.*

Amabile, T. M., & Gryskiewicz, S. S. (1988). Creative human resources in the R&D laboratory: How environment and personality impact innovation. In R. L. Kuhn (Ed.), *Handbook for creative and innovative managers.* New York: McGraw-Hill.

Amabile, T. M., Hennessey, B. A., & Grossman, B. S. (1986). Social influences on creativity: The effects of contracted-for reward. *Journal of Personality and Social Psychology, 50,* 14–23.

Andrews, F. M. (1975). Social and psychological factors which influence the creative process. In I. A. Taylor & J. W. Getzels (Eds.), *Perspectives in creativity.* Chicago: Aldine.

Barron, F. (1955). The disposition toward originality. *Journal of Abnormal and Social Psychology, 51,* 478–485.

Berglas, S., Amabile, T. M., & Handel, M. (1979). *An examination of the effects of verbal reinforcement on creativity.* Paper presented at the meeting of the American Psychological Association, New York.

Campbell, D. (1960). Blind variation and selective retention in creative thought as in other knowledge processes. *Psychological Review, 67,* 380–400.

Crutchfield, R. S. (1955). Conformity and character. *American Psychologist, 10,* 191–198.

Crutchfield, R. S. (1959). Personal and situational factors in conformity to group pressure. *Acta Psychologica, 15,* 386–388.

Crutchfield, R. S. (1962). Conformity and creative thinking. In H. Gruber, G. Terrell, & M. Wertheimer (Eds.), *Contemporary approaches to creative thinking.* New York: Atherton.

Csikszentmihályi, M. (1975). *Beyond boredom and anxiety.* San Francisco: Jossey-Bass.

Deci, E. L. (1971). Effects of externally mediated rewards on intrinsic motivation. *Journal of Personality and Social Psychology, 18,* 105–115.

Deci, E. L., & Ryan, R. M. (1985). *Intrinsic motivation and self-determination in human behavior.* New York: Plenum.

Feldman, D. (1980). *Beyond universals in cognitive development.* Norwood, NJ: Ablex.

Findlay, C. S., & Lumsden, C. J. (1988). The creative mind: Toward an evolutionary theory of discovery and innovation. *Journal of Social and Biological Structures.*

Getzels, J., & Csikszentmihályi, M. (1976). *The creative vision: A longitudinal study of problem-finding in art.* New York: Wiley Interscience.

Golann, S. E. (1963). Psychological study of creativity. *Psychological Bulletin, 60,* 548–565.

Gordon, W. W. (1961). *Synectics: The development of creative capacity.* New York: Harper & Row.

Guilford, J. P. (1956). The structure of intellect. *Psychological Bulletin, 53,* 267–293.

Harter, S. (1978). Effectance motivation reconsidered: Toward a developmental model. *Human Development, 21*, 34–64.

Harter, S. (1981). A new self-report scale of intrinsic versus extrinsic orientation in the classroom. *Developmental Psychology, 17*, 300–312.

Helson, R. (1965). Childhood interest clusters related to creativity in women. *Journal of Consulting Psychology, 29*, 352–361.

Hennessey, B. A. (1989). The effect of extrinsic constraints on children's creativity while using a computer. *Creativity Research Journal, 2*, 151–168.

Hennessey, B. A., & Amabile, T. M. (1987). *Creativity and learning.* Washington, DC: National Education Association.

Hennessey, B. A., Amabile, T. M., & Martinage, M. (in press). Immunizing children against the negative effects of reward. *Contemporary Educational Psychology.*

Hogarth, R. (1980). *Judgement and choice.* Chichester: John Wiley.

Hughes, T., & McCullough, F. (Eds.). (1982). *The journals of Sylvia Plath.* New York: Dial.

Isen, A. M., Daubman, K. A., & Nowicki, G. P. (1987). Positive affect facilitates creative problem solving. *Journal of Personality and Social Psychology, 52*, 1122–1131.

Isen, A. M., Johnson, M. M. S., Mertz, E., & Robinson, G. F. (1985). The influence of positive affect on the unusualness of word associations. *Journal of Personality and Social Psychology, 48*, 1–14.

Isen, A. M., Means, B., Patrick, R., & Nowicki, G. P. (1982). Some factors influencing decision-making strategy and risk-taking. In M. S. Clark & S. T. Fiske (Eds.), *Affect and cognition: The 17th Annual Carnegie Symposium on Cognition.* Hillsdale, NJ: Lawrence Erlbaum.

Izard, C. (1977). *Human emotions.* New York: Plenum.

Kruglanski, A. W., Friedman, I., & Zeevi, G. (1971). The effects of extrinsic incentive on some qualitative aspects of task performance. *Journal of Personality, 39*, 606–617.

Kruglanski, A. W., Stein, C., & Riter, A. (1977). Contingencies of exogenous reward and task performance: On the "minimax" principle in instrumental behavior. *Journal of Applied Social Psychology, 7*, 141–148.

Lepper, M. R., & Greene, D. (1978). *The hidden costs of reward.* Hillsdale, NJ: Lawrence Erlbaum.

Lepper, M. R., Greene, D., & Nisbett, R. (1973). Undermining children's intrinsic interest with extrinsic rewards: A test of the "overjustification" hypothesis. *Journal of Personality and Social Psychology, 28*, 129–137.

MacKinnon, D. W. (1962). The nature and nurture of creative talent. *American Psychologist, 17*, 484–495.

McKinnon, D. W. (1975). IPAR's contribution to the conceptualization and study of creativity. In I. Taylor & J. Getzels (Eds.), *Perspectives in creativity.* Chicago: Aldine.

McGraw, K. O. (1978). The detrimental effects of reward on performance: A literature review and a prediction model. In M. R. Lepper & D. Greene (Eds.), *The hidden costs of reward.* Hillsdale, NJ: Lawrence Erlbaum.

McGraw, K. O., & Fiala, J. (1982). Undermining the Zeigarnik effect: Another hidden cost of reward. *Journal of Personality, 50*, 58–66.

McGuire, W. (1973). The yin and yang of progress in social psychology. *Journal of Personality and Social Psychology, 26*, 446–456.

Newell, A., Shaw, J., & Simon, H. (1962). The processes of creative thinking. In H. Gruber, G. Terrell, & M. Wertheimer (Eds.), *Contemporary approaches to creative thinking*. New York: Atherton.

Newell, A. & Simon, H. (1972). *Human problem solving*. Englewood Cliffs, NJ: Prentice-Hall.

Nystrom, H. (1979). *Creativity and innovation*. London: John Wiley.

Osborn, A. (1963). *Applied imagination: Principles and procedures of creative thinking*. New York: Scribner.

Pames, S. (1967). *Creative behavior guidebook*. New York: Scribner.

Pittman, T. S., Emery, J., & Boggiano, A. K. (1982). Intrinsic and extrinsic motivational orientations: Reward-induced changes in preference for complexity. *Journal of Personality and Social Psychology, 42*, 789–797.

Pretty, G. H., & Seligman, C. (1983). Affect and the overjustification effect. *Journal of Personality and Social Psychology, 46*, 1241–1253.

Reeve, J., Cole, S. G., & Olsen, B. C. (1986). Adding excitement to intrinsic motivation research. *Journal of Social Behavior and Personality, 1*, 349–363.

Ryan, R. M. (1982). Control and information in the intrapersonal sphere: An extension of cognitive evaluation theory. *Journal of Personality and Social Psychology, 43*, 450–461.

Salancik, G. (1975). *Retrospective attribution of past behavior and commitment to future behavior*. Unpublished manuscript, University of Illinois.

Simon, H. (1966). Scientific discovery and the psychology of problem solving. In *Mind and cosmos: Essays in contemporary science and philosophy*. Pittsburgh: University of Pittsburgh Press.

Simon, H. (1967). Understanding creativity. In C. Gowan, G. D. Demos, & E. P. Torrance (Eds.), *Creativity: Its educational implications*. New York: John Wiley.

Simon, H. (1978). Information-processing theory of human problem-solving. In W. K. Estes (Ed.), *Handbook of learning and cognitive processes: Vol. 5. Human information processing*. Hillsdale, NJ: Lawrence Erlbaum.

Simonton, D. K. (1975). Sociocultural context of individual creativity: A transhistorical time-series analysis. *Journal of Personality and Social Psychology, 32*, 1119–1133.

Simonton, D. K. (1984). *Genius, creativity, and leadership: Historiometric inquiries*. Cambridge, MA: Harvard University Press.

Simonton, D. K. (1988). Creativity, leadership, and chance. In R. J. Sternberg (Ed.), *The nature of creativity*. New York: Cambridge University Press.

Simonton, D. K. (in press). *Scientific genius: A psychology of science*. Cambridge: Cambridge University Press.

Stein, M. I. (1974). *Stimulating creativity* (Vol 1). New York: Academic Press.

Thurstone, L., & Chave, E. (1929). *The measurement of attitude*. Chicago: University of Illinois Press.

Torrance, E. P. (1966). *Torrance Tests of Creative Thinking: Norms-technical manual*. Princeton, NJ: Personnel.

Wallas, G. (1926). *The art of thought*. New York: Harcourt, Brace.

Walster, E., Aronson, V., Abrahams, D., & Rottman, L. (1966). Importance of physical attractiveness in dating behavior. *Journal of Personality and Social Psychology, 4*, 508–516.

Watson, J. D. (1968). *The double helix*. New York: Atheneum.

White, R. (1959). Motivation reconsidered: The concept of competence. *Psychological Review, 66*, 297–323.

34.   WEIRDER THAN FICTION: THE REALITY AND MYTHS OF CREATIVITY

Joseph V. Anderson

WHEN OPPORTUNITY KNOCKS

A.C. Markkula had a nice life. As marketing manager for Intel Corporation, a major semi-conductor manufacturer, he had an interesting job, a cushy salary, and the recognition of his peers at conferences and conventions. Then one day in 1977 he opened his door and there stood Steve, a scruffy looking flake, who'd dropped out of college, flirted with fruitarianism and Hare Krishna, and spent a year in India contemplating his navel and the ultimate verities. Now Steve was storming back into reality with the claim that he'd discovered a bonafide wizard, plus a secret of the universe. He'd sold his VW bus for $1,300 and set up a venture to spread a special form of information across the globe and now, Steve said, he'd chosen Markkula to be his special agent. All Markkula had to do was quit his job, hand over a quarter of a million dollars, and get to work. And though Markkula wouldn't get paid, he'd have the right to be an equal partner in the venture.[1]

Creativity knocks on the door of our psyche every day. But it does so in the strangest forms: as flakes with messages from God, as weird ideas that wake us from slumber, and as strange visions that vaguely materialize when we're wide awake and otherwise quite sane. Sometimes, it even rises from a sea of numbers that stare back at us from a screen or printed page.

But more often than not, we send it away. We slam the door, go back to sleep, or rub our eyes incredulously, then return to what we were doing. That's a sane, and safe, response. But in doing so we rob ourselves of a part of ourselves—the part that's able to leap tall buildings at a single bound. Why do we do that?

We turn our back on creativity because, well frankly, because it's weird. It beckons us to the precipice of illogical danger, like turning over your life savings to a fruitarian on a quest. But ask yourself this—what makes such ventures weird? For the most part, we do. It's weird because no one else is doing it. Or because there's no guarantee it'll work. Or, most often, it's weird because "I can't do that, because …".

More often than not, the "because" we generate is a bunch of poppycock that we've been sucked into believing, such as, "I'm not creative enough to pull that off, no matter how good it sounds." Well if old A.C. Markkula had succumbed to that self-imposed obstacle, I'd still be writing my articles in longhand. Instead, he walked out the door with that odd-ball and took that grand leap of faith that carried him beyond the boundaries of vocation, family, and logic. That's how he hooked up with Steven Jobs and met the world's bonafide wizard, Stephen Wozniak. Markkula had just joined Apple computer company, which still operated out of Wozniak's garage. And Markkula made Steve's dream come to life. He chased that weird apparition because he believed he had it within himself to muster the creativity required. And he saw his own objections and timidity for what they were—poppycock. So he grabbed the poppy by its privates and gave it a heave. And the rest, as they say, is history. We can do the same.

Source: © Academy of Management Executive, 1992 Vol. 6 No. 4, pp 40–47.

All we need to do is separate reality from the myths that plague us. The biggest myth that constraints us is that creativity is too big for us to handle. The next biggest myth is that we only get creative by bearing down on a problem, through stringent systems, organizational re-design and personal struggle. As it turns out, these two grand myths are mostly hot air, and it is time to deflate them. We need to cut creativity down to size. And we need to substitute the commandment to be creative with the permission to do so.

First, a Look at Reality

Creativity is nothing more than going beyond the current boundaries, whether those are boundaries of technology, knowledge, social norms or beliefs. So Star Trek (boldly going where no man has gone before) certainly qualifies. And so does Beethoven's 5th symphony. But we lose sight of the fact that a host of mundane acts are equally as creative. Lengthening a hem beyond what the pattern calls for is no less creative than Beethoven's transition to a new kind of music. Both started from an existing framework. And both take the existing practice a step farther than the norm. Think about that for a while.

Creativity is nothing more than seeing and acting on new relationships, thereby bringing them to life. Like combining man's two chief needs, sustenance and safety, into a single fruit that guards the house, is incredibly loyal and plops itself into your cereal bowl. Al Capp invented that prototype long ago in his comic strip "Li'l Abner." It was called a Schmoo. Odd? Yes. Unreasonable? Nope. Just new and shocking, because it violated the laws of nature.

That little poo-poo of Mother Nature is a central point. The laws of nature are merely boundaries. And they've been violated before. Like the law that one body can not occupy two places at the same time. In essence, that law was violated thousands of years ago, with the first letter. One's thoughts could be in Athens, and in Corinth, at the same time. And if we take Descartes at his word, "I think, therefore, I am" the person simultaneously existed in both places since their thoughts did. The

telephone and live TV are simply better violations of the same law, because the thoughts are truly simultaneous whereas the letter writer had probably forgotten the thought by the time it got to Corinth. For letters, phones, telegraphs, and TV's to be invented someone had to believe that even the laws of nature could, in effect, be broken.

Yes, But Can I Do It? Now that we've established the concept of creativity, do you recognize it? Probably so. Have you experienced it? Most of us say "no" because we've never done anything big with it. We've never written a symphony, much less a hit song. We've never painted the Cystine [sic] Chapel, much less our own house. We never really invented anything. So we're likely to sit back and content ourselves with identifying creativity rather than practicing it. That makes us as useless as a drama critique . . . all talk and no action. The fact of the matter is we've all been creative. We just never labeled it as such, because we didn't understand the various types of creativity. We can rectify that problem pretty quickly.

The Types of Creativity. In essence, there are only three broad types of creativity. You can make things, you can combine things, or you can change things.

Creation is the activity we usually think of when someone says creativity. It is the act of making something out of nothing. With fervid apologies to physicists and their theory of atomic displacement, it *is* possible to make something out of nothing. Beethoven faced a blank page and made the immortal 5th symphony spring to life. Shakespeare did the same with *Othello* and a host of other masterpieces. The Wright brothers filled an empty sky with planes. And on and on it goes. Creation, is without question, creativity. But it is not the whole, nor is it even the most important type. There are others of equal import.

Synthesis is the act of relating two or more previously unrelated phenomena. Take a cake. Take a shovel. Put them side by side and stare at them. Boom! The cake server is born. It's a miniature shovel. That's synthesis. The first wheel was the product of creation. So was the first axle and the first box. But until someone came along and synthesized them into the cart, mankind didn't get much good out of the three components. Synthesis is the core of society's advancement. Creation is nice, but synthesis is the real engine of survival and prosperity. Have you ever performed synthesis? Did you ever fill a pie tin with mud instead of batter? Ever fill a balloon with water instead of air. Did you ever put Tuesday together with going to the beach rather than going to work? Congratulations. You synthesized. And that puts you in the same league as Thomas Edison. He never created anything in his whole life. All he did was suck the brains of others and synthesized like crazy. So whadayathink? You creative?

Modification is the act of altering something that already exists so that it can: (a) perform its function better, (b) perform a new function (c) perform in a different setting, or (d) be used by someone new. Putting pontoons on an airplane doesn't change the function of the plane (take off, fly, land), but it certainly broadens the settings in which it can perform its function. Moving a hose to the back end of a vacuum cleaner changes the whole function of the machine, from sucking to blowing. And something as simple as lowering a water fountain, or adding a foot stool opens its use to a whole new group, unattended children.

The remaining point to be made here is that creation, synthesis and modification overlap so much that it is difficult to separate them in reality. The folks at Etonic aggressively stumbled on creativity by deciding to play barefoot in the park at midnight. There in the blackness of night their senses took over and rediscovered the incredible lightness of being naked of foot, and the ability to pivot equally well on toe or heel. And that unlocked their "Catalyst" shoe, the revolutionary light shoe with a two piece sole. The Catalyst had never existed before. So in that respect it represented cre-

ation. But in essence it was just a modification, one that came via synthesis, putting tennis with bare feet, rather than with shoes.

The reality, therefore, is this. Each of us has the gift of creativity, in one form or another. So don't fret if a symphony isn't within you. You have one of the other gifts. And the only thing it takes to release them is for you to remove the self-imposed obstacles . . . the myths that confound us. And that just happens to be our next topic.

The Myths That Confound Us

The Missing Organ. Many people seem to think that creativity is like a mystic organ, say an extra pancreas or enlarged hypothalamus gland, that only a few people possess. In all honesty, they may be correct when it comes to true creation. However, that is a minuscule part of functional creativity, easily swamped by the contribution of synthesis and modification. And the latter two are not dependent on mysticism, revelation, or even an extra organ. All they require is open eyes and the willingness to act on what you see. If you ever hid food under your pillow you've got what it takes for those. You went beyond the boundary of Mom's social order, and you synthesized like crazy—associating food with a bed instead of with a table.

The Need for Genius. Many people also believe that creativity is the result of the *amount* of intelligence that one possesses. Clinical and field studies, however, fail to support this hypothesis. Verifiable geniuses (as measured by IQ tests and similar instruments) tend to do very well for themselves vocationally, but they usually do so as corporate vice presidents shuffling paper. They haven't made much of a dent in terms of making creative contributions to the world.[2] A solid "C" student with curiosity and determination usually makes a bigger impact on the world. Edison, Einstein, and even Theodore Geisel (otherwise known as "Dr. Seuss") were all lackluster students.

The key is not how much intelligence you have, but the type of intelligence, and your willingness to use it. Steven Jobs was a back alley hustler with street smarts, not an intellectual. His "genius" was the ability to dream dreams, then connive and cajole others into cooperation.

Wozniak was his first victim, and once he was under wing Jobs convinced lawyers and ad agencies to work for nothing more than the promise of future payments, and Markkula to risk everything he had. Jobs rightfully earned the title as the father of Apple, despite the fact that he was neither a technical nor marketing wizard. He was just a jack-of-all-trades in both, with a whole lot of chutzpa.

The Need for Chutzpa. Does it follow then than chutzpa is a requirement for creativity? No. Walter Middy, you may recall, was an outward milquetoast at the same time that his imagination was running rampant across the globe. Creativity can easily bloom without the social courage and hustle we call chutzpa. But there is a big difference between dreaming an idea and using it. And at that point chutzpa comes screaming back on stage. Without the outward hustle and courage it brings, ideas stay on the drawing board or get lost in the dark recesses of the mind. Consequently, we'd have to acknowledge that while creativity can bloom for anyone, it only bears fruit for the chutzpatic gardener. So reality provides a simple truth. The meek creative simply needs to form a partnership with an adrenal hustler. "Steve Wozniak, meet Steve Jobs. Now go make millions."

The Solitary Magician. Another myth is that the creative person exists in a vacuum, locked in his garage with God as the only source of inspiration. It makes a great movie script, but usually misses the mark in terms of reality.

Take a look at electricity. Frenchmen came up with the first spark maker and discovered alternating current. Germans invented the Leyden jar and the vacuum pump. Italians came up with the wet-cell and storage batteries. A Dane was the intellectual source of much of electric theory. Then Ben Franklin, perhaps the world's most under-rated creator, was the world's foremost authority on electric theory for a considerable time. An Austrian invented the first electric-powered machine. And an academic just down the road from Edison at Rensaller Institute of Technology was blissfully inventing capacitors, alternators, generators, and filters for his own entertainment.[3]

So when Thomas Edison sat alone in his workshop and "invented" the light bulb, he was hardly alone. Every one of those other folks was crammed into the shadows. They represented the ninety-nine percent perspiration Edison advocated—knowing the trail of research. In fact, Edison had been a regular visitor in Professor Henry Rowland's office, the American academic blissfully puttering away in his lab.

Creativity and Nobility. Since we tend to envision the creative person locked in his garage with God, we tend to see creativity as the progeny of sacred union. Sometimes it may be exactly that, but usually not. In fact, there are numerous indications that creativity is the product of someone you'd like to throw in jail.

In 1860 a group of investors paid young Johnnie to make a field investigation of the commercial viability of petroleum. He thought it was a sure fire winner. So he lied through his teeth. He told the investors it was a loser, put every penny of his own funds into petroleum, and aced them out of the market. Then he went on to invent most of the competitive practices that are now illegal. Before he was a philanthropist, John D. Rockefeller was a crook. But he was also marvelously creative, and the industry still bears his mark in terms of production, distillation, and distribution.

And if you want larceny with a grin, look at Samuel Slater. In 1790 he stole the trade secrets of mass production in England and sold himself to the highest bidder in America, boldly violating every aspect of British patent and copyright law, thereby putting America on the map as an industrial nation. But Sam redeemed himself. He and his wife were the originators of Sunday School in America. And ironically, at the same time he was violating the British, he was the leading advocate of the legislation that established America's own patent and copyright laws.[4] You have to sit back and admire that type of gall.

The list goes on and on, but the point is that creativity isn't very pristine. In fact, it sometimes emanates from the dark side of our personality. That's unsettling if you see business as a quaint tea party. It's intuitively obvious if you recognize it as trench warfare.

So with a nod to Freud, the first place you may want to check for ideas is your id. The second place you'll want to check is the id of thy neighbor. At it's worst, creativity involves outright theft on a grand scale. At its best, it is a form of unconscious plagiarism. If God accompanies us to the garage, he usually sits there and tells us what our neighbors are doing. So don't be timid about where you look or what you use. Any idea is fair game as a starting point. Even if its protected, it can inspire a useful offshoot. Apple hasn't really "created" anything. But it's been brilliant at synthesis and modification.

Purity of Heart Is to Will One Thing. That's a quote from Kierrkegard, a prominent and very dead theologian. They might be wise words to a religious aesthetic but they are the kiss of death to someone trying to be creative. No matter how creative you might be, you need to pull your head out of the sand and see what else is going on.

Surprisingly enough, though, many firms don't use the ideas and technologies that are readily available. It has been suggested that this is due to an "NIH syndrome" (not invented here), which seems to be equal parts pompous disdain, proprietary fastidiousness, and uncertainty about how to exploit new knowledge.

Bell & Howell was once a major name in every upscale home. Its eight millimeter movie cameras were the bane and blessing of every family gathering and the chronicler of American family history. By 1972 more than one million cameras were being sold each year, but by 1981, sales had plummeted by almost ninety percent and Bell & Howell became a name used only in nostalgia and *Trivial Pursuit*. The simplicity of video swept the market-

place, and Bell & Howell ignored the new idea. Now the marketplace ignores Bell & Howell.[5]

Revelation and Creativity. Michelangelo professed that he never created a sculpture. He simply stared at the block of marble until God showed him the statue that was trapped within. Then all Mike did was get the gravel out of the way. Wouldn't it be nice to have just such a direct line to the almighty? The fact of the matter is that Michelangelo's profession was probably on a par with Oral Robert's recent proclamation that God said his supporters better cough up $8,000,000 or their favorite healer was kaput.

In reality, if a line exists at all, it's so indirect and convoluted that one is reminded of Mark Twain's words, "Lord, if you forgive the little jokes I play on you, I'll forgive the great big ones you play on me." The bulk of creativity comes to the surface by accident, or initially mis-directed.

Alexander Graham Bell didn't get a direct commission from on high to create an instrument for carrying conversations between New York and Paris. He was dinking around trying to invent a hearing aid for his deaf fiance. In 1795 Nicholas Joseph Cugnot dabbled with an abject failure, a steam-driven cannon carriage for the French army. Men comfortably walk at three to four miles per hour. The gun carriage zipped along at two miles per hour and had to stop every 300 yards to rebuild a head of steam. But it was the first automobile, in disguise. In 1842, Dr. John Gorrie became mentally ill and died, because the medical industry refused to embrace his cure for malaria, which happened to be the first air-conditioner. So keep your eyes open and realize that the best application of your idea might be worlds away from your current focus.

External Validity and Creativity. The previous stories shoot a hole in a major myth that hamstrings us— if Mom doesn't tack it on the refrigerator, it doesn't count as art. More often than not we let others decree whether we are creative or not. And when that happens, we're in trouble. Either we stop trying, or we join John Gorrie in a padded cell.

The fact of the matter is that most creative acts are initially rejected, ignored or belittled. Bell was laughed off the stage at his first demonstration of the phone. Van Gogh never sold a painting—the ones that now go for eight million dollars. It was just about a century before Cugnot's car resurfaced in Henry Ford's factory, and it took just as long for Gorrie's machine to become the air conditioner.

Simply put, the rest of the world doesn't immediately embrace creativity. So if you rely on their judgment you'll never get out of the starting blocks. Remember, creativity exists if:

a. a new thing comes into being (creation);

b. two previously unrelated things are joined (synthesis);

c. or, if a thing is improved or gains a new application (modification).

That's it. The total list of requirements. Notice that the list does not say "Creativity exists only if someone else says 'My how creative'." Once you realize that, you become your own arbiter of creativity. Blanch DuBois may have been "dependent on the kindness of strangers" in *A Streetcar Named Desire*, but you don't have to be. In other words, stop chasing after the "moms" of the world looking for approval, and spend your time actually being creative. You'll stay sane, and the world will benefit from your work.

If It Ain't Big, It Ain't Creativity. And now we get to the crux of the matter. We surgically gut our latent creativity by setting incredibly high benchmarks, such as "it's only creative if it changes the world." So if we've never written a symphony, or invented a product, or designed a marketing plan that captured seventy-seven percent of the yuppie market, we look despairingly in the mirror at the slack-jawed drone that gazes back, and condemn ourselves to a life of drab obedience to those who have.

In the process we forget that moving a desk so that work flows smoother is also creativity. It's modification. And creativity also blooms when we re-design a job description so that related tasks are given to the same person. That's synthesis. It's even creativity when we cut our losses on a worthless industrial adhesive by slapping it on the back of our secretary's note pad so she can stick our messages where we'll see them. We call that bit of creation the 3-M "Post-It" notes.

And when you get right down to it, our notion of bigness and importance is usually the opposite of reality. The much bally-hooed creation of the Saturn car company by GM is small potatoes, infinitely unimportant. The car still has four wheels, still uses an internal combustion engine, people still ride inside it, and so on. It's big in terms of dollars, but frankly, it doesn't change the world a bit. What does? The lowly tin can. Now that's something to praise. It revolutionized the world. It changed food production and storage, made armies and individuals more mobile, and virtually eliminated botulism. The flush toilet is another one. Urban mortality rates plummeted as a result.

As it turns out, creativity usually resides in the seemingly small potatoes of corporate and individual life. Or should we say peanuts? George Washington Carver was probably the most prolific creator in America's history, making Edison look like a tortoise in terms of the number of products created. And Carver did it all by looking at one little insignificant thing—the peanut.

So start seeing creativity in your own peanuts: the reporting procedure that could be improved, the sales territory that can be redesigned, the new vendor or purchasing procedure, or the tasks that can be re-designed.

And Now for a Parting Shot

But what if you're trying to get creativity out of other people, and not just trying to be creative yourself? You start by confronting the reality and myths we've just covered. Then you add two more things.

First—realize that no structure, process, incentive system or management reorganization is going to make your firm creative, unless you first help the individuals within those structures and systems unlock their willingness to try. And that isn't done at arm's length. You've got to crawl into the trenches and be a cheerleader and seducer. Hold up a mirror for your people and help them see their own creative potential by identifying it for them.

The best creativity motivator I ever met was an old curmudgeon that ran one of the production shops at a naval shipyard. When someone finished a job ahead of schedule (with no defects) he jumped on a workbench with airhorn and megaphone in hand and treated the entire shop to an absolutely obscene drinking song in celebration. The sight of the grumpy old S.O.B. making a fool of himself was so ridiculous, and the instigator received so many kudos and free drinks, that everyone busted a hump to be the next cause of hilarity. Creativity ravished the shop floor, and no problem was insurmountable. They had less down time, less turnover, and higher productivity than any other unit.

Sometimes, our desire for professionalism is so strong that we make the affirmation process needlessly convoluted and diluted. When a kid takes their artwork to Mom, they want a hug and a kiss—an emotional reaction. Given the current climate, a hug and kiss at work will land you in jail, or on the Supreme Court—but some other kind of emotional reaction is certainly called for. So loosen up. Managers prosper from borrowing some inspirational tactics from the art of leadership. And that, in itself, is the creative act of synthesis.

Second—while you're holding that mirror, keep a careful eye on the images they see, because they'll initially need some help separating the reality from the poppycock.

- Remind them that creativity exists in the small and mundane things of life, as well as in the big things

- Remind them that creativity is more than creation. Celebrate synthesis and modification as well.

- Encourage them to look around—to transfer ideas from other areas, and to look for seemingly absurd applications of what they've already got.

- In short, help them see that they have the seed of creativity in themselves already.

And while you're at it, do the same for yourself.

NOTES

1. This, and subsequent information on Markkula and Apple, comes from Robert F. Hartley, *Marketing Successes* (New York: John Wiley & Sons Inc., 1985) 200–213.

2. Lewis Terman, father of the American IQ test, discovered this rather enlightening factoid in a 60-year study of 1,528 measurable geniuses. Cited by Leslie Dorman in "Original Spin," *Psychology Today*, August 1989, 47–52.

3. The historical information on electricity and other forms of technology comes from *The People's Chronology*, James Trager, ed. (New York: Holt, Rinehart and Winston, 1979). In addition to being an entertaining ammunition dump for *Trivial Pursuit*, it is a fascinating guide to the progression of knowledge. You'd be well served to buy a recent edition.

4. *The People's Chronology*, James Trager, ed. (New York: Holt Rinehart and Winston, 1979), again.

5. Ann Hughey, "Sales of Home Movie Equipment Falling as Firms Abandon Market, Video Grows," *Wall Street Journal*, March 17, 1982, 25.

Managing Organizational Innovation

The innovator makes enemies of all those who prospered under the old order, and only lukewarm support is forthcoming from those who would prosper under the new ... because men are generally incredulous, never really trusting new things unless they have tested them by experience.

Niccolo Machiavelli, The Prince

35.   THE POLITICAL NATURE OF INNOVATION

Peter J. Frost and Carolyn P. Egri

As observed long ago by Machiavelli, the introduction of an innovation or change continues to induce and become the focus of political activity in modern society and its organizations. It is in these disputes over the ambiguous means and ends of an envisioned change that the process of innovation becomes political. How then, does an innovation emerge and survive whatever conflict it engenders? Under what conditions and when does organizational politics flourish in the innovation process? Research evidence indicates that political gamesmanship is most likely to be positively linked with the degree of originality, with the degree of perceived risk, and with the complexity of the situation. Perhaps the most vulnerable time of the innovation process is during the implementation stage when the dysfunctional nature of organizational politics is most often highlighted. It is responsible for, among other things, unnecessary delays, excessive conflict, compromised outcomes, and sometimes, ultimate failure.

The main theme throughout studies in which these results are observed is on the "problem" of the social and political dynamics engendered by inno-

From: P. Frost, V. Mitchell, & W. Nord (Eds.), *Organizational Reality: Reports from the Firing Line,* Harper Collins, 1992, pp. 449–460.

vation. Consistent with the general pro-innovation bias found in society, these resistances to innovation are generally regarded by managers as threats rather than opportunities. For those managers who are more entrenched in an organization (either by virtue of age, seniority or through the benefits accorded them by the status quo) the messiness, disorder and "muddling through" required of the innovation process can be particularly distasteful, thereby resulting in avoidance or resistance.

To illustrate the tangle and complexity of the innovation process and its political nature, we present several case studies which describe the process in some detail. There do not appear to be as many studies of innovation which deal with the politics of innovation. Most common treatments of innovation either do not address process or gloss over or truncate its detail in the interest of limited space or because the authors are addressing other questions.

THE TRIALS OF PRODUCT CHAMPIONS AND SPONSORS— NASA MOONLANDER MONITOR

The case of the development of the NASA Moonlander Monitor is one which illustrates the integral role an innovation champion and his/her managerial sponsors can play in the development of a new product. It is also an example of how innovators can successfully be mavericks within an organizational culture which, while posing at the surface level a number of obstacles to such initiatives, is supportive of innovation and change in its deep structure.

As a young engineer at Hewlett-Packard, Chuck House proved to be instrumental in the development and application of oscilloscope technology for new venues (Pinchot, 1985). Initial impetus for the project was provided by the Federal Aviation Administration, which identified the need for an improved airport control tower monitor. Although the Hewlett-Packard monitor did not meet the FAA's specification for a high resolution picture and subsequently lost out to competitors, there

were features of their prototype which struck House as worthy of further investigation. House believed that the size (smaller and lighter than other models), speed (20 times as fast), energy efficiency and brighter (but fuzzier) picture of his group's monitor was a significant technological breakthrough—although one which had yet to find its niche in the marketplace.

In the course of his efforts to demonstrate the merits of his team's model, House proved to be a political gamesman who operated as a maverick by violating a number of organizational rules and boundaries. His first foray into the political arena involved conducting his own market research on potential applications. To gather such information, House personally showed the monitor prototype to 40 computer manufacturers and potential customers in an organizationally unsanctioned trip from Colorado to California. In doing so, not only was he violating functional organizational boundaries by circumventing the marketing department but he was also violating a cardinal Hewlett-Packard security rule which forbade the showing of prototypes to customers. However, based on the marketing information collected during his trip, House was able to gain a temporary reprieve from senior management for his project. During the next 18 months, the project team continued development work in the lab and on-site with customers.

The next obstacle to the continuation of the project came during the annual division review by senior management. This review was influenced to a large degree by a marketing department telephone survey which projected that there was only a total demand for 32 monitors. The resistance and lack of creative initiative of the marketing group (perhaps motivated by House's previous incursion into their territory) was evident in the manner in which the survey was conducted. As Pinchot (1985: 26–27) reports: "Chuck argued that marketing had failed to understand his strategy for marketing the product. They had called only upon oscilloscope customers, the only customers they knew. New applications required new customers, Chuck explained. Besides, the device was difficult to describe: Because it was new, only demonstrations could uncover its saleability." Marketing's forecast of demand for the monitor prevailed over House's group's projections which were based on direct operating feedback from customers (and were, to some extent, obtained through organizationally illegitimate means). Not only was House's project threatened by the lack of administrative innovation by the marketing group, his project did not have the support of the chief corporate engineer who favored an alternate technology.

The conclusion of the divisional review was that, in light of the apparent lack of market demand and technological support from others in the organization, the only rational action was to abort the project. In corporate founder David Packard's words: "When I come back next year I don't want to see that project in the lab!" (Pinchot, 1985: 27).

It is at this point that House's political gamesmanship was put to the test. Unwilling to accept this decision, House "chose" to reinterpret Packard's pronouncement to mean that the project would be out of the lab in one year's time but in production, not on the scrapheap. With the covert support of his boss Dar Howard, the tactic of covering up development costs of the project from budget restrictions started in earnest as House's team raced to complete the project in one year when the normal length of time would be two. In the face of continuing opposition from the marketing department, House gained additional support by convincing interested potential customers to personally call on his superiors and argue for the project.

Fortunately for House and his team, they made their deadline and when Packard returned one year later, the monitor was indeed in the marketplace. Packard was reported to be both amused and impatient with this obvious re-interpretation of his order but perhaps indicative of his own maverick origins, he now supported the obviously successful project. Rather than being punished for their insubordination, House and his team were now given permission to continue to develop additional applications, among them the eventual use of the oscilloscope monitor for the NASA Moon Mission, the medical monitor used in the first artificial heart transplant, and a large-screen oscilloscope which was used as part of an Emmy-award-winning special effects system. Without the committed championship of House and the sponsorship of his immediate superiors, these landmark innovations could have easily been the victims of opposing political forces.

DESIGNING POLITICAL BATTLES TO BUILD A NEW COMPUTER

In his Pulitzer-prize-winning book, *The Soul of a New Machine*, Tracy Kidder (1981) treats us to a detailed account of the trials of the design engineer in the highly competitive computer industry. He also gives us an inside look at how competitive political contests can be surreptitiously orchestrated by senior managers to promote innovation.

Data General prided itself on its maverick culture—a culture which could be directly traced back to its founding members, three young computer engineers who left DEC in 1968 to set up shop in a former beauty parlour. Within ten years, Data General was on the Fortune 500 list and had carved out its niche in the minicomputer market. However, by 1976, Data General was also sorely in need of a new product, namely, a 32-bit minicomputer which was comparable, but better, than those recently introduced by their competitors.

The political stage was set by senior executives headed by CEO Ed de Castro when they announced that Data General would build a new research and development facility in North Carolina. It was here, they publicly announced, that major research would be conducted to develop the needed 32-bit minicomputer. The important Fountainhead Project (FHP) was transferred to the new location along with 50 of the most talented DG engineers and technicians. Meanwhile, among those who remained behind in Westborough, Massachusetts, were Tom West and his small Eclipse group. Their previous project had been cancelled in favor of the FHP—Data General could not afford to fund two major competing projects. Instead, West was assigned to revamp the lower priority 16-bit Eclipse. Although de Castro never put it in writing, West received tentative approval to transform the Eclipse into a 32-bit minicomputer as the rechristened Eagle project. Technically, the Eclipse group was not to do any groundbreaking developments—that was the territory of North Carolina's FHP. How West and his managers were able to do just that in record time is a testament to skillful team building and political acumen.

The first priority was to keep a low profile so as not to appear to be in competition with FHP. This political strategy was justified by West as follows:

You gotta distinguish between the internal promotion to the actual workers and the promoting we did externally to other parts of the company. Outside the group I tried to low-key the thing. I tried to dull the impression that this was a competing product with North Carolina. I tried to sell it externally as not much of a threat . . . It was just gonna be a fast, Eclipse-like machine. This was the only way it was gonna live. We had to get the resources quietly, without creating a big brouhaha, and it's difficult to get a lot of external cooperation under those circumstances." (Kidder, 1981: 47)

Part of this low profile strategy was physical. The Eclipse group was located in the cramped basement quarters of Westborough headquarters where even the air conditioning didn't work properly. This resulted in both physical and social isolation from the rest of the company, all the better to facilitate covering up their real agenda for the Eagle project. The Eclipse group's low profile was also facilitated by the type of engineers recruited for the project. West and his lieutenant Carl Alsing hired recent engineering graduates not only for their excellent academic credentials but also for their willingness to work long hours and their unbridled enthusiasm for computer design work. By doing so, the group was ensured a low profile in that there were few who would see them as competition for the higher priced and proven talent in North Carolina.

One example of the lengths to which Eclipse group members went to avoid appearing to be in competition with FHP or encroaching on their territory is how computer architect Steve Wallach got his job done. If there was a computer instruction which deviated from the approved parameters of the Eagle project and might be construed as infringing on the FHP project, Wallach would work with his friends in System Software on the item. When finished, he would then ask his friends to write a memo requesting inclusion of the controversial instruction into the Eagle—thus avoiding any charges that the Eclipse group was going outside of approved project parameters.

Throughout the project, team members were constantly negotiating with support groups for their assistance. The competition for resources was difficult for the Eclipse group as Kidder (1981: 112) relates: "The game was fixed for North Carolina and all the support groups knew it." Through personal contacts and persuasive skills they were able to gain the needed resources.

What is particularly interesting in this case is that many of the engineers on the Eclipse team were unaware of the full extent of West's role in ensuring survival of the project. It was all part of his managerial style which was to stay separate from the team and to run interference with other corporate bodies in order that his engineering team could be creatively free. West also benefitted from having a management sponsor in Vice-President of Engineering Carl Carman who authorized the project and the money to recruit staff. Fortuitously, the FHP reported to a different Vice-President so there was no internal organizational conflict for Carman.

Finally, in a classic David vs. Goliath scenario, the small Eclipse group overcame all organizational and technical obstacles to deliver the 32-bit minicomputer ahead of North Carolina. This was a tale of a maverick group operating effectively within a maverick culture. For de Castro, it was a relatively low cost exercise in creative insurance so that Data General would have the desired product.

AN OUTSIDER DOING BATTLE WITH THE DEEP STRUCTURE: THE DVORAK SIMPLIFIED KEYBOARD

The case of the Dvorak Simplified Keyboard (DSK) is one which clearly demonstrates how self-interested political actors can effectively forestall a demonstrably beneficial technological change. When invented in 1873, the current universal "QWERTY" typewriter keyboard was designed to prevent typists from striking two adjoining keys in quick succession. Otherwise, the keys would "jam" together in the basket of a machine which relied on the forces of gravity to pull the keys back to their original positions. Technological improvements to the typewriter (the introduction of spring-loaded keys at the turn of the century and later, the invention of electric typewriters) overcame the jamming problem but the original keyboard remained. Enter Dr. August Dvorak, education professor, who through scientific time and motion studies developed a new keyboard configuration which would enable typists to work faster, more accurately (50% fewer mistakes) and with less physical strain to gain productivity improvements ranging from 35% to 100% (Dvorak, Merrick, Dealey, & Ford, 1936). Additionally, Dvorak proved that typists could learn their skill in one-third of the time it took to learn on the QWERTY keyboard. Why then, aren't we all (present authors included) typing on this technologically superior invention?

Perhaps the chief culprits in resisting this technological innovation were the typewriter manufacturers who had considerable financial interests in retaining the traditional keyboard. During the 1930s when Dvorak introduced his invention, there was little incentive for typewriter manufacturers to convert over to a keyboard which would increase typist productivity thereby conceivably resulting in fewer sales. Furthermore, they would be required to pay royalties on Dvorak's patented invention.

Rejected by the manufacturers, Dvorak then reasoned that publicity at the World Typewriting Championships would help generate public demand for his invention. From 1934 to 1941, DSK-trained typists did indeed win the top typing awards at these competitions. However, the championships were sponsored by the manufacturers who, faced with these embarrassing outcomes, worked to deny Dvorak the publicity he sought. When publishing contest results, they only listed the names of the winning typists, not the machines they used in competition. An attempt by contest officials to ban DSK typists from competition was aborted when Dvorak threatened to advise the newspapers. Dvorak was even forced to hire security guards to protect his machines during the contests when it was discovered that they had been sabotaged.

The manufacturers were also skillful in networking with the American National Standards Institute. As members of the ANSI Keyboard Committee, they were able to prevent inclusion of the DSK into the national standards manual. Dvorak's attempts to gain a government contract for his typewriters were also unsuccessful. Despite the demonstrated superiority of the DSK in experimental tests conducted in the U.S. Navy and the General Services Administration, both rejected the possibility of a conversion. The rationale was that the measurable costs of replacing obsolete equipment and retraining typists outweighed the intangible future benefits of productivity improvements. This was a surprising conclusion since the trial results showed an average productivity increase of 74% with retraining costs being amortized over 10 days. Then in the ultimate covering up political tactic, the U.S. Navy assigned the DSK test results a security classification.

It is no wonder that, after 30 years of political battles to fulfil his dream, a frustrated Dr. Dvorak told Parkinson: "I'm tired of trying to do something worthwhile for the human race. They simply don't want to change!" (Parkinson, 1972: 18)

But as this account of innovation politics suggests, it is not all humans who resist change but rather those interest groups who stand to lose their financial stake if the innovation is implemented.

THE POWER OF VESTED INTERESTS TO FRUSTRATE NEW IDEAS: HELPING AUTISTIC CHILDREN

As related by Graziano (1969) in his account of a mental health innovation, the realm of interorganizational innovation is often the scene for political action at the deep structural level. Set in the 1960s, this account shows how the entrenched interests of a medical establishment (expert in the psychoanalytic treatment of such patients) actively resisted acknowledging or experimenting with a new technique (behavioral modification) to treat autistic children. The power of the professional elite is demonstrated by their ability to effectively maintain the status quo of local mental health services while circumventing efforts of an opposing group to gain local funding for an alternative treatment.

At a fundamental level, the two opposing interest groups were aligned into one which was supported by the medical profession versus one which was community-based. On the side of the entrenched power elite in the mental health community were the private-practice psychiatrists who operated the local clinics and dominated the local Mental Health Association. How they were able to parlay their position to influence other institutional actors (the local university and the "United Agency" fund-raising organization) is particularly interesting in this drama of innovation. In opposition to this coalition for the status quo was the Association for Mentally Ill Children (ASMIC), which was a lay group comprised of the parents of those autistic children who had not been helped by the psychoanalytic methodology (either because they had not responded to this course of treatment or had parents who could not afford the expensive private clinics). The ASMIC had employed a psychologist skilled in this new approach (remember that the time was the early 1960s when behavior modification was still a relatively radical new theory) to assist them in their attempt to change the system. However the integral role in which organizational politics plays in the course of innovation is highlighted by Graziano's (1969: 10) comment that: "The *conception* of innovative ideas in mental health depends upon creative humanitarian and scientific forces, while their *implementation* depends, not on science or humanitarianism, but on a broad spectrum of professional or social politics."

Although both groups initially worked together for four years in a local clinic offering both methodologies, the subsequent struggles over the resources to be allocated to each program and evaluation of the therapeutic effectiveness of each led to their separation.

Operating independently, the ASMIC tried repeatedly to gain financial support for their alternative approach. Once outside the mainstream of the medical establishment though, they encountered political resistance orchestrated by the local private clinics at both the surface and deep structure levels. An ASMIC proposal to the local university to try an experimental pilot project testing the merits of the behavioral modification methodology was rejected on two counts—it was too radical and it was not supported by the local mental health community.

Attempts to gain independent funding for their project from the local community funding agency ("United Agency") were first delayed and finally rejected after three years of efforts by the ASMIC to comply with the agency's demands. The influence of the established clinics (which were also funded by the United Agency) could be surmised to have played a role in the construction of these obstacles to implementation. Even though the ASMIC had garnered enough funds (from the parents of the autistic children and latterly from the State Department of Mental Health) to operate at a minimal level of service, the United Agency's rationale for withholding funds proved to be innovative in their own right. First there was the criticism that the program was first only a "paper proposal"; then after six months of operation, the United Agency contended that the program had been in operation "too brief a time on which to base a decision." After another year, the funding application was rejected because it had not been "professionally evaluated"; with a positive State Department of Mental Health evaluation in hand, the ASMIC program was then deemed to be a "duplication of services"; with state endorsement that it was a nonduplicated service, the United Agency declared that state financial support was required; and finally, with a state grant in hand, the United Agency rejected the application outright because the AS-MIC had been "uncooperative" by not providing confidential information on clients' names, addresses, and fathers' places of employment.

AUTOMATICALLY CONTROLLED MACHINE TOOLS—AN OBJECT OF DEEP STRUCTURE POLITICS

That class conflict and the ideology of progress inform the institutions, ideas, and social groups which determine the design and use of a particular technology is the basic thesis of Noble's (1984) analysis of machine tool automation in manufacturing production. This case illustrates how deep structure politics were used to preserve and extend the control and power of the sectional interests of the owner/managerial, scientific technical and military communities at the expense of those of workers. The capacity of a societal ideology to influence not only the choice of a technology but also to frame (in a pre-emptive manner) that decision in terms of the criteria and assumptions which are used, demonstrates the covert and subtle nature of deep structure power games.

Following WW II, there were two viable avenues by which machine tool automation could proceed. The first was Record Playback (R/P) which built on the skills and knowledge of machinist craftsmen thereby enhancing their traditional power base in the production process. In R/P, automatic control of a machine tool was achieved via a taped program which recorded the movements of the machine operator. It required a skilled machinist to make the initial program and any subsequent changes and ad-

justments to it. The second option was Numerical Control (N/C) technology in which the tape was programmed not by repeating a machinist's movements but by using scientific engineering methods. This in turn resulted in the assignment of machine programming responsibilities to staff engineers and technicians.

At a fundamental level, what did each technological approach represent? By removing the critical programming function from the shopfloor, N/C extended managerial control over production start-up, pace, and maintenance. In contrast, the R/P approach would be a continuation of the current sharing of production control with the skilled workers on the shopfloor. The overwhelming choice of industrial management was to pursue the N/C technological approach. The primary motive for this managerial decision was that it enabled management to regain control over production.

This impetus for the assertion of managerial control was only reinforced by the growing unionization of the American blue-collar workforce during the 1950s which (when coupled with the union movement's ideological alliance with Communist ideals) served to elevate managerial perceptions of threat. Support for this observation can be found in the fate of R/P systems which were developed in a number of large firms such as General Electric and the Ford Motor Company. Despite positive preliminary test results (based on production efficiency and cost criteria) corporate management consistently cancelled these experiments in favor of more complex engineer controlled N/C systems. Significantly, the decision at GE was made during a period of labor union unrest.

Managerial interests were also influenced and supported by the actions of other societal interest groups which preferred the N/C technology. The power of the scientific and military communities in channeling the course of machine tool automation should not be underestimated. The military underwrote much of the research and development costs of N/C projects in the university labs. MIT, at the forefront of computer microelectronic research, was an early advocate of N/C technology. Not only did

N/C research provide MIT with a promising venue for applications of their new-found computer technology, but it also was consistent with an ideological bias for the superiority of formal educational expertise (needed to program N/C tapes) over layman experience (the basis of R/P technology).

SOME LESSONS FROM THE TRENCHES

Very briefly, we can draw some inferences from the experiences of innovators in these organizations. These propositions need to be tested in other settings and under conditions in which their effects can be carefully identified and analyzed. For the time being, we think it is useful for managers and others to consider the following lessons.

Lesson 1: Product innovation success within organizational settings requires a combination of both product *and* administrative innovation.

A good idea or product is simply not enough to guarantee successful implementation and diffusion within and outside an organization. For example, Hewlett-Packard's NASA Moonlander Monitor was a technological innovation which was almost terminated by a lack of administrative innovation. The information House gained from hands-on development with customers enabled him to modify the monitor to meet their needs while generating demand for the end-product. In this case and others, reliance on standard operating procedures are often insufficient to meet the unique requirements of new products or ideas.

Lesson 2(a): When a proposed innovation is congruent with the organizational and societal deep structure, political activity remains primarily on the surface, is benign or at a low level. Consequently, the probability of the acceptance and diffusion of such an innovation is enhanced with the support of the deep structure.

Lesson 2(b): A proposed innovation which threatens power relationships at the deep structure level evokes the full breadth and depth of opposing political forces, strategies and tactics.

Consequently, the probability of acceptance and diffusion of such an innovation is significantly reduced.

These propositions focus on the type and range of political tactics which emerge or are elicited when a proposed innovation either confirms or threatens existing power relationships. As evidenced in the cases of the Dvorak Simplified Keyboard, the mental health innovation and those areas of ICI which resisted OD initiatives, when those interests which benefit from maintaining the status quo perceive an innovation to be a threat, the politics of change are both numerous and powerful. What results is a mismatched contest where the deep structure frames the rules of the game and to a large extent preordains the outcome. The metaphor of a "corporate immune system" is a useful one in understanding the dynamics of this response. As Pinchot (1985, p. 189) relates:

When you start something new, the system naturally resists it. It is almost as if the corporation had an immune system which detects anything that is not part of the status quo and surrounds it. If you are to survive, you will have to lull this immune system into ignoring you. You will have to appear to be part of the corporate self, rather than identified as a foreign body.

Although Pinchot focuses on the intraorganizational arena, we believe that the same "immune system" can be activated in the interorganizational and societal realms. As outsiders or newcomers to the arenas in which they were trying to introduce their changes, Dvorak and the ASMIC were easily allocated the role of unwanted invaders by a system which perceived few, if any, benefits to influential system members through effecting a change to the status quo.

At ICI, the OD change agents were also perceived to be outsiders to the production process. However the success of Ripley and Bridge's program in the Agricultural Division could be traced to their strategy of first developing a strong, coherent program for change independent of the corporate system before attempting to enter it and then, to work within the system in a nonthreatening manner. They started low in the organizational structure and built support in an incremental way. In contrast, the OD programs in the other areas were more visible and did not have the strength of unity in either philosophy or personnel to withstand the opposition.

When the proposed innovation or change is consistent and/or supports existing power relationships, the politics remain at the more manageable surface level. The contests at Hewlett-Packard and at Data General were against a backdrop of a unity of interests between innovators and the corporate ethic. These innovators were secure in the knowledge that the organizational mission was to be at the forefront of their technology—a deep structure which desired technological change for competitive purposes. They also benefitted from cultures with a deep structure mythology of hero-founders who were mavericks in their own right. By acting as mavericks themselves, they were only continuing the organizational tradition and could count on a degree of understanding of their actions at the highest corporate levels. Opposition to these product innovations were of a more traditional and restricted nature in terms of internal power plays, managing line vs. staff territories and gaining the necessary resources for development. As corporate insiders, these innovators could draw on their past experience and that of others in the organization to gauge how best to proceed—which political tactics had succeeded in the past, which had failed, the relative risks involved, who were the power players and who were not.

For administrative innovations, political gamesmanship played a major role in the eventual success or failure of the proposed change. Success often hinged on the innovator's ability to marshall a wide range of supportive political tactics at both the surface and deep structure levels. Ripley and Bridge at ICI's Agricultural Division proved to be politically adept at numerous influence tactics. Review of these successful administrative innovations reveals that there was a minimal number of opposing political games, either at the surface or deep structure levels.

Administrative failures at ICI present a contrasting picture. The tactics of appealing to higher authority and appealing to reason proved to be ineffective against the deep structure games of a resistant organization. These OD change agents were effectively pre-empted by divisional managements which denied that any change to the status quo was needed and rejected the claim that these staff persons had a right to be involved in any change process.

Lesson 3: Within organizations, the political strategy of "asking for forgiveness" is limited to only the initial phases of the conception and development of a product innovation. For the adoption and diffusion of a new product, the innovator must "seek and secure permission" of the organization.

We note in these case studies of innovation there are two distinct types of political strategies—that of "asking for forgiveness" and that of "seeking and securing permission." "Asking for forgiveness" occurs when an innovator proceeds to the point of adoption without official organizational knowledge and/or sanction. It is an independent course of action often marked by secrecy and the furtive seconding or transfer of corporate resources. Alternatively, the strategy of "seeking and securing permission" usually encompasses the political strategies of developing champions and sponsors and of building networks and coalitions. Neglecting to do so may threaten the long term viability of an innovation.

In our view, asking for forgiveness is a viable strategy when pursuing product innovation. Seeking and securing permission is a more viable strategy when pursuing administrative innovations. It is possible to hide a product innovation from potential naysayers in the important fragile early phases of that innovation. Social and administrative innovations, on the other hand, depend more immediately on corporate interdependencies for their successful implementation. Thus it becomes important for the innovator to both seek *and* secure permission from organizational actors in a variety of positions and levels to ensure success. In the long run, product innovations move from the laboratory to implementation and thus to integration with other organizational routines and procedures. This entails a shift to a greater emphasis on the permission rather than the forgiveness strategy.

These accounts of innovation demonstrate the integral role political strategy plays in both promoting and suppressing innovation. If the proposed change threatens the self-interests of a powerful dominant coalition (as in the mental health innovation, the Dvorak keyboard, and machine tool automation), we find that the emergence of a technological innovation is a tenuous one. In these cases, the full breadth of deep structure and surface politics is elicited to preserve prevailing power relationships. Apparently, rationality is subsumed in these high stakes interorganizational and societal level battles for survival of the fittest. On the other hand, if there is no perceived fundamental threat, the political activity remains on the surface and can be more readily managed by prospective innovators.

REFERENCES

Dvorak, A.; Merrick, N. L.; Dealey, W. L.; and Ford, G. C. (1936). *Typewriting Behavior: Psychology Applied to Teaching and Learning Typewriting*. New York: American Book Company.

Graziano, A. M. (1969). "Clinical Innovation and the Mental Health Power Structure: A Social Case History," *American Psychologist 24*(1), 10–18.

Kidder, T. (1981). *The Soul of a New Machine*. New York: Avon Books.

Noble, D. F. (1984). *Forces of Production*. New York: Knopf.

Parkinson, R. (1972). "The Dvorak Simplified Keyboard: Forty Years of Frustration," *Computers and Automation 21*(11), 18–25.

Pinchot, J. III (1985). *Intrapreneuring*. New York: Harper and Row.

36. MANAGING INNOVATION: CONTROLLED CHAOS

James Brian Quinn

Management observers frequently claim that small organizations are more innovative than large ones. But is this commonplace necessarily true? Some large enterprises are highly innovative. How do they do it? Can lessons from these companies and their smaller counterparts help other companies become more innovative?

This article proposes some answers to these questions based on the initial results of an ongoing 2½ year worldwide study. The research sample includes both well-documented small ventures and large U.S., Japanese, and European companies and programs selected for their innovation records. More striking than the cultural differences among these companies are the similarities between innovative small and large organizations and among innovative organizations in different countries. Effective management of innovation seems much the same, regardless of national boundaries or scale of operations.

There are, of course, many reasons why small companies appear to produce a disproportionate number of innovations. First, innovation occurs in a probabilistic setting. A company never knows whether a particular technical result can be achieved and whether it will succeed in the marketplace. For every new solution that succeeds, tens to hundreds fail. The sheer number of attempts—most by small-scale entrepreneurs—means that some ventures will survive. The 90% to 99% that fail are distributed widely throughout society and receive little notice.

On the other hand, a big company that wishes to move a concept from invention to the marketplace must absorb all potential failure costs itself. This risk may be socially or managerially intolerable, jeopardizing the many other products, projects, jobs, and communities the company supports. Even if its innovation is successful, a big company may face costs that newcomers do not bear, like converting existing operations and customer bases to the new solution.

By contrast, a new enterprise does not risk losing an existing investment base or cannibalizing customer franchises built at great expense. It does not have to change an internal culture that has successfully supported doing things another way or that has developed intellectual depth and belief in the technologies that led to past successes. Organized groups like labor unions, consumer advocates, and government bureaucracies rarely monitor and resist a small company's moves as they might a big company's. Finally, new companies do not face the psychological pain and the economic costs of laying off employees, shutting down plants and even communities, and displacing supplier relationships built with years of mutual commitment and effort. Such barriers to change in large organizations are real, important, and legitimate.

The complex products and systems that society expects large companies to undertake further compound the risks. Only big companies can develop new ships or locomotives; telecommunication networks; or systems for space, defense, air traffic control, hospital care, mass foods delivery, or nationwide computer interactions. These large-scale projects always carry more risk than single-product introductions. A billion-dollar development air-craft, for example, can fail if one inexpensive part in its 100,000 components fails.

Clearly, a single enterprise cannot by itself develop or produce all the parts needed by such large new systems. And communications among the various groups making design and production decisions on components are always incomplete. The probability of error increases exponentially with complexity, while the system innovator's control over decisions decreases significantly—further escalating potential error costs and risks. Such forces inhibit innovation in large organizations. But proper management can lessen these effects.

OF INVENTORS & ENTREPRENEURS

A close look at innovative small enterprises reveals much about the successful management of innovation. Of course, not all innovations follow a single pattern. But my research—and other studies in combination—suggest that the following factors are crucial to the success of innovative small companies:

Need Orientation. Inventor-entrepreneurs tend to be "need or achievement oriented."[1] They believe that if they "do the job better," rewards will follow. They may at first focus on their own view of market needs. But lacking resources, successful small entrepreneurs soon find that it pays to approach potential customers early, test their solutions in users' hands, learn from these interactions, and adapt designs rapidly. Many studies suggest that effective technological innovation develops hand-in-hand with customer demand.[2]

Experts and Fanatics. Company founders tend to be pioneers in their technologies and fanatics when it comes to solving problems. They are often described as "possessed" or "obsessed," working toward their objectives to the exclusion even of family or personal relationships. As both experts and fanatics, they perceive probabilities of success as higher than others do. And their commitment allows them to persevere despite the frustrations, am-

biguities, and setbacks that always accompany major innovations.

Long Time Horizons. Their fanaticism may cause inventor-entrepreneurs to underestimate the obstacles and length of time to success. Time horizons for radical innovations make them essentially "irrational" from a present value viewpoint. In my sample, delays between invention and commercial production ranged from 3 to 25 years.[3] In the late 1930s, for example, industrial chemist Russell Marker was working on steroids called sapogenins when he discovered a technique that would degrade one of these, diosgenin, into the female sex hormone progesterone. By processing some ten tons of Mexican yams in rented and borrowed lab space, Marker finally extracted about four pounds of diosgenin and started a tiny business to produce steroids for the laboratory market. But it was not until 1962, over 23 years later, that Syntex, the company Marker founded, obtained FDA approval for its oral contraceptive.

For both psychological and practical reasons, inventor-entrepreneurs generally avoid early formal plans, proceed step-by-step, and sustain themselves by other income and the momentum of the small advances they achieve as they go along.

Low Early Costs. Innovators tend to work in homes, basements, warehouses, or low-rent facilities whenever possible. They incur few overhead costs; their limited resources go directly into their projects. They pour nights, weekends, and "sweat capital" into their endeavors. They borrow whatever they can. They invent cheap equipment and prototype processes, often improving on what is available in the marketplace. If one approach fails, few people know; little time or money is lost. All this decreases the costs and risks facing a small operation and improves the present value of its potential success.

Multiple Approaches. Technology tends to advance through a series of random—often highly intuitive—insights frequently triggered by gratuitous interactions between the discoverer and the outside world. Only highly committed entrepreneurs can tolerate (and even enjoy) this chaos. They adopt solutions wherever they can be found, unencumbered by formal plans or PERT charts that would limit the range of their imaginations. When the odds of success are low, the participation and interaction of many motivated players increase the chance that one will succeed.

A recent study of initial public offerings made in 1962 shows that only 2% survived and still looked like worthwhile investments 20 years later.[4] Small-scale entrepreneurship looks efficient in part because history only records the survivors.

Flexibility and Quickness. Undeterred by committees, board approvals, and other bureaucratic delays, the inventor-entrepreneur can experiment, test, recycle, and try again with little time lost. Because technological progress depends largely on the number of successful experiments accomplished per unit of time, fast-moving small entrepreneurs can gain both timing and performance advantages over clumsier competitors. This responsiveness is often crucial in finding early markets for radical innovations where neither innovators, market researchers, nor users can quite visualize a product's real potential. For example, Edison's lights first appeared on ships and in baseball parks; Astroturf was intended to convert the flat roofs and asphalt playgrounds of city schools into more humane environments; and graphite and boron composites designed for aerospace unexpectedly found their largest markets in sporting goods. Entrepreneurs quickly adjusted their entry strategies to market feedback.

Incentives. Inventor-entrepreneurs can foresee tangible personal rewards if they are successful. Individuals often want to achieve a technical contribution, recognition, power, or sheer independence, as much as money. For the original, driven personalities who create significant innovations, few other paths offer such clear opportunities to fulfill all their economic, psychological, and career-goals at once. Consequently, they do not panic or quit when others with solely monetary goals might.

Availability of Capital. One of America's great competitive advantages is its rich variety of sources to finance small, low-probability ventures. If entrepreneurs are turned down by one source, other sources can be sought in myriads of creative combinations.

Professionals involved in such financings have developed a characteristic approach to deal with the chaos and uncertainty of innovation. First, they evaluate a proposal's conceptual validity: If the technical problems can be solved, is there a real business there for someone and does it have a large upside potential? Next, they concentrate on people: Is the team thoroughly committed and expert? Is it the best available? Only then do these financiers analyze specific financial estimates in depth. Even then, they recognize that actual outcomes generally depend on subjective factors, not numbers.[5]

Timeliness, aggressiveness, commitment, quality of people, and the flexibility to attack opportunities not at first perceived are crucial. Downside risks are minimized, not by detailed controls, but by spreading risks among multiple projects, keeping early costs low, and gauging the tenacity, flexibility, and capability of the founders.

BUREAUCRATIC BARRIERS TO INNOVATION

Less innovative companies and, unfortunately, most large corporations operate in a very different fashion. The most notable and common constraints on innovation in larger companies include:

Top Management Isolation. Many senior executives in big companies have little contact with conditions on the factory floor or with customers who might influence their thinking about technological innovation. Since risk perception is inversely related to familiarity and experience, financially oriented top managers are likely to perceive technological innovations as more problematic than acquisitions that may be just as risky but that will appear more familiar.[6]

Intolerance of Fanatics. Big companies often view entrepreneurial fanatics as embarrassments or troublemakers. Many major cities are now ringed by companies founded by these "nonteam" players—often to the regret of their former employers.

Short Time Horizons. The perceived corporate need to report a continuous stream of quarterly profits conflicts with the long time spans that major innovations normally require. Such pressures often make publicly owned companies favor quick marketing fixes, cost cutting, and acquisition strategies over process, product, or quality innovations that would yield much more in the long run.

Accounting Practices. By assessing all its direct, indirect, overhead, overtime, and service costs against a project, large corporations have much higher development expenses compared with entrepreneurs working in garages. A project in a big company can quickly become an exposed political target, its potential net present value may sink unacceptably, and an entry into small markets may not justify its sunk costs. An otherwise viable project may soon founder and disappear.

Excessive Rationalism. Managers in big companies often seek orderly advance through early market research studies or PERT planning. Rather than managing the inevitable chaos of innovation productively, these managers soon drive out the very things that lead to innovation in order to prove their announced plans.

Excessive Bureaucracy. In the name of efficiency, bureaucratic structures require many approvals and cause delays at every turn. Experiments that a small company can perform in hours may take days or weeks in large organizations. The interactive feedback that fosters innovation is lost, important time windows can be missed, and real costs and risks rise for the corporation.

Inappropriate incentives. Reward and control systems in most big companies are designed to min-imize surprises. Yet innovation, by definition, is full of surprises. It often disrupts well-laid plans, accepted power patterns, and entrenched organizational behavior at high costs to many. Few large companies make millionaires of those who create such disruptions, however profitable the innovations may turn out to be. When control systems neither penalize opportunities missed nor reward risks taken, the results are predictable.

THE STUDY

(A questionnaire and poll of experts identified several outstanding innovative large companies in Europe, the United States, and Japan for study. These companies had more than $1 billion in sales and programs with at least tens of millions of dollars in initial investment and hundreds of millions of dollars in ultimate annual economic impact. Interviews and secondary sources were used and cross-checked to establish management patterns. Wherever possible, cases on these companies and ventures were written and will be released for public use. Case studies of Sony Corporation, Intel Corporation, Pilkington Brothers, Ltd., and Honda Corporation are already available from the author.)

HOW LARGE INNOVATIVE COMPANIES DO IT

Yet some big companies are continuously innovative. Although each such enterprise is distinctive, the successful big innovators I studied have developed techniques that emulate or improve on their smaller counterparts' practices. What are the most important patterns?

Atmosphere and Vision. Continuous innovation occurs largely because top executives appreciate innovation and manage their company's value system and atmosphere to support it. For example, Sony's founder, Masaru Ibuka, stated in the company's "Purposes of Incorporation" the goal of a "free, dynamic, and pleasant factory. . . where sincerely motivated personnel can exercise their technological skills to the highest level." Ibuka and Sony's chairman, Akio Morita, inculcated the "Sony spirit" through a series of unusual policies: hiring brilliant people with nontraditional skills (like an opera singer) for high management positions, promoting young people over their elders, designing a new type of living accommodation for workers, and providing visible awards for outstanding technical achievements.

Because familiarity can foster understanding and psychological comfort, engineering and scientific leaders are often those who create atmospheres supportive of innovation, especially in a company's early life. Executive vision is more important than a particular management background—as IBM, Genentech, AT&T, Merck, Elf Aquitaine, Pilkington, and others in my sample illustrate. CEOs of these companies value technology and include technical experts in their highest decision circles.

Innovative managements—whether technical or not—project clear long-term visions for their organizations that go beyond simple economic measures. As Intel's chairman, Gordon Moore, says: "We intend to be the outstandingly successful innovative company in this industry. We intend to continue to be a leader in this revolutionary [semiconductor] technology that is changing the way this world is run." Genentech's original plan expresses a similar vision: "We expect to be the first company to commercialize the [rDNA] technology, and we plan to build a major profitable corporation by manufacturing and marketing needed products that benefit mankind. The future uses of genetic engineering are far reaching and many. Any product produced by a living organism is eventually within the company's reach."

Such visions, vigorously supported, are not "management fluff," but have many practical implications. They attract quality people to the company and give focus to their creative and entrepreneurial drives. When combined with sound internal operations, they help channel growth by concentrating attention on the actions that lead to profitability, rather than on profitability itself. Finally, these visions recognize a realistic time frame for innovation and attract the kind of investors who will support it.

Orientation to the Market. Innovative companies tie their visions to the practical realities of the marketplace. Although each company uses techniques adapted to its own style and strategy, two elements are always present: a strong market orientation at the very top of the company and mechanisms to ensure interactions between technical and marketing people at lower levels. At Sony, for example, soon after technical people are hired, the company runs them through weeks of retail selling. Sony engineers become sensitive to the ways retail sales practices, product displays, and nonquantifiable customer preferences affect success. Similarly, before AT&T's recent divestiture, Bell Laboratories had an Operating Company Assignment Program to rotate its researchers through AT&T and Western Electric development and production facilities. And it had a rigorous Engineering Complaint System that collected technical problems from operating companies and required Bell Labs to specify within a few weeks how it would resolve or attack each problem.

From top to bench levels in my sample's most innovative companies, managers focus primarily on seeking to anticipate and solve customers' emerging problems.

Small, Flat Organizations. The most innovative large companies in my sample try to keep the total organization flat and project teams small. Development teams normally include only six or seven key people. This number seems to constitute a critical mass of skills while fostering maximum communication and commitment among members. According to research done by my colleague, Victor McGee, the number of channels of communication increases as $n[2^{(n-1)} - 1]$. Therefore:

For team size	=	1	2	3	4	5	6	7	8	9	10	11
Channels	=	1	2	9	28	75	186	441	1016	2295	5110	11253

Innovative companies also try to keep their operating divisions and total technical units small—below 400 people. Up to this number, only two layers of management are required to maintain a span of control over 7 people. In units much larger than 400, people quickly lose touch with the concept of their product or process, staffs and bureaucracies tend to grow, and projects may go through too many formal screens to survive. Since it takes a chain of yeses and only one no to kill a project, jeopardy multiplies as management layers increase.

Multiple Approaches. At first one cannot be sure which of several technical approaches will dominate a field. The history of technology is replete with accidents, mishaps, and chance meetings that allowed one approach or group to emerge rapidly over others. Leo Baekelund was looking for a synthetic shellac when he found Bakelite and started the modern plastics industry. At Syntex, researchers were not looking for an oral contraceptive when they created 19-nor-progesterone, the precursor to the active ingredient in half of all contraceptive pills. And the microcomputer was born because Intel's Ted Hoff "happened" to work on a complex calculator just when Digital Equipment Corporation's PDP8 architecture was fresh in his mind.

Such "accidents" are involved in almost all major technological advances. When theory can predict everything, a company has moved to a new stage, from development to production. Murphy's law works because engineers design for what they can foresee; hence what fails is what theory could not predict. And it is rare that the interactions of components and subsystems can be predicted over the lifetime of operations. For example, despite careful theoretical design work, the first high performance jet engine literally tore itself to pieces on its test stand, while others failed in unanticipated operating conditions (like an Iranian sandstorm).

Recognizing the inadequacies of theory, innovative enterprises seem to move faster from paper studies to physical testing than do noninnovative enterprises. When possible, they encourage several prototype programs to proceed in parallel. Sony pursued 10 major options in developing its videotape recorder technology. Each option had two to three subsystem alternatives. Such redundancy helps the company cope with uncertainties in development, motivates people through competition, and improves the amount and quality of information available for making final choices on scale-ups or introductions.

Developmental Shoot-Outs. Many companies structure shoot-outs among competing approaches only after they reach the prototype stages. They find this practice provides more objective information for making decisions, decreases risk by making choices that best reflect marketplace needs, and helps ensure that the winning option will move ahead with a committed team behind it. Although many managers worry that competing approaches may be inefficient, greater effectiveness in choosing the right solution easily outweighs duplication costs when the market rewards higher performance or when large volumes justify increased sophistication. Under these conditions, parallel development may prove less costly because it both improves the probability of success and reduces development time.

Perhaps the most difficult problem in managing competing projects lies in reintegrating the members of the losing team. If the company is expanding rapidly or if the successful project creates a growth opportunity, losing team members can work on another interesting program or sign on with the winning team as the project moves toward the marketplace. For the shoot-out system to work continuously, however, executives must create a climate that honors high-quality performance whether a project wins or loses, reinvolves people quickly in their technical specialties or in other projects, and accepts and expects rotation among tasks and groups.

At Sony, according to its top R&D manager, the research climate does not penalize the losing team: "We constantly have several alternative projects going. Before the competition is over, before there is a complete loss, we try to smell the potential outcome and begin to prepare for that result as early as possible. Even after we have consensus, we may wait for several months to give the others a chance. Then we begin to give important jobs [on other programs] to members of the losing groups. If your team doesn't win, you may still be evaluated as performing well. Such people have often received my 'crystal award' for outstanding work. We never talk badly about these people. Ibuka's principle is that doing something, even if it fails, is better than doing nothing. A strike-out at Sony is OK, but you must not just stand there. You must swing at the ball as best you can."

Skunkworks. Every highly innovative enterprise in my research sample emulated small company practices by using groups that functioned in a skunkworks style. Small teams of engineers, technicians, designers, and model makers were placed together with no intervening organizational or physical barriers to developing a new product from idea to commercial prototype stages. In innovative Japanese companies, top managers often worked hand-in-hand on projects with young engineers. Surprisingly, *ringi* decision making was not evident in these situations. Soichiro Honda was known for working directly on technical problems and emphasizing his technical points by shouting at his engineers or occasionally even hitting them with wrenches!

The skunkworks approach eliminates bureaucracies, allows fast, unfettered communications, permits rapid turnaround times for experiments, and instills a high level of group identity and loyalty. Interestingly, few successful groups in my research were structured in the classic "venture group" form, with a careful balancing of engineering, production, and marketing talents. Instead they acted on an old truism: introducing a new product or process to the world is like raising a healthy child—it needs a mother (champion) who loves it, a father (authority figure with resources) to support it, and pediatricians (specialists) to get it through difficult times. It may survive solely in the hands of specialists, but its chances of success are remote.

Interactive Learning. Skunkworks are as close as most big companies can come to emulating the highly interactive and motivating learning environment that characterizes successful small ventures. But the best big innovators have gone even farther. Recognizing that the random, chaotic nature of technological change cuts across organizational and even institutional lines, these companies tap into multiple outside sources of technology as well as their customers' capabilities. Enormous external leverages are possible. No company can spend more than a small share of the world's $200 billion devoted to R&D. But like small entrepreneurs, big companies can have much of that total effort cheaply if they try.

In industries such as electronics, customers provide much of the innovation on new products. In other industries, such as textiles, materials or equipment suppliers provide the innovation. In still others, such as biotechnology, universities are dominant, while foreign sources strongly supplement industries such as controlled fusion. Many R&D units have strategies to develop information for trading with outside groups and have teams to cultivate these sources.[7] Large Japanese companies have been notably effective at this. So have U.S. companies as diverse as Du Pont, AT&T, Apple Computer, and Genentech.

An increasing variety of creative relationships exist in which big companies participate—as joint venturers, consortium members, limited partners, guarantors of first markets, major academic funding sources, venture capitalists, spin-off equity holders, and so on. These rival the variety of inventive financing and networking structures that individual entrepreneurs have created.

Indeed, the innovative practices of small and large companies look ever more alike. This resemblance is especially striking in the interactions between companies and customers during development. Many experienced big companies are relying less on early market research and more on interactive development with lead customers. Hewlett-Packard, 3M, Sony, and Raychem frequently introduce radically new products through small teams that work closely with lead customers. These teams learn from their customers' needs and innovations, and rapidly modify designs and entry strategies based on this information.

Formal market analyses continue to be useful for extending product lines, but they are often misleading when applied to radical innovations. Market studies predicted that Haloid would never sell more than 5,000 xerographic machines, that Intel's microprocessor would never sell more than 10% as many units as there were minicomputers, and that Sony's transistor radios and miniature television sets would fail in the marketplace. At the same time, many eventual failures such as Ford's Edsel, IBM's FS system, and the supersonic transport were studied and planned exhaustively on paper, but lost contact with customers' real needs.

A STRATEGY FOR INNOVATION

The flexible management practices needed for major innovations often pose problems for established cultures in big companies. Yet there are reasonable steps managers in these companies can take. Innovation can be bred in a surprising variety of organizations, as many examples show. What are its key elements?

An Opportunity Orientation. In the 1981–1983 recession, many large companies cut back or closed plants as their "only available solution." Yet I repeatedly found that top managers in these companies took these actions without determining firsthand why their customers were buying from competitors, discerning what niches in their markets were growing, or tapping the innovations their own people had to solve problems. These managers foreclosed innumerable options by defining the issue as cost cutting rather than opportunity seeking. As one frustrated division manager in a manufacturing conglomerate put it: "If management doesn't actively seek or welcome technical opportunities, it sure won't hear about them."

By contrast, Intel met the challenge of the last recession with its "20% solution." The professional staff

agreed to work one extra day a week to bring innovations to the marketplace earlier than planned. Despite the difficult times, Intel came out of the recession with several important new products ready to go—and it avoided layoffs.

Entrepreneurial companies recognize that they have almost unlimited access to capital and they structure their practices accordingly. They let it be known that if their people come up with good ideas, they can find the necessary capital—just as private venture capitalists or investment bankers find resources for small entrepreneurs.

Structuring for Innovation. Managers need to think carefully about how innovation fits into their strategy and structure their technology, skills, resources, and organizational commitments accordingly. A few examples suggest the variety of strategies and alignments possible:

- Hewlett-Packard and 3M develop product lines around a series of small, discrete, freestanding products. These companies form units that look like entrepreneurial start-ups. Each has a small team, led by a champion, in low-cost facilities. These companies allow many different proposals to come forward and test them as early as possible in the marketplace. They design control systems to spot significant losses on any single entry quickly. They look for high gains on a few winners and blend less successful, smaller entries into prosperous product lines.

- Other companies (like AT&T or the oil majors) have had to make large system investments to last for decades. These companies tend to make long-term needs forecasts. They often start several programs in parallel to be sure of selecting the right technologies. They then extensively test new technologies in use before making systemwide commitments. Often they sacrifice speed of entry for long-term low cost and reliability.

- Intel and Dewey & Almy, suppliers of highly technical specialties to OEMs, develop strong technical sales networks to discover and understand customer needs in depth. These companies try to have technical solutions designed into customers' products. Such companies have flexible applied technology groups working close to the marketplace. They also have quickly expandable plant facilities and a cutting-edge technology (not necessarily basic research) group that allows rapid selection of currently available technologies.

- Dominant producers like IBM or Matsushita are often not the first to introduce new technologies. They do not want to disturb their successful product lines any sooner than necessary. As market demands become clear, these companies establish precise price-performance windows and form overlapping project teams to come up with the best answer for the marketplace. To decrease market risks, they use product shoot-outs as close to the market as possible. They develop extreme depth in production technologies to keep unit costs low from the outset. Finally, depending on the scale of the market entry, they have project teams report as close to the top as necessary to secure needed management attention and resources.

- Merck and Hoffman-LaRoche, basic research companies, maintain laboratories with better facilities, higher pay, and more freedom than most universities can afford. These companies leverage their internal spending through research grants, clinical grants, and research relationships with universities throughout the world. Before they invest $20 million to $50 million to clear a new drug, they must have reasonable assurance that they will be first in the marketplace. They take elaborate precautions to ensure that the new entry is safe and effective, and that it cannot be easily duplicated by others. Their structures are designed to be on the cutting edge of science, but conservative in animal testing, clinical evaluation, and production control.

These examples suggest some ways of linking innovation to strategy. Many other examples, of course, exist. Within a single company, individual divisions may have different strategic needs and hence different structures and practices. No single approach works well for all situations.

Complex Portfolio Planning. Perhaps the most difficult task for top managers is to balance the needs of existing lines against the needs of potential lines. This problem requires a portfolio strategy much more complex than the popular four-box Boston Consulting Group matrix found in most strategy texts. To allocate resources for innovation strategically, managers need to define the broad, long-term actions within and across divisions necessary to achieve their visions. They should determine which positions to hold at all costs, where to fall back, and where to expand initially and in the more distant future.

A company's strategy may often require investing most resources in current lines. But sufficient resources should also be invested in patterns that ensure intermediate and long-term growth; provide defenses against possible government, labor, competitive, or activist challenges; and generate needed organizational, technical, and external relations flexibilities to handle unforeseen opportunities or threats. Sophisticated portfolio planning within and among divisions can protect both current returns and future prospects—the two critical bases for that most cherished goal, high price-earnings ratios.

AN INCREMENTALIST APPROACH

Such managerial techniques can provide a strategic focus for innovation and help solve many of the timing, coordination, and motivation problems that plague large, bureaucratic organizations. Even more detailed planning techniques may help in guiding the development of the many small innovations that characterize any successful business. My research reveals, however, that few, if any, major innovations result from highly structured planning systems. Within the broad framework I have described, major innovations are best managed as incremental, goal-oriented, interactive learning processes.[8]

Several sophisticated companies have labeled this approach "phased program planning." When they see an important opportunity in the marketplace (or when a laboratory champion presses them), top managers outline some broad, challenging goals for the new programs: "to be the first to prove whether rDNA is commercially feasible for this process," or "to create an economical digital switching system for small country telephone systems." These goals have few key timing, cost, or performance numbers attached. As scientists and engineers (usually from different areas) begin to define technical options, the programs' goals become more specific—though managers still allow much latitude in technical approaches.

As options crystallize, managers try to define the most important technical sequences and critical decision points. They may develop "go, no go" performance criteria for major program phases and communicate these as targets for project teams. In systems innovations, for example, performance specifications must be set to coordinate the interactions of subsystems. Successful companies leave open for as long as possible exactly how these targets can be achieved.

While feeding resources to the most promising options, managers frequently keep other paths open. Many of the best concepts and solutions come from projects partly hidden or "bootlegged" by the organization. Most successful managers try to build some slacks or buffers into their plans to hedge their bets, although they hesitate to announce these actions widely. They permit chaos and replication in early investigations, but insist on much more formal planning and controls as expensive development and scale-up proceed. But even at these later stages, these managers have learned to maintain flexibility and to avoid the tyranny of paper plans. They seek inputs from manufacturing, marketing, and customer groups early. Armed with this information, they are prepared to modify their plans even as they enter the marketplace. A European executive describes this process of directing innovation as "a somewhat orderly tumult that can be managed only in an incremental fashion."

Why Incrementalism?

The innovative process is inherently incremental. As Thomas Hughes says, "Technological systems evolve through relatively small steps marked by an occasional stubborn obstacle and by constant random breakthroughs interacting across laboratories and borders."[9] A forgotten hypothesis of Einstein's became the laser in Charles Townes's mind as he contemplated azaleas in Franklin Square. The structure of DNA followed a circuitous route through research in biology, organic chemistry, X-ray crystallography, and mathematics toward its Nobel Prize-winning conception as a spiral staircase of matched base pairs. Such rambling trails are characteristic of virtually all major technological advances.

At the outset of the attack on a technical problem, an innovator often does not know whether his problem is tractable, what approach will prove best, and what concrete characteristics the solution will have if achieved. The logical route, therefore, is to follow several paths—though perhaps with varying degrees of intensity—until more information becomes available. Not knowing precisely where the solution will occur, wise managers establish the widest feasible network for finding and assessing alternative solutions. They keep many options open until one of them seems sure to win. Then they back it heavily.

Managing innovation is like a stud poker game, where one can play several hands. A player has some idea of the likely size of the pot at the beginning, knows the general but not the sure route to winning, buys one card (a project) at a time to gain information about probabilities and the size of the pot, closes hands as they become discouraging, and risks more only late in the hand as knowledge increases.

Political and Psychological Support

Incrementalism helps deal with the psychological, political, and motivational factors that are crucial to project success. By keeping goals broad at first, a manager avoids creating undue opposition to a new idea. A few concrete goals may be projected as a challenge. To maintain flexibility, intermediate steps are not developed in detail. Alternate routes can be tried and failures hidden. As early problems are solved, momentum, confidence, and identity build around the new approach. Soon a project develops enough adherents and objective data to withstand its critics' opposition.

As it comes more clearly into competition for resources, its advocates strive to solve problems and maintain its viability. Finally, enough concrete information exists for nontechnical managers to compare the programs fairly with more familiar options. The project now has the legitimacy and political clout to survive—which might never have happened if its totality has been disclosed or planned in detail at the beginning. Many sound technical projects have died because their managers did not deal with the politics of survival.

Chaos Within Guidelines

Effective managers of innovation channel and control its main directions. Like venture capitalists, they administer primarily by setting goals, selecting key people, and establishing a few critical limits and decision points for intervention rather than by implementing elaborate planning or control systems. As technology leads or market needs emerge, these managers set a few—most crucial—performance targets and limits. They allow their technical units to decide how to achieve these, subject to defined constraints and reviews at critical junctures.

Early bench-scale project managers may pursue various options, making little attempt at first to integrate each into a total program. Only after key variables are understood—and perhaps measured and demonstrated in lab models—can more precise planning be meaningful. Even then, many factors may remain unknown; chaos and competition can continue to thrive in the pursuit of the solution. At defined review points, however, only those options that can clear performance milestones may continue.

Choosing which projects to kill is perhaps the hardest decision in the management of innovation. In the end, the decision is often intuitive, resting primarily on a manager's technical knowledge and familiarity with innovation processes. Repeatedly, successful managers told me, "Anyone who thinks he

can quantify this decision is either a liar or a fool. . . . There are too many unknowables, variables. . . . Ultimately, one must use intuition, a complex feeling, calibrated by experience. . . .We'd be foolish not to check everything, touch all the bases. That's what the models are for. But ultimately it's a judgment about people, commitment, and probabilities. . . . You don't dare use milestones too rigidly."

Even after selecting the approaches to emphasize, innovative managers tend to continue a few others as smaller scale "side bets" or options. In a surprising number of cases, these alternatives prove winners when the planned option fails.

Recognizing the many demands entailed by successful programs, innovative companies find special ways to reward innovators. Sony gives "a small but significant" percentage of a new product's sales to its innovating teams. Pilkington, IBM, and 3M's top executives are often chosen from those who have headed successful new product entries. Intel lets its Magnetic Memory Group operate like a small company, with special performance rewards and simulated stock options. GE, Syntex, and United Technologies help internal innovators establish new companies and take equity positions in "nonrelated" product innovations.

Large companies do not have to make their innovators millionaires, but rewards should be visible and significant. Fortunately, most engineers are happy with the incentives that Tracy Kidder calls "playing pinball"—giving widespread recognition to a job well done and the right to play in the next exciting game.[10] Most innovative companies provide both, but increasingly they are supplementing these with financial rewards to keep their most productive innovators from jumping outside.

MATCH MANAGEMENT TO THE PROCESS

Management practices in innovative companies reflect the realities of the innovation·process itself. Innovation tends to be individually motivated, opportunistic, customer responsive, tumultuous, nonlinear, and interactive in its development. Managers can plan overall directions and goals, but surprises are likely to abound. Consequently, innovative companies keep their programs flexible for as long as possible and freeze plans only when necessary for strategic purposes such as timing. Even then they keep options open by specifying broad performance goals and allowing different technical approaches to compete for as long as possible.

Executives need to understand and accept the tumultuous realities of innovation, learn from the experiences of other companies, and adapt the most relevant features of these others to their own management practices and cultures. Many features of small company innovators are also applicable in big companies. With top-level understanding, vision, a commitment to customers and solutions, a genuine portfolio strategy, a flexible entrepreneurial atmosphere, and proper incentives for innovative champions, many more large companies can innovate to meet the severe demands of global competition.

NOTES

1. David McClelland, *The Achieving Society* (New York: Halsted Press, 1976); Gene Bylinsky, *The Innovation Millionaires* (New York: Scribner's, 1976).

2. Eric von Hippel, "Get New Products From Customers," HBR March–April 1982, p. 117.

3. A study at Battelle found an average of 19.2 years between invention and commercial production. Battelle Memorial Laboratories, "Science, Technology, and Innovation," Report to the National Science Foundation, 1973; R.C. Dean, "The Temporal Mismatch: Innovation's Pace vs. Management's Time Horizon," *Research Management*, May 1974, p. 13.

4. Business Economics Group, W.R. Grace & Co., 1983.

5. Christina C. Pence, *How Venture Capitalists Make Venture Decisions* (Ann Arbor, Mich.: UMI Research Press, 1982).

6. Robert H. Hayes and David A. Garvin, "Managing as if Tomorrow Mattered," HBR May–June 1982, p. 70; Robert H. Hayes and William J. Abernathy, "Managing Our Way to Economic Decline," HBR July–August 1980, p. 67.

7. In *Managing the Flow of Technology* (Cambridge: MIT Press, 1977), Thomas J. Allen illustrates the enormous leverage provided such technology accessors (called "gatekeepers") in R&D organizations.

8. For a further discussion of incrementalism, see James Brian Quinn, "Managing Strategies Incrementally," *Omega* 10, no. 6 (1982), p. 613; and *Strategies for Change: Logical Incrementalism* (Homewood, Ill.: Dow Jones-Irwin, 1980).

9. Thomas Hughes, "The Inventive Continuum," *Science 84*, November 1984, p. 83.

10. Tracy Kidder, *The Soul of a New Machine* (Boston: Little, Brown, 1981).

37. UNLEARNING THE ORGANIZATION

Michael E. McGill and John W. Slocum, Jr.

The first step to learning is to challenge those ways of thinking that worked so well in the past.

For years, the morning scene at the San Diego Zoo has been the same. A convoy of buses releases streams of schoolchildren eager for a face-to-face learning encounter with a mountain gorilla, reticulated boa, or sulphur-crested cockatoo. These days, the lunch-box-toting kids are likely to be joined by briefcase-toting executives from Sony, Pacific Bell, or Northern Telecom. They have come for a face-to-face learning experience with the Tiger River or Gorilla Tropics team. The San Diego Zoo, long acclaimed for its innovative presentation of animals in their natural habitats, is now drawing attention as a prototype learning organization.

The zoo has dedicated itself to becoming not a modern-day menagerie, but an organization that educates visitors about animals and their habitats, and that propagates conservation. This learning mission has led zoo managers to design new formats, such as Tiger River and the Gorilla Tropics—total environment areas that house the most natural displays possible. It has also led the zoo to find new ways of coordinating the complex work required in these formats. To bring together a wide variety of skills and functions, the zoo makes extensive use of cross-functional teams. Managers and employees find they are more productive than ever, with teams setting their own budgets and schedules and participating in hiring processes. The goal of becoming an educational organization has also led to the development of a new approach toward visitors, who

keep coming back because they learn something new with each visit. A trip to the San Diego Zoo has also become the latest outing for managers who are serious about creating learning organizations.

Frustrated by changes upon changes that have produced little improvement, managers have been drawn to the concept of organization learning—the process by which they become aware of the qualities, patterns, and consequences of their own experiences, and develop mental models to understand these experiences. Learning organizations discover what is effective by reframing their own experiences and learning from that process. Learning organizations are self-aware, introspective organizations that constantly scan their environments. By contrast, other organizations merely adapt. They attend only to those experiences that may redirect them toward their goals, and encourage their managers to make only those changes that fit the current structure. It is increasingly evident that adapting is an inadequate response to today's turbulent competitive environment. Learning is imperative. But few organizations truly learn from experience.

In this article, we differentiate four kinds of organization learning and describe the associated policies, practices, and possibilities for action.

THE KNOWING ORGANIZATION: BY THE BOOK

The knowing organization is the oldest of organization models. Its lineage can be traced to concepts

The authors would like to thank Joan Brett, Marshall Sashkin, Randy Schuler, Chuck Snow, and Al Vicere for their constructive comments on an earlier draft of this manuscript. The Bureau of Business Research at the Cox School, Southern Methodist University, provided funding for this research project.

From *Organizational Dynamics*, Autumn, 1993, pp. 67–79.

dating from the early 20th century: England's Adam Smith and his division of labor, German sociologist Max Weber's "bureaucracy," American engineer Frederick W. Taylor and his "scientific management," General Motors executives Mooney and Riley's "principles of management," and French theorist Henri Fayol's "administrative theory." These management theorists shared the belief that whatever there was to do, there was one best way to do it—a best way to do a job, a best way to manage employees, and a best way to organize tasks. Further, they believed that the best way was either known or knowable—hence, the knowing organization.

Knowing organizations have been and continue to be among the most successful of American businesses. Walt Disney, UPS, Toys-R-Us, 4-Day Tire Stores, Blockbuster Video, Avis, U-Carco, and thousands of other companies have discovered something that works, committed it to memory, and repeated it over and over . . . and over again. At Disneyland in Anaheim, DisneyWorld in Orlando, Tokyo Disneyland in Japan, and EuroDisney in Paris, the spiel on the Jungle Boat River Cruise is exactly the same—ad libs included—albeit in different languages. UPS drivers are given detailed route instructions—order of stops, length of red lights, even recommended length of stride! Blockbuster Video pioneered the display of tapes "live" on the shelf, three-day rentals, and bar coding to track inventory and speed checkout. It parlayed these formulas to become the largest and most successful video rental company in the world.

The most visible and successful of all knowing organizations is McDonald's. In any of the 13,000-plus McDonald's worldwide, consumers experience firsthand the best of what knowing organizations have to offer—efficiency, predictability, and control—in production and customer service. From his earliest days selling milkshake machines in San Bernardino, California, McDonald's founder, Ray Kroc, made a religion of (and a fortune from) discovering and duplicating the best way to manufacture and market fast food. Operations manuals spell out what every employee needs to know to perform his or her task in an efficient manner.

Employees know exactly how to draw milkshakes, grill hamburgers, and fry potatoes. The manuals specify cooking times for all products and temperature settings for all equipment, as well as standard portions on every food item, down to the quarter ounce of onions placed on each hamburger patty.

Kroc was not satisfied with seeking knowledge about "the best way" in manuals, curricula, and classroom training. Nor was he willing to rely totally on people (read teenagers) and their potential for unpredictability. McDonald's "engineered in" knowledge designing machines that make it virtually impossible to overcook the hamburgers, underserve the amount of fries, or shortchange the customer. In short, the food at McDonald's can be prepared and served only in the way that McDonald's knows is best.

The distinguishing characteristics of knowing organizations have changed little from the ideal, machine-like models of 100 years ago. The philosophy of a knowing organization is rationality; it values efficiency above all. Knowing organizations focus on standardized policies, procedures, rules, and regulations, and they do things "by the book." A manager's primary responsibility is to control employees' behavior by enforcing the rules. Customers of knowing organizations must either accept service by the rules or do business elsewhere.

Knowing organizations change in reaction to changes in their environment, making incremental improvements to existing processes, products, services, or technologies—improvements that are always within the boundaries of the company's proven track record. Inasmuch as these changes are not the product of learning, they often have little to do with the root causes of business problems.

Knowing organizations—with their high level of control, enforced conformity, routine behaviors, and risk-avoidance—are "learning disadvantaged." Their need to know gets in the way of their ability to learn from their experience. What was once "the best way" becomes simply "the company way." These organizations—often described as adaptive or single-loop—can be successful only so long as the nature of the marketplace (the technology, competition, customer demand, regulation, and other environmental forces) remains relatively mature and static. That is, knowing organizations can be successful so long as they don't *need* to learn. Real learning would require managers to give up control, predictability, and efficiency, and to open the organization up to an examination of its own experience.

THE UNDERSTANDING ORGANIZATION: VIRTUE IN VALUES

In the 1980s, many once-successful knowing organizations sensed the need to do things differently. With foreign competition eroding market share, customers demanding higher quality and more personalized service, and technology changing at an ever-increasing pace, these companies became aware that a continued focus on the one best way was not a sure way to succeed. The challenge that knowing organizations faced was twofold. On the one hand, they urgently needed to search for alternatives to established routines in order to preserve their identity; on the other, they could not allow their new responses to cast doubt upon their ability to know, or dilute their capacity for predicting and controlling others' behaviors. Many companies chose to address these challenges by pursuing only those changes compatible with the basic culture of the company, its core values and beliefs.

Bank of America is an excellent example of a company that eschewed knowing in favor of understanding. Founded by A. P. Giannini to provide banking services for the Italian immigrants of San Francisco, the bank, in its early years, pioneered many service innovations intended to make banking more "customer friendly." Advertising, branch banking, and inviting buildings attracted thousands of small, personal accounts and forced competitors to respond. At the same time, Giannini took corporate-level risks, such as backing bond and loan programs for projects as diverse as the Golden Gate Bridge and Walt Disney's movie, "Snow White and the Seven Dwarfs." The Bank of America discovered a great many things that worked over the years, and by

the late 1970s and early 1980s, it had institutionalized these discoveries, creating bureaucratic routines. Its resulting efficiency and predictability gave rise to a new set of assumptions: Don't risk failure; take a short-term view; don't be frank when evaluating products or programs; seniority is more important than performance; study a new idea to death; protect your own turf. In the 1980s, however, business reversals, a loss of market share, and a hostile takeover attempt left Bank of America in a weakened position, just when it needed to respond to increased competition in a deregulated market. What it had "known" no longer worked.

Rather than responding with new rules and regulations, Bank of America chose to reemphasize its core values and to promote change via a new, widespread comprehension of its original company culture. Its core values included putting the customer first and respecting, recognizing, and rewarding both customers and bank employees. The culture change began with the CEO. Via meetings, publications, and training programs, the company communicated the new culture throughout the organization. Coupled with a change in business strategy and an aggressive acquisition program, the new culture returned Bank of America to a position of banking preeminence.

In recent years, the same story has been repeated in hundreds of companies, from *Fortune* 500 giants to small family owned and operated firms. In the 1980s, corporate culture was to companies what the "one best way" had been for the previous 100 years. Culture offered predictability and control, not through excessive regimentation, but through a fundamental understanding of what the company valued. Strong-culture companies, like Digital Equipment, IBM, Apple, and Johnson & Johnson, were exalted, examined, and emulated. Procter & Gamble's value-based culture, in particular, was often cited as a key to that company's success. The company's founder, William Cooper Procter, set forth Procter & Gamble's most basic core value in straightforward terms: "Always try to do what is right." Other values embraced by Procter & Gamble—including "The customer is important," and "Things don't just happen, you make customer interests our own"—have served as a model for many companies.

The understanding, strong-culture organization guides strategy and action by using a set of core values, described by some as the "ruling myth." A ruling myth's function is to give meaning to experience, but it can also constrain the organization from taking action. Strong-culture organizations, such as GM, IBM, and Sears, tend to build moats around their castles to protect themselves from real learning. Sears and GM thought their economies of scale protected them from competition; IBM thought that since it had installed so much equipment, its customers would be forced to seek out IBM compatibility in their next orders. In these organizations, the culture surrounding the decision-making process was all-consuming.

For example, Sears spelled out procedures for decision making in an elaborate library of bulletins that storehoused the glory days of past years. The worshipping of retired "heroes" who were dedicated to maintaining the majesty of the culture fostered a practice of selecting internal "long-service" candidates for the CEO position. The company's strong culture hindered each successive CEO and other top managers from executing radical improvements. In the early 1970s, when its growth slipped as Kmart and Wal-Mart grew, Sears did not recognize the change going on in customer preferences, and did not develop a strategy to address it. Ignoring this change, it opened its monument to its past, the Sears Tower, in 1973.

The very nature of a strong-culture organization limits its capacity to learn from its experience. The philosophy of an understanding organization is that a clear statement of assumptions and basic beliefs is an adequate and appropriate guide to action for managers and employees. Understanding organizations maintain that their values should be comprehended by all employees and should be evident in every action taken. Management practices are intended to clarify, communicate, and reinforce the company's culture. As one Sears manager said, "God forbid there should be a problem that comes up for which there isn't a bulletin. That means the problem's new." For their part, employees are supposed to let their understanding of the company's culture guide their behaviors. Oftentimes, the culture encourages them to learn about their own jobs and divisions, but not about the relationships among other jobs and divisions. The understanding organization wants its customers to experience the company's cultural values in all interactions, which are peppered with references to the company's long history and years of commitment to core values. Customers can expect to be reminded of how much they are "valued by the company," regardless of what their immediate experience tells them.

An understanding organization can appreciate only those changes that are consistent with its core values or ruling myth. Change occurs within a circumscribed context. Companies involved in promoting their own culture are unlikely to be open to enhancing and expanding experiences, as learning requires; they cannot escape the rule of their own myths.

THE THINKING ORGANIZATION: FROM ANALYSIS TO ACTION

The banners appeared on Monday in the break areas and cafeterias of every store in the company: "T.L.C.," printed in bold red letters. Speculation was rife among employees as to what T.L.C. meant and, more specifically, what it meant for them. "Tender Loving Care" seemed too obvious and not at all corporate. Some thought the company was going the discount route with "Totally Low Cost." Most agreed it could mean "Too Little Commission" but probably didn't. Whatever it meant, T.L.C. was clearly the newest management campaign at Foley's Department Store, the Dallas-based retailer owned by Federated Department Stores. By the second week, when T.L.C. lapel pins were being passed out to all sales associates, interest had peaked. Management held meetings in every store detailing Foley's new customer service program, "T.L.C.—Think Like a Customer." In the ensuing weeks, more T.L.C. banners, along with coffee mugs, pencils, and memo pads, appeared throughout the stores.

The T.L.C. program was Foley's response to declining sales and eroding market share. Originally known as Sanger-Harris, this full-line department store had ridden the crest of the Southwest's dynamic growth, adding stores and chalking up successive years of sales growth. With the economic downturn of the Southwest, the fortunes of Sanger-Harris also turned. The continued slump, the aggressive entry of Target, Wal-Mart, and other discounters into the market, and the pressure to meet Federated's aggressive targets spurred Foley's to reestablish its role in the marketplace. The T.L.C. campaign was a carefully orchestrated rollout of a company-wide effort to refocus employee attention on the customer. At the same time, the company implemented major cost-cutting measures. It closed stores, let sales associates go, consolidated departments, and discontinued merchandise lines. As one employee observed, "T.L.C. was absolutely necessary. With fewer stores, fewer goods, and fewer associates, we got fewer customers. Those of us who were left had to think like customers because there were no customers around to tell us what they were thinking!"

The T.L.C. campaign at Foley's represents the best and worst of the problem-solving management practices that have become so popular in recent years. On the positive side, these practices result in quick diagnosis of a business problem, focused analysis, and mobilization of resources for a concentrated program of action. Business executives are trained to identify, analyze, and fix problems as they occur. Many management-sponsored programs, such as new customer service initiatives, support the value of this training. But what was lacking in Foley's approach, and in much of the problem-solving practiced by thinking organizations, is a more comprehensive understanding of causes, a willingness to experiment, and an ability to foresee problems and develop integrative possibilities that do not yet exist. A reliance on reactive programs to solve business problems foreshortens managerial perspective and frustrates learning.

Customer service programs are often problem-solving run amok. Every company seems to have made a crusade out of telling customers just how important they are. Customer service comment cards are placed on tables at restaurants, in cars at the service garage, and in the pockets of jackets back from the cleaners. Customer service "800" phone lines have become a requisite for retailers and manufacturers alike. However, as customers have learned, the mere adoption of a customer service solution is not evidence that a company has learned about customer service, any more than Band-Aids are cures for cuts.

The fault of today's problem-solving orientation is also apparent in areas other than customer service. Most of the currently popular quality programs are too often piecemeal efforts—quick fixes—that are not directed at fundamental problems. Moreover, they are primarily directed at the shop-floor level. David A. Garvin, a former member of the Board of Overseers of the Malcolm Baldrige National Quality Award, has observed, "Many . . . companies are still using packaged programs or off-the-shelf solutions: employee suggestion programs, customer surveys, or statistical process control packages that they have purchased from outside vendors. They remain customers of quality management, not creators, and have yet to put a personal stamp on their programs. Deployment is incomplete outside of manufacturing or operations, and lower level activities are not fully aligned with strategic goals."

"Packaged," "off-the-shelf," "incomplete," "not fully aligned." These criticisms also apply to other currently popular solutions to business problems—such as just-in-time inventory, fast cycle time, or empowered teams. The problem is not with the programs per se, since many have resulted in success stories; instead, the problem lies with companies thinking that these practices are solutions, and believing they have learned to solve their business problems. The awareness-analysis-action orientation of thinking/problem-solving companies is in itself limiting. As Matthew Kiernan has observed, "Such a linear approach virtually precludes the ability to step back and ask more fundamental, difficult, and useful questions."

According to the philosophy of the thinking/ problem-solving organization, if experience says it's broke, fix it and fix it fast, but don't focus on *why* it breaks. Management practices are programmed into discrete and identifiable solutions to fit the varieties of business problems. For example, thousands of organizations are engaged in some kind of total quality management (TQM) program. These programs typically require supervisors to spend five days learning about statistical quality control. Their bosses then get a two-day overview, and senior management receives a one-hour briefing.

Further, there is a premium on a manager's ability to sell company programs to employees and customers. Employees are expected to enthusiastically embrace and enact each new program, which is announced with great fanfare and hailed by managers as a sure-cure. Employee commitment and involvement—but only regarding the solution at hand—is encouraged. Many programs are begun simultaneously, sometimes at cross-purposes and typically without any systemic integration. Employees and customers alike often grow weary of "the solution of the month."

THE LEARNING ORGANIZATION: ENHANCING EXPERIENCE

In today's turbulent times, every organization is afforded a rich competitive experience, but few organizations profit from it; those that do are learning organizations. Learning organizations process both *the experience* and *the way the organization experiences it*. Drawing on the work of Peter Senge and Chris Argyris, as well as our own research, we can identify several organizational and behavioral characteristics of learning organizations. Many are evident at Home Depot.

Once inside the doors of a Home Depot store, you know you are dealing with a very different kind of company. A few feet from the entrance is a makeshift classroom, with bleacher seating, a chalk-board/bulletin-board, and a work table. As often as four times a day, Home Depot staff or supplier representatives conduct clinics for customers, teaching them how to install a pedestal sink, rewire an electric outlet, build a fence, or do any number of home improvement projects. Throughout these 100,000-plus square feet warehouse/stores are "Depot Dan" displays, which demonstrate the steps of various "how-to" projects and are positioned near the necessary materials and tools. Orange-aproned salespeople are hired not only for their product knowledge, but, as President Arthur M. Blank notes, for their ability "to raise the customer's enthusiasm about a project." As one customer said, "The salespeople at Home Depot are coaches and cheerleaders all in one. You feel like you have a partner on your project."

But the focus on learning at Home Depot is not geared just toward the customer. Before Home Depot opens a new store, employees receive nearly four weeks of training. The retailer also holds quarterly Sunday-morning meetings for its 23,000 employees, using satellite TV hook-ups in each store. Known as "Breakfast with Bernie and Arthur" (the company's founders), these meetings inform employees about the past quarter's performance and the company's growth plans and allow employees to phone the company's top executives to ask questions. The company's in-house TV station also produces programs designed to instill the Home Depot "service spirit" in new stores and their employees.

While customers learn a lot from Home Depot, they also do their share of teaching. For example, contractors asked for special checkout areas near the lumber racks; Home Depot obliged and found that the measure speeded "front-of-the-store" checkout. In some stores, Home Depot is experimenting with a bridal registry, because customers buying starter homeowner kits for newlyweds suggested the idea. Customers also taught Home Depot that selling paint and wallpaper wasn't enough—they needed decorating help too. Chairman Bernard Marcus commented on the importance of continuous customer testing: "One of the biggest lessons we learned was that we had to listen to our customers, whether they had requests on specific kinds of merchandise, needed help or counsel, or just wanted to complain. Now it's like a religion in our company." The religion is practiced through continuous testing/experimenting with merchandising ideas.

With this teaching/learning orientation, Home Depot has become the dominant force in the $115 billion home improvement industry. Founded in Atlanta in 1979 by Bernard Marcus and Arthur M. Blank (both of whom had been fired by once-rival Handy Dan), Home Depot today has more than 200 stores, sales over $6 billion, and profits of over $300 million. The chain's aggressive expansion plans call for 525 stores nationwide by the year 2000. Walter Johnson, senior editor of *Do-It-Yourself Retailing*, the publication of the National Retail Hardware Association, predicts, "Statistically, if Home Depot continues to rack up its current growth rate, and the market keeps up its 4.6 percent annual rate, Home Depot could virtually own the home improvement business by the year 2000."

The key to Home Depot's phenomenal success is its commitment to learning from every aspect of the organization's experience. In fact, any company today with a sustainable strategic advantage—an ability to ensure a competitive edge over the long run via protection, perpetuation, and/or replacement—has achieved that position through dedicating its people, policies, and practices to learning from experience. The San Diego Zoo, Home Depot, Sony, 3M, Wal-Mart, Heinz, Southwest Airlines, Levi Strauss, Motorola, and Honda all have shown that their advantage *is* their capacity to learn.

The philosophy at Home Depot, as at all learning organizations, is to maximize the learning that can be achieved from every company interaction with employees, customers/clients, vendors, suppliers, and even competitors. The company makes a conscious effort to learn from every experience, not just about the experience—be it a sale, a delivery, or a management meeting—but about the way the company collects, processes, and uses information.

The primary responsibility of management and the focus of management practices in a learning organization is to create and foster a climate that promotes learning. Management's task is not to control or be a corporate cheerleader or crisis handler; it is to encourage experimentation, create a climate for open communication, promote constructive dialogue, and facilitate the processing of experience. When management accomplishes this, employees share a commitment to learning. In a learning organization, employees are responsible for gathering, examining, and using the information that drives the learning process. They must be boundary spanners, working across functional departments and divisional lines to mine the experience of customers, suppliers, and even competitors. They must conscientiously expose failures and constructively promote dissent when their experience warrants disagreeing with the company line.

As the San Diego Zoo and Home Depot demonstrate, learning organizations bring a teaching/learning orientation to their relationship with the customer. This orientation is reflected in their open, ongoing dialogue with their customers. The learning organization believes in informing the customer and being informed by the customer—not via the occasional focus group, customer survey, or blitzkrieg campaign, but through a continuous conversation that enhances the experience of both parties.

Nowhere are the differences between the learning organization and its knowing, understanding, and thinking antecedents more evident than in their approaches to change. Because of its commitment to continuous improvement through experimentation, the learning organization always has a great many changes underway. Since there are so many changes, no one change is viewed as a panacea. Some are bound to fail. The organization's entire approach to change is one of acceptance and normalcy. Change is an input that leads to learning. By viewing each change as a hypothesis to be proven and by examining the results of each experiment, the learning organization ensures that change enhances its experience, and thus promotes learning.

	KNOWING	**UNDERSTANDING**	**THINKING**	**LEARNING**
Philosophy	Dedication to the one best way: • Predictable • Controlled • Efficient	Dedication to strong cultural values which guide strategy and action. Belief in the "ruling myth."	A view of business as a series of problems. If it's broke, fix it fast.	Examining, enhancing, and improving every business experience, including how we experience.
Management Practices	Maintain control through rules and regulations, "by the book."	Clarify, communicate, reinforce the company culture.	Identify and isolate problems, collect data, implement solutions.	Encourage experiments, facilitate examination, promote constructive dissent, model learning, acknowledge failures.
Employees	Follow the rules, don't ask why.	Use corporate values as guides to behavior.	Enthusiastically embrace and enact programmed solutions.	Gather and use information; constructively dissent.
Customers	Must believe the company knows best.	Believe company values insure a positive experience.	Are considered a problem to be solved.	Are part of a teaching/learning relationship, with open, continuous dialogue.
Change	Incremental, must be a fine tuning of "the best way."	Only within the "ruling myth."	Implemented through problem-solving programs, which are seen as panaceas.	Part of the continuous process of experience-examine-hypothesize-experiment-experience.

FIGURE 37.1 Organizational Approaches to Experience.

A COMPARISON OF APPROACHES

Figure 37.1 shows the key characteristics of each of the four types of organizations discussed above, drawn from dialogues with practicing managers. The continued use of experience as a way to improve is essential for any organization to survive.

Processing experience is not natural, however, for knowing organizations, which have institutionalized the continuity of reporting relationships and relations with their customers, suppliers, and others. For these firms, even mundane changes can become prohibitively costly. As we have indicated, managers in knowing organizations develop practices over time that protect the organization from pressure from outside influences, whatever their merit. Closed off from its own experience, the knowing organization has no forum or faculties for the kind of processing that learning requires.

Few people would question the assumption that an organization's culture impacts its employees, customers, and other key stakeholders. In the 1980s, many understanding organizations developed strong cultures that thwart learning. For them, culture is a metaphor for understanding their employees' behaviors. Rituals, stories, jargon, and physical settings are all instruments that can hinder their ability to detect and develop the mechanisms that learning requires. Opening up an organization's culture and boundaries is hard; in addition, many an understanding organization's ruling myth ensures that the company "spin" is applied to any information that crosses organizational boundaries. For them, the purpose of processing experience is to promote the culture.

The central argument advanced by managers using the thinking approach is that their adoption of the latest business practices is evidence of their ability to learn. Employees are encouraged to find out what the problems are and to help figure out the solutions; top managers are there to offer options and alternatives to those seeking advice. The organization confronts numerous problems and solutions as it seeks to respond effectively to seemingly ceaseless change. So consumed is the problem-solving organization by its constant problem-solving that it fails to appreciate the need to examine experience, to ask, "Why, with so many solutions, do we still have problems?"

A learning organization is qualitatively different from knowing, understanding, and thinking organizations. Its managers and members *behave* differently. We believe that several core behaviors are evident in learning organizations: openness, systemic thinking, creativity, personal efficacy, and empathy. These behaviors occur not simply because the organization believes learning is desirable, and not because it has adopted a learning mission/vision. Rather, these behaviors are part of the conscientious and consistent implementation and integration of management practices that promote learning; they are the result of the organization's culture, strategy, structure, information technology, reward systems, staffing, and leadership. To adopt these practices, however, managers must set aside much of what they have heretofore believed to be true about creating effective organizations.

UNLEARNING THE ORGANIZATION

If we, as owners, managers, employees, and observers, are to build learning organizations, we must first concern ourselves with *unlearning the organization*. It is not an easy task. We are comfortable in these conventional organization environments—we have trained in them, we have succeeded in them, and we feel protected by them. But many types of organizations, and the behaviors they promote, have outlived their usefulness. Organizations are designed to control employees' behaviors, yet individuals are intrinsically curious and want to experiment. For an organization to unlearn, it needs to free managers and their organizations from seven roadblocks that hinder learning, and embrace new practices.

Learning Culture

A learning organization has a culture and value set that promotes learning. A learning culture is characterized by its clear and consistent (1) openness to experience; (2) encouragement of responsible risk-taking; and (3) willingness to acknowledge failures and learn from them. A learning culture is not so much captured in a "Sloganeered" mission statement crafted by a consulting firm; instead, it is evident in the everyday practices of a company—its rites and rituals, the heroes it reveres, the legends it retells. In a company with a learning culture, everyone—management, employees, customers, and suppliers—sees opportunities to learn and grow. Groups engage in active dialogue and conversation, not discussions. These conversations are reflective, as opposed to argumentative, and they are guided by leaders who facilitate the building of strong relationships among key stakeholder groups. It is clear to us that to instill a learning culture, managers must set aside their penchant for discussion, embracing conversations and dialogues instead. To create conditions that foster conversation and dialogue, they must realize that face-to-face meetings are more functional than E-Mail or the distribution of computer printouts. A dialogue provides a forum for people to talk and think about problems together. E-Mail and fax are "lean" communications media that help a manager "tell" others what to do, but do not encourage experimentation and learning. Dialogue requires a "rich" media (face-to-face meetings), so that people can build shared visions and reflect on their own ways of looking at the world.

Continuous Experimentation

Strategy in a learning organization is predicated upon a recognition and acceptance that learning is the only source of sustainable strategic advantage. As such, management is committed to continuous experimentation as a means of institutionalizing learning. The low-cost strategy of Wal-Mart and the differentiator business strategy of JC Penney simply set the parameters for learning to occur. A strategy is an outcome of the learning process.

Learning companies unlearn "grand programs" in favor of smaller efforts and systematic abandonment. They relentlessly pursue new solutions to problems that their own product or service has just solved. Whenever Sony introduces a new product, for example, it simultaneously sets a "sunset" date on which it will deliberately abandon that product. This immediately triggers work on developing replacement offerings. The object is to create three new products for every one that is phased out: (1) an incrementally improved old product; (2) a new spinoff product from the original (e.g., the Sony Walkman from the portable tape recorder); and (3) an entirely new innovation. With so many experiments underway, some are bound to fail. In a learning organization, failure is expected, even desirable. The measure of strategic planning is necessarily flexibility and the conscious consideration of contingencies.

Network Intimacy

The structural characteristics of learning organizations are permeability, flexibility, and network intimacy. All boundaries in a learning organization are highly permeable, which maximizes the flow of information and opens the organization to its experiences. Learning organizations create the means for recognizing and embracing ideas that originate outside the company. The lines between management and employees, between departments, between employees and customers, between the company and its vendors, and even between the company and its competitors are blurred. The organization's structure is based on the need to learn; the driving organizing principle is to put the necessary resources in the hands of the people who need them. As tasks, needs, and people change, the structure changes so that customers and employees alike face minimal inconveniences. Network intimacy, closeness, and openness between management, employees, customers, competitors, and the community make it possible for the learning organization to constantly monitor changing needs and people. The idea of structure as a fixed, formal definition of how people and tasks are related must be unlearned; structure must be thought of as a process.

Information Systems

It is perhaps axiomatic that a learning organization is effective to the degree that the information it learns from is accurate. More to the point, information in a learning organization must be accurate, timely, available to those who need it, and presented in a format that facilitates its use. In most learning organizations, the tests of information and information systems are simply (1) How does this information add value to the decision process? and (2) How can it get to the people who need it? Home Depot, for example, excels in giving the customer the precise information he or she wants. Learning organizations must combine detailed product knowledge with operational flexibility so they can respond to almost any need. Thus, they must be open to external data regarding the industry, markets, competition, and customers, and must channel that information to the appropriate employees without a managerial "spin." Further, internal information processes must be neither so cluttered nor so cumbersome that information is generated for information's sake. To create this kind of information system, managers need to unlearn most of their current operating beliefs about who needs to know what—and when and why.

Reward Systems

Reward systems in the learning organization recognize and reinforce learning. This means that pay and promotion practices are tied to risk-taking, flexibility, continuous improvement, and other behaviors that learning organizations require. More than this, it means that punishments for failure and dissent are eliminated. In most organizations today, not only are risk-taking and dissent not encouraged, but they are severely punished and generally regarded by employees and managers alike as "career enders." By contrast, learning organizations encourage dissent. Management believes that intellectual diversity enhances and improves experience. Unlearning the traditional response of denigrating dissent, and learning to encourage diversity for maximum learning, is one of the key challenges facing managers in learning organizations.

Human Resource Practices

Does a learning organization, with its learning culture, experimental approach to strategy, open information systems, flexible structure, and encouragement of diversity require a different kind of employee? Yes. A learning organization must select people not for what they know, but for whether they are able to learn. We believe the ability to learn is in great supply in the workforce. The problem is that organizations, by their failure to unlearn, frustrate and squelch employees' learning abilities. John Reed, CEO of Citicorp, has said, "We know how to hire smart people and put them in the organization. But that doesn't produce a smart organization. We have to put more of our energy into building and creating smart organizations by capitalizing on our smart people."

Leaders' Mandate

The role of leadership in unlearning and learning cannot be overstated. Jack Welch, respected CEO of General Electric, presents a learning perspective on the question of retirement. Welch says he continually asks himself, "Are you regenerating? Are you dealing with new things? When you find yourself in a new environment, do you come up with a fundamentally different approach? That's the test. When you flunk, you leave." In many ways, Welch has captured the test of leadership in a learning organization: regenerating, dealing with new things, coming up with fundamentally different approaches.

Despite the general ease with which leaders and managers today call themselves members of "learning organizations," the actual building and maintaining of a learning organization is a Herculean task. The demands of this task run counter to most of what is currently believed about managing organizations. Learning organizations must be willing to uncover their assumptions about themselves and their environment. Thus, organizational learning is about more than simply acquiring new knowledge and insights; it requires managers to unlearn old practices that have outlived their usefulness and discard ways of processing experiences that have worked in the past. Unlearning makes way for new experiences and new ways of experiencing. It is the necessary precursor to learning.

A FINAL WORD

We've drawn most of our examples of learning organizations from major corporations. These examples are particularly illustrative because they deal with products and practices familiar to many of us. However, there is nothing about the learning organization, its characteristics, or its managers that makes it exclusively a big-company phenomenon. The behaviors required for unlearning and learning can be exhibited by all of us, whatever our involvement in organization life. Each of us has the opportunity to create, in our own lives and spheres of influence, learning behaviors and learning organizations. There are many agendas to choose from; the action begins with our own unlearning.

SELECTED BIBLIOGRAPHY

The materials about the San Diego Zoo were taken from Rahul Jacob, "Absence of Management," *American Way*, February 15, 1993, pp. 38–40. For other articles on learning organizations, see Thomas Kochan and Michael Useem, *Transforming Organizations* (New York: Oxford University Press, 1992); Chris Argyris, "Education for Leading-Learning," *Organizational Dynamics*, Winter 1993, pp. 5–17; Michael McGill, John Slocum, and David Lei, "Management Practices in Learning Organizations," *Organizational Dynamics*, Summer 1992, pp. 5–17; Peter M. Senge, *The Fifth Discipline: Five Practices of the Learning Organization* (New York: Doubleday, 1990); Curtis Ventriss and Jeff Luke, "Organizational Learning and Public Policy: Towards a Substantive Perspective," *American Review of Public Administration*, December 1988, pp. 337–357; Mathew Kiernan, "The New Strategic Architecture: Learning to Compete in the Twenty-First Century," *Academy of Management Executive*, February 1993, pp. 7–21; and Bob Hedberg, "How Organizations Learn to Unlearn," in *Handbook of Organization Design*, Paul Nystrom and William Starbuck, eds. (New York: Oxford University Press, 1981, Vol. 1, pp. 3–27). The entire issue of *Organization Science*, 1991, Vol. 2, was dedicated to theoretical expositions of learning organizations.

For readings on knowing organizations, Don Hellriegel and John W. Slocum, Jr.'s book *Management*, 6th edition (Reading, MA: Addison-Wesley, 1992, pp. 38–64) provides a good summary. Also see Paul Adler, "Time and Motion Regained," *Harvard Business Review*, January–February 1993, pp. 97–108.

For penetrating insights into how corporate cultures impact the behaviors of managers in their firms, see John Kotter and James Heskett, *Corporate Culture and Performance* (New York: The Free Press, 1992); Harrison Trice and Janice Beyer, *The Cultures of Work Organizations* (Englewood Cliffs, NJ: Prentice-Hall, Inc., 1993); Carol J. Loomis, "Dinosaurs?", *Fortune*, May 3, 1993, pp. 36–42; and Susan Cartwright and Cary Cooper, "The Role of Cultural Compatibility in Successful Organizational Marriage," *Academy of Management Executive*, May 1993, pp. 57–70.

Quality is Personal: A Foundation for Total Management by Harry Roberts and Bernard Sergesketter (New York: The Free Press, 1993) provides excellent insights into many practices of thinking organizations.

The material on how Home Depot delivers service has been experienced personally by the authors. Patricia Sellers, "Companies that Serve You Best," *Fortune*, May 31, 1993, pp. 74–88 details how Home Depot and other organizations have learned to serve their customers.

Leadership and Change

38. PATHFINDING, PROBLEM SOLVING, AND IMPLEMENTING: THE MANAGEMENT MIX

Harold J. Leavitt

Every couple of decades managers and academics scratch their heads and once again ponder some tough old questions like these: What is managing *really* all about? What are managers doing right? What are they doing wrong? What should they *really* be trying to do?

Even though such questions will never be finally answered, they are healthy, indicative of a recurrent readiness to change and to experiment. This time around, they seem especially important, driven partly by anxiety and uncertainty about what it will take to cope with the volatile, complex, and fast-changing world that lies ahead.

This small book tries to focus more clearly on questions of this kind, and to suggest partial and temporary answers to some of them. It begins with a simple three-part description of what the managing process looks like in the late 1980s. Those three parts then serve as handles for examining where American management has gone right and gone wrong in recent years, and what kinds of corrections and changes seem to be in order.

The book's general argument is that we have unintentionally neglected the visionary, pathfinding part of the managing process over the last 20 years. We have, at our peril, put most of our energies into two other areas—into planful, analytic, systematic methods of problem solving and into the action and people-oriented implementing parts of managing. Only since the early 1980s have the bills from that neglect of pathfinding become obvious. We are right now in a healthy but hectic period of repayment, regrouping, and renewal.

This first chapter outlines the three-part model of the managing process and briefly describes each of the three parts. The main purpose of the chapter is to lay the groundwork for understanding why the neglect of pathfinding by managers and educators alike has come close to costing us our managerial shirts.

The three parts into which this model divides managing are these: #1 pathfinding, #2 problem solving, and #3 implementing.

Reprinted from Harold Leavitt, *Corporate Pathfinders* (Homewood, Ill.: Dow Jones-Irwin, 1986), pp. 1–24.

Consider them in reverse order, starting with #3 *implementing*, because that one is such a pervasive element of our image of the modern manager. For here lies the macho mover-and-shaker part of the managing process, as well as the office politics and manipulative parts, and even the participative, human relations parts. It is this implementing side of managing that shows up most often in soap opera managers and in movie versions of the manager. Implementing is about *action*, about getting things done through people, making things happen. Implementing is getting the bricks laid, the services rendered, and the product delivered. Implementing is *doing* things *through others*. Managers are people who get things done. They persuade, cajole, influence, command.

But managing is not just about implementing. It is also about *problem solving*. Managers have to organize, plan, and make decisions. Good managing takes some IQ points as well as some capacity to get things done. Managing means taking hold of complex, messy, ill-defined problems and converting them into organized, systematized forms. Managers have to make rational decisions about products, people, and markets; they have to allocate scarce resources sensibly. Managers must be thinkers as well as doers. They have to make order out of chaos.

Behind both the problem solving and implementing parts of managing, there lurks still another part of the process, the much fuzzier, less observable #1 part, here called *pathfinding*. Pathfinding is the major focus of this book, and while ephemeral and hard to measure, it is an incontrovertibly real and critical part of the managing process.

#1 pathfinding is about getting the right questions rather than the right answers. It is about making problems rather than solving them. It is *not* about figuring out the best way to get there from here, nor even about making sure that we get there. It is rather about pointing to where we ought to try to go.

#1 pathfinding, that is, is about mission, purpose, and vision; #2 problem solving is about analysis, planning, and reasoning; and #3 implementing is about doing, changing, and influencing. Our model of managing is about those three critical sets of activities and about the back-and-forth interactions among the three.

The model is pictured in Figure 38.1.

The wavy vertical lines are there to show that the boundaries between the pieces are often foggy, and to suggest that movement from any one to any other can be both difficult and critical. It is not enough, that is, for the manager to be competent in one of these three, or even in all three at once. The manager had also better be skillful at moving across the harsh terrain that often separates them.

That three-part view of managing can (and will) be applied at several levels. For the individual manager, the three parts can be treated as three styles of managing. Some managers, that is, use predominantly pathfinding styles; others are problem solvers; still others are implementers. Most of us mix the three styles, presumably to fit appropriate situations. But are we really that flexible? Can we learn new styles late in life? How? Aren't the three parts of managing mutually contradictory?

At that same individual level, educational questions arise. In the education of managers, should we

A Model of the Managing Process		
#1	#2	#3
Pathfinding	Problem Solving	Implementing

FIGURE 38.1 A Model of the Managing Process.

try to teach a blend of all three and shoot for "balanced excellence"? Have business schools taught any pathfinding at all? Could they? Or should they try? Later chapters examine such questions from an individual perspective.

The three parts—pathfinding, problem solving, and implementing—can also be looked at from an organizational perspective. Do organizations need pathfinding individuals? In what proportions? At the top? Throughout the organization? Should the three parts of the process be specialized, with each the responsibility of a particular group or level? Should we let R&D, for example, do the pathfinding, while engineering does the problem solving and sales does the implementing? Or should the CEO be the pathfinder, with the staff people the problem solvers and all the rest the implementers?

Do large ongoing organizations need more pathfinding types? Won't that erode discipline and lead to anarchy? How can the individualistic, high-risk pathfinding style be integrated into the participative kind of implementation that has grown so prevalent in recent years?

This three-part model can be considered at a societal level as well. To what extent is pathfinding part of the heritage of most Western nations? Has some of that heritage been lost? Have recent educational policies and practices encouraged or suppressed pathfinding tendencies? Has the growth of very large organizations discouraged individualistic pathfinding? Do the cultures of most organizations, especially large and old ones, need a good shot of pathfinding style—a mood of urgency, a push toward innovation, a salient sense of mission?

IMPLEMENTING

Let's add a little meat to these bones by looking at each part of that three-part model in more depth. Again we start at the #3 end.

Implementing is not done by managers alone. Each of us implements all the time, whether or not we wear managerial hats. We mow the lawn, drive the car, fix the lamp, cook the dinner. But when implementing is part of the managing process, it has a couple of attributes that distinguish it from implementing in nonmanagerial settings.

First, managerial implementing is always done through other people. That's of course not at all a new idea. My old mentor Douglas McGregor used to define all of managing that way: "Managing is getting things done through people." While in other parts of life we can often implement our own decisions, managing human organizations invariably requires convincing other people to mow our lawns and cook our dinners. Implementing in organizations almost always requires the manager to persuade or command or manipulate or force other people to change their present behavior, to do what the manager wants done instead of what those people are now doing. *Managerial implementing is therefore a highly social activity.*

Second, managerial implementing involves changing other people's behavior, and therefore *it is a highly emotional activity.* Everything the social sciences know about changing behavior says that people change for emotional reasons far more than for rational reasons. It's love, hate, greed, loyalty, jealousy, and passion, much more than cool, pure reason, that drive us to change our ways. So the implementing part of managing has more to do with people's hearts than with their brains. It is not through logic and rationality that we persuade our employees to improve quality or increase productivity. It is through pride or ambition or loyalty. Getting people to do what you want them to do is much more a gutsy than an intellectual process.

But what's new? Hasn't that always been the case? Yes, but in our new world of knowledge and information, the role of emotionality has, paradoxically, gotten bigger, not smaller. In the old world of mostly physical arm-and-leg work, and in the social environment of those days, implementing was mostly focused on the fear-provoking emotionality of command and control or on the emotionality of paternalistic protectionism. In today's more professional, more educated, and more egalitarian organizational world, implementing becomes an issue of persuasion, negotiation, and inspiration rather than of command or protection.

Skill in working with human emotionality is not only rare in managers; it is often seen as "unmanagerial." Recent generations of young managers have, in general, been taught to use their heads much more than their hearts. They are supposed to learn to be rational, objective, hardheaded, professional. But when managers try to influence emotional human beings with exclusively rational tools, trouble starts.

Where and how, then, does one learn implementing skills? Imagine a teenager asking you something like that. "I really like that implementing stuff. I'd love to learn how to win friends and influence people. But how do I learn to become a great implementer? What should I study? What occupation should I try?"

It is not very difficult to identify some occupations in which implementing skills are critical to effective performance. How about direct selling? Or line supervision in a manufacturing plant? Surely platoon leaders in the Marine Corps had also better learn to be pretty good at implementing. They are helped along, of course, by rank, military structure, and all the rest, but in the last analysis it's the platoon leader who has to get those 50 marines to take that hill.

Litigating lawyers had better understand emotional implementing too. They have to persuade judges and jurors, to cajole and browbeat and sweet-talk witnesses. The litigators I have encountered in American law firms are killers, competitors. They are often singled out by other lawyers as a special subgenus of the legal species. Litigators worry about whether to select younger women for this jury or whether they would be better off with older men. They focus on the idiosyncrasies and characteristics of the opposing lawyers and on those of the judge. They work on people's prejudices and impulses, just as a very good salesperson does.

The band of occupations that can offer a young person practice in implementing is very broad indeed. It includes not only second lieutenants, lobbyists, and salespeople but also psychiatrists, counselors, organizational development people, and others in the "helping professions." Whether they acknowledge it or not, the members of these professions too try to change people's behavior by largely emotional means.

So what may seem like a collection of very strange bedfellows fits into this implementing part of the world of managing. Two bonds tie them all together. First, in all the varied kinds of managerial implementing, *human emotionality is the essence* from which change is made.

Second, most members of these implementing occupations think *small*. They think about people singly or in small numbers. For most skilled managerial implementers, human beings are *real*. They have names, faces, personalities, individual idiosyncrasies. They are not masses or statistics or hired hands, as they often are for extreme #2 problem solvers. So it should come as no surprise that when #3 implementers try to design large organizations, they usually want to use small groups as their building blocks, piling up pyramids composed of many small human units.

Problem Solving

Let's turn now for a closer look at the #2 problem solving piece of the managing process. If the key word for #3 implementing is *action*, then the key word for #2 problem solving is *analysis*. Problem solving (at least as we in the Western world see it) is about reason and logic. It is about orderly, systematic approaches to problems. It is about planning and coordinating.

We know a good deal about how to teach problem solving skills, much more than we know about how to teach implementing skills. Indeed, that's what most education is all about. Reading, writing, and arithmetic are all analytic problem solving skills. A caricature of the complete #2 problem solver does not look at all like the fast-moving, fast-talking caricature of the implementer. The problem solver casts an intellectually reserved shadow. The image is of the steel-trap mind poring over the printout by lamplight, figuring out the right answer, the logical solution, the defensible decision, the optimal strategy.

If that inquiring teenager likes the #2 problem solving image and asks you where a young person ought to go for training to become a great problem solver, the answer should be quite easy. One good place to go is the Modern American Business School. Something like 80 percent of the contemporary MBA curriculum has been focused on the #2 analytic problem solving part of managing. That's the place to learn about linear programming, systems analysis, operations research, and econometric methods, about how to build marketing models and how to do financial analyses. Look at the catalog of any MBA school. The course titles use the word *analysis* again and again: Financial Analysis, Market Analysis, Decision Analysis, Economic Analysis. Go to business school to learn to program what has previously been unprogrammable.

But business school is only one of the places where the young person can learn how to do analytic problem solving. He or she might also try engineering or accounting or management consulting or tax law. All of those professions require high levels of analytic skills. They require logic, consistency, and orderliness. While it's likely that members of those professions are sometimes talented in other ways too, analytic skill remains a sine qua non for competence in all of them.

Given all of that emphasis on analysis and logic, it is no surprise that all-out #2 types take a dim view of emotionality. While for #3 implementers emotionality is the raw material of change, for orthodox #2s that same emotionality is likely to be seen as noise in the system, as a sign of human imperfection. In a few million years the full rationality that God so clearly intended will evolve. Real men aren't emotional. So one of the trouble spots in the managing process is located at the junction of #2 and #3, where rational problem solvers meet emotional implementers.

Notice too that analytic occupations carry very high status in Western society, in contrast to the somewhat lower status usually ascribed to many of the implementing occupations, such as selling or manufacturing management. It's OK for your son

or daughter to enter any one of them. And they pay well too. Among MBA students, for example, it has been the jobs in consulting and financial analysis that have been viewed as the most desirable ones, at least until recently. Selling has been viewed as low class, and manufacturing as too dirty.

A caveat: While much of the problem solving part of managing can be learned through quantitative, analytic training, not *all* of it can be picked up that easily. There is, as every manager knows, more to real-world problem solving than can be found in the problem sets at the end of the chapters in the accounting text. There is more uncertainty in the real world, more unforeseeable variability. So such words as *judgment, experience, wisdom,* and *good sense* have stayed on our recruiting checklists, even as #2-type academics seek ways of making them unnecessary.

PATHFINDING

If implementing includes large emotional components and if problem solving includes large rational and analytic components, how can one characterize the #1 pathfinding part of the managing process? The central issue of pathfinding is not influence or persuasion, nor is it reasoning or systematic analysis. The key word here is *mission.* The pathfinding part of managing is the homeland of the visionary, the dreamer, the innovator, the creator, the entrepreneur, and the charismatic leader. The central questions are very difficult and often unaddressed: How do I decide what I want to be when I grow up? What should this organization try to become if it could become anything imaginable? What do we really want to do with this company?

The #1 pathfinding world is highly personal and subjective, with answers, where there are any, emerging more from within the self than from a diagnosis of what's out there. Pathfinding is the ephemeral part of managing that deals with values, aesthetics, and beliefs. Putting faith before evidence, pathfinders often violate #2 problem solving precepts. But they also build new worlds.

Do we even need such soft, subjective stuff to manage the modern organization? The answer is unequivocally yes, whether we derive it from social or political or organizational observation. The pathfinding role has always been a critical driving force in the rise of human institutions. From the founding of the United States to the development of IBM to the birth pangs of that new little start-up company, the beliefs and visions of a few stubborn souls have always driven innovation and development.

By far the best illustration of a pathfinding statement that I can offer is familiar to all Americans. It is the second sentence of the American Declaration of Independence: "We hold these truths to be self-evident, that all men are created equal, that they are endowed by their Creator with certain unalienable Rights, that among these are Life, Liberty and the pursuit of Happiness."

What an assertive, pathfinding declaration that is! It must have driven the #2 problem solvers of the day absolutely wild. All men are created equal? How do you know? What's the genetic evidence? "Rights" like "Liberty" or "the pursuit of Happiness"? How do you measure such stuff? "Self-evident" truths? No evidence required? No data to support them? And could anyone, even armed with the most clear and potent evidence, have changed those Founding Fathers' minds? They weren't to be distracted by mere facts!

The pathfinders whom most of us would cite as memorable are also necessarily skillful as implementers. We only remember them if other people have joined up with their visions. Visionaries who do *not* influence others to follow them are simply forgotten. Or if they are remembered at all, they are remembered as impractical dreamers, not as men and women of vision. Indeed, that almost defines a *charismatic leader*: A charismatic leader is a #1 pathfinder who is also successful at #3 implementing—someone with a sense of mission who can also get others to join in.

Pathfinders need not be heroes. They are not always lovable or even smart. People with unusual ideas, strong commitments, and deep beliefs may also be intransigent, single-minded, unforgiving, or simply stupid. It's not just the good guys, the Jesus Christs and Martin Luther Kings, who qual-

ify as pathfinders. Some great pathfinders were more than a bit unpleasant; some were very bad fellows. Adolf Hitler belongs in that set, as does Jim Jones of Jonestown in Guyana, and probably so too do many of the robber barons of European and American industrial history.

In business, the pathfinders are easiest to spot among entrepreneurs and founders of companies. Watson of IBM, Hewlett and Packard, Land of Polaroid, and Freddie Laker were all people dedicated to building their dreams into realities. Such pathfinders are not always pleasant or friendly, and they may not be successful in the long run, but they are all stubborn, committed believers with strong, clear notions of good and bad.

Pathfinders also turn up in old established companies, but less frequently. When they do, they inject new mission and purpose into old organizations. In the early 1980s Lee Iacocca, for example, may have done just that at Chrysler, and Carlson at SAS. In both cases they have turned around their companies' spirits as well as their P&Ls.

To what education and which professions, then, should we direct young people who decide that pathfinding is what excites them?

It's much harder to answer that question for #1 pathfinding than it was for #2 problem solving or #3 implementing. Pathfinders seem far easier to identify than to develop. Perhaps we should point young people in directions quite unrelated to the contemporary management scene. We could suggest that they seek their fortunes among artists and architects, or among philosophers and religionists, or among theoretical physicists; or perhaps we should recommend a broad liberal education, if such a thing still exists.

Indeed, one can argue that management education as we now practice it would do very little to enhance pathfinding abilities. Our methods of educating and developing new managers have not only neglected pathfinding; they have often downright clobbered it. While problem solvers and implementers, whether in companies or in universities, fight like the devil with one another, they also share a common interest (sometimes unconscious) in keeping the pathfinders out.

For obvious reasons, #2 problem solvers don't want stubborn, intractable, impractical visionaries around. Pathfinders can seldom offer (and seldom care to offer) hard evidence for their choices; and hard evidence is the essence of modern problem solving. Pathfinders often ignore the rules, or act impulsively, or wave off what they see as trivial details.

Here in northern California's Silicon Valley one version of the clash between #1 and #2 styles has occurred several times in recent years. It happens as small companies succeed and grow larger. At some point, the venture capitalists or other investors convince the #1-type founders that their now chaotic organization needs discipline and control. So a #2-type COO is brought aboard. Occasionally the marriage works, but frequently the freewheeling #1 style of the founder is just too disruptive for the control-oriented #2 manager (or vice versa), so sparks fly, heads roll, and energy is diverted from the main target just when it is needed most.

#3 implementers are also likely to feel cool toward those unmalleable, individualistic pathfinders. Contemporary #3 types are particularly oriented toward teamwork, consensus, and cooperation among an organization's members. No matter how positively we may value such styles, they do not fit neatly with the stubborn, determined individualism of pathfinders. #1 pathfinders often become team leaders, but they are seldom good team players.

OUTSTANDING PATHFINDERS, PROBLEM SOLVERS, AND IMPLEMENTERS: SOME EXAMPLES

Occasionally rare and unique personalities turn up who leave their mark in history almost entirely as implementers, or problem solvers, or pathfinders. They are so good at that one part of managing that it completely overshadows the other two. It's worth identifying a few such extraordinary people, people known to almost all of us, to help draw a clearer picture of the differences among the three parts.

Who, for example, among great public figures familiar to all of us, is the implementer par excellence? Who is preeminent among the problem solvers? Who are the outstanding pathfinders?

Certainly one ideal nominee for an Oscar among implementers would be Lyndon Baines Johnson, at least that part of him that keeps coming through in his biographies. Implementing can be done in many ways, and Johnson's was only one way. He was so good at it, however, and it was so central to his managing style that he serves as an excellent example.

As president, Johnson was certainly not considered by most observers to have been a particularly great #2 intellect, nor a great planner or organizer. Neither was he regarded as a great #1 visionary pathfinder. He did, the reader will remember, try to establish a mission for America, his Great Society, but that notion somehow never took hold, perhaps because many Americans weren't sure he really believed in it himself.

But Johnson will always be remembered as a top-notch implementer. His skill at twisting the arms and stroking the egos of congressmen was legendary. He could shuffle greed, love, fear, and sentimentality to get what he wanted. He could make compromises, negotiate workable solutions. He could get it done. In one sense, he was a very good planner too. He did his homework before taking on the people he wanted to influence. He learned all about their children and their lovers and their hobbies and their hangups. And he used whatever tactics were needed to do the job. He got things implemented through people.

The stories left behind from the Johnson presidency reflect those characteristics. Johnson's memorable quotations were invariably pragmatic and earthy. One of his favorites: "Don't spit in the soup; we all have to eat."

On one occasion, the story goes, an aide came to him to ask, "Mr. President, why are you climbing into bed with Joe Smith, who has always been your enemy? For years that guy has been trying to destroy you, and now you seem to be forming an alliance with him." Johnson is said to have replied,

"I'd rather have him inside the tent pissing out than outside pissing in."

No statesmanlike rhetoric here. Those Johnsonisms are not likely to make *The World's Great Quotations*, but they catch Johnson's pragmatic emphasis on doing what one has to do to get the damn job done. And they surely also illustrate his awareness of the relevance of human emotionality in the implementing process. Typical of the approach of excellent implementers, these quotations illustrate two key characteristics of #3 skill—attention to emotionality and attention to the individual.

After some hesitation, I have decided to include one more remark that has been ascribed, truly or falsely, to President Johnson. The remark is worth reporting, not because it is off-color, but because it so clearly demonstrates Johnson's faith that implementing is what *really* counts. "When you grab 'em by the balls," the remark goes, "their hearts and minds will soon follow." Translated, that would read, "If you catch people where their #3 emotions are, then the #2 rationality and their #1 values will adapt themselves to fit." In this rather cynical ideology, emotionality dominates both logic and morality. While Johnson's application of that ideology looks especially manipulative, the ideology itself underlies the practice of many other types of implementers.

It's not too difficult to find other examples of excellent implementers. During World War II General George Patton was a flamboyant example, out there at the head of his troops, his twin pearl-handled revolvers at his side. And Ronald Reagan has shown extraordinary skill at social influence, both through his mastery of the media and in face-to-face dealings with congressmen. Remember, for example, how, early in his first term, he got those AWAC planes for the Saudis? While commentators were insisting that he couldn't possibly push the deal through, he did. And the newspapers talked about how his personal charm had swung the votes his way. Incidentally, was any #1 mission involved in that deal? Or was any of the deal part of a grand #2 plan? Most observers seemed to feel that in that case #3 was all there was.

Doesn't Lee Iacocca belong on any list of great recent managerial implementers? He may be good at #1 and #2 as well, but his affable personal implementing style and his effective exploitation of the emotional aspects of managing have been extraordinary.

Each of us could probably make a private list of "implementers I have known"—from a particular teacher who counseled and guided us, to the company tactician who always seemed to know just when to push hard and when to back off, to that extraordinary sales rep who somehow made those impossible sales, to the negotiator who always seemed to get a better deal than anyone else.

If Johnson serves as a caricature of the extreme and skillful implementer, who can similarly exemplify the far-out problem solver? The epitome of rational, analytic intelligence? The person who could decompose very complex problems and then reassemble them into a clear controllable form? Does your vice president for finance fit the mold? Or your chief industrial engineer? How about David Stockman, recently the director of the U.S. Budget Bureau?

One public figure of a couple of decades ago who fitted that image perfectly, at least by media stereotype, was Robert McNamara during his tenure as U.S. secretary of defense. The later McNamara of the World Bank appears much more mellow than did the earlier Department of Defense version. McNamara in those early years was much admired by many of his contemporaries chiefly because of his brilliantly orderly, systematic, and rational mind. In contrast to the stories about LBJ (under whom McNamara served), the stories about McNamara reflect just those #2 qualities. Here's one:

McNamara is attending a presentation at which the presenter shows slide after slide full of graphs and charts and numbers. At the 105th slide, McNamara says, "Stop! Slide number 105 contradicts slide number 6." And sure enough, he is right! Everyone in attendance is awed by his capacity to order and process such massive quantities of information. Some Washington veterans still count

McNamara as the greatest civil servant of his time. They usually cite his incisive, analytic, logical qualities as the main reason.

However, at least as the stories go, the McNamara of those DOD days was not nearly as effective in implementing his decisions as he was in making them, and history books are not likely to picture him as a great visionary (though that is probably quite unjust). There are Washington old-timers who still turn beet red with anger at the mention of his name. When they calm down enough to say why, it is almost always to complain that he tried to "take over," to reduce other people's autonomy. Some generals in Vietnam and some legislators in Washington, themselves pretty good #3 implementers, viewed him as an intruder into their autonomous territories and resisted those carefully worked-out controls imposed from the Pentagon.

While it is difficult to identify senior managers who manifest extreme #2 posture in these late 1980s, such managers were less rare in the 60s and 70s. In those years, executives like Roy Ash at Litton Industries and Harold Geneen at ITT were seen as the very model of modern managers—brilliant, tough, systematic, coldly rational.

Analytic think tanks like the Rand Corporation flourished in those decades too. And small analytic-planning groups played a powerful role in France. The stereotype of the cool analytic MBA also came into its own in that period too, and it became so popular with managers that the number of such MBAs multiplied, as did the number of business schools that produced them. The 1960s and 70s were the decades when corporate staffs grew fat and great conglomerates roamed the earth.

Examples of #1 pathfinders, however, seem to turn up throughout human history. They include great religious figures like Jesus and Mohammed; leaders of nations like Mahatma Gandhi, Vladimir Ilyich Lenin, Charles de Gaulle, Lee Kuan Yew, and Golda Meir; and pioneers in the professions like Florence Nightingale and Sigmund Freud.

Other less attractive personages also belong on the pathfinder list: Adolf Hitler, Muammar al-Qaddafi, Napoleon Bonaparte, and Attila the Hun. My favorite candidate for recent top-of-the-line pathfinder is Dr. Martin Luther King, Jr. His most remembered phrase is "I have a dream." That's as pathfinding a phrase as one can imagine. Of course, Dr. King must be counted as a great implementer as well. Followers flocked to act upon his dream. He too changed behavior by emotional means, though he used a style quite different from President Johnson's.

Just for practice, imagine how differently either Robert McNamara or Lyndon Johnson, given the same intent as King's, might have approached the same problem of changing race relations in America.

McNamara would have worked out a grand strategy, wouldn't he? He would have been sure that all of the staff work had been done, the information gathered and analyzed, the contingencies planned for. He would have done an admirably professional job.

President Johnson's approach? Perhaps he would have identified the key players, figured out which people really had the power. Then perhaps he would have worked on those people, one at a time, using every weapon that he could muster to line them up—from the prestige of his office, to promises of support for their pet projects, to personal persuasion.

Would either of them have shown the passionate, resolute, self-sacrificing style used by Dr. King? I think not.

In the corporate world, pathfinders are, thank heaven, not yet an entirely endangered species. They can most often (but not always) be found among founders of companies, in part because successful founders are apt to get more public attention than second- or third-generation managers.

Some recent examples: Messrs. Hewlett and Packard seem to have truly committed themselves to a clear set of organizational values. They have captured and transmitted much of their intent with the phrase "the H-P way." That phrase really means something to H-P people everywhere. It describes a style of openness, honesty, and mutual support and respect reminiscent of the best of small-town America. At Apple Computer, in contrast, Steve Jobs and Company tried to pursue a very different vision—a brash, innovative, almost arrogant organizational culture. Some observers saw that pursuit as a somewhat flaky new children's crusade; for others, it was a youthful cultural revolution, ideally appropriate to its time, its place, and its product.

But in older companies too, pathfinders arise. Pehr Gyllenhammer at Volvo has pushed long, hard, and effectively for a more humane and productive alternative to the old assembly line. He has argued saliently for keeping most of Volvo's operations in its native Sweden despite high labor costs, because he believes in fighting the productivity battle in more positive ways than by escaping to cheap labor overseas.

So Volvo has tried to stay competitive (and so far it has worked) by innovating in both the technology and the sociology of production—building quality cars and trucks with small teams, using appropriate tools, and even modifying the design of its products to fit coherently into the total system. So far, it's doing pretty well.

Ren McPherson, at Dana Corporation, has also successfully pushed his vision of people-based productivity into an otherwise unglamorous old auto parts company. He too did it by using personal passion and determination, injecting pride and enthusiasm into the organization.

In all of these cases the pathfinding leaders have backed up their own pathfinding leadership with effective #3 participative-type implementation, providing us with living examples of successful marriages between #1 and #3. In later chapters that #1–#3 relationship gets a closer look, and so do some of the obstacles that frequently beset such marriages.

Surely the reader can (and should) add to this list from personal experience. Pathfinders—dedicated, purposive people—are not to be found only among the famous and infamous, or only at the tops of large organizations. Small entrepreneurial companies are very often led by people with such dedication to particular visions and values, and deep

within large organizations, often in the face of enormous bureaucratic roadblocks, the dedicated champions of new ideas and important causes still make their voices heard.

DOES THE MANAGERIAL WORLD NEED MORE PATHFINDING?

There are some persuasive arguments on both sides of the question of the importance of pathfinding, especially in large organizations. On the pro side:

- Innovations are almost always the products of pathfinding individuals and small groups, almost never the products of large, highly structured bureaucracies.

- Breakthroughs in any field typically emerge from a combination of thorough understanding of the existing rules *and* a risk-taking readiness to break out of them, to march to different drummers.

- One can also cite the usual broader arguments: the knowledge explosion, ever faster technological change, a crowded and small organizational world. For those reasons and more, organizations need both innovation and direction. They need a constant flow of innovations in products and services because competitors will kill them if they stand still. Intercontinental airplanes knock off passenger liners. Slide rules give way to calculators. Transistors not only destroy vacuum-tube makers but also displace old ways of building watches, radios, and computers. Organizations need direction and purpose lest they be lost in the buffeting storms of competition, regulation, and social change. And individuals need purpose lest *they* be lost in meaningless ennui. The pathfinding part of managing is about both innovation and purpose.

- But let's not try to justify #1 by using only #2-type arguments. There are powerful #1-type reasons for building more pathfinding into Western management. Pathfinding is our heritage, in the United States and almost all other Western countries. Our traditions and our self-esteem commit us to changing the world, to developing the new and the better. Independence, achievement, and daring are integral to our value systems. Pathfinding is what we claim to believe in. We should build it into ourselves and our organizations just because it is our heritage, and just because we believe it is good.

- Just in case the hardheaded reader wants a more practical reason to supplement all of that sentimental junk, here's one: Our traditions of individualism, of independent effort, of starting new fires may just constitute one of our few comparative advantages over the Japanese, with their traditions of conformity, obedience, and self-subordination.

Perhaps it's appropriate here to cite just a few arguments against pushing the pathfinding idea too far:

- How can you run a company full of independent, rule-breaking, intractable pathfinders? That's an invitation to anarchy.

- It's always (well, almost always) been the well-organized, disciplined army that wins the war. Precision and planfulness, not vision and stubbornness, make the difference between success and failure.

- Those imaginative dreamers are a dime a dozen. They're almost always unrealistic and impractical. They bite off more than they can chew, and they won't spit it out no matter how obvious it is that they're wrong. They can kill a company by stubbornly refusing to abandon their dogmatic beliefs.

- The job of managers is to understand the world as it exists and to deal with it, not to take on the impossible job of making it over.

39. MANAGING WITH POWER

Jeffrey Pfeffer

It is one thing to understand power—how to diagnose it, what are its sources, what are the strategies and tactics for its use, how it is lost. It is quite another thing to use that knowledge in the world at large. And putting the knowledge of power and influence into action—managing with power—is essential for those who seek to get things accomplished:

"There's a thing you learn at Data General, if you work here for any period of time," said West's lieutenant of hardware, Ed Rasala, "that nothing happens unless you push it."[1]

Computers don't get built, cities don't get rebuilt, and diseases don't get fought unless advocates for change learn how to develop and use power effec-tively. We saw that in the early 1980s the blood banks resisted testing for transfusion-transmitted AIDS, and even denied that a contaminated blood supply was a serious health risk. The 1980s saw an increase in the political skill of the AIDS lobby, and its tactics are now being borrowed by others:

Women with breast cancer are taking a lesson from AIDS advocacy groups and using political action to urge the Federal and state governments to pay more attention to their disease. "They showed us how to get through to the government. . . . They took on an archaic system and turned it around while we have been quietly dying."[2]

Women's health issues are sorely underfunded compared to the proportion of women in the popula-

---

From *Managing with Power*. Boston: Harvard Business School Press, 1992, pp. 337–345.

tion, a situation that is likely to change if, and only if, power and influence are brought to bear on, and more importantly, *in* those organizations that fund medical research and regulate the pharmaceutical and medical industries.

In corporations, public agencies, universities, and government, the problem is how to get things done, how to move forward, how to solve the many problems facing organizations of all sizes and types. Developing and exercising power require having both will and skill. It is the will that often seems to be missing. Power and influence have a negative connotation. We hound politicians from office, and try to bring down those institutions or individuals that seek to do things differently or better. I wonder how many of us would have had the nerve or the courage to do what the young Henry Ford II did when the company that bears his name was in trouble in the 1940s?

Ford Motor Company was founded by Henry Ford II's grandfather. Although the elder Ford had tremendous engineering genius, and the Model T truly transformed the country, in his later years he was rigid, inflexible, autocratic, and virtually destroyed the company by failing to incorporate new technology and styling. Ford saw a criticism of the Model T as a criticism of him personally, so the competitive threat of Chevrolet was met with price cutting—eight times from 1920 to 1924, twice more in 1926.[3] Even after the Model A was introduced in 1927, the company continued to decline. Henry Ford, originally surrounded by bright engineers and innovative managers, soon surrounded himself with bodyguards and strongmen, including the notorious Harry Bennett, who carried a gun and who would, on occasion, take target practice while talking with visitors.

Even the brief triumph of the Model A did not halt the downward spiral of the company. Henry Ford remained locked in the past. He grew more erratic and finally senile. At the end of his life he believed that World War II did not exist, that it was simply a ploy made up by the newspapers to help the munitions industry. . . . It was a spectacular self-destruction, one that would never again be matched in a giant American corporation.[4]

By the time of World War II, the federal government actually considered taking over the company, because it was in such desperate managerial and financial condition that it could fail at any time, and the government badly needed its wartime production capabilities. In 1943, Secretary of the Navy Frank Knox discharged a 26-year-old Henry Ford II from the Navy. He had a bigger, more important job to do—to take over and then save the Ford Motor Company. Henry's father, Edsel Ford, had died of stomach cancer that same year at the age of 49. Although described as both gentle and brilliant, he had been totally dominated by the elder Ford, and had never played a major role in the company. The company had destroyed the second generation of Fords, and there were people who would have been quite happy to do the same thing with the third generation.

As Ford had grown older and more senile, effective control of the company had passed to the hands of Harry Bennett, head of the dreaded Ford Service Department, which was effectively a secret police force of hoodlums, gangsters, and ex-policemen, who exercised control through physical force. One story had it that when an employee violated the company's policy against smoking, Bennett personally shot the cigar from the man's mouth. With Edsel gone, and Henry Ford increasingly infirm, the only thing keeping Bennett from control of Ford was Henry Ford II.

Although Ford was in the company, with the title of vice president, Bennett constantly belittled him (as he had his father, Edsel). Moreover, the elder Ford had drawn up a codicil to his will, which stipulated that at his death, control of the company would pass to a 10-person board of directors, not including Henry Ford II, for 10 years. Henry was incensed, and threatened to resign unless the will was changed. He also warned that he would inform the company's dealers about the firm's sorry condition. Henry's mother (Edsel's widow), Eleanor Clay Ford (related to the Hudson department store family), insisted that Henry II be given control of the company or she would sell her stock. Henry's grandmother (and the elder Ford's wife), Clara

Bryant Ford, backed Eleanor. On September 20, 1945, Henry Ford II became president of Ford Motor Company. The next day this decision was ratified by the board of directors.

Henry Ford immediately fired Bennett—after 29 years in the company, much of it as its effective boss, he was out. Inheriting a company with no financial controls and in managerial disarray, losing $10 million a month, Ford hired financial experts, including Arjay Miller, to straighten out the company's books and records, and Ernie Breech, from Bendix, to help with the management. In the first several months in control, Ford fired more than 1,000 executives, including many of Bennett's cronies. By 1949, Ford had instituted a pension plan with the United Auto Workers Union, the first in the industry, and brought out an all–new automobile. In 1950, the company earned a profit of $265 million. Ford and his recent hires had turned the company around, but it had taken courage and a willingness to take on some pretty tough people inside the organization to do it. Henry Ford II had managed with power.

What does it mean, to manage with power?

First, it means recognizing that in almost every organization, there are varying interests. This suggests that one of the first things we need to do is to diagnose the political landscape and figure out what the relevant interests are, and what important political subdivisions characterize the organization. It is essential that we do not assume that everyone necessarily is going to be our friend, or agree with us, or even that preferences are uniformly distributed. There are clusters of interests within organizations, and we need to understand where these are and to whom they belong.

Next, it means figuring out what point of view these various individuals and subunits have on issues of concern to us. It also means understanding why they have the perspective that they do. It is all too easy to assume that those with a different perspective are somehow not as smart as we are, not as informed, not as perceptive. If that is our belief, we are likely to do several things, each of which is disastrous. First, we may act contemptuously toward those who disagree with us—after all, if they aren't as competent or as insightful as we are, why should we take them seriously? It is rarely difficult to get along with those who resemble us in character and opinions. The real secret of success in organizations is the ability to get those who differ from us, and whom we don't necessarily like, to do what needs to be done. Second, if we think people are misinformed, we are likely to try to "inform" them, or to try to convince them with facts and analysis. Sometimes this will work, but often it will not, for their disagreement may not be based on a lack of information; it may, instead, arise from a different perspective on what our information means. Diagnosing the point of view of interest groups as well as the basis for their positions will assist us in negotiating with them and in predicting their response to various initiatives.

Third, managing with power means understanding that to get things done, you need power—more power than those whose opposition you must overcome—and thus it is imperative to understand where power comes from and how these sources of power can be developed. We are sometimes reluctant to think very purposefully or strategically about acquiring and using power. We are prone to believe that if we do our best, work hard, be nice, and so forth, things will work out for the best. I don't mean to imply that one should not, in general, work hard, try to make good decisions, and be nice, but that these and similar platitudes are often not very useful in helping us get things accomplished in our organizations. We need to understand power and try to get it. We must be willing to do things to build our sources of power, or else we will be less effective than we might wish to be.

Fourth, managing with power means understanding the strategies and tactics through which power is developed and used in organizations, including the importance of timing, the use of structure, the social psychology of commitment and other forms of interpersonal influence. If nothing else, such an understanding will help us become astute observers of the behavior of others. The more we understand power and its manifestations, the better will be our clinical skills. More fundamentally, we need to understand strategies and tactics of using power so that we can consider the range of approaches available to us, and use what is likely to be effective. Again, as in the case of building sources of power, we often try not to think about these things, and we avoid being strategic or purposeful about employing our power. This is a mistake. Although we may have various qualms, there will be others who do not. Knowledge without power is of remarkably little use. And power without the skill to employ it effectively is likely to be wasted.

Managing with power means more than knowing the ideas discussed in this book. It means being, like Henry Ford, willing to do something with that knowledge. It requires political savvy to get things done, and the willingness to force the issue.

For years in the United States, there had been demonstrations and protests, court decisions and legislative proposals attempting to end the widespread discrimination against minority Americans in employment, housing, and public accommodations. The passage of civil rights legislation was a top priority for President Kennedy, but although he had charisma, he lacked the knowledge of political tactics, and possibly the will to use some of the more forceful ones, to get his legislation passed. In the hands of someone who knew power and influence inside out, in spite of the opposition of southern congressmen and senators, the legislation would be passed quickly.

In March 1965, the United States was wracked by violent reactions to civil rights marches in the South. People were killed and injured as segregationists attacked demonstrators, with little or no intervention by the local law enforcement agencies. There were demonstrators across from the White House holding a vigil as Lyndon Johnson left to address a joint session of Congress. This was the same Lyndon Johnson who, in 1948, had opposed federal antilynching legislation, arguing that it was a matter properly left to the states. This was the same Lyndon Johnson who, as a young congressional secretary and then congressman, had talked conservative to conservatives, liberal to liberals, and was said

by many to have stood for nothing. This was the same Lyndon Johnson who in eight years in the House of Representatives had introduced not one piece of significant legislation and had done almost nothing to speak out on issues of national importance. This was the same Lyndon Johnson who, while in the House, had tried instead to enrich himself by influencing colleagues at the Federal Communications Commission to help him both obtain a radio station in Austin, Texas, and change the operating license to make the station immensely profitable and valuable. This was the same Lyndon Johnson who, in 1968, having misled the American people, would decide not to run for re-election because of both his association with the Vietnam War and a fundamental distrust of the presidency felt by many Americans. On that night Johnson was to make vigorous use of his power and his political skill to help the civil rights movement:

With almost the first words of his speech, the audience . . . knew that Lyndon Johnson intended to take the cause of civil rights further than it had ever gone before. . . . He would submit a new civil rights bill . . . and it would be far stronger than the bills of the past. . . . "their cause must be our cause, too," Lyndon Johnson said. "Because it is not just Negroes, but really it is all of us, who must overcome the crippling legacy of bigotry and injustice. . . . And we shall overcome."[5]

As he left the chamber after making his speech, Johnson sought out the 76-year-old chairman of the House Judiciary Committee, Emmanuel Celler:

"Manny," he said, "I want you to start hearings tonight."

"Mr. President," Celler protested, "I can't push that committee or it might get out of hand. I am scheduling hearings for next week."

. . . Johnson's eyes narrowed, and his face turned harder. His right hand was still shaking Celler's, but the left hand was up, and a finger was out, pointing, jabbing.

"Start them this week, Manny," he said. "And hold night sessions, too."[6]

Getting things done requires power. The problem is that we would prefer to see the world as a kind of grand morality play, with the good guys and the bad ones easily identified. Obtaining power is not always an attractive process, nor is its use. And it somehow disturbs our sense of symmetry that a man who was as sleazy, to use a term of my students, as Lyndon Johnson was in some respects, was also the individual who almost single-handedly passed more civil rights legislation in less time with greater effect than anyone else in U.S. history. We are troubled by the issue of means and ends. We are perplexed by the fact that "bad" people sometimes do great and wonderful things, and that "good" people sometimes do "bad" things, or often, nothing at all. Every day, managers in public and private organizations acquire and use power to get things done. Some of these things may be, in retrospect, mistakes, although often that depends heavily on your point of view. Any reader who always does the correct thing that pleases everyone should immediately contact me— we will get very wealthy together. Mistakes and opposition are inevitable. What is not inevitable is passivity, not trying, not seeking to accomplish things.

In many domains of activity we have become so obsessed with not upsetting anybody, and with not making mistakes, that we settle for doing nothing. Rather than rebuild San Francisco's highways, possibly in the wrong place, maybe even in the wrong way, we do nothing, and the city erodes economically without adequate transportation. Rather than possibly being wrong about a new product, such as the personal computer, we study it and analyze it, and lose market opportunities. Analysis and forethought are, obviously, fine. What is not so fine is paralysis or inaction, which arise because we have little skill in overcoming the opposition that inevitably accompanies change, and little interest in doing so.

Theodore Roosevelt, making a speech at the Sorbonne in 1910, perhaps said it best:

It is not the critic who counts; not the man who points out how the strong man stumbles, or where the doer of deeds could have done them better. The credit belongs to the man who is actually in the arena, whose face is marred by dust and sweat and blood; who strives valiantly; who errs, and comes short again and again; because there is not effort without error and shortcoming; but who does actually strive to do the deeds; who knows the great enthusiasms, the great devotions; who spends himself in a worthy cause, who at the best knows in the end the triumphs of high achievement and who at the worst, if he fails, at least fails while daring greatly, so that his place shall never be with those cold and timid souls who know neither victory nor defeat.[7]

It is easy and often comfortable to feel powerless— to say, "I don't know what to do, I don't have the power to get it done, and besides, I can't really stomach the struggle that may be involved." It is easy, and now quite common, to say, when confronted with some mistake in your organization, "It's not really my responsibility, I can't do anything about it anyway, and if the company wants to do that, well, that's why the senior executives get the big money—it's their responsibility." Such a response excuses us from trying to do things; in not trying to overcome opposition, we will make fewer enemies and are less likely to embarrass ourselves. It is, however, a prescription for both organizational and personal failure. This is why power and influence are not the organization's last dirty secret, but the secret of success for both individuals and their organizations. Innovation and change in almost any arena require the skill to develop power, and the willingness to employ it to get things accomplished. Or, in the words of a local radio newscaster, "If you don't like the news, go out and make some of your own."

NOTES

1. Tracy Kidder, *Soul of a New Machine* (Boston: Atlantic-Little, Brown, 1981), 111.

2. Jane Gross, "Turning Disease Into a Cause: Breast Cancer Follows AIDS," *New York Times* (January 7, 1991): A1.

3. David Halberstam, *The Reckoning* (New York: William Morrow, 1986), 90.

4. Ibid., 91.

5. Robert A. Caro, *Means of Ascent: The Years of Lyndon Johnson* (New York: Alfred A. Knopf, 1990), xix–xx.

6. Ibid., xxi.

7. Richard M. Nixon, *Leaders* (New York: Warner Books, 1982), 345.

40. BEYOND THE CHARISMATIC LEADER: LEADERSHIP AND ORGANIZATIONAL CHANGE

David A. Nadler and Michael L. Tushman

Like never before, discontinuous organization change is an important determinant of organization adaptation. Responding to regulatory, economic, competitive and/or technological shifts through more efficiently pushing the same organization systems and processes just does not work.[1] Rather, organizations may need to manage through periods of both incremental as well as revolutionary change.[2] Further, given the intensity of global competition in more and more industries, these organizational transformations need to be initiated and implemented rapidly. Speed seems to count.[3] These trends put a premium on executive leadership and the management of system-wide organization change.

There is a growing knowledge base about large-scale organization change.[4] This literature is quite consistent on at least one aspect of effective system-wide change—namely, executive leadership matters. The executive is a critical actor in the drama of organization change.[5] Consider the following examples:

Don Hambrick and Charles O'Reilly made valuable suggestions on earlier versions of this article. The article is partially based on research conducted under the sponsorship of Columbia University's Innovation and Entrepreneurship Research Center and its Executive Leadership Research Center. A version of this article appeared in M. Tushman, C. O'Reilly, and D. Nadler, eds., *The Management of Organizations: Strategy, Tactics, and Analyses* (New York, NY: Harper & Row, 1989).

From *California Management Review*, Vol 32, No 2, Winter 1990, pp 77–97. © 1990 by, The Regents of the University of California *CMR*, Volume 32, Number 2, Winter 1990.

At Fuji-Xerox, Yotaro Kobayashi's response to declining market share, lack of new products, and increasing customer complaints was to initiate widespread organization change. Most fundamentally, Kobayashi's vision was to change the way Fuji-Xerox conducted its business. Kobayashi and his team initiated the "New Xerox Movement" through Total Quality Control. The core values of quality, problem solving, teamwork, and customer emphasis were espoused and acted upon by Kobayashi and his team. Further, the executive team at Fuji instituted a dense infrastructure of objectives, measures, rewards, tools, education and slogans all in service of TQC and the "New Xerox." New heroes were created. Individuals and teams were publicly celebrated to reinforce to the system those behaviors that reflected the best of the new Fuji-Xerox. Kobayashi continually reinforced, celebrated, and communicated his TQC vision. Between 1976–1980, Fuji-Xerox gained back its market share, developed an impressive set of new products, and won the Demming prize.[6]

Much of this Fuji-Xerox learning was transferred to corporate Xerox and further enhanced by Dave Kearns and his executive team. Beginning in 1983, Kearns clearly expressed his "Leadership Through Quality" vision for the corporation. Kearns established a Quality Task Force and Quality Office with respected Xerox executives. This broad executive base developed the architecture of Leadership Through Quality. This effort included quality principles, tools, education, required leadership actions, rewards, and feedback mechanisms. This attempt to transform the entire corporation was initiated at the top and diffused throughout the firm through overlapping teams. These teams were pushed by Kearns and his team to achieve extraordinary gains. While not completed, this transformation has helped Xerox regain lost market share and improve product development efforts.[7]

At General Electric, Jack Welch's vision of a lean, aggressive organization with all the benefits of size but the agility of small firms is being driven by a set of interrelated actions. For example, the "work-out" effort is a corporate-wide endeavor, spearheaded by Welch, to get the bureaucracy out of a large-old organization and, in turn, to liberate GE employees to be their best. This effort is more than Welch. Welch's vision is being implemented by a senior task force which has initiated workout efforts in Welch's own top team as well as in each GE business area. These efforts consist of training, problem solving, measures, rewards, feedback procedures, and outside expertise. Similarly, sweeping changes at SAS under Carlzon, at ICI under Harvey-Jones, by Anderson at NCR, and at Honda each emphasize the importance of visionary leadership along with executive teams, systems, structures and processes to transfer an individual's vision of the future into organizational reality.[8]

On the other hand, there are many examples of visionary executives who are unable to translate their vision into organization action. For example, Don Burr's vision at People Express not only to "make a better world" but also to grow rapidly and expand to capture the business traveller was not coupled with requisite changes in organization infrastructure, procedures, and/or roles. Further, Burr was unable to build a cohesive senior team to help execute his compelling vision. This switch in vision, without a committed senior team and associated structure and systems, led to the rapid demise of People Express.

Vision and/or charisma is not enough to sustain large-system change. While a necessary condition in the management of discontinuous change, we must build a model of leadership that goes beyond the inspired individual; a model that takes into account the complexities of system-wide change in large, diverse, geographically complex organizations. We attempt to develop a framework for the extension of charismatic leadership by building on the growing leadership literature,[9] the literature on organization evolution,[10] and our intensive consulting work with executives attempting major organization change.[11]

ORGANIZATIONAL CHANGE AND RE-ORGANIZATION

Organizations go through change all the time. However, the nature, scope, and intensity of organizational changes vary considerably. Different kinds of organizational changes will require very different kinds of leadership behavior in initiating, energizing, and implementing the change. Organization changes vary along the following dimensions:

- *Strategic and Incremental Changes*—Some changes in organizations, while significant, only affect selected components of the organization. The fundamental aim of such change is to enhance the effectiveness of the organization, but within the general framework of the strategy, mode of organizing, and values that already are in place. Such changes are called *incremental changes*. Incremental changes happen all the time in organizations, and they need not be small. Such things as changes in organization structure, the introduction of new technology, and significant modifications of personnel practices are all large and significant changes, but ones which usually occur within the existing definition and frame of reference of the organization. Other changes have an impact on the whole system of the organization and fundamentally redefine what the organization is or change its basic framework, including strategy, structure, people, processes, and (in some cases) core values. These changes are called *strategic organizational changes*. The Fuji-Xerox, People Express, ICI, and SAS cases are examples of system-wide organization change.

- *Reactive and Anticipatory Changes*—Many organizational changes are made in direct response to some external event. These changes, which are forced upon the organization, are called *reactive*. The Xerox, SAS and ICI transformations were all initiated in response to organization performance crisis. At other times, strategic organizational change is initiated not because of the need to respond to a contemporaneous event, but rather because senior management believes that change in anticipation of events still to come will provide competitive advantage. These changes are called *anticipatory*. The GE and People Express cases as well as more recent system-wide changes at AL-COA and Cray Research are examples of system-wide change initiated in anticipation of environmental change.

If these two dimensions are combined, a basic typology of different changes can be described (see Figure 40.1).

Change which is incremental and anticipatory is called *tuning*. These changes are not system-wide redefinitions, but rather modifications of specific components, and they are initiated in anticipation of future events. Incremental change which is initiated reactively is called *adaptation*. Strategic change initiated in anticipation of future events is called *reorientation*, and change which is prompted by immediate demands is called *re-creation*.[12]

Research on patterns of organizational life and death across several industries has provided insight into the patterns of strategic organizational change.[13] Some of the key findings are as follows:

- *Strategic organization changes are necessary.* These changes appear to be environmentally driven. Various factors—be they competitive, technological, or regulatory—drive the organization (either reactively or in anticipation) to make system-wide changes. While strategic organization change does

	Incremental	Strategic
Anticipatory	**Tuning**	**Re-orientation**
Reactive	**Adaptation**	**Re-creation**

FIGURE 40.1 Types of Organizational Changes.

not guarantee success, those organizations that fail to change, generally fail to survive. Discontinuous environmental change seems to require discontinuous organization change.

• *Re-creations are riskier.* Re-creations are riskier endeavors than reorientations if only because they are initiated under crisis conditions and under sharp time constraints. Further, re-creations almost always involve a change in core values. As core values are most resistant to change, re-creations always trigger substantial individual resistance to change and heightened political behavior. Re-creations that do succeed usually involve changes in the senior leadership of the firm, frequently involving replacement from the outside. For example, the reactive system-wide changes at U.S. Steel, Chrysler, and Singer were all initiated by new senior teams.

• *Re-orientations are associated more with success.* Re-orientations have the luxury of time to shape the change, build coalitions, and empower individuals to be effective in the new organization. Further, re-orientations give senior managers time to prune and shape core values in service of the revised strategy, structure, and processes. For example, the proactive strategic changes at Cray Research, AL-COA, and GE each involved system-wide change as well as the shaping of core values ahead of the competition and from a position of strength.

Re-orientations are, however, risky. When sweeping changes are initiated in advance of precipitating external events, success is contingent on making appropriate strategic bets. As re-orientations are initiated ahead of the competition and in advance of environmental shifts, they require visionary executives. Unfortunately, in real time, it is unclear who will be known as visionary executives (e.g., Welch, Iacocca, Rollwagen at Cray Research) and who will be known as failures (e.g., Don Burr at People Express, or Larry Goshorn at General Automation). In turbulent environments, not to make strategic bets in associated with failure. Not all bets will pay off, however. The advantages of re-orientations derive from the extra implementation time and from

the opportunity to learn from and adapt to mistakes.[14]

As with re-creations, executive leadership is crucial in initiating and implementing strategic re-orientations. The majority of successful re-orientations involve change in the CEO and substantial executive team change. Those most successful firms, however, have executive teams that are relatively stable yet are still capable of initiating several re-orientations (e.g., Ken Olsen at DEC and An Wang at Wang).

There are, then, quite fundamentally different kinds of organizational changes. The role of executive leadership varies considerably for these different types of organizational changes. Incremental change typically can be managed by the existing management structures and processes of the organization, sometimes in conjunction with special transition structures.[15] In these situations, a variety of leadership styles may be appropriate, depending upon how the organization is normally managed and led. In strategic changes, however, the management process and structure itself is the subject of change; therefore, it cannot be relied upon to manage the change. In addition, the organization's definition of effective leadership may also be changing as a consequence of the re-orientation or re-creation. In these situations, leadership becomes a very critical element of change management.

This article focuses on the role of executive leadership in strategic organization change, and in particular, the role of leadership in re-orientations. Given organization and individual inertia, re-orientations can not be initiated or implemented without sustained action by the organization's leadership. Indeed, re-orientations are frequently driven by new leadership, often brought in from outside the organization.[16] A key challenge for executives facing turbulent environments, then, is to learn how to effectively initiate, lead, and manage re-orientations. Leadership of strategic re-orientations requires not only charisma, but also substantial instrumental skills in building executive teams, roles, and systems in support of the change, as well as institutional skills in diffusing leadership throughout the organization.

THE CHARISMATIC LEADER

While the subject of leadership has received much attention over the years, the more specific issue of leadership during periods of change has only recently attracted serious attention.[17] What emerges from various discussions of leadership and organizational change is a picture of the special kind of leadership that appears to be critical during times of strategic organizational change. While various words have been used to portray this type of leadership, we prefer the label "charismatic" leader. It refers to a special quality that enables the leader to mobilize and sustain activity within an organization through specific personal actions combined with perceived personal characteristics.

The concept of the charismatic leader is not the popular version of the great speech maker or television personality. Rather, a model has emerged from recent work aimed at identifying the nature and determinants of a particular type of leadership that successfully brings about changes in an individual's values, goals, needs, or aspirations. Research on charismatic leadership has identified this type of leadership as observable, definable, and having clear behavioral characteristics.[18] We have attempted to develop a first cut description of the leader in terms of patterns of behavior that he/she seems to exhibit. The resulting approach is outlined in Figure 40.2, which lists three major types of behavior that characterize these leaders and some illustrative kinds of actions.

The first component of charismatic leadership is *envisioning*. This involves the creation of a picture of the future, or of a desired future state with which people can identify and which can generate excitement. By creating vision, the leader provides a vehicle for people to develop commitment, a common goal around which people can rally, and a way for people to feel successful. Envisioning is accomplished through a range of different actions. Clearly, the simplest form is through articulation of a compelling vision in clear and dramatic terms. The vision needs to be challenging, meaningful, and worthy of pursuit, but it also needs to be credible. People must believe that it is possible to succeed in the pursuit of the vision. Vision is also communicated in other ways, such as through expectations that the leader expresses and through the leader personally demonstrating behaviors and activities that symbolize and further that vision.

The second component is *energizing*. Here the role of the leader is the direct generation of energy—motivation to act—among members of the organization. How is this done? Different leaders

---

Envisioning
- Articulating a compelling vision
- Setting high expectations
- Modeling consistent behaviors

Energizing
- Demonstrating personal excitement
- Expressing personal confidence
- Seeking, finding, & using success

Enabling
- Expressing personal support
- Empathizing
- Expressing confidence in people

FIGURE 40.2 The Charismatic Leader.

engage in energizing in different ways, but some of the most common include demonstration of their own personal excitement and energy, combined with leveraging that excitement through direct personal contact with large numbers of people in the organization. They express confidence in their own ability to succeed. They find, and use, successes to celebrate progress towards the vision.

The third component is *enabling*. The leader psychologically helps people act or perform in the face of challenging goals. Assuming that individuals are directed through a vision and motivated by the creation of energy, they then may need emotional assistance in accomplishing their tasks. This enabling is achieved in several ways. Charismatic leaders demonstrate empathy—the ability to listen, understand, and share the feelings of those in the organization. They express support for individuals. Perhaps most importantly, the charismatic leader tends to express his/her confidence in people's ability to perform effectively and to meet challenges.

Yotaro Kobayashi at Fuji-Xerox and Paul O'Neil at ALCOA each exhibit the characteristics of charismatic leaders. In Kobayashi's transformation at Fuji, he was constantly espousing his New Xerox Movement vision for Fuji. Kobayashi set high standards for his firm (e.g., the 3500 model and the Demming Prize), for himself, and for his team. Beyond espousing this vision for Fuji, Kobayashi provided resources, training, and personal coaching to support his colleagues' efforts in the transformation at Fuji. Similarly, Paul O'Neil has espoused a clear vision for ALCOA anchored on quality, safety, and innovation. O'Neil has made his vision compelling and central to the firm, has set high expectations for his top team and for individuals throughout ALCOA and provides continuous support and energy for his vision through meetings, task forces, video tapes, and extensive personal contact.

Assuming that leaders act in these ways, what functions are they performing that help bring about change? First, they provide a psychological focal point for the energies, hopes, and aspirations of people in the organization. Second, they serve as powerful role models whose behaviors, actions and personal energy demonstrate the desired behaviors expected throughout the firm. The behaviors of charismatic leaders provide a standard to which others can aspire. Through their personal effectiveness and attractiveness they build a very personal and intimate bond between themselves and the organization. Thus, they can become a source of sustained energy; a figure whose high standards others can identify with and emulate.

Limitations of the Charismatic Leader

Even if one were able to do all of the things involved in being a charismatic leader, it might still not be enough. In fact, our observations suggest that there are a number of inherent limitations to the effectiveness of charismatic leaders, many stemming from risks associated with leadership which revolves around a single individual. Some of the key potential problems are:

- *Unrealistic Expectations*—In creating a vision and getting people energized, the leader may create expectations that are unrealistic or unattainable. These can backfire if the leader cannot live up to the expectations that are created.

- *Dependency and Counterdependency*—A strong, visible, and energetic leader may spur different psychological response. Some individuals may become overly dependent upon the leader, and in some cases whole organizations become dependent. Everyone else stops initiating actions and waits for the leader to provide direction; individuals may become passive or reactive. On the other extreme, others may be uncomfortable with strong personal presence and spend time and energy demonstrating how the leader is wrong—how the emperor has no clothes.

- *Reluctance to Disagree with the Leader*—The charismatic leader's approval or disapproval becomes an important commodity. In the presence of a strong leader, people may become hesitant to disagree or come into conflict with the leader. This may, in turn, lead to stifling conformity.

• *Need for Continuing Magic*—The charismatic leader may become trapped by the expectation that the magic often associated with charisma will continue unabated. This may cause the leader to act in ways that are not functional, or (if the magic is not produced) it may cause a crisis of leadership credibility.

• *Potential Feelings of Betrayal*—When and if things do not work out as the leader has envisioned, the potential exists for individuals to feel betrayed by their leader. They may become frustrated and angry, with some of that anger directed at the individual who created the expectations that have been betrayed.

• *Disenfranchisement of Next Levels of Management*— A consequence of the strong charismatic leader is that the next levels of management can easily become disenfranchised. They lose their ability to lead because no direction, vision, exhortation, reward, or punishment is meaningful unless it comes directly from the leader. The charismatic leader thus may end up underleveraging his or her management and/or creating passive/dependent direct reports.

• *Limitations of Range of the Individual Leader*—When the leadership process is built around an individual, management's ability to deal with various issues is limited by the time, energy, expertise, and interest of that individual. This is particularly problematic during periods of change when dif-

ferent types of issues demand different types of competencies (e.g., markets, technologies, products, finance) which a single individual may not possess. Different types of strategic changes make different managerial demands and call for different personal characteristics. There may be limits to the number of strategic changes that one individual can lead over the life of an organization.

In light of these risks, it appears that the charismatic leader is a necessary component—but not a sufficient component—of the organizational leadership required for effective organizational re-organization. There is a need to move beyond the charismatic leader.

INSTRUMENTAL LEADERSHIP

Effective leaders of change need to be more than just charismatic. Effective re-orientations seem to be characterized by the presence of another type of leadership behavior which focuses not on the excitement of individuals and changing their goals, needs or aspirations, but on making sure that individuals in the senior team and throughout the organization behave in ways needed for change to occur. An important leadership role is to build competent teams, clarify required behaviors, built in measurement, and administer rewards and punishments so that individuals perceive that behavior consistent

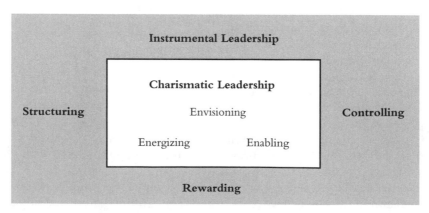

FIGURE 40.3 Instrumental Leadership.

with the change is central for them in achieving their own goals.[19] We will call this type of leadership *instrumental leadership*, since it focuses on the management of teams, structures, and managerial processes to create individual instrumentalities. The basis of this approach is in expectancy theories of motivation, which propose that individuals will perform those behaviors that they perceive as instrumental for acquiring valued outcomes.[20] Leadership, in this context, involves managing environments to create conditions that motivate desired behavior.[21]

In practice, instrumental leadership of change involves three elements of behavior (see Figure 40.3). The first is *structuring*. The leader invests time in building teams that have the required competence to execute and implement the re-orientation[22] and in creating structures that make it clear what types of behavior are required throughout the organization. This may involve setting goals, establishing standards, and defining roles and responsibilities. Re-orientations seem to require detailed planning about what people will need to do and how they will be required to act during different phases of the change. The second element of instrumental leadership is *controlling*. This involves the creation of systems and processes to measure, monitor, and assess both behavior and results and to administer corrective action.[23] The third element is *rewarding*, which includes the administration of both rewards and punishments contingent upon the degree to which behavior is consistent with the requirements of the change.

Instrumental leadership focuses on the challenge of shaping consistent behaviors in support of the re-orientation. The charismatic leader excites individuals, shapes their aspirations, and directs their energy. In practice, however, this is not enough to sustain patterns of desired behavior. Subordinates and colleagues may be committed to the vision, but over time other forces may influence their behavior, particularly when they are not in direct personal contact with the leader. This is particularly relevant during periods of change when the formal organization and the informal social system may lag behind the leader and communicate outdated messages or reward traditional behavior. Instrumental

leadership is needed to ensure compliance over time consistent with the commitment generated by charismatic leadership.

At Xerox, for example, David Kearns used instrumental leadership to further enliven his Leadership Through Quality efforts.[24] Beyond his own sustained behaviors in support of the Leadership Through Quality effort, Kearns and his Quality Office developed a comprehensive set of roles, processes, teams, and feedback and audit mechanisms for getting customer input and continuous improvement into everyday problem solving throughout Xerox. Individuals and teams across the corporation were evaluated on their ability to continuously meet customer requirements. These data were used in making pay, promotion, and career decisions.

The Role of Mundane Behaviors

Typical descriptions of both charismatic and instrumental leaders tend to focus on significant events, critical incidents, and grand gestures. Our vision of the change manager is frequently exemplified by the key speech or public event that is a potential watershed event. While these are important arenas for leadership, leading large-system change also requires sustained attention to the myriad of details that make up organizational life. The accumulation of less dramatic, day-to-day activities and mundane behaviors serves as a powerful determinant of behavior.[25] Through relatively unobtrusive acts, through sustained attention to detail, managers can directly shape perceptions and culture in support of the change effort. Examples of mundane behavior that when taken together can have a great impact include:

- allocation of time; calendar management
- asking questions, following up
- shaping of physical settings
- public statements
- setting agendas of events or meetings
- use of events such as lunches, meetings, to push the change effort

- summarization—post hoc interpretation of what occurred
- creating heroes
- use of humor, stories, and myths
- small symbolic actions, including rewards and punishments

In each of these ways, leaders can use daily activities to emphasize important issues, identify desirable behavior, and help create patterns and meaning out of the various transactions that make up organizational life.

The Complementarity of Leadership Approaches

It appears that effective organizational re-orientation requires both charismatic and instrumental leadership. Charismatic leadership is needed to generate energy, create commitment, and direct individuals towards new objectives, values or aspirations. Instrumental leadership is required to ensure that people really do act in a manner consistent with their new goals. Either one alone is insufficient for the achievement of change.

The complementarity of leadership approaches and the necessity for both creates a dilemma.[26] Success in implementing these dual approaches is associated with the personal style, characteristics, needs, and skills of the executive. An individual who is adept at one approach may have difficulty executing the other. For example, charismatic leaders may have problems with tasks involved in achieving control. Many charismatic leaders are motivated by a strong desire to receive positive feedback from those around them.[27] They may therefore have problems delivering unpleasant messages, dealing with performance problems, or creating situations that could attract negative feelings.[28]

Only exceptional individuals can handle the behavioral requirements of both charismatic and instrumental leadership styles. While such individuals exist, an alternative may be to involve others in leadership roles, thus complementing the strengths and weaknesses of one individual leader.[29] For example,

in the early days at Honda, it took the steadying, systems-oriented hand of Takeo Fujisawa to balance the fanatic, impatient, visionary energy of Soichiro Honda. Similarly, at Data General, it took Alsing and Rasala's social, team, and organization skills to balance and make more humane Tom West's vision and standards for the Eclipse team.[30] Without these complementary organization and systems skills, Don Burr was unable to execute his proactive system-wide changes at People Express.

The limitations of the individual leader pose a significant challenge. Charismatic leadership has a broad reach. It can influence many people, but is limited by the frequency and intensity of contact with the individual leader. Instrumental leadership is also limited by the degree to which the individual leader can structure, observe, measure and reward behavior. These limitations present significant problems for achieving re-orientations. One implication is that structural extensions of leadership should be created in the process of managing re-orientations.[31] A second implication is that human extensions of leadership need to be created to broaden the scope and impact of leader actions. This leads to a third aspect of leadership and change—the extension of leadership beyond the individual leader, or the creation of institutionalized leadership throughout the organization.

INSTITUTIONALIZING THE LEADERSHIP OF CHANGE

Given the limitations of the individual charismatic leader, the challenge is to broaden the range of individuals who can perform the critical leadership functions during periods of significant organizational change. There are three potential leverage points for the extension of leadership—the senior team, broader senior management, and the development of leadership throughout the organization (see Figure 40.4).

Leveraging the Senior Team

The group of individuals who report directly to the individual leader—the executive or senior team—

is the first logical place to look for opportunities to extend and institutionalize leadership. Development of an effective, visible, and dynamic senior team can be a major step in getting around the problems and limitations of the individual leader.[32] Examples of such executive teams include the Management Committee established at Corning by Jamie Houghton or Bob Allen's Executive Committee at AT&T. Several actions appear to be important in enhancing the effectiveness of the senior team.

- *Visible Empowerment of the Team*—A first step is the visible empowerment of the team, or "anointing" the team as extensions of the individual leader. There are two different aspects to this empowerment: objective and symbolic. Objective empowerment involves providing team members with the autonomy and resources to serve effectively. Symbolic empowerment involves communicating messages (through information, symbols, and mundane behaviors) to show the organization that these individuals are indeed extensions of the leader, and ultimately key components of the

leadership. Symbolic empowerment can be done through the use of titles, the designation of organizational structures, and the visible presence of individuals in ceremonial roles.

- *Individual Development of Team Members*—Empowerment will fail if the individuals on the team are not capable of executing their revised leadership roles. A major problem in re-orientations is that the members of the senior team frequently are the product of the very systems, structures, and values that the re-orientation seeks to change. Participating in the change, and more importantly, leading it, may require a significant switching of cognitive gears.[33] Re-orientations demand that senior team members think very differently about the business and about managing. This need for personal change at the most senior level has implications for the selection of senior team members (see below). It also may mean that part of the individual leader's role is to help coach, guide, and support individuals in developing their own leadership capabilities. Each individual need not (and should not) be a "clone" of the individ-

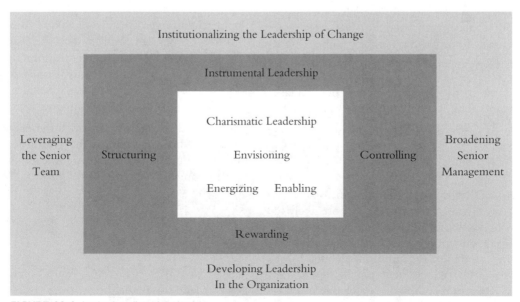

FIGURE 40.4 Institutionalized Leadership.

ual leader; but each should be able to initiate credible leadership actions in a manner consistent with their own personal styles. Ultimately, it also puts a demand on the leader to deal with those who will not or can not make the personal changes required for helping lead the re-orientation.

• *Composition of the Senior Team*—The need for the senior team to implement change may mean that the composition of that team may have to be altered. Different skills, capabilities, styles, and value orientations may be needed to both lead the changes as well as to manage in the reconfigured organization.[34] In fact, most successful re-orientations seem to involve some significant changes in the make-up of the senior team. This may require outplacement of people as well as importing new people, either from outside the organization, or from outside the coalition that has traditionally led the organization.[35]

• *The Inducement of Strategic Anticipation*—A critical issue in executing re-orientations is strategic anticipation. By definition, a re-orientation is a strategic organizational change that is initiated in anticipation of significant external events. Re-orientation occurs because the organization's leadership perceives competitive advantage from initiating change earlier rather than later. The question is, who is responsible for thinking about and anticipating external events, and ultimately deciding that re-orientation is necessary? In some cases, the individual leader does this, but the task is enormous. This is where the senior team can be helpful, because as a group it can scan a larger number of events and potentially be more creative in analyzing the environment and the process of anticipation.

Companies that are successful anticipators create conditions in which anticipation is more likely to occur. They invest in activities that foster anticipation, such as environmental scanning, experiments or probes inside the organization (frequently on the periphery), and frequent contacts with the outside. The senior team has a major role in initiating, sponsoring, and leveraging these activities.[36]

• *The Senior Team as a Learning System*—For a senior team to benefit from its involvement in leading change, it must become an effective system for learning about the business, the nature of change, and the task of managing change. The challenge is to both bond the team together, while avoiding insularity. One of the costs of such team structures is that they become isolated from the rest of the organization, they develop patterns of dysfunctional conformity, avoid conflict, and over time develop patterns of learned incompetence. These group processes diminish the team's capacity for effective strategic anticipation, and decreases the team's ability to provide effective leadership of the re-orientation.[37]

There are several ways to enhance a senior team's ability to learn over time. One approach is to work to keep the team an open system, receptive to outside ideas and information. This can be accomplished by creating a constant stream of events that expose people to new ideas and/or situations. For example, creating simulations, using critical incident techniques, creating near histories, are all ways of exposing senior teams to novel situations and sharpening problem-solving skills.[38] Similarly, senior teams can open themselves to new ideas via speakers or visitors brought in to meet with the team, visits by the team to other organizations, frequent contact with customers, and planned informal data collection through personal contact (breakfasts, focus groups, etc.) throughout the organization. A second approach involves the shaping and management of the internal group process of the team itself. This involves working on effective group leadership, building effective team member skills, creating meeting management discipline, acquiring group problem-solving and information-processing skills, and ultimately creating norms that promote effective learning, innovation, and problem solving.[39]

David Kearns at Xerox and Paul O'Neil at ALCOA made substantial use of senior teams in implementing their quality-oriented organization transformations. Both executives appointed senior quality task forces composed of highly respected senior executives. These task forces were charged with developing the corporate-wide architecture of the change effort. To sharpen their change and quality skills these executives made trips to Japan and to other experienced organizations, and were involved in extensive education and problem-solving efforts in their task forces and within their own divisions. These task forces put substance and enhanced energy into the CEO's broad vision. These executives were, in turn, role models and champions of the change efforts in their own sectors.

As a final note, it is important to remember that frequently there are significant obstacles in developing effective senior teams to lead re-orientations. The issues of skills and selection have been mentioned. Equally important is the question of power and succession. A team is most successful when there is a perception of common fate. *Individuals have to believe that the success of the team will, in the long run, be more salient to them than their individual short-run success.* In many situations, this can be accomplished through appropriate structures, objectives, and incentives. But these actions may fail when there are pending (or anticipated) decisions to be made concerning senior management succession. In these situations, the quality of collaboration tends to deteriorate significantly, and effective team leadership of change becomes problematic. The individual leader must manage the timing and process of succession in relation to the requirements for team leadership, so that conflicting (and mutually exclusive) incentives are not created by the situation.[40]

Broadening Senior Management

A second step in moving beyond individual leadership of change is the further extension of the leadership beyond the executive or senior team to include a broader set of individuals who make up the senior management of the organization. This would include individuals one or two levels down from

the executive team. At Corning, the establishment of two groups—the Corporate Policy Group (approximately the top 35) and the Corporate Management Group (about the top 120)—are examples of mechanisms used by Houghton to broaden the definition of senior management. This set of individuals is in fact the senior operating management of most sizeable organizations and is looked upon as senior management by the majority of employees. In many cases (and particularly during times of change) they do not feel like senior management, and thus they are not positioned to lead the change. They feel like participants (at best) and victims (at worst). This group can be particularly problematic since they may be more embedded in the current system of organizing and managing than some of the senior team. They may be less prepared to change, they frequently have molded themselves to fit the current organizational style, and they may feel disenfranchised by the very act of developing a strong executive team, particularly if that team has been assembled by bringing in people from outside of the organization.

The task is to make this group feel like senior management, to get them signed up for the change, and to motivate and enable them to work as an extension of the senior team. Many of the implications are similar to those mentioned above in relation to the top team; however, there are special problems of size and lack of proximity to the individual charismatic leader. Part of the answer is to get the senior team to take responsibility for developing their own teams as leaders of change. Other specific actions may include:

- *Rites of Passage*—Creating symbolic events that help these individuals to feel more a part of senior management.
- *Senior Groups*—Creating structures (councils, boards, committees, conferences) to maintain contact with this group and reinforce their sense of participation as members of senior management.
- *Participation in Planning Change*—Involving these people in the early diagnosing of the need to

change and the planning of change strategies associated with the re-orientation. This is particularly useful in getting them to feel more like owners, rather than victims of the change.

• *Intensive Communication*—Maintaining a constant stream of open communication to and from this group. It is the lack of information and perspective that psychologically disenfranchises these individuals.

Developing Leadership in the Organization

A third arena for enhancing the leadership of re-organizations is through organizational structures, systems, and process for leadership development consistent with the re-orientation. Frequently leadership development efforts lag behind the re-orientation. The management development system of many organizations often works effectively to create managers who will fit well with the organizational environment that the leadership seeks to abandon. There needs to be a strategic and anticipatory thinking about the leadership development process, including the following:

• *Definition of Managerial Competence*—A first step is determining the skills, capabilities, and capacities needed to manage and lead effectively in the re-orientation and post re-orientation period. Factors that have contributed to managerial success in the past may be the seeds of failure in the future.

• *Sourcing Managerial Talent*—Re-orientations may require that the organization identify significantly different sources for acquiring leaders or potential leaders. Senior managers should be involved in recruiting the hiring. Because of the lead time involved, managerial sourcing has to be approached as a long-term (five to ten years) task.

• *Socialization*—As individuals move into the organization and into positions of leadership, deliberate actions must be taken to teach them how the organization's social system works. During periods of re-orientation, the socialization process ought to lead rather than lag behind the change.

• *Management Education*—Re-orientation may require managers and leaders to use or develop new skills, competencies, or knowledge. This creates a demand for effective management education. Research indicates that the impact of passive internal management education on the development of effective leaders may be minimal when compared with more action-oriented educational experiences. The use of educational events to expose people to external settings or ideas (through out-of-company education) and to socialize individuals through action-oriented executive education may be more useful than attempts to teach people to be effective leaders and managers.[41]

• *Career Management*—Research and experience indicate that the most potent factor in the development of effective leaders is the nature of their job experiences.[42] The challenge is to ensure that middle and lower level managers get a wide range of experiences over time. Preparing people to lead re-orientations may require a greater emphasis on the development of generalists through cross-functional, divisional, and/or multinational career experiences.[43] Diverse career experiences help individuals develop a broad communication network and a range of experiences and competences all of which are vital in managing large-system change. This approach to careers implies the sharing of the burden of career management between both the organization and the employee as well as the deliberate strategy of balancing current contribution with investment for the future when placing people in job assignments.[44]

• *Seeding Talent*—Developing leadership for change may also require deliberate leveraging of available talent. This implies thoughtful placement of individual leaders in different situations and parts of the organization, the use of transfers, and the strategic placement of high-potential leaders.[45]

Perhaps the most ambitious and most well-documented effort at developing leadership throughout the organization is Welch's actions at GE. Welch has used GE's Management Development Institute at Crotonville as an important lever in the transformation of GE. Based on Welch's vision of a lean, competitive, agile organization with businesses leading in their respective markets, Crotonville has been used as a staging area for the revolution at GE. With Welch's active involvement, Crotonville's curriculum has moved from a short-term cognitive orientation towards longer-term problem solving and organization change. The curriculum has been developed to shape experiences and sharpen skills over the course of an individual's career in service of developing leaders to fit into the new GE.[46]

SUMMARY

In a world characterized by global competition, deregulation, sharp technological change, and political turmoil, discontinuous organization change seems to be a determinant of organization adaptation. Those firms that can initiate and implement discontinuous organization change more rapidly and/or prior to the competition have a competitive advantage. While not all change will be successful, inertia or incremental change in the face of altered competitive arenas is a recipe for failure.

Executive leadership is the critical factor in the initiation and implementation of large-system organization change. This article has developed an approach to the leadership of discontinuous organization change with particular reference to re-orientations—discontinuous change initiated in advance of competitive threat and/or performance crisis. Where incremental change can be delegated, strategic change must be driven by senior management. Charismatic leadership is a vital aspect of managing large-system change. Charismatic leaders provide vision, direction, and energy. Thus the successes of O'Neil at ALCOA, Welch at GE, Kearns at Xerox, and Rollwagen and Cray are partly a function of committed, enthusiastic, and passionate individual executives.

Charisma is not, however, enough to effect large-system change. Charismatic leadership must be bolstered by instrumental leadership through attention to detail on roles, responsibilities, structures, and rewards. Further, as many organizations are too large and complex for any one executive and/or senior team to directly manage, responsibility for large-system change must be institutionalized throughout the management system. The leadership of strategic organization change must be pushed throughout the organization to maximize the probability that managers at all levels own and are involved in executing the change efforts and see the concrete benefits of making the change effort work. O'Neil, Welch, Kearns, and Rollwagen are important catalysts in their organizations. Their successes to date are, however, not based simply on strong personalities. Each of these executives has been able to build teams, systems, and managerial processes to leverage and add substance to his vision and energy. It is this interaction of charisma, attention to systems and processes, and widespread involvement at multiple levels that seems to drive large-system change.

Even with inspired leadership, though, no re-orientation can emerge fully developed and planned. Re-orientations take time to implement. During this transition period, mistakes are made, environments change and key people leave. Given the turbulence of competitive conditions, the complexity of large-system change and individual cognitive limitations, the executive team must develop its ability to adapt to new conditions and, as importantly, learn from both its successes and failures. As organizations can not remain stable in the face of environmental change, so too must the management of large-system change be flexible. This ability of executive teams to build-in learning and to build-in flexibility into the process of managing large-system organizational change is a touchstone for proactively managing re-orientations.

REFERENCES

1. R. Solow, M. Dertouzos, and R. Lester, *Made in America* (Cambridge, MA: MIT Press, 1989).

2. See M.L. Tushman, W. Newman, and E. Romanelli, "Convergence and Upheaval: Managing the Unsteady Pace of Organizational Evolution," *California Management Review*, 29/1 (Fall 1986):29–44.

3. E.g., K. Imai, I. Nonaka, and H. Takeuchi, "Managing the New Product Development Process: How Japanese Companies Learn and Unlearn," in K. Clark and R. Hayes, *The Uneasy Alliance* (Cambridge, MA: Harvard University Press, 1985).

4. E.g., A. Pettigrew, *The Awakening Giant: Continuity and Change at ICI* (London: Blackwell, 1985); J.R. Kimberly and R.E. Quinn, *New Futures: The Challenge of Managing Corporate Transitions* (Homewood, IL: Dow Jones-Irwin, 1984); Y. Allaire and M. Firsirotu, "How to Implement Radical Strategies in Large Organizations," *Sloan Management Review* (Winter 1985).

5. E.g., J. Gabbaro, *The Dynamics of Taking Charge* (Cambridge, MA: Harvard Business School Press, 1987); L. Greiner and A. Bhambri, "New CEO Intervention and Dynamics of Deliberate Strategic Change," *Strategic Management Journal*, 10 (1989): 67–86; N.M. Tichy and M.A. Devanna, *The Transformational Leader* (New York, NY: John Wiley & Sons, 1986); D. Hambrick, "The Top Management Team: Key to Strategic Success," *California Management Review*, 30/1 (Fall 1987):88–108.

6. Y. Kobayashi, "Quality Control in Japan: The Case of Fuji Xerox," *Japanese Economic Studies* (Spring 1983).

7. G. Jacobson and J. Hillkirk, *Xerox: American Samurai* (New York, NY: Macmillan, 1986).

8. For SAS, see J. Carlzon, *Moments of Truth* (Cambridge, MA: Ballinger, 1987); for ICI, see Pettigrew, op. cit.; for NCR, see R. Rosenbloom, *From Gears to Chips: The Transformation of NCR in the Digital Era* (Cambridge, MA: Harvard University Press, 1988); for Honda, see I. Nonaka, "Creating Organizational Order Out of Chaos: Self-Renewal in Japanese Firms," *California Management Review*, 30/3 (Spring 1988):57–73.

9. Gabbaro, op. cit.; H. Levinson and S. Rosenthal, *CEO: Corporate Leadership in Action* (New York, NY: Basic Books, 1984); Greiner and Bhambri, op. cit.

10. Tushman et al., op. cit.; R. Greenwood and C. Hinings, "Organization Design Types, Tracks, and the Dynamics of Strategic Change," *Organization Studies*, 9/3 (1988):293–316; D. Miller and P. Friesen, *Organizations: A Quantum View* (Englewood Cliffs, NJ: Prentice-Hall, 1984).

11. D.A. Nadler and M.L. Tushman, "Organizational Framebending: Principles for Managing Re-orientation," *Academy of Management Executive*, 3 (1989):194–202.

12. For a more detailed discussion of this framework, see Nadler and Tushman, ibid.

13. Tushman et al., op. cit.; Greiner and Bhambri, op. cit.; Greenwood and Hinings, op. cit.; B. Virany and M.L. Tushman, "Changing Characteristics of Executive Teams in and Emerging Industry," *Journal of Business Venturing*, 1 (1986):261–274; M.L. Tushman and E. Romanelli, "Organizational Evolution: A Metamorphosis Model of Convergence and Re-orientation," in B.M. Staw and L.L. Cummings, eds., *Research in Organizational Behavior*, 5 (Greenwich, CT: JAI Press, 1985), pp. 171–222.

14. J. March, L. Sproull, and M. Tamuz, "Learning from Fragments of Experience," *Organization Science* (in press).

15. R. Beckhard and R. Harris, *Organizational Transitions* (Reading, MA: Addison-Wesley, 1977).

16. See R. Vancil, *Passing the Baton* (Cambridge, MA: Harvard Business School Press, 1987).

17. J.M. Burns, *Leadership* (New York, NY: Harper & Row, 1978); W. Bennis and B. Nanus, *Leaders: The Strategies for Taking Charge* (New York, NY: Harper & Row, 1985); N.M. Tichy and D. Ulrich, "The Leadership Challenge: A Call for the Transformational Leader," *Sloan Management Review* (Fall 1984); Tichy and Devanna, op. cit.

18. D.E. Berlew, "Leadership and Organizational Excitement," in D.A. Kolb, I.M. Rubin, and J.M. McIntyre, eds., *Organizational Psychology* (Englewood Cliffs, NJ: Prentice-Hall, 1974); R.J. House, "A 1976 Theory of Charismatic Leadership," in J.G. Hunt and L.L. Larson, eds., *Leadership: The Cutting Edge* (Carbondale, IL: Southern Illinois University Press, 1977); Levinson and Rosenthal, op. cit.; B.M. Bass, *Performance Beyond Expectations* (New York, NY: Free Press, 1985); R. House et al., "Personality and Charisma in the U.S. Presidency," Wharton Working Paper, 1989.

19. Hambrick, op. cit.; D. Ancona and D. Nadler, "Teamwork at the Top: Creating High Performing Executive Teams," *Sloan Management Review* (in press).

20. V.H. Vroom, *Work and Motivation* (New York, NY: John Wiley & Sons, 1964); J.P. Campbell, M.D. Dunnette, E.E. Lawler, and K. Weick, *Managerial Behavior, Performances, and Effectiveness* (New York, NY: McGraw-Hill, 1970).

21. R.J. House, "Path-Goal Theory of Leader Effectiveness," *Administrative Science Quarterly*, 16 (1971):321–338; G.R. Oldham, "The Motivational Strategies Used by Supervisors: Relationships to Effectiveness Indicators," *Organizational Behavior and Human Performance*, 15 (1976):66–86.

22. See Hambrick, op. cit.

23. E.E. Lawler and J.G. Rhode, *Information and Control in Organizations* (Pacific Palisades, CA: Goodyear, 1976).

24. Jacobson and Hillkirk, op. cit.

25. Gabbaro, op. cit.; T.J. Peters, "Symbols, Patterns, and Settings: An Optimistic Case for Getting Things Done," *Organizational Dynamics* (Autumn 1978).

26. R.J. House, "Exchange and Charismatic Theories of Leadership," in G. Reber, ed., *Encyclopedia of Leadership* (Stuttgart: C.E. Poeschel-Verlag, 1987).

27. M. Kets de Vries and D. Miller, "Neurotic Style and Organization Pathology," *Strategic Management Journal* (1984).

28. Levinson and Rosenthal, op. cit.

29. Hambrick, op. cit.

30. T. Kidder, *Soul of the New Machine* (Boston, MA: Little, Brown, 1981).

31. These are discussed in Nadler and Tushman, op cit.

32. Hambrick, op. cit.

33. M. Louis and R. Sutton, *Switching Cognitive Gears* (Stanford, CA: Stanford University Press, 1987).

34. C. O'Reilly, D. Caldwell, and W. Barnett, "Work Group Demography, Social Integration, and Turnover," *Administrative Science Quarterly*, 34 (1989):21–37.

35. Hambrick, op. cit.; Virany and Tushman, op. cit.

36. See D. Ancona, "Top Management Teams: Preparing for the Revolution," in J. Carroll, ed., *Social Psychology in Business Organizations* (New York, NY: Erlbaum Associates, in press).

37. Louis and Sutton, op. cit.

38. March et al., op. cit.

39. See also C. Gersick, "Time and Transition in Work Teams," *Academy of Management Journal*, 31 (1988):9–41; Ancona and Nadler, op. cit.

40. See Vancil, op. cit.

41. N. Tichy, "GE's Crotonville: A Staging Ground for Corporate Revolution," *Academy of Management Executive*, 3 (1989):99–106.

42. E.g., Gabbaro, op. cit.; V. Pucik, "International Management of Human Resources," in C. Fombrun et al., *Strategic Human Resource Management* (New York, NY: John Wiley & Sons, 1984).

43. Pucik, op. cit.

44. M. Devanna, C. Fombrun, and N. Tichy, "A Framework for Strategic Human Resource Management," in C. Fombrun et al., *Strategic Human Resource Management* (New York, NY: John Wiley & Sons, 1984).

45. Hambrick, op. cit.

46. Tichy, op. cit.